The Cambridge Handbook of Phonology

Phonology – the study of how the sounds of speech are represented in our minds – is one of the core areas of linguistic theory, and is central to the study of human language. This state-of-the-art handbook brings together the world's leading experts in phonology to present the most comprehensive and detailed overview of the field to date. Focusing on the most recent research and the most influential theories, the authors discuss each of the central issues in phonological theory, explore a variety of empirical phenomena, and show how phonology interacts with other aspects of language such as syntax, morphology, phonetics, and language acquisition. Providing a one-stop guide to every aspect of this important field, *The Cambridge Handbook of Phonology* will serve as an invaluable source of readings for advanced undergraduate and graduate students, an informative overview for linguists, and a useful starting point for anyone beginning phonological research.

PAUL DE LACY is Assistant Professor in the Department of Linguistics, Rutgers University. His publications include *Markedness: Reduction and Preservation in Phonology* (Cambridge University Press, 2006).

The Cambridge Handbook of Phonology

Edited by **Paul de Lacy**

CAMBRIDGE UNIVERSITY PRESS
Cambridge, New York, Melbourne, Madrid, Cape Town, Singapore, São Paulo

Cambridge University Press
The Edinburgh Building, Cambridge CB2 2RU, UK

Published in the United States of America by Cambridge University Press, New York

www.cambridge.org
Information on this title: www.cambridge.org/9780521848794

© Cambridge University Press 2007

First published 2007

Printed in the United Kingdom at the University Press, Cambridge

A catalogue record for this book is available from the British Library

ISBN-13 978-0-521-84879-4 hardback
ISBN-10 0-521-84879-2 hardback

Contents

Contributors

John D. Alderete, Assistant Professor, Department of Linguistics, Simon Fraser University.

Arto Anttila, Assistant Professor, Department of Linguistics, Stanford University.

Diana Archangeli, Professor, Department of Linguistics, University of Arizona.

Eric Baković, Assistant Professor, Linguistics Department, University of California, San Diego.

Ricardo Bermúdez-Otero, Lecturer, Department of Linguistics and English Language, University of Manchester.

Barbara Bernhardt, Associate Professor, School of Audiology and Speech Sciences, University of British Columbia.

Paula Fikkert, Associate Professor, Department of Dutch Language and Culture, Radboud Universiteit Nijmegen.

Stefan A. Frisch, Assistant Professor, Department of Communication Sciences and Disorders, University of South Florida.

Matthew Gordon, Associate Professor, Department of Linguistics, University of California, Santa Barbara.

Carlos Gussenhoven, Professor, Department of Linguistics, Radboud Universiteit Nijmegen and Queen Mary, University of London.

T. A. Hall, Assistant Professor, Department of Germanic Studies, Indiana University, Bloomington.

John Harris, Professor, Department of Phonetics and Linguistics, University College London.

René Kager, Professor, Utrecht Institute of Linguistics OTS (Onderzoeksinstituut voor Taal en Spraak), Utrecht University.

John Kingston, Professor, Department of Linguistics, University of Massachusetts Amherst.

Paul de Lacy, Assistant Professor, Department of Linguistics, Rutgers, The State University of New Jersey.

John J. McCarthy, Professor, Department of Linguistics, University of Massachusetts Amherst.

Alan Prince, Professor II, Department of Linguistics, Rutgers, The State University of New Jersey.

Douglas Pulleyblank, Professor, Department of Linguistics, University of British Columbia.

Keren Rice, Professor, Department of Linguistics, University of Toronto.

Joseph Paul Stemberger, Professor, Department of Linguistics, University of British Columbia.

Donca Steriade, Professor, Department of Linguistics and Philosophy, Massachusetts Institute of Technology.

Bruce Tesar, Associate Professor, Department of Linguistics, Rutgers, The State University of New Jersey.

Hubert Truckenbrodt, Assistent, Seminar für Sprachwissenschaft, Universität Tübingen.

Suzanne Urbanczyk, Associate Professor, Department of Linguistics, University of Victoria.

Adam Ussishkin, Assistant Professor, Department of Linguistics, University of Arizona.

Moira Yip, Professor, Department of Phonetics and Linguistics; Co-director, Centre for Human Communication, University College London.

Draga Zec, Professor, Department of Linguistics, Cornell University.

Acknowledgements

For a book of this size and scope it is probably unsurprising that many people contributed to its formation.

At Cambridge University Press, I owe Andrew Winnard a great deal of thanks. The idea for The Cambridge Handbook of Phonology was his, and it was a pleasure developing the project with him. My thanks also to Helen Barton for providing a great deal of editorial help throughout the process.

One of the most exhausting jobs was compiling, checking, and making consistent the seventeen hundred references. I am very grateful to Catherine Kitto and Michael O'Keefe for dealing with this task, and to Jessica Rett for contributing as well.

Of course, without the contributors, this volume would not exist. My thanks to them for meeting such difficult deadlines and responding so quickly to my queries.

A number of people commented on the initial proposal for this book, and every chapter was reviewed. My thanks go to: three anonymous reviewers, Crystal Akers, Akinbiyi Akinlabi, Daniel Altshuler, Eric Baković, Ricardo Bermúdez-Otero, Lee Bickmore, Andries Coetzee, José Elías-Ulloa, Colin Ewen, Randall Gess, Martine Grice, Bruce Hayes, Larry Hyman, Pat Keating, Martin Krämer, Seunghun Lee, John McCarthy, Laura McGarrity, Chloe Marshall, Nazarré Merchant, Jaye Padgett, Joe Pater, Alan Prince, Jessica Rett, Curt Rice, Sharon Rose, Elisabeth O. Selkirk, Nina Topintzi, Moira Yip, and Kie Zuraw. Of the reviewers, I must single out Kate Ketner and Michael O'Keefe: they carefully reviewed several of the articles each, provided the perspective of the book's intended audience, and also contributed a large number of insightful comments. There are also several times as many people again who 'unofficially' reviewed chapters for each author – my thanks to all those who in doing so contributed to this handbook.

Finally, I thank my colleagues and friends for advising and supporting me in this exhausting endeavour: Colin Ewen, Jane Grimshaw, John McCarthy, Alan Prince, Curt Rice, Ian Roberts, Moira Yip, and my colleagues in the linguistics department at Rutgers. Finally, I thank my family – Mary and Reg for their unfailing support, and Sapphire and Socrates for their help with editing. Most of all I thank Catherine, whose encouragement and support were essential to my survival.

Introduction: aims and content

Paul de Lacy

Introduction

Phonological theory deals with the mental representation and computation of human speech sounds. This book contains introductory chapters on research in this field, focusing on current theories and recent developments.

1 Aims

This book has slightly different aims for different audiences. It aims to provide concise summaries of current research in a broad range of areas for researchers in phonology, linguistics, and allied fields such as psychology, computer science, anthropology, and related areas of cognitive science. For students of phonology, it aims to be a bridge between textbooks and research articles.

Perhaps this book's most general aim is to fill a gap. I write this introduction ten years after Goldsmith's (1995) *Handbook of Phonological Theory* was published. Since then, phonological theory has changed significantly. For example, while Chomsky & Halle's (1968) *The Sound Pattern of English* (*SPE*) and its successors were the dominant research paradigms over a decade ago, the majority of current research articles employ Optimality Theory, proposed by Prince & Smolensky (2004). Many chapters in this book assume or discuss OT approaches to phonology.

Another striking change has been the move away from the formalist conception of grammar to a functionalist one: there have been more and more appeals to articulatory effort, perceptual distinctness, and economy of parsing as modes of explanation in phonology. These are just two of the many developments discussed in this book.

2 Website

Supplementary materials for this book can be found on the website: http://handbookofphonology.rutgers.edu.

3 Audience and role

The chapters are written with upper-level undergraduate students and above in mind. As part of a phonology course, they will serve as supplementary or further readings to textbooks. All the chapters assume some knowledge of the basics of the most popular current theories of phonology. Many of the chapters use Optimality Theory (Prince & Smolensky 2004), so appropriate background reading would be, for example, Kager's (1999) textbook *Optimality Theory*, and for the more advanced McCarthy's (2002) *A Thematic Guide to Optimality Theory*.

Because it is not a textbook, reading the book from beginning to end will probably not prove worthwhile. Certainly, there is no single common theme that is developed step-by-step throughout the chapters, and there is no chapter that is a prerequisite for understanding any other (even though the chapters cross-reference each other extensively). So, the best use of this book for the reader is as a way to expand his/her knowledge of phonology in particular areas after the groundwork provided by a textbook or phonology course has been laid.

This book is also not a history of phonology or of any particular topics. While it is of course immensely valuable to understand the theoretical precursors to current phonological theories, the focus here is limited to issues in recent research.

4 Structure and content

The chapters in this book are grouped into five parts: (I) conceptual issues, (II) prosody, (III) segmental phenomena, (IV) internal interfaces, and (V) external interfaces.

The 'conceptual issues' part discusses theoretical concepts which have enduring importance in phonological theory: i.e. functionalist vs. formalist approaches to language, markedness theory, derivation, representation, and contrast.

Part II focuses on the segment and above: specifically prosodic structure, sonority, and tone. Part III focuses on subsegmental structure: features and feature operations. The chapter topics were chosen so as to cover a wide range of phenomena and fit in with the aims of phonology courses. However, while the areas in Parts II and III are traditionally considered distinct, the boundaries are at least fluid. For example, Gussenhoven

(Ch.11) observes that research on tone and intonation seems to be converging on the same theoretical devices, so the tone–intonation divide should not be considered a theoretically significant division. In contrast, some traditionally unified phenomena may consist of theoretically distinct areas: Archangeli & Pulleyblank (Ch.15) observe that there may be two separate types of harmony that require distinct theoretical mechanisms. Nevertheless, the division into discrete phenomena is inevitable in a book of this kind as in practice this is how they are often taught in courses and conceived of in research.

Part IV deals with 'internal interfaces' – the interaction of the phonological component with other commonly recognized modules – i.e. phonetics (Kingston Ch.17), syntax (Truckenbrodt Ch.18), and morphology (Ussishkin Ch.19 and Urbanczyk Ch.20).

Part V focuses on a variety of areas that do not fit easily into Parts I–IV. These include well-established areas such as diachronic phonology (Bermúdez-Otero Ch.21), areas that have recently grown significantly (e.g. language acquisition – Fikkert Ch.23) or have recently provided significant insight into phonological theory (e.g. free variation – Anttila Ch.22, learnability – Tesar Ch.24, phonological impairments – Bernhardt & Stemberger Ch.25).

Practical reasons forced difficult decisions about what to exclude. Nevertheless, as a number of phonologists kindly offered their views on what should be included I hope that the topics covered here manage to reflect the current concerns of the field.

While phonological research currently employs many different transcription systems, in this book an effort has been made to standardize transcriptions to the International Phonetic Alphabet (the IPA) wherever possible: http://www2.arts.gla.ac.uk/IPA/index.html.

Chart of the International Phonetic Alphabet
(revised 1993, updated 1996)

THE INTERNATIONAL PHONETIC ALPHABET (revised to 2005)

CONSONANTS (PULMONIC)   © 2005 IPA

	Bilabial	Labiodental	Dental	Alveolar	Postalveolar	Retroflex	Palatal	Velar	Uvular	Pharyngeal	Glottal
Plosive	p b			t d		ʈ ɖ	c ɟ	k ɡ	q ɢ		ʔ
Nasal	m	ɱ		n		ɳ	ɲ	ŋ	N		
Trill	ʙ			r					ʀ		
Tap or Flap		ⱱ		ɾ		ɽ					
Fricative	ɸ β	f v	θ ð	s z	ʃ ʒ	ʂ ʐ	ç ʝ	x ɣ	χ ʁ	ħ ʕ	h ɦ
Lateral fricative				ɬ ɮ							
Approximant		ʋ		ɹ		ɻ	j	ɰ			
Lateral approximant				l		ɭ	ʎ	ʟ			

Where symbols appear in pairs, the one to the right represents a voiced consonant. Shaded areas denote articulations judged impossible.

CONSONANTS (NON-PULMONIC)

Clicks	Voiced implosives	Ejectives
ʘ Bilabial	ɓ Bilabial	ʼ Examples:
ǀ Dental	ɗ Dental/alveolar	pʼ Bilabial
ǃ (Post)alveolar	ʄ Palatal	tʼ Dental/alveolar
ǂ Palatoalveolar	ɠ Velar	kʼ Velar
ǁ Alveolar lateral	ʛ Uvular	sʼ Alveolar fricative

OTHER SYMBOLS

ʍ Voiceless labial-velar fricative   ɕ ʑ Alveolo-palatal fricatives
w Voiced labial-velar approximant   ɺ Voiced alveolar lateral flap
ɥ Voiced labial-palatal approximant   ɧ Simultaneous ʃ and x
ʜ Voiceless epiglottal fricative
ʢ Voiced epiglottal fricative   Affricates and double articulations can be represented by two symbols joined by a tie bar if necessary.   k͡p t͡s
ʡ Epiglottal plosive

VOWELS

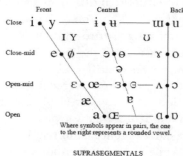

Where symbols appear in pairs, the one to the right represents a rounded vowel.

SUPRASEGMENTALS

ˈ Primary stress
ˌ Secondary stress   ˌfoʊnəˈtɪʃən
ː Long   eː
ˑ Half-long   eˑ
˘ Extra-short   ĕ
| Minor (foot) group
‖ Major (intonation) group
. Syllable break   ɹi.ækt
‿ Linking (absence of a break)

DIACRITICS   Diacritics may be placed above a symbol with a descender, e.g. ŋ̊

̥ Voiceless	n̥ d̥	̤ Breathy voiced	b̤ a̤	̪ Dental	t̪ d̪
̬ Voiced	s̬ t̬	̰ Creaky voiced	b̰ a̰	̺ Apical	t̺ d̺
ʰ Aspirated	tʰ dʰ	̼ Linguolabial	t̼ d̼	̻ Laminal	t̻ d̻
̹ More rounded	ɔ̹	ʷ Labialized	tʷ dʷ	̃ Nasalized	ẽ
̜ Less rounded	ɔ̜	ʲ Palatalized	tʲ dʲ	ⁿ Nasal release	dⁿ
̟ Advanced	u̟	ˠ Velarized	tˠ dˠ	ˡ Lateral release	dˡ
̠ Retracted	e̠	ˤ Pharyngealized	tˤ dˤ	̚ No audible release	d̚
̈ Centralized	ë	̴ Velarized or pharyngealized	ɫ		
̽ Mid-centralized	e̽	̝ Raised	e̝ (ɹ̝ = voiced alveolar fricative)		
̩ Syllabic	n̩	̞ Lowered	e̞ (β̞ = voiced bilabial approximant)		
̯ Non-syllabic	e̯	̘ Advanced Tongue Root	e̘		
˞ Rhoticity	ɚ a˞	̙ Retracted Tongue Root	e̙		

TONES AND WORD ACCENTS

LEVEL		CONTOUR	
e̋ or ˥	Extra high	ě or ˩˥	Rising
é ˦	High	ê ˥˩	Falling
ē ˧	Mid	e᷄ ˦˥	High rising
è ˨	Low	e᷅ ˩˨	Low rising
ȅ ˩	Extra low	e᷈ ˧˩˧	Rising-falling
↓	Downstep	↗	Global rise
↑	Upstep	↘	Global fall

This chart is provided courtesy of the International Phonetics Association, Department of Theoretical and Applied Linguistics, School of English, Aristotle University of Thessaloniki, Thessaloniki 54124, GREECE.

1

Themes in phonology

Paul de Lacy

1.1 Introduction

This chapter has two aims. One is to provide a brief outline of the structure of this book; this is the focus of Section 1.1.1. The other – outlined in Section 1.1.2 – is to identify several of the major themes that run throughout.

1.1.1 Structure

Several different factors have influenced the contents and structure of this Handbook. The topics addressed reflect theoretical concerns that have endured in phonology, but they were also chosen for pedagogical reasons (i.e. many advanced phonology courses cover many of the topics here). There were also 'traditional' reasons for some aspects of organization. While these concerns converge in the main, there are some points of disagreement. For example, there is a traditional distinction between the phonology of lexical tone and intonation, hence the separate chapters by Yip (Ch.10) and Gussenhoven (Ch.11). However, Gussenhoven (11.7) comments that theoretically such a division may be artificial.

Consequently, it is not possible to identify a single unifying theoretical theme that accounts for the structure of this book. Nevertheless, the topics were not chosen at random; they reflect many of the current concerns of the field. In a broad sense, these concerns can be considered in terms of representation, derivation, and the trade-off between the two. 'Representation' refers to the formal structure of the objects that the phonological component manipulates. 'Derivation' refers to the relations between those objects.

Concern with representation can be seen throughout the following chapters. Chomsky & Halle (1968) (*SPE*) conceived of phonological representation as a string of segments, which are unordered bundles of features. Since then, representation has become more elaborate. Below the segment, it is widely accepted that features are hierarchically organized (see discussion and references in Hall Ch.13). Above the segment, several layers of constituents are now commonly recognized, called the 'prosodic hierarchy' (Selkirk 1984b). Figure (1) gives a portion of an output form's representation; it categorizes the chapters of this book in terms of their representational concerns. There is a great deal of controversy over almost every aspect of the representation given below – Figure (1) should be considered a rough expositional device here, not a theoretical assertion; the chapters cited should be consulted for details.

(1)

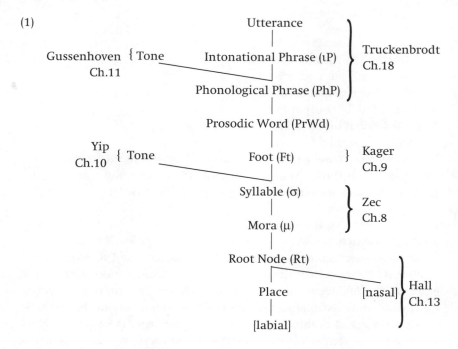

Harris (Ch.6) should be added to the chapters cited in (1); Harris' chapter is concerned with broader principles behind representation, including the notion of constituency, whether certain sub-constituents are phonologically prominent (i.e. headedness), and hierarchical relations.

   Not represented in (1) is the interaction between constituents. For example, de Lacy (Ch.12) examines the interaction of tone, the foot, and segmental properties. Similarly, a part of Kager (Ch.9) is about the relation between the foot and its subconstituents. At the segmental level, three chapters are concerned with the interaction of segments and parts of segments: Baković (Ch.14), Archangeli & Pulleyblank (Ch.15), and Alderete & Frisch (Ch.16). For example, Baković's chapter discusses the pressure for segments to have identical values for some feature (particularly Place of Articulation).

   Figure (2) identifies the chapters that are concerned with discussing the interaction of different representations. For example, Truckenbrodt (Ch.18) discusses the relation of syntactic phrases to phonological phrases. Ussishkin (Ch.19) and Urbanczyk (Ch.20) do the same for the relation of morphological

and phonological structure. Kingston (Ch.17) discusses the relation of phonological to phonetic structures.

(2) **Syntax**   **Morphology**

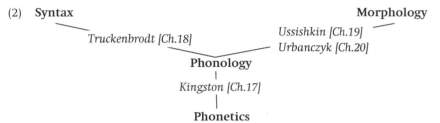

Truckenbrodt [Ch.18]   Ussishkin [Ch.19]
                                        Urbanczyk [Ch.20]
                  Phonology
                Kingston [Ch.17]

                  Phonetics

There is also a 'derivational' theme that runs through the book chapters.
McCarthy (Ch.5) focuses on evidence that there are relations between
morphologically derived forms, and theories about the nature of those
relations. Discussion of derivation has traditionally focused on the relation
between input and output forms, and between members of morphological
paradigms. However, the traditional conception of derivation has been
challenged in Optimality Theory by McCarthy & Prince's (1995a, 1999)
Correspondence Theory – the same relations that hold between separate
derivational forms (i.e. input~output, paradigmatic base~derivative) also
hold in the same output form between reduplicants and their bases; thus
Urbanczyk's (Ch.20) discussion of reduplication can be seen as primarily
about derivation, in this broadened sense.

   Of course, no chapter is entirely about the representation of constituents;
all discuss derivation of those constituents. In serialist terms, 'derivation of
constituents' means the rules by which those constituents are constructed.
In parallelist (e.g. Optimality Theoretic) terms, it in effect refers to the
constraints and mechanisms that evaluate competing representations.

   There is a set of chapters whose primary concerns relate to both representation and derivation: Prince (Ch.2), Gordon (Ch.3), Rice (Ch.4), and
Steriade (Ch.7) discuss topics that are in effect meta-theories of representation and derivation. Gordon (Ch.3) examines functionalism – a name for a
set of theories that directly relate to or derive phonological representations
(and potentially derivations) from phonetic concerns. Rice (Ch.4) discusses
markedness, which is effectively a theory of possible phonological representations and derivations. Steriade (Ch.7) discusses the idea of phonological contrast, and how it influences representation and derivation.

   Rice's discussion of markedness makes the current tension between
representation- and derivation-based explanations particularly clear.
Broadly speaking, there have been two approaches to generalizations like
"an epenthetic consonant is often [ʔ]". One assigns [ʔ] a representation that
is different (often less elaborate) than other segments; the favouring of
epenthetic [ʔ] over other segments is then argued to follow from general
derivational principles of structural simplification. The other is to appeal
to derivational principles such as (a) constraints that favour [ʔ] over every
other segment and (b) no constraint that favours those other segments over

[?]; [?] need not be representationally simple (or otherwise remarkable) in this approach. These two approaches illustrate how the source of explanation – i.e. derivation and representation – is still disputed. The same issue is currently true of subsegmental structure – elaborated derivational mechanisms may allow simpler representational structures (Yip 2004).

Part V of this book contains a diverse array of phonological phenomena which do not fit easily into the themes of representational and derivational concerns. Instead, their unifying theme is that they are all areas which have been the focus of a great deal of recent attention and have provided significant insight into phonological issues; this point is made explicitly by Fikkert (Ch.23) for language acquisition, but also applies to the other areas: diachronic phonology (Bermúdez-Otero Ch.21), free variation (Anttila Ch.22), learnability (Tesar Ch.24), and phonological disorders (Bernhardt & Stemberger Ch.25). There are many points of interconnection between these chapters and the others, such as the evidence that phonological disorders and language acquisition provide for markedness.

Standing quite apart from all of these chapters is Prince (Ch.2). Prince's chapter discusses the methodology of theory exploration and evaluation.

In summary, no single theoretical issue accounts for the choice of topics and their organization in this book. However, many themes run throughout the chapters; the rest of this chapter identifies some of the more prominent ones.

1.1.2   Summary of themes

One of the clearest themes seen in this book is the influence of Optimality Theory (OT), proposed by Prince & Smolensky (2004).[1] The majority of chapters discuss OT, reflecting the fact that the majority of recent research publications employ this theory and a good portion of the remainder critique or otherwise discuss it.[2] However, one of the sub-themes found in the chapters is that there are many different conceptions and sub-theories of OT, although certain core principles are commonly maintained. For example, some theories employ just two levels (the input and output), while others employ more (e.g. Stratal OT – McCarthy 5.4). Some employ a strict and totally ordered constraint ranking, while others allow constraints to be unranked or overlap (see Anttila 22.3.3 and Tesar 24.4 for discussion). Theories of constraints differ significantly among authors, as do conceptions of representation (see esp. Harris Ch.6).

Another theme that links many of the chapters is the significance of representation and how it contributes to explanation. The late 1970s and 1980s moved towards limiting the form of phonological rules and elaborating the representation by devices such as autosegmental association, planar segregation, lack of specification, and feature privativity. In contrast, Harris (6.1) observes that the last decade has seen increased reliance on constraint form and interaction as sources of explanation. Constraint interaction as an explanatory device appears in many of the chapters. Section 1.3 summarizes the main points.

Section 1.4 discusses the increasing influence of Functionalism in phonology, a theme that is examined in detail by Gordon (Ch.3). Reference to articulatory, perceptual, and parsing considerations as a source of phonological explanation is a major change from the Formalist orientation of *SPE* and its successors. This issue recurs in a number of chapters, some explicitly (e.g Harris 6.2.2, Steriade 7.5), and in others as an implicit basis for evaluating the adequacy of constraints.

Of course, the following chapters identify many other significant themes in current phonological theory; this chapter focuses solely on the ones given above because they recur in the majority of chapters and are presented as some of the field's central concerns.

1.2   The influence of Optimality Theory

Optimality Theory is explicitly discussed or assumed in many chapters in this volume, just as it is in a great deal of current phonological research ('current' here refers to the time of writing – the middle of 2005). This section starts by reviewing OT's architecture and core properties. The following sections identify particular aspects that prove significant in the following chapters, such as the notion of faithfulness and its role in derivation in Section 1.2.1, some basic results of constraint interaction in Section 1.2.2, and its influence on conceptions of the lexicon in Section 1.2.3. The sections identify some of the challenges facing OT as well as its successes and areas which still excite controversy. The relation of OT to other theories is discussed in Section 1.2.4.

OT Architecture

OT is a model of grammar – i.e. both syntax and phonology (and morphology, if it is considered a separate component); the following discussion will focus exclusively on the phonological aspect and refer to the model in (3).

(3)   *OT architecture*

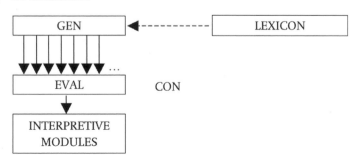

For phonology, the GEN(erator) module takes its input either directly from the lexicon or from the output of a separate syntax module. GEN creates a possibly infinite set of candidate output forms; the ability to elaborate on the input without arbitrary restraint is called 'freedom of analysis'. In Prince & Smolensky's original formulation, every output candidate literally contained the input; to account for deletion, pieces of the input could remain unparsed (i.e. not incorporated into prosodic structure) which meant they would not be phonetically interpreted. Since McCarthy & Prince (1995a/1999), the dominant view is that output candidates do not contain the input, but are related to it by a formal relation called 'correspondence'; see Section 1.2.1 for details (cf. Goldrick 2000).

One significant restriction on GEN is that it cannot alter the morphological affiliation of segments ('consistency of exponence' – McCarthy & Prince 1993b). In practice it is common to also assume that GEN requires every output segment to be fully specified for subsegmental features, bans floating (or 'unparsed') features (except for tone – Yip 10.2.2, Gussenhoven 11.5.1), and imposes restrictions on the form of prosodic and subsegmental structure (though in some work they are considered violable – e.g. Selkirk 1995a, Crowhurst 1996, cf. Hyde 2002).

The EVAL(uator) module determines the 'winner' by referring to the constraints listed in CON (the universal constraint repository) and their language-specific ranking. Constraints are universal; the only variation across languages is (a) the constraints' ranking, and (b) the content of the lexicon. The winner is sent to the relevant interpretive component (the 'phonetic component' for phonology – Kingston Ch.17).

There are two general types of constraint: Markedness and Faithfulness. Markedness constraints evaluate the structure of the output form, while Faithfulness constraints evaluate its relationship to other forms (canonically, the input – see McCarthy Ch.5).[3] As an example, the Markedness constraint ONSET is violated once for every syllable in a candidate that lacks an onset (i.e. every syllable that does not start with a non-nuclear consonant – Zec 8.3.2). [ap.ki] violates ONSET once, while [a.i.o] violates it three times. The Faithfulness constraint I(nput)O(utput)-MAX is violated once for every input segment that does not have an output correspondent: e.g. /apki/ → [pi] violates IO-MAX twice (see Section 1.2.1 for details).

In each grammar the constraints were originally assumed to be totally ranked (although evidence for their exact ranking may not be obtainable in particular languages); for alternatives see Anttila (Ch.22). Constraints are violable; the winner may – and almost certainly will – violate constraints. However, the winner violates the constraints 'minimally' in the sense that for each losing candidate L, (a) there is some constraint K that favors the winner over L and (b) K outranks all constraints that favor L over the winner (a constraint 'favors' x over y if x incurs fewer violations of it than y); see Prince (2.1.1) for details.

Tableaux

The mapping from an underlying form to a surface form – a 'winner' – is represented in a 'tableau', as in (4). The aim here is to describe how to read a tableau, *not* how to determine a winner or establish a ranking: see Prince (2.1.1) for the latter.

The top left cell contains the input. The rest of the leftmost column contains candidate outputs. The winner is marked by the 'pointing hand'. C_3 outranks C_4 (shorthand: $C_3 \gg C_4$), as shown by the solid vertical line between them (C_1 outranks C_3, and C_2 outranks C_3, too). The dotted line between C_1 and C_2 indicates that no ranking can be *shown* to hold between them; it does not mean that there is no ranking.

Apart from the pointing hand, the winner can be identified by starting at the leftmost constraint in the tableau and eliminating a candidate if it incurs *more* violations than another contending candidate, where violations are marked by *s. For example, $cand_4$ incurs more violations than the others on C_1, so it is eliminated from the competition, shown by the '!'. C_2 likewise rules out $cand_3$. While $cand_4$ incurs fewer violations of C_3 than $cand_1$, it has already been eliminated, so its violations are irrelevant (shown by shading). C_3 makes no distinction between the remaining candidates as they both incur the same number of violations; it is fine for the winner to violate a constraint, as long as no other candidate violates the constraint *less*.

Another point comes out by inspecting this tableau: $cand_1$ incurs a proper subset of $cand_2$'s violation marks. Consequently, $cand_2$ can never win with any ranking of these constraints – $cand_1$ is a 'harmonic bound' for $cand_2$ (Samek-Lodovici & Prince 1999). Harmonic bounding follows from the fact that to avoid being a perpetual loser, a candidate has to incur fewer violations of some constraint for every other candidate; $cand_2$ doesn't incur fewer violations than $cand_1$ on any constraint.

(4)   *A 'classic' tableau*

/input/	C_1	C_2	C_3	C_4
☞ (a) $cand_1$			*	*
(b) $cand_2$			*	* *!
(c) $cand_3$		*!		*
(d) $cand_4$	*!			

In some tableaux a candidate is marked with ☛ or ☜: these symbols indicate a winner that should not win – i.e. it is ungrammatical; in practical terms it means that the tableau has the wrong ranking or is considering the wrong set of constraints. In some tableaux, ☠ is used to mark a winner that is universally ungrammatical – i.e. it never shows up under any ranking; it indicates that there is a harmonic bound for the ☠-candidate.

The tableau form in (4) was introduced by Prince & Smolensky (2004) and is the most widely used way of representing candidate competition. Another method is proposed by Prince (2002a), called the 'comparative tableau'; it is used in this book by Prince (Ch.2), Baković (Ch.14), and Tesar (Ch.24).

The comparative tableau represents competition between pairs of candidates directly, rather than indirectly through violation marks. The leftmost column lists the winner followed by a competitor. A 'W' indicates that the constraint prefers the desired winner (i.e. the winner incurs fewer violations of that constraint than its competitor), a blank cell indicates that the constraint makes no preference, and an L indicates that the candidate favors the loser.

It is easy to see if a winner does in fact win: it must be possible to rearrange columns so that every row has at least one W before any L. Rankings are also easy to determine because on every row some W must precede all Ls. It's therefore clear from tableau (5) that both C_1 and C_2 must outrank C_3, and that C_1 must outrank C_4. It's also clear that it's not possible to determine the rankings between C_1 and C_2, C_2 and C_4, and C_3 and C_4 here. Harmonic bounding by the winner is also easy to spot: the winner is a harmonic bound for a candidate if there are only W's in its row (e.g. for the winner and $cand_2$ – it's harder to identify harmonic bounding between losers).

The comparative tableau format is not yet as widely used as the classic tableau despite having a number of presentational and – most importantly – analytical advantages over the classic type, as detailed by Prince (2002a).

(5) *A comparative tableau*

/input/	C_1	C_2	C_3	C_4
winner~cand$_2$				W
winner~cand$_3$		W	L	
winner~cand$_4$	W		L	L

Comparative tableaux can be annotated further if necessary: *e* can be used instead of a blank cell, and subscript numbers can indicate the number of violations of the loser in a particular cell (or even the winner's vs. loser's violations). The winner need not be repeated in every row: the top leftmost cell can contain the input→winner mapping, or the second row can contain the winner and its violations and the other rows can list the losers alone (i.e. just '~ *loser*' instead of '*winner~loser*').

Bernhardt & Stemberger (1998) propose another way of representing tableaux that is similar to the classic form; see Chapter 25 for details.

Core principles

Prince & Smolensky (2004) identify core OT principles for computing input→output mappings, including freedom of analysis, parallelism, constraint violability, and ranking. As they observe, many theories of CON and representation are compatible with these principles. Consequently, a great deal of work in OT has focused on developing a theory of constraints; for proposals regarding other principles, see Section 1.2.4.

The dominant theories before OT – *SPE* and its successors – employed rules and a 'serial' derivation. For them, the input to the phonological component underwent a series of functions ('rules') that took the previous output and produced the input to the next until no more rules could apply. For example, /okap/ would undergo the rule $C \rightarrow \emptyset/\_]_\sigma$ to produce [oka] which would then serve as the input to the rule $V \rightarrow \emptyset/_\sigma[\_$ to produce [ka]. Rule-based derivation is described in detail in McCarthy (Ch.5). In contrast, the winner in OT is determined by referring to the constraint hierarchy and by comparison with (in principle) the entire candidate set (McCarthy & Prince 1993b:Ch.1§1).

Certainly, other theories had and have since proposed such concepts as constraints and two- or three-level grammars (e.g. Theory of Constraints and Repair Strategies – Paradis 1988; Harmonic Phonology – Goldsmith 1993a, Two-level Phonology – Koskenniemi 1983, Karttunen 1993; Declarative Phonology – Scobbie 1992, Coleman 1995, Scobbie, Coleman, and Bird 1996). However, OT's combination of these ideas and the key notions of constraint universality, ranking, and violability proved to have wide and almost immediate appeal.

The following sections discuss aspects of the theory that recur or are assumed in many of the following chapters. Section 1.2.1 discusses derivation, correspondence, and faithfulness. Section 1.2.2 discusses the form of the constraint component CON and some important constraint interactions while Section 1.2.3 examines OT's influence on the concept of the lexicon. Section 1.2.4 discusses the several different versions of OT that currently exist and their relation to other extant phonological theories.

1.2.1 Derivation and faithfulness

A concept that recurs throughout the following chapters is 'faithfulness' – it is discussed explicitly by McCarthy (Ch.5) and faithfulness constraints are used in many of the discussions of empirical phenomena.

In *SPE* and the theories that adopted its core aspects of rules and rule-ordering, there is no mechanism that requires preservation of input material. If input /abc/ surfaces as output [abc], the similarity is merely an epiphenomenon of rule non-application: either all rules fail to apply to /abc/, or the rules that apply do so in such a way as to inadvertently produce the same output as the input.

McCarthy & Prince (1995a, 1999) propose a reconceptualization of identity relations. Segments in different forms can stand in a relation of 'correspondence'. For example, the segments in an input $/k_1æ_2t_3/$ and winning faithful output $[k_1æ_2t_3]$ are in correspondence with one another, where subscript numerals mark these relations. Equally, the segments in an unfaithful pair, $/k_1æ_2t_3/ \rightarrow [d_1ɔ_2g_2]$, still correspond with one another, even though in this case two segments have metathesized and all have undergone drastic featural change. In keeping with 'freedom of analysis', correspondence relations can vary freely among candidates. For example, input $/k_1æ_2t_3/$ has the outputs $[k_1æ_2t_3]$, $[k_1æ_2]$ (deletion of $/t/$), $[k_1æ_2t_3i]$ (epenthesis of [i]), $[k_1t_3æ_2]$ (metathesis of $/æt/$), $[k_1æ_{2,3}]$ (coalescence of $/æ/$ and $/t/$ to form $[æ̡]$), and combinations such as $[t_3æ_2]$ (metathesis of $/æt/$ and deletion of $/k/$) and forms that are harmonically bounded (i.e. can never win) such as $[k_3æ_3t_2]$, and so on.

Constraints on faithfulness regulate the presence, featural identity, and linear order of segments. The ones proposed in McCarthy & Prince (1995a) that appear in this book are given in (6).

(6) *Faithfulness constraint summary (from McCarthy & Prince 1995a)*
  (a) Faithfulness constraints on segmental presence (e.g. Zec 8.3.2)
  Max   "Incur a violation for each input segment x such that x has no output correspondent." (Don't delete.)
  Dep   "Incur a violation for each output segment x such that x has no input correspondent." (Don't epenthesize.)
  (b) Faithfulness constraints on featural identity (e.g. Steriade 7.4.3)
  Ident[F]   "Incur a violation for each input segment x such that x is $[αF]$ and x's ouput correspondent is $[-αF]$." (Don't change feature F's value.)
  (c) Faithfulness constraints on linear order (e.g. de Lacy 12.6)
  Linearity   "For every pair of input segments x,y and their output correspondents x',y', incur a violation if x precedes y and y' precedes x'." (No metathesis.)
  (d) Faithfulness constraints on one-to-many relationships (e.g. Yip 10.3.3)
  Uniformity   "Incur a violation for each output segment that corresponds to more than one input segment." (No coalescence.)

McCarthy & Prince (1995a, 1999) argue that correspondence relations can also hold within candidate outputs, specifically between reduplicative morphemes and their bases. Consequently, the candidate $[\underline{p_1a_2}p_1a_2t_3a_4]$, where the underlined portion is the reduplicant, indicates that the reduplicant's [p] corresponds to the base's [p], and the reduplicant's [a] to the base's. This proposal draws a direct link between the identity effects seen in input→output mappings and those in base-reduplicant relations. Other elaborations of faithfulness are discussed in Section 1.2.2.

Parallelism

Faithfulness relates to the concept of parallelism: there is essentially a 'flat derivation' with the input related directly to output forms. As the chapters show, a lot of the success and controversy over parallelism arises in 'local' and 'non-local' interactions. One success is in its resolution of ordering paradoxes found in rule-based approaches. For example,

Ulithian's reduplication of /xas/ surfaces as [kakkasi] (Sohn & Bender 1973:45). Coda consonants assimilate to the following consonant, preventing the output from being *[xasxasi]. However, the form does not become the expected *[xaxxasi] because [xx] is banned. Instead, the resulting output is [kakkasi] – this form avoids [xx], satisfies the conditions on codas, and at the same time ensures that the reduplicant is as similar to the base as possible by altering the base's consonant from /x/ to [k].

The ordering paradox can be illustrated by a serialist rule-based analysis in (7). For the reduplicant to copy the base's [k] in [kakkasi], copying would have to be ordered *after* gemination and consequent fortition; however, reduplication *creates* the environment for gemination and fortition.

(7) *A serialist approach to Ulithian reduplication*

    INPUT: /RED+xasi/

    (a) REDUPLICATION: xas.xa.si

    (b) GEMINATION: xax.xa.si

    (c) [xx] FORTITION: *[xak.ka.si]

In contrast, Correspondence Theory (CT) provides an explanation by positing an identity relationship between the base and reduplicant. In tableau (8), CODACOND requires a coda consonant to agree with the features of the following consonant (after Itô 1986). *[xx] bans geminate fricatives. To force the input /x/ to become [k], both CODACOND and *[xx] must outrank IO-IDENT[continuant], a constraint that requires input-output specifications for continuancy to be preserved. Together, CODACOND and *[xx] favor the candidates with a [kk] – i.e. the winner [kak-kasi] and loser *[xak-kasi]. The crucial distinction between these two is that [kak-kasi]'s reduplicant copies its base's continuancy better than *[xak-kasi]'s. In short, the reason that [kak-kasi] wins is due to a direct requirement of identity between base and reduplicant (cf. discussion in Urbanczyk 20.2.6).

(8) *Ulithian reduplication in OT*

/RED-xasi/	CODA COND	*[xx]	BR-IDENT [continuant]	IO-IDENT [continuant]
(a) kak-kasi~xas-xasi	W		L	L
(b) kak-kasi~xax-xasi		W	L	L
(c) kak-kasi~xak-kasi			W	

Global conditions

Other aspects of faithfulness and parallelism have resulted in a great deal of controversy. One involves 'locality of interaction': a rule/constraint seems to apply at several places in the derivation (globality) or only once (opacity).

'Global rules' or 'global conditions' are discussed in detail by Anderson (1974): global conditions recur throughout a serial derivation. An example that I am familiar with is found in Rarotongan epenthesis (Kitto & de Lacy 1999). There is a ban on [ri] sequences, and this ban recurs throughout the derivation. So, while the usual epenthetic vowel is [i] (e.g. [kaːɾiti] 'carrot', [meneti] 'minute', [naeroni] 'nylon'), to avoid a [ri] sequence the epenthetic vowel after [ɾ] is a copy of the preceding one: e.g. [peːɾe] 'bail', [ʔamaɾa] 'hammer', [poːɾo] 'ball', [vuɾu] 'wool'. In serialist terms, the condition on [i] epenthesis seems straightforward: Ø → [i]/C$^{[-rhotic]}$__#, followed by a rule Ø → V$_i$ /V$_i$ɾ__#. The problem is that the ban on [ri] 'recurs' in the context [. . .iɾ]: if copying the vowel would result in a [ri] sequence, [a] is epenthesized as a last resort (e.g. [piɾa] 'bill', *[piɾi]). Consequently, the second rule needs to be reformulated as Ø → V$_i$ /[¬i]ɾ__#, followed by Ø → [a] elsewhere. These rules miss the point entirely: there is a constraint on [ri] sequences that continually guides epenthesis throughout the derivation.

   In OT, global conditions are expressed straightforwardly. A constraint on [ri] sequences outranks the constraints that would permit [ri]. The constraint M(¬i) is a shorthand for the constraints that favour [i] over all other vowels; AGREE(V) requires vowels to harmonize (Baković Ch.14, Archangeli & Pulleyblank Ch.15). In tableau (9), *[ri] is irrelevant because there is no [ɾ]; so the constraint M(¬i) favours [i] as the epenthetic vowel. In tableau (10), *[ri] blocks the epenthesis of [i], so the 'next best' option is taken – vowel harmony; this is one of the situations in which *[ri] blocks epenthesis. Tableau (11) illustrates the other: when harmony would produce an [ri] sequence, it is blocked and [a] is epenthesized instead.

(9)   *Epenthesize [i] after non-[ɾ]*

/menet/	*ri	M(¬i)	AGREE(V)
(a) meneti~menete		W	L
(b) meneti~meneta		W	

(10)   . . . *except when [i] epenthesis would result in [ri], then copy*

/vuːɾ/	*ri	M(¬i)	AGREE(V)
(a) vuːɾu ~ vuːɾi	W	L	W
(b) vuːɾu ~ vuːɾa			W

(11)   . . . *unless copying would create [ri], in which case epenthesize [a]*

/piːɾ/	*ri	M(¬i)	AGREE(V)	M(¬a)
(a) piːɾa ~piːɾi	W	L	L	W
(b) piːɾa~piːɾe				W

Opacity

OT's success in dealing with global rules raises a problem. In a sense, the opposite of a global rule is one that applies in only one place in the derivation but not elsewhere, even when its structural description is met. Such cases are called 'opaque' and can be broadly characterized as cases where output conditions are not surface true. For example, an opaque version of Rarotongan epenthesis would have *ri apply only to block default [i]-epenthesis after [r]; it would not block harmony, so allowing /pir/→[piri]. As McCarthy (5.4) discusses opacity in detail, little will be said about the details here (also see Bermúdez-Otero 21.3.2 for an example). Suffice to say that it is perhaps the major derivational issue that has faced OT over the past several years and continues to attract a great deal of attention. It has motivated a number of theories within OT, listed in McCarthy (Ch.5), and a number of critiques (e.g. Idsardi 1998, 2000). It is only fair to add that while opacity is seen as a significant challenge for OT, it also poses difficulties for a number of serialist theories: McCarthy (1999, 2003c) argues that serialist theories allow for unattested types of opaque derivation, where the input undergoes a number of rules that alter its form only for the output to end up identical to the input (i.e. 'Duke of York' derivations).

In summary, McCarthy & Prince's (1995a, 1999) theory that there is a direct requirement of identity between different derivational forms and even within forms has resulted in many theoretical developments and helped identify previously unrecognized phonological regularities. The opacity issue remains a challenge for OT, just as ordering paradoxes and global conditions pose problems for serialist rule-based frameworks.

1.2.2   Constraints and their interaction

Like many of the chapters in this book, a great deal of recent phonological research has been devoted to developing a theory of constraints. This Section discusses the basic constraint interactions and subtypes of faithfulness constraint that appear in the following chapters. The form of markedness constraints is intimately tied to issues of representation and Formalist/Functionalist outlook; these are discussed in Section 1.3 and Section 1.4 respectively.

Faithfulness

Many of the chapters employ faithfulness constraints that are elaborations of those in (6), both in terms of their dimension of application and environment-specificity.

McCarthy & Prince (1995a,1999) proposed that faithfulness relations held both on the input-output (IO) dimension and between bases and their reduplicants (BR) (see Urbanczyk Ch.20) for more on BR faithfulness). In its fundamentals, McCarthy & Prince's original conception of faithfulness

relations have remained unchanged: i.e. the core ideas of regulating
segmental presence, order, and identity are still at the core of faithfulness.
However, the dimensions over which faithfulness has been proposed to
apply have increased. Correspondence relations within paradigms have
been proposed by McCarthy, (1995, 2000c, 2005) and Benua (1997) (see
McCarthy 5.5), from inputs to reduplicants by Spaelti (1997), Struijke
(2000a/2002b) and others cited in Urbanczyk (20.2.6), and correspondence
relations within morphemes have been explored by Kitto & de Lacy (1999),
Hansson (2001b), and Rose & Walker (2004) (see Archangeli & Pulleyblank
15.3).

Others have proposed that there are environment-specific faithfulness
constraints. For example, Beckman's (1997, 1998) 'positional faithfulness'
theory proposes that constraints can preserve segments specifically in
stressed syllables, root-initial syllables, onsets, and roots (also see Casali
1996, Lombardi 1999). For example, ONSET-IDENT[voice] is violated if an
onset segment fails to preserve its underlying [voice] value, as in /aba/ →
[a.pa] (but not /ab/→ [ap]) (see e.g. Steriade 7.4.3, Baković 14.4.3). There is
currently controversy over whether positional faithfulness constraints are
necessary, or whether their role can be taken over by environment-specific
markedness constraints (Zoll 1998). For further elaborations on the form of
faithfulness constraints in terms of environment, see Jun (1995, 2004),
Steriade (2001b), and references cited therein.

In addition, some work seeks to eliminate particular faithfulness constraints, such as Keer (1999) for UNIFORMITY and Bernhardt & Stemberger
(1998) and (25.3.4) for DEP.

A significant controversy relates to segment- and feature-based faithfulness. In McCarthy & Prince's (1995a) proposal, only segments could stand
in correspondence with each other; a constraint like IDENT[F] then regulates featural identity as a property of a segment. In contrast, Lombardi
(1999) and others have proposed that features can stand directly in correspondence – a constraint like MAX[F] requires that every input feature have
a corresponding output feature. The difference is that the MAX[F] approach
allows features to have a life of their own outside of their segmental
sponsors. Consequently, the mapping /pa/→[a] does not violate IDENT[labial],
but does violate MAX[labial]. For tone, MAX[Tone] constraints seem to be
necessary (Yip 10.3, Myers 1997b), but for segments, it is common to use
IDENT[Feature]. For critical discussion, see Keer (1999:Ch.2), Struijke (2000a/
2002b:Ch.4), de Lacy (2002a§6.4.2), and Howe & Pulleyblank (2004).

Interactions of markedness and faithfulness

The source of much phonological explanation in OT derives from constraint interaction. At its most basic, the interaction of faithfulness and
markedness determines whether input segments survive intact in the
output (e.g. FAITH(α) » *α) or are eliminated (*α » FAITH(α)). In constraint
terms, this is putting it fairly crudely: there are subtleties of constraint

interaction that can prevent elimination of underlying segments in different contexts. For example, Steriade (7.4.3) shows how the general ranking $*\beta\gamma \gg *\alpha \gg$ IDENT[α] prevents an otherwise general /α/→[β] mapping before γ (i.e. 'allophony').

One theme that the chapters here lack is explicit discussion of constraints on inputs. This is because interactions of faithfulness and markedness constraints preclude the need for restrictions on the input ('richness of the base' – Prince & Smolensky 2004: Sec. 9.3). For example, there is no need to require that inputs in English never contain a bilabial click /⊙/; the general ranking $*⊙ \gg$ FAITH[⊙] will eliminate clicks in all output environments.

Turning to more subtle consequences of constraint interaction, a number of the following chapters employ a consequence of OT: the decoupling of rule antecedents and consequents. A rule like α→β describes both the 'problem' – i.e. α, and the 'solution' – i.e. β. In contrast, a constraint like $*\alpha$ identifies the problem without committing itself to any particular solution. $*\alpha$ could be satisfied by deleting α or altering α to β, for example. The proposal that the same constraint can have multiple solutions – both cross-linguistically and even in the same language – is called 'heterogeneity of process, homogeneity of target' (HoP-HoT – McCarthy 2002c: Sec 1.3.2).[4] Examples are found in various chapters: Baković (14.3) discusses the many ways that AGREE[F] can be satisfied, including assimilation, deletion, and epenthesis, with some languages employing more than one in different environments, Yip (10.3.3) shows how the OCP – a constraint on adjacent identical tones – can variously force tone deletion, movement, and coalescence in different languages, and de Lacy (12.6) shows how constraints that relate prosodic heads to sonority and tone can motivate metathesis, deletion, epenthesis, neutralization, and stress 'shift'.

While HoP-HoT has clearly desirable consequences in a number of cases, one current challenge is to account for situations where it over-predicts. For example, Lombardi (2001) argues that a ban on voiced coda obstruents can never result in deletion or epenthesis, only neutralization (e.g. such a ban can force /ab/ to become [ap] but never [a] or [a.b<u>i</u>]). This situation of 'too many solutions' is currently an area of increasing debate in OT (Lombardi 2001, Wilson 2000, 2001, Steriade 2001b, Pater 2003, de Lacy 2003b, Blumenfeld 2005).

Another consequence of constraint interaction is the Emergence of the Unmarked (TETU): a markedness constraint may make its presence felt in limited morphological or phonological environments (see e.g. Rice 4.5.1, 4.5.2, Urbanczyk 20.2.4). For example, a number of languages have only plain stops (e.g. Māori – Bauer 1993), so constraints against features like aspiration ($*^{h}$) must exist and in Māori outrank IDENT[^{h}]. In other languages where aspiration can appear fairly freely, IDENT[^{h}] outranks $*^{h}$. In contrast, in Cuzco Quechua $*^{h}$ has an 'emergent' effect – while aspirated stops appear in roots, they do not appear at all in affixes. Beckman (1997§4.2.3) shows that this pattern can be accounted for by the ranking Root-Ident[^{h}] » *^{h} » Ident[^{h}], where Root-Ident[^{h}] is a positional faithfulness constraint that preserves aspiration in root segments only. Steriade (Ch.7) provides details.

TETU has provided insight into many areas of phonology. However, there are some challenging issues related to it. One is that in some languages, TETU results in a segment that is otherwise banned. For example, Dutch has an epenthetic [ʔ] in onsets, even though [ʔ] is otherwise banned in the language. For discussion, see Łubowicz (2003:Ch.5).

1.2.3   The lexicon

The chapters make both explicit and implicit assumptions about the form of the lexicon and the sort of information it provides in OT. The lexicon has been traditionally seen as the repository of 'unpredictable information' – it contains morphemes (or words) and their unpredictable properties, such as their morphological and syntactic categories, their phonological content, and their semantic content. Two ongoing issues with the lexicon are (a) where to store unpredictable information and (b) how much predictable information to store. In post-*SPE* phonology, the dominant view was to put all unpredictable information into the lexicon and to try to minimize predictable information. From the opposite point of view, Anderson (1992) proposed that at least some lexical items could effectively be expressed as rules.

Ussishkin (Ch.19) adopts a popular middle ground in OT, with some unpredictable aspects of morphemes implemented as constraints. For example, McCarthy & Prince (1993a) propose constraints such as Align-L(*um*, stem), which requires the left edge of the morph of the Tagalog morpheme *um* to align with the left edge of a stem (i.e. be a prefix); this approach is discussed in detail by Ussishkin (19.3.2). So, whether a morpheme is prefixing or suffixing is not expressed in the lexicon as a diacritic that triggers a general concatenative rule (e.g. Sproat 1984), but as a morpheme-specific constraint.

The idea that unpredictable lexical information can be expressed as a rule/constraint is not due to OT, but OT has allowed expression of such information by constraints to be straightforward, and it is now widely assumed (cf. Horwood 2002). It is also debatable how much lexical information should be expressed as a constraint: Golston (1995) and Russell (1995) argue that even morphemes' phonological material should be introduced by constraint.

In *SPE*, as much predictable information was eliminated from the lexicon as possible and given by rule. For example, if medial nasal consonants always have the same place of articulation as the following consonant, pre-consonantal nasals in lexical entries were not specified for Place of Articulation. This idea was adapted in underspecification theories of the 1980s and 1990s. The explanatory power of *SPE* and its later rule-based successors partly relied on the fact that the input to the phonology was restricted in predictable ways.

In contrast, Prince & Smolensky's (2004) principle of 'Richness of the Base' (RoB) forces this idea to be reconsidered. Because OT eschews constraints on input forms, a language's grammar must be able to account for every conceivable input, so whether underlying lexical forms lack predictable information or not becomes almost irrelevant with RoB. Consequently, a great deal of work in OT and in the chapters here assumes that lexical entries are fully specified for phonological information (cf. Itô et al. 1995, Inkelas et al. 1997, Artstein 1998). The irrelevance of the specification of predictable information in the lexicon does not indicate any greater level of complexity in OT. In fact, the principle it relies on – the lack of restrictions on inputs – has allowed resolution of some long-standing problems (e.g. the Duplication Problem – McCarthy 2002c§3.1.2.2).

Finally, a large amount of work in OT has re-evaluated the formal expression of morphological relatedness. As McCarthy (5.5) discusses, Correspondence Theory has been extended to account for phonological similarities among morphologically related words, such as the syllabic nasal in 'lighten' [laɪtn̩] and 'lightening' [laɪtn̩ɪŋ] (cf. 'lightning' [laɪtnən], *[laɪʔnən] – in the formal register of my dialect of New Zealand English) (e.g. Benua 1997). This issue is discussed more fully by McCarthy (5.5).

In short, the lexicon in OT is different in significant ways from the lexicon in previous work. Some unpredictable information has been moved out of the lexicon and expressed as constraints, and some predictable information is commonly assumed to remain in the lexicon. The formal expression of 'morphological relatedness' and paradigms has changed fundamentally as part of the development of Correspondence Theory; it is no longer necessary to appeal to a serial derivation to account for phonological similarities between morphologically related words.

1.2.4 OT theories and other theories

One point that emerges from surveying the chapters in this volume is that it is misleading to imply that there is a single unified theory of OT that everyone adheres to. It is more accurate to say that there is an OT framework and many OT sub-theories.

Almost every aspect of OT has been questioned. For example, McCarthy & Prince's (1995a, 1999) theory of GEN with Correspondence is fundamentally different from the Containment model of Prince & Smolensky (2004). There are also fundamentally different approaches to the constraint component CON: some view constraints from a Functionalist perspective and others from a Formalist one (see Section 1.3). In addition, some approaches see each constraint as independently motivated, while others attempt to identify general schemas that define large classes of constraints (e.g. McCarthy & Prince's 1993a ALIGN schema (Ussishkin 19.2.1), Beckman's

1997 positional faithfulness schema, and markedness schemas in a variety of other work). The concept of a totally ordered and invariant ranking has been questioned from several perspectives (see Anttila Ch.22 for details). Wilson (2000) proposes an EVAL that is fundamentally different from Prince & Smolensky's (2004) (cf. McCarthy 5.4, 2002b). McCarthy (2000b) examines – but does not advocate – a Serialist OT theory (also Rubach 2000). Finally, a number of proposals involving more than two levels have been put forward recently (see McCarthy 5.4).

In addition, the core principles of OT are compatible with aspects of other theories. For example, Harris & Gussmann (1998) combine representational elements of Government Phonology with OT. Some key features of the rule-based Lexical Phonology have been recast in an OT framework (see McCarthy 5.5).

In summary, there are many subtheories of OT, there are mixtures of OT and other theories' devices, and there also are a number of other theories that are the focus of current research (e.g. Government Phonology in Scheer 1998, 2004; Declarative Phonology – Coleman 1998, Bye 2003, and many others). Nevertheless, it is clear from the chapters here that Prince & Smolensky's (2004) framework has had a profound impact on the field and helped to understand and reconceptualize a wide variety of phonological phenomena.

1.3   Representation and explanation

Harris (6.1) observes that "recent advances in derivational theory have prompted a rethink of . . . representational developments." Comparison of the chapters in Goldsmith's (1995a) *Handbook* with the ones here underscores this point: here there is less appeal to specific representational devices and more reliance on constraints and their interaction to provide sources of explanation.

To give some background, in Autosegmental Phonology (Goldsmith 1976b, 1990) and Metrical Phonology (see Hayes 1995, Kager Ch.9 for references) the aim throughout the 1980s and early 1990s was to place as much of the explanatory burden as possible on representation with very few operations (e.g. relinking and delinking of association lines, clash and lapse avoidance). In contrast, constraint interaction in OT allows ways to analyze phonological phenomena that do not rely on representational devices.

Markedness and representation
An example is found in the concept of Markedness, which has been a central issue in phonological theory since the Prague School's work in the 1930s (Trubetzkoy 1939, Jakobson 1941/1968). It is the focus of Rice's chapter (Ch.4) in this handbook, and markedness theory is explicitly discussed in many others (e.g. Zec 8.5, de Lacy Ch.12, Fikkert Ch.23, Bernhardt & Stemberger 25.2.1).

'Markedness' refers to asymmetries in linguistic phenomena. For example, it has often been claimed that epenthesis can produce coronals, but never labials or dorsals (e.g. Paradis & Prunet 1991b and references cited therein). Coronals are therefore less marked than labials and dorsals, and this markedness status recurs in many other processes (e.g. neutralization). In general, phonological phenomena such as neutralization and epenthesis are taken to produce exclusively unmarked feature values.[5]

SPE's approach to markedness was to define feature values – *u* for unmarked and *m* for marked – which were interpreted by special 'marking conventions' which essentially filled in a phonetically interpretable value of '+' or '−' (*SPE*:Ch.9). *SPE*'s approach was therefore essentially representational: markedness follows from the form of feature values. After *SPE*, a more elaborate theory of representation and markedness developed in the Autosegmental Theory of representation (Goldsmith 1976a, 1990), and in theories of underspecification (e.g. Kiparsky 1982b, Archangeli 1984) and privativity (e.g. Lombardi 1991) (see Harris 6.3, Hall 13.2). The unmarked feature value was indicated by a lack of that feature; for example, coronals had no Place features at all (articles in Paradis & Prunet 1991b, Avery & Rice 1989, Rice 1996, also see Hall Ch.13). Coupled with the view that neutralization is feature deletion, the fact that neutralization produces unmarked elements is derived.

While the representational approach to markedness has continued in OT work (for recent work – Causley 1999, Morén 2003), Prince & Smolensky (2004) and Smolensky (1993) opened up an entirely different way of conceiving of the concept (its most direct precursor is in Natural Generative Phonology – Stampe 1973). Instead of relying on representation, constraint ranking and form is central: coronals are not marked because they are representationally deficient, but because all constraints that favour dorsals and labials over coronals are universally lower-ranked than those constraints that favor coronals over other segments: i.e. ||*DORSAL »» *LABIAL »» *CORONAL ||, where '»»' indicates a ranking that is invariant from language to language. There is no need to appeal to the idea that coronals lack Place features in this approach: they are the output of neutralization because other options – labials and dorsals – are ruled out by other constraints (for examples of fixed ranking, see Zec 8.5, Yip 10.3.2, de Lacy 12.2.2).

The idea of universally fixed rankings is found in the opening pages of Prince & Smolensky (2004); its success at dealing with markedness hierarchies in the now famous case of Imdlawn Tashlhiyt Berber syllabification is probably part of the reason that OT's influence spread so quickly (see Zec 8.5.1 for discussion). Recent approaches to markedness in OT have rejected universally fixed rankings; they instead place restrictions on constraint form to establish markedness relations (see de Lacy Ch.12). However, the principle is the same: markedness relations are established by ranking and constraint form, not by representational devices.

The OT ranking/constraint form approach to markedness has been widely accepted in current work, but the representational theory also remains popular: the two approaches are often even employed together. As discussed in Harris (Ch.6), the debate continues as to where the balance lies.

Representation in current theory

The chapters identify and exemplify a number of reasons why there was a shift towards explanation through constraint interaction. One function of representation was to express markedness; as explained above, from the first, Prince & Smolensky (2004) showed how to capture markedness effects with constraint interaction. Similarly, much of the theory of representation relied on, or at least employed, serial derivations. For example, assimilation was seen as a three-step process of delinking a feature, adding an association to a nearby feature, then deleting the stray feature (also see Harris 6.3.3). With a two-level approach to grammar, the concepts of delinking and reassociation have no clear counterpart (though see Yip Ch.10 and the discussion below).

In many of the chapters here, Correspondence Theory is used instead of representational devices. For example, reduplication was seen in Marantz (1982) and McCarthy & Prince (1986) as a series of associations followed by delinking due to a ban on crossed association lines; Urbanczyk (Ch.20) shows how reduplication can be analyzed using correspondence – another type of relation entirely. Representation was also relied on to express dependency relations. For example, if a feature F always assimilates whenever feature G does, then F was assumed to be representationally dependent on G. Harris (6.3.3) observes that Padgett's (2002) work shows that at least some dependency relations between features and classhood can be expressed through constraint interaction and do not rely on an explicit representational hierarchy of features (also see Yip 2004).

Of course, it is crucial for any theory of phonology to have a well-defined restrictive theory of representation. However, OT has allowed the burden of explanation to move from being almost exclusively representation-based to being substantially constraint-based.

In fact, while most recent work in OT has focused on constraint interaction, a good deal has examined or employed representational devices as a crucial part of explanation. For example, Beckman (1997, 1998) employs an OT version of Autosegmental phonology to deal with assimilation. Cole & Kisseberth (1994) propose Optimal Domains theory, which certainly relies less on representational devices than its predecessors but crucially refers to a representational notion of featural alignment. McCarthy (2004a) proposes a theory of representation that builds on autosegmental concepts. Interestingly, the representation of tone has been least affected by the move to OT. Very little has changed in representational terms: pre-OT notions such as multiply-linked (i.e. spread and contour) tones, floating tones, and tonal non-specification are commonly used in OT work – see Yip (Ch.10) for details.

One reason for the lack of in-depth discussion of representation is that it has become common to focus on constraint interaction and violations in OT work, while there has been less necessity to provide explicit definitions of constraint form. An example is the AGREE[F] constraint (Lombardi 1999, Baković 2000), defined by Baković (14.1) as "Adjacent output segments have the same value of the feature *x*." The constraint is defined in this way because the definition aims to express the *effect* of the constraint (i.e. how it assigns violations) rather than providing a formal structural description. If one wishes to completely formalize the definition, though, it is necessary to deal with representational issues: what does the term "have the same value" mean? In formal terms, is this phrase necessarily expressed as a multiply-associated feature? Or can it be expressed through correspondence relations? These issues are receiving more attention in recent work.

In summary, much of the burden of explanation has shifted from representational devices to constraint interaction. However, many of the representational devices that were developed in the 1980s remain integral to current phonological analyses, as exemplified by the detailed prosodic structures used by Zec (Ch.8), Kager (Ch.9), Yip (Ch.10), Gussenhoven (Ch.11), and Truckenbrodt (Ch.18), and the feature structure discussed by Hall (13.2). As the authors discuss, justification for the structures remains despite the effects of constraint interaction.

1.4   Functionalism

Gordon (Ch.3) observes that "the last decade has witnessed renewed vigor in attempting to integrate functional, especially phonetic, explanations into formal analyses of phonological phenomena." Functionalist principles are discussed in many of the chapters in this book (including Rice 4.7, Harris 6.2.2, Zec 8.6, Steriade 7.3, Yip 10.4.2, Hall 13.2, Baković 14.4.1, Alderete & Frisch 16.3, Kingston 17.3, Bermúdez-Otero 21.4, Anttila 22.3.3, 22.4, Fikkert 23.2). This section provides some background to both Functionalist and Formalist approaches to phonology (also see McCarthy 2002c§4.4).

Gordon (Ch.3) identifies a number of core principles in Functionalist approaches to phonology. A central concept is expressed by Ohala (1972:289): "Universal sound patterns must arise due to the universal constraints or tendencies of the human physiological mechanisms involved in speech production and perception". Many researchers have advocated a Functionalist approach (e.g. Stampe 1973, Ohala 1972 et seq., Liljencrants & Lindblom 1972, Archangeli & Pulleyblank 1994, Bybee 2001 and many others), but it is only recently that Functionalist theories employing OT-like frameworks have gained a great deal of popularity, as documented by Gordon (Ch.3) (also see the articles in Gussenhoven & Kager 2001, Hume & Johnson 2001, and Hayes et al. 2004; Flemming 1995, Jun 1995, Boersma 1998, Kirchner 1998, 2001, Gordon 1999, 2002b, and many others). Research has focused on issues such as how concepts such as markedness are grounded in concepts of articulatory ease and perceptual distinctiveness, and how to express these influences in constraint form.

The property common to all current Functionalist approaches is the idea that phonological effects (especially markedness) are not due to innate constraints or constraint schemas. Instead, one Functionalist view (called 'Direct Functionalism' here) holds that constraints are constructed by mechanisms that measure articulatory effort and perceptual distinctiveness (and perhaps also parsing difficulty). Constraints are defined in units that directly record this effort and distinctiveness; consequently, the approaches use finely differentiated units (e.g. real numbers) not used in traditional conceptions of phonology (see Harris 6.2.2 for discussion, also Anttila 22.3.3 and Tesar 24.4).

Another view combines direct functionalism with the idea that the phonological component is limited in terms of its expressive power. In this view, constraints are constructed with reference to articulation and perception, but they must be expressed in terms of a small set of phonological primitives: i.e. "phonological constraints tend to ban phonetic difficulty in simple, formally symmetrical ways" (Hayes 1999§6.2). The phonological primitives may not be well-adapted to expressing phonetic categories, so there may be various mismatches.

Distinct from these views is the 'diachronic functionalist' approach (Ohala 1971 et seq., Blevins 2004). Blevins' approach in particular potentially allows the phonological component to generate virtually any sound pattern (Gordon 3.5). However, not every sound pattern survives diachronic transmission equally well. Consequently, markedness effects are due to the process of language learning, and explanation for diachronic change and synchronic processes are the same. Diachronic functionalism is discussed by Gordon (3.5), so will not be examined further here.

1.4.1   The Formalist approach

A great deal of current phonological work has its roots in Formalist approaches (see Chomsky 1966 for phonology specifically, Chomsky 1965 et seq., and more recently Hale & Reiss 2000b). In OT, the Formalist approach is responsible for the assumption that all constraints or constraint schemas are innate.

The Formalist approach does not necessarily rule out functional grounding in constraints. As Chomsky & Lasnik (1977§1.2) discuss, Formalist approaches can assume a 'species-level' functionalism: this is the idea that a particular constraint has been favoured in evolution because it helps with articulation, perception, or parsing. For example, Chomsky & Lasnik suggest that the syntactic constraint *[$_{NP}$NP TENSE VP] is innate, and has survived because it simplifies parsing (p.436).

The implication of the Formalist approach for phonology is that derivation, representation, and constraints can have 'arbitrary' aspects – i.e. they may not directly aid (and could even act against) reduction of articulatory effort and increase in perceptual distinctiveness. However, it is not surprising to find that some (or even many) mechanisms or constraints do serve to aid in articulation, perception, and processing; this functional grounding would be seen as following from 'species-level' adaptations or 'accident', through fortuitous random mutation or exaptation.

With 'species-level functionalism', it may seem that the Formalist and Functionalist approaches would have very similar effects. However, the difference resides in the Formalist possibility for arbitrary phonological structures, hierarchies, and constraints. For example, Zec (8.5) and de Lacy (12.2) employ the sonority hierarchy as a central part of their analyses of prosodic structure, yet determining the phonetic basis of sonority – and therefore its articulatory and perceptual value – has proven notoriously difficult (Parker 2002 and references cited therein). It seems that the sonority hierarchy is at least partially arbitrary (i.e. without functional motivation), and only partially adapted to aiding articulation and perception; this sort of mismatch is expected in the Formalist approach. Of course, the difficulty in identifying arbitrariness is that we may simply not be looking at the right articulatory, perceptual, or parsing property.

Also expected in the Formalist view is the idea that there could be arbitrary (and even functionally non-sensical) restrictions on phonological processes. An example is found in tone- and sonority-driven stress, discussed in de Lacy (Ch.12). Longer segments (e.g. long vowels, diphthongs) often attract stress, and there are plausible functional reasons for such attraction (Ahn 2000). In fact, this attraction may (partially) account for the attraction of stress to high sonority vowels like [a] because they typically have a longer inherent duration than low sonority vowels like [i], [u], and [ə]. However, in many languages there is a correlation between tone level and vowel duration: the lower the tone, the longer the vowel (e.g. Thai – Abramson 1962). Thus, low-toned [à] is longer than high-toned [á], and so on. If low tone increases duration, and stress is attracted to longer elements, functional reasoning should lead us to believe that stress will be attracted to low tone over high tone. However, this is *never* the case: stress always prefers high-toned vowels to low-toned ones. Of course, there may be some other functional reason for favouring high-toned stressed syllables, but given the fact that languages can vary as to which functional factor they favour (i.e. through ranking), it is surprising that *no* language favours stressed low-toned vowels over high-toned ones (cf. functional approaches to vowel inventories, where articulatory and perceptual factors can conflict, but one can take precedence over the other in particular languages).

To summarize, support for the Formalist view (with 'species-level functionalism') can be sought in phonological arbitrariness and Competence–Performance mismatches.

1.4.2 Challenges

Gordon (3.1) observes that one reason for the increase in Functionalist popularity is OT's formalism: OT can be easily adapted to expressing gradient phenomena; it also provides a framework for expressing the concept of 'tendency' through constraint ranking. However, it is important to emphasize that OT is not an inherently Functionalist theory, and some Functionalist versions of OT depart significantly from Prince & Smolensky's (2004) proposals (e.g. versions of Stochastic OT – see discussion and references in Anttila 22.3.3, McCarthy 2002c: Sec. 4.4).

Another reason may be that the Formalist explanation for sound patterns is seen by some as insufficiently profound. For example, the fact that dorsals are more marked than coronals receives the explanation that *DORSAL universally outranks *CORONAL in a Formalist approach, and this universal ranking is innate. In other words, the constraint ranking is an axiom of the theory. Yet there is clearly a good articulatory reason for this ranking – dorsals require more articulatory effort than coronals (if effort is measured from rest position), and there may be perceptual reasons as well. A Functionalist approach makes a direct connection between the substantive facts and the formalism.

A further reason is skepticism about the ability of species-level functionalism to account for phonological facts. For example, how could the fixed ranking *DORSAL »» *CORONAL evolve? A fixed ranking *DORSAL »» *CORONAL would have to appear through a random mutation (or exaptation), then provide some advantage that a speaker who had to learn their ranking did not have (e.g. faster learning). Identifying the exact advantage (whether survival or sexual) is challenging. There may also be the issue of plausibility, though as Pinker & Bloom (1990) have observed, tiny advantages can have significant influence over time. On the other hand, natural selection is not the only force in biological evolution.

The problem that Formalist approaches face is not that they lack explanation, but that it is difficult to provide proof. Little is understood about the biology of phonological evolution, and so evolutionary arguments are hard to make (though see Hauser, Chomsky, and Fitch 2002 for discussion and references). Given the burgeoning popularity of Functionalist approaches, the onus currently seems to be on the Formalist approach to close the 'plausibility gap' and identify clearly testable predictions that differ from Functionalist ones.

There are also challenges for the Functionalist perspective. For the diachronic Functionalist view, one challenge is to account for cases where a diachronic change has no synchronic counterpart, and why there are unattested synchronic grammars which could easily be created by a series of natural diachronic changes (Kiparsky 2004). Mismatches also pose a challenge for the 'direct' Functionalist point of view, as do cases of arbitrariness (as in the sonority hierarchy), as all constraints and markedness hierarchies should be tied directly into Performance considerations.

Functionalist approaches have already had a significant impact on phonological theory. There are many works that explicitly advocate Functionalist principles (cited in Section 1.3 above). It is also commonplace in recent publications to see a constraint's validity evaluated by whether it is related to a decrease in articulatory effort or helps in perception or parsing. For example, in a widely-used textbook, Kager (1999a:11) comments that "phonological markedness constraints should be *phonetically grounded* in some property of articulation and perception". Of course, a Formalist perspective does not accept the validity of such statements. In the immediate future, I think it is likely that the Functionalist perspective will continue to gain ground, but also that there will be increasing dialogue between the various Formalist and Functionalist approaches and increased understanding of the implications of Formalist tenets in phonology.

1.5   Conclusions

The preceding sections have attempted to identify some of the major theoretical themes that appear throughout the following chapters. Of course, there are many others in the following chapters that are not covered here (e.g. the role of contrast in phonology – Steriade Ch.7, Rice 4.6). Fikkert (23.1) comments that for language acquisition there has been an increase in research and resources, and Tesar (Ch.24) discusses the growing field of learnability. As detailed in the chapters in Part V, areas of phonology that have traditionally been under-studied or seen as peripheral (e.g. free variation – Anttila Ch.22) are having a significant influence on central issues in the field.

The chapters in this Handbook show that phonological theory has undergone enormous theoretical changes compared with ten years ago, and it continues to change rapidly. It is probably for this reason that none of the chapters in this book attempt to make predictions about the broad issues that will dominate phonology in the next ten years. Perhaps the only safe bet is that any prediction about the future of phonology will be wildly inaccurate.

Notes

My thanks to all those who commented on this chapter in its various incarnations: José Elías-Ulloa, Kate Ketner, John McCarthy, Nazarré Merchant, Michael O'Keefe, and Alan Prince.
1 Prince & Smolensky's manuscript was originally circulated in 1993. A version is available online for free at the Rutgers Optimality Archive (ROA): http://roa.rutgers.edu/, number 537.
2 From inspecting several major journals from 1998 to 2004, around three-quarters of the articles assumed an OT framework, and many of the others compared their theories with an OT approach.

3 There is currently an ambiguity in the term 'markedness'. In OT, 'mark-edness' refers to a type of constraint. 'Markedness' also refers to a concept of implicational or asymmetric relations between phonological segments and structures (see Section 1.3 and Rice Ch.4).

4 The opposite is identified and exemplified by Ketner (2003) as 'hetero-geneity of target, homogeneity of process', where the same process is used to satisfy a number of different conditions.

5 There is a great deal of controversy over the role of markedness in phonology. For example, Blevins (2004) proposes that markedness effects can be ascribed to diachronic change, and Hume (2003) rejects the idea that there are any markedness asymmetries (at least with respect to Place of Articulation). Rice (4.7) and de Lacy (2006§1.3) re-evaluate the scope of markedness effects, arguing for recognition of a strict division between Competence and Performance. There has also been an ongoing re-evalu-ation of the empirical facts that support markedness. While there is much debate about which markedness asymmetries exist at the moment, it is at least clear that many traditional markedness diagnostics are not valid (e.g. Rice 4.6; also Rice 1996 et seq., de Lacy 2002a, 2006, Hume & Tserdanelis 2002).

Part I

Conceptual issues

2

The pursuit of theory

Alan Prince

2.1   The Theory is also an object of analysis

Common sense is often a poor guide to methodology. Any theory presents us with two fundamental and often difficult questions:

— What *is* it?
— How do you *do* it?

The first of these arises because a theory is the totality of its consequences. It must be given as the set of its defining conditions, and we may polish them, ground them, tailor them to meet various expectations, but unless we have mapped out what follows from them, the theory remains alien territory. Newton's theory of gravitation can be written on a postcard, and we might like to think of it as nothing more than what makes apples fall straight to earth and planets follow simple repetitive paths, but its actual content is strange beyond imagining and still under study hundreds of years after it was stated.[1] Once formulated, a theory has broken definitively with intuition and belief. We are stuck with its consequences whether we like them or not, anticipate them or not, and we must develop techniques to find them.

The second question arises because the internal logic of a theory determines what counts as a sound argument within its premises. General principles of rigor and validation apply, of course, but unless connected properly with the specific assumptions in question, the result can easily be oversight and gross error. Here's an example: in many linguistic theories developed since the 1960s, violating a constraint leads directly to ungrammaticality. A parochial onlooker might get the intuition that violation is somehow ineluctably synonymous with ill-formedness, in the nature of things. A grand conclusion may then be thought to follow:

(1)   "... the existence of phonology in every language shows that Faithfulness [in Optimality Theory] is at best an ineffective principle that might well be done without." (Halle 1995b).

'Phonology' here means 'underlying-surface disparity'. Each faithfulness constraint forbids a certain kind of input–output disparity: *case closed*. But no version of Optimality Theory (OT) has ever been put forth that lacks a full complement of Faithfulness constraints, because their operation – their minimal violation, which includes satisfaction as a special case – is essential to the derivation of virtually every form. The intuition behind the attempted criticism, grounded in decades of experience, is that well-formed output violates no constraints; but this precept is theory-bound and no truth of logic. It just doesn't apply to OT, or to any theory of choice where constraints function as criteria of decision between flawed alternatives.

2.1.1   Optimality Theory as it is

A more telling example emerges immediately from any attempt to work within OT. At some point in the course of analyzing a given language, we have in hand a hypothesized constraint set and a set of analyses we regard as optimal. We now face the *ranking problem*: which constraint hierarchies (if any) will produce the desired optima as actual optima?

Any sophisticated problem-solver's key tactic is to identify the simplest problem that contains the elements at play, solve it, and build up from there. Let's deploy it incautiously: since the smallest possible zone of conflict involves two constraints and two candidates (one desired optimal), gather such 2×2 cases and construct the overall ranking from the results.[2] But the alert should go up: no contact has been made with any basic notion of the theory. We actually don't know with any specificity what it is about the necessities of ranking that we can learn from such a limited scheme of comparison. A wiser procedure is to scrutinize the definition of optimality and get clear about what it is that we are trying to determine. A rather different approach to the ranking problem will emerge. What, then, does 'optimal' actually mean in OT? Let us examine this question with a certain amount of care, which will not prove excessive in the end.

Optimality is composite: the judgment of hierarchy is constructed from the judgment of individual constraints. Proceeding from local to global, definition begins with the 'better than' relation over a single constraint, proceeds to 'better than' over a constraint hierarchy, and then gets optimality out of those relations.

In the familiar way, one candidate is better than another on a constraint if it is assigned fewer violations by that constraint.

(2)   *'Better than' on a constraint*
       For candidates a,b and constraint C, $a \succ_C b$ iff $C(a) < C(b)$.

Here we have written $a \succ_C b$ for 'a is better than b on C', and $C(x)$ for the (nonnegative) number of violations C assigns to candidate x.

To amalgamate such individual judgments, we impose a linear ordering, a 'ranking', written $\gg$, on the constraint set, giving a constraint hierarchy.

(We say C_1 *dominates* C_2 if $C_1 \gg C_2$.) Using that order, and using the definition of 'better than' on a constraint just given, we define the notion 'better than on a hierarchy'.

As usual, we will say that one candidate is better than another on a hierarchy if it is better *on the highest-ranked constraint that distinguishes the two*. (This concise formulation is due to Grimshaw 1997; a constraint is said to 'distinguish' two candidates when it assigns a different number of violations to them; that is, when one is better than the other on that constraint.)

(3) *'Better than' on a constraint hierarchy.*
     For candidates *a,b* and constraint hierarchy H,
     $a \succ_H b$ iff there is a constraint C in H that distinguishes *a, b*, such that
          (1) $a \succ_C b$
     and (2) no constraint distinguishing *a* and *b* dominates C.

To be optimal is to be the best in the candidate set, and to be the best is to have none better.

(4) *'Optimal'*
     For a candidate *q*, a candidate set K, with $q \in K$, and a hierarchy H, *q* is *optimal* in K according to H, iff there is no candidate $z \in K$ such that $z \succ_H q$.

Now that we know what we're looking for, we can sensibly ask the key question: what do we learn about ranking from a comparison of two candidates (one of them a desired optimum)?

Since optimality is globally determined by the totality of such comparisons, and we are looking at just one of them, the best we can hope for is to arrive at conditions which will ensure that our desired optimum is *better than* its competitor on the hierarchy. This leads us right back to definition (3), and from it, we know that some constraint preferring the desired optimum must be the highest-ranked constraint that distinguishes them. The constraints that threaten this state of affairs are those that *dis*prefer the desired optimum: they must all be outranked by an optimum-preferring constraint. Let's call this the 'elementary ranking condition' (ERC) associated with the comparison.

(5) *Elementary ranking condition*
     For $q,z \in K$, a candidate set, and S, a set of constraints, some constraint in S preferring *q* to *z* dominates all those preferring *z* to *q*.

Any constraint ranking on which candidate *q* betters *z* must satisfy the ERC. (To put it non-modally: candidate *q* is better than *z* over a ranking H of S if and only if the ranking H satisfies the ERC (5).) The ERC, then, tells us exactly what we learn from comparing two candidates.

To make use of this finding, we must first calculate each constraint's individual judgment of the comparison. A constraint measures the desired

optimum against its competitor in one of just three ways: better, worse,
same. We indicate these categories as follows, writing '$q{\sim}z$' for the comparison between desired optimum q and competitor z.

(6)   *Constraint C assesses the comparison q vs. z.*

Comparative relation	Violation pattern	Gloss
$C[q{\sim}z] = \mathbf{W}$	$C(q) < C(z)$	'C prefers the desired optimum'
$C[q{\sim}z] = \mathbf{L}$	$C(q) > C(z)$	'C prefers its competitor'
$C[q{\sim}z] = \mathbf{e}$	$C(q) = C(z)$	'C does not distinguish the pair'

Now consider a distribution of comparative values that could easily result
from some such calculation. For illustrative purposes, imagine that the
entire constraint set contains six constraints:

(7)   *Typical two-candidate comparison*

	C_1	C_2	C_3	C_4	C_5	C_6
$q{\sim}z$	L	e	W	W	e	L

The relevant associated ERC declares this: C_3 *or* C_4 dominates *both* C_1 and C_6.
   In any ranking of these constraints on which q is better than z, this
condition must be met.
   We now have the tools to examine the intuition that $2{\times}2$ comparison is
the building block of ranking arguments. First, consider shrinkage of the
candidate set. In order to narrow our focus to just 2 candidates, we exclude
all the others from view. This is entirely legitimate: the hierarchical evaluation of a pair of candidates is determined entirely by the direct relation
between them. Some other candidates may exist that are better than either,
or worse than either, or intermediate between them, but no outsiders have
any effect whatever on the head-to-head pair-internal relation. This fundamental property has been called 'contextual independence of choice'
(Prince 2002b:iv), and is related to Arrow's 'irrelevance of independent
alternatives' (Arrow 1951:26). It is not a truth of logic, inherent in the
notion of 'comparison' or 'choice', but the premises of OT succeed in
licensing it. (It is also fragile: modify those premises and it can go away,
as it does in the Targeted-Constraint OT of Wilson 2001.)
   Now consider the role of the constraint set, where we find no such
comfort. The form of the ERC in no way privileges 2-constraint arguments:
all L-assessing constraints must be dominated, and *some* W-assessing constraint must do the domination. If we omit an L-assessing constraint from
the calculation, the resulting ERC is incomplete, and it is no longer true
that any hierarchy satisfying it will necessarily yield the superiority of the
desired optimum (though the converse *is* true); further conditions may be
required. Leaving out C_1 from tableau (7), for example, deprives us of the
crucial information that C_1 must be dominated; if it is not, then undesired
z betters q.

If we happen to omit a W-assessing constraint, the associated ERC can mistakenly exclude a successful hierarchy, leading to false assertions that cannot be remedied by merely obtaining further information. This is more dangerous than L-omission when we are arguing from optimum–suboptimum pairs to the correct ranking, as when dealing with the 'ranking problem' in the course of analysis. In tableau (7), for example, we have two W-assessors, C_3 and C_4. If negligence leads us to omit C_3, say, we are tempted to the conclusion that C_4 *must* dominate C_1 and C_6. This is not sound in itself, and depending on other circumstances, it could easily turn out that C_4 lies at the bottom of the correct hierarchy, dominating nothing, with C_3 doing the work of domination demanded by (7).[3]

The logic of the theory, then, allows us to discard from any particular comparison only the neutral e-assessing constraints. Tableau (7) shrinks to 2×4, and no further. In the literature, correct handling of the ERC is not ubiquitous, and omission of constraints often rests optimistically on intuitions about relevance and likely conflict. But pairwise (or intuitively restricted) examination of constraint relations has no status. This is not a matter of convenience, taste, typography, notation, presentation, or luck. We must *do* the theory as it dictates, even in the face of common sense.

2.1.2 Using the Evaluation Metric

Let us turn to a case where reliance on intuition leads to an interesting failure to appreciate what the theory actually claims. Consider the phonological theory put forth in *The Sound Pattern of English* (*SPE*: Chomsky & Halle 1968). A vocabulary is given for representing forms and for constructing rules, which are to apply in a designated order (some cyclically) to produce outputs from lexical items. Any sample of language data, even a gigantic one, is consistent with a vast, even unbounded, number of licit grammars. Which one – note the titular definite article – is correct? It is crucial to find a formal property that distinguishes the correct grammar, if linguistic theory is to claim realism and, more specifically, if it is to address the acquisition problem, even abstractly. (It is less crucial for linguistic practice, since linguists can, and indeed must, argue for grammars on grounds of evidence unavailable to the learner.) The well-known proposal is that grammars submit to evaluation in terms of their length, which is measured in terms of the number of symbols they deploy (Chomsky 1965: 37–42; *SPE* p.334). Shorter is better, and the shortest grammar is hypothesized to be the real one. The *SPE* statement runs as follows:

(8) "The 'value' of a sequence of rules is the reciprocal of the number of symbols in its minimal representation." (*SPE* p.334, ex. (9))

Ristad (1990) has noted a potentially regrettable consequence: the highest valued sequence of rules will have no rules in it at all. We therefore make the usual emendation, left tacit (I believe) in *SPE*: that we must also take account of the number of symbols expended in the lexicon. The length of the entire Lexicon+Rule System pairing determines the values we are comparing. A rule earns its keep by reducing the size of the lexicon.

The Evaluation Metric thus defined is entirely coherent (given a finite lexicon) and, as asserted by Chomsky & Halle, "provides a precise explication for the notion 'linguistically significant generalization'. . ." which is subject to empirical test. It seems to be the case, however, that there are literally no instances where the Evaluation Metric was put to use as defined. That is: no analysis in the entire literature justifies a proposed Lexicon+Rule System hypothesis by showing it to have the best evaluation of all those deemed possible by the theory. Is there even a case where the value was calculated?

The reason is not far to seek. Though defined globally, the metric was always interpreted locally. Typically, this was at the level of the rule:

(9)   ". . . the number of symbols in a rule is inversely related to the degree of linguistically significant generalization achieved in the rule." (*SPE* p.335)

But could even be extended to rule-internal contents:

(10)   ". . . the 'naturalness' of a class . . . can be measured in terms of the number of features needed to define it." (*SPE* p.400).

Of course, nothing of the sort can legitimately be asserted without building considerable bridgework between the global metric and the behavior of the local entities out of which the grammar is composed. One has the intuition, perhaps, that it can't hurt to economize locally, and therefore that one is compelled to do so. But it can easily happen in even moderately complex optimization systems that a local splurge yields a global improvement by yielding drastic simplifications elsewhere. In a highly interactive system, the results of global optimization can be all but inscrutable locally.

We can see the local–global relation playing out variously in the other examples discussed above. The idea that Faithfulness is useless when violated represents a kind of hyperlocalism focused on one candidate and one constraint; of course, nothing follows. The local relation between 2 candidates, by contrast, is preserved intact in any set of candidates that contains them, including the entire candidate set. A relation between 2 *constraints*, though, has no such local-to-global portability to the entire constraint set. What is the situation, then, with the intuitive rule-focused evaluation of *SPE* phonologies?

A question not easily answered, alas: it isn't at all clear what the 'local interpretation' might be, or how it would replace the global interpretation. To evaluate, we must compare whole grammars with different lexica, different rules, and different numbers of rules. This provides no difficulty for the global metric, which doesn't see rules or lexica at all. The local interpretation wants to compare rules, though, and so must have rules in hand and some way of finding correspondences between them across grammars to render them comparable. This appears feasible for sets of adjacent rules, under the same lexicon, which perform identical mappings and collapse under the notational conventions; but beyond that . . . obscurity.

Stepping back from the theory, I'd suggest that the actual practice was largely based on discovering contingencies in the data, assuming that they must be reflected in rules of a specific type, and then setting out to simplify the assumed rule-types through notational collapse, ordering, and some fairly local interactional analysis; all under lexical hypotheses that sought a single underlying form for each morpheme. This is reasonable tactically, but it is a far cry from using the theory itself to compute (deterministically) which licit grammar is being evidenced by the data, and, as noted, it never involved using the theory (nondeterministically) to prove that the correct grammar had been obtained. Some such procedure of grammar discovery could even be legitimated, in principle or in part, by results clarifying the conditions under which it produces the Evaluation Metric optimum.

Overall, the effect of acting as if there were a "local interpretation" was not negative. Under its cover, attention was focused on processes, representations, their components and interactions, leading to substantive theories of great interest. Nevertheless, the divergence between theory and practice deprived the theory of the essential content that it claimed. Much effort was expended in fending off opponents who had, it seems, little knowledge of the theory they were criticizing, a faulty grasp of optimization, and little feel for how empirical consequences are derived from the actual assumptions of a theory as opposed to some general impression of them. One such defensive/offensive statement is the following:

(11)   "It should be observed in this connection that although definition (9) [rephrased as (8) above] has been referred to as the 'simplicity' or 'economy criterion,' it has never been proposed or intended that the condition defines 'simplicity' or 'economy' in the very general (and still very poorly understood) sense in which these terms usually appear in the philosophy of science. The only claim that is being made here is the purely empirical one . . ."[4] (*SPE* pp.334–5)

We grant, of course, that the *SPE* theory is abstractly empirical in the way it characterizes linguistic knowledge, and note that the contemporary research style has profited enormously from the unprecedented daring exhibited in staking out territory where none before had imagined it possible. What's missing, though, is the sense of any *particular* empirical claim or set of claims which has been identified and tested against the facts. Worse, the failure to use the theory of evaluation means that we literally do not know what such a claim is. This is Newton's *Principia* without the equations, or with equations that have never been solved. Many rules and rule systems were put forth to describe many language phenomena; but in no case can we be sure that the system proposed is the one projected by the Evaluation Metric. But it is only the optimal system that contains the claims to test.

The Evaluation Metric imbroglio is directly due to a failure to apply the definition to the practice of the theory. The definition provided a formal front for the activities of the researcher, which proceeded on a separate, intuitive track. As with the example of erroneous but commonly applied beliefs about ranking, it is not satisfactory to point defensively to the success of some practitioners in developing interesting theories under false premises. "A long habit of not thinking a thing wrong, gives it a superficial appearance of being right, and raises at first a formidable outcry in defence of custom" (Paine 1776). We must do better.

2.2   What is real and what is not

One need only glance at the formal literature leading up to generative grammar to grasp that we are the beneficiaries of a fundamental change in perspective. Aiming in *Methods in Structural Linguistics* (1951) for "the reduction of linguistic methods to procedures" (p.3), Zellig Harris introduces his proposals with this modest remark:

(12)   "The particular way of arranging the facts about a language which is offered here will undoubtedly prove more convenient for some languages than for others." (Harris 1951:2)

He does not intend, however, to impose a "laboratory schedule" of analytical steps that must be followed sequentially, and he characterizes the value of his methodology in this way:

(13)   "The chief usefulness of the procedures listed below is therefore as a reminder in the course of the original research, and as a form for checking or presenting the results, where it may be desirable to make sure that all the information called for in these procedures has been validly obtained." (Harris 1951:1-2)

These are to be "methods which will not impose a fixed system upon various languages, yet will tell more about each language than will a mere catalogue of sounds and forms."

The goal, then, is to produce useful descriptions, to be judged by such criteria as accuracy, convenience, reliability, responsiveness to variation, and independence from observer bias. No one can sensibly dispute the importance of these factors in empirical investigation of any kind. What further ends is linguistic description intended to serve? Historical linguistics and dialect geography, phonetics and semantics, the relation of language to culture and personality, and the comparison of language structure with systems of logic are cited as areas of study that will profit from "going beyond individual descriptive linguistic facts" to "the use of complete language structures" (p.3).

Largely absent from this program is a sense that the focus of study is a real object, evidenced by the arranged facts but not reducible to them, about which one makes statements that are (because it is real) *right* or *wrong* – as opposed to convenient or awkward, useful or irrelevant to one's parochial purposes. Descriptive, synchronic linguistics is a conduit for pipelining refined information to various disciplines that make use of language data. Chomsky changes all that, of course, by identifying an object that linguistics is to be *about* – competence, I-language, the internal representation of linguistic knowledge. This move is set in the context of rival conceptions of mental structure:

(14)   ". . . empiricist speculation has characteristically assumed that only the procedures and mechanisms for the acquisition of knowledge constitute an innate property of the mind. . . . On the other hand, rationalist speculation has assumed that the general form of a system of knowledge is fixed in advance as a disposition of the mind, and the function of experience is to cause this general schematic structure to be realized and more fully differentiated." (Chomsky 1965:51–52)

The ground has been shifted so fundamentally that both poles of this opposition lie outside the domain in which Harris places himself, where 'knowledge' of language is not at issue. Nevertheless, there is a clear affinity between Harris's interest in methods and the empiricist focus on 'procedures and mechanisms'. Note, too, the force of the Evaluation Metric idea in this context, since it severs the choice of grammar completely from methods and procedures of analysis: the correct grammar is defined by a formal characteristic it has, not as the result of following certain procedures.

To pursue the issue further into linguistics proper, let us distinguish heuristically between 'Theories of Data' (TODs), which produce analyses when set to work on collections of facts, and 'Free-Standing Theories' (FSTs), which are sufficiently endowed with structure that many predictions and properties can be determined from examination of the theory alone.

A near-canonical example of a TOD is provided by the Rumelhart-McClelland model of the English past tense (Rumelhart & McClelland 1986; examined in Pinker & Prince 1988). This is a connectionist network which can be trained to associate an input activation pattern with an output activation pattern. When trained on stem/past-tense pairs, it will produce, to the best of its ability, an output corresponding to the past tense of its input. No assumptions are made about morphology or phonology, regular or irregular, although a structured representational system (featural trigrams) is adopted which allows a word to be represented as a pattern of simultaneous activation. This is a fully explicit formal theory, which operates autonomously. And, once trained, a model will make clear predictions about what output is expected for a given input, whether that input has been seen before or not. It makes limited sense, however, to query it in advance of training, looking for guidance as to what the structure of human language might be; and a trained model is not really susceptible to fine-grained analytic dissection *post hoc* either, due to the complexity of its internal causal structure. The model only takes on predictive structure when it has been exposed to data, and that predictive structure can only be investigated by presenting it with more data.

Examples of Free-Standing Theories are not difficult to find. A theory that spells out a sufficiently narrow universal repertory of structures, constraints, or processes, and explicitly delimits their interactions, will generate an analytically investigable space of possible grammars. Clear examples range from early proposals like that of Bach (1965), Stampe (1973), Donegan & Stampe (1979) to parametrized theories in syntax and those in phonology like Archangeli & Pulleyblank (1994), Halle & Vergnaud (1987), Hayes (1995), as well as many others; Optimality Theory (Prince & Smolensky 2004) falls into the Free-Standing class, both in the large and in domain-specific instantiations of constraint sets. Such theories are in no way limited to symbol-manipulation; the Dynamic Linear Model of stress and syllable structure (Goldsmith and Larson 1990, Larson 1992, Goldsmith 1994, Prince 1993), which computes with numbers, is as canonical an example of an FST as one could imagine, as we will see below in Section 3.2.

The distinction is heuristic and scalar, because theories may be more and less accessible to internal analysis, and may require more or fewer assumptions about data to yield analytical results.[5] Even a dyed-in-the-wool TOD like the Rumelhart-McClelland model admits to some analysis of its representational capacities, and Pinker & Prince mount a central argument against it in terms of its apparent incapacity to generalize to variables like 'stem' which range over lexical items regardless of phonetic content (Pinker & Prince 1988, Prince & Pinker 1988; Marcus 2001). Nevertheless, it is clear that Optimality Theory, for example, or parametrized theories of linguistic form, will admit a deeper and very much more thorough explication in terms of their internal structure.

The distinction between Theories of Data and Free-Standing Theories cross-cuts the empiricist/rational distinction that Chomsky alludes to in the passage quoted above. On the empiricist side, 'procedures and methods for the acquisition of knowledge' can be so simple as to admit of detailed analysis, like that afforded to the two-layer 'perceptron' of Rosenblatt (1958) in Minsky & Papert (1969), which treats it as an FST and achieves a sharp result. But the major step forward in connectionist theory in the 1980s is generally agreed to have been the advance from linear activation functions to differentiable nonlinear activation functions, which in one step enormously enriched the class of trainable networks and rendered their analysis far more difficult.[6] On the rationalist side, *SPE*-type phonology has a TOD character, and investigation of its fundamental properties has shown its general finite-state character (Johnson 1972) but, to my knowledge, little of research-useful specificity.

It is perhaps not surprising that many recent versions of linguistic theory developed under the realist interpretation of its goals should fall toward the FST end of the spectrum. If the aim is to discover a 'system of knowledge' that is separate from the encounter with observables, then unless a hypothesized system has discernible properties and significant predictivity, it is unlikely to be justifiable. To the extent that it is data-dependent, and usable mostly for modeling data rather than predicting general properties, it must face off with other TODs, particularly those offering powerful mechanisms for induction and data representation. (If compressing the lexicon is the supreme goal of phonology, expect stiff competition from the manufacturers of WinZip™ and the like.) Within the ever-expanding palette of choices available to cognitive science, it seems unlikely that rationalist theory will beat statistical empiricism on its native turf. The argument must be that the object of study is not what empiricism assumes it to be. But this must be shown; and is best shown by the quality of the theories developed from rationalist assumptions.

In the absence or failure of such theories, linguistics must recede to a Harris-like position: it might serve as a helpful guide to scientists who (for whatever reason) wish to study phenomena where language plays some role, a map of the terrain but no part of the terrain itself. What's real would be the general data-analyzing methods of empiricist cognitive science, for which language has no special identity or integrity, along with whatever results such methods obtain when applied to the data, linguistic or other, that is fed to them.

In phonology proper, representational theory has moved from the undifferentiated featural medium of *SPE* to the deployment of special structures keyed to the properties of different phenomenal domains, leading naturally (though not inevitably) to contentful FSTs of those domains. Increasing the structural repertory is a two-edged sword. Poorly handled, taken as an add-on to available resources, it can turn out to be no more than a profusion of apparatus that enriches descriptive possibilities, leading to TOD. More interestingly configured, it can yield narrow, predictive theories; but these will contain significant built-in content and hence tend toward the FST side of the spectrum.

In this context, the surprise is not the emergence of the FST but the persistence of what we might call the 'Descriptive Method' (DM) – data description as the primary analytical methodology for determining the content of a theory. For a TOD, this is virtually inevitable; there may be no other way to get an inkling of the theory's character. As soon as an FST is given, though, its consequences are fully determined by its internal structure.

Yet by far the dominant approach to probing linguistic FSTs consists of confronting them with specific data. This can be done haphazardly or with reference to a few inherited 'favorite facts', or it can be done with prodigious vigor and problem-solving prowess, as in for example Hayes (1995). Although parametric theories are plentiful, few indeed are those whose 'exponential typology' of parameter settings has been laid out in full or studied in depth.

This places linguistic theory in an odd position. The axioms or defining conditions of a theory provide a starting place, not an endpoint: a theory is the totality of its consequences. With an FST, these are available to us analytically, and claims about the theory can be decided with certainty. If we decline to pursue the consequences analytically, we impose on ourselves a limited and defective sense of what the theory actually is. This then unnecessarily distorts both further development and theory comparison. Rational arguments about two theories' comparative success, for example, depend on a broad assessment of their properties; lacking that, such discussions not infrequently descend into the cherry-picking of isolated favorable and unfavorable instances.[7] What we might call the 'Analytical Method' is essential for determining the systematic content of theory. It is particularly valuable for delimiting the negative space of prohibitions into which the Descriptive Method does not venture, but it is equally essential for finding the structure of a theory's predictions of possibility.

2.3   Following the Analytical Method

Analysis of Free-Standing Theories is often driven by the most basic formal questions. Perhaps the most fundamental thing we must ask of a proposed theory is — 'does it *exist*?' That is: do the proposed defining conditions actually succeed in defining a coherent entity?[8] Closely related is the question of *under what conditions* the theory exists: what conditions are required for it to give a determinate answer or an answer that makes sense formally?[9] A natural extension of such concerns, for linguistic theories, is the question of whether the theory is *contentful* in that it excludes certain formally sensible states-of-affairs from description. It might seem to some that such questions are arid and of limited interest, since (on this view) most formal deficiencies will not show up in practice, and in the empirical hurly-burly those that do can be patched over. We have already seen how, contrary to such expectations, commanding the answers to drily fundamental questions (e.g. what *is* optimality?) is essential to the most basic acts of data-analysis. Here we examine two cases that show the very tangible value of asking the abstract questions about a theory's content and realm of existence.

2.3.1   Harmonic Ascent

Let us first consider Optimality Theory in the large. Moving beyond the barebones definition of optimality, let us endow the constraint set with some structure: a distinction between Markedness constraints, which penalize configurations in the output, and Faithfulness constraints, which each demand identity of input and output in a certain respect by penalizing any divergence from identity in that respect. Assume that the Markedness/Faithfulness distinction partitions the constraint set, so that any licit constraint belongs to one of the categories; let's call the theory so defined 'M/F-OT'. This gives us perhaps the simplest feasible OT linguistic theory, assuming the usual generative phonological architecture in which the grammar maps a lexical form (input) to a surface form (output). We may now ask if the theory achieved at this level of generality is *contentful*, or if it requires further structure to attain predictions of interest. Exactly this question is taken up in Moreton (2004a), and the results he obtains are illuminating.[10]

To begin, we note that OT has a property that we might call 'positivity' which it shares with certain other multiple-criterion decision-making systems, though by no means all.[11] Broadly speaking, a 'positive' system will be one in which a candidate can do well globally only by doing well locally. If a *winning* candidate does poorly on some criteria in comparison to some particular competitor, we can infer, in a positive system, that it must be doing better than its competitor on some other criteria. OT's positivity comes immediately from the way it defines 'optimal': we know that if on some *hierarchy* it happens that q is better than z, then there is some particular *constraint* on which q is better than z on (namely, the highest ranked constraint that distinguishes them). Now widen the focus: suppose we know that the inferior candidate z is (perversely) better than q on some designated subset D of the constraints, ranked as in the hierarchy as a whole. Clearly, since q is the overall superior candidate, it must be that q is better than z on some particular constraint, and that constraint must belong to *the complement set* of D.

Applying this observation to M/F-OT, we find that if q, the superior candidate, is worse than z on the Faithfulness subhierarchy, then q must be better than z on the Markedness subhierarchy (and vice versa). This observation gains particular force because it is commonly the case that there is a fully faithful candidate (FFC) in the candidate set. The FFC has a tremendous advantage, because it satisfies every F constraint and nothing can beat it over the Faithfulness constraints, no matter how they are ranked. It follows that any non-faithful mapping – any mapping introducing faithfulness-penalized input–output disparity – can be optimal only if it is superior to the FFC on grounds of Markedness. Since the FFC is essentially a copy of the input, this means that in an unfaithful mapping, the output must be less marked than (the faithful copy of) the input, when it exists. We can call this property 'harmonic ascent', using the term 'harmonic' to refer to the opposite of 'markedness'.

(15)   *Harmonic Ascent*

Suppose for $y \neq x$, $x \rightarrow y$ is optimal for some hierarchy H, where $x \rightarrow x$ is also a candidate.

Then for H|M, the subhierarchy of M constraints ranked as they are in H, it must be that $y \succ x$ on H|M.

Sloganeering, we can say: if things do not stay the same, they must get better (markedness-wise). See Lemma (26) of Moreton (2004a) for details.

This property severely restricts the mappings that M/F-OT can execute. A first consequence is that there can be no *circular chain shifts*. This is easiest to see in the case of the smallest possible circle: imagine a grammar that takes input /x/ to distinct output [y] and input /y/ to output [x]:

$$x \rightarrow y$$
$$y \rightarrow x$$

(An example would be a grammar mapping /pi/ to [pe] and /pe/ to [pi].) This pair of mappings cannot be accommodated in one grammar under M/F-OT, because the 'better than' relation is a strict order. By Harmonic Ascent, the optimality of $x \rightarrow y$ requires $y \succ x$ on the Markedness subhierarchy. But $y \rightarrow x$ requires $x \succ y$. One form cannot be both *better than* and *worse than* another.

More generally, any chain shift involving a cycle cannot be expressed. For example:

(16)   *Impossible chain-shift in OT*

Mapping	Markedness Relation
$x \rightarrow y$	$y \succ x$
$y \rightarrow z$	$z \succ y$
$z \rightarrow x$	$x \succ z$

Here the argument is just one step more complicated. Putting all the implied Markedness relations together, we have $x \succ z \succ y \succ x$. Since 'better than' is transitive, asymmetric, and (hence) irreflexive, this set of relations is impossible: it yields $x \succ x$, as well as both $x \succ y$ and $y \succ x$.

A second consequence follows from this fact: there is an end to getting better. If OT is to exist at all, no constraint can portray the candidate set as an unbounded upward-tending sequence of better and better forms (see note 9). This, taken with Harmonic Ascent, rules out the endless shift:

(17)   *Impossible endless shifts in OT*

$$x_1 \rightarrow x_2$$
$$x_2 \rightarrow x_3$$
$$x_3 \rightarrow x_4$$
$$\ldots$$
$$x_k \rightarrow x_{k+1}$$
$$\ldots$$

Of these consequences, the second seems clearly right. There is, I believe, no phonological process that, for example, adds a syllable to every input. Actual augmentation processes aim to hit some target (like bimoraicity or bisyllabicity) which is clearly relatable to Markedness constraints on prosodic structure. There is no sense in which longer is better regardless of the outcome (McCarthy & Prince 1993b, Prince & Smolensky 2004).

The first is perhaps more interesting because it characterizes rather than merely excludes. Chain shifts are well-attested, and almost always noncircular. Moreton & Smolensky (2002) review some 35 segmental cases, of which 3 are doubtful, 4 inferred from distribution, and 28 robustly evidenced by alternations; none are circular. The famous counter-example is the 'Min tone circle' of Taiwanese (Xiamen, Amoy) tone sandhi, examined in Moreton (1999, 2004a) and much discussed in the literature (see e.g. Chen 1987, 2000, Yip 2002 and references therein). The details of the case, Moreton argues, are such that it does not invite analysis in terms of "simple, logical, plausibly innate constraints," and, as a phenomenon that is "synchronically speaking, completely arbitrary and idiosyncratic," it must be understood as a nonphonological "paradigm replacement" (Moreton 2004a:159), an intriguing possibility in need of further specification (but see Mortensen 2004 for more cases and a different view). In the end, if the circular cases prove to fall under special generalizations outside the reach of core phonology, then the prediction is vindicated. At this point, the matter must be regarded as somewhat unsettled, absent a compelling analysis of the tone circle.

Whatever the fate of circularity, it remains remarkable that a theory as simple as M/F-OT, at a level of analysis that lacks any characterization of constraints other than the formal, should show a property like Harmonic Ascent, which governs and severely restricts what it can do. We need theories that have such properties if we are to establish the rationalist perspective that Chomsky enunciated in his foundational work. The Descriptive Method of theory investigation, and its typically particularized results, can give no hint that such a property is obtainable without stipulation. Equally remarkable is the abstractness of the question that led to its discovery: 'what limitations does the theory place on the mappings a grammar can accommodate?' One might expect the answer to be so negative ('no limit') or so abstract (for example, registering them with respect to automata theory) that no obvious practical consequences ensue. Theoretically, we learn that expanding the repertoire of constraint types to include *anti*-Faithfulness constraints (Alderete 1999b, 2001b) is more than an aesthetic complication; if unrestricted, it imperils the core emergent property of M/F-OT. And empirically, we find ourselves steered directly toward an entirely central phenomenon and informed that it is not merely of descriptive interest, but that its character actually determines the kind of theory we can have.

A further consequence of major analytical significance follows immediately from Moreton's work. Suppose we have a chain shift, [1] $x \rightarrow y$, [2] $y \rightarrow z$; this can only be obtained by preventing x from going all the way to z. We know from [2] that z is better than y on the Markedness subhierarchy. Thus, only Faithfulness can prevent x from leaping all the way to z; it is futile to seek a Markedness explanation for the fact that x halts at y.

More exactly, the ungrammatical candidate $^*x \rightarrow z$, which we wish to avoid, is better on Markedness than licit $x \rightarrow y$, but to lose, it must be *worse* on Faithfulness. This means that we need a Faithfulness constraint forbidding $^*x \rightarrow z$ *which does not forbid* $x \rightarrow y$. The analysis of M/F-OT not only tells us in general terms that circular shifts are disallowed; it specifically characterizes the kind of Faithfulness constraints that must exist if *non*circular chain shifts are to be admitted. It is far from trivial to develop a respectable theory of Faithfulness that contains such constraints; see, for example, Kirchner (1996), Gnanadesikan (1997), Moreton & Smolensky (2002), Mortensen (2004); and for other approaches, Alderete (1999b), (2001b) for antifaithfulness, and Łubowicz (2003), who aims to put the issue entirely outside the M/F distinction.

2.3.2 The Barrier Models

Goldsmith and Larson have proposed a spreading-activation account of linguistic prominence, which they have vigorously pursued through encounters with many attested patterns of stress and syllable structure — the Descriptive Method (Goldsmith & Larson 1990, Larson 1992, Goldsmith 1994). The model is, however, entirely self-contained as a formal object and susceptible to treatment as a Free-Standing Theory whose key properties can be determined analytically (Prince 1993 – henceforth IDN).[12] The aim of this section is to illustrate once again, in a very different context, how pursuing the basic formal questions leads not to an exercise in logical purification, but quite directly to properties of notable empirical significance.

The model works like this: the basic structure is a sequence of N 'nodes', each of which carries an 'activation' level, represented numerically. This gives it the power to represent ordinal properties of segments and syllables like sonority and prominence. Each node also has an unvarying bias, which may be interpreted as the intrinsic sonority or prominence of the linguistic unit that it represents. Rather than make a single calculation over these values to determine the output activation, the model calculates repeated interactions between adjacent nodes — the same mode of interaction repeated over and over. When the process converges on stable values, the model has calculated an activation profile that corresponds to a prominence structure such as a stress pattern or assignment of syllable peaks and margins. Nodes which bear greater activation than their closest neighbors – local maxima – are interpreted as having peaks of prominence.[13] Since the updating scheme is linear and iterative, we will call it the Dynamic Linear Model (DLM).

The neighborly interaction is mediated by two numerical parameters, which we designate L and R, each of which governs the character of the interaction in one of the two directions. The parameter L governs leftward spreading of activation; R, rightward spreading. Diagramatically, we can portray the situation like this:

(18) *DLM Network*

$$
\begin{array}{ccccccccc}
 & R & & R & & R & & R & \\
N_1 & \underset{\leftarrow}{\overset{\rightarrow}{}} & N_2 & \underset{\leftarrow}{\overset{\rightarrow}{}} & N_3 & \underset{\leftarrow}{\overset{\rightarrow}{}} & \cdots & \underset{\leftarrow}{\overset{\rightarrow}{}} & N_n \\
| & L & | & L & | & L & & L & | \\
B_1 & & B_2 & & B_3 & & & & B_n
\end{array}
$$

The model starts out with each node bearing zero activation. In the first step, each node gains the activation donated by its own bias; and then the serious trading begins. At each stage, the new activation of a node is determined from the current activation of its neighbors taken together with its own intrinsic bias level. The update scheme, in which we write a_k for the activation of N_k, can be represented like this:

(19) $a_k \leftarrow \frac{1}{2}\,L \cdot a_{k+1} + \frac{1}{2}\,R \cdot a_{k-1} + B_k$

A node's own current activation plays no role in determining its next state: only its bias, which never changes. Since L, R, and B_k are all constants, this is a linear scheme: each node's new activation is a weighted sum of its neighbor's activations, with its own bias added in.

Here are some examples to give a sense of how it works. Suppose we start out with a bias sequence (1,1,1,1,1,1), representing a string of 6 undifferentiated syllables. Let L=R= −1. The result is approximately (1.1, −0.3, 1.4, −0.6, 1.7, −0.9). This may look like nothing more than a mess of numbers, but the significant fact is the location of the local maxima – those nodes greater than their neighbors (or neighbor, if at an edge). Marking those, we see that the DLM has calculated this mapping, which we write using x for 'unstressed' and X for 'stressed': x x x x x x → X x X x X x

A familiar kind of alternating pattern has been imposed.

Now suppose we start out with a bias sequence (0,0,1,0,0,0) and set L=1.333 and R=.75. The result comes out approximately like this: (2.0, 3.0, **3.4**, 1.9, 1.0, 0.4). Identifying the one maximum (bolded), we see that this is the Input → Output relation:

   x x X x x x → x x X x x x

which is naturally interpreted to express a case in which an accent marked in the lexical input has been preserved on the surface.

If we alter the L,R parameters, we get a different result: for L=1.6, R=.635, we get approximately (2.9, **3.7**, 3.4, 1.6, 0.7, 0.2). The significant configuration now centers on the second entry, and we have portrayed the map

   x x X x x x→ x X x x x x

in which an underlying accent has been over-ridden.

A variety of linguistic and nonlinguistic patterns may be produced from such experimentation, suggesting the value of further systematic research.[14] What, then, are the general properties of the theory? At this point, two paths diverge. We may follow the Descriptive Method, with Goldsmith and Larson, aiming to deal with a wide range of known prominence phenomena in specific languages by finding L, R values and biases that will accommodate them. Or we may attempt to see what we can learn by interrogating the formal structure of theory, trying to classify its parameter space and look for characterizing properties.[15]

Let's start with one of the most fundamental questions we can ask: under what conditions does the theory *exist*? In the context of an iterative scheme like the DLM, this question takes a clear and exact form: when does the model converge, producing stable finite values as output? Specifically, what values of the parameters L and R lead to convergence? The fine-grained convergence limit is tied to a specific model's length in nodes; but generalizing over all models, we have this pleasing result, which will prove quite useful: if the absolute (unsigned) value of the product L·R is less than or equal to 1, any model of any length will converge.

(20)   *Convergence of the DLM*
       Any Dynamic Linear Model M_n with $|LR| \leq 1$ converges, for all n, n the number of nodes in the model.[16] (IDN:53)

From the descriptive point of view, this result has its uses – it tells us where not to look for parameter values – though, in practical terms, if we start our search near zero for both L and R, an astute prospector armed with a spreadsheet program ought to be able to find suitable values experimentally, when they exist. Analytically, its interest emerges when we ask a further question, targeted at finding the content of the theory in its realm of existence: given L, R, and a sequence of biases, is there a *formula* that describes the output of the iterative scheme? The goal is not merely to shorten the process of calculation (pointless in the Excel™ era), but to have a characterization of the model's output that may be scrutinized for general properties.

For the vast majority of networks, 'solving the model' in this way is not an option, and the Descriptive Method is essential to finding out what's going on; this is why we classified the Rumelhart & McClelland model as a TOD, and why people tend to think of network models as TOD on arrival. But the simple structure of the DLM renders it amenable to analysis.

Because the function computed by the DLM is linear in the biases, it is natural formally to inquire about the fate of bias sequences that consist entirely of 0's except for a single 1. Any other sequence can be built up from a weighted sum of such basic sequences. Here linguistics lines up happily with algebra – it is also linguistically natural to regard such sequences as representing a form with a single lexical accent.

We want to describe the value assumed by each node, given that the 'underlying accent' occurs in a certain place. The local maximum in the output, which is fully determined by these values, is where the surface accent lies. Calculation produces a formula which is a bit messy though not intractable (involving hyperbolic sines and cosines and the occasional complex number; see IDN:62). But a remarkable simplification occurs when we restrict the parameters to the curves LR=1, on which convergence is universally guaranteed.[17] Because of their simplicity, we may call these the 'Canonical Models'. The Canonical Models come in two kinds. Either L and R are both negative, in which case we have alternation of prominence, as we always do when both parameters are negative; or both parameters are positive.

The behavior of the general DLM when both L and R are positive is straightforward: accent is culminative, with a single maximum occurring in the activation function.[18] The same will be true in the Canonical Models. But when we seek the location of that maximum in the Canonical Models, a striking property emerges: there is a *window* at one edge or the other into which the surface accent must fall.

Given any value of R greater than 1, the surface accent can fall no further than a certain distance from the right edge, regardless of where the underlying accent is placed. The same is true for L (corresponding to values of R less than 1), with respect to the beginning of the word. Within the window, underlying accent is preserved. Outside the window, it is lost and in its place, as it were, the accent shows up at the inner edge of the window – the closest unit to the underlying accent that can be surface-accented.

We can name each model by the farthest internal location at which an accent can fall, (given single accented input), indicating by subscript the edge it measures from: thus, 3-Model$_R$ is the model in which the accent can fall no further into the string than the 3rd node from the end. Let us call these Canonical Models the 'barrier models', since in a k-Model, the kth node provides a kind of barrier beyond which surface accent may not venture. The parameter space divides up as in Table (21). NB: the cited ranges *exclude* the end points.

(21)   *Right Barrier Models*

Model #	"range" of R			Length of Range	Accent no further from end than
1-Model$_R$	∞	to	2	∞	final syllable
2-Model$_R$	2	to	3/2	1/2	penult
3-Model$_R$	3/2	to	4/3	1/6	antepenult
4-Model$_R$	4/3	to	5/4	1/12	preantepenult
5-Model$_R$	5/4	to	6/5	1/20	prepreantepenult
...		...		...	
j-Model$_R$	$j/(j-1)$	to	$(j+1)/j$	$1/j(j-1)$	$(\text{pre})^{j-3}$ antepenult

Symmetrically, the Left Barrier Models determine a window at the *beginning* of the string. The Right Barrier Models charted above occupy the parameter span where $R \in (1, \infty)$. The Left Barrier Models lie within the positive line segment $L \in (1, \infty)$, or equivalently $R \in (0,1)$, since $R=1/L$.[19]

This result is multiply remarkable. First, the barrier/windowing behavior is fully emergent from assumptions which make no mention of anything like that property. The alternating pattern that comes about when L and R are both negative has a kind of resonance with structural formulations like *CLASH (Kager 9.2.1). Both, in their different ways, seek to suppress prominence on adjacent units. And when L and R are both positive, it is perhaps not naively expected that the result should be a single maximum in the activation function, but it doesn't seem like an unusual outcome. It is the particularity of the windowing effect, and its lack of reducibility to some obvious local characteristic of the network, that makes it surprising.

Second, it is remarkable that the parameter ranges are valid for any length of string.[20] The number of nodes plays a role in the formula describing the output, and in other situations it figures in empirically anomalous dependencies (IDN:17). In this case, though, we have conditions that are valid across all forms, fully independent of form size.

Third, although nontrivial barrier/windowing behavior, with non-peripheral accents allowed, goes on outside the Canonical Models, it is restricted to a relatively small portion, a little less than 1/6, of the parameter space in the first quadrant. This means that random prospecting could easily miss it. Crucial to finding it is investigation along the hyperbola LR=1; but this curve presents itself as particularly interesting only because of its role in delimiting convergence.[21] The abstract, airless-seeming question with which we began – under what conditions does the model exist? – has led us right to one of its central properties.

Finally, it is striking that this fundamental result connects directly with a major phenomenon in stress and accent systems. The DLM overshoots the mark in a couple of respects – it is totally left-right symmetric, and allows windows of any size, while known windowing systems typically range up to no more than 3 syllables in length at the end of words, and 2 syllables at the beginning.[22] Whatever the remaining questions, the model opens the way to an entirely novel account of the windowing effect, unlike anything seen before. This renders the DLM worth studying alongside the other contentful accounts of prosodic structure that occupy linguistic attention, while vindicating the analytic method that reveals its structure.

2.4   Description and descriptivism

In a recent essay, Larry Hyman asks and answers the question "Why Describe African Languages?" (Hyman 2004). He argues that there is irreducible value in describing "complex phenomena using the ordinary tools of general linguistics," and that this goal stands in opposition to, and is at least as worthy as, developing grammars within current "theories [that] are not description-friendly," such as Minimalism and OT.

With the main thrust of his argument there can be little dissent: deep empirical work discovering the facts and generalizations of human languages is the very basis of linguistics, and it is essential that there be sound descriptions to convey them to the community of researchers. Why then the question? In part, Hyman's concern is driven by disciplinary attitudes toward 'theory' and 'description' – where, it seems, a certain class of person expects one to make a 'theoretical contribution' in every outing and will disdain or suppress work that lacks that key ingredient.[23] As for what a 'theoretical contribution' might be, Hyman cites an unidentified commentator:

(22)   "The shared belief of many in the field appears to be that a paper making a theoretical contribution must (a) propose some new mechanism, which adds to or replaces part of some current theory, or (b) contradicts some current theory. Papers that do neither, or those that do either but in a relatively minor way, are not looked at as making a theoretical contribution." Quoted in Hyman (2004:25).

This is very much a matter of 'mind your labels' – and we shouldn't be led to abandon the idea of 'theoretical contribution' because an obtunded version is instrumental in the intercollegial jostling and jousting of the field. In the present context, where a theory is taken to be an object in grave need of explication and analysis, it should be clear that an authentic 'theoretical contribution' can involve deepening the understanding of a theory's consequences or of the proper methods of using it, without a hint of replacement or contradiction.[24] We reject the 'shared belief' identified in the quote, and deny the privileged status it accords to certain types of work, to advocate a broader though not boundaryless account of what a contribution, including a 'theoretical contribution', may be. Hyman's move, by contrast, is to argue toward a unification of theory with description, neutralizing the distinction: "description and theory are very hard to disentangle – and when done right, they have the same concerns" (p.25). He goes on to clarify:

(23)   "Description is *analysis* and should ideally be

(a)   rigorous . . .
(b)   comprehensive . . .
(c)   rich . . .
(d)   insightful . . .
(e)   interesting . . ." (Hyman 2004:25)

No one would dispute either the importance of the cited criteria or the claim that they apply to theory as well as description. A closer look, though, is profitable, and suggests some important divergences. Criteria (c), (d), and (e) are contentful but difficult to assess intersubjectively, and perhaps connect more closely with Harris's 'convenience' than with questions of truth and falsity. We therefore focus on (a) *rigor* and (b) *comprehensiveness*.

Of rigor, the key remark is the one made in Section 1 above: there is no general sense of rigor that can be directly applied without regard for the specific assumptions at play in a given case. Work is therefore required. To design a successful ranking argument, as in our example, you must build from the actual definition of 'optimality'. It is necessary to ask 'what can be learned from the comparison of two candidates, one assumed optimal?' If the Evaluation Metric is to be employed seriously, you must inquire about the relation between local reduction of symbol consumption and the eventual global symbol count of the entire grammar. To achieve 'rigor', there is a range of questions that must be asked about the theory itself, and these questions differ in character from those asked of data (e.g. what is the distribution of downstepped high tone in Bangangte Bamileke?) or of the data-analysis relation (e.g. how are floating tones interpreted? how are they manipulated in Bangangte Bamileke?).[25] And different methods are required to answer them.[26]

Comprehensiveness – the inclusion of all relevant material – is a systematic notion and therefore presupposes a notion of 'system' which delimits relevance. Just like rigor, then, it takes on different colorations in different contexts. Contrast the questions to be asked and the techniques required to attain and evaluate, say, a full account of a language's verbal paradigm[27] with those used to derive and characterize the consequences of a formal theory. It makes sense to classify these as different 'contributions', if we are classifying things, though the inevitable ensuing scuffle to hierarchize them socially is better explicated by primatology than by the philosophy of science.

In the present context, the interpretation of *comprehensiveness* also marks an important divide between appropriate strategies for descriptive work and for theory development. Much can be gained theoretically by explicitly failing to be comprehensive over the data in ways that would be absurd descriptively. The study of idealized, delimited problems is a familiar and essential tool for exploring theories. At the grand level: the de Sitter cosmology imagines a universe that lacks matter entirely (it expands); Schwarzschild solves the field equations of General Relativity under the assumption of strict spherical symmetry of matter distribution (local collapse can result).[28] To cite a case considerably humbler and closer to home: much can be learned by working with a simplified Jakobsonian typology of syllable structure (Clements & Keyser 1983, Prince & Smolensky 2004), although it would be grossly inappropriate to claim comprehensiveness for a *description* of natural language syllable patterns that overlooks long vowels, diphthongs, and intrasyllabic consonant clusters.

Investigation of theories, even via the Descriptive Method, is tied to the availability of research strategies that idealize and delimit, deferring comprehensiveness. In the case of FST, this is particularly crucial because it opens up possibilities for obtaining analytical results when the general situation is complex and its structure obscure. Attitudes toward comprehensiveness therefore play a subtle but central role in estimating the relative promise of different research directions. One line of thinking finds expression in "Why Phonology is Different" (Bromberger and Halle 1989). The authors are concerned to justify their belief that phonology is intrinsically not amenable to being understood as the interaction of universal principles, distinguishing it in their view from syntax; the key, they argue, is the availability of stipulated language-specific rule-ordering in phonology alone:

(24) "Rule ordering is one of the most powerful tools of phonological description, and there are numerous instances in the literature where the ordering of rules is used to account for phonetic effects of great complexity." (Bromberger & Halle 1989: 59).

The perspective here is determinedly descriptive; the theory is to be justified by its ability to portray "complex" cases, for which much "power" is thought to be needed. There is no hint of an ambition to find and derive general properties of the language faculty, and consequently no willingness to tolerate the local costs of such ambition — idealization; plurality of theoretical lines; openness to ideas that limit rather than expand descriptive options; empirical lacunae and anomalies; admission of uncertainty. Their argument continues:

(25) "Until and unless these accounts are refuted and are replaced by better-confirmed ones, we must presume that Principle (7) [extrinsic ordering – AP] is correct." (Bromberger & Halle 1989:59).

One can only admire the authors' willingness to take on the entire literature in an area before rejecting its premises, but there are sound reasons why this strategy has never had much purchase on the field, which has been more notable for innovation than uniformity. At bottom, providing unsteady foundations, is an unexamined notion of 'confirmation', without which such qualifiers as 'better-confirmed' and 'correct' risk vacuity. More concretely, there are so many active, promising lines of investigation into every aspect of the enterprise, from the nature of the data to the identity of the targets of explanation, that it seems premature to shut them down on the basis of a presumption.

Whatever the ultimate status of their imperative, its interest in the present context is its orthogonality to the kind of theoretical concerns we have been probing. There is no sense in their work that a theory is an opaque object, whose content and proper handling must be discovered before we can declare success and failure, even descriptively, or compare it properly with other theories. Supreme is the goal of 'accounting for', and given a disposition to regard the facts as a fixed body, the approach merges with classic descriptivism. The real threat to their favored theory, then, is not provided by those versions of generative phonology which pursue very different explanatory goals, but rather by statistical empiricism, which also avails itself of 'powerful tools' to gain even more comprehensive models of their data.

2.5   Conclusion

The encounter with fact is essential to the validation, falsification, and discovery of theories. But as soon as a theory comes into existence, it must also be encountered on its own terms. A theory cannot even be faced with fact – we cannot *do* it properly – if we don't know how to construct valid arguments from its premises. And since a theory's content is the set of its consequences, which are typically far from legible in its defining conditions, we are obliged to interrogate its structure to find out what it *is*. Asking the fundamental formal questions, and finding or developing techniques to answer them, is an irreplaceable aspect of linguistic research that identifies the major predictions and particularly meaningful empirical challenges associated with a theory.

Linguistic theory has shown a notable tendency to develop what we have called Free-Standing Theories, those which have an internal structure susceptible to detailed analysis independent of the factual encounter. The reasons for doing so may be, as suggested above, intrinsic to the realist project, since rationalist theories require an abstract object of study whose existence is likely to be justifiable only in terms of deep, non-obvious properties. In the absence of such properties, empiricist inductivism exerts a strong claim to the territory.

It is reasonable to ask, then, why the 'Analytic Method' of confronting theories on their own terms does not play a more conspicuous role in the current ecology of the field, which could be argued to conserve, largely, an intuitive methodology more properly rooted in the descriptive ambitions of pre-generative work. An important factor may be the sense that formal analysis can be successfully replaced by approaches more closely allied to facts and to techniques for dealing with facts – 'the ordinary tools of general linguistics'. Invaluable in empirical assessment of claims, the Descriptive Method has often been taken as the primary mode of exploring a theory's structure and content, where it has severe limitations. Adhered to strictly, it cannot distinguish between a superset theory ("too powerful") and a proper subset theory; it has no particular relation to a theory's systematic properties; and it is unable to provide certainty in the assessment of claims about predictions and exclusions.

A more recent development which is sometimes taken to provide a feasible substitute for analysis is 'grounding' – in the case of phonology, pointing to phonetics as supporting the correctness of theoretical assertions. In much work, the term has a specific well-defined sense which gives it theoretical status (Archangeli & Pulleyblank 1994, Hayes 2004a:299), but it also leads a second, more fluid life as a motivator and recipient of intuitive appeals. Some of this may be discerned in the following statement from Hayes (2004a:291), who is asking "what qualifies a constraint as an authentic markedness principle?":

(26)   "The currently most popular answer, I think, relies on typological evidence: a valid constraint 'does work' in many languages, and does it in different ways.

    However, a constraint could also be justified on functional grounds. In the case of phonetic functionalism, a well-motivated phonological constraint would be one that either renders speech easier to articulate or renders contrasting forms easier to distinguish perceptually. From the functionalist point of view, such constraints are a priori plausible, under the reasonable hypothesis that language is a biological system that is designed to perform its job well and efficiently." (Hayes 2004a:291).

But the symmetry is illusory. A constraint, in the intended sense, is a principle within a theory and, like any other principle in any other theory, is justified by its contribution to the consequences of that theory. Since OT is a theory of grammar, the consequences are displayed in the grammars predicted and disallowed – 'typological evidence'. A constraint which cannot be justified on those grounds cannot be justified. Further, 'justifying' a constraint functionally (or in any other extrinsic way) can have no effect whatever on its role within the theory. A constraint, viewed locally, can appear wonderfully concordant with some function, but this cannot supplant the theory's logic or compel the global outcome ('efficiency') that is imagined to follow from the constraint's presence, or even make it more likely.

A ranking argument based on two candidates, one desired optimal, remains valid whether the constraints are grounded or not; and in Targeted Constraint OT, where grounding is invoked to support the notion of targeting (Wilson 2001:156–160), such two-candidate arguments lose their validity because of the formal structure of the theory, and phonetic function cannot restore it. The property of Harmonic Ascent cannot be abrogated, amended, or influenced by grounding or its lack. The choice of *Markedness* constraints, no matter how grounded, cannot by itself predict grammatical behavior, because mappings are determined by the interaction of Markedness with Faithfulness constraints, whose properties are crucial to the range of possible outcomes.

When stated explicitly (p.299), Hayes's 'inductive grounding' is not an exercise in the plausible,[29] but a concrete proposal for the generation of certain kinds of constraints from specific data, which relies on finding the local maxima in a certain space of possibilities. Its fate is in the hands of geometry and logic. As an actual theory, it has left behind any hopes that attended its conception and birth, and now lives in the realm of the issues explored here.

Such considerations suggest a bright future for linguistic research as it grows beyond its origins. Analysis is deaf to our desires, but it can tell us what we want to know, if we know how to ask.

Notes

I'd like to thank Paul Smolensky, John McCarthy, Jane Grimshaw, Bruce Tesar, Jean-Roger Vergnaud, Vieri Samek-Lodovici, Chaim Tannenbaum, Seth Cable, Naz Merchant, and Adrian Brasoveanu for interactions which have shaped and re-shaped my views on the matters addressed here. Thanks to Paul de Lacy for valuable comments on an earlier draft.

1 Saari (2005) is a recent study. To get a sense of what can happen, see Ekeland (1988), esp. pp. 123–131.

2 The intuition gets a boost from previous analytical practice: in ordering rules, the analyst typically looked at two rules at a time (and that worked, didn't it?).

3 If an erroneously truncated ERC has excluded the correct hierarchy, there will be further information that contradicts it, yielding the impression that no correct hierarchy exists. Even if the erroneous ranking condition has not excluded the correct hierarchy, it produces a distorted account of the explanatory force of the various constraint relations in it.

4 Interestingly, the actual on-the-ground interpretation of the Evaluation Metric may have been closer to the loose general sense of 'be simple' than to the formal definition of evaluation.

5 At a considerably more abstract level, there is much to be said about the capacities and dynamics of connectionist networks, see Smolensky et al. (1996) for a large-scale multi-perspective overview.

6 See Rumelhart & McClelland (1986), McClelland et al. (1986a). The general view taken there is that "the objects referred to in macrostructural [i.e. symbolic –AP] models of cognitive processing are seen as approximate descriptions of emergent properties of the microstructure" (McClelland, Rumelhart, and Hinton 1986:12). Smolensky and Legendre (2005) develop a very different view, according exact reality to both continuous (micro) and discrete (macro) processing as distinct levels.

7 Interestingly, competition often provokes localized analysis of a rival theory, treated as an FST, even in the context where the favored theory is being laid out and investigated by the Descriptive Method. To cite merely one example: in Halle and Vergnaud (1987), an important synthetic work that brings together much prior theory under the unifying rubric of the bracketed grid (Hammond 1984), there is an argument against one of Hammond's proposals, based on an apparently false consequence derived from it (p.75). Halle & Vergnaud's system is well and even elegantly formalized, yet due to their reliance on the Descriptive Method, we have little idea of the scope of their own predictions, some of which may involve equally disturbing pathologies.

8 Nonexistence isn't the worst thing that can happen. Yang-Mills theory, for example, is said to be basic to modern particle physics, but is not known to 'exist' mathematically, i.e. to have coherent foundations. The Clay Institute offers $1,000,000 for showing its 'existence': http://www.claymath.org/millennium/Yang-Mills_Theory.

9 For example, the theory of multiplication and division exists; but you can't divide by zero. Similarly, if you are computing probabilities, they must not be less than 0 or greater than 1. To move nearer to our concerns, note that it is crucial for OT that there be at least one *best* element in the candidate

set. Suppose that a constraint was posited to offer *rewards* rather than penalties, as all do now. Let the putative constraint LONG give a reward of +1 for each syllable that a form contains. Then there is no candidate that has the maximal value on LONG, and were the constraint asked to produce the class of forms that do maximally well on it, no output would be defined. If such a constraint is admitted, the theory ceases to exist.

10 The presentation of Moreton's results given here will be considerably more qualitative than Moreton's own, and will diverge in some points of perspective. See Moreton (2004a) for a scrupulous rendering of the details.

11 'By no means all'—this innocuous phrase hides the difficulty, in many circumstances where ordinal preference is involved, of finding a system that has the property. Common sense intuition fails dramatically here. See Saari (2001), for example, to make contact with the vast literature emerging from Arrow (1951).

12 Discussion is based on "In defense of the number *i*" (Prince 1993 – IDN), improved notationally and formally in a few respects.

13 Although the model operates internally on numbers, it does not strive to compute an empirically-determined numerical value; its interpreted output is fully discrete and indeed binary, discriminating only peaks from nonpeaks.

14 Such experimentation with the parameters of a theory is a part of what we are calling the Analytic Method, though here we are emphasizing the aspects of analysis that yield provable results.

15 In noting this methodological divergence, we are of course not asserting that only one path should be pursued.

16 For a specific length N, we have convergence iff $|LR| < 1/\cos^2(\pi/(N+1))$, which is always greater than 1. If L and R have the same sign, a model diverges to infinity at and beyond the limiting value; if they have different signs, the model enters an oscillatory regime of period 4 at the limiting value, and diverges to infinity beyond it.

17 The resulting formula turns out to involve the product of two linear terms, each reflecting distance to the edge, and an exponential term based on either of the L or R parameters, whose exponent reflects the distance between the underlying accent and the node whose value is being computed. Schematically, we can write it like this, using $a_k[j]$ to mean the value of the *j*th node in the output vector whose input has a '1' in position k and zeroes elsewhere:

$$a_k[j] = C \cdot \text{dist-k\#}(j) \cdot \text{dist-j\#}(k) \cdot R^{\text{dist}(j,k)}$$

where C is a length-based constant $2/(n+1)$, the 'tilt' $\sqrt{(R/L)} = R$, dist-k#(j) gives the unsigned distance of j from the edge where k is not in the j-to-edge path, dist-j#(k) *mutatis mutandis*; dist(j,k) is the signed distance $(j - k)$ between j and k.

18 Caveat: what we are calling a 'maximum' can be spread across two adjacent nodes that have identical activation values.

19 For R=L=1, we simply reproduce the input accent, no matter where it is located, on any string of any length; this is the ∞-Model. The behavior at the other end points of the ranges is not entirely welcome: we get adjacent pairs of nodes with equal activation at the window boundary when the input accent lies at or beyond the barrier. In the R Models, for example, when R=2, we get equal activation on the final and penult when the input accent is penult or earlier. When R=3/2, we get equal activation on penult and antepenult when the input accent is antepenult or earlier.

20 Hence the celebratory appellation *Theorema Egregium* applied to its announcement (IDN:85).

21 In the original formulation of the model, the Canonical Models were defined by LR=1/4, which is even less obvious as a condition to pursue.

22 One could imagine that the drastic shrinking of the parameter range with increase in window size might support a more detailed account of the empirical restrictions, at least in part (IDN:91).

23 Stepping through the looking glass, we can easily discern the antitype who demands an 'empirical contribution' as the prerequisite for admissibility.

24 Just as in certain regions of physics, to risk an extravagant comparison, finding a solution to a known equation, or a method for solving a type of equation, can net a Nobel Prize or an office at the Institute for Advanced Study.

25 The questions are drawn from Hyman's discussion of Voorhoeve (1971).

26 Those methods require analysis and development in themselves, since they call on statistics, formal language theory, ordinal preference theory, recursive function theory, logic, and so on.

27 This casual and overly certain-sounding allusion to 'verbal paradigm' should remind us that the categories of the presupposed 'system' are almost always under contention, and can be wrong, leading to failure of comprehensiveness and the missing of generalizations. Is a phonological description comprehensive without reference to aspects of speech perception and speech production? Is a syntactic analysis comprehensive that overlooks pragmatics? In some such cases, the answer must be *yes*, or we are done for; but which?

28 Interestingly, Einstein neither expected nor was happy with these results. Pais (1983) is the authoritative account of the life and works, though its perspective has been somewhat outdated by the intense subsequent growth (unexpected, perhaps, by Pais) of black hole studies and String Theory with its higher-dimensional space-times.

29 Terms like 'plausible' or 'reasonable' seem to diagnose what we might call 'conceptual orientation' in the discourse participants. The implicit contrast is with *possible* — if something is said to be X-ologically possible, the implication is that we know enough about the theory of X-ology to calculate with it; the comforts of the X-ologically *plausible* are those of intuition and common-sense.

3

Functionalism in phonology

Matthew Gordon

3.1 Introduction

This chapter discusses the role of functional factors in shaping sound systems. There has been a great deal of work exploring the articulatory, perceptual, and processing underpinnings of phonology. In particular, the last decade has witnessed renewed vigor in attempting to integrate functional, especially phonetic, explanations into formal analyses of phonological phenomena. This program of phonetically-driven phonology has been spurred by the advent of Optimality Theory, which can be adapted to model gradient and contingent phenomena using constraints.

While an overarching appreciation for the role of phonetic and other functional factors unites all work within phonetically-driven phonology, there are disparate areas of research and viewpoints represented in the framework. Some work focuses principally on the role of articulation, other research attaches primary importance to perception, while other work appeals to processing factors. Some research focuses on the role of phonetic factors in predicting cross-linguistic markedness patterns, whereas other research explores correlations between phonetics and phonology on a language-specific basis. Approaches within phonetically-driven Optimality Theory also differ in terms of the predicates manipulated by the constraints; some favour analyses in which constraints are expressed using discrete phonological constructs while others assume that continuous phonetic variables are directly encoded in the constraints. Some researchers assume that phonetic considerations alone are sufficient to predict phonological patterns, while others assume that raw phonetic factors are mediated by measures of phonological simplicity.

The structure of this chapter is as follows. Section 3.2 discusses early work exploring the phonetic motivations behind phonological patterns. Section 3.3 focuses on the formal modelling of phonetic factors within phonetically-driven OT. Other non-phonetic considerations relevant to

phonology, including processing and frequency effects, are explored in
Section 3.4. Section 3.5 examines evidence for the synchronic productivity
of phonetic knowledge in phonological systems. Section 3.6 summarizes
the chapter.

3.2   The groundwork for phonetically-driven phonology

There has long been interest in the role of phonetic and functional factors
in shaping phonological systems. Functional motivations (not necessarily
phonetic in nature) behind phonological patterns were proposed by linguists
throughout the last century often from a diachronic perspective (e.g.
Jakobson 1931, Firth 1948, Martinet 1968). A substantial body of research
conducted during the last three decades of the twentieth century by phoneticians explored phonetic motivations for recurring patterns in sound inventories. In one of the earlier works in this research program, Liljencrants and
Lindblom (1972) advance the hypothesis that vowel inventories are guided
by a preference for vowels to be maximally distinct from each other in
the perceptual domain. In order to quantify perceptual distinctness, they
convert formant values expressed in Hertz in the acoustic dimension to
a perceptual measure of frequency calculated in mels. As hypothesized,
Liljencrants and Lindblom find a fairly close match between frequently
occurring vowel systems and perceptual distinctness (also see Kingston
17.3.2).

   Later work by Lindblom and Maddieson (1986) builds on Liljencrants
and Lindblom's perceptually based approach by attributing some role to
articulatory factors in forging sound systems. Focusing on consonants, they
propose a model in which languages prefer perceptually divergent sounds
within regions of similar articulatory difficulty. Languages first exploit the
subspace consisting of articulatorily simpler sounds, choosing sounds
within the simple articulatory space that are maximally distinct from a
perceptual standpoint. Once the articulatorily basic subspace is perceptually saturated, inventories are expanded through introduction of more
complex articulations. Space within this second tier of articulatory difficulty
is then carved up according to perceptual distinctness until no more
sounds may be added without jeopardizing other distinctions. At this point,
any inventory expansion necessitates exploitation of the most difficult articulatory subspace. In this way, perceptual and articulatory factors conflict:
maximizing perceptual distinctness comes at the price of greater articulatory difficulty, while minimizing articulatory effort reduces perceptual
distinctness. This conflict between maximization of perceptual differentiation
and minimization of articulatory complexity is a recurring theme of much
work in phonetically-driven phonology.

   Other work by various phoneticians tackles the phonetic motivations,
both articulatory and perceptual, behind various phonological phenomena

(see Ohala 1997 for an overview). Much of this work is appealed to by later researchers working within the framework of formal phonetically-driven phonology.

3.3 Optimality Theory and phonetic motivations in phonology

The advent of Optimality Theory (Prince and Smolensky 2004) in the 1990s sparked a large body of research attempting to integrate phonetic explanations directly into the OT formalism as constraints on naturalness. An important precursor to this work is Archangeli and Pulleyblank's (1994) analysis of ATR vowel harmony, in which they argue that interactions between the feature [ATR] and height and backness features are grounded in phonetic factors (see Hall 13.6.3). For example, the [−ATR] specification of low vowels is attributed to the retracted position of the tongue root during their production.

Early work in phonetically-driven OT follows Archangeli and Pulleyblank in attempting to ground implicational statements of markedness, typically contextually governed, in acoustic and articulatory factors. It argues that a phonetically-informed model of phonology is both more explanatory and offers better empirical coverage than alternative approaches not appealing to phonetics. Sections 3.3.1–3.3.4 discuss some representative works in phonetically-driven OT. The interested reader is also referred to other related literature including Kaun (1995), Jun (1996a), Myers (1997a), Boersma (1998, 2003), Gafos (1999, 2002), Steriade (2001a), Padgett (2003a), Côté (2004), and Hayes et al. (2004).

3.3.1 Universal perceptibility hierarchies in phonetically-driven OT: the case of laryngeal neutralization

Steriade's (1999b) account of laryngeal neutralization provides a cogent example of the formal implementation of phonetically-driven phonology using OT. Steriade's work explores the hypothesis that observed implicational hierarchies in laryngeal neutralization sites correspond closely to hierarchies of perceptual salience: laryngeal contrasts are maintained in positions where they are less perceptible only if the same contrasts also exist in contexts of greater salience.

To illustrate the basic patterns in need of explanation, languages such as Classical Greek and Lithuanian have voicing contrasts in obstruents only when they immediately precede sonorants (i.e. vowels and sonorant consonants): e.g. Lithuanian [áukle] 'governess' vs. [auglingas] 'fruitful', [akmuó] 'stone' vs. [augmuó] 'growth'. The voicing contrast is neutralized to voiceless word-finally and to the voicing specification of a following obstruent word-medially: e.g. /daúg/→ [daúk] 'much' /atgal/ → [adgal] 'back' vs. /dégti/→ [dékti]

'burn-inf.' Other languages are less stringent in their minimal requirements of salience for voicing contrasts to be preserved. Thus, in Hungarian,
a voicing contrast in obstruents is found not only in presonorant position
but also word-finally. Yet another neutralization pattern, still less stringent
than the other two, is found in many varieties of Arabic and allows for
voicing contrasts not only in presonorant position and word-finally but
also after a sonorant. Finally, the possibility of voicing contrasts occurring
in all contexts, including when not adjacent to either a preceding or following
sonorant is attested in Khasi.

We thus have a hierarchy of voicing neutralization sites, as in (1), where
languages differ in their cut-off points between permissible and impermis-
sible locations for voicing contrasts in obstruents. Note that the division
between languages lacking voicing contrasts and those only allowing contrasts in presonorant position is included for the sake of completeness.

(1) *Hierarchy of environments for laryngeal neutralization*

voicing contrasts allowed   voicing contrasts disallowed

◄──►

nowhere   pre-   word-   post-   pre-   everywhere
          sonorant   finally   sonorant   obstruent

Steriade observes that perceptual considerations predict the hierarchy of
neutralization sites. Neutralization is more likely in contexts where laryngeal features are difficult to implement in a perceptually salient manner.
Drawing on the results of studies on the perception of voicing (e.g. Raphael
1981, Slis 1986), Steriade suggests that the perceptual salience of laryngeal
features in different environments depends on the acoustic properties
associated with those environments. The accurate perception of obstruents,
in particular stops, relies heavily on cues realized on transitions from the
obstruents to adjacent vowels. Focusing on voicing, these contextual cues
include the following: (a) burst, which is less intense for voiced obstruents
than for voiceless ones, (b) voice-onset-time, which is negative for voiced
stops and either zero or positive for voiceless stops, as well as (c) fundamental
frequency and first formant values during adjacent vowels, both of which
are lower in proximity to voiced obstruents. Internal cues to obstruents (i.e.
properties temporally aligned with the consonant constriction itself) are
less numerous and generally less salient perceptually; these internal cues
to laryngeal features include voicing (present for voiced obstruents but
not for voiceless ones) and closure duration (typically shorter for voiced
obstruents than for voiceless ones).

Presonorant position is superior to preobstruent or final position for
realizing a laryngeal contrast saliently, since several transitional cues are
present: voice-onset-time, the burst, and fundamental frequency and first
formant values at the offset of the consonant. Final position is better
than preobstruent position since obstruents are more likely in this context
to have an audible release burst in addition to internal voicing cues.

Preobstruent position is worst from a perceptual standpoint, since the only cues to laryngeal features in this position are the internal cues of voicing, and if audibly released, closure duration.

Steriade posits a series of constraints whose ranking is fixed based on scales of perceptibility: constraints banning a laryngeal feature in a less salient context are ranked above constraints banning that laryngeal feature in a more salient context. A faithfulness constraint requiring preservation of underlying laryngeal features is interleaved on a language-specific basis to predict the laryngeal neutralization pattern characteristic of a given language. This schema (slightly modified from Steriade's analysis) is depicted in (2) for the feature [voice].

(2) *Ranking of constraints governing voicing contrasts*

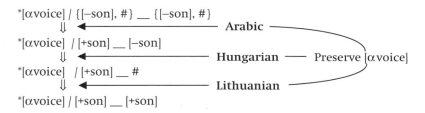

Steriade characterizes her constraints in terms of [F], where F stands for the relevant laryngeal feature, in this case [voice]. She adopts this notation rather than one referring to either a positive or negatively stated feature, arguing that the perceptibility of the laryngeal contrast is at stake rather than only a positively or only a negatively specified feature value. This analysis is also consistent with the fact that laryngeal neutralization characteristically produces laryngeally unspecified consonants whose surface properties are those that are easiest to implement in a particular environment, voiced when preceding a voiced sound and voiceless when preceding a voiceless sound or in final position, where aerodynamic considerations militate against voicing.

The fact that the output of laryngeal neutralization is context dependent indicates that Steriade's constraints are not wholly reliant on perceptual factors. Rather, Steriade suggests that the constraints refer to the ratio of effort required to implement a contrast in a perceptually salient manner: contrasts are more likely to be banned in contexts in which great effort must be expended for minimal perceptual rewards.

Steriade observes that Lombardi's (1995b) syllable-based theory of neutralization fails to explain many of the patterns in (1). In Lombardi's account, laryngeal neutralization affects consonants in coda position of a syllable, since coda position is unable to license independently linked laryngeal features. The Hungarian type pattern, whereby voicing contrasts are limited to final position and to presonorant position cannot be explained with reference to the coda, since word-final obstruents are codas and are thus erroneously expected to undergo neutralization parallel to word-medial obstruents. Nor is it descriptively adequate to say that word-final consonants are extraprosodic and thus not codas, since word-final consonants are prosodically active in the calculation of the minimal word requirement, which is CVC in Hungarian. Similarly, in Lithuanian, only a subset of coda consonants (those occurring before obstruents and word-finally) undergo neutralization. It is thus insufficient to state simply that codas undergo neutralization in Lithuanian.

3.3.2   Language specificity in phonetic conditioning factors: the case of syllable weight

While Steriade's work focuses on the explication of universal contextual markedness scales, other work within phonetically-driven OT tackles the issue of whether cross-linguistic variation in phonological patterns is also predictable on phonetic grounds. In his study of weight-sensitive stress, Gordon (2002b) tests the hypothesis that closed syllables have different phonetic properties in languages in which they are phonologically heavy (e.g. Finnish) from languages in which they are light (e.g. Khalkha Mongolian). As a starting point in the study, Gordon suggests that languages tend to adopt weight distinctions that are phonetically sensible, where a distinction's phonetic effectiveness is a function of the degree to which it offers maximal separation of heavy and light syllables.

Gordon tests various potential parameters along which phonetic effectiveness can be quantified, ultimately finding that a measure of perceptual energy (i.e. loudness integrated over time) of the rime matches up well with weight distinctions in a number of languages. Crucially, languages that treat CVC as light differ from those that treat CVC as heavy in the relative phonetic effectiveness of different distinctions. In languages with heavy CVC, the inclusion of CVC in the set of heavy syllables improves the degree of phonetic separation of heavy and light syllables relative to other candidate distinctions, in particular the distinction that treats only CVV and not CVC as heavy. In languages with light CVC, on the other hand, treating CVC as a heavy syllable type reduces the phonetic effectiveness relative to other weight distinctions. Gordon's work builds on earlier work by Broselow et al. (1997) exploring language-specific correlations between syllable weight and phonetic properties. However, Broselow et al. find a close correlation between coda weight and a simple measure of phonetic duration in languages with light CVC (Malayalam in their study) and heavy CVC (Hindi and Arabic). They find that vowels in closed syllables are substantially shorter than their counterparts in open syllables in Malayalam, unlike in the examined languages with heavy CVC. They suggest that the shortening of vowels in closed syllables in Malayalam is attributed to mora sharing between the coda consonant and the nucleus. In languages with heavy CVC there is no mora sharing between a nucleus and a coda, in keeping with the absence of a phonetic distinction in vowel length between open and closed syllables.

Besides the difference between Gordon and Broselow et al.'s studies in the phonetic parameters found to correlate with weight, the two works differ in the nature of the relationship assumed to obtain between phonetics and phonology. Broselow et al. take the position that languages tailor their phonetic systems to enhance the realization of phonological weight. Gordon, on the other hand, pursues the hypothesis that weight systems are constructed on the basis of a language's phonetic properties.

These two models of the phonetics–phonology interface are difficult to tease apart since they both predict a correlation between phonetics and phonology. One way to tease apart the two hypotheses is to look for an independent and language-specific property of languages that could explain the observed phonetic patterns independent of weight. Gordon claims that the match between the phonetics and phonology of weight is attributed to a more basic property of languages: syllable structure. He finds that languages that treat CVC as heavy have a higher proportion (in type frequency) of relatively intense codas (including sonorants and voiced consonants) than languages that treat CVC as light. Gordon suggests that the large number of high intensity codas in languages with heavy CVC increases the aggregate energy profile of CVC, thereby increasing the likelihood that it will be phonologically heavy. The observed indirect link between syllable structure and phonological weight criterion would be accidental in a model that assumes that phonology only influences but is not influenced by phonetics.

3.3.3 Phonological simplicity in phonetically-driven phonology
3.3.3.1 Simplicity in syllable weight

Gordon's work on weight explores another factor that emerges as relevant in quantitative studies of phonetically-driven phonology. He finds that certain hypothetical weight distinctions in fact provide a closer match to the phonetic map than some of the actual attested distinctions. For example, in Khalkha Mongolian, a distinction treating only long vowels and syllables containing /a/ followed by a coda nasal (CVV, CaN heavy) is phonetically superior to all other weight distinctions including the exploited distinction between heavy CVV and all other syllables. Gordon suggests that there is a bias against the {CVV, CaN} heavy distinction and others like it even if they are phonetically effective, since such distinctions manipulate highly asymmetrical weight categories. In the case of the {CVV, CaN} heavy distinction, reference must be made to multiple phonological dimensions: vowel length, vowel quality, and type of coda. Attested phonological dimensions are simpler in terms of the dimensions they manipulate, either number of timing positions in the case of the distinction that treats both CVV and CVC heavy, vowel length, or vowel quality. Gordon thus proposes that languages employ a criterion of phonological simplicity in addition to the criterion of phonetic effectiveness when evaluating potential weight distinctions: in his model, languages adopt the phonetically most sensible among the distinctions that do not exceed a complexity threshold, which Gordon tentatively formulates with reference to the number of associations between timing slots and features.

3.3.3.2   Simplicity in obstruent voicing patterns

Gordon's appeal to a notion of phonological simplicity is shared with work by Hayes (1999) on the phonetic naturalness of obstruent voicing. Based on results from an aerodynamic modelling experiment, Hayes finds that the relative naturalness of stop voicing is contingent upon a number of factors, two of which I focus on here: place of articulation and the context in which the stop occurs. First, ease of voicing is correlated with frontness of the constriction. Bilabials facilitate voicing because they are associated with a relatively large oral cavity, which delays the equalization of oral and subglottal pressure that triggers cessation of vocal fold vibration. Velars, on the other hand, inhibit voicing since pressure builds up rapidly behind the closure thereby eliminating the necessary aerodynamic conditions for voicing. The second factor that predicts ease of voicing is the context in which the stop occurs. Voicing is facilitated in a postnasal context where the raising of the velum for the nasal increases the size of the cavity behind the oral closure and the potential for some air leaking through the nasal cavity delays the cessation of voicing. Voicing is slightly more difficult following a non-nasal sonorant, still more difficult in initial position (where low subglottal pressure inhibits voicing), and most difficult after an obstruent (where intraoral pressure is already high). Combining the two dimensions of frontness and environment yields a matrix of stop voicing naturalness (expressed in arbitrary units based on aerodynamic modelling) as in (3), where larger numbers indicate increased difficulty of voicing.

(3)   *Phonetic map of obstruent voicing*

Environment	[b]	[d]	[g]
[−son]__ (after obst)	43	50	52
#__ (initial)	23	27	35
[+son, −nas]__ (after non-nasal sonorant)	10	20	30
[+nas]__ (after nasal)	0	0	0

While Hayes finds that cross-linguistic patterns of stop voicing line up well with the aerodynamic modelling results, phonologies of individual languages for the most part are sensitive to only one of the dimensions relevant for predicting voicing ease: either context or place of articulation. For example, Latin bans voiced obstruents after another obstruent while Dakota's only voiced stop is the bilabial [b]. Strikingly absent are systems that are simultaneously sensitive to environment and place of articulation in predicting stop voicing patterns, even if these patterns are phonetically well-grounded. For example, we do not find languages that ban all voiced stops after an obstruent, both /b/ and /d/ but not /g/ in initial position, and /g/ but not /b/ and /d/ after a non-nasal sonorant.

Hayes suggests that the explanation for this gap in attested patterns lies in their complexity relative to other slightly less phonetically natural but nevertheless more symmetrical patterns. Hayes' procedure for integrating complexity and naturalness differs from Gordon's in assuming that phonetic naturalness is compared across constraints that are formally similar in terms of the features they manipulate (differing only in the substitution of a single predicate, such as switching feature values, addition or loss of feature, and so on). The phonetically most natural of the constraints within each family of closely related constraints are those that are exploited by actual languages. A crucial difference between Hayes' metric of simplicity and the one adopted by Gordon is that phonetic effectiveness in Hayes' approach is only evaluated across formally similar constraints, unlike in Gordon's work which assumes that phonetic effectiveness is compared across all potential constraints regardless of their formal similarity.

3.3.4 Continuous phonetic variables and constraint formulation: the case of contour tones

The works discussed up to this point have in common that their constraint formulation relies on discrete phonological entities – i.e. features, timing positions, syllables. However, some work in phonetically-driven OT has posited constraints referring directly to continuous phonetic variables, such as duration, frequency, and distance. The incorporation of gradience into the formal analysis has proved beneficial in at least two areas. First, certain phenomena appear to be sensitive to finer-grained distinctions than traditional discrete representations are able to differentiate. Second, the application of many processes is dependent on speech rate, a factor that is not easily modelled using conventional phonological categories.

Zhang's (2002, 2004) analysis of contour tone distributions implements a set of constraints referring to continuous phonetic dimensions. Drawing on a cross-linguistic survey of contour tones in 187 languages, Zhang finds that certain syllables are more conducive to supporting contour tones than others. The first relevant dimension concerns the rime. Contour tones most prefer to dock on syllables containing a long vowel (CVV), followed by short vowel syllables ending in a sonorant coda (CVR). Contour tones on short vowel open syllables and on short vowel syllables ending in a coda obstruent are comparatively rare. Zhang also finds that many languages preferentially allow contour tones on stressed syllables but not on unstressed syllables. Another predictor is syllable position: final syllables are more likely to tolerate tonal contours than non-final syllables. Finally, some languages are sensitive to the number of syllables in a word, such that shorter words are more receptive to carrying contour tones than longer words.

Zhang proposes that all of these distributional skewings are sensible if one considers the phonetic requirements of tone. Tonal information is recoverable from not only the fundamental frequency, but also from the lower harmonics, which occur at frequency multiples of the fundamental. Sonorants are far better suited to carrying tone than obstruents due to their more energetic harmonic structure. Vowels are ideal carriers of tone since they have the greatest intensity in their harmonic structure. Because contour tones require a greater duration than simple tones to be executed in a perceptually recoverable manner, Zhang argues that it is not surprising that many languages restrict contour tones to CVV and others limit contours to CVV and CVR. It also follows that stressed vowels, final vowels, and vowels in shorter words should be better equipped to support contour tones. Stressed vowels are characteristically longer than unstressed vowels, final vowels are longer than non-final vowels, and vowels are longer in shorter words than in longer words.

Zhang posits a formula for predicting the ability of a syllable to carry a contour tone: $C_{\text{CONTOUR}} = a \cdot \text{Dur}(V) + \text{Dur}(R)$. According to this formula, the contour tone carrying ability is a function of the duration of a sonorant coda plus the duration of the vowel multiplied by some value (a) greater than one, which reflects the greater ability of a vowel to support a contour relative to a sonorant consonant. The actual value of a is not crucial for present purposes (see Zhang 2002 for discussion).

Whether a given syllable can support a contour tone or not is a function of the C_{CONTOUR} value for the rime and the type of contour involved. Thus, rising tones require larger C_{CONTOUR} values than falling tones since they take longer to execute, and complex tones require larger C_{CONTOUR} values than contour tones since there are more tonal targets to reach. Formally, the tone bearing ability of different syllables is captured through a family of constraints of the form *CONTOUR(T)–$C_{\text{CONTOUR}}(R)$, where a tone T is banned for a rime possessing an insufficiently large C_{CONTOUR} value to support the tone. These constraints interact with faithfulness constraints requiring that underlying tones surface, PRES(T), and constraints banning excess length in the rime beyond that minimally required in a given prosodic context, *DUR. Parallel to the CONTOUR(T)–$C_{\text{CONTOUR}}(R)$ constraints, both PRES(T) and *DUR refer to continuous values reflecting in the case of PRES(T) the degree to which a surface tone is perceptually divergent from its corresponding input and, in the case of *DUR the amount of the durational difference between the surface rime and the duration characteristic of a given prosodic position when not supporting a tonal contour.

Depending on the ranking of these three constraints relative to each other different output patterns emerge. If all members of both the PRES(T) and *DUR families outrank the relevant *CONTOUR(T)–$C_{\text{CONTOUR}}(R)$ constraint for a given contour tone, then that underlying tonal contour will surface

without any lengthening of the rime to accommodate the tone. If all the
*DUR constraints are undominated and *CONTOUR(T)–C$_{contour}$(R) has priority
over some but not all PRES(T) constraints, the tonal contour will be reduced
in order to allow for its effective realization. If *CONTOUR(T)–C$_{contour}$(R) and
*DUR outrank all PRES(T), the contour will be completely eliminated.
Yet another possibility is for at least some of the *DUR constraints to be
outranked by *CONTOUR(T)–C$_{contour}$(R) and PRES(T). This produces different
patterns of lengthening to accommodate the contour tone, where the
degree of lengthening depends on which of the *DUR constraints are outranked. A final possibility is a compromise between preserving vestiges of
the underlying tonal contour and minimizing lengthening to accommodate
the contour; this pattern reflects the ranking of *CONTOUR(T)–C$_{contour}$(R)
above some but not all PRES(T) and *DUR constraints.

An advantage of an analysis employing constraints referring to continuous variables is its ability to more closely capture surface forms than
formal analyses using less finely grained discrete predicates. For example,
non-neutralizing lengthening of a short vowel in order to accommodate a
contour tone can be represented in Zhang's approach. In a moraic analysis,
lengthening in a language with contrastive vowel length can be captured
in terms of mora count only if it neutralizes the underlying length distinction. Furthermore, the number of distinctions relevant to the phonology
often exceeds the number that can be represented in traditional discrete
phonological models. Thus, differences in the ability of various syllable
types to carry contour tones are typically captured using moras, such that
contour tones can be decomposed into level tones, each of which must be
associated with its own mora. However, because the number of moras is
limited by phonemic contrasts in length and segment count, certain tonal
distribution facts cannot easily be accommodated by moraic models. For
example, Zhang cites Mende as a language in which long vowels can carry
the complex tone LHL in monosyllabic words but not in longer words.
Similarly short vowels can carry both LH and HL contours in monosyllables,
only HL contours in the final position of longer words and no contours in
other environments. This type of pattern which makes reference to both
type of contour and syllable count cannot be captured by a moraic model,
in which mora count is consistent across different syllable positions and
different word lengths. In Zhang's direct phonetics approach, the Mende
patterns emerge naturally since both number of syllables and syllable
position influence the same phonetic variable – duration – which is referred
to by a single constraint family. The difference between rising LH and
falling HL tones also is predicted given that rising tones characteristically
take longer to execute than falling tones.

Despite the descriptive richness permitted by a formal approach
appealing directly to phonetics, there are some assumptions that such an
analysis must make. First, because constraints refer to continuous phonetic
properties rather than discrete phonological entities in Zhang's approach,

it must be assumed that speakers normalize across different speech rates and styles. If this were not the case, then a constraint such as *CONTOUR(T)–$C_{CONTOUR}$(R) could potentially be violated by a form at fast speech rates but honored by the same form in slower speech, thereby yielding different phonologies at different speech rates. Zhang thus assumes that the values manipulated by constraints are determined on the basis of some canonical speech rate and style.

On the other hand, despite the apparent consistency found across speech rates, certain phenomena are rate dependent and suggest the need for constraints referring to absolute durations imposed by physiological limitations. For example, Kirchner (2004) discusses the OT modelling of lenition processes dependent on speech rate in Florentine Italian.

Another issue that a direct phonetics approach must address is the fact that the set of attested contrasts in any language is a small subset of those logically predicted to occur given a set of constraints manipulating continuous variables. To account for this fact, Flemming (1995, 2004) and Kirchner (1997) suggest that the set of contrasts is limited by considerations of perceptual distinctness such that phonetic differences must be sufficiently salient if they are to be exploited as a phonological contrast. For example, Flemming assumes a family of constraints governing the perceptual distance between different formants. These MINDIST constraints compete with constraints requiring that articulatory effort be minimalized in keeping with Lindblom's (1986, 1990c) Theory of Adaptive Dispersion, which assumes that phonological systems are the result of compromise between the conflicting goals of increasing the number of phonological contrasts while simultaneously minimizing articulatory effort and maximizing perceptual distinctiveness.

3.4   Other functional factors in phonology

3.4.1   Speech processing and phonology

In addition to purely phonetic factors, there are other functional considerations that appear to play a role in shaping phonological systems. One such factor is the mechanism of speech processing. In work investigating consonant co-occurrence restrictions in Arabic roots, Frisch et al. (2004) and Frisch (2004) suggest that similar consonants are avoided because they are more easily confused in both perception and production than dissimilar consonants. In order to make explicit this confusion, Frisch assumes Dell's (1986) connectionist model of phonological encoding in which different levels of phonological structure (e.g. features, segments, syllable position, word) are represented as distinct but interlinked tiers each consisting of activation nodes. A node associated with a given property is activated upon hearing or planning utterances containing that property or, in gradient fashion, other similar properties. For example, the activation node corresponding to the segment /k/ is strongly activated by any word containing the sound /k/ and less strongly activated by the occurrence of a word containing a different voiceless stop. Because featurally similar segments overlap in their activation patterns, there is potential for them to be mistaken for each other. Frisch et al. (2004) quantify similarity in terms of number of natural classes shared by the segments in question. Segments that share a greater number of natural classes are more similar to each other and thus less likely to co-occur in the same root.

Hansson (2001a) offers a processing-based account of long distance consonant harmony. In a typology of consonant harmony system, Hansson finds a strong bias toward anticipatory harmony cross-linguistically. Observing that the same directional bias is also found in child language and speech error data, he suggests that consonant harmony is motivated by the same mechanisms underlying speech planning. Walker (2003a) finds evidence for the relevance of speech planning in shaping consonant harmony systems from a psycholinguistic experiment in which segment transposition errors are induced through priming. She finds that segments that are homorganic are more likely to be transposed in keeping with a homorganicity requirement on harmonizing consonants found in certain languages with consonant harmony.

3.4.2 Frequency in phonology

One of the factors relevant in many connectionist models of speech processing is word frequency; nodes associated with more frequent properties have lower thresholds of activation required for firing. As a result, frequent items are more likely to be produced or perceived when activated by items sharing similar properties. The relevance of frequency effects in speech production and perception finds independent support from psycholinguistic studies and plays an important role in Bybee's (2001) model of phonology. Bybee assumes that words may have different phonological representations in the mental lexicon according to their frequency. More frequent words are pronounced differently from less frequent words; in particular, they tend to undergo phonological reduction. For example, a relatively common word like 'summary' is more likely to lack a vowel in the second syllable (i.e. [sʌmɹi]) than a less frequently occurring word such as 'summery' (i.e. [sʌmǝɹi]). Similarly, deletion of word-final coronal stops following another consonant is more common in high frequency words than in low frequency words (Bybee 2000). In Bybee's model, these reduction phenomena gradually become incorporated into the lexicon leading to different distributions in surface pronunciation.

Pierrehumbert (2001) attempts the difficult job of quantitatively modelling these gradient frequency effects using an exemplar-based model (see also Goldinger 1996, Johnson 1997, Wedel 2004). Following other exemplar models, Pierrehumbert assumes that each phonological category is stored in memory as a group of exemplars of that category. Each exemplar possesses an activation strength that is determined as a function of two properties. First, more recently heard tokens possess greater activation levels than tokens heard longer ago. Second, tokens that are too similar to be perceptually distinguished are stored as a single token with an increased activation level relative to tokens heard fewer times. When an input datum is processed, it is categorized according to the perceptual proximity and the activation level of nearby exemplars. In speech production, a speaker randomly selects an exemplar (where sociolinguistic factors may constrain the set of exemplars being targeted for production) from the cloud of tokens associated with the targeted category. Frequency effects are modelled by assuming a hypoarticulation bias in speech production, such that each token is produced slightly lenited relative to its target exemplar. If one assumes that words and not just individual phonemes are represented as exemplar clouds, the frequent use of a word will gradually lead to a shifting of its exemplar set in the direction of increased lenition in keeping with the synchronic lenition effect associated with increased word frequency.

3.5   The synchronic vs. diachronic role of phonetics in phonology

One of the major outstanding issues in work on the phonetics–phonology interface concerns the question of whether phonetic considerations play an active role in synchronic phonologies or whether phonetic factors merely are at work on the diachronic level gradually causing languages to drift in the direction of greater phonetic naturalness. This evolutionary perspective on the role of phonetics in phonology has been espoused by a number of researchers (e.g. Ohala 1981, Hyman 2001a, Blevins 2004, Blevins and Garrett 2004). Given that phonetically unnatural patterns exist in various languages, the position that phonetic factors govern all synchronic properties would appear to be untenable. Rather, the existence of seemingly phonetically unmotivated phenomena suggests that speakers have the ability to acquire patterns that could not be learned through phonetic experience. Thus, a phonetically-informed synchronic model of phonology must assume that the acquisition process entails both inductive learning through exposure to the ambient language as well as phonetic experimentation to determine which patterns are articulatorily easy to implement and perceptually recover.

   In practice, it is difficult to find evidence that teases apart the synchronic vs. evolutionary view of phonetically-driven phonology. One promising avenue of investigation employs psycholinguistic experiments to determine whether speakers actively employ phonetic criteria in grammaticality judgments. This line of research, which is in its infancy, involves presenting listeners with phonological patterns differing in their phonetic naturalness and then observing how well the listeners acquire the presented patterns. If speakers were sensitive to phonetic considerations in constructing a grammar, they would be predicted to master phonetically natural patterns more easily than phonetically unmotivated patterns. If, on the other hand, phonetically natural patterns were not more easily acquired, the evolutionary view of phonetically-driven phonology would find support.

Recent research using psycholinguistic experiments has addressed this issue. In one experiment, Pycha et al. (2003) presented listeners who are native speakers of English with one of three artificially constructed patterns of vowel harmony. Crucially, because English does not have vowel harmony, results could not be attributed to interference from pre-existing knowledge of a harmony system. In one condition, the presented forms illustrated a phonetically natural rule of palatal harmony of the type found in many natural languages (e.g. Finnish) in which suffixes have two allomorphs varying in backness depending on the backness of the root vowel. In another condition, listeners were given forms instantiating a phonetically unnatural process of palatal disharmony in which the suffixal vowel has the opposite backness values of the root vowel. Finally, the third pattern involved an arbitrary type of palatal harmony in which certain vowels (i, æ, ʊ) trigger a front vowel suffix, while others (ɪ, u, a) trigger a back vowel suffix. Both the phonetically natural harmony process and the phonetically unnatural disharmony process are formally simple in terms of manipulating a single phonological predicate, the backness value. The arbitrary rule of harmony, on the other hand, is formally complex since it requires reference simultaneously to height and backness of the vowels conditioning harmony in the suffix.

After a training session in which examples of harmony were presented aurally, listeners were asked for their grammaticality judgments on a series of novel forms differing in their well-formedness according to the learned harmony rule. Results indicated difficulty in acquiring the formally complex and arbitrary rule of vowel harmony, as the correctness of listeners' grammaticality judgments hovered at chance levels for this type of harmony, significantly worse than performance for the other two types of harmony systems. Pycha et al. also found that the percentage of correct responses for listeners exposed to the phonetically natural harmony system was greater than for speakers presented with the phonetically unnatural but formally simple alternation. This difference, however, did not reach statistical significance, though the authors suggest that significance could be reached given a larger subject pool.

Using a somewhat different experimental paradigm, Wilson (2003b) also attempted to address the role of naturalness in the acquisition process. Listeners were presented with one of two different nasal harmony processes. In one condition, listeners heard tokens containing a suffix with two allomorphs, [-na] and [-la], where the occurrence of each was conditioned by the nasality of the final consonant of the stem following a well attested and natural type of nasal harmony system found in natural languages: a nasal consonant triggered the [-na] variant whereas an oral consonant triggered the [-la] variant. The other group of listeners were given forms in which the [-na] allomorph was triggered by a final dorsal consonant and the [-la] allomorph was conditioned by a non-dorsal consonant, a less natural and unattested type of harmony system. After a training session in which the relevant grammar was illustrated, listeners were presented novel forms either conforming or failing to conform to the patterns from the training session, and asked whether they had heard these forms previously or not. Wilson found that listeners were far more accurate in recognizing forms conforming to the phonetically more natural rule of nasal harmony conditioned by the nasality of the final root consonant than the rule conditioned by the dorsality of the final consonant. In a follow-up experiment, listeners were presented with forms illustrating a process of nasal disharmony in which a nasal consonant in the root triggered the non-nasal [-la] allomorph. Nasal disharmony is attested in several languages (Alderete 1997, Suzuki 1998). In keeping with the results of Pycha et al. (2003), listeners were better able to recognize grammatical forms illustrating disharmony than another group of listeners exposed to an arbitrary rule in which the [-la] allomorph was conditioned by a dorsal consonant in the root. Wilson does not make a direct comparison of results for the nasal harmony and nasal disharmony conditions.

Zhang and Lai (2005) also delved into the relative productivity of phonetically motivated and phonetically unmotivated processes in their study of Mandarin tone sandhi. Mandarin possesses two types of tone sandhi, one with a much clearer phonetic motivation than the other. The phonetically natural sandhi involves simplification of the complex dipping (213) tone to a simple falling (21) tone in a phrasal context preceding another word with either a high level (55) tone, a rising (35) tone, or a falling (51) tone. This type of sandhi is presumably the natural result of truncating the tone in a phrase-medial context in which there is less time to execute all three tonal targets required for the canonical realization of the dipping tone. The phonetically less natural tone sandhi changes the dipping tone to a rising (35) tone before an immediately following dipping tone. Zhang and Lai presented subjects pairs of words, in which the first contained the dipping tone and the second contained one of four tones, three of which trigger the phonetically natural sandhi and one, the dipping tone, which triggers the less natural sandhi. The pairs of words differed in that, for some, both words were real, for others both were artificial, and, for still others, only one of the two words was real. Subjects were asked to apply tone sandhi immediately upon presentation of the word pairs. Results indicate that the temporal lag between the presentation of the words and the speakers' application of sandhi was greater in the case of the less natural sandhi for both real and nonce words. Furthermore, among the nonce words, the more natural sandhi was produced with greater phonetic accuracy in terms of contour shape than the less natural sandhi process. Zhang and Lai's results are thus consistent with the view that phonetically natural phenomena have a privileged status in terms of ease of acquisition.

In summary, rigorous research into the synchronic productivity of phonetic conditioning factors is still in its early stages. Results are not completely conclusive but thus far offer some support for the view that speakers have access to phonetic knowledge in constructing phonologies.

3.6 Conclusions

Exploration of the functional bases for phonological patterns is a productive area of research since many cross-linguistic distributional facts about phonology appear to be explainable in terms of independent biases in speech articulation, perception, and processing. Many of these functional factors have been incorporated into formal phonological analyses using the constraint-based framework of Optimality Theory. Despite important advances in our understanding of the role of functional factors in shaping phonological systems, there are still critical questions remaining to be answered about how and whether phonetic and processing explanations should be implemented in formal models of phonology reflecting synchronic linguistic knowledge.

Note

The author gratefully acknowledges the helpful comments provided by Paul de Lacy, Bruce Hayes and Michael O'Keefe.

4

Markedness in phonology

Keren Rice

4.1 Introduction

The concept of markedness in linguistics came to prominence in the twentieth century, and continues to play a central role in the discipline. A number of important questions arise about markedness in phonological theory. The most basic ones are: What is markedness? What are its diagnostics? What role does it play in a phonological system, if any? Can markedness be characterized universally in terms of substance, or is it language-particular, or are there both universal and language-specific aspects to it?

This chapter concentrates on features and markedness in phonology. Markedness is a contentious subject in phonology. The chapter focuses on the evidence for a view of featural markedness that relates to contrast; see Lombardi (2002) and de Lacy (2002a, 2006), for example, for alternative views. It begins with an examination of the ways in which the term markedness is used in phonology (Sections 4.2, 4.3, 4.4), and then surveys the commonly used markedness diagnostics (Section 4.5) and some of the factors that must be taken into account to understand markedness (Sections 4.6, 4.7).

4.2 Defining markedness

The term markedness is used in phonology to capture the central observation that not all elements in a phonological system are of equal status. The term was introduced by Trubetzkoy (1939/1969) to refer to relations between elements of a phonological class (e.g. place of articulation, phonation types) on a language-particular basis. Over the years, the use of this term has grown and expanded in many ways so that today, while the notion of markedness is core to phonological theory, capturing exactly what it means is not straightforward. The terms in (1) are often used to define the opposition between marked and unmarked. These terms are placed into two groups with non-phonological criteria in (1a) and phonological criteria in (1b).

(1) *Markedness terms*

	marked	unmarked
(a)	less natural	more natural
	more complex	simpler
	more specific	more general
	less common	more common
	unexpected	expected
	not basic	basic
	less stable	stable
	appear in few grammars	appear in more grammars
	later in acquisition	earlier in acquisition
	early loss in language deficit	late loss in language deficit
	implies unmarked feature	implied by marked feature
	harder to articulate	easier to articulate
	perceptually more salient	perceptually less salient
	smaller phonetic space	larger phonetic space
(b)	subject to neutralization	result of neutralization
	unlikely to be epenthetic	likely to be epenthetic
	trigger of assimilation	target of assimilation
	remains in coalescence	lost in coalescence
	retained in deletion	lost in deletion

These characterizations of the marked/unmarked dichotomy are drawn from many sources, from Jakobson (1941/1968) and Trubetzkoy (1939/1969) through current linguistic dictionaries (e.g. Trask 1996, Crystal 2003), encyclopedia articles (Kean 1992), and textbooks (e.g. Kenstowicz 1994, Roca 1994, Spencer 1996, Kager 1999a), works on phonological theory (e.g. Greenberg 1966, Anderson 1985, Harris 1994, Archangeli and Pulleyblank 1994, Blevins 2004), to writings on the theory of markedness (e.g. Battistella 1990, Mohanan 1991, Steriade 1995, Rice 1999a, 2002, Lombardi 2002, de Lacy 2002a, 2006).

Most of the aspects of markedness in (1) have their first substantial articulation in work of the Prague School, starting with Trubetzkoy (1939/1969). Jakobson (1941/1968) proposes that markedness constrains phonological inventories, systems, and rules and plays a role in determining sound change and the order of acquisition of sounds; relative frequency, combinatorial capacity, and assimilatory power of features are determined by the priority relationships within the universal feature hierarchy that he proposed.

It is worthwhile to divide the characteristics in (1) into two sets. Those in (1b) relate to phonological markedness, called 'structural markedness' by Bybee

(2001), and refer to phonological systems. Those in (1a) refer to what Anderson (1985) terms 'natural markedness' and what Bybee (2001) calls 'frequency markedness'; these relate in large part to the phonetic basis of an opposition.

4.3   A simple example of markedness

Markedness can be illustrated in a straightforward way with respect to syllable structure. There is general agreement that CV syllables are unmarked with respect to syllable shape (e.g. Clements and Keyser 1983, Clements 1990, Blevins 1995). Evidence for this claim comes from several sources. A primary one is that many languages do not permit syllables with codas or complex onsets (e.g. Hawaiian [Austronesian, United States], Elbert and Pukui 1979); those that do permit syllables with codas and complex onsets also allow CV syllable shapes (e.g. English). Based on implication, CV syllables are considered to be unmarked: the existence of, for instance, CVC syllables or of V syllables in a language implies the existence of CV syllables in that language, but not vice versa.

Markedness with respect to syllable shape is of little debate within phonological theory (see, however, Breen and Pensalfini 1999 on Arrernte [Arandic, Australia] for discussion of a language with no onsets, thus providing a counterexample to the generalization that the CV syllable is cross-linguistically unmarked), with discussion centering on the precise mechanisms for capturing the agreed upon facts. Agreement that the CV syllable is unmarked relative to other syllable shapes is based primarily on cross-linguistic implication, but also on criteria such as frequency, naturalness, and early emergence in language acquisition.

4.4   Markedness and phonological features

While the notion of markedness pervades all aspects of phonology, perhaps the most challenging work on this topic is in the domain of featural markedness. It is often said, for instance, that coronals are unmarked with respect to other places of articulation (e.g. Paradis and Prunet 1991b), that nasals are unmarked with respect to other sonorants (e.g. Rice and Avery 1991), that voiceless obstruents are unmarked with respect to voiced obstruents (e.g. Lombardi 1991), that high tone is unmarked with respect to low tone (e.g. Pulleyblank 1986), that high and low vowels are unmarked with respect to mid vowels (e.g. Beckman 1997). Maddieson (1984) provides empirical foundations for these generalizations. What are the foundations of such observations? Are these valid as cross-linguistic generalizations? If so, how are they best captured?

In terms of phonological criteria, the observation that leads to the positing of featural markedness has to do with the fact that asymmetries between features within a class exist. These asymmetries may be of various types. Perhaps the clearest example comes from a study of the patterning of consonantal place of articulation, with a focus on coronal asymmetries; see, for instance, the articles in Paradis and Prunet (1991b). The coronal place of articulation is proposed as the unmarked place with respect to labial and dorsal places of articulation for several reasons. First, there are phonological reasons, with coronal consonants patterning asymmetrically to other places of articulation. For instance, coronals have a different distribution from labials and velars – they may be epenthetic and may result from neutralization, while labials and velars are argued to not show such patterning; in addition, coronals may be the target of asymmetric assimilation while labials and velars are triggers rather than targets. Second, there are natural markedness reasons: all languages have coronal segments, coronal places of articulation occur more frequently than other places of articulation, coronals are early in acquisition, coronals are considered to be articulatorily and perceptually simple. Similarly, high and low vowels are often proposed to be unmarked with respect to mid vowels. Phonologically, high vowels are common in epenthesis and often result from neutralization; in addition, high vowels are frequent in inventories and, generally, the presence of mid vowels in an inventory implies the presence of high vowels.

4.5   The phonological diagnostics for featural markedness

Three major types of phonological diagnostics are used to determine markedness relations within a feature class. One diagnostic is the phenomenon known as 'the emergence of the unmarked' – the unmarked pole of a featural opposition emerges under certain conditions (McCarthy and Prince 1994). The emergence of the unmarked is found in neutralization and epenthesis. A second markedness diagnostic is the opposite of the emergence of the unmarked, what I will call 'the submergence of the unmarked' or 'the triumph of the marked' or 'the masking of the unmarked' (see Rice 1999a, 2002); it is also called 'markedness preservation,' 'faithfulness to the marked,' and 'preservation of the marked' in de Lacy (2002a, 2006). A third diagnostic is 'the transparency of the unmarked,' where unmarked features pattern as if they were absent with respect to non-local assimilation, allowing assimilation to pass through them; marked features are blockers. Each of these is exemplified in the following sections.

4.5.1   The emergence of the unmarked 1: neutralization

Neutralization, either passive or active, is perhaps the most widely acknowledged diagnostic for the unmarked pole of an opposition. For instance, in many languages, voiced and voiceless obstruents are distinguished in morpheme-, word-, or syllable-initial positions, but not in corresponding final positions, where the distinction between voiced and voiceless is neutralized, usually to voiceless. Voicelessness is considered to be the unmarked member, as it is the value found in final position. Vietnamese [Mon-Khmer, Vietnam] is an example: in the Hanoi dialect (Thompson 1965), morphemes can begin with stops /b, t, t^h, d, c, k, g/ but only /p, t, c, k/ can end morphemes – the voicing contrast is suspended morpheme-finally. This is called 'passive neutralization' because there are no alternations that show underlying voiced stops turning into voiceless ones; the evidence for neutralization is distributional. In other languages, neutralization is active: alternations indicate that voiced and voiceless obstruents are allowed in a position in the lexicon, but these are neutralized in that position in the output, as in well-known cases such as German, Russian, and Turkish; see, for instance, Lombardi (1991) on final devoicing. For example, Turkish [Altaic, Turkey] has active neutralization of obstruents to voiceless in syllable-final position, as shown by the following forms: /kanad/ → [ka.nat] 'wing', /kanad-lar/ → [ka.nat.lar] 'wings', cf. /kanad-ɨ/ → [ka.na.dɨ] 'his wing'; compare /sanat/ → [sa.nat] 'art', /sanat-ɨ/ → [sa.na.tɨ] 'his art', /sanat-lar/ → [sa.nat.lar] 'arts' (Underhill 1976:3). Likewise, laryngeal features [spread glottis] and [constricted glottis] may be contrastive in morpheme-/word-/syllable-initial position but neutralize finally, as in Korean [Korean, Korea], where phonological lax, aspirated and tensed stops are phonetically lax syllable-finally (e.g. /ap^h/ 'front' → [ap], cf. [ap^h-ɛ] 'front-locative' without neutralization and [ap.-t'o] 'front also' with syllable-final neutralization – Yoonjung Kang, personal communication, June 2005). Coronal place of articulation is often considered unmarked among places of articulation. This can hold lexically – for example, in Finnish [Uralic, Finland], consonants are restricted to coronal place if they are the first member of a cluster or are word-final (e.g. Yip 1991) or it can be a consequence of active neutralization (e.g. Basque [Basque, Spain] – Hualde 1991:83).

4.5.2 The emergence of the unmarked 2: epenthesis

Epenthetic segments are not present in a lexical entry, but are added to satisfy surface constraints on well-formed prosodic structures (e.g. Itô 1986). Their absence from lexical representations makes epenthetic segments strong candidates for unmarked features as insertion might be expected to provide the least marked features, a paradigm example of the emergence of the unmarked. While the most common epenthetic consonant is probably a laryngeal, either glottal stop or [h] (Lombardi 2002), stops can be epenthetic. Epenthetic stops tend to be voiceless and coronal (e.g. Axininca Campa [Arawakan, Peru], Payne 1981; Odawa [Algonquian,

Canada], Piggott 1974), the features of their classes that are generally considered to be unmarked.[1]

4.5.3 The submergence of the unmarked 1: asymmetries in assimilation

A phonological argument for distinguishing marked from unmarked features comes from the existence of asymmetries in trigger/target patterning in assimilation. Some features serve as assimilation triggers within their class but not as targets; others serve as targets but not as triggers. A well-known example of coronal unmarkedness from Korean is given in (2).

(2) *Korean place of articulation assimilation* (Yoon-Jung Kang, personal communication, March 2005)[2]

(a)	coronal-labial	ko/t + p/alo	→ ko[pp']alo	'straight'
		a/n + p/aŋ	→ a[mp']aŋ	'inner room'
(b)	coronal-dorsal	pa/t + k/o	→ pa[kk']o	'to receive and'
		ha/n + k/aŋ	→ ha[ŋg]aŋ	'the Han river'
(c)	labial-coronal	pa/p + t/o	→ pa [pt']o	'rice also'
		su/m + t/a	→ su [mt']a	'hide'
(d)	dorsal-coronal	i/k + t/a	→ i[kt']a	'ripe'
		ka/ŋ + t/o	→ ka[ŋd]o	'robber'

The coronal is a target, optionally assimilating to other places of articulation (2a, b), but is not a trigger (2c, d). The labial and dorsal, on the other hand, are triggers, giving their place features (2a, b), but not targets, as they are not affected by assimilation (2c, d). The coronal place of articulation is considered to exhibit unmarked patterning, while the labial and dorsal illustrate marked patterning. Korean also exhibits an asymmetry between labials and dorsals, with labials optionally assimilating to dorsals (ə/p+k/o → ə[pk']o 'carry something on the back and' but not vice versa (a/k+p/o → a[kp']o 'musical score'); thus labials can be considered to be unmarked with respect to dorsals.

In assimilation, the marked features within a class are active – these features transmit to other segments; the unmarked features are passive, or inert – these do not transmit but are overridden by other features.

4.5.4 The submergence of the unmarked 2: deletion and coalescence

Submergence of the unmarked arguments for markedness asymmetries based on coalescence and symmetrical deletion are also found. In these processes, marked features within a class are maintained and unmarked features lost. For instance, in Modern Greek vowel deletion, the higher vowel on a hierarchy is retained (e.g. Mackridge 1985: 34). Modern Greek has a standard five-vowel inventory: /i e a o u/. In vowel-vowel sequences, a front vowel deletes when it is adjacent to a back vowel regardless of the order of the vowels. The fact that a back vowel is maintained over a front vowel indicates that its place feature is marked with respect to that of the front vowel; see de Haas (1988) for discussion of this phenomenon in Ancient Greek.

4.5.5   The transparency of the unmarked: non-local assimilation

Another diagnostic for determining markedness is transparency: unmarked features may be transparent to assimilation, resulting in non-local assimilation, while marked features are blockers. Vowel harmony may be allowed to cross laryngeals but not other places of articulation, suggesting that laryngeals are unmarked in place while other consonantal places of articulation are marked (Steriade 1987); vowel harmony crosses the coronal place of articulation in Guere [Niger Congo], but not others, implying that coronal is unmarked among the places of articulation (Paradis and Prunet 1989).

4.6   Complications

If everything were as presented in Section 4.5, phonological markedness theory should be uncontroversial – the linguist's job would be to identify the appropriate substantive properties (features and classes) and the asymmetries within a class. In fact, the features identified as unmarked in the previous discussion – for instance, coronal for consonantal place, voicelessness for obstruents – are often considered to be universally unmarked with respect to the other features in their class. This line of research is taken by many researchers. For instance, Lombardi (2002:221) proposes a place of articulation markedness hierarchy as follows: *LABIAL, *DORSAL » *CORONAL » *PHARYNGEAL. This hierarchy specifies that pharyngeal places of articulation are the least marked place of articulation, and labial and dorsal places of articulation are the most marked. One would expect then, that in emergence-of-the-unmarked contexts, less marked place of articulation features would result. Beckman (1997:14) proposes a height hierarchy for vowels, *MID » *HIGH, *LOW. This hierarchy states that high and low vowels are less marked in height than are mid vowels. All other things being equal, high and low vowels are preferred to mid vowels.

Featural markedness continues as an area of study because it is not as simple as this. At least two reasons for this can be identified. First, at least superficially – the expected features within a class are not always the ones that emerge where they are expected. Basically, emergence-of-the-unmarked diagnostics do not yield the same results cross-linguistically, suggesting that there is not a single universally unmarked consonant or vowel in phonological terms. Instead, which feature of a class patterns as least marked depends, to some degree, on other factors. In particular, the contrasts within an inventory may be implicated in determining unmarked patterning. Even controlling for contrasts, variation on the phonological diagnostics outlined in Section 4.5 exists cross-linguistically. The following sections examine these points.

Second, while the phonological diagnostics outlined in Section 4.5 are, in large part, agreed upon by various linguists concerned with markedness, there are subtle points of debate. For instance, de Lacy (2002a, 2006) distinguishes two types of neutralization. He considers neutralization to be a valid diagnostic for markedness under the following condition: given two elements /x/ and /y/, /y/ is more marked than /x/ if /x/ and /y/ neutralize to produce [x]. On the other hand, if /y/ undergoes neutralization but /x/ does not, then markedness relationships cannot be determined. De Lacy (2002a, 2006) further argues that consonant epenthesis is a valid markedness diagnostic while vowel epenthesis is not, and assimilation triggers present evidence for markedness while assimilation undergoers do not.

These debates keep the study of markedness a lively one. In the next sections I focus on the first reasons for the debates, namely the fact that the diagnostics do not converge on a single feature within a class as unmarked cross-linguistically.

4.6.1   Contrast: variation in the unmarked depending upon inventory

Trubetzkoy (1939/1969) proposes that which feature within a class patterns as unmarked can vary depending upon the system in which the feature occurs. Battistella (1990:13–14), in a discussion of Jakobson's contributions to the understanding of markedness, compares the vowel systems of Turkish (/i, e, y, œ, ɨ, a, u, o/) and Cayapa [Barbacoan, Ecuador] (/i, e, u, o/), commenting that the [i]'s in the two systems "differ in the function of the features that define them, even though they might be pronounced identically – the Turkish /i/ must be defined as high, nonback, and nonround, while the Cayapa /i/ is simply high and nonback." Using Battistella's features, one might expect different patternings in these languages with respect to [round], with it functioning actively in Turkish but not in Cayapa.

The fact that a single feature within a class cannot be uniquely defined as unmarked can be illustrated using vowel place. In a system with a three-way place opposition in vowels, with front, central, and back vowels (e.g. /i, ɨ, u/ as high vowels), the central vowel patterns as unmarked with respect to phonological criteria – the central vowel serves as a target for assimilation and never as a trigger. Tunica [Gulf, United States, extinct] illustrates this, with front, central, and back vowels in the low range and front and back vowels in the mid and high range. See Haas (1941, 1946) for the original analysis and Odden (1991) for a recent interpretation. Tunica has the vowel inventory shown in (3).

(3)   *Tunica vowel inventory*

i		u
e		o
ɛ	a	ɔ

The central vowel [a] is an assimilation target, taking on the place of a preceding vowel. If the first vowel is front and the second vowel is /a/, [ɛ] results (4a); if the first vowel is back and the second is /a/, [ɔ] results (4b).

(4)   *Tunica vowel assimilation* (Haas 1946: 342)

     (a)   /mɛ/ 'search' + /ʔaki/ 'she is' → [mɛʔɛki] 'she searched'
     (b)   /po/ 'see' + /ʔaki/ 'she is'   → [po-ʔɔki] 'she saw'

While /V-(C)a/ results in a low vowel of the same place of articulation as the first vowel, in words with the reverse sequence of vowels /a-(C)V/, /a/ simply deletes with no effect. Thus the central vowel is a target and not a trigger while the front and back vowels are triggers and not targets. With respect to submergence of the unmarked, the central vowel patterns as unmarked.

In addition, emergence-of-the-unmarked diagnostics point to the unmarkedness of the central vowel. Vowels neutralize to central vowels, as in the reduction of unstressed vowels to schwa in English; see, for instance, Crosswhite (2001). Central vowels can be epenthetic, as in Chaha [Semitic, Ethiopia] (Rose 1993), another case of the emergence of the unmarked. See Rose (1993), de Lacy (2002a, 2006), Lombardi (2003), and Rice (forthcoming) for discussion of the typology of epenthetic vowels.

Not all vowel systems include central vowels. In a system without a central vowel, it makes no sense to say that the central vowel is the least marked, yet such systems may show phonological markedness asymmetries. The Greek deletion described above is an example of a submergence-of-the-unmarked asymmetry between front and back vowels, with the back vowel patterning as marked and the front vowel as unmarked. Emergence-of-the-unmarked diagnostics also do not converge on central vowels as unmarked, as front vowels, like central vowels, can be epenthetic (e.g. Yawelmani [Penutian, United States] – Newman 1944) and the target of neutralization.

Similar facts are seen with vowel height. 'Metaphony' refers to a process found in Spanish [Romance] dialects that raises vowels in height; Dyck's (1995) study finds that metaphony is triggered only by a high vowel that is in opposition with a mid vowel at its place of articulation. In asymmetric systems with /i e a u/ in trigger position, only /i/ is a possible metaphony trigger while the other phonetically high vowel, [u], never triggers metaphony; in the asymmetric /i a o u/ inventory in trigger position, on the other hand, only /u/ is a possible trigger. In the first instance, the high vowel /i/ is opposed to the mid vowel /e/, while the high vowel /u/ has no mid counter-part; in the second case, the high vowel /u/ has a mid counterpart /o/, while the high vowel /i/ is missing a mid counterpart. Thus, the patterning of /i/, for instance, is not fixed with respect to markedness criteria; its patterning as a trigger for high harmony depends upon what it is opposed to in height.

In conclusion, one factor that creates cross-linguistic variation in mark-edness patterning is the system of contrasts in the language. On the one hand, something may pattern as unmarked if it is present, but in its absence something else patterns as unmarked. Alternatively, a feature may pattern as marked if some contrast is present, but as not marked in the absence of that contrast. Overall, as contrasts vary, the particular feature or features of a class that pattern as unmarked also vary. A theory of featural markedness must be able to account for variation in the pres-ence of different contrasts.

4.6.2   The absence of contrast: variation in the emergence of the unmarked

Variation is also found in the absence of contrast, either lexically or as a result of neutralization. For instance, Australian languages often have a single series of stops, and these stops are generally realized as voiceless and unaspirated. However, a range of variation in their realization exists both between and within languages – in some languages the stops are usually voiced, but are voiceless in some contexts; in others they are often spir-antized between sonorants. See Hamilton (1996) for discussion and refer-ences. Spanish exhibits variation between voiced stops and voiced fricatives/approximants in different contexts. Whether the stop or the continuant is found depends on environment, and it is not possible to speak of one as being less marked than the other in any absolute sense, but only in terms of syntagmatic context.

In many cases, free, or non-contextual, variation in the realization of a particular lexical representation can occur in a single position. In some Slave [Athapaskan, Canada] dialects, what is reconstructed as Proto-Athapaskan *n is realized variably as [d], [n], or [nd] in the same position (Rice 1989, 1993). In Manipur [Sino-Tibetan, India], [n] and [l] vary freely syllable-finally, but con-trast elsewhere (Bhat and Ningomba 1997). In White Mountain Apache [Athapaskan, United States], a coronal (dental) and a velar stop occur stem-finally in free variation (Rice 1996). In Algonquin [Algonquian, Canada], [u] and [o] are in free variation phonetically, at least in stressed position. Ahtna [Athapaskan, United States] (Kari 1990) has variation between [ts]/[tʃ], [s]/[ʃ], etc. In Māori [Austronesian, New Zealand] (Bauer 1993) the stops /p t k/ are voiceless with variable aspiration. In Manam [Austronesian, Papua New Guinea], final nasals are realized as either labial or velar (Lichtenberk 1983) in an active neutralization process. Only nasals occur word-finally in Manam, and these neutralize in absolute word-final position to either [m] or [ŋ];

Lichtenberk reports that these are in free variation (1983:30), with [ŋ] seeming to be more frequent than [m]. Some examples are given in (5).

(5)   *Free variation in word-final nasals in Manam*

(a)   /daŋ/ → da[m] *or* da[ŋ] 'water' (30)

cf.   mata-daŋ   -ígu

eye   -water-1sg.adnominal

'my tears'

(b)   /zem/ 'chew'

bua   u   -ze[m] -Ø

or bua   u   -ze[ŋ] -Ø

betel nut   1sg.realis-chew   -3pl.obj

'I chewed betelnuts' (30)

cf. búa   ú   -zem -i

betel nut   1sg.realis -chew -3sg.obj

'I chewed a betel nut' (30)

(c)   /ʔan/ 'eat'

udi   go   -á[ŋ]   -Ø

or udi   go   -ʔá[m]   -Ø

banana 2sg.irrealis-eat   -3pl.obj

'eat the bananas!' (31)

cf. údi   gó   -ʔan   -i

banana 2sg.irrealis-eat   -3sg.obj

'eat the banana!' (31)

The examples discussed above illustrate that, in the absence of a contrast, variation in phonetic realization is possible. It is thus difficult to identify a single feature within a class as unmarked based on neutralization, given the possibility of variation in phonetic implementation. Instead, markedness is only relevant when there is contrast.

The existence of variation in the absence of contrast is reinforced in cross-linguistic surveys of both active and passive neutralization. For instance, in languages that allow only a single nasal place of articulation in word-final position, some allow only coronals (e.g. Finnish – Yip 1991), some only velars (e.g. Japanese – Vance 1987), and some only labials (e.g. Central Eastern Tundra Nenets [Uralic] – Salminen 1998). Active neutralization in Manam is illustrated in (5) above, with either a labial or a velar nasal resulting. Similarly with stops, some languages allow only a coronal place of articulation in word-final position (e.g. Finnish – Yip 1991), some only a velar (e.g. East Finnmark Saami, Karasjok dialect [Uralic]; Nielsen 1926), and some only a labial (e.g. Nimboran [Indonesia] – Anceaux 1965). Likewise, in languages which allow word-final stops but do not permit laryngeal contrasts, some languages allow only voiceless unaspirated stops (e.g. Sekani [Athapaskan, United States] – Hargus 1988), some only voiceless aspirated stops (e.g. Klamath [Penutian, United States] – Barker 1964; San Marcos dialect of Misantla Totonac [Totonacan, Mexico] – MacKay 1999), some only glottalized stops (e.g. Yecuatla dialect of Misantla Totonac – MacKay 1999) and some only voiced stops (e.g. Somali [Cushitic, Africa] – Saeed 1999).

Variation in emergence of the unmarked features in epenthesis is also found. Briefly, epenthetic vowels can be front, central, or back in place and high, mid, or low in height; epenthetic consonants are drawn from laryngeal, coronal, labial, and velar places of articulation; they can be obstruents or sonorants. For instance, the vowel [i] is epenthetic in Yawelmani [Penutian, United States] (Newman 1944, Archangeli 1984), and [u] in Seediq [Atayalic, Taiwan] (Holmer 1996); [e] is found in many Spanish dialects, and schwa in Sekani (Hargus 1988); [a] is epenthetic in Takelma [Penutian, United States, extinct] (Sapir 1922). With consonants too, languages differ in quality of an epenthetic segment. For instance, Balochi [Indo-European, Pakistan] is reported to have epenthetic [h], [w], and [j], depending on dialect (Elfenbein 1997).

Neutralization and epenthesis, the emergence-of-the-unmarked diagnostics, thus do not appear to converge on a single feature on any phonological dimension, either language-internally or cross-linguistically, leading one to question these diagnostics as indicators of phonological markedness. Rather, in these cases where contrasts do not exist, statistically the features classified as unmarked (see Section 4.5) predominate, but in no featural class is there a single feature which patterns uniformly as phonologically unmarked cross-linguistically. As remarked earlier, this claim is a controversial one; see Lombardi (2002) and de Lacy (2002a, 2006) for an alternative perspective.

4.6.3   Variation in markedness in the presence of similar contrasts

When languages have different contrasts, cross-linguistic variation in what features show marked and unmarked patterning is found (Section 4.6.1). Similarly, in the absence of contrast, cross-linguistic variation in emergence-of-the-unmarked diagnostics exists (Section 4.6.2). These findings lead one to question whether it is possible to identify in a substantive sense universal unmarked features. To pursue this question, it is necessary to examine languages with similar inventories to see if variation is found, or if cross-linguistic convergence occurs.

Place of articulation in consonants is particularly interesting in this regard. In a language with a two-way contrast in place of articulation in a particular position, no predictions can be made about which of the two places will be an assimilation trigger and which a target. For instance, while it is common in languages with a coronal-labial contrast in target position for the coronal to assimilate to the labial (e.g. Koyra Chiini [Nilo-Saharan, Africa] – Heath 1999), languages exist in which the labial assimilates to the coronal (e.g. Seri [Hokan, Mexico] – Marlett 1981). In languages with a three-way consonantal place of articulation contrast in a particular position, labial, coronal, and velar, two places of articulation, coronal and velar, can pattern as unmarked with respect to submergence-of-the-unmarked tests. In Korean, the coronal patterns asymmetrically to the other places of articulation in being a target, as in (2), while in Chukchi [Chukotko-Kamchatkan, Siberia], it is the velar that serves as an assimilation target, as in (6) (Krause 1980, Kenstowicz 1986, Odden 1987a).

(6) *Chukchi Place assimilation*

    (a) velar is assimilation target

        (i) te[ŋ]-əlʔ-ən   'good' (Kenstowicz 81)

        (ii) ta[m]-pera-k   'to look good' (Kenstowicz 81)

        (iii) ta[n]-ləmŋəl   'good story' (Kenstowicz 81)

        (iv) /ga-ŋəpe-lin/ → ga[mp]e-lin   'got off' (Kenstowicz 82)

    (b) labials and coronals are not assimilation targets

        (i)   /na-mə-k-ə-kn/ → na[mk]-əkn 'often' (Kenstowicz 82)

        (ii) ɣa-[n-p]er-w-len   'decorated' (Kenstowicz 82)

If a coronal subplace is added to a basic labial, coronal, velar system, then generally only the velar patterns as assimilator. This is illustrated by Serbian [Slavic] (Morén 2006), which has a final contrast between labial, apical coronal, laminal coronal, and velar nasal places of articulation. The velar assimilates to the exclusion of the others. Similar patterning is found in Polish [Slavic] (Czaykowska-Higgins 1993) and Gujarati [Indo-Iranian, India] (Cardona 1965).

Other two-way contrasts also often allow for variation in the substance of what patterns as unmarked. With respect to manner of articulation, in the submergence of the unmarked, either stops or continuants can show unmarked patterning. First, stops may assimilate to the manner of articulation of continuants. Sudanese Arabic [Semitic] illustrates assimilation of a stop to a fricative of the same place of articulation; specifically, assimilation occurs when the consonants share place of articulation.

(7) *Sudanese Arabic* (Kenstowicz 1989 from Hamid 1984)

    (a) (i)   kitaa[b]   'book'
          (ii)   kitaa[f] faṭhi   'Fathi's book'
          (iii) kitaa[p] samiir   'Samiir's book'
    (b) (i)   bi[t]   'girl'
          (ii)   bi[t] fariid   'Fariid's girl'
          (iii) bi[s] saamya   'Saamya's girl'
          (iii) ʔal-bi[ʃ] ʃaafat   'the girl saw'

The D-effect in many Athapaskan languages provides evidence that continuants can show unmarked patterning and stops marked patterning. This process coalesces a stop /t/ with a following fricative in certain environments, creating a stop with the place of articulation of the fricative. This is seen in Ahtna, as in the example in (8) (Kari 1990:25).

(8)   *Ahtna D-effect*

   /s-t-ʁoɬ/ → [sqoɬ] 'it broke' (Ahtna, Lower dialect)

In a language with a stop/continuant contrast in a particular position, either the continuant (Sudanese Arabic) or the stop (Ahtna) can show marked patterning.

   These examples point to the following conclusion: within a featural class, it may not be possible to identify a single feature of an opposition as unmarked cross-linguistically in terms of its phonological patterning, but the feature which patterns as unmarked can differ from language to language.

4.6.4   How much variation is possible?

Given the variation in what can pattern as unmarked in both emergence-of-the-unmarked and submergence-of-the-unmarked phonological diagnostics, one might conclude that it is not possible to develop a theory of phonological markedness based on phonological processes. However, the variation is not without limit. The table in (9) provides information about a few featural classes and which elements within the class can potentially serve as unmarked based on asymmetric assimilation. See Rice (1999a, 2002, forthcoming) for details.

(9)   *Variation in least marked place of articulation based on contrast*

class	contrast	possible unmarked units
vowel place	front, central, back	central
vowel place	front, back	front or back
vowel place	front, central	central
vowel height	high, low	high or low
consonant place	labial, velar, coronal	coronal, or velar
consonantal place	labial, velar, coronal 1, coronal 2	velar
consonantal manner within obstruents	stop, continuant	stop, or continuant
laryngeal features	voiced, voiceless aspirated, voiceless glottalized, voiceless unaspirated	voiceless unaspirated

While feature classes differ somewhat in their properties, generally in classes with a two-way opposition (e.g. vowel place in the absence of a central vowel, consonantal manner, two-height vowel systems), either one of the two poles of the opposition can pattern as unmarked with respect to submergence-of-the-unmarked diagnostics, while in classes with a larger number of oppositions (e.g. consonantal place of articulation with a three-way contrast, vowel place in the presence of a central vowel, laryngeal), not all features can pattern as unmarked. Despite the variation, then, cross-linguistic generalizations exist.

4.6.5 Summary

A study of phonological markedness reveals a number of complexities. On the one hand, language-particular variation in the substance of what can be marked and unmarked exists based on emergence of the unmarked and submergence of the unmarked diagnostics, especially with respect to the emergence-of-the-unmarked diagnostics of neutralization and epenthesis. The absence of contrast leaves the substantive phonetic realization of a particular sound unconstrained from a phonological perspective. Nevertheless, there are tendencies, examined in Section 4.7. On the other hand, submergence-of-the-unmarked diagnostics show that there is a universal basis for phonological markedness, with the range of variation related to the nature of the inventory. While two languages with identical surface contrasts within a class may differ in how they pattern with respect to submergence-of-the-unmarked diagnostics, this variation is not without limit: it is constrained, with only certain features demonstrating unmarked patterning in a given set of contrasts.

It thus appears that the most frequently cited phonological diagnostic for markedness, neutralization, is not useful in singling out one or two features within a class as universally unmarked from a phonological perspective, as both within and between language variation arises (see de Lacy 2002a, 2006) for an alternative perspective). Further, assimilation facts suggest that there is cross-linguistic uniformity but this generally occurs only in the presence of sufficient contrast within a class; see Jun (1995), Lombardi (2002, 2003), and de Lacy (2002a, 2006) for alternative interpretations. In order to account for such patterns, universal grammar must offer constraints on phonological markedness, but these must be sufficiently flexible to allow for some language-particular choices. Given that a close investigation of phonological markedness diagnostics points to a large degree of variation, one might ask if there are other reasons why linguists have such strong intuitions about featural markedness in terms of substantive content.

4.7 Other markedness diagnostics: implication and frequency

The markedness diagnostics that are most commonly mentioned in the literature are the non-phonological ones in (1), especially implication and frequency.

Implication is a diagnostic that is often cited in the literature: a feature X is more marked than a feature Y if the presence of X implies the presence of Y. For instance, statistically if a language contains a voiced obstruent, it also has a voiceless obstruent. Interpreted in terms of markedness, this implication means that voiceless obstruents are unmarked with respect to voiced obstruents. Similarly, the presence of plain coronals in an inventory is generally implied by the presence of other places of articulation. (Note that there are counterexamples. Hawaiian lacks a coronal stop, but has labial and velar stops although it has a coronal nasal.) Similar findings exist in other classes. For instance, with rare exception, languages have nasals but may lack liquids, making nasals the unmarked sonorant. (Again, counterexamples exist as a few languages have been reported to be without nasal sonorants. These include Quileute [Chemakuan, United States] – see Powell 1975 and Maddieson 1984.) Generally if a language has mid vowels it has high vowels, leading to the conclusion that high vowels are unmarked with respect to low vowels. (Counterexamples exist. For instance, Alabama [Muskogean, United States] is reported to have an [e a o] vowel system, without high vowels (Maddieson 1984)). Implication was appealed to in the discussion of syllables: most languages have CV syllables, while not all have CVC syllables, making CV less marked than CVC.

Unmarked features are also often identified by frequency: unmarked features occur more frequently than marked features. Frequency can be investigated both language-internally and cross-linguistically. For example, Hamilton (1996) argues for the markedness of non-coronals in final position in Australian languages on the basis of both implication and frequency. Australian languages with final labials and/or velars have final coronals; in addition, in languages with more than coronals in this position, coronals are of greater frequency than non-coronals. Maddieson (1984) investigates cross-linguistic frequencies as well, reinforcing the conclusion that unmarked features/segments are more frequent than marked ones. For instance, plain coronals occur more in more languages than do other places of articulation – in Maddieson (1984:35), 263 languages have plain voiceless bilabials, 309 plain voiceless dental/alveolars, and 283 plain voiceless velars.

It is often assumed that phonological markedness diagnostics and natural markedness diagnostics converge to yield the same results. However, this is not always so. Recall from Section 4.6.1 that if a central vowel occurs in a system, it has unmarked phonological characteristics, all other things being equal. One might expect that central place should be implied by other places and be the most frequent place cross-linguistically. However, this is not the case judging from inventories. Maddieson lists 40 languages with a high central vowel, while 271 have the vowel /i/ and 254 the vowel /u/. Thus phonetically central place is neither implied by other places nor is it frequent cross-linguistically compared to other vowel places at this height. Taken in this way, implication and phonological evidence cannot be used to reinforce one another – the evidence that central vowel place is unmarked with respect to phonological patterning is strong, but is not reinforced by implication and frequency. Implication and phonological diagnostics diverge in other cases. For instance, based on implication and cross-linguistic frequency, coronal place is considered to be un-marked, but, as discussed in Section 4.6.2, any place of articulation can appear in a neutralization position, and more than just coronal place of articulation is available as an assimilation target in asymmetric assimilation, as in Chukchi, discussed in Section 4.6.3.

Implication faces a complication when learnability issues are considered. Consider a child acquiring a language. The child does not know, for in-stance, that a dental or alveolar stop appears in almost all languages (316 languages in Maddieson's survey; p.32) while a uvular stop occurs in only some languages (47 in Maddieson 1984). As the child has input only from the language(s) to which s/he is exposed, no direct source is available to inform her/him that uvulars imply dentals/alveolars. Similarly, a child acquiring a language with only voiceless stops may not be aware of the existence of voiced stops; even the occurrence of both voiced and voiceless stops in a language is not in itself an indication of which is the marked pole phonolo-gically. Frequency too faces a similar complication in that there is no reason to believe that a child has access to cross-linguistic frequencies. In short, implication cannot be determined on the basis of an individual grammar.

Other factors require consideration with respect to frequency as a marked-ness diagnostic. The criteria for counting must be firmly established – Trask (1996), following Lass (1984:132), states that the marked segment has lower text-frequency, while Battistella (1990:48) claims that frequency refers to frequency of contexts rather than text frequency. Position may make demands on the kind of material that appears there. The term *position* is broadly defined – for instance, initial versus final position can refer to a morphological domain like stem or morpheme, a prosodic domain like syllable or foot, types of morphemes such as stem and affix, and subtypes of affixes such as derivation or inflection. Each of these positions, and others, may have its own set of constraints. For instance, in stem-initial position in Navajo [Athapaskan, United States], voiceless aspirated stops and affricates appear more frequently than voiceless unas-pirated stops and affricates, although based on implication and cross-linguistic frequency as well as on language-internal phonological evidence, voiceless unaspirated stops would be considered to be less marked than voiceless aspirated stops. In Australian languages, all allow a contrast be-tween labial, dorsal, and laminal coronals stem-initially, but not all allow apicals in this position. In stem-final position, all Australian languages with final consonants permit coronals; only some permit labials and dorsals in this position. Within the coronals, if laminals can appear, then apicals can as well. Both implicational and frequency are related to position, and no general statements can be made. The masking of the unmarked discussed in Section 4.5 affects frequency counts computed on surface representations, as unmarked things are submerged in favour of marked elements.

Phonological markedness and natural markedness thus do not necessarily assess the same thing, and one must be cautious in using the results of phonological markedness and natural markedness to reinforce one another.

4.8   Conclusion

Phonologists tend to have strong intuitions about markedness, and the word is commonly found in the phonology literature, both technically, as in markedness constraints in Optimality Theory, and informally, where its particular sense is often left undefined. In certain domains (e.g. syllable structure), overall agreement exists on what is marked and what unmarked. However, featural markedness is murkier. Using emergence and submergence of the unmarked as diagnostics, cross-linguistic variation exists in what can pattern as unmarked, although the variation is not without limit. In this sense, phonological markedness criteria underdetermine the actual substantive patterning, even in a particular system. Natural markedness criteria including language-particular and cross-linguistic frequency, ease of articulation, perceptual salience, and likely historical and social factors as well, work together to determine the tendencies toward certain phonetic outputs. Variation in substantive markedness results from an interplay between phonological and non-phonological factors.

What are the theoretical consequences of this variation? Are substantive markedness relations universal? Or do they vary depending on language-particular factors and, if so, how much? How are the phonological diagnostics, which yield variant results, to be interpreted? Are the phonological diagnostics even understood, given the debate that exists on how they are defined? To what degree should markedness theory be based on phonetic principles such as ease of articulation and salience of perception (e.g. Flemming 1995, Ní Chiosáin and Padgett 2001)? Are the markedness facts best captured by fixed universal scales (e.g. Prince and Smolensky 2004)? Or are they better accounted for structurally (e.g. Avery and Rice 1989)? Is markedness in phonology a consequence of a more general linguistic, or cognitive, facility? More radically, is the notion of phonological markedness to be abandoned altogether (e.g. Hume and Tserdanelis 2002, Hume 2004)? The issues surrounding markedness do not appear to be ones that will find quick solutions, and markedness promises to provoke lively debate for some time to come.

Notes

Thank you to the phonology group at the University of Toronto for discussion of many of the ideas in this article. Special thanks are due to Peter

Avery and Bill Idsardi. This work was partially funded by the Social Science and Humanities Research Council of Canada research grant #410-03-0913 to B. Elan Dresher and Keren Rice and by the Canada Research Chair in Linguistics and Aboriginal Studies. This article grows out of earlier work (see Rice 1999a,b, 2002), and many of the ideas are more fully developed in Rice (forthcoming).

1 Laryngeal place of articulation ([h], glottal stop) is also considered to be unmarked; see, for instance, Lombardi (2002) and de Lacy (2002a, 2006). The discussion in this chapter focuses on the labial, coronal, and dorsal places of articulation, and the relationship between them.

2 The data in (2) also illustrate processes that tense and voice stops; these are not relevant to the present discussion.

5

Derivations and levels of representation

John J. McCarthy

5.1   Introduction

In the theory of generative phonology, the phonological grammar of a language is regarded as a function from underlying to surface forms: /kæt+z/ → [kæts] 'cats'. Underlying and surface form are known as *levels of representation*, and the mapping between them is a *derivation*. This chapter describes the rationale for positing distinct levels of representation, various views of how many and what kind of levels of representation there are, and the nature of the derivations that link different levels of representation.

5.2   Levels of representation

In structuralist phonology of the first half of the twentieth century (see Joos 1957 for many examples), three levels of representation were recognized. One level, called *allophonic* or *phonetic*, offers a more or less accurate transcription of the actual speech event: [kʰæʔts] *cats*. At the *phonemic* level, only contrasting speech sounds are represented: /kæts/. At the *morphophonemic* level, every morpheme has a unique representation: //kæt-P//, where //P// is a morphophoneme that abstracts over the plural allomorphs /-z/, /-s/, /-əz/, /-ən/ (*oxen*), /-ɹən/ (*children*), /-iː-/ (*geese*), etc.

In the theory of generative phonology (Chomsky and Halle 1968 – hereafter *SPE*), the *surface* level has approximately the same properties as the structuralists' allophonic level (though see Kingston (Ch.17) for discussion of some of the difficulties in pinning down the properties of the surface level). Generative phonology differs from structuralism, however, in denying that there are separate phonemic and morphophonemic levels, since positing this distinction leads to missed generalizations (Anderson 1985, Halle 1959). At generative phonology's *underlying* level, every morpheme has a unique representation, except for suppletion. Underlying representations are composed of the same elements as surface representations, bundles of distinctive features, rather than phonetically uninterpretable symbols like the morphophoneme //P//. The English regular plural morpheme is /-z/, with suppletive alternants like /-ən/ or /-iː-/ listed lexically.

When a morpheme alternates non-suppletively, its underlying representation must be discovered by the analyst and the learner. In paradigms like German [bʊnt]/[bʊntə] 'multicolored/pl.' and [bʊnt]/[bʊndə] 'federation/pl.', distinct underlying representations are required because there are distinct patterns of alternation: /bʊnt/ 'multicolored' vs. /bʊnd/ 'federation'. In theory and in actual practice, as we will soon see, the relationship between the hypothesized underlying representation and the observed paradigm is sometimes less transparent than this.

Some recent research explores alternatives to positing an underlying level of representation. These approaches are *monostratal* in the sense that they recognize only a single level of representation, the surface form. In Declarative Phonology (Scobbie, Coleman, and Bird 1996), the work of underlying representations is done by constraints that describe morphemes. These descriptions are crucially incomplete in the case of alternating morphemes: e.g. for German [bʊnt]/[bʊndə] a constraint requires a final alveolar stop but says nothing about its voicing. Another monostratal approach seeks to express phonological generalizations purely in terms of relations between surface forms (e.g. Albright 2002, Burzio 2002). In German, for example, final [t] in one paradigm member is allowed to correspond with non-final [d] in another member.

In this context, it is worth reviewing why generative phonology posits an underlying level of representation (see Kenstowicz and Kisseberth 1979: Ch.6 for an accessible overview of the evidence). The main argument comes from paradigms where the relationships among surface forms make sense only when mediated by an underlying form that is distinct from all of the surface forms. Schane's (1974) Palauan example in (1) is a well-known case.

(1) *Palauan Vowel Reduction*

Underlying	Present Middle	Future Participle (conservative)	Future Participle (innovative)	gloss
/daŋob/	[mə-'daŋəb]	[də'ŋob-l]	[dəŋə'b-all]	'cover opening'
/teʔib/	[mə-'teʔəb]	[tə'ʔib-l]	[təʔə'b-all]	'pull out'

Because unstressed vowels reduce to [ə] and there is only one stress per word, disyllabic roots like 'cover' and 'pull out' never show up with more than one surface non-schwa vowel. The hypothesized underlying representations /daŋob/ and /teʔib/ record the quality of the vowels as they appear when stressed. These underlying representations incorporate all of the unpredictable phonological information about these morphemes. In generative phonology, the underlying representation of a root is the nexus of a set of related words, so it must contain sufficient information to allow the surface forms of those words to be derived by the grammar of the language.

In discussing the number and types of levels of representation that different theories allow, it is useful to introduce a distinction between what might be called designated and nondesignated levels. The designated levels are landmarks in a phonological derivation with special restrictions on their content or unique roles to play, particularly as the interface to other grammatical components. The nondesignated levels are usually not thought of as levels of representation at all; they are unremarkable points in the derivation lying intermediate between the designated levels.

Generative phonology in the *SPE* tradition recognizes only two designated levels of representation, underlying form and surface form, but it allows for any number of nondesignated levels intermediate between the underlying and surface levels. These nondesignated levels are the result of sequential application of phonological rules. *SPE* requires that all phonological rules apply sequentially. Therefore, if a language has n rules in its grammar, it has $n-1$ intermediate representations, each of which is a potentially distinct way of representing the linguistic form that is being derived. In Palauan, for example, there is an intermediate level at which stress has been assigned but vowel reduction has not yet applied: /daŋob-l/ → da'ŋobl → [də'ŋobl]. Indeed, *SPE* requires rules to apply sequentially even when simultaneous application would produce the same result (an exception is made for certain rules that can be conflated using *SPE*'s abbreviatory devices, which then must apply simultaneously). *SPE*'s intermediate levels do not have any special or unique roles, however; they are simply a side-effect of the way that rules apply, and so they will be referred to as nondesignated.

The theory of Lexical Phonology is firmly situated in the *SPE* tradition of rule application, but it imposes more structure on the grammar and increases the number of designated levels of representation (Kaisse and Hargus 1993, Kaisse and Shaw 1985, Kiparsky 1985, Mohanan 1982, among many others). In Lexical Phonology, the phonological grammar is organized, at a minimum, into separate lexical and postlexical modules, called strata. The output of the postlexical stratum is the surface representation, but the output of the lexical stratum is a designated intermediate level of representation with its own special properties. One of these properties, for example, is *structure preservation*, the requirement that the segments and structures occurring at this level be the same as those that are allowed in underlying representation. Depending on the language and on the specific version of Lexical Phonology applied to it, there may also be additional designated intermediate levels, such as a word-level stratum lying between the lexical and postlexical strata.

The theory of Lexical Phonology inherits from *SPE* the idea of sequential rule application and the resulting nondesignated levels of representation.

Alternative theories have been developed, however, in which sequential rule application is discarded but Lexical Phonology's modular structure is retained. These systems typically recognize just three levels, underlying, lexical or word, and surface. Approaches of this type include Harmonic Phonology (Goldsmith 1993a), Cognitive Phonology (Lakoff 1993), and Stratal Optimality Theory (5.4).

Apart from monostratal theories, the minimum number of levels of representation is of course two, underlying and surface. Finite-state phonological models, including a finite-state reduction of *SPE*, have this two-level property (Kaplan and Kay 1994, Karttunen 1993). More importantly for present purposes, Optimality Theory, as it was originally proposed by Prince and Smolensky (2004), maps underlying representations to surface representations with no intermediate levels.

5.3 Derivations

With the exception of monostratal theories, all current phonological models assume that the grammar maps underlying representations to surface representations. This mapping is called a *derivation*. Theories differ significantly in how complex derivations can be and in how derivations are organized internally.

The *SPE* approach to derivations retains considerable currency because it is often assumed even in contemporary theories that have moved far beyond *SPE*'s original hypotheses about rules and representations (e.g. Hayes 1995). In *SPE*, the grammar consists of an ordered list of rules. The rules are applied in a strict sequence, with the output of rule i supplying the input to rule $i+1$. As was noted in Section 5.2, the outputs of individual rules constitute nondesignated levels of representation intermediate between underlying and surface form. The sole exception to this strict sequentiality is cyclic rule application, in which certain rules are allowed to reapply to successively larger grammatical constituents. (More will be said about cyclicity in Section 5.5.)

In *SPE*, the ordering of rules is *extrinsic*, which means that it is imposed on the rules by the grammar and cannot be predicted from rule form or function. From about 1969 through 1980, a voluminous literature developed around the question of whether some or even all aspects of rule ordering could be predicted (see Iverson 1995 for a brief survey or Anderson 1974 and Kenstowicz and Kisseberth 1977:chs.4,6 for more extensive discussion). A particular focus of attention in this period was the functional relationship between pairs of interacting rules: does one rule *feed* or *bleed* the other (Kiparsky 1968, 1976)?

Rule A is said to feed rule B if A creates additional inputs to B. If A in fact precedes B, then A and B are in feeding order (if B precedes A, then they are in counterfeeding order, to be discussed in Section 5.4). An example of feeding order is the interaction between vowel and consonant epenthesis in Classical Arabic. Words that begin with consonant clusters receive prothetic [ʔi] (or [ʔu], if the next vowel is also [u]). As (2) shows, vowel epenthesis before a word-initial cluster (= rule A) creates new inputs to [ʔ] epenthesis (= rule B) before syllable-initial vowels.

(2) *Feeding order in Classical Arabic*

Underlying	/dˤrib/	'beat! (m.sg.)'
Vowel epenthesis	idˤrib	
[ʔ] epenthesis	ʔidˤrib	
Surface	[ʔidˤrib]	

In the *SPE* model, the phonological grammar of Classic Arabic must include a statement to the effect that vowel epenthesis precedes [ʔ] epenthesis. In some revisions of that model (such as Anderson 1974, Koutsoudas, Sanders, and Noll 1974), this ordering statement was regarded as superfluous on the grounds that feeding order is unmarked or natural. In what sense is feeding order natural? If rules are allowed to apply freely at any point in the derivation when their structural descriptions are met, then the result will be the same as (2). Feeding orders maximize rule applicability. They also help to ensure that rules enforce generalizations that are surface-true: in Arabic, no syllable starts with a vowel because [ʔ] epenthesis applies freely.

Rule A is said to bleed rule B if A eliminates potential inputs to B. If A in fact precedes B, then A and B are in bleeding order (if B precedes A, then they are in counterbleeding order, also to be discussed in Section 5.4). For example, in a southern Palestinian variety of Arabic, progressive assimilation of pharyngealization is blocked by high front segments, among them [i]. When the vowel [i] is epenthesized into triconsonantal clusters, it also blocks assimilation, as shown in (3a) (Davis 1995). Example (3b) is provided for comparison, since it shows progressive assimilation applying when it is unimpeded by intervening [i].

(3) *Bleeding order in southern Palestinian Arabic*

		(a) /batˤnha/	(b) /batˤn-ak/
Underlying		'her stomach'	'your (m.sg.) stomach'
Vowel epenthesis		batˤinha	—
Progressive assimilation		—	batˤnˤaˤkˤ
Regressive assimilation		bˤaˤtˤinha	bˤaˤtˤnˤaˤkˤ
Surface		[bˤaˤtˤinha]	[bˤaˤtˤnˤaˤkˤ]

This is a bleeding order: epenthesis eliminates some opportunities for progressive assimilation to apply. In the *SPE* model, the phonological grammar of Palestinian Arabic must include a statement to the effect that vowel epenthesis precedes progressive assimilation. Bleeding orders do not maximize rule applicability: on the contrary, the bleeding order in (3a) robs progressive assimilation of a chance to apply. But bleeding orders do help to ensure that rules state surface-true generalizations: the effect of the bleeding order in (3a) is that progressive assimilation does not traverse any surface [i] vowel, regardless of whether it is present in the input or derived by rule.

As these remarks suggest, feeding and bleeding interactions have something in common: when feeding and bleeding orders are in effect, structures derived by a rule are treated exactly the same as structures that were already present in underlying representation. For example, the derived initial vowel in the intermediate representation [idˤrib] is treated the same as the underlying initial vowel in /al-walad-u/ 'the boy (nom.sg.)'; both trigger [ʔ] epenthesis, yielding [ʔidˤrib] and [ʔalwaladu]. Likewise, epenthetic and non-epenthetic [i] equally block progressive assimilation in Palestinian Arabic, as shown by (3a) and /sˤiħħa/ → [sˤiħħa] 'health'. In feeding and bleeding interactions, what you see is what you get: when derived and underived structures are identical, they exhibit identical phonological behavior. This is emphatically not the case with counterfeeding and counterbleeding interactions, which will be discussed in Section 5.4.

Because simple feeding and bleeding interactions yield surface-true generalizations, the intermediate derivational stage is superfluous. Therefore, examples like (2) and (3) can be readily accommodated in theories that posit much shallower derivations than the *SPE* model. Although the discussion here will focus on Optimality Theory, much the same can be said about any of the other approaches mentioned at the end of Section 5.2.

The central idea of OT is that constraints on linguistic forms are ranked and violable. Constraints come in two types: markedness constraints impose restrictions on surface representations, and faithfulness constraints require identity in the mapping from underlying to surface form. In feeding-type interactions, two markedness constraints are active, with both dominating antagonistic faithfulness constraints. In the Classical Arabic example (2), the active markedness constraints are *COMPLEX, which prohibits tautosyllabic clusters, and ONSET, which prohibits vowel-initial syllables. Both dominate the faithfulness constraint DEP, which militates against epenthesis. The ranking argument is given in (4).

(4)   *COMPLEX, ONSET » DEP

/dˤrib/	*COMPLEX	ONSET	DEP
☞ (a) ʔidˤrib			**
(b) idˤrib		*!	*
(c) dˤrib	*!		

Because satisfying *COMPLEX creates a condition that puts ONSET in peril, as shown by candidate (4b), there is no need to go through an intermediate step where vowel epenthesis has occurred but consonant epenthesis has not. It is enough to say that surface forms must satisfy both of these constraints, even at the expense of unfaithfulness to the input.

When two rules contradict one another, at least in part, their relationship does not fit the simple feeding/bleeding classification. An example comes from Nuuchahnulth, formerly known as Nootka (Sapir and Swadesh 1978). This language has a process that rounds velars and uvulars when they follow round vowels (5a), as well as a process that unrounds velars and uvulars at the end of a syllable (5b). When a velar or uvular consonant is preceded by a round vowel and also falls at the end of a syllable, these two rules are in conflict, a conflict that the *SPE* model resolves by ordering them as in (5c). The result is that consonants surface as nonround when they both follow a round vowel and precede a syllable boundary (indicated by a period/full stop).

(5)   *Nuuchahnulth (un)rounding*

(a)   Rounding

	Underlying	/ħaju-qi/	'ten on top'
	Rounding	[ħa.ju.qʷi]	(cf. [hi.ta.qi] 'on top')

(b)   Unrounding

	Underlying	/ɬakːʷ-ʃitɬ/	'to take pity on'
	Unrounding	[ɬaːk.ʃitɬ]	(cf. [ɬaː.kʷiq.nak] 'pitiful')

(c)   Interaction

	Underlying	/m'uːq/	'throwing off sparks'
	Rounding	m'uːqʷ	(cf. [m'o.qʷak] 'phosphorescent')
	Unrounding	[m'uːq]	

Pullum (1976) dubs this a *Duke-of-York derivation*, after the English nobleman who, in a nursery rhyme, orders his men up a hill and then down again (also see Kenstowicz and Kisseberth 1977:171ff.) These rules are in a mutual feeding relationship, and it is not possible for both of them to state surface-true generalizations. Under *SPE* assumptions, the 'truer' rule is the one that is ordered last, syllable-final unrounding.

In OT, because constraints are ranked and violable, there is no need to go through an intermediate stage where the consonants become rounded, only to lose that rounding later in the derivation. The Nuuchahnulth situation involves conflict between two markedness constraints, one requiring that velars and uvulars be nonround at the end of a syllable (call it *Kʷ]ₛ), and the other requiring that they be round after a round vowel (call it *uK). Faithfulness to rounding is ranked below both of these markedness constraints. The ranking argument is shown in (6).

(6) $^{*}K^{w}]_{\sigma} \gg {^{*}}uK \gg$ IDENT(ROUND)

/m'uːq/	$^{*}K^{w}]_{\sigma}$	*uK	IDENT(round)
☞ (a) m'uːq		*	
(b) m'uːqʷ	*!		*

The Nuuchahnulth example further illustrates why OT, in its original conception, maps underlying representations directly to surface representations, without intermediate levels. In the *SPE* model, ordering is a way of establishing priority relationships among rules, and in a case like Nuuchahnulth it is the last rule that has priority in the sense that it states a surface-true generalization, even though the earlier rule does not. In OT, priority relationships among constraints are established by ranking them, and (6) shows that ranking can replace at least some applications of rule ordering. The strongest claim, then, is that OT can dispense with ordering and all of its trappings, including intermediate derivational steps. This claim is not uncontroversial (see Section 5.4).

The discussion in this section suggests that sequential rule application is unnecessary, at least for feeding and bleeding interactions. The evidence of counterfeeding and counterbleeding interactions will be discussed in Section 5.4, but first it is necessary to remark on certain conceptual arguments that have been made in support of sequential rule application.

One of these conceptual arguments holds that sequential rules accurately model a system of mental computation (Bromberger and Halle 1997). The failure of the Derivational Theory of Complexity showed that this idea is very far off the mark, at least in syntax (Fodor, Bever, and Garrett 1974); the same seems to be true in phonology (Goldsmith 1993b). Indeed, if the goal of generative grammar is to construct competence models (Chomsky 1965), then it is a category mistake to ask whether these models faithfully replicate mental computation.

Another argument offered in favor of sequential rule application is that it makes sense in terms of language history (Bromberger and Halle 1989): the ordering of synchronic rules matches the chronology of diachronic sound changes. The problem with this view is that it somewhat misconceives the diachronic situation. If generation X+1 innovates a sound change, they do not simply add a rule onto the end of generation X's phonological grammar – they cannot, since generation X+1 obviously does not have direct access to generation X's grammar. In other words, generation X+1's learning is informed exclusively by X's productions, as filtered through the X+1 perceptual system. X's productions offer only indirect evidence of X's grammar, subject to well-known limitations like the absence of negative evidence. From this perspective, we neither expect nor do we necessarily observe that grammars change by accreting rules at the end of the ordering.

5.4　Opacity

If rule A feeds rule B but they are applied in the order B precedes A, then these rules are said to be in *counterfeeding* order. For example, in a variety of Bedouin Arabic (Al-Mozainy 1981, McCarthy 2006), there are processes raising short /a/ to a high vowel in nonfinal open syllables (= rule A) and deleting short high vowels in nonfinal open syllables (= rule B). These processes are in a feeding relationship, since raising has the potential to create new inputs to deletion. But their order is actually counterfeeding, as shown in (7).

(7)　*Counterfeeding order in Bedouin Arabic*

Underlying	(a)	/dafaʕ/ 'he pushed'	(b)	/ʃarib-at/ 'she drank'
Deletion		–		ʃarbat
Raising		difaʕ		–
Surface		[difaʕ]		[ʃarbat]

High vowels derived by raising (7a) are treated differently from underlying high vowels (7b); only the underlying high vowels are subject to deletion. In a feeding order like (2), derived and underlying structures behave alike, but in a counterfeeding order they behave differently.

The same is true of *counterbleeding* order, where rule A bleeds rule B but they are applied in the order B precedes A. In this same Arabic dialect, there is also a process palatalizing velars when they are adjacent to front vowels. Deletion (= rule A) bleeds palatalization (= rule B), since deletion can remove a high front vowel that would condition velar palatalization. But their order is counterbleeding, as shown in (8).

(8)　*Counterbleeding order in Bedouin Arabic*

Underlying	(a)	/haːkim-iːn/	(b)	/t-ha-kum-in/
Palatalization		haːkʲimiːn		–
Deletion		[haːkʲmiːn]		[t-hakm-in]
		'ruling (m.pl)'		'they (f.) rule'
		(cf. [haːkʲim]		(cf. [t-hakum]
		'ruling (m.sg.)')		'you (m.sg.) rule')

High front vowels, even when they are absent from surface forms, induce adjoining velars to palatalize. Example (8b) shows the necessary contrast: a velar is not palatalized in a virtually identical surface context that is derived from a different underlying source with a back rather than a front vowel.

The result of counterfeeding and counterbleeding interactions is phonological *opacity*. Kiparsky (1976) defines opacity as in (9).

(9) *Opacity*

A phonological rule P of the form $A \rightarrow B \mid C\_\_D$ is **opaque** if there are surface structures with any of the following characteristics:
  (a) instances of A in the environment $C\_\_D$.
  (b) instances of B derived by P that occur in environments other than $C\_\_D$.
  (c) instances of B not derived by P that occur in the environment $C\_\_D$.

Clause (9c) describes all processes of neutralization and so it is not relevant to our concerns here. We will focus then on clauses (9a) and (9b).

In the derivation /dafaʕ/ → [difaʕ] (7a), the deletion rule is opaque under clause (9a) of this definition: there are instances if [i] (=A) in an open syllable (=$C\_\_D$). Typically, counterfeeding order produces opacity of this type, in which surface forms contain phonological structures that look like they should have undergone some rule but in fact did not.

In the derivation /ħaːkimiːn/ → [ħaːkʲmiːn] (8a), the palatalization rule is opaque under clause (9b) of this definition: there are instances of [kʲ] (=B) derived by palatalization that are not in this rule's context, adjacent to a front vowel (=$C\_\_D$). Typically, counterbleeding order produces opacity of this type, in which surface forms contain derived phonological structures without the context necessary for them to be derived.

Counterfeeding and counterbleeding interactions supply the best (arguably, the only) evidence for language-particular rule ordering. It is not surprising, then, that skepticism about stipulated rule ordering stimulated efforts to deny that opaque interactions involve living phonological processes. According to the proponents of Natural Generative Phonology (Hooper [Bybee] 1976, 1979, Vennemann 1974), real phonological rules must state surface-true generalizations and they must be unordered. They therefore maintain that opaque processes are merely the lexicalized residue of sound changes that are no longer productive — the commonly-used phrase is that they are not "psychologically real". In fact, much if not all of the abstractness controversy of the 1970s, which dealt with proposed limits on the degree of disparity between underlying and surface representations (see Kenstowicz and Kisseberth 1977:Ch.1, 1979:Ch.6), was really an argument about opacity, since underlying forms are abstract precisely because opaque rules operate on them.

Certainly, there have been dubious analyses based on opaque rules and excessively abstract underlying forms (*SPE*'s /rixt/ → [raːjt] *right* comes to mind – Chomsky and Halle 1968:233–4), but complete denial of opaque interactions is an overreaction. The Bedouin Arabic example is instructive. Al-Mozainy (1981) presents several arguments that the opaque processes in this language are alive and productive. First, they are active in borrowed words. Second, high vowel deletion applies productively across word boundaries (10), which means that it cannot be lexicalized.

(10) *Phrase-level deletion in Bedouin Arabic*

/ʃaːrib al-maː/	[ʃaːrb alma]	'drinking the water'
/tiʕtˤuːnih al-musayʕiːdiː/	[tiʕtˤuːnh almseːʕiːdi]	'you give it to the one from the clan of Musa'ʕīd'

Third, the most compelling evidence that raising is productive comes from a secret or play language. Although raising generally affects short /a/ in a non-final open syllable, there are phonological conditions under which it regularly fails to apply: after a guttural consonant ([ʔ], [h], [ħ], [ʕ], [χ], [ʁ]), or before a guttural consonant or coronal sonorant ([l], [r], [n]) that is itself followed by [a]. Bedouin Arabic has a secret language that permutes the consonants of the root, and this will sometimes alter the conditions necessary for raising. When this happens, the vowel raises or not in exact conformity with these generalizations (11):

(11) *Raising alternations in a secret language*

difaʕ	fidaʕ	
	daʕaf	No raising before guttural + [a]
	faʕad	"
	ʕadaf	No raising after guttural
	ʕafad	"

Fourth, the secret language data show that palatalization is also productive, even though it is opaque. In sum, the opaque phonology of Bedouin Arabic is also its living phonology. (For further examples of processes that are productive yet opaque, see Donegan and Stampe 1979.)

If opacity is an authentic property of phonology, then any successful phonological theory must be able to accommodate it, at least in robust instantiations like Bedouin Arabic. Theories of the *SPE* variety, with as many levels of representation as there are rules, have no difficulty with opacity, as we have seen. The challenge, then, is to account for opacity within theories whose resources are more limited. There is certainly no consensus about how best to do this, but there are several promising lines of on-going research.

The most direct line of attack on the opacity problem is to retain something like the basic rule-ordering mechanism but limit the theory to three or four designated levels of representation, with no nondesignated levels. For example, Harmonic Phonology (Goldsmith 1993a) and Cognitive Phonology (Lakoff 1993) recognize just three levels of representation, called morphophonemic (M), word (W), and phonetic (P). The M and P levels are equivalent to underlying and surface representation, respectively; the innovation is to recognize a unique intermediate level, W. Processes that occur in the M→W mapping necessarily precede processes that occur in the W→P mapping, so limited effects of rule ordering can be achieved.

Stratal Optimality Theory obtains opaque interactions similarly (Kiparsky 2000, 2003, McCarthy and Prince 1993b, Rubach 2000, and contributions to

Hermans and van Oostendorp 1999 and Roca 1997a, among many others). Stratal OT is also called OT/LP because of its connection with the rule-based theory of Lexical Phonology. The basic idea is that a succession of OT grammars is linked serially, with the output of one grammar constituting the input to the next one. These grammars are distinct, which in OT means that they contain different rankings of the same universal constraint set. Each of these grammars corresponds to one of the strata of Lexical Phonology; this includes one or more lexical strata, a word stratum, and a postlexical stratum, which altogether define at least three levels of representation. As in Harmonic Phonology and Cognitive Phonology, opaque interactions are obtained by the intrinsic ordering between these grammar modules.

The counterbleeding interaction of palatalization and deletion in (8) will serve to illustrate Stratal OT in action. This interaction requires that the /k/ → [kʲ] unfaithful mapping occurs in a stratum earlier than the /i/ → Ø unfaithful mapping. If the /k/ → [kʲ] mapping is the result of a ranking that holds in the word stratum, then the constraint ranking responsible for deletion must not obtain until the postlexical stratum. This system is illustrated with the tableaux in (12). In these tableaux, deletion of high vowels is assumed to be a response to the markedness of high vowel nuclei under *NUC/[HI], following Gouskova (2003); velar palatalization is attributed to the cover constraint PAL, which prohibits sequences of a plain velar and a front vowel.

(12) *Stratal OT approach to opacity in Bedouin Arabic*

(a) Word stratum: PAL, MAX » *Kʲ » IDENT(back); MAX » *NUC/[HI]

/ħa:kim-i:n/	PAL	MAX	*Kʲ	*NUC/[HI]	IDENT(back)
☞ (a) ħa:kʲimi:n			*	**	*
(b) ħa:kimi:n	*!			**	
(c) ħa:kmi:n		*!		*	
(d) ħa:kʲmi:n		*!	*	*	*

(b) Postlexical stratum: IDENT(back) » *Kʲ; *NUC/[HI] » MAX

/ħa:kʲimi:n/	IDENT(back)	PAL	*NUC/[HI]	*Kʲ	MAX
(a) ħa:kʲimi:n			**!	*	
(b) ħa:kimi:n	*!	*!	**!		
(c) ħa:kmi:n	*!		*		*
☞ (d) ħa:kʲmi:n			*	*	*

The word stratum (12a) requires the ranking PAL » *Kʲ » IDENT(back), which is necessary to explain why palatalized velars occur only in contiguity with (underlying) front vowels. It also requires the ranking MAX » *NUC/[HI]. This ranking prevents deletion in the word stratum, since if deletion were allowed then the transparent form *[ħa:kmi:n] would win. In the postlexical stratum (12b), two rerankings are necessary. The ranking of *NUC/[HI] and MAX must be reversed so that deletion takes place in the postlexical phonology. The other reranking, that of IDENT(back) and *K^j, is necessary to prevent depalatalization of the previously palatalized velar. Since the input to the postlexical stratum is the output of the word stratum, IDENT(back) is protective of the derived [k^j] in the word-stratum output / postlexical-stratum input [ħaːk^{j}imiːn].

Stratal OT's approach to opacity is a significant departure from the original theory of Lexical Phonology, which recognized two possible sources of opaque ordering: the intrinsic ordering of rules that are assigned to different strata, and the extrinsic ordering of rules within a stratum. Stratal OT makes a much stronger claim: all opaque interactions are reducible to processes that occur transparently in different strata. It remains to be seen whether this claim survives empirical scrutiny, including the challenge presented by extant Lexical Phonology analyses that require within-stratum opaque ordering, such as Kiparsky's (1984) analysis of Icelandic (also see Noyer 1997:515, Paradis 1997:542, Roca 1997b:14ff., Rubach 1997:578 for various critical remarks).

Stratal OT and rule-based Lexical Phonology agree on a different claim: if independent criteria require that two processes be assigned to different strata, then the ordering of those processes is forced by the intrinsic ordering of the strata. In Lexical Phonology, there were many criteria that tended to segregate processes by stratum, such as structure preservation or the strict cycle. Stratal OT has abandoned nearly all of these principles, but one remains: the stratum determines the domain of a process. Processes that can apply between words are necessarily postlexical, whereas processes that are word-bounded are necessarily assigned to the lexical or word strata. The counterfeeding interaction in (7) presents a direct challenge to this claim. Raising is word-bounded; except for a few fixed expressions like /baːrak alˤlˤah fiːk/ → [baːrˤik alˤlˤah fiːk] 'may Allah bless you', raising does not occur across word boundaries even when an open syllable is created by syllabifying a word-final consonant as an onset when the next word begins with a vowel. Deletion is a phrase-level process (10), so it must be assigned to the postlexical stratum, as we have already noted. Since the word stratum where raising occurs precedes the postlexical stratum where deletion occurs, raising should feed deletion, resulting in derivations like /samiʕ-t/ →$_{Word}$ [simiʕt] →$_{Postlex}$ *[smiʕt] 'you (m.sg.) heard'. The correct form is [simiʕt], since raising does not in fact feed deletion. Furthermore, there is no straightforward way to salvage the analysis, since the failure is one of principle. For deletion to be in a counterfeeding relationship with any other process, that process must be assigned to a stratum later than deletion's stratum, but since deletion is a phrase-level process, there is no later stratum. It would seem, then, that no analysis is possible within the assumptions of Stratal OT.

Targeted constraints (Wilson 2000), comparative markedness (McCarthy 2002a, 2003a), sympathy (McCarthy 1999, 2003b), and virtual phonology

(Bye 2001) also rely on a third representation, neither underlying nor surface, to support the analysis of opacity in OT. These various approaches differ from each other and from Stratal OT in how they organize the grammar and how they identify that third form, but at a sufficiently distant level of abstraction they share this point of similarity.

Space does not permit a thorough review of these approaches, their advantages, and their limitations, so a brief sketch will have to suffice, using as an example the counterfeeding interaction of raising and epenthesis in Bedouin Arabic. Raising occurs in open syllables, but open syllables derived by epenthesis do not condition raising: /gabr/ → [gaburˤ], *[giburˤ] 'a grave'. The third form that indirectly influences the outcome is *[gabrˤ], an output representation that lacks the epenthetic vowel. Targeted constraints are inherently comparative, and *[gabrˤ] is the basis for comparison by a constraint that says, in effect, that a word without a final cluster is more harmonic than an otherwise identical word with that cluster, so [gaburˤ] ≻ *[gabrˤ]. In comparative markedness, the constraint responsible for raising asks whether [a] is in an open syllable in the fully faithful candidate *[gabrˤ]. Sympathy theory looks to the candidate that is most harmonic except that it obeys Dep, and this too is *[gabrˤ]. Virtual phonology selects *[gabrˤ] as the third or 'virtual' form using markedness and faithfulness constraints that are indexed to the virtual evaluation. In short, these various theories share the assumption that the form *[gabrˤ], *qua* output, exerts indirect influence over the outcome of harmonic evaluation, so that opaque [gaburˤ] triumphs over transparent *[giburˤ]. (For critical discussion of targeted constraints, see McCarthy (2002b); of comparative markedness, see the various rejoinders appearing in *Theoretical Linguistics* 29 (2003); of sympathy, see Itô and Mester (2001), Kiparsky (2000), and McMahon (2000a).)

Another general strategy for attacking the opacity problem is to allow rules or constraints to have simultaneous access to different levels of representation. A classic *SPE* phonological rule has an elementary form of this property: its structural description is met at some (nondesignated) level of representation, and its structural change creates the next level of representation after that. Variations on this scheme can accommodate differences between transparent and opaque interactions. For example, Harmonic and Cognitive Phonology provide a system of two-level rules (also see Karttunen 1993, Koskenniemi 1983). A two-level rule can specify a structural description that must be met by its input, its output, or both. In Bedouin Arabic, for example, the structural description of raising requires that the affected vowel be in an open syllable in the input (13a), since open syllables derived by vowel epenthesis do not condition raising: /gabr/ → [gaburˤ] 'a grave'. On the other hand, the transparent interaction of vowel and consonant epenthesis in (2) shows that the structural description of consonant epenthesis must be met in the output (13b).

(13)   *Some two-level rules*

By their very nature, faithfulness constraints in OT have access to two levels of representation, and so it is not surprising that extensions of the basic faithfulness theory have been applied to opacity. Constraint conjunction is a mechanism for combining constraints: the constraint $C = [A \& B]_\delta$ is violated if and only if some constituent or sequence of type δ violates both A and B. The conjunction of two faithfulness constraints produces a type of faithfulness constraint that can be applied to counterfeeding opacity. For example, [IDENT(low) & DEP]$_{ADJ\text{-}\sigma}$ is violated if a vowel is raised and a vowel is epenthesized in adjacent syllables. Ranked appropriately, this constraint will rule out the mapping /gabr/ → *[gibur$^\varsigma$] while still allowing /dafaʕ/ → [difaʕ], where there is no nearby epenthesis. The problem with local conjunction is that it rules out the cooccurrence of unfaithful mappings in close proximity, but mere proximity is not the source of opacity. Rather, counterfeeding opacity involves unfaithful mappings that crucially *interact* with one another; what is forbidden is for epenthesis to create the open syllable that conditions raising. The difference between proximity, which has no apparent linguistic relevance, and interaction, which is the basis for opacity, becomes clear once it is realized [IDENT(low) & DEP]$_{ADJ\text{-}\sigma}$ is violated not only in the interacting case *[gibur$^\varsigma$], where epenthesis creates the open-syllable context for raising, but also when epenthesis occurs in the preceding syllable, where it does not interact with raising. This prediction of the local-conjunction model is not only typologically implausible – in known cases of counterfeeding opacity, interaction and not proximity is essential – but also factually incorrect in Bedouin Arabic, as shown by examples like /tˤarad ʁanam-i/ → [tˤaradiʁnim-i] 'I pursued my sheep'. Here, the first underlined [i] is epenthetic and the second is the result of raising, showing that there is no prohibition on raising a vowel when there is epenthesis in the preceding syllable.

Another way of allowing simultaneous access to two levels of representation is to fold them into a single level of representation (for a monostratal approach to opacity within Declarative Phonology, see Bye 2003). The development of nonlinear phonology in the 1970s offered ways of making distinctions between underlying and derived structures that would otherwise be identical, and Prince and Smolensky's (2004) PARSE/FILL model of faithfulness exploits this possibility. One assumption of this model is that segments are never literally deleted; rather, they remain present in the segmental string but are unpronounced because they are not incorporated into prosodic structure. The lingering presence of the underlying but unpronounced segment offers opportunities for the transparent analysis of opaque interactions. In the Bedouin Arabic counterbleeding case (8), for instance, the winning candidate has an unsyllabified [<i>] that transparently induces palatalization of the preceding velar: [ħaːkʲ<i>miːn]. (For further developments along these general lines, see Goldrick (2000).)

Finally, it is worth noting that opaque interactions contribute in a backhanded way to maintaining the transparency of the input-output relation. For example, the speaker of Bedouin Arabic who hears [gaburˤ] can legitimately infer that the [u] is epenthetic, since that is why the preceding [a] is not raised. Kaye (1974, 1975) and Kisseberth (1973) discussed such functional motivations for opacity, and Lubowicz (2003) has developed an OT-based system in which opacity serves to preserve underlying contrasts.

This review of opacity does not exhaust a very rich topic, and future developments can surely be expected. There is a need for a body of solidly supported examples of phonological opacity, similar to Bedouin Arabic, and for greater understanding of the nature of and limits on opaque interaction.

5.5 Cyclicity

In *SPE*, the strict linear order of phonological rules admits of a single exception: cyclic rule application. Certain rules are designated as cyclic – in *SPE*, these are the English stress rules – and this causes them to apply repeatedly to successively larger morphological or syntactic constituents. The cycle accounts for transderivational similarities like those in (14), from American English:

(14) *Transderivational similarities*
  (i)   Monomorphemic words like ˌKalamaˈzoo and ˌWinnepeˈsaukee show the normal stress pattern when three light syllables precede the main stress. Derived words like acˌcrediˈtation and iˌmagiˈnation deviate from this pattern under the influence of acˈcredit and iˈmagine.
  (ii) A closed, sonorant-final syllable is normally unstressed in pre-stress position: ˌserenˈdipity, ˌgorgonˈzola, ˌPennsylˈvania. But the same kind of syllable is stressed in the derived words ˌauˌthenˈticity and ˌconˌdemˈnation under the influence of ˌauˈthentic and conˈdemn.

In *SPE*, the aberrant stress of the derived words is explained by their bracketing and cyclic application of stress. The stress rules first apply on the inner constituents of [accredit]ation or [authentic]ity and then on the outer constituents. The primary stress assigned on the first cycle becomes a secondary stress on the second cycle, when a new primary stress is assigned later in the word. Monomorphemic *Kalamazoo* and *serendipity* have no inner cycle, so they show the effects of just a single pass through the stress rules.

Cyclic rule application has also been invoked to account for prosodic closure effects that have no obvious transderivational motivation. In Axininca Campa, for example, /V+V/ sequences at stem+suffix juncture are syllabified by epenthesizing [t] (Payne 1981): /i-N-koma-i/ → [iŋ.ko.ma.ṭi] 'he will paddle'; /i-N-koma-ako-i/ → [iŋ.ko.ma.ṭa.ko.ṭi] 'he will paddle for'. Since *[iŋ.ko.mai] and *[iŋ.ko.maː.koi] are phonotactically possible in this language, the problem comes down to explaining why a syllable like [mai] is forbidden just in case [ma] and [i] come from different morphemes. Spring (1990) proposes an analysis based on cyclic syllabification: the stem [iŋ.ko.ma] is fully syllabified on the inner cycle, and on the outer cycle affixal [i] is by assumption barred from joining any pre-existing syllable, forcing it to join with epenthetic [t] to become syllabified. Cyclic syllabification explains why vowel-final stems are closed under syllabification. Because Axininca Campa does not allow final codas, consonant-final stems cannot be closed under syllabification. Instead, the final consonant remains extrasyllabic until affixal /-i/ is added on the next cycle, at which point they join to form a syllable: /i-N-t͡ʃʰik-i/ →$_{1st\ cyc.}$ [iɲ.t͡ʃʰi.<k>] →$_{2nd\ cyc.}$ [iɲ.t͡ʃʰi.ki]. Hence, consonant-final stems are not prosodically closed.

Cyclic effects of both types have attracted a great deal of recent attention, particularly in OT. Three basic approaches can be identified and will be discussed in turn. It should be noted that these approaches are not necessarily inconsistent with one another; they may be complementary, each with its own proper analytic domain.

Closest to the *SPE* model are those accounts that regard transderivational relationships as fundamentally asymmetrical: if word or stem A exerts an influence on the phonology of word or stem B, then B cannot exert an influence on A. Typically, A and B stand to one another as base and derivative, like *authentic* and *authenticity*. This can be accomplished by combining an *SPE*-style cycle with an OT grammar, taking the output of the grammar, adding an affix, and then returning the result to the grammar as a new input. It can also be done with *output-output faithfulness* constraints, which require that related words resemble one another, just as ordinary faithfulness constraints demand identity between input and output (Benua 1997, Kager 1999b, Pater 2000b). A strength of output-output faithfulness is its restrictiveness, limiting cyclic effects to transderivational relationships between actually existing words. A weakness is the need to stipulate the asymmetry with a principle of 'base priority'.

More distant from *SPE* and Stratal OT are approaches that allow symmetric transderivational effects: word B can also influence the phonology of word A even if, morphologically, B is derived from A. Burzio (1994) and Kenstowicz (1996) were early advocates of this view; Downing, Hall, and Raffelsiefen (2005) is a recent anthology containing much relevant work. Symmetric transderivational effects seem to be important in inflectional paradigms. Morphologically, paradigms lack the obvious base/derivative structure of derivational morphology. In the Classical Arabic perfective verb paradigm (15), for example, there is little reason to see one form as more basic than the others:

(15)   *Classical Arabic perfective paradigm of* ktb *'write'*

	singular	plural
1st	katabtu	katabna:
2nd masc.	katabta	katabtum
2nd fem.	katabti	katabtunna
3rd masc.	kataba	katabu:
3rd fem.	katabat	katabna

The transderivational effect exhibited by the Arabic paradigm involves the impossibility of having a verb stem with a long vowel in the second syllable (McCarthy 2005). Some members of the paradigm have suffixes that begin with consonants, such as [katabtu], and other members have suffixes that begin with vowels, such as [kataba]. If it were possible to have a verb stem with a long vowel in the second syllable, then its paradigm would necessarily have a vowel length alternation, because long vowels are shortened in closed syllables: the paradigm for the hypothetical stem /taba:k/ would include [tabaktu], [taba:ka], etc. But there are no such verbal paradigms in the language, indicating that some constraint rules out vowel length alternations within paradigms. In other words, [taba:ka] is ill-formed because it differs in vowel length from its paradigmatic relative [tabaktu], or more generally the stems with vowel-initial suffixes must accommodate themselves, as regards vowel length, to the stems with consonant-initial suffixes, where vowel length is excluded for phonological reasons. It is problematic to suggest, as a strict commitment to asymmetry would demand, that some stem with a consonant-initial suffix just happens to be the base from which all other stems are derived. Rather, information about phonological form flows freely in any direction within a paradigm, even between forms with no obvious base/derivative relationship.

Finally, prosodic closure phenomena like the one in Axininca Campa are amenable to analysis using alignment constraints (McCarthy and Prince 1993a). Alignment constraints require that the edges of morphological and prosodic constituents coincide. One such constraint, ALIGN-R(stem, σ), says that the rightmost segment in every stem must be final in some syllable. In Axininca Campa, it crucially dominates DEP, so it is able to compel consonant epenthesis (16):

(16)   ALIGN-R(stem, σ) ≫ DEP

/i-N-koma-i/	ALIGN-R(stem, σ)	DEP
☞ (a) iŋ.ko.ma|.ti		*
(b) iŋ.ko.ma|i	*!	

The failed candidate (16b) has an unaligned stem that ends in mid-syllable (the right edge of the stem is indicated by the vertical bar). The winner (16a) lines up the stem and syllable exactly at the expense of epenthesizing a consonant. Though decisive in /V+V/ junctures like this, ALIGN-R(stem, σ) is crucially dominated by a restriction on coda consonants, CODA-COND. That is why there is no consonant epenthesis in /C+V/ juncture (17):

(17) CODA-COND ≫ ALIGN-R(stem, σ)

/i-N-t͡ʃʰik-i/	CODA-COND	ALIGN-R(stem, σ)	DEP
☞ (a) iɲ.t͡ʃʰi.k‖i		*	
(b) iɲ.t͡ʃʰik‖.t̲i̲	*!		*

Cyclic or transderivational relationships are one aspect of the larger topic of how phonology interfaces with the other grammatical components, morphology and syntax (see Ussishkin Ch.19, Urbanczyk Ch.20, Truckenbrodt Ch.18). Cyclicity also has connections with the opacity problem, connections that are made quite explicitly in Stratal OT.

5.6 Conclusion

This chapter has explored the concept of level of representation and the closely related idea of a derivation that connects the different levels of representation with one another. These are areas of on-going, productive research activity. As this work continues, we may expect to see some consensus emerging about the basic questions: How many and what kind of levels of representation are there? Are serial derivations a central property of phonology, and if so what are their properties? What is the range and character of opacity phenomena, and how are they best analyzed? How do morphological structure and morphological relatedness impinge on phonology?

6

Representation

John Harris

6.1   Introduction

In building theories of phonological grammar, researchers focus on two main areas of enquiry, broadly definable as representation and derivation. Representational theory concerns itself with the structure and content of phonological forms – the sound shape of morphemes. Derivational theory concerns itself with relations between different forms – for example between the lexical and output forms of a morpheme, or between different alternants of a morpheme.

Although the areas of representation and derivation are distinguishable in the round, there is a fair degree of overlap. During the 1980s, much work in phonology was directed towards constraining derivational theory by enriching the representational component. A recurring theme of this chapter will be that recent advances in derivational theory have prompted a rethink of some of these representational developments.

Phonological representations contain two fundamentally different types of information. One type involves segment-specific properties that map in a relatively stable manner to differences in phonetic quality. Examples include coronality, frication and voicing. The other type involves structural or prosodic relations between segments within phonological strings and is expressed in a phonetically relative way, particularly along the parameters of intensity, duration and pitch. Examples include stress prominence, length and syllabic affiliation.

A linear model of phonological representation is one in which segmental and prosodic properties are not formally distinguished. Representations in early generative theory can be characterised as linear in this sense: both types of information were phonologically encoded in terms of features (as in *SPE* – Chomsky & Halle 1968). A phonological form was conceived of as a linear string of segments, each of which was specified for an unordered bundle of features. It is now generally agreed that the segmental and prosodic aspects of phonological representations are subject to distinct organising principles and should be kept formally distinct (Goldsmith 1976a, Halle & Vergnaud 1982). Features are reserved for segmental information, while prosodic information is encoded in terms of constituent structure. The resulting model of representation is nonlinear: the two types of information are deployed on separate levels and linked to one another in ways that are not monotonic.

For the purposes of this chapter, it will be convenient to discuss the segmental and prosodic aspects of representations separately. Section 6.3 reviews different responses to a range of questions concerning the nature of segmental form. Are features defined in articulatory or auditory-acoustic terms? How many values does each feature bear? Can particular values remain unspecified? Are features hierarchically organised? Section 6.4, on prosodic form, discusses different approaches to syllable structure, metrical (stress) representation, constituent headedness and licensing. We will start, however, by exploring two fundamental questions for representational theory (Section 6.2). One is whether phonological representations are categorical or directly reflect the sort of gradient phonetic detail encountered in speech. The other is whether the design of phonological representations helps explain recurrent properties of languages' sound systems.

6.2   The nature of phonological representation

6.2.1   Are phonological representations categorical?

Phonological representations form part of the grammar that encapsulates the linguistic knowledge of a listener-talker. Their basic function is to service the sound aspect of the link between speech sounds and linguistic meanings. The phonological form of a morpheme serves to distinguish the morpheme from others in the lexicon and provides the material that enables it to be made phonetically manifest.

The manner in which phonological forms are produced by talkers and perceived by listeners involves continuously varying phonetic parameters. For example, individual productions of the *p* in 'pat', 'happen', 'apart' and the *b* in 'bat', 'rabbit', 'about' can be arrayed along a continuum of values for Voice Onset Time (VOT, the interval between the release of a plosive and the start of vocal-fold vibration in a following vowel). The knowledge underlying this kind of behaviour in speech, it is generally agreed, must at some level be coded in a form that is also continuous. On the other hand, there are certain aspects of sound patterning in language that are clearly categorical. For example, the use of sound contrasts to distinguish one morpheme from another typically operates in a binary fashion. Thus, while there are many different degrees of VOT in the phonetic realisation of labial stops in English, only a two-way phonological distinction can be made in any particular phonological environment (as in 'pat' vs. 'bat'). The contrasts employed in individual languages form systems that are organised into discrete sound classes. The same categorical organisation is evident in the way sound classes are affected by phonological processes and distributional restrictions.

A number of important questions arise at this point. Is the phonological form of a morpheme represented in a continuous or categorical fashion? If continuous, how do we account for the categorical aspects of sound patterning? If categorical, how is the form mapped to continuous phonetics? A fairly standard response to these questions, dating back to *SPE*, is embodied in the model of representational levels depicted in (1) (also see Bermúdez-Otero 21.3.1).

(1)

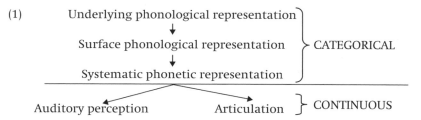

In this arrangement, phonological representations are categorical, in the sense that they are composed of discrete entities such as segments, binary features and syllables. These entities are sparsely specified at an underlying level, where phonological forms contain only the information that is minimally necessary to distinguish one morpheme from another. Phonological derivation produces surface forms in which non-distinctive specifications have been filled in. On their way to continuous phonetic interpretation, surface forms transit through a categorical buffer, variously known as the systematic phonetic or categorical phonetic level (see Keating 1990a). Here binary feature specifications are translated into scalar values; for example, [voice] is mapped to [nvoice] (Ladefoged & Vennemann 1973).

The model in (1) has been increasingly called into question in the recent literature. One challenge is linked to the emergence of constraint-based theory, which has highlighted a problem arising from having distinct types of representation at an underlying level (input) and on the surface (output). Constraints that evaluate the goodness of fit between a given output form and its lexical input are generally assumed to be no different from constraints that evaluate the correspondence between different output forms (McCarthy & Prince 1995a, Benua 1997). This argues strongly against having different degrees or types of specification in inputs and outputs. We return to this point in the discussion of feature underspecification below. A radical response is to dispense with the distinction between underlying and surface representation altogether (as in Declarative Phonology; see Scobbie, Coleman & Bird 1996 and the references there).

Much output-oriented theory continues to assume the existence of a categorical phonetic level, which phonological forms pass through once constraints have done their evaluative work (see for example Goldsmith 1993a, McCarthy & Prince 1993b, Mohanan 1995). However, a simpler alternative is to assume that phonological forms map directly to the continuous values of articulation and auditory perception (see for example Pierrehumbert 1990). Combining direct phonetic mapping with a rejection of an underlying-surface distinction results in a pared-down model in which there is only one type of categorical representation.

Another challenge to the standard model has come from work on speech perception which questions the very notion that phonological forms are categorical (also see Bermúdez-Otero 21.4). There is significant empirical support for the view that the sound shapes of morphemes are stored in a listener-talker's mental lexicon as a cloud of exemplars accumulated in episodic memory (Pierrehumbert 2001, 2002). The exemplars are labelled in terms of regions on a cognitive map that is an analogue representation of physical phonetics. On the face of it, this is a radical departure from how phonologists traditionally think of phonological forms. The exemplar model is arguably better equipped than familiar categorical models to account for variable aspects of speech behaviour. For example, sound changes that take place within the speech of individuals over the course of their lifetimes are consistent with the notion that exemplar clouds are incrementally updated in the light of ongoing linguistic experience (Kirchner 1999).

However, there are several respects in which the exemplar and categorical models might be said to converge. At least as applied to human speech, exemplar theory acknowledges that the sound shapes of morphemes are decomposable into smaller entities. There is after all a wealth of evidence bearing this out, coming not just from the recurrent sound patterns that are the staple of phonological theory but also from 'external' sources, including speech errors (Fromkin 1988), language games (Bagemihl 1995) and poetic devices such as rime and alliteration (Fabb 1997). These smaller entities, the labelled regions of the internalised phonetic map, figure in the structural description of processes that affect sets of target morphemes. To a large extent, the labels correspond to the categories of traditional phonological description. Moreover, within the cloud of specific memories associated with a typical morpheme, there will be one region where the population of exemplars is at its densest. This can be understood as providing the basis of a prototype for the morpheme's sound shape. It can be argued that the categorical representations of traditional phonological theory are abstractions corresponding to prototypes of this sort.

6.2.2   Do phonological representations explain anything?

Phonological representations encode the conventionalised knowledge that allows the listener-talker to receive and transmit linguistic messages by sound. On the simplest interpretation of a grammar as being dedicated to specifically linguistic knowledge, this would be an exhaustive definition of what phonological representations are for. According to this view, the phonological form of a morpheme serves only the two functions mentioned above: to distinguish the morpheme from others in the lexicon, and to enable it to be phonetically expressed. In fact, since the earliest days of generative phonology, it has been widely assumed that the ingredients of representations – and in particular features – play an important additional role, namely to help explain the patterned behaviour of languages' sound systems. Much of the argumentation for particular versions of feature theory is based on this thinking. For example, particular sets of place features have been proposed on the grounds that they provide a more satisfactory explanation of assimilation than available alternatives (see especially the references on feature geometry below).

Most of the patterns in question have a basis in phonetic naturalness. Attempting to provide a representational explanation for them is thus founded on the premise that phonological grammars contain not just conventionalised knowledge but also 'natural' knowledge. That is, listener-talkers are assumed to have a tacit appreciation of the speech-based pressures that help determine the design of their phonological systems. The supposed link between conventionalised and natural knowledge is rarely explicitly motivated in the phonological literature (a notable exception is Hayes 2004a). It certainly cannot be taken for granted. There is no *a priori* reason to believe that knowing what a possible form is in your language presupposes knowing about the forces that shape the material out of which forms are constructed (for differing views on this issue, see Prince Ch.2 and Gordon Ch.3).

Without a commitment to the notion that grammars contain natural knowledge, arguments for the phonetic plausibility of particular representational proposals lose a good deal of force. Arguments of this sort are unlikely to sway those who take the view that explanations of sound patterns belong not in a theory of grammar but rather in a theory of language change (John J. Ohala 1995, Blevins 2004).

In any event, the standard representational machinery employed to model conventionalised phonological knowledge is simply not sufficient to the task of explaining the natural bases of sound patterns. Familiar features such as [coronal], [continuant] and [voice] can characterise the binarity of phonological contrasts, but they are too coarse-grained to characterise the continuously varying phonetic parameters that need to be referred to when seeking natural explanations of phonological behaviour.

A recent approach to this problem takes the radical step of rejecting the assumption that there exist distinct types of representation, one for continuous phonetics and another for categorical phonology. What is proposed instead is that the representational space within which the sound shape of morphemes is defined is phonetically continuous in its entirety (Flemming

1995, 2001, Kirchner 1998, 2004, Steriade 1999c). Dimensions of contrast are represented in terms of analogue parameters such as formant frequency, degree of jaw lowering and duration. The categorical behaviour of contrasts emerges from the manner in which grammar-internal constraints act on these continuous parameters. The relevant constraints are motivated by communicative pressures, some of which are in competition with one another. The main types of constraint can be summarised as 'maximise the number of contrasts in the system', 'maximise the auditory-perceptual distance between contrasts' and 'minimise the expenditure of articulatory effort'. When these constraints are ranked in particular ways, they impose discreteness on otherwise continuous phonetic parameters.

One of the claimed advantages of this approach is that it provides a unified account of phonologisation, the historical process by which variable and phonetically continuous effects such as coarticulation and target undershoot become phonologically entrenched as categorical effects such as harmony and lenition. The transition is modelled as a reranking of the relevant constraints. The claim that these constraints are functionally 'live' commits this overall approach to the view that grammars encompass natural phonological knowledge. The approach provides us with our first specific example of how developments in derivational theory can spark a radical reappraisal of the nature of phonological representation.

6.3   Segmental representation

There is a considerable body of evidence supporting the conclusion that the basic components of segmental representation are smaller than the phoneme. For example, phonological processes and distributional restrictions typically refer to recurrent classes of sounds rather than to individual phonemes. These same sound classes recur as dimensions of contrast in languages' consonant and vowel systems. The simplest explanation is that the sound classes in question share certain natural properties – features – which define the targets for the rules or constraints responsible for this patterned behaviour (see Hall Ch.13 for a review of commonly accepted segmental features). Here we may review current thinking about phonological features by asking a number of fundamental questions about them. Are they appropriately defined in articulatory or auditory-acoustic terms? Are they specified in binary terms? Are they organised within segments in any particular way? Do all of the feature specifications associated with a particular segment have to be consistently present?

6.3.1   Articulatory vs. auditory-acoustic features

Let us first consider the question of whether features should be defined in articulatory or auditory-acoustic terms from the viewpoint of how they code conventionalised phonological knowledge. For some time, the mainstream view has been that features are either primarily or exclusively defined in terms of the articulatory movements of the talker. In frameworks that can trace a direct lineage to *SPE* feature theory, the definitions are primarily articulatory in orientation. Each feature is initially defined in terms of some vocal-tract configuration, for which some acoustic correlate is then also assumed (Halle & Clements 1983). The best established framework with an exclusively articulatory orientation is Articulatory Phonology, in which the units of segmental representation are vocal-tract gestures (Browman & Goldstein 1989, 1992).

The more closely wedded to articulation a feature framework is, the more obviously it must subscribe to some version of the notion that listeners perceive speech in terms of the articulatory movements of talkers. Either the listener internally resynthesises the movements that are likely to have produced the speech sounds they hear, as claimed in the Motor Theory of Speech Perception (Liberman & Mattingly 1985), or they literally perceive the movements themselves, as in Direct Realist theory (Fowler 1986). Neither of these theories has been widely accepted in the speech perception literature, where the prevalent view remains that in speech 'we hear sounds rather than tongues' (Ohala 1996).

With regard to the perception–production relation in speech, there is a well established imbalance in favour of perception. Listeners listen, while talkers both talk and listen (in monitoring their own output); perception precedes production in phonological acquisition; articulatory impairment is no barrier to normal speech perception, while deafness is a barrier to normal speech production. At least as far as the representation of conventionalised phonological knowledge is concerned, this asymmetry strongly favours a specification of features in terms that are either primarily or exclusively auditory-perceptual rather than articulatory. This is the view embodied in the earliest versions of modern feature theory, especially that of Jakobson and colleagues (Jakobson, Fant & Halle 1952).

However, the view that phonological grammars also contain natural knowledge necessitates a more encompassing approach to feature specification. Since the natural bases of phonological patterns call for both articulatory and auditory-acoustic explanations, it follows that the grammar has to make provision for both types of feature specification (Boersma 1998, Flemming 2001). It has been argued that this explanatory goal cannot be achieved by simply taking standard articulatory features and supplementing them with acoustic definitions but requires distinct sets of features, one for production and another for perception. Examples of phonological affinities between segment classes that cannot be adequately accounted for in terms of articulatory specifications include velars and labials, retroflex consonants and round vowels, and labio-dental and dental fricatives (Flemming 1995). Each of these pairs can only be satisfactorily captured by means of auditory-acoustic features (such as the Jakobsonian feature [grave] for velars and labials).

6.3.2 Valency

The categorical nature of phonological oppositions typically manifests itself in a binary fashion. Even those contrastive dimensions that are phonetically scalar, such as vowel height or VOT, can usually be shown to exhibit binary phonological behaviour. If a given contrast is viewed as balanced or equipollent, it makes sense to specify the feature that defines the contrast in terms of two independent values. This results in bivalent specifications such as [+coronal] vs. [−coronal]. Alternatively, a contrast can be viewed as privative, in the sense that one member possesses the relevant feature while the other lacks it, resulting in monovalent specifications such as [coronal] vs. zero. In Prague-School phonology, it was assumed that some contrasts were equipollent, while others were privative (Anderson 1985: Ch.4). In current theory, this view survives in feature frameworks that incorporate both bivalent and monovalent features (see Clements & Hume 1995). In *SPE*, features are uniformly bivalent, and there are frameworks in which all features are monovalent (see for example Anderson & Ewen 1987, Hulst 1989, Avery & Rice 1989).

There are clear empirical differences between the two conceptions of feature valency (for discussion and references, see Ewen & Hulst 2001). Most of the literature on this point has focused on the issue of whether both terms of a contrast are phonologically active. *Ceteris paribus* (in particular, given a common set of features), monovalency predicts a significantly smaller number of active sound classes than bivalency. With a bivalent feature, rules or constraints can target either the plus value or the minus value (not to mention both values simultaneously). With monovalency, only the feature itself can be targeted (on the understanding that rules or constraints cannot refer to the absence of anything). The class of segments lacking the feature is predicted to be phonologically inert; that is, it should be unable to trigger or block processes. In the case of [labial] or [round] for example, bivalency predicts that some processes can target the class of round vowels, while others can target non-round. In this instance, the evidence comes down firmly in favour of monovalency (Steriade 1987). For example, while rounding harmony is widely attested in different languages, there are no clear-cut examples of unrounding harmony (Clements & Hume 1995).

In the case of certain features, however, it has been argued that monovalency is empirically underpowered. For example, defining [voice] as a monovalent feature specific to prevoiced obstruents correctly predicts that active voicing assimilation will only occur in languages with consonants of this type (Iverson & Salmons 1995, Lombardi 1995a). However, it fails to predict that voiceless obstruents can also sometimes be active in such languages (Wetzels & Mascaró 2001). The response from proponents of monovalency has usually been to enrich the feature set, either by drafting in extra features or by exploiting other representational resources (such as dependency, on which more below). In cases such as this, the *ceteris paribus* rider ceases to apply.

A related point of comparison between monovalency and bivalency concerns the issue of whether a given feature specification has a clearly identifiable phonetic signature. Monovalent frameworks are constrained by the requirement that every feature be phonetically definable in this way. The issue is not so clear-cut with bivalency, because there are two rather different ways of viewing the phonetic manifestation of a minus value: either it lacks any phonetic signature of its own, or it possesses a phonetic signature that is the equipollent counterpart to that of its plus complement.

Both interpretations are implicit in *SPE*-derived feature theory, as can be illustrated by comparing standard definitions of [round] and [continuant]. When treated monovalently, [round] has a clearly specifiable phonetic manifestation – a low-frequency spectral peak resulting from the convergence of the first two formants. Under a bivalent treatment, the same definition can be applied to the plus value, but no equivalent definition is available for the minus value. That is, there is no single phonetic signature that unifies the class of non-round vowels. To put it concretely: the speech signal can contain a consistent auditory-acoustic cue to both [u] and [o], but no equivalent cue exists for [a] and [i]. The only way of providing a phonetic definition of the non-round set is to refer to an *absence* of the signature associated with the complement set (as, for example, Halle & Clements 1983 do). This effectively incorporates a monovalent design property into a supposedly bivalent model.

The situation is different with [±continuant]. Here the minus value does have a consistent phonetic signature – a radical reduction in acoustic energy produced by a medial constriction in the oral tract. A monovalent framework is obliged to recognise this in the form of an independent feature (equivalent to the Jakobsonian label [abrupt]).

There is little doubt that monovalency presents a potentially more restrictive model of feature specification than bivalency. While there continues to be disagreement about the extent to which this potential can be realised over an entire feature set, it is nevertheless fair to say that there is a core of features that are widely agreed to be monovalent. Examples for which this is true include [round], [nasal], [labial], [coronal] and [dorsal] (or differently labelled equivalents).

The fact that the same natural classes of sounds recur in the phonological regularities we encounter in the world's languages has usually been taken to mean that features of the sort just mentioned define universal categories of segmental representation. This view is radically different from the one adopted by Flemming (2001), Kirchner (2004) and others, reviewed in Section 6.2 above, according to which the categorical nature of segmental behaviour emerges from the effect of ranked constraints acting on continuous phonetic parameters. In a model of this type, the parameters can be thought of as analogue counterparts of the coarsely digitised categories of standard feature theory.

6.3.3   Hierarchical organisation

In *SPE*, it was assumed that the feature specifications for any given segment were combined in an unordered bundle. As a result of developments in non-linear theory during the 1970s and 1980s, it is now generally agreed that the featural content of representations is autosegmentally organised: each feature is deployed on a separate tier and is linked to syllabic positions or other feature tiers by means of association lines (see Hall Ch.13 for details; Goldsmith 1976a and the further references below). Autosegmental representation allows individual features to be independently accessed by phonological processes such as assimilation and deletion.

In an extension of non-linear theory, it has been proposed that autosegmental representations are hierarchically structured. Two types of hierarchical organisation have been proposed: one in which features are grouped under intermediate constituent nodes (feature geometry), and another in which features enter into head-dependent relations (for a review of the formal and empirical differences between the two types, see Ewen 1995).

Feature geometry is designed for the same general purpose as autosegmental representation – to explain recurrent properties of phonological processes such as assimilation, coalescence and deletion. More specifically it is motivated by the observation that features pattern into natural classes no less than segments do (see Clements 1985a, Sagey 1986 and the reviews in McCarthy 1988 and Clements & Hume 1995). In place assimilation, for example, place features tend to spread *en bloc*, while in debuccalisation the same set of features is subject to deletion. In linear theory, there was no way of representing this group behaviour other than by arbitrarily combining the features in question in the structural descriptions of individual rules. Nor can the behaviour be directly accounted for under an autosegmental arrangement in which each feature links independently to a given syllabic position (as in earlier autosegmental theory; see Goldsmith 1976a, Halle & Vergnaud 1982).

The geometric solution is to gather natural classes of features under intermediate class nodes. The best established of these nodes within geometric theory are the Root node, which represents the unity of the segment, and its daughters Laryngeal and Place (which dominates the major articulator nodes Labial, Coronal and Dorsal) (for a comparison of variations on this basic arrangement, see Clements & Hume 1995). Each node (which is inherently monovalent) defines a potential target for particular rules or constraints, which thereby access all of the daughter features simultaneously. Consider for example the fragment of the hierarchy representing labial place shown in (2a) (where x stands for a syllabic position).

(2)   (a)   x   (b)   x   (c)   x   x

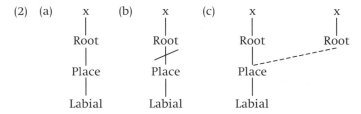

Debuccalisation is represented by the delinking operation depicted in (2b). Severing the association between the Place and Root nodes results in the deletion of any individual feature dominated by Place (in this instance Labial). Place assimilation is represented by the spreading operation shown in (2c). Inserting an association line between the Place node of one syllabic position and the Root of a neighbouring position results in the spreading of any individual Place feature.

Feature geometry is another example of a representational design that is having to be reconsidered in the light of more recent derivational developments. In Optimality Theory, feature classes can now be captured by constraints which refer directly to individual features that pattern into sets on the basis of phonetic criteria (Padgett 2002). This development arguably renders geometric class nodes superfluous.

Under an alternative conception of segment-internal organisation, features are viewed as entering into asymmetric relations that define contrasts and determine phonetic interpretation. This approach, which represents a radical departure from *SPE*-derived feature theory, extends to segmental structure the machinery of head-dependency exploited in prosodic structure and morphosyntax (see below). The longest-established version of this approach is Dependency Phonology, which is closely associated with a model of vowel quality based on the components | a | ('open'), | i | ('front') and | u | ('round') (Anderson & Ewen 1987, Hulst 1989; for related proposals, see Schane 1984, Kaye, Lowenstamm & Vergnaud 1985 and the review in Harris & Lindsey 1995). These define vowel contrasts by appearing alone or in combination with one another. Alone, the components define the corner vowels [a i u] as in (3a).

(3)   *Dependency Phonology vowel representations*

   (a)   SIMPLEX
      | i | = [i] | a | = [a] | u | = [u]
   (b)   ASYMMETRIC COMPOUNDS
      | i | | u |
        | = [e] | = [o]
      | a | | a |

      | a | | a |
        | = [æ] | = [ɒ]
      | i | | a |
   (c)   SYMMETRIC COMPOUNDS
      |i, a | = [ɛ] |i, a | = [ɔ]

In an asymmetric compound, one component acts as the head, the other as a dependent, as in (3b). Alternatively, two components may be mutually dependent, resulting in symmetric compounds such as those shown in (3c). Dependency relations help determine the phonetic expression of a compound, with a head component contributing more to the quality of a particular vowel than a dependent.

6.3.4   Partial specification

A notable design property of the AIU model is the ability of each component to be phonetically expressed in isolation (as the [a i u] vowels themselves). This is markedly different from *SPE*-derived theory, where a given feature value can only be expressed when it appears as part of a segment, in harness with a full span of other feature values. Some of these values will be distinctive, others redundant. The sole purpose of redundant values is to support the phonetic interpretation of the segment it belongs to. In certain cases, a redundant value can be said to 'enhance' the phonetic expression of a distinctive value; for example, [+round] can enhance [+back] (Stevens & Keyser 1989).

In early generative work, the lack of distinctive function in redundant values gave rise to the notion that they could be omitted from lexical representations and filled in by rule (Halle 1959). Later, the idea that phonological forms could be partially specified or underspecified in this way was adapted to give direct representational expression to other types of phonological phenomena, such as unmarked status or a failure to trigger or block phonological processes. For example, it has been argued that underspecifying coronal place enables us to capture its unmarked and often phonologically inert status (see the contributions to Paradis & Prunet 1991b). Much of the work on feature theory in the mid 1980s to mid 1990s focused on this issue (see for example Archangeli 1984, Archangeli & Pulleyblank 1986, 1994 and the review in Steriade 1995).

Particularly since the upsurge of interest in output-oriented theory in the early 1990s, the validity of underspecification has been increasingly called into question. There are various reasons for this. One has to do with the nature of output itself. A partially specified representation lacks a vital proportion of the ingredients necessary for it to be made phonetically manifest. As a result, it cannot be considered phonological output proper. There has been some attempt to accommodate underspecification within Optimality Theory by allowing economy-based constraints that ban redundant feature values to outrank phonetically-based constraints that demand full specification (Itô, Mester & Padgett 1995). Under these conditions, however, partially specified optimal candidates are not true output forms and have to be passed on to some post-constraint level where missing feature values are filled in. Put differently, supposedly output-oriented constraints are actually evaluating pre-output forms.

If authentic outputs are required to be fully specified, this renders under-specification irrelevant to one dimension of faithfulness in Optimality Theory, namely output–output correspondence. The degree of correspond-ence between morphologically related output forms can be gauged without reference to the possibility that some feature values may be missing from their inputs.

It might be concluded that predictable information, including redun-dant feature values, can at least be omitted from input forms (as in *SPE*) and then supplied by the phonological generator. However, there is no obvious advantage to allowing this kind of mismatch between input and output. The argument that underspecification directly captures the unmarked status of certain feature values is no longer persuasive once we adopt an output-oriented perspective (McCarthy & Taub 1992, Steriade 1995). This is mainly because markedness constraints only need to evaluate outputs. Moreover, at least in OT, there is an independent means of expressing markedness asymmetries among segment classes, namely by imposing universally fixed rankings on particular sets of markedness constraints (Prince & Smolensky 2004). The fixed-ranking solution is admittedly stipu-lative but probably no more so than deciding that coronal rather than some other place should be underspecified.

None of the problems associated with trying to adapt underspecification to output theory need arise in the case of the AIU model. The stand-alone interpretability of these components (and their consonantal equivalents – see for example Harris 2004) means that the model can dispense with anything resembling redundant feature values. Any component targeted by an output constraint is both distinctive and capable of being phonetic-ally expressed without the support of any other segmental material.

6.4   Prosodic structure

6.4.1   Syllable structure and the skeletal tier

In *SPE*, the syllabic affiliation of segments was represented linearly in terms of the feature [±syllabic]. By the late 1970s, however, it had become clear that syllable structure needed to be hierarchically represented, allowing for direct reference to the traditionally recognised sub-syllabic constituents of onset, rime, nucleus and coda (Kahn 1976, Harris 1983; for a review, see Blevins 1995 and Zec Ch.8). Arguments in favour of syllabic structure draw on a variety of sources of evidence, most particularly weight, prosodic morphology and phonotactic restrictions.

The terminal nodes of the syllabic hierarchy are positions that provide information about phonological weight. There is a significant body of evidence supporting the conclusion that weight relations are independ-ently coded in phonological representations. Some of this evidence demon-strates the ability of weight to remain stable in the face of changes or differences that affect the segmental content of forms. This is clearly illustrated in compensatory lengthening, where one segment expands to fill the vacuum left by the deletion of a neighbouring segment (see the contributions to Wetzels & Sezer 1986). Another type of evidence comes from the role of syllable weight in metrical structure, in particular where VV and VC sequences both count as heavy and thereby attract stress, despite the segmental differences between the second positions (Hayes 1995, Zec Ch.8, Kager Ch.9).

Facts such as these have been used to motivate an independent timing tier consisting of skeletal positions that code weight relations. There are two competing ways of formalising the skeletal tier, differing according to whether the positions take the form of x-slots (Levin 1985, Kaye, Lowen-stamm & Vergnaud 1990) or morae (Hyman 1985, McCarthy & Prince 1986) (for reviews, see Brockhaus 1995, Broselow 1995, Zec Ch.8). The simplest versions of the two models are depicted in (4) (where • stands for a feature-geometric root node).

(4) **(a)**   **(b)**

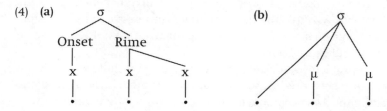

A necessary component of both models is the facility to distinguish that portion of the syllable which bears weight (the rime) from that which does not (the onset). In the x-slot model, this is achieved by granting the onset and rime formal constituent status, as shown in (4a). A heavy syllable is then defined as one with a branching rime. In the moraic model, only weight-bearing positions project morae (represented by μ in (4b)), thereby removing the need for independent onset and rime nodes. A heavy syllable is then defined as one that is bimoraic.

For many purposes, x-slot and moraic representations are notationally equivalent. For example, in both frameworks, compensatory lengthening is modelled as the spreading of a segment into a position from which some neighbouring segment has been delinked. However, there are several re-spects in which the two models can be separated on descriptive and ex-planatory grounds. For example, it has been argued that the moraic model is better able to explain a recurrent property of compensatory lengthening, namely that it only occurs in languages with a syllable weight contrast (Hayes 1989a). In languages of this type, a syllable-final consonant projects a mora ('weight by position') and thus presents a prosodic target for compensatory spreading in the event of its segmental content being de-leted. In languages without a weight contrast, a syllable-final consonant does not project a mora and thus cannot trigger lengthening. In the x-slot model, any rime-final consonant occupies a skeletal position regardless of whether it contributes to syllable weight. This wrongly predicts that compensatory lengthening should be able to occur in any language with closed syllables, even in those where a coda is otherwise weightless.

On the other hand, there are phenomena that the x-slot model is better placed to capture. One has to do with the statement of phonotactic restrictions, which are widely assumed to be syllabically conditioned. Take for example the consonant cluster restrictions traditionally described in terms of sonority sequencing preferences: a rising sonority slope is favoured within complex onsets ([pl], [tr], etc.), while a falling slope is favoured in syllable contacts ([mp], [lt], etc.) (Selkirk 1982a). In the x-slot model, these restrictions can be uniformly expressed in terms of relations between adjacent positions on the skeletal tier. In the moraic model, restrictions on syllable contact can only be expressed in a heterogeneous fashion, by referring simultaneously to moraic and syllabic nodes. ('A root node attached to a mora prefers to be of a higher sonority when followed by a root node attached to a syllabic node.') However, it is clear that this criticism loses considerable force if phonotactic restrictions are deemed to be conditioned by factors other than syllable structure.

Recent work on phonotactics has spawned a reaction against syllable structure. This rejects two of the widely held assumptions about restrictions on consonant clusters mentioned above, namely that they are (i) conditioned by syllabic position and (ii) driven by sonority sequencing constraints (Steriade 1999c, Blevins 2003). The restrictions are instead claimed to emerge from differences in the facility with which consonants can project auditory-acoustic cues in different phonological contexts defined linearly in terms of segments and word boundaries (see also Jun 2004). The reaction against sonority is based largely on the fact that, despite its long history in phonological theory, it remains resistant to a clear phonetic definition (Ohala 1990a). The main evidence against syllable-based phonotactics involves cases where the same restrictions on consonant clusters occur in what are claimed to be different syllabic configurations, either in different languages or even in different word positions within the same language. For example, in Cypriot Greek, word-internal heterosyllabic clusters of the form fricative plus stop ([ft], [st], [xt]) can appear both word-internally and word-initially. Under a standard syllable-based analysis, the first context is heterosyllabic, while the second is tautosyllabic.

An alternative reaction to phonotactic parallels such as these is to conclude that, rather than undermining syllabic analysis *per se*, they force a radical rethink of what syllable structure looks like. If phonotactic evidence is taken as a reliable guide to syllabic affiliation, it follows that the same type of cluster should be uniformly syllabified no matter where it appears in a word. In the Cypriot Greek case, if it is correct to treat [ft], [st], [xt] as heterosyllabic word-internally, then the same clusters must also be heterosyllabic when word-initial. This gives rise to a model that departs from the traditional assumption that every word edge necessarily defines a syllable edge (a view taken for granted in much of the literature; see Blevins 1995). The assumption is in any event problematic for syllable theory, since it implies that conditions on phonological regularities that are expressed in terms of syllable boundaries can be more simply expressed in terms of word boundaries – precisely the view embodied in the rejection of syllable structure in *SPE*.

In contrast, defining syllable structure independently of word structure allows for the possibility of misalignment between the two types of edge. A syllable can overhang the left edge of a word, as in the Cypriot Greek case where, under this analysis, the first member of [ft], [st], [xt] clusters occupies a coda not only word-internally but also word-initially. Similarly, misalignment can occur at the right edge of a word, where a word-final consonant occupies an onset followed by a silent nucleus (see Gussmann 2002: Ch.5 for a review of this position). The second configuration is consistent with segment extrametricality, where a word-final consonant does not contribute to the weight of a preceding rime (Hayes 1982).

6.4.2   Head-dependency relations in prosodic structure

In earlier linear theory, relations of stress prominence were represented in terms of the scalar-valued feature [stress]. Since the mid 1970s, it has generally been accepted that stress is more adequately represented relationally, in terms of metrical structure. Two main modes of metrical representation have been proposed, grids and constituents (Liberman & Prince 1977, Hayes 1995). The grid represents the rhythmic structure of a phonological string as a sequence of alternating strong and weak beats located on stressable elements (syllables or morae). The basic metrical constituent, the foot, consists of one stressed element optionally combined with one unstressed element (in some models more than one). These devices, initially employed in rule-based treatments of word stress, continue to figure prominently in more recent, constraint-based work.

In frameworks incorporating metrical constituency, stress is largely determined by rules, parameters or constraints that control the design and location of feet (Halle & Vergnaud 1987, Hayes 1995, McCarthy & Prince 1993b). For a given language, this helps decide such questions as the following. Are feet minimally binary? Is binarity based on a mora or syllable count? Does prominence fall on the left of the foot (the trochaic pattern) or on the right (iambic)? Must all syllables be parsed into feet? Are feet oriented towards the left edge of the word or the right? Does main stress in the word fall on the leftmost or rightmost foot?

The asymmetric distribution of prominence within the foot and the word has given rise to the notion that metrical constituency displays head-dependency relations. In early metrical work, this was expressed by labelling each branch of a constituent as strong or weak (Liberman & Prince

1977), a mode of representation that was then extended to syllable structure (Kiparsky 1979). What emerges from these developments is a unified conception of a prosodic hierarchy (Selkirk 1982b, Nespor & Vogel 1986, McCarthy & Prince 1986), in which asymmetric relations are discernible at all levels of structure. A nucleus heads a rime; a rime heads a syllable; a prominent syllable heads a foot; a foot containing a main-stressed syllable heads a prosodic word.

Dependency relations came to assume increasing importance in various prosodic theories, most obviously in Dependency Phonology itself and its direct off-shoots (Anderson & Ewen 1987, Hulst 1989). In a related development, prosodic relations are expressed in terms of government, defined as an asymmetric relation holding between two positions that are adjacent at some level of prosodic projection (Kaye, Lowenstamm & Vergnaud 1990). In the case of syllabic structure, government involves adjacency at the level of the skeletal tier, being left-headed within constituents and right-headed between constituents. For example, within an onset such as [pl] the first position governs the second, while the reverse directionality holds in a coda-onset sequence such as [mp]. These constituent-based relations correlate with segmental-distributional asymmetries, with a governor being able to support a greater range of contrasts than its governee. Nuclei, the heads of syllables, project to higher levels of prosodic structure, where they enter into governing relations with one another, involving adjacency within domains such as the foot and word. At these levels of projection, government is implicated in a range of phenomena including stress and vowel syncope.

Much of the work on prosodic dependency draws explicit parallels with constituency and headedness in syntax (see also Levin 1985). However, there are clearly limits on how far this programme can be pushed. This point can be briefly illustrated by considering two design properties of syntactic structure – recursion and accessibility – that have no direct analogues in phonology (Neeleman & Koot, to appear). There is some evidence of limited recursion in sentence-level prosody, where there are circumstances under which one phonological phrase can arguably be embedded in another (Selkirk 1995a). However, generally speaking, nothing directly equivalent to full-blooded syntactic recursion is found in phonology. It is certainly not attested below the level of phrasal phonology. For example, there is no evidence that one syllable can embed within another. As to accessibility, feature percolation in syntax is subject to a constraint whereby information in a given node can only be read by nodes immediately above it or below it. Metrical structure clearly does not respect this constraint, as can be illustrated by the distinction between main and subsidiary stresses. Under certain circumstances, main stress prominence can only be assigned to a particular syllable by comparing it to some other stressed syllable within the same domain. This is what happens in the English rhythm rule, where main stress shifts away from the right edge of a word, in order to avoid a clash with a main stress in a following word, as in *sìxtéen* vs. *síxtèen mén* (Prince 1983). In this case, for the head syllable of a foot to be projected as a head at word level, it needs to be compared with the head of a neighbouring foot. The metrical head thus has to access information in a sister node, in violation of accessibility.

A notion related to prosodic dependency is that of licensing, also initially borrowed from syntax. The term is used in two senses in phonology. One refers to the link between prosodic structure and segmental content: a syllabic position is said to license the features with which it is associated (Itô 1986, Itô, Mester & Padgett 1995, Lombardi 1999, Walker 2001). In its other use, the term refers to certain types of relation within prosodic structure. For example, an onset is sometimes described as being licensed by a following nucleus, a coda by a following onset (Charette 1991). Combining these two interpretations of licensing results in a unified model of representation, in which differences in the ability of individual positions to license segmental material are directly determined by the licensing relations they contract with other positions within prosodic structure (Harris 1997, Dresher & Hulst 1998). In this way, phonological representations transparently record the fact that prosodic heads (for example stressed syllables) support a greater array of segmental contrasts than dependent positions. Segmental asymmetries of this type can be thought of as direct representational responses to constraint rankings that require contrasts to be faithfully preserved in prominent positions (Beckman 1997).

Expanding the role of dependency or licensing relations in prosodic theory inevitably renders constituency increasingly redundant. This development reaches a logical conclusion in work that reduces the prosodic aspect of phonological representations to a linear string of positions that are bound to one another by means of dependency or licensing relations (see Scheer 1998 and the references there).

6.5   Conclusion

The sound shape of a morpheme is classically thought of as being represented in terms of a dichotomy between the phonological and the phonetic. The phonological aspect is 'abstract', fully categorical and contains only the information necessary to fulfil the symbolic function of distinguishing the morpheme from others in the lexicon. The phonetic aspect is 'concrete', closer to the continuously varying values of speech and contains the information necessary to allow the morpheme to be heard and pronounced. This view sits most comfortably with an input-oriented model of derivation, in which abstract underlying forms are converted into concrete surface forms.

Ongoing developments in linguistic theory and speech science are rendering this view increasingly untenable. Advances in output-oriented derivational theory are progressively subverting the notion of an under-lying-surface distinction in phonology. Moreover, categorical patterning in languages' sound systems can no longer be taken as immediate proof that phonological or phonetic forms are themselves represented in terms of categorical entities. The patterns can instead be seen as emerging from a complex interaction of forces in the mind-body of the listener-talker that help shape the acquisition, long-term storage and on-line implementation of phonological knowledge – forces emanating from the areas of auditory perception, speech production, lexical memory, morphosyntax and so forth.

So where does this leave the categories traditionally applied to the description of phonological representation – the features, syllables and feet discussed in the preceding sections? They still have an important heuristic value as descriptors to be used in the building and experimental testing of models of phonological grammar. But researchers these days are increasingly likely to view categorical behaviour as an emergent rather than an inherent property of these descriptors. There is a growing reluc-tance to embrace the classically generative view that the entities of phono-logical representation are predefined categories of universal grammar.

Note

Thanks to Paul de Lacy and Michael O'Keefe for valuable comments on an earlier draft.

7

Contrast

Donca Steriade

7.1 Introduction: basic notions and outline

Phonological representations are composed of discrete building blocks, drawn from a finite, universal set. The building blocks are feature values and segments. In the representation of any utterance, feature values are linked to each other by relations such as precedence and constituency, and form *phonemes,* or combinations of substantially overlapping features. The same relations group phonemes into larger syntagmatic units, such as syllables. Phonemes *contrast* with each other: a difference between a phoneme pair, embedded in otherwise identical contexts, normally has the potential to convey a meaning difference. This potential for contrast is not actualized in every context: when pairs of phonemes systematically fail to contrast in some position, their contrast has been *neutralized*. A phoneme has contextual variants – *allophones* – which differ from each other in feature composition. Being contextually predictable, differences between allophones cannot convey meaning and thus are *non-contrastive*. Necessarily then, features that differentiate only allophones, not phonemes, are non-contrastive. Based on the universal set, each grammar defines its inventory of phonemes and the contrastive features from which its phonemes are built. Together, the phonemes and contrastive features can be thought of as language-specific alphabets of phonological categories. Universal constraints place limits on the composition of such alphabets.

The contents of the preceding paragraph are widely assumed in pre-generative, structuralist phonology (Sapir 1933, Trubetzkoy 1939, Hockett 1955). A subset of these ideas plays a role in early generative phonology (Chomsky and Halle 1968); virtually all have informed Lexical Phonology (Kiparsky 1982a, 1985; Mohanan 1982) and continue to influence current phonological thinking. Insofar as they can be conceived of as empirical hypotheses, these ideas are increasingly under debate. In particular, the following have been called into question: the notion of a small and universal set of features and of segment-sized feature combinations; the reality of segments in mental representations; the very existence of a clear cut between contrastive and non-contrastive categories – or of categories *tout court* – in individual grammars. Not all these debates can be discussed in this space. Lindblom (1990b), Pierrehumbert (2003a), Johnson (2004), and Port and Leary (2005) provide some important perspectives on these issues that differ substantially from the assumptions of most working phonologists. Only three broad questions are discussed below, selected for the role they play in the current analytical literature: by what formal mechanisms and at what juncture in the mapping from UR to SR are phonemic alphabets defined (Sections 7.2 and 7.3); what inventories does the grammar define: sounds, features, contrasts (Sections 7.4, 7.5, 7.6); and what factors condition neutralization (Sections 7.3, 7.4, and 7.5, passim).

7.2   Contrast beyond segments

The notions of phoneme and allophone refer to segment-sized units, but the issue of contrast arises in similar terms with larger domains and with non-featural properties. Precedence can differentiate phoneme strings – e.g. /task/ vs. /taks/ – and occasionally pairs of single phonemes (e.g. prenasalized /^{n}d/ vs. post-nasalized /d^n/). Like feature-sized properties, precedence can be contrastive, as above, or can be thought of as non-contrastive (cf. McCarthy 1989 on V-C precedence).

   The relation of temporal overlap (Browman and Goldstein 1992; Sagey 1988) can also be viewed in terms of contrast and neutralization. The extent and consistency of overlap is what distinguishes a bundle of features forming a single segment from a cluster (Byrd 1996;): /$\widehat{kp}$/ vs. /kp/. A few languages contrast unit phonemes C^j, C^w, C^h, C' with corresponding Cj, Cw, Ch, C? clusters: Indo-European, for instance, is reconstructed as having both /k^w/ and /kw/ (Ernout and Meillet 1967:200); Yokuts contrasts /t?/ with the ejective /t'/ (Newman 1944). More frequently, however, this kind of contrast is neutralized: thus, it's not obvious what unit Latin or English <qu> spells – C^w or Cw – but it is clear that it doesn't contrast in either language with *the other* thing. In Takelma, heteromorphemic combinations of C+h merge with C^h (Sapir 1922:43); the same compression of sequenced articulations into segment-sized units functions on a much larger scale in Mazateco (Steriade 1994). It appears that small differences in degree of overlap between otherwise identical articulations are insufficiently distinct to signal a contrast like /k^w/ vs. /kw/ (Wright 1996). Thus whether a phoneme class is included in a phoneme inventory depends frequently on whether the language permits a certain cluster, and conversely, whether a language permits a certain cluster depends on whether the inventory contains the relevant phoneme. (More likely, both issues depend on the inter-gestural timing relations prevalent in the language – Browman and Goldstein 1992.) Then not only does the notion of contrast extend beyond the segmental domain but also segment-internal contrasts – e.g. /k/ vs. /k^w/ – can't be separately analyzed from non-segmental contrast – e.g. /kw/ vs. /k^w/ – since some clusters give rise to segments. This diminishes the prospects for a separate statement of a language's phonemic alphabet that's somehow analytically prior to the statement of sequence phonotactics. A point we return to below is the role of the factor of *sufficient distinctness* in predicting the existence of contrasts, whether segment internal or not.

7.3   Laws constraining phonemic sets

The composition of phonemic sets is lawful and obeys universal constraints. The best understood are laws of asymmetric implication, or *implicational universals*: if certain segments are selected, then certain other segments also are. Thus if front rounded /y/ is present, then so is front unrounded /i/; but /i/ does not symmetrically imply /y/ (Jakobson 1941/ 1968; Maddieson 1984). Similarly, if nasalized vowels are present then nasal consonants also are. It is widely assumed, and explicitly so in OT work, that such typological observations have counterparts in the competence of individual speakers: so, not only is there no hypothetical language with a vowel inventory of {y, u, ø, o, a} – as against {i, u, e, o, a} – but, this assumption goes, such systematic gaps arise from a property present in each speaker's grammar and thus are independent of the segmental alphabet the grammar generates. This property could be a ranking between constraints on features (Prince and Smolensky 2004) or a ranking between constraints on contrasts (Flemming 2002, 2004); or a set of filters (i.e. inviolable constraints) activated only in a specific order (Chomsky and Halle 1968:410; Calabrese 1995).[1] Some of these options are discussed below.

There are less well-understood but more general laws which underlie individual implicational constraints in the formation of segmental alphabets. These involve the notions of dispersion and feature economy. *Dispersion* (Lindblom 1990b; Flemming 2004; Gordon 3.3.4) is a relation between pairs of sounds: the general idea here is that contrasting pairs separated by small distances in auditory space (e.g. /ɛ/ and /e/) imply the existence of other contrasting pairs, separated by a larger distance (e.g. /a/ and /i/). *Feature economy* (Clements 2003) is the tendency to minimize the ratio of features over segments in an alphabet. Thus the alphabet in (1) makes a more economic use of features (here [labial], [coronal], [dorsal], [−continuant], [±voice], [±nasal]) than the one in (2), which generates the same number of segments by combining more features, or than (3), which combines the same features as (1), but yields fewer segments[2].

(1) {p t k b d g m n ŋ}
(2) {p tʰ k' β ɾ g w n̪ ŋ}
(3) {b t ŋ}

These examples (adapted from Lindblom 1990b) suggest that dispersion and feature economy are, to an extent, conflicting forces: more economic alphabets have less well separated members, because fewer features distinguish them. The more surprising aspect of the comparison between (1), (2) and (3) is that feature economy and dispersion are insufficient to characterize the typology of segmental alphabets. That's because (2) and (3), which achieve vastly better dispersion at the cost of some decrease in economy, are unattested and probably impossible alphabets; in contrast, (1) is widely attested. If an unconstrained tug-of-war between dispersion and economy had been sufficient to characterize the notion of possible alphabet, it would be difficult to exclude (2) and (3). This is a point we will return to.

7.4 Underlying and derived alphabets

7.4.1 Early generative grammar

The interest in modeling the grammatical process that selects phoneme sets is recent. Structuralist and early generative analyses postulate without comment an underlying segment inventory for each language. The assumptions of lexical minimality (minimizing lexically stored information: Chomsky and Halle 1968:381; Steriade 1995:114) and feature economy (as defined above) play an implicit role in these cases. To illustrate the role of feature economy, Kenstowicz and Kisseberth (1979) argue that the underlying vowel set of Yawelmani Yokuts is (4a), as against (4b), which is closer to surface structures. The reason is, in part, that (4a) is "more symmetrical" (1979:206). Cast in feature economy terms, the point is that (4a) makes maximal use of [±long], [±high] and [±round] and eliminates the superfluous use of [±low] implicit in (4b).

(4) *Yawelmani Yokuts vowel inventories (Kenstowicz & Kisseberth 1979)*

    (a) Underlying: /a i o u;   aː iː oː uː/
    (b) Surface: [a e i o u;   aː eː oː]

Similar arguments are given by Chomsky and Halle (1968:203) for deriving surface [ʌ] from /u/ in English, by Mohanan and Mohanan (1984) for deriving Malayalam [r] from /t/, among many others. In all these cases, the feature economy arguments are supported by evidence from alternations. How speakers organize their phonemic alphabet when the evidence from feature economy and alternations fails to converge is unknown.

    In early generative models, the assumption of lexical minimality has the effect of reducing the underlying alphabet to the minimal sound set needed to express surface differences between distinct morphemes. This requires then the elimination of allophonic variants from lexical entries: the American English allophone set {[tʰ], [t̚], [ʔt], [ɾ]} for instance, would have to be reduced in the lexicon to one sound. What should the features of this sound be? Here too lexical minimality works to dictate that only those features minimally necessary to distinguish lexical items should be used. So, if [±spread glottis] does not distinguish lexical items, the lexical /t/ sound will be entered as *underspecified* for aspiration: it will bear no value for that feature. How (and whether) learners proceed to eliminate predictable feature values from lexical entries is an unresolved question: so, given that [±round] and [±back] are mutually predictable in the glides /w/ and /j/, do learners represent /w/ and /j/ as [+round] and [−round], respectively, or as [+back] and [−back]? See Dresher, Piggott and Rice (1994) for some proposals. Some doubt that lexical minimality is a useful guideline in constructing lexical entries, noting that the empirical evidence for underspecification is limited and open to a variety of interpretations (Mohanan 1991, Steriade 1995).

In Chomsky and Halle's model, the set of surface speech sounds is the result of the rules of grammar applying in sequence to representations composed, initially, of underlying segments. No regularities characterize the surface inventory. The possibility that a distinct alphabet might be defined at any derivational stage other than the underlying form – e.g. at a "systematic phonemic level" – is explicitly rejected (1968:11) for lack of empirical support. As they note, "the issue is whether the rules of grammar must be so constrained as to provide, at a certain stage of generation, a system of representation meeting various proposed conditions."

7.4.2 **Lexical Phonology and Structure Preservation**

It is the recognition of just such an intermediate stage of generation that distinguishes the theory of Lexical Phonology (LP; Kiparsky 1982a, 1985; Mohanan 1982) from early generative phonology and from parallelist versions of Optimality Theory. This intermediate level is the output of the lexical component (for whose attempted definitions see Kaisse and Shaw 1985; contributions to Hargus and Kaisse 1993). Here is a clear statement of this position, from Mohanan and Mohanan (1984:575): "Lexical Phonology incorporates three levels of phonological representation: underlying, lexical and phonetic. The lexical 'alphabet' consisting of the 'lexical phonemes' need not be identical to the underlying alphabet consisting of the underlying phonemes." The argument for recognizing the lexical alphabet as distinct from the underlying and phonetic ones is that speakers' judgments of identity and distinctness are rendered at the lexical level: "listeners perceive speech sounds in terms of the grid provided by the lexical alphabet of the languages they speak" (Mohanan and Mohanan 1984:596). For instance, Malayalam dental [n̪], a non-underlying segment, is generated lexically in stem-initial position.

(5)   /n/ → n̪ / [stem_

Dental [n̪] is said to be non-underlying because it is in complementary distribution with alveolar [n] stem internally. The rule generating it is said to be lexical because it is conditioned by a morphological factor, the stem boundary. The Malayalam pair [n]-[n̪] is reportedly perceived as clearly distinct by Malayalam speakers. By contrast, the English [n]-[n̪] segments – with [n̪] as in [tɛn̪θ] – are not perceived as distinct by English speakers: the rule generating [n̪] is said to be postlexical and that excludes [n̪], on this view, from the lexical grid of English, explaining the distinctness judgments[3].

Even if we grant that judgments of distinctness identify a level of representation intermediate between UR and SR, there may be other ways to look at the specific data cited. For the comparison of Malayalam and English [n̪], what may be relevant is people's tendency to compensate for the effect of context, in speech and other forms of sensory perception: the dental articulation of Malayalam stem initial [n̪] cannot be attributed to a neighboring dental and that's perhaps why [n̪]'s dentality is accurately perceived. By contrast, English [n̪] arises only next to the overtly dental [θ] and thus its dentality can be parsed out of [n̪]'s percept (cf. Gow 2001, for experimental evidence on related points). This scenario also explains why English [ŋ] is perceived as distinct from [n] (Harnsberger 1999). The assimilation of [ŋ] from /n/ is the same process that creates [n̪] before [θ]. But in [ŋ]'s case, the conditioning /g/ disappears word finally, in most English dialects (/long/ → [lɔŋ]): in /g/'s absence, the velarity of [ŋ] becomes salient, because it can't be attributed to the context. On this interpretation, the lexical–postlexical distinction need not be invoked in comparing English and Malayalam [n̪]. It is, in any case, difficult to invoke it: [ŋ] and [n̪] result from the same English assimilation process, but give rise to different judgments of distinctness relative to [n].

Very little empirical work addresses LP's intuition that distinctness judgements tap the lexical – as against the underlying or surface – level: see Whalen et al. (1997) and Jones (2002) on English subjects' ability to judge the contextual appropriateness of allophonic aspiration in English voiceless stops; Paradis and La Charité (2005) and Kenstowicz (2003) on whether L1 allophonic distinctions affect loan adaptation; and some of the contributions to Daniels and Bright (1996) on the derivational level tapped by writing systems. Sapir's (1933) anecdotes about his native informants' spelling preferences are frequently cited as proof of 'phonemic' as against 'phonetic' perception, but their evidence is limited and not clearly about the lexical as against the underlying level.

There are further noteworthy aspects of LP that concern contrast and allophony. First, work in LP (e.g. Kiparsky 1985, Borowsky 1989) introduces filters that jointly characterize an underlying phoneme set. The lexical inventory is defined as the set of sounds obtained by subtracting the feature combinations prohibited by lexical filters from all phoneme-sized combinations otherwise sanctioned by feature theory. To expand on an earlier example, classical LP can characterize the phonemic inventory of English in terms of conditions like (6), which prohibit /ŋ/, /ɲ/, /ɱ/, /n̪/ in lexical entries.

(6) (a) */ŋ/: *[+nasal, dorsal];   (c) */ɱ/: *[+nasal, labiodental]
     (b) */ɲ/: *[+nasal, coronal,–anterior]   (d) */ṉ/: *[+nasal, +distributed]

Being barred by (6) from lexical entries, [ŋ], [ɲ], [ɱ], [ṉ] surface only where the rules of English grammar derive them from other segments. This explains their predictable distribution: [ŋ] surfaces only before [k], [g] – where it is traceable to /ng/, /nk/ – or where the grammar could have eliminated an underlying /g/; [ɲ], [ɱ], [ṉ] appear, optionally, only before homorganic consonants, where place assimilation might have generated them.

Unique to LP is the idea that a subset of the lexical filters constrains the effect of rule application in the lexical component. This is the hypothesis of Structure Preservation (Kiparsky 1985). English assimilates /n/ to any following stop but this process applies differently depending on whether the output is [m] as against [ŋ], [ɲ], [ɱ], [ṉ]. Word-internal applications yielding [m] are unrestricted and obligatory – cf. **i[np]ermissible*, **e[nb]ed*. That's as predicted by Structure Preservation: /m/ is a member of the lexical inventory in English, no lexical filter prohibits it, so if place assimilation is to apply at all it will generate at least [m]. But applications yielding [ɲ], [ɱ], [ṉ] are optional and absent from slow, careful speech (cf. well-formed *i[nf]allible, e[nf]old*) as are, in certain cases, those yielding [ŋ] (see Borowsky 1989 for the details). Much of this picture is also exactly as predicted by Structure Preservation, based on the blocking effect of the filters in (6) on lexical rule applications. The LP claim is that these sounds could arise only post-lexically, where place assimilation is optional and rate-dependent.

The evidence for Structure Preservation highlights a fundamental drawback of SPE's views on phonemic alphabets: if constraints characterizing possible phonemes hold exclusively of UR's, then why should rules be blocked from generating, *in derived representations*, sounds absent from the underlying set? Concretely: what is the connection between the absence from English URs of /ɱ/, /ṉ/, /ɲ/ – or more neutrally put, their predictable distribution – and the fact that word-internal place assimilation avoids creating these sounds? The same type of question arises in relation to vowel harmony (Kiparsky 1985), metaphony (Calabrese 1995), lenition (Everett 2003), epenthesis (Steriade 1995), and consonant mutation (Lieber 1984) to name only a few processes. There is substantial evidence that alphabet constraints like (6) *can* restrict derived representations. Sometimes they block rules from applying: the constraint against *[ɨ] blocks Finnish harmony from spreading [+back] onto /i/ (Kiparsky 1985). Sometimes they trigger repair processes: the prohibition against high lax vowels in Salentino is expressed when metaphony raises an underlying /ɛ/ not to *[ɪ], as expected, but to [iɛ] (Calabrese 1995). (By contrast /e/ is allowed to raise to [i], without diphthongization to [ie], because tense high vowels are permitted.) It is then inaccurate to say that constraints on alphabets – like (6), or Finnish *ɨ and Salentino *ɪ – only apply to define the underlying inventory:

some of these constraints are *persistent* (Myers 1991) and prohibit the same feature combinations throughout much or all of the derivation.

Structure Preservation also raises a question for LP: how early in the derivation does allophonic differentiation take place? Recall that the assumption of lexical minimality, which LP shares, causes the underlying phoneme inventory to be stripped of contextual variants and segments to be lexically represented as underspecified for predictable features. LP enforces both of these policies through the use of lexical constraints and Structure Preservation, an idea whose benefits were seen above. The problem arises when distinct allophones are generated by processes that have lexical characteristics. The diagnostic tests of lexical status have undergone constant revision but interaction with cyclic morphology has always been on this list (cf. most recently Itô and Mester 2003). It is just such an interaction that we observe in the processes generating nasalized allophones in (7) and (8):

(7)   *Sundanese (Cohn 1989, after Robins 1957)*

(a) Underlying	(b) After nasal harmony	(c) Infixed, surface	
/miasih/	mĩãsih	m-ãr-ĩãsih	'love-pl.'

(8)   *Madurese (Stevens 1968)*

(a) Underlying	(b) After nasal harmony	(c) Reduplicated, surface	
/nejat/	nẽj̃ãt	j̃ãt-nẽj̃ãt	'intentions'

The nasalized vowels of these languages arise through nasal harmony, which spreads nasality from nasals onto contiguous strings of vowels (and glides, in Madurese). Since nasalized vowels are contextually predictable, lexical minimality excludes them from the lexicon. A lexical filter like *[+nasal, +continuant] used for this purpose will prohibit the underlying contrast between, say /a/ and /ã/. In turn, Structure Preservation will prevent sounds prohibited by this filter from arising in the lexical component. But this is problematic, because the phonology of words created through infixation (in (7)) and reduplication (in (8)) must be computed based on the forms that have undergone nasal harmony (cf. (7b), (8b)). This *cyclic* interaction between morphology and phonology is viewed as diagnosing lexical processes. It follows then that the nasalized allophones are derived by lexical processes.

There are other instances of allophonic processes whose outputs are cyclically transmitted to derived words (Borowsky 1993, Benua 1997, Steriade 2000) and this entire body of evidence suggests the need to revise aspects of LP, such as the idea of a boundary separating lexical from postlexical phonology. However, Structure Preservation cannot be abandoned altogether, because an aspect of it is needed to explain the effect of filters like (6) on derived structures.

7.4.3 Contrast and allophony in OT

The most radical modification of the idea of lexical filters is Optimality Theory's (Prince and Smolensky 2004) move to take Structure Preservation and stand it on its head. While LP views filters like (6) as constraining URs and then rule applications, up to an ill-defined derivational juncture, OT proposes that the function of filters is to directly constrain surface representations, with only an indirect effect on URs. The surface orientation of filters immediately explains why place assimilation has difficulty generating surface [ɱ], [ɲ], [n̪] in English words and why harmony and metaphony can't generate Finnish [ɨ] or Salentino [ɪ]: it is filters on surface structure that prohibit these sounds. The grammar's job is not to first define possible well-formed inputs and then proceed to deform them through rules: it is to characterize the class of well-formed outputs, regardless of their underlying source.

Here are the main lines of an OT analysis for each of the processes reviewed thus far. First, the discussion of nasalized vowel allophones (as in (7), (8)) illustrates the fact that certain sound qualities must be allowed to occur but must not contrast: for instance Sundanese [ã] is permitted, but not in contexts where [a] is. The surface occurrence of [ã] is made possible by ranking *[+nasal, +continuant] below the constraint that triggers nasal harmony: *[+nasal][−cons, −nasal]. The lack of contrast between [ã] and [a] is due, in part, to the effect of *[+nasal, +continuant]: this penalizes all nasal vowels, wherever they occur and whatever their source. (9) illustrates both aspects of the analysis:

(9)   *Sundanese: markedness constraints result in neutralization*

/ana/	*[+nasal][−cons, −nasal]	*[+nasal, +continuant]
(a) ana	*!	
☞ (b) anã		*
(c) ãnã		* *!

The basic ranking is justified by the comparison of (9a) and (9b). Candidate (9c) illustrates in part how the allophonic distribution of [a] and [ã] is analyzed: for each [ã] that does not follow a nasal segment – e.g. the initial [ã] in (9c) – a better candidate exists that replaces this [ã] by oral [a]. The modified candidate – (9b) – better satisfies *[+nasal, +continuant] without violating *[+nasal] [−cons, −nasal]. The idea then is to make it impossible for [ã] to surface *anywhere except where mandated by the higher ranked phonotactic.* To repeat: higher ranked *[+nasal][−cons, −nasal] ensures that no [a] surfaces after nasals and the lower ranked *[+nasal, +continuant] ensures that no [ã] surfaces anywhere else. Under these conditions, contrast between [a] and [ã] is impossible. The opposite ranking yields a different kind of complementary distribution between [a] and [ã], namely systems that exclude nasalized vowels, like English.

The next aspect of the analysis of allophony in OT concerns the role of faithfulness. Phonotactics alone cannot describe the difference between

French, where nasal and oral vowels contrast (Cohn 1989), or Acehnese, where they contrast under stress (Durie 1985), vs. English or Sundanese, where their distribution is predictable. For French and Acehnese, the nasal vowels surface because they are protected by faithfulness to inputs like /ã/. The relevant constraint is IDENT *[±nasal] in V's Input-to-Output* (IO): pairs of UR-SR vowels standing in correspondence have identical values for nasality (McCarthy & Prince 1995a). IDENT [±nasal] in V's (IO) must be ranked above *[+nasal, +continuant] to allow the French nasal vowels to surface (10):

(10)   *French: Preservation of underlying nasality results in a surface contrast*

/ã/ 'year'	IDENT[±nasal] in V's (IO)	*[+nasal, +continuant]
☞ (a) ã		*
(b) a	*!	

For Sundanese or English, IDENT [±nasal] in V's (IO) is *inactive*: it is outranked by *[+nasal, +continuant] and therefore any underlying nasal vowel will either be oralized, to satisfy *[+nasal, +continuant], or will accidentally preserve its nasality, when required by a phonotactic constraint (like the one triggering nasal harmony), rather than because of faithfulness to the underlying form.

A factorial typology of allophony involving vowel nasality is given in (11).

(11)   *Factorial typology of nasal vowel allophony*

(a)   Nasal and oral vowels contrast in all environments
      IDENT[±nas] in V's (IO) » *[+nas, +cont], *[+nas][–cont, –nas]

(b)   Nasal vowels neutralize to oral in all environments
      *[+nas, +cont] » IDENT[±nas] in V's (IO), *[+nas][–cont, –nas]

(c)   Vowels must be nasal after nasal consonants; elsewhere they neutralize to oral
      *[+nas][–cont, –nas] » *[+nas, +cont] » IDENT[±nas] in V's (IO)

(d)   Vowels must be nasal after nasal consonants; elsewhere they contrast
      *[+nas][–cont, –nas] » IDENT[±nas] in V's (IO) » [nas, cont]

(e)   Some systems predicted to be impossible:
      (i) Oral vowels neutralize to nasal vowels in all environments
      (ii) Vowels contrast for nasality after a nasal consonant, but neutralize
      elsewhere

This result can be generalized in interesting ways. Kirchner (1997) shows that the contrastive status of any feature F – that is, F's ability to differentiate lexical items in surface forms – is determined in an OT grammar by the position of the IDENT F IO constraint in the constraint hierarchy (see also Itô, Mester and Padgett 1995). Inactive IDENT F IO yields a strictly allophonic distribution for the feature. A grammar in which IDENT F IO outranks some conflicting phonotactic constraints, but not all, describes the case in which F is contrastive for some segments – or some segments in some contexts – but not across the board.

As Kirchner (1997) and Goldsmith (1995b:9–13) note, contrastiveness never functions as an on/off switch in grammars (cf. also Kager 2003). Rather, "phonological systems exert varying amounts of force on the specification of the feature F" (Goldsmith 1995b:12) resulting in a cline from the standard contrastive status, to intermediate states of "modest asymmetry, not yet integrated semi-contrasts, just barely contrastive [features]," all the way to standard allophony and complementary distribution. The variable position of faithfulness constraints like IDENT F relative to conflicting phonotactics is well suited to formalize Goldsmith's gradual cline from contrast to allophony.

The distribution of Acehnese nasality (Durie 1985) is a particularly good example of this cline. Here, nasal vowels contrast under stress with oral vowels: ['bɛ̃h] 'a calf's cry', [ca'hɛ̃ʔt] 'sever with a knife attached to the end of a pole', ['pĩ˞ʔp] 'to suck' (Durie 1985:15–27). After nasal segments, stressed and stressless vowels and glides are nasalized by a rule comparable to that of Sundanese: [mã'ɲɛ̃t] 'corpse'; [mã'w̃ʌ̃] 'rose'; [paŋli'mã] 'army leader'; [p-un-ã'ɹoh] 'food delicacies', cf. [pa'ɹoh] 'to eat'. Stressless vowels can be nasal only through nasal harmony and are predictably oral elsewhere: no forms like *[pã'ɹoh] occur. The analysis of this system involves a *positional faithfulness constraint* (Casali 1996, Beckman 1998): the constraint requires identity for the value of the feature [±nasal] between pairs of correspondent vowels, in which the surface vowel is stressed. This is abbreviated as IDENT [±nasal] in 'V (IO). (12) illustrates how stressed vowels preserve their nasality.

(12) *Acehnese: Positional faithfulness allows contrast in stressed syllables*

/cahɛ̃ʔt/	IDENT[±nasal] in 'V (IO)	*[+nasal, +continuant]
(a) ca'hɛʔt	*!	
☞ (b) ca'hɛ̃ʔt		*

IDENT [±nasal] in 'V (IO) must be outranked by *[+nasal][–cons, –nasal] to allow stressed vowels to undergo nasal harmony. To demonstrate this, we use [mã'ɲɛ̃t] 'corpse', whose original form (in a borrowing from Arabic) was [ma'jit]. (13) models one step in the mapping of [ma'jit] to [mã'j̃ɛ̃t], from which present-day [mã'ɲɛ̃t] must have resulted.

(13)

/majit/	*[+nasal][–cons, –nasal]	IDENT[±nasal]/in 'V (IO)
(a) mã'jɛt	*!	
☞ (b) mã'j̃ɛ̃t		*

The interest of Acehnese is that its vocalic nasality is contrastive, but not unrestrictedly contrastive: it does not contrast outside of the stressed syllable. Even under stress, a vowel is not protected by its contrastive orality from undergoing harmony. An analytical system (such as those reviewed in Steriade 1995; cf. also Dresher, Piggott and Rice 1994) in which contrastive status for F results in full specification for both values of F and where full specification blocks rules like harmony will have some difficulty with this case. Its OT analysis is simple:

(14)

$$*[+\text{nasal}][-\text{cons}, -\text{nasal}] \gg \frac{\text{IDENT}[\pm\text{nasal}]}{\text{in 'V(IO)}} \gg *[+\text{nasal}, +\text{continuant}] \gg \frac{\text{IDENT}}{[\pm\text{nasal}]}$$

The further ascent of IDENT [±nasal] in 'V (IO) above *[+nasal][−cons, −nasal] describes Guaraní (Kiparsky 1985 and references there), where stressed vowels are both distinctively nasal *and* protected from undergoing nasal harmony. This entire range of attested options seems compatible only with the constraint system whose factorial typology was shown in (11).

Section 7.2 noted that segmental features are not the only contrastive properties in a phonological system: relations like precedence and temporal overlap, and in addition non-segmental features like tone, and global properties like stress or relative prominence, signaled by a variety of phonetic means, all represent potential sources of lexical distinctions. The difference between contrastive and allophonic status for all these properties can be formalized in the same terms as above, given the necessary faithfulness and conflicting phonotactic constraints.

The notion of *derived contrast* (Harris 1990) is also definable in terms of phonotactics-faithfulness rankings. A phonological property +P that is predictable by reference to both morphosyntactic and phonological information, may appear to contrast with −P, if the contribution of the morphosyntax is ignored. Thus Malayalam [a-n̪a], with predictably dental stem-initial [n̪], may appear to contrast − if we overlook the silent stem boundary − with [ana], with stem medial alveolar [n]. Similarly, the nasal [ĩ] of the infixed Sundanese form [m-ār-ĩãsih] 'love-pl' ((7) above) contrasts with the oral [i] of monomorphemic [mãrios]. In a rule-based phonology, derived contrasts are created by letting allophonic rules apply cyclically: a later cycle inherits the allophones generated by the immediately preceding one. So the infixation cycle /m-ar-ĩãsih/ inherits the effects of nasal harmony from the previous cycle /mĩãsih/. As seen above, this move is problematic in LP if cyclicity is restricted to the lexical component and if allophony is excluded from it. The OT approach to cyclic effects is described in McCarthy (Ch.5) and makes use of *output-to-output (OO) faithfulness* constraints, as against the *IO faithfulness* constraints, whose interactions with phonotactics define non-derived contrast. What is strictly relevant to derived contrasts is that in a system where IDENT F IO is inactive, IDENT F OO may be active, by outranking a critical phonotactic constraint. Forms like Sundanese [m-ãr-ĩãsih] are generated by letting IDENT [±nasal] OO » *[+nas, +cont]; in the same system, the ranking *[+nas, +cont] » IDENT [±nas] IO describes the predictable status of vocalic nasality stem internally (Benua 1997). There is no contradiction here: the two types of faithfulness constraints are distinct, because they relate distinct pairs of representations, and thus can occupy different places in the constraint hierarchy.

7.4.4   Richness of the Base and Lexicon Optimization

Two distinct ideas underlie the notion of Richness of the Base, summarized by Prince and Smolensky (2004:191) as "for the purposes of deducing the possible outputs of a grammar, [. . .] all inputs are possible." One of these is the distinction between the Lexicon *sensu stricto*, containing the actual entries a subject happens to know, vs. the full set of potential lexical entries. The example in (13) – showing how Arabic [majit] surfaces as [mãjɛ̃t] in Acehnese - illustrates this distinction. An L2 word like [majit] is necessarily absent from the L1 lexicon: but the grammar must still characterize its realization as a well-formed L1 word, if this form is borrowed. If the surface L1 pattern displays a certain regularity – e.g. "every contiguous string of vowels and glides following a nasal is nasalized; and no stressless nasalized vowels and glides occur elsewhere" – the right grammar will guarantee this output pattern, no matter what the input is. This idea is not specific to OT: any generative grammar is responsible for mapping to surface not only entries in the Lexicon in the narrow sense, but those from the unrestricted list of potential inputs.

The second component of Richness of the Base, as currently understood, is the strictly parallelist idea of a one-step mapping from any potential lexical entry, *sensu lato*, to the surface form. This hypothesis rejects conditions holding specifically of lexical entries, because they amount to a two-step filtering of potential inputs: one step eliminates impossible UR's, while the subsequent step, the derivation proper, maps the residue to well-formed SR's. The theory of Stratal OT (Kiparsky 2006) and variants of it (Itô and Mester 2003) which distinguish lexical from postlexical constraint hierarchies have roughly this multi-step property, dictated by empirical considerations, such as the analysis of opacity (see McCarthy 5.4). In principle, then, any form that is an input to the grammar may be underspecified for some or all features, or might contain all manner of redundant phonological information, or a mix of redundant and underspecified material. To require either systematic underspecification of features in lexical entries, or systematic full specification amounts to a condition on inputs; such requirements are rejected by the second component of Richness of the Base on the parallelist grounds outlined above and, one may add, because the necessity for any such conditions on lexical entries is yet to be proven.

In practice, however, the related hypothesis of Lexicon Optimization (Prince and Smolensky 2004:ch.9) does have an effect on how certain inputs are lexically represented. The idea is that non-alternating phonological properties – say the aspiration of initial [kʰ] in [kʰæt] – are always present in the lexical entry, for the following reason: the right grammar will guarantee the surface occurrence of [kʰ] in [kʰæt] no matter whether [kʰ] or [k] is present underlyingly, but the advantage of the identity mapping /kʰæt/ → [kʰæt] over /kæt/ → [kʰæt] is that the former avoids a faithfulness violation (IDENT [±aspiration]). Lexicon Optimization yields (approximately) opposite results on the issue of underlying specification compared to lexical minimality: non-alternating redundant information will always end up lexically listed. Here too, one can think of empirical work that could test this hypothesis, including lines of research of the sort cited in Section 7.4.2.

7.5   Constraints on contrast

Both LP's lexical filters and the surface-oriented filters of OT are constraints on sounds and sound sequences. When interacting with rules (in LP) or faithfulness (in OT) these filters indirectly generate patterns of contrast, allophonic variation and neutralization. The alternative explored by Flemming's (1995, 2002, 2004) Dispersion Theory of Contrast (DTC; see also Padgett 2001, 2003b and references there) is that certain core constraints refer directly to properties of the *relation of contrast*, namely its distinctiveness, rather than to the quality of the sounds standing in contrast. To understand how properties of sounds differ from properties of contrasts, imagine three tonal inventories, each contrasting a relatively lower tone with one relatively higher tone: using Chao's (1930) numbers, the inventories are {2, 4}, {3, 5} and {1, 5}. Each inventory differs from the others in the absolute height of one or both tones, and thus in the properties of the sounds involved; but the first two inventories are equivalent in the relative spacing of the tones ({2, 4} and {3, 5}) and thus in the distinctiveness of the contrast defined. The third inventory ({1, 5}) requires a greater distance between contrasting tonal values: it defines a better separated, more distinctive, tonal contrast.

The following is an example (adapted from Flemming 2004:250ff. and Flemming and Johnson 2004) where reference to contrast rather than sound properties is necessary. To characterize the fact that most varieties of English lack [ɨ], other accounts (e.g. Calabrese 1995) include rules or constraints about the properties of this sound, such as *[+high, +back, −round]. The activity of such a filter is independent of that of filters on [i], [u], [y]: in other words, a standard system decides whether to let [ɨ] in, regardless of what other sounds [ɨ] will coexist with. The DTC differs on this because it predicts the absence of [ɨ] by reference to the distinctiveness of the contrasts that would exist, if [ɨ] were allowed. Specifically, the DTC singles out the effect [ɨ] would have on decreasing the distance in perceptual space (here F2) between the pairs [ɨ]-[u], [ɨ]-[i]: these involve smaller distances in F2 compared to that between [u] and [i]. So removing [ɨ] is beneficial, not because [ɨ] possesses any inherently bad quality, but because the contrasts it would necessarily enter into would be less distinctive. (At the same time, removing [ɨ] is detrimental, because the system is left with one fewer expressive category. The formal account of dispersion, outlined below, exploits the conflict between expressiveness and dispersion in characterizing the typology.)

The DTC predicts then that the grammatical status of a sound will change depending on the system of contrasts it's embedded in: [ɨ] has detrimental effects on a system containing [i] and [u], but it fares well as the unique vowel. It is from this type of prediction that the DTC draws significant empirical support. The vowel system of American English illustrates this (15): stressed syllables contain [i] and [u], [ɪ] and [ʊ], along with other vowels, but not [ə]; stressless final syllables contain [i], [o] and [ə], again without [ɨ]; whereas stressless non-final syllables contain a single vowel quality and that is [ɨ][4] (Flemming and Johnson 2004).

(15)   *American English vowel distribution*

stressed	ɪ ʊ i u	ɑ æ ɔ ɛ ʌ e o
stressless final	i o	ə
stressless non-final	ɨ	

The striking fact in (15) is that in any given context we find either an F2 contrast such as [i]-[o], or, if no such contrast exists, then [ɨ]. That's exactly what the DTC predicts: in the absence of contrast, there's nothing wrong with [ɨ].

Dispersion alone does not predict that [ɨ] is *necessary* in a one-vowel system, only that it's a possible choice there. The factor that specifically favors [ɨ] is articulatory: CɨC sequences, for most choices of Cs, avoid steep articulatory transitions better than other CVCs. This applies to stressless medial syllables, as in (15), because those are typically very short, and steep transitions relate to short durations (Flemming 2004:250ff.).

The phenomena supporting the DTC are the typology of enhancement and neutralization. Both require that the grammatical system evaluate the distinctiveness of contrasts, in addition to articulatory properties of individual sounds. Thus Flemming shows that neutralization is triggered by contrasts that are insufficiently separated (see also Barnes 2002, Bradley 2001, Crosswhite 2001, Padgett 2001, 2002, Steriade 1999b, 2001b), so its proper formalization should involve explicit comparison of candidate inventories based on the distinctiveness of their contrasts. *Enhancement* (cf. Stevens et al. 1986) is the alternate remedy for insufficiently distinctive contrasts: if x and y contrast on some dimension D_1, but are insufficiently separated on D_1, their contrast can be enhanced by making them differ also on some other dimension D_2. For instance, a voicing contrast (e.g. {t, d}) is frequently enhanced by duration and F0 differences on neighboring vowels (Kingston and Diehl 1994). A significant finding is that *only contrasts are enhanced* (Kingston and Diehl 1994:436ff; Flemming 2004:258ff): Tamil [d], a contextually voiced co-allophone of [t], does not receive the F0 properties that enhance voicing in the contrastive /d/ of English. This observation can be modeled only if the grammatical system tells apart an allophonic voicing difference from a voicing contrast. The formalization of the DTC does exactly that.

The DTC uses two classes of novel constraints: constraints that favor maximizing the number of contrasting categories on specific auditory dimensions (e.g. closure duration; F2; VOT; loudness) and those that favor maximally distinct contrasting categories. Their format is illustrated in (16)–(17), using the example of backness (F2) as a dimension of contrast. Flemming's original statements are reformulated in minor ways.

(16)   *Constraints on contrast numbers:* MAX-*Contrast*
     i.   There are at least 2 distinct categories on the F2 dimension.
    ii. There are at least 3 categories on the F2 dimension.

(17)   *Constraints on minimal distance between contrasting categories:* MINDIST
     i.   MinDist=F2:1 Any two categories on the F2 dimension differ by at least 1 unit.
    ii. MinDist=F2:4 Any two categories on the F2 dimension differ by at least 4 units.

The basic idea of this system is that distance between contrasting categories on a dimension is inversely related to the number of categories defined on it. The MINDIST:F2 constraints penalize less well separated contrasts and thus, indirectly, systems in which more contrasting categories are packed into the space of F2. The MaxContrast:F2 constraints push in the opposite direction. Assuming for this illustration that there are at most 6 potential categories definable on the F2 value of high vowels ({i ɨ ị i ɯ u}), an inventory that selects just the F2 extremes {i, u} ensures a distance of 4 units between these categories and thus satisfies both (17.ii) and (17.i). The selection of {i ɨ u} reduces this distance to 1, so this system satisfies only (17.i), but it provides better satisfaction for the MAX-Contrast constraints: both (17.i) and (17.ii) are satisfied by this inventory. Contextual neutralization – e.g. the collapse of a larger vowel inventory into a small one in specific contexts – is formalized through the interaction of these constraints with constraints on articulatory effort. Thus the reduction in medial stressless syllables of the entire vowel inventory to a contextually variable vowel centered on [i] is attributed to the drastic decrease in duration that accompanies lack of stress, as sketched above. So the feature composition of sounds is an emergent property in the DTC: it emerges from the interplay of dispersion (MinDist), expressiveness (MaxContrast) and avoidance of articulatory effort.

7.6 Interactions between dimensions of contrast

Different dimensions of possible contrast interact in the case of enhancement (as in the example of voicing and vocalic F0 above) or in the related case of *a displaced contrast,* where a contrast on one dimension migrates to a related dimension (e.g. a voicing contrast, possibly enhanced by vocalic F0, becomes just a tonal contrast; Halle and Stevens 1971 Hombert et al. 1979). The notion of displaced contrast has also been used by Łubowicz (2003) to explore certain benefits of opacity (cf. McCarthy 5.4).

A more challenging sort of interaction between contrast dimensions is raised by the phenomenon of feature economy mentioned in (7.3, cf. Clements 2003). It was observed there that feature economy competes with dispersion, but that the competition is limited in certain ways, since it fails to yield certain highly uneconomical systems, such as {p tʰ k' β ɾ ɡ w n̪ ŋ}. The effect of feature economy in a grammar is currently unformalized – no constraint enforces it – but it is interesting to observe that feature economy relates to an unexplored property of Flemming's MAXCONTRAST constraints. This is mentioned here in the belief that these issues will eventually receive a unified resolution.

Originally the MaxContrast constraints were formulated as specific to individual dimensions of contrast, as seen in (17). A problem that arises with the original formulation was that the system is not encouraged to "fully cross" its contrasts: so the inventory (18) satisfies MaxContrast:F1=3 (i.e. "have at least three vowel height categories") as well as the less fully crossed (19) and (20) do.

(18) {a e o i u, ã ẽ õ ĩ ũ}
(19) {a e o i u, ã ĩ ũ}
(20) {a e o i u, ʌ̃}

Intuitively, MaxContrast:F1=3 should be satisfied only by (18): in (19) and (20) the height categories in the nasal system have been reduced to two and one, respectively. But if what is required is that just somewhere in the system there be three height degrees, that's equally true of all of (18)–(20). Moreover, the dispersion constraints are better satisfied by (20) as nasal vowels tend to be realized with wider formant bandwidths, so, under this interpretation, (18) and (19) are harmonically bounded by (20). That's incorrect: all three systems are instantiated, and (20), the least economical, in Clements's sense, is also by far the least well attested (Ruhlen 1978).

The problem is solved by the modified version of MaxContrast which appears in Flemming (2004:240), and which is no longer dimension specific: there is now a single MaxContrast constraint that is better satisfied by systems possessing more segments overall. However, it is feasible to evaluate this constraint only if we limit ourselves to a segment inventory. When we step into the larger world of sequential contrasts, accentual contrasts, contrasts in syllable numbers, and so on, it is no longer clear what kinds of additional expressions will provide an equal or better satisfaction of MaxContrast compared to simply adding novel segment types. It was suggested earlier (Sec. 7.2) that the distinction between segmental and non-segmental contrasts is somewhat artificial: for this reason, among others, the real resolution to the problem posed by (18)–(20) does not seem to lie in setting aside the inventory of *segmental* contrasts and evaluating globally its expressiveness. Perhaps a more interesting solution will emerge if a revised formalization of the DTC evaluates numbers of contrastive categories on individual featural dimensions, as the original formalization did, but takes on the problem of incorporating into the grammar the violable requirement of feature economy. Feature economy – not contrast numbers – is probably the factor that allows systems to prefer (18) to (19) and both to (20).

7.7 Conclusion

This chapter has surveyed the transition from the early generative conception of an alphabet of contrasting phonemes, defined on underlying representations, to the Optimality Theoretic idea that phonemic alphabets are the result of the interaction between surface oriented constraints with faithfulness conditions. In the last sections, we have reviewed work demonstrating that neutralization and enhancement are triggered by insufficient distinctiveness, or insufficient separation in perceptual space between contrasting sounds. Grammars that evaluate the degrees of distinctiveness of candidate inventories must perform certain global comparisons – such as that of (18) to (19) to (20). The relation between such evaluations and the more familiar evaluation of mappings from UR to SR in individual utterances remains to be explored. It does appear clear from this review that there is no substitute to recognizing the role of systemic constraints – dispersion and economy – in the organization of contrast systems.

Notes

I would like to thank Paul de Lacy and Ania Łubowicz for comments on the chapter; and Adam Albright and Edward Flemming for enlightening discussion of its contents.

1 These differences on *how* to model the relation between typology and individual competence are minor in comparison with the debate on *whether* typology and grammar stand in any kind of direct relation: cf. Blevins (2004). This topic is more general than that of contrast and will not be further addressed here.

2 The notions of symmetry and pattern congruity discussed in the structuralist literature (Hockett 1955:159) reduce to feature economy.

3 In an AXB classification experiment reported by Harnsberger (1999), Malayalam subjects judged [n̪] to be *more* similar to [n] than American English subjects. This result could be an artefact of the experimental conditions, but it highlights the need for solid evidence on the distinctness judgments serving as the empirical basis of the lexical level.

4 More precisely, stressless non-final vowels are realized in a region in F1-F2 space whose center is [i]. As with other reduced vowels, there is considerable contextual variation here.

Part II

Prosody

8

The syllable

Draga Zec

8.1 Introduction

The syllable has a central role in phonological theory as a constituent that represents phonologically significant groupings of segments. It is needed to account for pervasive cross-linguistic similarities among permissible segment sequences, which are crucially recurrent. The syllable is also used as a descriptive tool in the traditional accounts of sound patterns, as well as patterns of poetic meter.

The syllable is an abstract phonological constituent without clear phonetic correlates (Ladefoged and Maddieson 1996). Stetson's (1928) chest pulse theory – once considered the standard physiological characterization of the syllable – was shown by Ladefoged (1967) to be largely unsubstantiated. Even segmental sonority – a central concept in explaining the organization of the syllable – is highly phonologized (Parker 2002).

Phonological representations in general, and the syllable in particular, are best characterized in output-oriented frameworks. Our frame of reference will be Optimality Theory (henceforth OT), a theory of constraint interactions in grammar developed in Prince and Smolensky (2004 [1993]) and further refined in McCarthy and Prince (1995a). However, we bring in earlier theoretical insights from both rule-based and constraint-based approaches that have crucially advanced the understanding of the syllable as a phonological unit. The chapter is organized as follows. Section 8.2 begins with evidence for the syllable as a domain of segment sequencing. Evidence for the linear organization of the syllable is presented in Section 8.3, and for its hierarchical organization in Section 8.4. The role of sonority in the organization of the syllable is extensively discussed in Section 8.5. At relevant points the range of variation displayed by this phonological unit is expressed in terms of implicationally based typologies.

8.2   The syllable as the domain of segment sequencing

The syllable is an organizing principle for grouping segments into sequences, as argued by Hockett (1955), Haugen (1956), Fudge (1969), Kahn (1976), Selkirk (1982a), and others. The distribution of segments is highly constrained: in any given language, the set of occurring sequences presents only a fraction of the much larger set that would result from a free concatenation of members of its segment inventory. In order for the grammar to account for restrictions on segment distribution, an obvious move is to posit a constituent that serves as a domain of phonotactics. While more than one candidate has been proposed for this role, strong evidence points to the syllable, a prosodic unit "larger than the segment and smaller than the word" (Kahn 1976:20).

In the simple case, word initial and word final sequences are also syllable initial and syllable final, respectively, and should occur medially. To take a case from Kahn (1976:57), *atktin* [ætktɪn] is not a possible word in English. There are four ways this word could be divided into syllables: [æ.tktɪn], [æt.ktɪn], [ætk.tɪn], [ætkt.ɪn]. However, none of these produce both syllable-initial and syllable-final sequences that are possible word-initial/final sequences. For example, in [æt.ktɪn] [kt] is never found at the beginning of a word, and in [ætk.tɪn], [tk] is never found word-finally. This case provides an important insight: the stated generalization would be lost if *atktin* were ruled out by a mechanism that makes no reference to the syllable.[1] In sum, words and sometimes longer sequences are exhaustively parsed into syllables, so that the sequencing principles that characterize the syllable naturally extend to larger constituents.

As a useful point of comparison, we turn to an alternative perspective. The domain of sequencing generalizations initially assumed in the generative paradigm was the morpheme: with the phonological representations reduced to feature matrices and morphological boundaries, generalizations pertaining to segment sequencing could make reference to morphological constituents alone (Chomsky & Halle 1968). With no other types of entities larger than the segment admitted into the grammar, the absence of forms like *atktin* was expressed by morpheme structure constraints (MSCs), also known as lexical redundancy rules (Chomsky and Halle 1968). This case requires MSCs stating that no morpheme begins in *kt*, ends in *tk*, or medially contains *tkt*. Of course, these restrictions fail to capture Kahn's generalization about the nature of medial clusters in this frame of reference.

The syllable is thus a representational device that encompasses principles of segment sequencing. The 'Broadcast American' English morpheme 'syllable', for example, will be exhaustively parsed into licit substrings of segments, each dominated by a σ node:

(1)

While it will suffice for capturing some aspects of the syllable, this simple representation will be replaced by a more elaborate one in Section 8.4.

In sum, once the principles of syllable organization are properly stated, they subsume most of the generalizations about segment sequencing. While languages differ in how these universal principles are manifested, they differ in constrained and predictable ways, as we shall see in Section 8.3.

8.3   Basic syllable shapes

8.3.1   Typology

Under minimal assumptions, the principal subparts of the syllable are the nucleus and the two margins, the onset and the coda. The nucleus contains the most sonorous segment, where sonority is an abstract property of a segment discussed further in Section 8.5. The sequence in (2a) corresponds to a syllable with all three principal subparts, (2b) contains only the onset and the nucleus, (2c) contains the nucleus and the coda, and (2d) only the nucleus. Segments typically occurring in the nucleus are represented as V, and those typically in the margins as C.[2] V does not necessarily refer to 'vowel'. In some languages, the V slot can also be occupied by a consonant: for example, in (1) the final syllable has an [l] in the V slot.

(2)   (a)   CVC
      (b)   CV
      (c)   VC
      (d)   V

Our discussion will be based on the typology of syllable inventories originally stated in Jakobson (1962) and elaborated in Clements and Keyser (1983) and Prince and Smolensky (2004). This typology is based on syllable inventories attested across languages. It belongs to the class of substantive universals, and includes the implicational relations that hold among specific syllable shapes. The CV syllable figures in all language-specific inventories, and has a special status as the least marked syllable shape.

While inventories of syllable shapes in specific languages may vary widely, a given inventory always corresponds to a possible language type. A syllable has to contain a nucleus, and this of course is also the property of all syllable shapes in (2). Language types whose syllables have onsets but no codas are listed in (3). The onset is obligatory in (3a), as in Senufo (Kientz 1979)[3], and optional in (3b), as in Fijian (Schütz 1985, Dixon 1988, Hayes 1995 and the references therein).

(3)   *Systems without codas*
      (a) Onsets are required: CV
      (b) Onsets are optional: CV, V

Next, in a number of languages, syllables possess all three subparts, which yields two further types; the onset is obligatory in (4a), as in Temiar (Benjamin 1976) and Cairene Arabic (McCarthy 1979b), but not in (4b), as is the case in Turkish (Clements and Keyser 1983).

(4)   *Systems that allow codas*
      (a) Onsets are required: CV, CVC
      (b) Onsets are optional: CV, V, CVC, VC

Note that there are no dependencies between constituents. If a language requires onsets, it does not ban or require codas, and vice versa. As mentioned above, Fijian bans codas and onsets are optional, while Senufo bans codas while onsets are required. Similarly, codas are allowed in Arabic and Turkish, and onsets are obligatory in the former and optional in the latter. However, implicational relations hold across, as well as within, syllable inventories, and crucially reflect an asymmetry between the left and right margins: onsets are highly desirable, and codas are dispreferred. The desirability of onsets is shown by the fact that every language allows syllables with onsets; no language has only onsetless syllables. In contrast, codas are avoided in many languages, and they are never required in all environments: there is no language that has (C)VC syllables but no (C)V syllables.

In sum, (3) and (4) exhaust the possible language types projected from the basic syllable shapes in (2). For example, there is no language type with CV and VC syllables, to the exclusion of V and CVC; or with V and CVC syllables, to the exclusion of CV and VC. Moreover, while there is a clear asymmetry between onsets and codas, no dependencies hold between them. If it were the case that, say, a syllable with a coda must have an onset, we would have the non-occurring type CV, V, CVC.

The number of types is further proliferated by the number of segments allowed in either of the margins. The onset may include more than one consonant, yielding the additional types in (5). 'CC' stands for 'more than one consonant'; some languages allow three or more segments in the margin (e.g. English [splæt] 'splat', [sɪksθs] 'sixths'). Crucially, an implicational relation holds between, say CCV and CV or CVCC and CVC; if the former is present in the inventory, so is the latter. More generally, if n consonants are allowed in an onset, then so are m consonants where $1 \leq m \leq n$; the same is true of codas except that m may also be zero.

(5)   *Systems that allow complex onsets*
      (a) Codas are banned: CV, CCV
      (b) Codas are optional: CV, CCV, CVC, CCVC

Further types can be posited with syllables that allow complex codas, or both complex onsets and codas.

If more than one consonant is allowed in a margin, there is in principle no limit to the number permitted; however, limits are set by co-occurrence restrictions on adjacent segments as convincingly argued in Clements

Table 8.1. *Typology of syllable shapes*

onset	coda	onset cluster	coda cluster	inventory	language
R	O	O	O	(C)CV(C)(C)	Totonak
			X	(C)CV(C)	Dakota
		X	O	CV(C)(C)	Klamath
			X	CV(C)	Temiar
R	X	O	–	(C)CV	Arabela
		X	–	CV	Senufo
O	O	O	O	(C)(C)V(C)(C)	English
			X	(C)(C)V(C)	Spanish
		X	O	(C)V(C)(C)	Finnish
			X	(C)V(C)	Turkish
O	X	O	–	(C)(C)V	Pirahã
		X	–	(C)V	Fijian

R = required, O = optional, X = banned
- Codas are never required
- Onset clusters are never required
- Coda clusters are never required
- Onsets are never banned

and Keyser (1983), Steriade (1982) and McCarthy and Prince (1986), among others (see Section 8.5 for further discussion). The claim thus is that languages crucially differ in allowing at most one, or more than one, consonant at the margin; no language will impose a maximum of, say, two such consonants.

Finally, the onset/coda asymmetry is evidenced in yet another respect: a VCV sequence is cross-linguistically syllabified as V.CV rather than VC.V, a phenomenon known as onset maximization.

The typology of syllable shapes presented in this section is summarized in Table 8.1. Each of the twelve types is exemplified either by cases already mentioned here, or by cases from the detailed survey in Blevins (1995: 217–219).[4]

8.3.2 Formal account

The universal properties of syllable inventories identified in Section 8.3.1 and the implicational relations that hold within and across them have guided both rule-based and constraint-based formal accounts of the syllable.

Rule-based approaches typically include structure building rules responsible for the construction of nuclei, onsets and codas (Kahn 1976, Steriade 1982, Clements and Keyser 1983, Levin 1985, Hayes 1989a). While rules for constructing nuclei and onsets invariably figure in the rule systems of specific languages, the coda rule is present only in languages with inventories as in (4). Moreover, onset and coda rules may apply only once or iteratively, which differentiates languages with multiple margin consonants, as in (5), from those that allow only one margin consonant. Further rules supply an onset consonant in language types (3b) and (4b) if lexical forms do not provide one; or insert a nucleus into sequences of consonants that cannot be syllabified. Onset maximization is captured by rule ordering: the onset rule is always ordered before the coda rule, so the intervocalic consonant in a VCV sequence is invariably included in the onset.

However, because of its representational nature the syllable is most adequately characterized in output-oriented frameworks. Such approaches rely on mechanisms such as templates or constraints. They have emerged as part of the general shift of emphasis in phonological theory from rules to representations. For template-based approaches, see Kiparsky (1979, 1981), Selkirk (1982a), and McCarthy and Prince (1986); for early constraint-based approaches, see Itô (1986, 1989). We proceed to show how the range of possible syllable shapes and syllable inventories is characterized by a set of output constraints, in the spirit of Prince and Smolensky's (2004) OT account.

The following constraints on syllable form are sufficient to capture the basic syllable shapes, as well as their relative markedness:

(6) *Constraints on syllable form* (after Prince & Smolensky 2004):
   (a) Nuc   Syllables must have nuclei.
   (b) Ons   Syllables must have onsets.
   (c) ¬Cod   Syllables may not have a coda.

All basic syllable shapes conform to Nuc, which is never violated. This suggests that Nuc may be a principle of Gen, derivable from conditions imposed by the Prosodic Hierarchy. Ons and ¬Cod capture the ways in which syllable shapes minimally differ. Ons penalizes the absence of an onset while ¬Cod penalizes the presence of a coda. This asymmetry in the very statement of Ons and ¬Cod captures the empirically established difference in the status of the two margins. Thus, V violates Ons, CVC violates ¬Cod, and VC violates both Ons and ¬Cod. The universal CV syllable shape emerges as the least marked by virtue of satisfying all constraints on syllable form, so its unmarked status is derived in the theory.

Constraints on syllable form in (6) belong to the general class of markedness constraints in OT. They crucially interact with faithfulness constraints: Max, which prohibits segment deletion, and Dep, which prohibits segment insertion, as stated in (7):

(7) *Faithfulness constraints* (from McCarthy & Prince 1995a)
   (a) Max   An input segment has a correspondent in the output.
              (No deletion)
   (b) Dep   An output segment has a correspondent in the input.
              (No epenthesis)

The range of syllable inventories found in languages is characterized through interactions between markedness and faithfulness constraints. If only markedness constraints had a say, all syllables in all languages would be CV because this is the only syllable type that satisfies all constraints in (6).[5] Further syllable shapes are admitted under the pressure to preserve input segments. Thus, the range of syllable inventories in (3)–(4) will be captured through interactions of Ons and ¬Cod with the faithfulness constraints in (7). Ons and ¬Cod do not directly conflict with each other, so it is therefore not possible to rank them directly. Consequently, there are four general rankings between Ons, ¬Cod and the faithfulness constraints, with each ranking corresponding to one of the four language types in (3)–(4). {Max, Dep} indicates that at least one of Max and Dep must be in the ranking position indicated.

(8) *Basic syllable rankings*

    (a) CV   Ons, ¬Cod » {Max, Dep}

    (b) CV, V   ¬Cod » {Max, Dep} » Ons

    (c) CV, CVC   Ons » {Max, Dep} » ¬Cod

    (d) CV, CVC, V, VC   {Max, Dep} » Ons, ¬Cod

Section 8.3.3 shows how the constraints on syllable form motivate different types of unfaithfulness such as deletion and epenthesis.

We give tableaux for the rankings in (8b) and (8c). In (8b), the prohibition against codas overrides faithfulness but the demand for onsets does not, as shown in the two tableaux in (9). Epenthesis is the primary response to the syllable constraints in this system; this is due to having Max outrank Dep so no candidates are given with deletion (see Section 8.3.3 for further discussion).

(9) *CV, V*

(a)

/CVC/	¬Cod	Dep	Ons
CVC	*!		
☞ CV.CV̲		*	

(b)

/VC/	¬Cod	Dep	Ons
VC	*!		*
☞ V.CV̲		*	*
C̲V.CV̲		**!	

Ranking in (8c) yields the reverse situation: faithfulness is overridden by the demand for onsets, but not by the prohibition against codas (10).

(10) *CV, CVC*

/VC/	Ons	Dep	¬Cod
VC	*!		*
C̲V.CV		**!	
☞ C̲VC		*	*

The ranking in (8a) yields the simple CV shape as the optimal output no matter what sequence is submitted for evaluation; this is the expected outcome when constraints on syllable form outrank faithfulness constraints. However, with faithfulness constraints outranking markedness constraints (8d), the optimal output preserves the segmental content in lexical forms, so allowing any syllable shape.

Because the competition for the intervocalic consonant in a CVCV string is governed by ONS and ¬COD, the onset parse is bound to win over the coda parse, in accordance with the principle of onset maximization. Tableau (11) shows that [CVC.V] incurs a superset of [CV.CV]'s violations. This situation – known as 'harmonic bounding' – means that [CVC.V] can *never* beat [CV.CV] no matter what the ranking of the constraints identified here.[6]

(11)   /CVCV/→ [CV.CV]

/CVCV/	ONS	¬COD
☞ CV.CV		
CVC.V	*(!)	*(!)

Complex margins are regulated by the markedness constraints *COM-PLEX$_{ONS}$ and *COMPLEX$_{CODA}$ stated in (12).

(12)

    (a) *COMPLEX$_{ONS}$ Syllables must not have more than one onset segment.

    (b) *COMPLEX$_{Coda}$ Syllables must not have more than one coda segment.

The *COMPLEX constraints can be added to the rankings in (8), as in (13). The ranking in (13a) and (13b) calls for a further comment: with ¬COD » MAX, DEP, no coda consonants will be admitted regardless of how *COMPLEX$_{CODA}$ (parenthesised in these cases) is ranked. This is because of the general–special relation that holds between *COMPLEX$_{CODA}$ and ¬COD: if the former is violated, so is the latter.

(13)   *Syllable rankings with *COMPLEX *constraints*
    (a) CV   *COMPLEX$_{ONS}$, (*COMPLEX$_{CODA}$), ONS, ¬COD » {MAX, DEP}
    (b) CV, V   *COMPLEX$_{ONS}$, (*COMPLEX$_{CODA}$), ¬COD » {MAX, DEP} » ONS
    (c) CV, CVC   *COMPLEX$_{ONS}$, *COMPLEX$_{CODA}$, ONS » {MAX, DEP} » ¬COD
    (d) CV,CVC,V,VC   *COMPLEX$_{ONS}$, *COMPLEX$_{CODA}$ » {MAX, DEP} » ONS, ¬COD

With the constraints in (6), those in (12) capture three further situations: where (a) only onsets may be complex, (b) only codas may be complex, (c) both onsets and codas may be complex. For example, the ranking {MAX, DEP} » *COMPLEX$_{CODA}$, ¬COD licenses any number of coda consonants includ-ing none. In contrast, the ranking ONS » {MAX, DEP} » *COMPLEX$_{ONS}$ yields one or more onset consonants. The latter case is shown in (14).

(14) *CV,CCV*

/CCVV/	Oɴs	Dᴇᴘ	*Cᴏᴍᴘʟᴇx_{ONS}
CCV.V	*!		*
C<u>V</u>.CV.C<u>V</u>		* *!	
☞ CCV.C<u>V</u>		*	*

To conclude, the presented typology of syllable inventories is characterized by the different rankings of the sets of constraints in (6) and (12), including the ranking in (13). This same set of rankings also characterizes phonological processes driven by syllable well-formedness, as elaborated in Section 8.3.3.

8.3.3 Syllable-related phonological processes

Input strings may contain more or fewer segments than the syllable pattern of a language can accommodate. Such strings are resolved by phonological processes that either delete or insert segments. For example, in a language which prohibits codas, VCCV sequences are resolved either by supplying an extra nucleus as in (15a), or by leaving the offensive consonant unsyllabified as in (15b). The former is the case in Hua, in which consonant clusters are resolved by epenthesis, as in /aksi/ → [akəsi] 'sneezing' (Haiman 1980: 26); and the latter in Diola Fogny, in which consonant clusters are resolved by deletion, as in /ujukja/ → [ujuja] 'if you see' (Sapir 1965: 18).[7] The outlined V is epenthetic (and the same for outlined C).

(15) (a) *Hua*   (b) *Diola Fogny*

Such phonological processes are essential in 'coercing' segment strings to comply with the demands of syllable shapes, as argued among others by Selkirk (1981), LaPointe and Feinstein (1982), Levin (1985), and Itô (1986, 1989).[8]

Coercion is captured in OT by an interaction of constraints on syllable shapes with the faithfulness constraints Mᴀx and Dᴇᴘ. What strategy will be employed depends on the language specific ranking of Mᴀx and Dᴇᴘ. With Mᴀx » Dᴇᴘ, the repair strategy will be epenthesis, and with Dᴇᴘ » Mᴀx, the repair strategy will be segment deletion (cf. Prince and Smolensky 2004).

Repairs are crucially effected by a dominating markedness constraint: ONS, ¬COD or *COMPLEX. The same rankings that characterize syllable inventories in Section 8.3.2 also characterize the "coercion" of segment strings into syllable shapes. The two outcomes in (15) are generated by the ranking (13b), with undominated ¬COD. With MAX » DEP as in (16a), the winning candidate contains an epenthesized nucleus; with the reversed ranking in (16b), the winner has one less consonant than the input.

(16) (a) *Hua*

/VCCV/	¬COD	*COMPLEX_{ONS}	MAX	DEP
VC.CV	*!			
V.CV			*!	
V.CCV		*!		
☞ V.CV̱.CV				*

(b) *Diola Fogny*

/VCCV/	¬COD	*COMPLEX_{ONS}	DEP	MAX
VC.CV	*!			
☞ V.CV				*
V.CCV		*!		
V.CV̱.CV			*!	

We further inspect a case captured by the ranking in (13c), with all markedness constraints other than ¬COD at the top of the hierarchy. In Temiar, characterized by the MAX » DEP ranking, an initial consonant cluster is eliminated by epenthesis: /CCVC/ → [CV̱CVC]; /CCCVC/ → [CV̱CCVC], and /CCCCVC/ → [CV̱CV̱CCVC] (Benjamin 1976; Itô 1986, 1989). Tableau (17) presents the evaluation of the second case. The constraint *COMPLEX_{coda} is left out of the tableau as it is not relevant here.

(17) *Temiar*

/CCCVC/	ONS	*COMPLEX_{ONS}	MAX	DEP	¬COD
CCCVC		*!			*
V̱C.CCVC	*(!)	*(!)		*	* *
CVC			*!*		*
☞ CV̱C.CVC				*	* *

Finally, with ONS at the top of the hierarchy as in (13a) and (13c), /CVVC/ sequences are resolved by (a) deletion if DEP » MAX, yielding [CVC], or (b) by epenthesis under the reverse ranking, yielding [CVCVC].

In sum, the phonological processes that alter strings of segments under the pressure of constraints on syllable shapes may conspire to supply a nucleus or an onset, but never a coda. Moreover, the coda is the only subpart of the syllable that may be 'eliminated' by such processes, as in (16).

The asymmetry between the coda and other subparts of the syllable is further evidenced by prohibitions against specific classes of consonants in the coda. Thus, voiced segments are ousted from the coda in Polish, Russian and Catalan (Cho 1999, Lombardi 1991). Place features may be prohibited in the coda: all place features, as in Diola Fogny (Itô 1986), or a single place feature, like [dorsal] in Kiowa (Watkins 1984, Zec 1995). These facts are captured by coda constraints, proposed in Itô (1986). These positional markedness constraints are a special case of the more general ¬Cod. Examples are given in (18).[9]

(18)   *Positional markedness coda constraints*
     (a) Polish: ¬Cod/ [+voice]   No voiced segments in codas
     (b) Kiowa: ¬Cod/ [dorsal]   No dorsal segments in codas

The effect of constraints in (18) will be seen only if they outrank both the faithfulness constraints and ¬Cod. Thus, coda devoicing in Polish is captured by the ranking ¬Cod/ [+voice] » IDENT-IO[voice] » ¬Cod.

The phonological processes responsible for maintaining syllable shapes have been presented in broad outline here; further cases will be discussed in Section 8.5.

8.4   Representation of subsyllabic constituency

We now turn to the structural characterization of the syllable. Its principal subparts – the nucleus, the onset and the coda – need to be properly delimited; this can be accomplished only in a hierarchically organized syllable which includes subsyllabic structural positions. Drawing upon the moraic theory of subsyllabic constituency (Hyman 1985, McCarthy and Prince 1986, Hayes 1989a), one structural position will represent the nucleus and another will represent syllable weight. These structural positions will be justified in Sections 8.4.1 and 8.4.2 respectively; Section 8.4.3 focuses on how the two structural positions are integrated into the overall subsyllabic constituency.

8.4.1   Representing the nucleus

The simplest representation of the syllable is a flat structure with no subsyllabic constituency as in (1). Such a representation is sufficient for characterizing the syllable nucleus as long as the nuclear segment can be differentiated from those that precede or follow solely in terms of segment quality. This is the amount of structure assumed in Kahn (1976), with the *SPE* feature [syllabic] invoked to differentiate between the nucleus and the margins. Kahn's syllabification rules make direct reference to this feature: the nucleus rule targets a [+syllabic] segment, and the onset and coda rules target [−syllabic] segments. Another mode of differentiating between nuclear and non-nuclear segments in flat syllable structure is the CV timing tier, with V corresponding to the nucleus (Clements and Keyser 1983); in its formal essentials, this theory is very similar to the [syllabic] approach.

However, syllabicity is not an intrinsic property of segments: the feature [syllabic], unlike most segmental features, does not provide a partitioning of segments into those that are [+syllabic] and those that are [−syllabic]. How likely it is for a segment to be syllabic depends on its relative perspicuity, or sonority. This important property of segments will be invoked here briefly, but in-depth discussion will be left for Section 8.5. Segments are generally divided into those that gravitate towards the nucleus, such as vowels and those that gravitate towards margins, such as obstruents. However, many languages have so-called ambidextrous segments that may link either to the nucleus or to the margin. For example, in English [l] acts as the nucleus in *muscle* [mʌ.s̩l̩], where it occurs word finally after an obstruent; but not in *muscly* [mʌ.sli], where it is followed by a vowel. This case can be resolved in structural terms as in (19), with a subsyllabic structural position reserved for the nucleus. The nuclear node is construed as a mora, and represented as μ. The segment linked to a mora is more perspicuous than segments in its immediate environment. The less perspicuous segments, those at syllable margins, are linked directly to the σ node. Since [l] is more perspicuous than an obstruent, and less perspicuous than a vowel, it may be in the peak position only when none of the adjacent segments exceeds it in perspicuity, as in (19a), but not when this is the case, as in (19b).

(19)

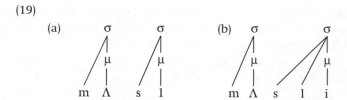

The constituency in (19) also accounts for vowel/glide alternations. High vowels tend to exhibit the dual behavior of linking either to the nucleus or to the margin; in the latter case they are realized as glides (Clements and Keyser 1983, Levin 1985, Guerssel 1986, Waksler 1990, Rosenthall 1994).[10] In Ait Seghrouchen Berber, for example, high vowels and glides are in complementary distribution: an underlying high vowel is realized as a vowel when adjacent to consonants, as in (20a), and as a glide in the vicinity of a vowel, as in (20b) (Guerssel 1986).

(20) *Ait Seghrouchen Berber*

    (a) /i-ru/ →   [iru]   'he cried'

         /u-mazan/ → [umazan] 'messenger'

    (b) /i-ari/ →   [jari]   'he writes'

         /u-ansa/→   [wansa]   'place'

The analysis of this case relies on the assumption that high vowels are less perspicuous than non-high vowels. Vowels are generally syllable peaks, and as such are linked to a mora, as in (21a). But when a high vowel is followed by another vowel, it links to the margin, to provide an onset, as in (21b).

(21) (a)   [iru] 'he cried'   (b)   [jari] 'he writes'

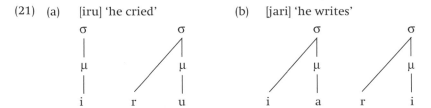

No such straightforward account is available by recourse to the *SPE* feature [+/−syllabic], with the interpretation that [+syllabic] "characterizes all segments constituting a syllable peak" (Chomsky and Halle 1968: 354).[11] In fact, it is precisely cases like Ait Seghrouchen Berber that have drawn attention to the inadequacies of this feature. The fact that high vowels are in some contexts [+syllabic] and in others [−syllabic] is beneficially reinterpreted in structural terms: [+syllabic] as linked to the nucleus and [−syllabic] as linked to a margin (Clements and Keyser 1983, Levin 1985, Rosenthall 1994).

8.4.2 Representing weight

Syllables are often classed as light or heavy; this bifurcation is useful for many purposes, most notably stress (Newman 1972, McCarthy 1979b, Steriade 1982, Clements and Keyser 1983, Zec 1988, Hayes 1989a, Kager (Ch.9), among others). Syllable weight and the phenomena directly related to it, such as segment length, are directly represented in structural terms by positing a second peak within the syllable. A light syllable includes a single peak, as in (22a); and a heavy syllable includes two peaks, as in (22b). The representation in (22) is thus consistent with the traditional interpretation of the mora as a measure of syllable weight (Trubetzkoy 1939).

(22) (a)   *Light*   (b)   *Heavy*

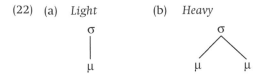

Moras have the dual function of serving both as subsyllabic constituents and as units of timing. In the former capacity, they characterize syllable weight, and in the latter, segment length.[12] We focus here on vowel length, which is captured in terms of structural positions within the syllable: a short vowel is associated with one mora, and a long one with two.[13] This mode of representing length highlights the parallelism between a long vowel and a diphthong, each being associated with two moras as in (23b) and (23c), in contrast to a short vowel as in (23a). Segment count need not correlate with mora count, and indeed it does not in the case of long vowels and diphthongs.

(23)

   (a) *Short vowel*   (b) *Long vowel*   (c) *Diphthong*

$$
\begin{array}{ccc}
\sigma & \sigma & \sigma \\
\mu & \mu\ \mu & \mu\ \mu \\
C\ \ V & C\ \ V & C\ \ V_i\ \ V_j \\
& & (V_i \neq V_j)
\end{array}
$$

The representation of vowel length in (23) serves as a blueprint for characterizing weight patterns across languages. If a syllable inventory includes only open syllables as in (3), syllables with short vowels are light and those with long vowels or diphthongs are heavy, as in (23). Syllable inventories which do include closed syllables (4), exhibit two cross-linguistically attested weight patterns that are captured straightforwardly in moraic terms. CVC syllables may pattern with CVV syllables as in (24) or with CV syllables as in (25).

(24)   *CV vs. CVV, CVC*

(25)   *CV, CVC vs. CVV*

  Heavy CVC syllables are bimoraic, as represented in (26); light CVC syllables are monomoraic, as represented in (27). In the former, but not in the latter case, CVV and CVC syllables exhibit a functional unity which is mirrored by their structural parallelism (McCarthy 1979b).

(26) (a) *Light*   (b) *Heavy*

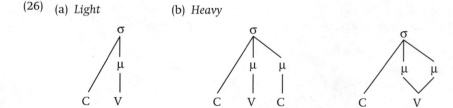

(27) (a) *Light* (b) *Heavy*

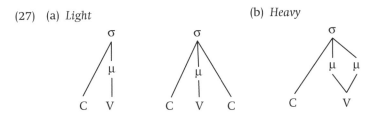

A detailed discussion of weight systems is postponed to Section 8.5. At this point, we briefly review some of the evidence brought to bear on the weight patterns in (24) and (25), and the assumed structural parallelisms in (26) and (27).

Heavy syllables attract stress. Thus, if the weight pattern is as in (24), stress will fall on CVV and CVC syllables but not on CV (e.g. Cairene Arabic – Mitchell 1960, McCarthy 1979b, Hayes 1995:67ff). If the weight pattern is as in (25), however, stress will be attracted to CVV syllables, to the exclusion of CV and CVC, as in Khalkha Mongolian (Zec 1995) and Lenakel (Lynch 1978, Hayes 1995:167ff).

The weight pattern in (24) is also supported by the widespread phenomenon of vowel shortening in closed syllables evidenced, for example, in Turkish (Clements and Keyser 1983), Kiowa (Watkins 1984) and in Chadic languages such as Hausa (Newman 1972). Languages that prohibit CVVC syllables point to the bimoraic status of CVC syllables, and to the ban on syllables with more than two moras. In sum, long vowels are blocked from closed syllables in order not to disrupt their bimoraicity. No such blocking of vowel length in closed syllables is expected in weight patterns as in (25), in which closed syllables do not differ in weight from corresponding open syllables.

Compensatory lengthening has typically been invoked as evidence in favor of the structural representation of syllable weight (Ingria 1980, Steriade 1982, Clements and Keyser 1983, Hayes 1989a). As shown in Latin, vowel lengthening compensates for the loss of the consonant under the second mora (Ingria 1980). Thus, a structural position is preserved under segment deletion, which argues for the structural unity of CVV and CVC syllables in Latin, as in (28).[14]

(28) *Latin: kasnus → ka:nus 'gray'*

8.4.3 Concluding remarks on subsyllabic constituency

To summarize, the syllable necessarily includes at least one peak, which stands for the nucleus, and may also include a second peak which marks it as heavy. The two peaks are represented as moras. One mora in a syllable is designated the 'head' (μ_h) in order to capture the asymmetries between the nuclear and the non-nuclear structural positions; this will be further justified in Section 8.5.

In (29) we present the range of structural options for the syllable estab-lished in this section. The descriptive categories for subparts of the syllable, the nucleus, the onset and the coda, now have clear structural counter-parts. Segments linked to the head mora are in the nucleus, while those linked to the second mora are weight-bearing (e.g. 29b). Segments at the left edge linked directly to the syllable node constitute the onset. The coda is of a hybrid nature: a consonant following a tautosyllabic vowel is either a weight-bearing segment linked to the second mora (29b) or a weightless segment linked directly to the syllable node as an appendix (29c).

(29)   (a)   (b)   (c)

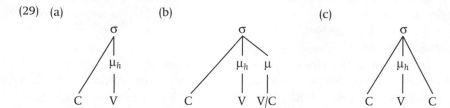

The constituency in (29) is to be construed as a relatively stable, universally available mode of organization. Variation remains within the bounds set up in Section 8.3 and whether the coda is moraic or an appendix. The status of the appendix is regulated by the following markedness constraint (30) which prohibits this position (adapted from Sherer 1994).

(30)   *APPENDIX   Incur a violation for each consonant in the appendix.

Thus, an appendix will be licensed if (30) ranks below the faithfulness constraints, as in (31a), but not under the reversed ranking in (31b):

(31)   (a) Appendix is licensed: {MAX, DEP} » *APPENDIX
       (b) Appendix is not licensed: *APPENDIX » {MAX, DEP}

What segment may appear under the second mora is part of the broader scheme which yields a typology of heavy syllables. This will be addressed in Section 8.5, and captured in terms of OT constraint interactions. We will take the strong position that the nuclear node is a defining structural property of the syllable, and as such is not subject to the whims of con-straint interactions.[15]

A brief comparison is in order at this point with the immediate predeces-sor of the moraic representation, given in (32). This more elaborate con-stituency includes structural positions for each relevant subpart of the syllable. The syllable node branches into the onset and the rime, and the latter further branches into the nucleus and the coda (Fudge 1969, Halle and Vergnaud 1980, Selkirk 1982a, Steriade 1982, Harris 1983, Levin 1985,

and many others). The obligatory subconstituents are the rime, and one of
its dependents, the nucleus.

(32)

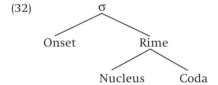

This constituency captures syllable weight in structural terms, by designat-
ing the rime as the weight domain: a heavy syllable has a branching rime,
as distinct from a light syllable whose rime does not branch. However,
because the rime is the domain of weight, it needs to be stipulated that
onsets are weightless, that is, that branching under the syllable node is not
relevant for the computation of weight (see McCarthy and Prince 1986 for a
broader discussion).

Arguments for the constituency in (32) are in effect arguments for the
rime constituent. Thus, according to Fudge (1969, 1987, 1989) and Selkirk
(1982a), the two immediate constituents of the syllable, the onset and the
rime, serve as domains of co-occurrence restrictions on pairs of adjacent
tautosyllabic segments: such restrictions are said to hold within the rime
but not across onsets and rimes. The validity of this argument has been
disputed by providing evidence that co-occurrence restrictions within the
syllable may cross the onset/rime divide (cf. Clements and Keyser 1983,
Davis 1989a). Moreover, arguments for the rime as a domain of phonological processes (Harris 1983, Steriade 1988c) are less than convincing,
since the proposed domain has a straightforward counterpart in a simpler
subsyllabic constituency, in particular, in the moraic constituency.

8.5 Sonority

In order to provide a fully refined characterization of segment sequencing
within syllables, including the characterization of both peaks and margins,
we invoke the sonority of segments. The relevance of sonority for the organization of the syllable has been noted in a wide range of literature, including
the early works of Sievers (1881), Jespersen (1904), Saussure (1916), as well as
Vennemann (1972), Kiparsky (1979, 1981), Hooper (1976), Steriade (1982),
Selkirk (1984a), Zec (1988), and Clements (1990), among others. For discussion about sonority's influence above the syllable, see de Lacy (Ch.12).

Sonority of segments is commonly represented by means of a scale like
(33), which corresponds to an ordering of segments ranging from those
highest in sonority, i.e. vowels, to those lowest in sonority, i.e. stops. We
give a fine-grained version of the scale, but group it into V(owels), L(iquids),
N(asals) and O(bstruents) which will suffice for the scope of our discussion.

(33)   *Sonority scale*
    V   low vowels
        mid vowels
        high vowels
    L   rhotics
        laterals
    N   nasals
    O   voiced fricatives
        voiced stops
        voiceless fricatives
        voiceless stops

An important issue is how sonority is to be represented in the grammar. There are at least two general views. According to one, sonority should be incorporated into the grammar as a multivalued feature [sonority] (or strength) with integers as standardly assumed values (Vennemann 1972, Hooper 1976:205–207, Selkirk 1984a, and others). Another view is that sonority classes can be characterized by the major class features (Kiparsky 1979, 1981, Clements 1990, Zec 1988, among others). That is, the values for the major class features, under a proper mode of computation, yield the sonority classes. Justification for the latter view is as follows: because the major class features are independently needed, having both the major class features and the multivalued feature [sonority] in the grammar would lead to duplication. See also de Lacy (2004) for a relevant discussion.

By taking into account the ordering in (33), the arrangement of segments within the syllable follows a clear pattern: the most sonorous segment occupies the nucleus, while the less sonorous ones occur towards the margins. Sonority thus steers the crucial aspects of syllable internal segment sequencing. To quote Clements (1990:299): "Sequences of syllables display a quasiperiodic rise and fall in sonority, each repeating portion of which may be termed a sonority cycle."

This patterning is due to two general modes of constraining sonority within the syllable. First, both the syllable and the mora are associated with thresholds on minimal sonority. In (34), segment s_2 is subject to the sonority threshold on the syllable, and s_3 to the sonority threshold on the mora. The two subsyllabic structural positions are thus differentiated from the margins by being more sonorous.

(34)

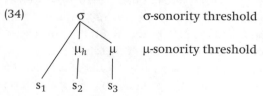

                σ σ-sonority threshold

           μ_h μ μ-sonority threshold

       s_1 s_2 s_3

The head of the syllable is the leftmost mora, which bears the h subscript, and the head of the mora is the segment it immediately dominates. The sonority threshold on moras affects all segments they dominate, while the sonority threshold on syllables affects segments dominated by the head mora. Sonority thresholds are thus encoded by virtue of the head relation, a mode of encoding prominence typically employed throughout the prosodic hierarchy.[16] We will henceforth refer to the head segment of the head mora as the syllabic segment, and to the head segment of the non-head mora as the moraic segment.

The second mode of constraining sonority is syntagmatic in nature. Constraints on sonority distance have the task to optimize the sonority slope between margins and peaks, both within and across syllables.

The two modes of constraining sonority conspire to give the syllable its characteristic sonority profile. We focus on sonority thresholds in Section 8.5.1, and on sonority distance in Section 8.5.2.

8.5.1 Sonority thresholds

The effect of sonority thresholds is to restrict the minimal sonority of the syllable and the mora, which is directly reflected in the sonority of the syllabic and moraic segments (compare (34)). This will be characterized in terms of the natural hierarchy of peaks, based on the sonority scale in (33) (Prince and Smolensky 2004). As shown in (35), a four-point peak hierarchy defines four sonority thresholds. In (35a) only vowels are above the sonority threshold, in (35b) vowels and liquids, in (35c) vowels, liquids and nasals, and in (35d), all segments are above the sonority threshold.

(35)   *Hierarchy of syllable peaks*

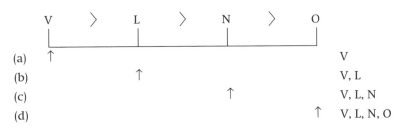

With this background, we turn to characterizing the minimal sonority thresholds on syllabicity and weight, addressed in Sections 8.5.1.1 and 8.5.1.2 respectively.

8.5.1.1 Sonority thresholds on the syllable peak

The sonority hierarchy of syllable peaks is given in (36). Any of the thresholds in (35) may define the set of syllabic segments in a language. As shown in (36), the set of syllabic segments includes vowels in Bulgarian, vowels and liquids in Slovak, vowels, liquids and nasals in English, and all segments in Imdlawn Tashlhiyt Berber (Zec 1988, 1995 and the references therein).

(36)   *Sonority threshold on syllabicity*

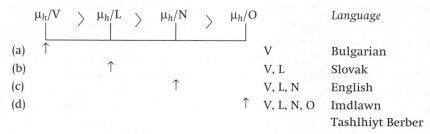

			Language
(a)	↑	V	Bulgarian
(b)	↑	V, L	Slovak
(c)	↑	V, L, N	English
(d)	↑	V, L, N, O	Imdlawn Tashlhiyt Berber

The sonority hierarchy of syllable peaks in (36) is incorporated into the grammar as a set of markedness constraints with a universally fixed ranking, as in (37) (Prince & Smolensky 2004). This set of constraints, while banning all segments from the nuclear position, places the strongest ban on the least sonorous segments, that is, obstruents, and the weakest on vowels.

(37)   *Constraints on syllabicity*

$$*\mu_h/O \gg *\mu_h/N \gg *\mu_h/L \gg *\mu_h/V$$

The cut-off points for individual languages will be determined by constraint interaction. In each language, some constraint, by virtue of its ranking, will delimit the class of segments above the sonority threshold:

(38)   *Syllabicity thresholds*

    (a)   Bulgarian: $*\mu_h/O \gg *\mu_h/N \gg *\mu_h/L \gg \mathcal{C} \gg *\mu_h/V$

    (b)   Slovak: $*\mu_h/O \gg *\mu_h/N \gg \mathcal{C} \gg *\mu_h/L \gg *\mu_h/V$

    (c)   English: $*\mu_h/O \gg \mathcal{C} \gg *\mu_h/N \gg *\mu_h/L \gg *\mu_h/V$

    (d)   IT Berber: $\mathcal{C} \gg *\mu_h/O \gg *\mu_h/N \gg *\mu_h/L \gg *\mu_h/V$

The interacting constraint $\mathcal{C}$ is typically a faithfulness constraint such as Max or Dep. To provide an illustration, we focus on the minimal difference between Bulgarian and Slovak, listed in (38a) and (38b) respectively, which we attribute to the agency of the faithfulness constraint Dep. The syllabic set in Slovak includes vowels, as in (39a), and liquids, as in (39b) (Pauliny 1961); syllable boundaries are marked by dots.

(39)   *Slovak syllabic segments*

    (a)   traː.va   'grass'

              kraː.sa   'color'

    (b)   kr̥v   kr̥.vi   'blood'

              vl̥k   vl̥.ka   'wolf'

Only vowels are syllabic in Bulgarian. This fact is seen in so-called 'liquid metathesis', illustrated in (40) (Scatton 1983). Schwa epenthesis occurs in the (a) forms as shown by the fact that its position varies – essentially, epenthetic [ə] seeks to appear inside a closed syllable. In contrast, underlying

/ə/ surfaces in the same position, regardless of its environment (i.e. the examples in (b)).

(40)

    (a)   *Epenthesis of schwa*

        (i) /krv/ → [krəv] 'blood'   cf. /krv-av/ → [kər.vav] 'bloody'

        (ii) /mlk/ → [mlək] 'silence!'   cf. /mlk-om/ → [məl.kom] 'silently'

    (b)   *Preservation of underlying schwa*

        (i) /bləf/ → [bləf] 'bluff'   cf. /bləf-ət/ → [blə.fət], *[bəl.fət]

        (ii) /vəlk/→[vəlk] 'wolf', *[vlək] cf. /vəlk-ət/ → [vəl.kət]

The vowel in the output forms of (a) appears to avoid syllabic liquids, as shown in tableau (41).

(41)   *Bulgarian: liquid nuclei are not possible*

/krv/	*μ_h/L	DEP	*μ_h/V
kr̩v	*!		
☞ krəv		*	*

In contrast, comparable inputs in Slovak have forms with syllabic liquids as optimal outputs, and with no faithfulness violations as in (42).

(42)   *Slovak: liquid nuclei are possible*

/krv/	DEP	*μ_h/L	*μ_h/V
☞ kr̩v		*	
krəv	*!		*

In sum, inputs of the shape CLC are treated differently in Bulgarian and Slovak, and this difference is captured by the minimal difference in constraint ranking in (38), with C instantiated as DEP.

However, when two adjacent segments are both above the sonority threshold and are thus competing for the nucleus role, the more sonorous one wins. Thus in Slovak, vocalic nuclei win over liquid nuclei, as shown in (43). The dominating constraint ONS insures that the less sonorous liquid is relegated to the margin.

(43)   *Slovak: vocalic nuclei are preferred over liquid nuclei*

/traː.va/	ONS	*μ_h/L	*μ_h/V
☞ traː.va			**
tr̩.aː.va	*!	*	**

Finally, the set of segments above the syllabicity threshold in Imdlawn Tashlhiyt Berber includes the entire segment inventory. This language illustrates the same point, but in a more forceful way. Because any segment may be syllabic, the selection of the nucleus crucially depends on the relative sonority of segments. This property of Imdlawn Tashlhiyt Berber is accentuated by Dell and Elmedlaoui's (1984) syllabification algorithm, as well as by Prince and Smolensky's (2004) well-known OT analysis. Tableau (44) illustrates the evaluation of two entirely consonantal forms. Not only ONS but also the faithfulness constraints MAX and DEP rank above the markedness constraints on syllabicity.

(44)   *Imdlawn Tashlhiyt Berber*

(a) [tz̩.dm̩t] 'gather wood'

/tzdmt/	ONS	MAX,DEP	*μ_h/O	*μ_h/N	*μ_h/L	*μ_h/V
☞ tz̩.dm̩t			*	*		
tz̩d.m̩t			* *!			
tz̩d.m̩t	*!		*	*		
tz̩.dm̩t	*!		*	*		
tz̩.dm̩.t̩	*!		* *	*		
taz.dm̩t		*!		*		*

(b) [tzm̩t] 'it (fem.) is stifling'

/tzmt/	DEP	*μ_h/O	*μ_h/N	*μ_h/L
tzm̩t		*!		
☞ tzm̩t			*	
tzm̩t̩		*!		
taz.mat	**!			

The rankings in (38) yield a typology of syllabicity thresholds, summarized in (45). The set of occurring types in (45a) could be more elaborate with a more elaborate sonority scale, but in any further type syllabic segments would cover a continuous range, including its sonorous end, as in (45a). In the excluded types in (45b), syllabic segments either fail to cover a continuous range of the sonority scale, as in (i), or cover a continuous range starting from the wrong end, as in (iii), or fail to start from the right end, as in (iv); note that none could follow from the rankings in (38).

(45)   *A typology of syllabicity thresholds*

(a) Predicted cases

	V	L	N	O
(i)	yes			
(ii)	yes	yes		
(iii)	yes	yes	yes	
(iv)	yes	yes	yes	yes

(b) Excluded cases

	V	L	N	O
(i)	yes			yes
(ii)	yes		yes	
(iii)			yes	yes
(iv)		yes	yes	
(v)		yes	yes	yes
(vi)	yes		yes	yes
(vii)	yes	yes		yes

One of the types excluded by the theory is attested: in languages such as Swahili, the set of syllabic segments includes vowels and nasals but not liquids, precisely as in (45bii) (Ashton 1944, Polome 1967). From an OT perspective, such discontinuities may well be due to further constraint interactions.

8.5.1.2 Sonority thresholds on the mora

In addition to characterizing syllabicity, the hierarchy of peaks in (35) also characterizes moraicity – the weight-bearing property of segments. Sonority conditions on moras may differ from those on the head mora. The sonority threshold on the head mora is usually more restrictive than the sonority threshold on the non-head mora: while the former may contain only vowels, the latter may contain vowels as well as less sonorous classes of segments. Specific cases of moraicity thresholds are listed in (46). In Khalkha Mongolian and Fijian only vowels are moraic (46a); in Kwak'wala and Gonja, only vowels and sonorant consonants (46c); and in Cairene Arabic, all segments are moraic (46d).

(46)   *Sonority threshold on weight*

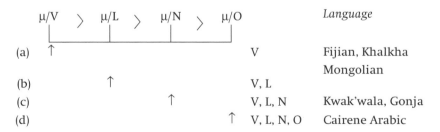

(a)	V	Fijian, Khalkha Mongolian
(b)	V, L	
(c)	V, L, N	Kwak'wala, Gonja
(d)	V, L, N, O	Cairene Arabic

The three classes of languages in (46) have different weight systems, as shown in (47):

(47)   *Weight systems*
    (a) Khalkha Mongolian, Fijian   heavy CVV
    (b) Kwak'wala, Gonja   heavy CVV, CVL, CVN
    (c) Cairene Arabic   heavy CVV, CVL, CVN, CVO

Supporting evidence is of the sort presented in Section 8.4.2. In all
languages listed in (47) other than Gonja, heavy syllables attract stress:
CVV syllables in Khalkha Mongolian (Street 1963) and Fijian (Dixon 1988,
Schütz 1985), syllables closed with a sonorant consonant in Kwak'wala
(Boas 1947, Grubb 1977), and all closed syllables listed in (47c) in Cairene
Arabic (Mitchell 1960, McCarthy 1979b, Hayes 1995). The weight-bearing
character of sonorants in Gonja is substantiated by their ability to be
associated with tone (Painter 1970).[17] Note the gap in (46b): no cases with
only liquids permitted in the weight-bearing position have been attested. It
is left for future research to determine whether this is an accidental gap, as
we are assuming at this point.

As with the sonority threshold on syllabicity, we posit a set of markedness constraints with a fixed ranking based on a natural hierarchy of
moraic peaks in (46). Given the ranked constraints in (48) all segments are
undesirable moraic heads, yet segments that are less sonorous are more
marked in this role (Morén 1999, Rosenthall & Hulst 1999).

(48) *Constraints on moraicity*
      $^*\mu/O \gg {}^*\mu/N \gg {}^*\mu/L \gg {}^*\mu/V$

The cut-off point for individual languages will be determined by constraint
interaction: some constraint $\mathcal{C}$ will delimit the class of segments above the
sonority threshold, as in (49).

(49) *Moraicity thresholds*
      (a) Khalkha Mongolian, Fijian: $^*\mu/O \gg {}^*\mu/N \gg {}^*\mu/L \gg \mathcal{C} \gg {}^*\mu/V$
      (b) Kwak'wala, Gonja: $^*\mu/O \gg \mathcal{C} \gg {}^*\mu/N \gg {}^*\mu/L \gg {}^*\mu/V$
      (c) Cairene Arabic: $\mathcal{C} \gg {}^*\mu/O \gg {}^*\mu/N \gg {}^*\mu/L \gg {}^*\mu/V$

In the case of the syllabicity threshold, $\mathcal{C}$ is typically instantiated by a
faithfulness constraint. In contrast, the sonority threshold on moraicity
can be delimited either by a faithfulness constraint or by *APPENDIX. It is
significant that the ranking schema in (49) characterizes not only the range
of cross-linguistically attested weight systems, but also the range of cross-
linguistically attested closed syllables. In order to demonstrate this, we
need to bring up again the fine structural differences that characterize
the right periphery of the syllable.

As noted in Section 8.4.3, the constraint *APPENDIX prohibits a weightless
(i.e. non-moraic) coda consonant, and crucially interacts with faithfulness
constraints. A weightless coda is prohibited if *APPENDIX is ranked above
the faithfulness constraints, and is licensed with *APPENDIX ranked lower
than the faithfulness constraints, as stated in (31) above. The former case is
presented in (50), and the latter in (52).

The ranking in (50) yields the set of heavy syllables listed in (47): CVV in Fijian, CVV, CVL and CVN in Gonja, and CVV, CVL, CVN, and CVO in Cairene Arabic.

(50) *Appendix* » {Max, Dep}
   (a) Fijian: $^*\mu/O$ » $^*\mu/N$ » $^*\mu/L$ » {Max, Dep} » $^*\mu/V$
   (b) Gonja: $^*\mu/O$ » {Max, Dep} » $^*\mu/N$ » $^*\mu/L$ » $^*\mu/V$
   (c) Cairene Arabic: {Max, Dep} » $^*\mu/O$ » $^*\mu/N$ » $^*\mu/L$ » $^*\mu/V$

Thus, a faithfulness constraint acts as a threshold delimiter if outranked by *Appendix*, and in this case syllables may be closed only with moraic segments. In Gonja, a syllable may be closed by a moraic nasal, as in (51a), but not by an obstruent, which is below the sonority threshold, as in (51b). This summarizes the situation in languages that do not license an appendix at the right edge of the syllable.

(51) *Gonja*

(a)

/CVN/	$^*\mu/O$	*Appendix*	Max	$^*\mu/N$
CV			*!	
CVN		*!		
☞ CVN$_\mu$				*

(b)

/CVO/	$^*\mu/O$	*Appendix*	Max	$^*\mu/N$
☞ CV			*	
CVO		*!		
CVO$_\mu$	*!			

If C is replaced by *Appendix*, as in (52), the range of heavy syllables is the same as in (50).

(52) Max, Dep » *Appendix*
   (a) Khalkha: $^*\mu/O$ » $^*\mu/N$ » $^*\mu/L$ » *Appendix* » $^*\mu/V$
   (b) Kwak'wala: $^*\mu/O$ » *Appendix* » $^*\mu/N$ » $^*\mu/L$ » $^*\mu/V$
   (c) (See below): *Appendix* » $^*\mu/O$ » $^*\mu/N$ » $^*\mu/L$ » $^*\mu/V$

However, the range of light closed syllables is considerably expanded. With *Appendix* as a threshold delimiter, the weightless coda is reserved for segments that are not sufficiently sonorous to sustain a mora: obstruents in Kwak'wala, and all consonants in Khalkha Mongolian. The evaluation of CVO and CVN inputs in Khalkha Mongolian is given in (53); and in Kwak'-wala, in (54).

(53) *Khalkha Mongolian*

(a)

/CVO/	*μ/O	*μ/N	*μ/L	*APPENDIX	*μ/V
CVO$_\mu$	*!				*
☞ CVO				*	*

(b)

/CVN/	*μ/O	*μ/N	*μ/L	*APPENDIX	*μ/V
CVN$_\mu$		*!			*
☞ CVN				*	*

(54) *Kwak'wala*

(a)

/CVO/	*μ/O	*APPENDIX	*μ/N	*μ/L	*μ/V
CVO$_\mu$	*!				*
☞ CVO		*			*

(b)

/CVN/	*μ/O	*APPENDIX	*μ/N	*μ/L	*μ/V
☞ CVN$_\mu$			*		*
CVN		*!			*

No example is supplied for (52c) as this pattern does not differ from (50c). It remains for future research to identify what, if anything, differentiates these two types of languages. One possibility is that the language filling this slot should grant special freedom to the occurrence of the appendix, and more generally, to complex codas.

The typology of weight systems is characterized by the ranking schema in (49), whether instantiated as (50) or (52). These rankings yield the range of predicted types in (55a), but exclude the cases in (55b).

(55) *Typology of heavy syllables*

(a) Predicted types

	HEAVY			LIGHT		
	CVL$_\mu$	CVN$_\mu$	CVO$_\mu$	CVL	CVN	CVO
(i)				yes	yes	yes
(ii)	yes				yes	yes
(iii)	yes	yes				yes
(iv)	yes	yes	yes			

(b) Excluded types

	HEAVY			LIGHT		
	CVL$_\mu$	CVN$_\mu$	CVO$_\mu$	CVL	CVN	CVO
(i)			yes	yes	yes	
(ii)		yes	yes	yes		
(iii)	yes		yes		yes	
(iv)		yes		yes		yes

Crucially, if a language has both light and heavy closed syllables, the former are closed with less sonorous consonants than the latter, as in (55aii) and (55aiii). The reversed situation, in (55bi) and (55bii), constitutes an impossible type. A further confounding factor is coda constraints, which restrict the occurrence of consonantal features in syllable final position (see Section 8.3.3). These constraints target both weight-bearing and weight-less consonants. That is, they may interact with both *APPENDIX and the constraints on moraicity thresholds (see Zec 1995). Thus, in a number of languages, syllables may be closed only by nasals, which could be either weightless, as in Axininca Campa (Payne 1981), or weight-bearing, as in Manam (Lichtenberk 1983). This however does not follow from the typologies posited here, and may well be due to the added effect of coda constraints (see Section 8.3.3). It is of interest that the situation in Manam, in which nasals, but not liquids, are moraic, is comparable with Swahili, in which nasals are syllabic, but liquids are not.

8.5.2　Constraints on sonority distance

Sonority sequencing is of a syntagmatic nature: how sonorous a segment needs to be depends not only on its structural role within the syllable but also on the sonority of its neighbors. Sonority sequencing is thus crucially relational, as is apparent in the following statement (56) (based on Selkirk 1984a:116):

(56)　*Sonority Sequencing Generalization (SSG)*
　　　For every pair of segments s and z in a syllable, s is less sonorous than z if

　　　　　(a)　(i) $s < z < Nucleus$
　　　　　　　or (ii) $Nucleus > z > s$
　　　or (b)　(i) $s < z$ and z is the nucleus
　　　　　　　or (ii) $z > s$ and z is the nucleus

　　Constraints on sonority distance may impose restrictions on the rise or fall in sonority that go beyond the minimal requirements of SSG. This is captured by Prince and Smolensky's (2004) natural hierarchy of margins, which is the mirror image of the peak hierarchy in (35). The best margins are obstruents, followed by nasals and liquids, with vowels being the worst margins. In (57) is given the sonority hierarchy of onsets, since our focus will be the left margin of the syllable:

(57)   Hierarchy of onsets: Ons/O $\rangle$ Ons/N $\rangle$ Ons/L

We address the sonority distance between the onset and the nucleus in Section 8.5.2.1, within a complex onset in Section 8.5.2.2, and in syllable contact in Section 8.5.2.3.

8.5.2.1 Sonority distance from onset to nucleus

All else being equal, constraints on syllabicity thresholds insure that syllable nuclei are more sonorous than onsets, as shown in Section 8.5.1.1. However, onsets may tend towards low sonority beyond the minimal requirement of being less sonorous than the neighboring nucleus. Thus, OV is better than NV, which in turn is better than LV, even though all conform to the SSG. While this preference seems less pronounced than the preference for high sonority peaks (and is certainly less well documented), it brings the important role of low onset sonority in the overall sonority profile of the syllable into relief.

Gnanadesikan (2004) furnishes evidence from a child language grammar, in which *snow* [snou] is simplified as [so] rather than [no]; and *please* [pliːz] as [piːz] rather than [liːz]. In both cases, the surviving consonant is lower in sonority than its competitor yet any consonant may occupy a simplex onset regardless of its sonority. A comparable situation is documented in Pāli: in cluster simplification, the consonant that is eliminated is more sonorous than the one that stays, and the one that stays is linked to the onset.[18]

Preference for low sonority onsets is captured by Prince and Smolensky's (2004) hierarchy of onsets in (58). This hierarchy of onsets yields markedness constraints on onset sonority, as proposed in de Lacy (2001). The set of onset sonority constraints in (57), with fixed ranking, makes obstruent onsets the least marked, and liquid onsets the most marked.

(58)   *Ons/L » *Ons/N » *Ons/O

This set of constraints captures the sonority rise at the left edge of the syllable, as stated in SSG. It also captures the tendency towards low sonority onsets beyond the requirements of SSG.

Interestingly, in a small number of languages, high sonority segments are entirely banned from the onset, as reported in de Lacy (2001) and Smith (2003). In Seoul Korean, for example, word-initial syllables may not begin with liquids, and word internally, liquids in the onset are also linked to the coda. The ranking *Ons-L » ident-IO[approx] » *Ons/N insures that nasal onsets will be protected, and that liquid onsets will be eliminated (i.e. /loin/ → [no.in] '(an) old man').

8.5.2.2 Sonority distance within a complex onset

SSG states the *relative* sonority within complex onsets: in a biconsonantal onset cluster, the second consonant should be more sonorous than the first, as in the Spanish forms *preso* [preso] 'prisoner' and *plano* [plano] 'flat'. However, [pn] and [ml] are not possible onset sequences in Spanish even though the second member of the cluster is more sonorous than the first (Harris 1983).

Cases like this are explained in terms of Minimal Sonority Distance (MSD) imposed on a pair of onset segments (Vennemann 1972, Hooper 1976, Steriade 1982, Selkirk 1984a, Levin 1985, Baertsch 2002). Given the scale in (59), [p] is separated from [l] by two intervals, while only one interval separates [p] from [n], and [m] from [l]. Because the minimal sonority distance in Spanish is at least two intervals, [pl] and [pr] are possible onset clusters, while [pn] and [ml] are not. In sum, any two consonants that are at least two intervals apart can form a complex onset.

(59) *Sonority Distance*

The range of values for MSD, based on the scale in (59), is given in (60). Sequences with flat sonority are given the value MSD0, sequences with the steepest rise, MSD2, and those with a less steep rise, MSD1.

(60) *Minimal Sonority Distance (MSD)*
      MSD0   OO, NN, LL
      MSD1   ON, NL
      MSD2   OL

Chukchee, which allows ON, NL, and OL onset clusters, provides an example of a language with the minimal sonority distance MSD1; clusters of lesser distance are broken by epenthesis (Bogoras 1922, Levin 1985). Bulgarian allows OO, NN, LL, ON, NL, and OL onset clusters, and so exemplifies a language whose minimal sonority distance is MSD0 (Scatton 1983). As already noted, the minimal sonority distance for Spanish is MSD2 as it allows only OL onset clusters (Harris 1983, Baertsch 2002).

Note that the markedness constraints on onset sonority in (58) are not sufficient to account for the facts of minimal sonority distance in onsets. The first member of an onset cluster tends towards low sonority, and this indeed is captured by the constraints in (58). However, the second member of an onset cluster tends towards high sonority, and this is what forms the basis for sonority distance within onsets. This suggests that the two members of an onset cluster may be subject to different sonority requirements; for a proposal based on this insight, see Baertsch (2002).

8.5.2.3 Sonority distance in syllable contact

Pairs of syllables that emerge as optimal under constraints on syllable shapes are further subject to the requirements of Syllable Contact (SC), which favors a sonority fall across syllable boundaries (Hooper 1976, Vennemann 1988, Davis 1998, Baertsch 2002, Gouskova 2001, 2004).

Phonological alternations may be driven by syllable contact, and one such case comes from Kirgiz. As shown by Gouskova (2001), word-initial clusters in loan words are resolved by epenthesis and the site of the epenthetic vowel is governed by syllable contact. Clusters of falling or flat sonority are preceded by the epenthetic vowel, as in (61a); clusters of rising sonority are broken by the epenthetic vowel as in (61b). Initial epenthesis in (61b) would have resulted in heterosyllabic clusters of rising sonority, which constitutes an intolerable syllable contact.

(61) *Kirgiz loanword adaptation*

	Russian	Kirgiz	gloss
(a) falling/flat sonority			
L.O	lʲvof	il.vop	city name
N.N	mnemonitʃeskij	um.nemonitʃeskij	'mnemonic'
(b) rising sonority			
*O.L	trupka	tu.rupke/*ut.rupke	'pipe'
*O.N	kniʃka	ki.neʃke/*ik.neʃke	'book'

Syllable contact effects are further exemplified in Sidamo. Input consonant sequences of descending sonority may form heterosyllabic clusters, as in (62a)–(62b), while input sequences of ascending sonority undergo metathesis (62c, d) (Gouskova 2004).[19]

(62) Syllable Contact in Sidamo

(a) /ful-te/	[ful.te]	'Your having gone out'	LO→LO
(b) /qaram-tino/	[qa.ran.ti.no]	'she worried'	NO→NO
(c) /hab-nemmo/	[ham.bem.mo]	'we forget'	*ON→NO
(d) /has-nemmo/	[han.sem.mo]	'we look for'	*ON→NO

The result of metathesis is an improvement in syllable contact: a heterosyllabic cluster of ascending sonority is converted into a cluster of descending sonority.

The scale in (63) provides an evaluation of syllable contact. Sequences of flat sonority are given the value SC0, sequences of rising sonority have positive values, and those that fall in sonority have negative values. Syllable contacts with positive values (italicized) are highly disfavored.

(63) *Syllable Contact (SC)*

SC +2			*OL*
SC +1		*ON, NL*	
SC 0	OO, NN, LL		
SC −1		LN, NO	
SC −2			LO

Both Kirgiz and Sidamo exhibit preference for clusters in the negative range of this scale, and no tolerance for clusters in the positive range. However, in contrast to these more restrictive cases, languages like Turkish admit all types of heterosyllabic clusters in (63) (see Baertsch and Davis 2001).

Syllable contact effects accentuate the already stated preference for low sonority onsets, and for high sonority moraic codas. According to a recent proposal in Gouskova (2004), syllable contact is to be captured by combining the effects of two sets of markedness constraints: constraints on moraicity threshold in moras, which favor high sonority in codas, and constraints on onset sonority, which favor low sonority in onsets (see also Baertsch 2002). Under this perspective light closed syllables do not participate in syllable contact effects, and it remains to be seen whether this is empirically substantiated.

8.6   Closing remarks

In this chapter, it has been shown that the syllable is a complex constituent, constrained in both linear and hierarchical terms, with sonority playing an overarching role. Moreover, the range of cross-linguistic variation is sufficiently restricted to be stated in terms of straightforward typologies along several dimensions, yet sufficiently varied to point at minimal structural differences across languages. Departures from the relatively simple picture presented here may be due to further constraint interactions, and are bound to emerge in detailed characterizations of syllables in specific languages. Constraints that make reference to morphological constituencies may affect the place of syllable boundaries (Prince and Smolensky 2004 and McCarthy and Prince 1993b), while constraints on phonological constituencies higher or lower than the syllable may affect syllable shapes or their weight properties (Rosenthall and Hulst 1999). It is left for future research to establish the range of such interfaces, and the range of structural variation that arises from them. Ultimately, the formal framework will need to encode a typology of such effects, delimiting the set of those that do occur from those that do not.

We have also shown that the constraints on syllable shapes and, in particular, those on sonority sequencing, go a long way in capturing segment sequencing in linguistic forms. In fact, the original motivation for positing the syllable was to account for segment phonotactics, as detailed in Section 8.2. This perspective has been challenged by Steriade (1999a) and Blevins (2003). Their alternative view is that accounts of segment phonotactics should be string-based rather than syllable-based. The supporting argument is largely based on the distribution of consonantal place and laryngeal features, which are subject to neutralization in certain environments. Steriade (1999a) and Blevins (2003) argue against the standard view that such neutralizations take effect in the coda and are to be captured by coda constraints (see Section 8.3.3). They specifically focus on cases of neutralization that cannot be subsumed under coda constraints, or any other constraints that make reference to the syllable. The overall claim is that phonotactics are rooted in perceptibility, and as such have a phonetic rather than structural basis. However, this argument is not sufficient to deny the syllable its important role in segment sequencing. The syllable should not be called upon to account for *all* segment phonotactics. Some aspects of segment sequencing are in fact not related to the syllable. Constraints on string-adjacent segments, so-called cluster constraints, have been proposed, for example, by Yip (1991). Crucially, cluster constraints operate in tandem with syllable-based constraints. In sum, rather than positing a single principle underlying phonotactic relations, it would be advantageous to tease apart those aspects of segment sequencing that are governed by the syllable from those governed by other forces, and then establish their mutual interactions.

Notes

I am grateful to Paul de Lacy for invaluable comments and suggestions; and to Seongyeon Ko, Rina Kreitman, and Jiwon Yun for their help in improving the manuscript.

1 However, the proposed parallelism between syllable edges and word edges may on occasion be obliterated by special effects reserved for word edges (Clements 1990, McCarthy and Prince 1995a, Beckman 1998).

2 Length of the nucleus, which is not relevant at this point, will be addressed in Section 8.4.

3 Senufo does have a small number of mostly borrowed forms that are vowel initial.

4 References for the cases from Blevins (1995): Totonac (MacKay 1999), Dakota (Shaw 1989), Klamath (Barker 1964), Arabela (Rich 1963), Spanish (Harris 1983), Finnish (Keyser and Kiparsky 1984, Prince 1983), Pirahã (Everett and Everett 1984).

5 In most rule-based analyses the emergence of the CV syllable as the least marked is captured by stipulation (e.g. by granting it the formal status of the core syllable – see Steriade 1982, Itô 1986).

6 Note that the syllabification of a VCV sequence is determined only by the markedness constraints Ons and ¬Cod. This either shows that input forms are not syllabified, or that faithfulness constraints cannot protect syllabification in input forms.

7 For the Hua facts, see Haiman (1980); while syllables in Hua are for the most part open, Haiman also reports that some may be closed by a glottal stop. The Diola Fogny facts are described in Sapir (1965), and analyzed in Steriade (1982), Itô (1986), and de Lacy (2002a), among others.

8 Specifically, epenthesis in (15a) was construed as supplying an 'unfilled' nucleus; and deletion in (15b) as 'stray erasure' of a segment that has not been parsed into a syllable. This perspective is echoed in the early version of OT faithfulness constraints, PARSE and FILL (Prince and Smolensky 2004), subsequently replaced by MAX and DEP (McCarthy & Prince 1995a).

9 Positional faithfulness provides an alternative perspective on the prohibition of features in codas: rather than being banned from the coda, segmental features are granted the privilege of occurrence in the onset (Lombardi 1995b, Beckman 1998).

10 Non-alternating glides also exist. Usarufa exhibits a contrast between [i] and [j], and [u] and [w], as in [aue] vs. [awe] (Levin 1985:81). Hyman (1985) proposes to analyze non-alternating glides as [+consonantal], to differentiate them from [–consonantal] alternating glides (see also Hayes 1989a).

11 The device of choice in cases of contextual syllabicity has been underspecification: segments that are syllabic are [+syllabic], those that are not syllabic are [–syllabic], while those whose syllabicity is predictable are [0 syllabic], with the feature value contextually supplied (as in Steriade 1982, Waksler 1990). See Levin (1985) and the references therein for arguments against this approach.

12 The timing component originally posited in phonological theory is the CV tier (McCarthy 1981), and the X tier (Levin 1985). Under both earlier views, every segment has its projection on the timing tier.

13 Capturing the length of geminate consonants in structural terms is less straightforward. Hayes' (1989a) proposal is that geminate consonants are heterosyllabic segments dominated by a mora and syllable node.

14 Gordon (1999, 2002b) presents an important challenge to the idea that syllable weight is computed solely in terms of mora count. He argues that the diagnostics for syllable weight distinctions may yield conflicting results in a single language, and that in some cases weight distinctions do not correlate with mora count.

15 Such a position may be too strong in light of studies such as Cho and King (2003) and Féry (2003) that argue for moraless syllables which occur under highly restricted circumstances. See also Hyman (1985) and Kiparsky (2003) and the references therein for cases which arguably need to be analyzed in terms of unsyllabified moras.

16 For the head relation within the prosodic constituency, see Liberman and Prince (1977), McCarthy and Prince (1993b), and Selkirk (1995a); and for the head relation within the syllable, see Kiparsky (1979, 1981), Zec (1988, 1995, 2003) and de Lacy (2002a, 2004).

17 See Zec (1995) for an analysis of these cases.

18 The situation in Pāli is in fact more complex. Pāli is characterized by massive cluster simplification in intervocalic position (Hankamer and Aissen 1974). These facts are analyzed either as deletion (e.g. Cho 1999)

or as coalescence, as in de Lacy's (2002a) detailed account. The consonant that survives is generally less sonorous than its competitor, as in /lag-no/ yielding [lagga] ([lag-a-ti] 'to attach'), or /kiɭ-na/ yielding [kiɳɳa] ([kir-a-si] 'to strew'). Although the surviving consonant is a geminate, its selection seems to be driven by the preference for low sonority onsets. Yet simplex onsets do not exhibit a comparable tendency towards low sonority.

19 This case has further complexities. Another repair strategy is assimilation: the input sequence /ful-nemmo/ becomes [ful.lem.mo] 'we go out' and /mar-nonni/ becomes [mar.ron.ni] 'they went.' For details, see Gouskova (2004).

9

Feet and metrical stress

René Kager

9.1 Metrical stress: introduction

9.1.1 What are stress languages?

In stress languages, one or more syllables in each word or phrase is said to be 'more prominent' than others. 'Prominence' is not an intrinsic property of stressed syllables, but a matter of relative strength between 'stronger' and 'weaker' syllables. Most stress languages distinguish only two degrees of stress: stressed and unstressed. Yet a further distinction among stressed syllables into primary and secondary stress is common, while some languages even display a three-way distinction into primary, secondary, and tertiary stress. Here we will use the IPA conventions for stress notation. Primary stress is indicated by a superscript vertical bar before the syllable carrying it, secondary stress by a subscript vertical bar. Consider, for example, the transcription for 'designate': ['dɛ.zɪɡ.ˌneɪt].

There is no unique phonetic property corresponding to stress, although it is cross-linguistically highly common for stressed syllables to have higher pitch levels, longer duration, and greater loudness than unstressed syllables. Tones tend to be attracted to stressed syllables (see Gussenhoven Ch.11, Yip Ch.10, and de Lacy Ch.12). Yet, stress is clearly different from tone in the sense that stress does not assimilate, neither locally between adjacent syllables, nor across longer distances. Cross-linguistically, relations between segmental properties and stress are common. The vowels of stressed syllables are prone to lengthen, while those of unstressed syllables may undergo reduction. Stressed syllables tend to license a larger set of vowels than unstressed syllables.

In 'free stress' languages, word stress is lexically contrastive, resulting in minimal pairs that differ in terms of stress alone (e.g. Russian ['baɡrɪtʲ] 'to spear fish' and [baˈɡrɪtʲ] 'to paint crimson'). In 'fixed stress' languages, stress is phonologically predictable, but a word's morphological structure may affect the location of stress. For example, suffixes may attract stress, repel it, or be stress-neutral. Also, prefixes may be included in the word stress domain or fall outside it. This chapter will focus on fixed-stress languages, and mostly ignore contrastive stress and morphological effects.

9.1.2 Cross-linguistic properties of stress

A number of properties of stress languages have been identified, some of which are universal. Among these properties, the following four are well-established.

9.1.2.1 Culminative stress

'Culminativity' means that there is one and only one maximally prominent peak within a stress domain. It is characteristic of stress languages for grammatical units (stems, words, or phrases) to have minimally one stressed syllable. This stress peak, the most prominent syllable in its gram-matical domain, typically serves as the anchoring point for intonational contours (see Gussenhoven Ch.11). At the word level, culminativity amounts to a stressability requirement, which many languages impose on content words (nouns, verbs, adjectives, or adverbs) while relaxing it for function words (articles, pronouns, prepositions, etc.), which are proso-dically dependent on content words (McCarthy & Prince 1986).

9.1.2.2 Demarcative stress

Stress can have a demarcative function: it signals the beginning and/or end of morphological boundaries. Cross-linguistically, stress tends to be attracted to syllables located near the edges of grammatical units, espe-cially the initial syllable. Since final syllables are exempted from stress in many languages, initial and prefinal syllables are, by far, the most favored locations of stress, followed by stress on the second and final syllable. Examples from Diyari (Austin 1981, Poser 1989) illustrate how stress may serve to highlight morphological structure. All morphemes, stems or suffixes, of length two or more syllables, are stressed on their initial syllable.

(1)   *Diyari: initial stress on all polysyllabic morphemes*

(a)	'kana-ni-ˌmata	'man' (loc. iden.)
(b)	'kana-ˌwara-ŋgu	'man' (pl. loc.)
(c)	'kana-ˌwara-ˌŋgundu	'man' (pl. abl.)
(d)	'jakalka-ˌjirpa-ˌmali-na	'to ask' (ben. recip. part.)

Observe how the minimal binarity requirement on stressibility serves to avoid stress on final syllables, as well as on adjacent syllables. This naturally leads us to the next property.

9.1.2.3   Rhythm

Stress languages show a preference for well-formed rhythmic patterns, where strong and weak syllables are spaced apart at regular intervals. This is manifested by avoidance of adjacent stressed syllables ('clash'), or by avoidance of strings of unstressed syllables ('lapse'). Nevertheless, stress languages vary in degree of rhythmicity. On one end of the spectrum, *bounded* languages occur, with perfectly alternating rhythms, oriented toward the left or right edge of the word. For example, Pintupi (Hansen & Hansen 1969) has stress on the initial syllable and following alternate non-final syllables, while Warao (Osborn 1966) stresses the prefinal syllable and alternate preceding syllables.

(2)   *Pintupi: stress on initial syllable and following alternate nonfinal syllables*

    (a) ˈtʲi.ˌli.ˌri.ŋu.ˌlam.pa.tʲu   'the fire for our benefit flared up'

    (b) ˈju.ma.ˌɹɪŋ.ka.ˌma.ra.ˌtʲa.ɹa.ka 'because of mother-in-law'

(3)   *Warao: stress on penultimate syllable and preceding alternate syllables*

    (a) ˌja.pu.ˌru.ki.ˌta.ne.ˈha.se   'verily to climb'

    (b) e.ˌna.ho.ˌro.a.ˌha.ku.ˈta.i   'the one who caused him to eat'

At the opposite end of the rhythmic spectrum we find *unbounded* languages which have one stress per word and no alternating rhythm, allowing long strings of unstressed syllables. Unbounded stress patterns are exemplified in (4)–(5) by Selkup and Western Cheremis. Selkup (Kuznecova et al. 1980, Walker 1997) stresses the rightmost heavy syllable (heavy syllables have long vowels in this language), and otherwise the initial syllable in forms lacking heavy syllables. Selkup is a so-called 'default-to-opposite-edge' system.

(4)   *Selkup: stress on rightmost heavy syllable, otherwise initial syllable*

    (a) L H L ˈH   qu.moː.qlɪ.ˈlɪː   'your two friends'

    (b) H ˈH L   uː.ˈcoː.mit   'we work'

    (c) L L LˈH   py.na.ki.ˈsəː   'giant!'

    (d) ˈL L L L   ˈqolʲ.cim.pa.ti 'found'

A 'default-to-same-edge' system occurs in Western Cheremis (Itkonen 1955, Walker 1997), where stress falls on the rightmost nonfinal strong (i.e. full-voweled) syllable and otherwise, in forms lacking nonfinal strong syllables, on the rightmost nonfinal syllable.

(5)   *Western Cheremis: stress on rightmost nonfinal strong syllable, otherwise penult*

    (a) ˈH L H   ˈβaʃ.tə.lam   'I laugh'

    (b) H ˈH L   oʃˈmaʃ.tə   'sand' (iness.)

    (c) L ˈL L   pə.ˈre.ʃəm   'I went in'

    (d) L ˈL H   ə.ˈmel.tem   'I throw my shade on'

9.1.2.4 Quantity-sensitivity

Stress prefers to lodge on syllables which have a certain degree of intrinsic prominence. Usually, the relevant property is syllable weight (moraic quantity, see Zec Ch.8). Long vowels and vocalic diphthongs are always bimoraic; coda consonants are mora-bearing on a language-specific basis, so (C)VC syllables may count as heavy in one language and light in another. Occasionally, stress is attracted by syllables which carry a high tone, or contain a vowel of high sonority (see de Lacy Ch.12). Stress attraction by heavy syllables was exemplified for unbounded languages by Selkup and Western Cheremis (4–5).

A striking case of a bounded quantity-sensitive pattern is found in Yidiɲ (Dixon 1977). In words containing an even number of syllables which lack long vowels, stress falls on all odd-numbered syllables (6a). When a long vowel occurs in an even-numbered syllable, stress falls on even-numbered syllables (6b). In words containing an odd number of syllables, the penultimate syllable is lengthened, and stress falls on even-numbered syllables (6c–d).

(6) Yidiɲ: *mutual dependence of stress and vowel length*

(a)	/gudaga-ni/	'gu.da.'ga.ni	'dog' (gen.)
(b)	/durgu:-nu-la/	dur.'gu:.nu.'la	'mopoke owl' (gen./loc.)
(c)	/gudaga/	gu.'da:.ga	'dog' (abs.)
(d)	/gudaga-gudaga/	gu.'da.gu.'da:.ga	'dog' (red.)

This example shows how the presence of stress depends on quantity, as well as how quantity can depend on stress. Yidiɲ lengthens the vowel of a stressed penultimate syllable, increasing its quantity. Another related cross-linguistically common strategy is consonant gemination in stressed syllables. Conversely, vowels in unstressed syllables tend to shorten, reduce, or even delete, thus decreasing their syllable weight, as in English /ætɒm/ 'atom' surfacing as ['ærəm] and [ə'tʰɒmək] 'atomic'. In sum, quantity-sensitivity amounts to an agreement between quantitative structure (patterns of light and heavy syllables) and metrical structure (groupings into weak and strong syllables).

Although usually a strict division into quantity-sensitive and quantity-insensitive systems is assumed, stress systems actually fall into finer-grained classes, showing various degrees of quantity-sensitivity, with a range of intermediate positions (Kager 1992a, b; Alber 1997).

9.2   The formal representation of stress

Our representational basis is *metrical phonology*, a theory whose central assumption is that stress is a relational property, represented by prominence relations between constituents in hierarchical structures (Liberman 1975; Liberman & Prince 1977; Hayes 1980). We use the metrical representation known as *constituentized grid* or *bracketed grid* (Hammond 1984; Halle & Vergnaud 1987; Hayes 1995), which combines the metrical grid with constituency.

9.2.1 The grid

The *metrical grid* forms a hierarchical representation of rhythm (Liberman 1975; Liberman & Prince 1977; Prince 1983; Selkirk 1984b), a succession of columns of grid elements of different height. Height of columns represents a syllable's relative prominence. Horizontally, the arrangement of grid elements represents rhythm, from which alternation, stress clash, and stress lapse can be read. As an example, consider the alternating stress pattern of *Apalachicola* [ˌæpəˌlætʃɪˈkoːlə]. Its grid analysis (7) contains six columns, each standing over a syllable. The first, third and fifth columns are taller than the second, fourth and sixth. The fifth column, indicating the grid's culminating peak, is taller than the first and third.

(7) PrWd-level   x
     Foot-level   x   x   x
     Syllable-level x   x   x   x   x   x
                    ˌæ. pə. ˌlæ. tʃɪ. ˈkoː. lə

This particular grid shows a perfect rhythmic alternation, since all strong foot-level beats are separated by a weak syllable-level beat.

   The grid, as a representation of rhythm, is essential in the description of word stress patterns. Languages strive towards a rhythmic alternation of strong and weak syllables, avoiding dis-rhythmic situations, known as 'stress clash' and 'lapse'. We define 'clash' as a situation of adjacent strong beats without an intervening weak beat at the next-lower level (Liberman 1975; Liberman & Prince 1977; Prince 1983; Selkirk 1984b).

(8) Clash   *n+1*   x x
             n   x x

'Lapse' is defined as the adjacency of two grid elements at level *n*, without either having a level *n+1* counterpart.

(9) Lapse   *n+1*
             n   x   x

'Rhythmic alternation' is defined as the absence of clash and lapse. Every two grid elements which are adjacent at level *n+1* must be separated by precisely one element at level *n*.

(10) Alternation   *n+1*   x   x   x
                    n   ... x x x x x x ...

Pure-grid variants of metrical theory, which involve no metrical constituency, were proposed by Prince (1983), Selkirk (1984b), and Gordon (2002a).

9.2.2 Metrical constituency

Metrical constituency refers to groupings of grid elements at low levels into higher-order elements. Constituency is formally represented by bracketing grid elements by pairs of parentheses (Hammond 1984, Halle & Vergnaud 1987, Halle & Idsardi 1995, Hayes 1995). Each constituent has an obligatory *head*, represented by a grid element at the next-higher level, plus an optional non-head, which has no corresponding mark at the next-higher level. By adding constituency to the grid in (7), we obtain a bracketed representation in (11).

```
(11)  PrWd-level                            x
      Foot-level      (x      x       x      )
      Syllable-level  (x   x) (x   x) (x   x)
                      ˌæ.  pə. ˌlæ. tʃɪ. ˈkoː.  lə
```

At the syllable level, pairs of grid elements are bracketed together by parentheses into three *metrical feet*: (æ.pə), (læ.tʃɪ), (koː.lə). Rhythmically strong syllables are called 'heads'. Strong-initial feet, as in (11), are called *trochees*. Each foot projects its head by a gridmark at the foot level. Elements at the foot level are similarly bracketed together in a single constituent, whose head is final in English. This projects a grid element at the Prosodic Word level, the culminative peak of the word.

Hayes (1995) uses a flattened bracketed grid representation, which collapses three layers into two. Within each constituent, the head is represented by an asterisk, the non-head by a dot.

```
(12)  (.        .          *     )
      (*    .) (*   .) (*     .)
      ˌæ.  pə. ˌlæ. tʃɪ. ˈkoː.  lə
```

Throughout this chapter, we will use even flatter representations, as exemplified in (13). Dots denote syllable boundaries; parentheses, foot boundaries; and square brackets, PrWd boundaries. Relative prominence is marked by IPA-style stress marks before syllables:

(13) [(ˌæ.pə).(ˌlæ.tʃɪ).(ˈkoː.lə)]

These informal representations are notationally equivalent with bracketed grids in (11) and (12).

9.2.3 An inventory of metrical feet

A central hypothesis of metrical theory is that there is a small universal inventory of foot types, and languages can only select types from this inventory. The particular foot inventory which we focus on (Hayes 1985, 1987, 1995; McCarthy & Prince 1986; Prince 1990) is based on converging evidence from a range of phenomena found in natural languages, including stress patterns, rhythmic lengthening and shortening, word minima, and templates in prosodic morphology. It contains three basic foot types, two of which are *trochaic* (head-initial), and one *iambic* (head-final). The quantity-insensitive *syllabic trochee* requires two syllables of indiscriminate weight. The quantity-sensitive *moraic trochee* has two light syllables, or a single heavy syllable. Finally, the quantity-sensitive *iamb* has three forms: two light syllables, a single heavy, or a light syllable plus a heavy syllable (14).

(14)   *licit forms*   *degenerate forms*

  (a) *Syllabic trochee*   (* .)   (*)

                  σ σ   σ

  (b) *Moraic trochee*   (* .)   (*)   (*)

                  σ σ   σ   σ

                  | | /\ |

                  μ μ   μ μ   μ

  (c) *Iamb*   (. *)   (*)   (. *)   (*)

                  σ σ   σ   σ σ   σ

                  | /\   /\ | | |

                  μ μ μ   μ μ   μ μ   μ

This foot inventory is *asymmetrical* in the sense that it imposes a sharp rhythmic distinction between iambs, whose preferred expansion (light-plus-heavy) is quantitatively uneven, and trochees, which are quantitatively even at the level of the syllable or mora. Another major element of the foot inventory is its distinguishing licit expansions, which meet the requirement of *binarity* at the level of the syllable or the mora, from degenerate expansions, which fall below the binary threshold. Many languages avoid degenerate feet altogether, while other languages allow them only in absolutely peripheral positions or under main stress (Kager 1989, 1993, 1995a; Kiparsky 1991; Hayes 1995, cf. Halle & Idsardi 1995).

We will use an informal notation for feet, where a syllable of indiscriminate weight is denoted by 'σ', a light syllable by 'L', and a heavy syllable by 'H'. The head of the foot is underlined (15).

(15)   *licit expansions*   *degenerate expansion*

  (a) *Syllabic trochee*   (<u>σ</u>σ)   (<u>σ</u>)

  (b) *Moraic trochee*   (<u>LL</u>)   (<u>H</u>)   (<u>L</u>)

  (c) *Iamb*   (L<u>H</u>)   (<u>H</u>)   (L<u>L</u>)   (<u>L</u>)

We now turn to a brief discussion of these foot types. For fuller exemplification of stress systems, see typological studies such as Hyman (1977), Hayes (1980, 1995), Halle & Vergnaud (1987), Elenbaas & Kager (1999), Gordon (2002a), and the papers in Goedemans, van der Hulst & Visch (1996).

9.2.3.1 Syllabic trochees

The syllabic trochee is exemplified in its most canonical, strictly binary form by languages which lack a syllable weight contrast altogether, such as Pintupi (16) and Warao (17), where the direction of metrification is rightward and leftward, respectively.

(16) *Pintupi (Hansen & Hansen 1969): syllabic trochees from left to right*

- Primary stress is initial.
- Secondary stresses fall on every odd-numbered non-final syllable.

(a) ('σσ)   'pa.ɳa   'earth'
(b) ('σσ)σ   'ɲu.ɳi.tʲu   'mother'
(c) ('σσ)(ˌσσ)   'ma.la.ˌwa.na   'through (from) behind'
(d) ('σσ)(ˌσσ)σ   'pu.liŋ.ˌka.la.tʲu   'we (sat) on the hill'
(e) ('σσ)(ˌσσ)(ˌσσ)   'tʲa.mu.ˌlim.pa.ˌtʲuŋ.ku   'our relation'
(f) ('σσ)(ˌσσ)(ˌσσ)σ   'tʲi.ḷi.ˌri.ɲu.ˌlam.pa.tʲu   'the fire for our benefit flared up'

(17) *Warao (Osborn 1966): syllabic trochees from right to left*

- Primary stress is penultimate.
- Secondary stress falls on alternate syllables counting back from the primary stress.

(a) ('σσ)   'ti.ra   'woman'
(b) σ('σσ)   ko.'ra.nu   'drink it!'
(c) (ˌσσ)('σσ)   ˌru.hu.'na.e   'he sat down'
(d) σ(ˌσσ)('σσ)   ji.ˌwa.ra.'na.e   'he finished it'
(e) (ˌσσ)(ˌσσ)(ˌσσ)('σσ)   ˌja.pu.ˌru.ki.ˌta.ne.'ha.se   'verily to climb'
(f) σ(ˌσσ)(ˌσσ)(ˌσσ)('σσ)   e.ˌna.ho.ˌro.a.ˌha.ku.'ta.i   'the one who caused him to eat'

The syllabic trochee also serves to analyse languages which possess a syllable weight contrast, but fully or partially ignore it in stress assignment. Languages of this type are rare (Kager 1992a,b), a case being Finnish (Carlson 1978, Hanson & Kiparsky 1996, Elenbaas & Kager 1999). Unstressed heavy syllables occur, so as to avoid clash, as well as (optionally) to avoid final stress. As shown by (18bii) and (18cii), optional alternative metrifications of (18bi) and (18ci), the syllabic trochee allows for a monosyllabic foot consisting of a single heavy syllable.

(18) *Finnish (Carlson 1978): syllabic trochees with variable quantity-sensitivity*

- Primary stress is initial.

- Secondary stress is variable, partly depending on syllable quantity, where closed syllables count as heavy.

(a) ('σσ) L   'pe.ri.jæ   'inheritor' (nom.)
(b) (i)   ('σσ) H   'ku.nin.gɑs   'king' (nom.)
     (ii) ('σσ) (ˌH)   'ku.nin.ˌgɑs
(c) (i)   ('σσ) (ˌσσ)   'ra.vin.ˌto.lɑt   'restaurants' (nom.)
     (ii) ('σσ) L (ˌH)   'ra.vin.to.ˌlɑt

Taking into account similar foot minima in other syllabic trochee languages, Hayes (1995) proposes to redefine the licit forms of the syllabic trochee as (σ σ) or (H), the so-called *generalized trochee*. As a result, all three foot types share a definition of the degenerate foot as a single light syllable (L).

9.2.3.2 Moraic trochees

The moraic trochee captures the idea that a single heavy syllable is quantitatively and metrically equivalent to two light syllables (Allen 1973; Halle & Vergnaud 1978; McCarthy 1979a; Prince 1983). It is exemplified by the pattern of Cairene Arabic (19), in particular the stressing of classical Arabic words in this dialect (Mitchell 1960). The foot bracketing is due to Hayes (1995).

(19)   *Cairene Arabic (Mitchell 1960): moraic trochees from left to right*

- Stress falls on the penult or antepenult, whichever is separated by an even number of syllables from the rightmost nonfinal heavy syllable or, if there is no heavy syllable, from the left edge of the word.
- Secondary stresses are phonetically covert.

(a)	(ˌLL) (ˈLL) L	ˌʃa.d͡ʒa.ˈra.tu.hu	'his tree'
(b)	(ˌLL) (ˌLL) (ˈLL)	ˌʃa.d͡ʒa.ˌra.tu.ˈhu.ma(a)	'their (dual) tree'
(c)	(ˌH) (ˌLL) (ˈLL)	ˌʔad.wi.ja.ˈtu.hu	'his drugs'
(d)	(ˌH) (ˌLL) (ˈLL) L	ˌʔad.wi.ja.ˈtu.hu.ma(a)	'their (dual) drugs'

The analysis brackets together pairs of moras into feet, going from left to right through the word. Note that heavy syllables cannot be split between feet. Also note that a licit bimoraic trochee cannot consist entirely of a single light syllable – hence the lack of final stress in (19a) and (19d). The theory restricts quantity-sensitive trochees to (LL) quantitatively balanced 'even' trochees, ruling out (HL) 'uneven' trochees.

Hayes (1995) observes that crucial distributional rhythmic evidence for the even trochee comes from rightward metrification, in particular from the parsing of a heavy syllable which is immediately followed by a string of light syllables. Even bimoraic trochees (H), (LL) predict the parsing in (20a), with a clash, while 'uneven' trochees (H), (HL), (LL) predict the rhythmically alternating (20b).

(20)   *left-to-right parsing*

    (a) even trochee   → (ˌH) (ˌLL) (ˈLL)   (ʔad).(wi.ja).(ˈtu.hu) 'his drugs'
    (b) uneven trochees → (ˌHL) (ˈLL) L   *(ʔad.wi).(ˈja.tu).hu

This context thus allows differentiation between an 'even' and 'uneven' parsing mode. On the basis of examples such as (20) from Cairene Arabic, Hayes rejects uneven trochees in favour of even trochees. Leftward moraic trochees could not, however, offer direct distributional evidence for the even trochee, since the even trochaic parsing ← (ˌH) L (ˌLL) (ˈLL) is, qua stress distribution, indistinguishable from the uneven parsing ← (ˌHL) (ˌLL) (ˈLL).

Unambiguous examples of right-to-left moraic trochees are rather difficult to obtain. Hayes (1995) analyzes languages such as Maithili (21) in this way.

(21)   *Maithili (Jha 1958): leftward moraic trochees*

(a)	(ˌLL) (ˈH) L	ˌa.dʰə.ˈlaːhə	'bad'
(b)	(ˌLL) (ˈLL)	ˌdʰa.nə.ˈhɒ.rə	(no gloss)
(c)	(ˌLL) (ˈH)	ˌpɑ.ʈə.ˈhiː	'thin'

(d) (‚H) (ꞌH) L   ‚de.ꞌkʰɑː.rə   ꞌseenꞌ
(e) (ꞌH) (‚LL)   ꞌgɑː.‚bʰi.nə   ꞌpregnantꞌ
(f) (ꞌH) (‚H)   ꞌsɑː.‚ɹiː   ꞌwomanꞌs garment or clothꞌ

Hayesꞌ argument for the even trochee in Maithili is indirect, and depends on the placement of primary stress in (21e–f). This involves *foot extrametricality*, a device rendering the final foot ineligible for primary stress placement. In Hayesꞌ analysis, foot extrametricality is triggered by a clash between the final footꞌs head syllable and the preceding syllable. Moreover, only absolutely final feet can ever be extrametrical, due to the *Peripherality Condition* on extrametricality (Harris 1983). If (HL) were a licit foot, forms such as (21d) would be wrongly predicted to undergo foot extrametricality, resulting in an initial primary stress [(ꞌH) (‚HL)]. Assuming the even parsing [(‚H) (ꞌH)L], the Peripherality Condition correctly blocks extrametricality.

9.2.3.3 Iambs

Iambs are exemplified by Hixkaryana, where foot structure is apparent from the lengthening of vowels in alternating open syllables. Word-final syllables are never lengthened, and can be assumed to remain unfooted. Hixkaryana (22) matches Cairene Arabic in having a rightward metrification. No primary–secondary stress difference is reported, so all stresses are marked with the primary stress symbol.

(22) *Hixkaryana (Derbyshire 1979): iambs from left to right*

- Stress falls on heavy syllables and on even-numbered non-final syllables in strings of open syllables. Stressed open syllables are rhythmically lengthened.

(a) /LLL/   → (LꞌH) L   to.ꞌroː.no   ꞌsmall birdꞌ
(b) /LLLL/   → (LꞌH) L L   a.ꞌtʃoː.wo.wo   ꞌwindꞌ
(c) /LLLLL/   → (LꞌH) (LꞌH) L   ne.ꞌmoː.ko.ꞌtoː.no   ꞌit fellꞌ
(d) /LLHL/   → (LꞌH) (ꞌH) L   kʰa.ꞌnaː.ꞌnih.no   ꞌI taught youꞌ
(e) /HLLL/   → (ꞌH) (LꞌH) L   ꞌak.ma.ꞌtaː.ri   ꞌbranchꞌ
(f) /HLLLL/   → (ꞌH) (LꞌH) L L   ꞌtoh.ku.ꞌrʲeː.ho.na   ꞌto Tohkuryeꞌ
(g) /HLLLLLLL/   → (ꞌH)(LꞌH)(LꞌH)(LꞌH)L ꞌtoh.ku.ꞌrʲeː.ho.ꞌnaː.ha.ꞌʃaː.ha ꞌfinally to Tohkuryeꞌ

The analysis features extrametricality of final syllables, which is highly common in iambic languages.

The iamb is not restricted to languages that have a weight distinction, as Araucanian shows (23).

(23) *Araucanian (Echeverría & Contreras 1965): iambs from left to right*

(a) (σꞌσ)   wu.ꞌle   ꞌtomorrowꞌ
(b) (σꞌσ) σ   ti.ꞌpan.to   ꞌyearꞌ
(c) (σꞌσ) (σ‚σ)   e.ꞌlu.mu.‚ju   ꞌgive usꞌ
(d) (σꞌσ) (σ‚σ) σ   e.ꞌlu.a.‚e.new   ꞌhe will give meꞌ
(e) (σꞌσ) (σ‚σ) (σ‚σ)   ki.ꞌmu.fa.‚lu.wu.‚laj   ꞌhe pretended not to knowꞌ

Hayes (1995) maintains that languages of this type, which have no syllable weight contrast, nor iambic lengthening, do not counter-exemplify the foot inventory. See Kager (1993) for further discussion.

Hixkaryana and Araucanian exemplify rightward metrification. The uneven parsing → (L'L) (L'L) (L'H) suits the uneven iamb, though not exclusively, since even iambs would predict the same stress distribution → (L'L) (L'L) L ('H). To test the prediction about the iamb's uneven shape, a quantity-sensitive case is needed with leftward metrification. Unfortunately, the leftward quantity-sensitive iamb is notoriously rare, the best known case being Tübatulabal (24).

(24) *Tübatulabal (Voegelin 1935): leftward iambs, degenerate feet allowed*

    (a) (L'L) (L'L)   wi.'taŋ.ha.'tal   'the Tejon Indians'
    (b) ('L) (L'L) (L'H) (L'L) 'wi.taŋ.'ha.ta.'laː.ba.'cu 'away from the Tejon Indians'
    (c) (L'H) ('L)   ha.'niː.'la   'the house' (obj.)
    (d) ('H) ('L) (L'H)   'taː.'ha.wi.'laːp   'in the summer'
    (e) ('L) (L'H) ('L) (L'L) 'a.na.'ŋiː.'ni.ni.'mut 'he is crying wherever he goes' (distr.)

The parsing has degenerate feet, just like leftward quantity-insensitive iambic languages, such as Weri (25). ([ľ] is described as a 'vibrant alveolar' by Boxwell & Boxwell 1966).

(25) *Weri (Boxwell & Boxwell 1966): leftward iambs, degenerate feet allowed*

    (a) (L'L)   ŋɪn.'tɪp   'bee'
    (b) (ˌL) (L'L)   ˌkʊ.ľɪ.'pʊ   'hair of arm'
    (c) (LˌL) (L'L)   ʊ.ˌlʊ.a.'mɪt   'mist'
    (d) (ˌL) (LˌL) (L'L)   ˌa.kʊ.ne.te'paľ   'times'
    (e) (LˌL) (LˌL) (L'L)   lɪ.ˌlɪ.ŋe.ˌwe.ľɪ.'aľ   'two ladders'
    (f) (ˌL) (LˌL) (LˌL) (L'L) ˌmoľ.mo.ˌľa.i.ˌmen.tɪ.'aľ 'two tomatoes'

That is, no languages are attested which have the same stress patterns as Tübatulabal and Weri, except that degenerate feet are disallowed. Here, the initial stress would be missing in odd-numbered forms, resulting in an initial lapse. The strong correlation between direction of parsing and minimum foot size in right-to-left iambic languages goes unexplained by current foot-based metrical theories. The iambic asymmetry is among the major theoretical issues in metrical phonology.

9.2.3.4 Alternative foot inventories

Alternative foot inventories have been proposed, which depart from asymmetric foot theory in more or less radical ways. Kager (1993), remaining otherwise close to the rhythmic assumptions of asymmetric theory, assumes a strictly binary foot inventory, including a bimoraic iamb. Arguments for the uneven trochees occur in Jacobs (1990, 2000), Rice (1992), van der Hulst & Klamer (1996), and Mellander (2001, 2004). Halle & Vergnaud (1987), Halle (1990), Halle & Kenstowicz (1991), Idsardi (1992), and Halle & Idsardi (1995) assume a symmetrical foot inventory in which grid elements and metrical brackets can be independently manipulated. 'Resolved' feet with branching heads are proposed by Dresher & Lahiri (1991) and Lahiri & Dresher (1999). Some theories allow overlapping foot constituents (Crowhurst & Hewitt 1995, Hyde 2002).

9.3   Metrification in Optimality Theory

This section presents an Optimality-Theoretic analysis (Prince & Smolensky 2004, McCarthy & Prince 1993a, b) of the preliminary metrical typology developed in Section 9.2. The discussion proceeds from binary quantity-insensitive systems to ternary systems, quantity-sensitive systems, and unbounded systems.

9.3.1   Binary quantity-insensitive systems

A binary system is one in which stressed and unstressed syllables alternate by binary intervals, so that all odd-numbered or even-numbered syllables, counting from the left edge or right edge of the word, are stressed. We start our survey with rhythmic patterns which involve light syllables only. Examples come from languages which lack syllable weight distinctions, as well as, occasionally, from languages which have such a distinction. In the typologically most common case, feet must be strictly binary and fall into a single sweep of metrification: such *uni-directional* patterns start from one edge, usually the left, and run to the opposite edge (9.3.1). The main departure from strict binarity concerns systems in which feet are allowed to be unary under duress (9.3.2); a departure from uni-directionality concerns systems in which metrification is *bi-directional*, being oriented toward both word edges (9.3.3).

We start by observing that foot type (trochee or iamb) will be selected by the relative ranking of two constraints, FTTYPE=TROCHEE and FTTYPE=IAMB, which determine the side of the head within a foot. Their ranking with respect to other stress constraints is of little importance, and for this reason, we leave these constraints out of consideration. Binary rhythm is enforced by two constraints. The first requires all syllables in a Prosodic Word to be parsed by feet, while the second imposes binarity on feet, excluding feet falling below the threshold (unary, degenerate feet) or above it (unbounded feet).

(26)   PARSE-SYL
       Syllables are parsed by feet.
(27)   FT-BIN
       Feet are binary under moraic or syllabic analysis.

While in words composed of an even number of syllables both constraints can be naturally met by an exhaustive parse, these constraints conflict in words that contain an odd number of syllables. In strictly binary patterns, such as Pintupi (28), unary feet are disallowed by top-ranked FT-BIN. However, this is achieved at the expense of exhaustive parsing, since any word with an odd number of syllables will contain an unfooted syllable, even when parsing is otherwise maximally tight.

(28) *Strictly binary feet (Pintupi):* FT-BIN » PARSE-SYL

/σ σ σ σ σ/	FT-BIN	PARSE-SYL
(a) (σ σ) (σ σ) (σ)	*!	
☞ (b) (σ σ) (σ σ) σ		*
(c) (σ σ) σ σ σ		* *!*

In alternating patterns which allow degenerate feet, as in candidate (28a), the ranking is reversed, as shown in Section 9.3.2.

Although the relative ranking of FT-BIN and PARSE-SYL determines whether feet are binary, the direction of parsing still needs to be settled. The classical OT analysis of directional metrification is based on a pair of foot alignment constraints, ALL-FT-LEFT and ALL-FT-RIGHT (McCarthy & Prince 1993a). For every foot, these constraints calculate the distance, *gradiently* expressed in syllables, between its left (right) edge and the left (right) edge of the word.

(29) *ALL-FT-LEFT*
       Align (Ft, L, PrWd, L)   "Every foot stands at the left edge of the PrWd."

(30) *ALL-FT-RIGHT*
       Align (Ft, R, PrWd, R)   "Every foot stands at the right edge of the PrWd."

The total number of violation marks equals the sum of all individual violations by feet. Consequently, when ALL-FT-L or ALL-FT-R is undominated, only one foot, standing at the absolute edge of the word, is allowed. The reverse ranking, with PARSE-SYL dominating ALL-FT-X (where X stands for either 'left' or 'right'), is required for alternating stress systems such as Pintupi and Murinbata.

(31) *Mini-typology: single foot versus multiple feet*

       (a) single foot systems: FT-BIN, ALL-FT-X » PARSE-SYL
       (b) alternating systems: FT-BIN » PARSE-SYL » ALL-FT-X

The analysis of Pintupi (32), with alternating stresses on non-final odd-numbered syllables, shows minimal violation effects of foot alignment, and the resulting left-to-right foot distribution:

(32) *Left-to-right binary feet in Pintupi*
       FT-BIN » PARSE-SYL » ALL-FT-L » ALL-FT-R

/ puliŋkalatʲu /	FT-BIN	PARSE-SYL	ALLFTL	ALLFTR
☞ (a) ('pu.liŋ).(ˌka.la).tʲu		*	**	*, ***
(b) ('pu.liŋ).ka.(ˌla.tʲu)		*	***!	***
(c) pu.('liŋ.ka).(ˌla.tʲu)		*	*, **!*	**
(d) ('pu.liŋ).ka.la.tʲu		**!*		***
(e) ('pu.liŋ).(ˌka.la).(ˌtʲu)	*!		**, ****	*, ***

Violation of ALL-FT-L is assessed gradiently: a violation mark is incurred for every syllable occurring between the left edge of a foot and the left edge of the word; for each candidate, violation marks for individual feet are summed. Violations are separated by commas above to make it easier to see which feet are responsible for which violations. The same syllable can be the cause of several violations – one for every foot it appears before. Candidate (32a) incurs a smaller number of marks than its closest competitor (32b), reflecting the minimal difference in the position of the rightmost feet. Since ALL-FT-L pulls all feet towards the left edge of the word, the unparsed syllable ends up in word-final position.

9.3.2 Mixed binary + unary systems

A departure from strict foot binarity resides in systems which allow degenerate feet (33).

(33) *Murinbata (Street & Mollinjin 1981): rightward trochees, degenerate feet allowed*

    (a) (′σσ)   ′mam.ŋe   'I/he/she said/did to her'
    (b) (′σσ)(ˌσ)   ′la.la.ˌma   'shoulder'
    (c) (′σσ)(ˌσσ)   ′wa.lʊ.ˌmʊ.ma   'blue-tongue lizard'
    (d) (′σσ)(ˌσσ)(ˌσ) ′pʰɛ.rɛ.ˌwɛ.rɛ.ˌtʲɛn 'season just before the "dry"'
    (e) (′σσ)(ˌσσ)(ˌσσ) ′ŋa.ram.ˌka.rʊ].ˌɲi.me 'we (excl.pc.f.) arrived'

By reversing the ranking of (28), exhaustive parsing is achieved at the expense of binarity, making (34a) the winning candidate.

(34) *Binary plus unary feet (Murinbata):* FT-BIN » PARSE-SYL

/σ σ σ σ σ/	PARSE-SYL	FT-BIN
☞ (a) (σ σ) (σ σ) (σ)		*
(b) (σ σ) (σ σ) σ	*!	
(c) (σ σ) σ σ σ	*!**	

Turning to the direction of metrification, we meet with a slight surprise. Both Pintupi and Murinbata have rightward metrification; however, as compared to Pintupi, Murinbata (35) requires the reverse ranking ALL-FT-R » ALL-FT-L (Green & Kenstowicz 1995).

(35) *Left-to-right mixed binary-plus-unary feet in Murinbata*
    PARSE-SYL » FT-BIN » ALL-FT-R » ALL-FT-L

/ pʰɛrɛwɛrɛtʲɛn /	PARSE-SYL	FT-BIN	ALL-FT-R	ALL-FT-L
☞ (a) (′pʰɛ.rɛ).(ˌwɛ.rɛ).(ˌtʲɛn)		*	*, ***	**, ****
(b) (′pʰɛ.rɛ).(ˌwɛ).(ˌrɛ.tʲɛn)		*	**, ***!	**, ***
(c) (′pʰɛ).(ˌrɛ.wɛ).(ˌrɛ.tʲɛn)		*	**, ***!*	*, ***

The leftward trochaic counterpart of Murinbata, with clash between the first two feet (35c), occurs in Biangai (Dubert & Dubert 1973). Iambic systems which allow degenerate feet also occur. The leftward iambic pattern was already exemplified by Weri (25). A case of rightward iambs, with a clash in odd-numbered forms, is exemplified by Ojibwa (36).

(36)   *Ojibwa (Kaye 1973, Piggott 1980): rightward iambs, degenerate feet allowed*

    (a)   (σ'σ) (ˌσ)   na.ˈga.ˌmo   'he sings'
    (b)   (σ'σ) (σˌσ)   ni.ˈbi.mo.ˌse   'I walk'
    (c)   (σ'σ) (σˌσ) (ˌσ)   ni.ˈna.ga.ˌmo.ˌmin   'we sing'

By varying three factors, namely foot type (trochee versus iamb), directionality (rightward versus leftward), and tolerance of degenerate feet, gradient foot alignment theory, like Hayes' (1995) rule-based framework, predicts eight uni-directional systems, which are tabulated below. The numbers of languages are taken from Gordon's (2002a) survey of quantity-insensitive stress languages.

(37)   *Overview of uni-directional systems*

	trochees (45 languages)		iambs (9 languages)	
	left-to-right (32 lgs)	right-to-left (13 lgs)	left-to-right (4 lgs)	right-to-left (5 lgs)
strictly binary feet (29 lgs)	('σ σ) (ˌσ σ) ('σ σ) (ˌσ σ) σ̲ Pintupi (final lapse) 14 languages	(ˌσ σ) ('σ σ) σ (ˌσ σ) ('σ σ) Warao (perfect grid) 12 languages	(σ'σ) (σˌσ) (σ 'σ) (σˌσ) σ Araucanian (perfect grid) 3 languages	(σˌσ) (σ 'σ) σ̲ (σ̲ ˌσ) (σ 'σ) *unattested* (initial lapse)
mixed binary + unary feet (25 lgs)	('σ σ) (ˌσ σ) ('σ σ) (ˌσ σ) (ˌσ) Murinbata (perfect grid) 18 languages	(ˌσ σ) ('σ σ) (ˌσ̲)(ˌσ̲ σ) ('σ σ) Biangai (initial clash) 1 language	(σ'σ) (σˌσ) (σ'σ) (σˌσ̲) (ˌσ̲) Ojibwa (final clash) 1 language	(σˌσ) (σ 'σ) (ˌσ) (σ ˌσ) (σ 'σ) Weri (perfect grid) 5 languages

Considered from a purely rhythmic viewpoint, this set of uni-directional patterns displays interesting properties. Exactly four patterns (38 languages) display perfect rhythmic alternation, allowing neither clash nor lapse. These 'perfect-grid' (PG) patterns are seen in Murinbata, Warao, Araucanian and Weri. The remaining patterns (16 languages) minimally deviate from rhythmic perfection, allowing small deviations in peripheral contexts, in particular a lapse in final position (Pintupi), or a clash between two secondary stresses at the left edge (Biangai) or at the right edge (Ojibwa). One predicted system, with strictly binary iambs going from right to left, remains unattested. This would involve a lapse on the initial syllables of odd-numbered forms, e.g. [σ (σˌσ) (σ'σ)]. Apparently, no languages occur that minimally deviate from the Perfect Grid by initial lapse. (See Section 9.3.5 for further discussion.)

All systems analysed thus far placed the primary stress on the foot at the edge where the iteration started. The position of the primary stress is governed by a pair of antagonistic alignment constraints, ALIGN-HEAD-L and ALIGN-HEAD-R.

(38) *ALIGN-HEAD-L*
      Align (PrWd, L, Head/PrWd, L)   "The PrWd begins with the primary stress foot."

(39) *ALIGN-HEAD-R*
      Align (PrWd, R, Head/PrWd, R)   "The PrWd ends with the primary stress foot."

When undominated, ALIGN-HEAD produces primary stress on a foot which is strictly initial or final in PrWd. More interesting are its effects under domination by a foot alignment constraint favouring the opposite edge, when the primary stress comes to lodge on the first or last of a sequence of feet. This places the primary stress on the foot at the opposite edge from where the iteration started. This occurs in languages such as Cairene Arabic (40), where word stress falls on the rightmost foot of a sequence that is laid down by a left-to-right metrification.

(40) *Word-stress-at-opposite-edge in Cairene Arabic*
      FT-BIN » PARSE-SYL » ALL-FT-L » ALL-FT-R

/ʃa.ja.ra.tu.hu/	FT-BIN	PARSE-SYL	ALL-FT-L	ALIGN-HEAD-R
☞ (a) (ˌʃa.ja).('ra.tu).hu		*	**	*
(b) (ˌʃa.ja).ra.('tu.hu)		*	***!	

An iambic counterpart of Cairene Arabic is Creek (Haas 1977, Hayes 1995).

9.3.3 Bidirectional systems

Thus far we have seen patterns that are laid down by a single sweep of metrification. Another, more complex kind of alternating pattern has a single foot fixed at one edge while remaining feet depart from the opposite edge. For strictly binary trochees, bi-directional patterns occur in Garawa (41) and Piro (42).

(41) *Garawa (Furby 1974): binary trochees; fixed foot at left edge plus alternating feet right to left*

(a) ('σσ)   'ja.mi   'eye'
(b) ('σσ) σ   'pun.ja.ḷa   'white'
(c) ('σσ) (ˌσσ)   'wa.cim.ˌpa.ŋu   'armpit'
(d) ('σσ) σ (ˌσσ)   'ka.ma.ḷa.ˌṛi.ɲi   'wrist'
(e) ('σσ) (ˌσσ) (ˌσσ)   'ja.ka.ˌla.ka.ˌlam.pa   'loose'
(f) ('σσ) σ (ˌσσ) (ˌσσ)   'ŋan.ki.ṛi.ˌki.rim.ˌpa.ji   'fought with boomerangs'

(g) ('σσ) σ (ˌσσ) (ˌσσ) (ˌσσ) 'na.ri.ŋin.ˌmu.ku.ˌɲi.na.ˌmi.ra 'at your own many'

(42) *Piro (Matteson 1965): binary trochees; fixed foot at right edge plus alternating feet left to right*

(a) ('σσ)	'wa.lo	'rabbit'
(b) σ ('σσ)	ru.'txi.txa	'he observes taboo'
(c) (ˌσσ) ('σσ)	ˌtʃi.ja.'ha.ta	'he cries'
(d) (ˌσσ) σ ('σσ)	ˌsa.lwa.je.'hka.kna	'they visit each other'
(e) (ˌσσ) (ˌσσ) ('σσ)	ˌpe.tʃi.ˌtʃʰi.ma.'tlo.na	'they say they stalk it'
(f) (ˌσσ) (ˌσσ) σ ('σσ)	ˌru.slu.ˌno.ti.ni.'tka.na	'their voices already changed'
(g) (ˌσσ) (ˌσσ) (ˌσσ) ('σσ)	ˌsa.ple.ˌwhi.ma.ˌmta.na.'tka.na	'they say he went along screaming again'
(h) (ˌσσ) (ˌσσ) (ˌσσ) σ ('σσ)	ˌka.xru.ˌka.kʰi.ˌma.nma.ta.'tka.na	'they were joking together then, it is said'

The fixed foot requires word-to-foot alignment, requiring that every PrWd begins or ends with a foot, as captured by the constraint pair below:

(43) ALIGN (PRWD, LEFT)
      Align (PrWd, L, Ft, L)   "Every PrWd begins with a foot."

(44) ALIGN-PRWD-RIGHT
      Align (PrWd, R, Ft, R)   "Every PrWd ends in a foot."

Tableau (45) illustrates the interaction of alignment constraints and PARSE-SYL for Garawa. In the interests of brevity, violations for ALL-FT-R and ALL-FT-L are expressed as numbers; "2, 5" means that one of the feet incurred two violations while another incurred five, to make a total of 7 violations of the constraint.

(45) *Bidirectional rhythm in Garawa*
      ALIGN-PRWD-L » PARSE-SYL » ALL-FT-R » ALL-FT-L

Input: /'ŋankiɾikirimpaji/	ALIGN-PRWD-L	PARSE-SYL	ALL-FT-R	ALL-FT-L
☞ (a) ('ŋan.ki).ɾi.(ˌki.rim)(ˌpa.ji)		*	2, 5	3, 5
(b) ('ŋan.ki).(ɾi.ki).(ˌrim.pa).ji		*	1, 3, 5!	2, 4
(c) ('ŋan.ki).ɾi.ki.rim.(ˌpa.ji)		**!*	5	5
(d) ŋan.('ki.ɾi).(ˌki.rim).(ˌpa.ji)	*!	*	2, 4	1, 3, 5

Bidirectional patterns which allow degenerate feet are rare. One trochaic case is Gosiute Shoshone (Miller 1996; as referred to by Gordon 2002a), which has a fixed secondary stress on the final syllable, and alternating stress on odd-numbered syllables. Two iambic cases are Tauya (MacDonald 1990) and Southern Paiute (Sapir 1930).

A factorial typology of systems with strictly binary feet arises when the ranking of foot alignment ALL-FT-X (with X being either Left or Right) is varied with respect to ALIGN-PRWD-X and PARSE-SYL. (FT-BIN remains undominated throughout the typology).

(46)   *Iterative binary systems*

(a) single foot systems:

          FT-BIN, ALIGN-PRWD-X, ALL-FT-X » PARSE-SYL

(b) unidirectional binary systems:

          FT-BIN, ALIGN-PRWD-X » PARSE-SYL » ALL-FT-X

(c) bidirectional binary systems:

          FT-BIN, ALIGN-PRWD-X » PARSE-SYL » ALL-FT-Y

Depending on the ranking of ALIGN-HEAD-X with respect to ALL-FT-X, systems have primary stress on the same side (as in Pintupi) or on the opposite side (as in Cairene Arabic).

Many languages impose the requirement that the final syllable must be *unstressed*: the PrWd must not end in a stressed syllable. In strictly binary trochaic systems, such as Pintupi, high-ranked FT-BIN already guarantees final non-stressability, but iambic systems need a special constraint to that effect. A stronger kind of nonfinality is the requirement that final syllables be *unfooted*: the PrWd must not end in a foot. (See again the Hixkaryana pattern in (22)). Both requirements are combined in Prince & Smolensky's version of NONFINALITY:

(47)   *NONFINALITY*

No prosodic head is final in PrWd.

This is the OT counterpart of 'extrametricality' in rule-based theory. The difference is, of course, that OT constraints are violable. NONFINALITY can give in to avoid violation of higher-ranking constraints, such as those enforcing quantity-sensitivity (see example under unbounded systems below) or minimal word requirements (see Section 9.4.2). For further discussion of NONFINALITY, see Hung (1994), Kager (1999a), and Hyde (2002).

9.3.4   Ternary systems

Thus far we have seen rhythmic patterns which were based on binary alternation, albeit occasionally obscured by clashes or lapses. Other languages have a 'ternary' style of alternation, where stresses fall on every third syllable, separated by two weak syllables. Ternary rhythmic patterns are exemplified by Cayuvava (48), where stresses fall on every third syllable, starting at the right edge.

(48)   *Cayuvava (Key 1961): antepenultimate syllable, leftward ternary rhythm*

(a) ('σσ)	'da.pa	'canoe'
(b) ('σσ)σ	'to.mo.ho	'small water container'
(c) σ('σσ)σ	a.'ri.po.ro	'he already turned around'
(d) σσ('σσ)σ	a.ri.'pi.ri.to	'already planted'
(e) (,σσ)σ('σσ)σ	,a.ri.hi.'hi.be.e	'I have already put the top on'
(f) σ(,σσ)σ('σσ)σ	ma.,ra.ha.ha.'e.i.ki	'their blankets'
(g) σσ(,σσ)σ('σσ)σ	i.ki.,ta.pa.re.'re.pe.ha	'the water is clean'
(h) (,σσ)σ(,σσ)σ('σσ)σ	,tʃa.a.di.,ro.bo.βu.'ru.ru.tʃe	'ninety-nine (first digit)'

Elenbaas & Kager (1999) extend the gradient foot alignment analysis to ternary rhythm. Their analysis incorporates the insight from Ishii (1996) that ternarity arises from the interaction of gradient alignment constraints (ALL-FT-X) and an anti-lapse constraint. However, Kager & Elenbaas deviate from Ishii (1996) in employing a grid-based anti-lapse constraint, instead of a foot-based one. Kager & Elenbaas refer to this constraint as *LAPSE, but we will rename it as:

(49) *LONG-LAPSE
      A weak beat must be adjacent to a strong beat or the word edge.

This constraint effectively bans sequences of three or more unstressed syllables (Gordon 2002a). With it ranked above ALL-FT-X, ternary rhythms are produced.

(50) *Ranking for ternarity*

      *LONG-LAPSE » ALL-FT-X » PARSE-SYL

Undominated *LONG-LAPSE restricts the maximal distance between stresses to two. The sub-ranking ALL-FT-X » PARSE-SYL, known from (46a), reduces the number of feet to the bare minimum needed to avoid long lapses. The result is a perfect ternary alternation. An example from Cayuvava (51) shows the activity of *LONG-LAPSE for a six-syllable word. (FT-BIN is assumed to be undominated.)

(51) *Ternarity in Cayuvava: words of length 3n*

/arihihibee/	*LONG-LAPSE	ALL-FT-L	ALL-FT-R	PARSE-SYL
(a) ('a.ri).hi.hi.be.e	*!**		4	****
(b) a.ri.hi.('hi.be).e	*!	3	1	****
☞ (c) (,a.ri).hi.('hi.be).e		3	1,4	**
(d) (,a.ri).(,hi.hi).('be.e)		2,4!	2,4	

A seven-syllable word shows how gradient alignment functions not only to reduce the number of feet, see (52e), but also to place the feet, compare (52c–d).

(52) *Cayuvava: words of length 3n+1*

/marahahaeiki/	*LONG-LAPSE	ALL-FT-L	ALL-FT-R	PARSE-SYL
(a) (,ma.ra).ha.ha.('e.i).ki	*!	4	1, 5	***
(b) (,ma.ra).ha.('ha.e).i.ki	*!	3	2, 5	***
☞ (c) ma.(,ra.ha).ha.('e.i).ki		1, 4	1, 4	***
(d) ma.ra.(,ha.ha).e.('i.ki)		2, 5!	3	***
(e) (,ma.ra).(,ha.ha).('e.i).ki		2, 4!	1, 3, 5	*

An eight-syllable word shows interaction between two gradient alignment constraints. Two candidates tie (53b–c) on the highest-ranking alignment constraint, so that the lower-ranking constraint steps in.

(53)   *Cayuvava: words of length 3n+2*

/ ikitaparerepeha /	*Long-Lapse	All-Ft-L	All-Ft-R	Parse-Syl
(a) i.(ˌki.ta).pa.('re.re).pe.ha	*!	1, 4	2, 5	****
☞ (b) i.ki.(ˌta.pa).re.('re.pe).ha		2, 5	1, 4	****
(c) (ˌi.ki).(ˌta.pa).re.('re.pe).ha		2, 5	1, 4, 6!	**
(d) (ˌi.ki).ta.(ˌpa.re).re.('pe.ha)		3, 6!	3, 6	**
(e) (ˌi.ki).(ˌta.pa).(ˌre.re).('pe.ha)		2, 4, 6!	2, 4, 6	

The interaction of two antagonistic alignment constraints is a typical feature of the OT analysis.

A mini-typology shows skeletal rankings for single foot, binary, and ternary systems.

(54)   *Mini-typology*

(a) single foot   : All-Ft-X » *Long-Lapse , Parse-Syl
(b) binary rhythm : *Long-Lapse , Parse-Syl » All-Ft-X
(c) ternary rhythm : *Long-Lapse » All-Ft-X » Parse-Syl

9.3.5 Quantity-sensitive systems

We now turn to stress systems which involve sensitivity to syllable weight. As compared to strings of light syllables only, mixed strings of light and heavy syllables are naturally subject to a larger set of stress-affecting factors, such as stress attraction by heavy syllables, repulsion of stress by light syllables, and stress-induced lengthening and shortening. Consequently, the typology becomes more complicated. We will focus on relatively straightforward patterns of moraic trochees and iambs, examples of which occur in Section 9.2.3, while leaving out of consideration more subtle effects of quantity-sensitivity. (See Alber 1997, Kager 1999a, Elenbaas 1999.)

Quantity-sensitivity is enforced mainly by the Weight-to-Stress Principle:

(55)   *Weight-to-Stress Principle (WSP)*
       Heavy syllables must be stressed. (If heavy, then stressed.)

This constraint is violated by any heavy syllable that is not prominent, either within or outside a foot. Hence, it expresses the conditional 'if heavy then stressed'. This is illustrated by Tübatulabal (56; see 24).

(56) *Right-to-left iambs in Tübatulabal*
WSP, Parse-Syl » All-Ft-L » Ft-Bin

/ hani:la /	WSP	Parse-Syl	All-Ft-L	Ft-Bin
☞ (a) (ha.'ni:).('la)			**	*
(b) (ha.'ni:).la		*!		
(c) ('ha).(ni:.'la)	*!		*	*

The power of gradient foot alignment is illustrated by example (57), which motivates the ranking All-Ft-L » Ft-Bin:

(57) Tübatulabal: *Even string of light syllables between the left edge and a heavy syllable*

/ witaŋhatala:bacu /	WSP	Parse-Syl	All-Ft-L	Ft-Bin
☞ (a) ('wi).(taŋ.'ha).(ta.'la:).(ba.'cu)			1, 3, 5	*
(b) (wi.'taŋ).(ha.'ta).('la:).(ba.'cu)			2, 4, 5!	

The reverse conditional, 'if stressed then heavy' is expressed by a gradient constraint, measuring degrees of syllable weight, indicated by |x|.

(58) *Peak Prominence (Pk-Prom)*
Peak(x) is more harmonic than Peak(y) if |x| > |y|.

This constraint correlates the size of a prominence peak (that is, the height of its grid column) with the quantity of the syllable which carries it. More concretely, it requires the tallest peak to lodge on the heaviest syllable. We will see applications below in unbounded stress systems.

9.3.6 Unbounded systems

Unbounded stress systems broadly fall into two classes: default-to-same-edge systems, exemplified by Western Cheremis in (5), and default-to-opposite-edge systems, as exemplified by Selkup in (4). The standard analysis (e.g. Prince & Smolensky 2004; Zoll 1996; Walker 1997; Baković 1998) is based on the interaction of alignment constraints, quantity-sensitivity constraints, and nonfinality constraints.

The analysis of default-to-same systems involves the core ranking Pk-Prom » Align-Head (59).

(59) *Default-to-same:* Pk-Prom » Align-Head

(a)

/H L H/	Pk-Prom	Align-Head-R
☞ (a) H L'H		
(b) H 'L H	*!	σ
(c) 'H L H		σ!σ

(b)

/L L L/	Pk-Prom	Align-Head-R
☞ (a) L L 'L	*	
(b) L 'L L	*	σ!
(c) 'L L L	*	σ!σ

In default-to-same systems, two types of nonfinality effects occur (Prince & Smolensky 2004; Walker 1997). First, nonfinality may hold for all final syllables, regardless of syllable weight. Such 'quantity-insensitive nonfinality' is found in Western Cheremis (60).

(60) *QI nonfinality (Western Cheremis):* NonFinality » Pk-Prom » Align-Head-R

(a)

HHL /oʃmaʃtə/	NonFinality	Pk-Prom	Align-Head-R
(a) oʃ.maʃ.'tə	*!	*	
☞ (b) oʃ.'maʃ.tə			σ
(c) 'oʃ.maʃ.tə			σσ!

(b)

LLH /əməltem/	NonFinality	Pk-Prom	Align-Head-R
(a) ə.məl.'tem	*!		
☞ (b) ə.'məl.tem		*	σ
(c) 'ə.məl.tem		*	σσ!

(c)

HLH /βaʃtəlam/	NonFinality	Pk-Prom	Align-Head-R
(a) βaʃ.tə.'lam	*!		
(b) βaʃ.'tə.lam		*!	σ
☞ (c) 'βaʃ.tə.lam			σσ

(d)

LLL /pərəʃəm/	NONFINALITY	PK-PROM	ALIGN-HEAD-R
(a) pə.rə.ˈʃəm	*!	*	
☞ (b) pə.ˈrə.ʃəm		*	σ
(c) ˈpə.rə.ʃəm		*	σσ!

Quantity-sensitive nonfinality is found in Sindhi (Khubchandani 1969, Walker 1997). If a word has only one heavy syllable (CVV, CVC), stress falls on it (61a, b). If a word has more than one heavy syllable, stress falls on the rightmost nonfinal heavy syllable (61c, d, e). In words composed of light syllables only, the penult is stressed (61f, g).

(61) *Sindhi: Quantity-sensitive non-finality*

(a) LH	ɗə.ˈgoː	'ox'
(b) HLL	ˈsəh.kə.ɳʊ	'to gasp'
(c) HLH	ˈoː.cɪ.toː	'sudden'
(d) HLLH	ˈmoː.kɪ.lɪ.ɳoː	'to be sent'
(e) HHH	kʰoː.ˈliːn.da	'they will open' (trans.)
(f) LL	ˈbʰɪ.tɪ	'wall'
(g) LLL	ʊ.ˈtʰə.lə	'inundation'

This is accounted for by re-ranking PK-PROM and NONFINALITY, so that stress falls on a final syllable if it is the only heavy syllable in the word (62).

(62) *QS nonfinality (Sindhi):* PK-PROM » NONFINALITY » ALIGN-HEAD-R

(a)

LH /ɗəgoː/	PK-PROM	NONFINALITY	ALIGN-HEAD-R
☞ (a) ɗə.ˈgoː		*	
(b) ˈɗə.goː	*!		σ

(b)

HLH /oːcɪtoː/	PK-PROM	NONFINALITY	ALIGN-HEAD-R
(a) oː.cɪ.ˈtoː		*!	
(b) oː.ˈcɪ.toː	*!		σ
☞ (c) ˈoː.cɪ.toː			σσ

(c)

LLL /ʊtʰələ/	PK-PROM	NONFINALITY	ALIGN-HEAD-R
(a) ʊ.tʰə.ˈlə	*	*!	
☞ (b) ʊ.ˈtʰə.lə	*		σ
(c) ˈʊ.tʰə.lə	*		σσ!

The analysis of default-to-opposite systems requires an additional constraint, which draws stress to the opposite edge of the word if there are no heavy syllables. This is a licensing constraint (Zoll 1996, Walker 1997), which bans stressed light syllables except in initial position.

(63)   ALIGN ('L, PrWd, L)
       A stressed light syllable ('L) must be PrWd-initial.

This constraint is illustrated in (64) for Selkup (Walker 1997):

(64)   *Default-to-same. Selkup: rightmost heavy, else initial*
       ALIGN ('L, PRWD, L) » ALIGN-HEAD-R

(a)

LHLH /qumo:qlɪlɪ:/	ALIGN('L, PRWD, L)	ALIGN-HEAD-R
☞ (a) qu.mo:.qlɪ.'lɪ:		
(b) qu.mo:.'qlɪ.lɪ:	*!	σ
(c) qu.'mo:.qlɪ.lɪ:		σ!σ
(d) 'qu.mo:.qlɪ.lɪ:		σ!σσ

(b)

LLH /pynakisə:/	ALIGN('L, PRWD, L)	ALIGN-HEAD-R
☞ (a) py.na.ki.'sə:		
(b) py.na.'ki.sə:	*!	σ
(c) py.'na.ki.sə:	*!	σσ
(d) 'py.na.ki.sə:		σ!σσ

(c)

LLLL /qolʲcimpati/	ALIGN('L, PRWD, L)	ALIGN-HEAD-R
(a) qolʲ.cim.pa.'ti	*!	
(b) qolʲ.cim.'pa.ti	*!	σ
(c) qolʲ.'cim.pa.ti	*!	σσ
☞ (d) 'qolʲ.cim.pa.ti		σσσ

The typology of default-to-opposite systems includes nonfinality effects, which will not be discussed.

Thus far, we have seen some virtues of rhythmic alignment constraints. However, the next section will expose certain problems for gradient alignment theory.

9.3.7   Revising classical alignment theory

Stress typology contains a well-known gap, already identified above: in strictly binary iambic systems, parsing is uniformly rightward (Kager 1993, 2001; Hayes 1995; McCarthy & Prince 1993b; Vijver 1998; Alber 2001; Hyde 2002). The classical theory, which assumes foot type (trochee or iamb) to be dissociated from foot distribution, predicts four strictly binary uni-directional patterns. Yet, only three patterns are attested, see

(37). This asymmetry cannot be attributed to a universal prohibition against leftward iambic parsing, since leftward iambs do in fact occur in languages such as Weri and Tübatulabal, which allow unary feet by the ranking PARSE-SYL » FT-BIN. In sum, an unexplained interdependence holds between foot type, foot binarity, and directionality of parsing. Kager (2001) observes that the missing pattern suffers from a rhythmic defect: it contains a *word-initial lapse*. Cross-linguistically, initial lapses are sharply disfavored, in contrast to final lapses, which widely occur in stress languages, for example in Pintupi. The lapse asymmetry is known from other rhythmic domains, in particular musical rhythm, where double upbeats are avoided (Lerdahl & Jackendoff 1983).

Kager proposes that parsing is controlled by local rhythmic configurations, rather than by gradient alignment. He introduces a set of *rhythmic licensing* constraints, which ban lapses everywhere except in one specific context. An example is in (65).

(65) LAPSE-AT-END
      Lapse must be adjacent to the right edge.

This constraint assigns one violation mark for each pair of unstressed syllables, except the final one. In a trochaic language like Pintupi, this attracts the unparsed syllable to the word end, giving the illusion of a directional, rightward parsing. ALL-FT-X is now dispensed with, while word-to-foot alignment is no longer gradient, and becomes categorical.

The factorial typology of the revised constraint set does not contain the iambic initial lapse pattern as this is 'harmonically bounded' (Samek-Lodovici & Prince 1999). If the violations of a candidate C_1 form a proper subset of those of another candidate C_2, then C_2 cannot be generated under any ranking of constraints in the set. The iambic initial lapse pattern (66b) is harmonically bounded by any iambic candidate which has the same number of feet, satisfies right-edge alignment, but in addition satisfies left-edge alignment.

(66) *Harmonic bounding of the initial lapse pattern*

/σ σ σ σ σ σ σ/	*LAPSE	LAPSE -AT-END	ALIGN -WD-L	ALIGN -WD-R
☞ (a) (σ'σ)σ̱(σ̱'σ)(σ'σ)	*	*		
(b) σ̱(σ'σ)(σ̱'σ)(σ'σ)	*	*	*!	

Although the initial lapse pattern (66b) is eliminated, the resulting iambic typology still contains a gap, since (66a), a bidirectional pattern, is also unattested. Nevertheless, the typology is more restrictive than the standard typology, which generates both gaps (66a–b).

In rhythmic licensing theory, the ranking in (67) produces the pattern of Pintupi:

(67) *Lapse-based analysis of Pintupi*

FT-BIN, ALIGN-WD-L, LAPSE-AT-END » PARSE-SYL, *LAPSE

/puliŋkalatʲu/	FT-BIN	ALIGN-WD-L	LAPSE-AT-END	PARSE-SYL	*LAPSE
☞ (a) (ˈpu.liŋ).(ˌka.la).tʲu				*	*
(b) (ˈpu.liŋ).ka.(ˌla.tʲu)			*!	*	*
(c) (ˈpu.liŋ).ka.la.tʲu			*!*	***	***
(d) pu.(ˈliŋ.ka).(ˌla.tʲu)		*!		*	
(e) (ˈpu.liŋ).(ˌka.la).(ˌtʲu)	*!				

Kager (2001) observes a second gap, which is more subtle, but equally puzzling as the iambic gap. In bidirectional systems, directional footing always starts from the edge opposite from the edge where the fixed foot lodges. This is shown for strictly binary trochaic systems in (68).

(68) *Overview of bidirectional trochaic systems with strictly binary feet*

	fixed foot right plus left-to-right	fixed foot left plus right-to-left
primary stress on fixed foot	(ˌσσ)(ˌσσ)(ˈσσ) (ˌσσ)(ˌσσ)σ(ˈσσ) Piro	(ˈσσ)(ˌσσ)(ˌσσ) (ˈσσ)σ(ˌσσ)(ˌσσ) Garawa
secondary stress on fixed foot	(ˈσσ)(ˌσσ)(ˌσσ) (ˈσσ)(ˌσσ)σ(ˌσσ) unattested	(ˌσσ)(ˌσσ)(ˈσσ) (ˌσσ)σ(ˌσσ)(ˈσσ) unattested

In the standard analysis, the edge specification of the fixed foot is independent of directionality of parsing, hence all four strictly binary bidirectional trochaic systems are predicted. These gaps cannot be attributed to a resulting mismatch between directionality of parsing and the End Rule (Hammond 1984, Hulst 1984), because languages exist that exhibit mismatches, such as Cairene Arabic. Nor can the gap be attributed to a mismatch between the edge of the fixed foot and the End Rule, since such mismatches occur in languages which allow unary feet, such as Southern Paiute. Why should there be interdependence between the edge of the fixed foot and the edge of the End Rule? Again, the restriction is stateable in terms of rhythmic targets: the lapse occurs immediately before the stress peak, as in Piro, or immediately after the peak, as in Garawa. This motivates another rhythmic licensing constraint.

(69) LAPSE-AT-PEAK
      Lapse must be adjacent to the peak.

As an example of a bidirectional system, consider the analysis of Garawa (70).

(70)   *Lapse-based analysis of Garawa*

ALIGN-WD-R, ALIGN-WD-L LAPSE-AT-PEAK » PARSE-SYL, LAPSE-AT-END

/'ŋankiɻikirimpaji/	ALIGN-WD-R	ALIGN-WD-L	LAPSE-AT-PEAK	PARSE-SYL	LAPSE-AT-END
☞ (a) ('ŋan.ki).ɻi.(ˌki.rim).(ˌpa.ji)				*	*
(b) ('ŋan.ki).(ˌɻi.ki).rim.(ˌpa.ji)			*!	*	*
(c) ('ŋan.ki).(ˌɻi.ki).(ˌrim.pa).ji	*!			*	

The unattested trochaic pattern (70b) is harmonically bounded by (70a). Consequences of the rhythmic licensing theory for quantity-sensitive systems need further investigation. (See Alber 2001 for some issues to be addressed.)

McCarthy (2003b) generalizes Kager's proposal to abandon gradient foot alignment so that all constraints become categorical. He re-evaluates cases that apparently require gradient alignment (unbounded stress and foot extrametricality), and finds no compelling evidence for gradient alignment. This conclusion is reinforced by work in computational phonology suggesting that formally, gradient constraint evaluation is a rather questionable device (Riggle 2004; Biró 2004; Heinz, Kobele & Riggle 2005). These modifications of classical foot alignment theory show an increased reliance on the grid, while remaining within representational assumptions of bracketed-grid theory. Taking the rhythmic perspective further, Gordon (2002a) develops a grid-only typology for quantity-insensitive stress, while Hyde (2002) questions one-to-one mapping between constituents and the grid. Probably, we will see a reassessment of the balance between rhythm and constituency in metrical phonology in the years ahead.

9.4   Feet in phonological domains and prosodic morphology

This section identifies evidence for metrical feet apart from stress patterns. Feet can be domains for phonological processes, minimal word conditions, and templates in morphologically-sensitive processes. Of course, feet within a language should be consistent – if the stress pattern requires iambs, then word minimality requirements should also demand iambs, and so on; this consistency of foot form within the same language is called the *metrical cohesion hypothesis* (Prince 1980; Hayes 1982, 1995; McCarthy & Prince 1986; Dresher & Lahiri 1991; cf. Gordon 1999). Among the non-stress phenomena to be discussed here are feet as domains for phonological processes, minimal word conditions, and templates in prosodic morphology.

9.4.1   Feet as phonological domains

Vowel lengthening and shortening are often sensitive to foot structure. For example, many languages display a process of rhythmic lengthening of vowels in alternating even-numbered syllables, often excluding the final syllable of the word. See Hixkaryana (22) for illustration. Rightward iambs, respecting nonfinality, account for the rhythmic distribution of vowel lengthening and the exclusion of final syllables, while supplying a rationale of vowel lengthening as filling the foot template (LH) to its maximal size.

Similarly, vowels in unstressed syllables undergo vowel reduction (licensing inside or outside the foot: Dutch (Kager 1989), Russian (Crosswhite 1999)).

Evidence for the even moraic trochee comes from various sources. Uneven sequences /HL/, when forced into a bimoraic foot, undergo trochaic shortening /HL/ → (LL) in Latin (Mester 1991) and Fijian (71a) (Dixon 1988, Prince 1990, Hayes 1995). Another strategy to attain bimoraic trochees is vowel breaking, as in Tongan (71b) (Churchward 1953, Mester 1991, Prince & Smolensky 2004, Hayes 1995).

(71)   *Two reactions to a sequence . . .HL#*

    (a) Fijian: trochaic shortening

        /siːβi/   [('si.βi)]   'to exceed'

    cf. /siːβi-ta/   [(ˌsiː).('βi.ta)] 'to exceed' (trans.)

    (b) Tongan: vowel breaking

        /huː/   [('huː)]   'to go in'

    cf. /huː-fi/   [hu.('u.fi)]   'to open officially'

Both languages avoid a heavy plus light sequence at the end of a word, and strive toward a situation in which a bimoraic trochee is right-aligned in the word.

Although the asymmetrical foot inventory accounts for an impressive set of quantitative changes in natural languages, it also meets with a number of challenges. For example, some trochaic languages display a process of stressed vowel lengthening, which typically affects the main stress, but sometimes alternating syllables (Mellander 2001, 2004). Iambic lengthening might thus be construed as a special case of the general process of stressed vowel lengthening, which is specifically enhanced in iambic feet due to lapse avoidance within the foot (Kager 1993), or domain-final lengthening (Revithiadiou & Vijver 1997; Vijver 1998). Another kind of evidence which challenges the uneven iamb comes from segmental processes which suggest metrification into bimoraic even iambs (LL), (H). The key example is fortition in Chugach Yupik (72) (Leer 1985, Kager 1993). All foot-initial consonants have a fortis realization (in lodd).

(72)   *Chugach Yupik fortition governed by even iambs*

   (a) /LLLL/   (a.ˈku).(t̪a.ˈmek)   *akutaq* (a food) (abl.sg.)
   (b) /LLLLLL/   (m̪a.ˈŋar).su.(qu.ˈta).(qu.ˈni)   'if he (refl.) is going to
                                                       hunt porpoise'
   (c) /HLH/   (ˈɑn).tʃi.(ˈquɑ)   'I'll go out'
   (d) /HLLH/   (ˈn̪ɑː).(m̪ɑ.ˈtʃi).(ˈquɑ)   'I will suffice'

Note especially how the parsing of (72c) deviates from the prediction of the uneven theory, [(H)(LH)].

Other phonological sources of evidence for metrical feet involve stress shifts after the deletion of stressed vowels (Halle & Kenstowicz 1991; Hayes 1995), foot boundaries creating opaque domains to further metrification (Free Element Condition; Steriade 1988a; Halle & Kenstowicz 1991), and tonal phenomena (see Yip Ch.10).

9.4.2   Minimal words

Another type of evidence for the metrical foot derives from minimal word effects. Many languages require stems to have a fixed minimum size, such as two syllables or a single heavy syllable, matching a binary *foot*. The requirement that a stem minimally equal a foot derives from the prosodic hierarchy, which requires every element at level *n* (here, the PrWd) to dominate at least one element at level *n-1* (here, a foot). The following constraint captures the relation between a morphological category (Stem) and a prosodic category (PrWd).

(73)   STEM=PRWD
       For every stem, there is a PrWd and the stem and PrWd's boundaries coincide

If FT-BIN is high-ranked, as can be verified in the stress system, it follows that the minimal word must be binary as well.

Strong evidence for word minima comes from languages which actively reinforce it by avoiding subminimal words. This may happen by means of epenthesis or lengthening in subminimal words, or by means of the blocking of otherwise general processes of deletion, where deletion would produce a subminimal (monosyllabic or monomoraic) word. Augmentation is illustrated by examples from Mohawk (epenthesis, 74a) and Levantine Arabic (lengthening, 74b):

(74)   *Epenthesis driven by the minimal word*
   (a)   Mohawk (Michelson 1981): /k-tat-s/ → [iktats] 'I offer'
   (b)   Levantine Arabic (Broselow 1995): /sʔal/ → [sʔaːl] 'ask' (m.sg.)
   (c)   Hixkaryana (Derbyshire 1979): /kʷaja/ → [kʷaːja] 'red and green
         macaw'

The Hixkaryana example in (74c) shows an interaction of subminimal lengthening with nonfinality. Since the final syllable cannot be footed, words of two light syllables undergo subminimal lengthening of the first syllable.

The blocking of apocope (i.e. deletion of word-final vowels) to avoid a subminimal word is illustrated by Lardil and Estonian (75).

(75)   *Apocope blocked if it would result in a sub-minimal word*

　　　(a) Lardil (Wilkinson 1988)
　　　　　/majara/　　→ [majar]　'rainbow'
　　　　　/kela/　　　→ [kela]　'beach'　　　　　　　　　　*[kel]

　　　(b) Estonian (Prince 1980)
　　　　　/tænava/　　→ [tænav]　'street' (nom.sg.)
　　　　　/kana/　　　→ [kana]　'chicken' (nom.sg.)　　　*[kan]
　　　　　/koi/　　　　→ [koi]　'clothes-moth' (nom.sg.)　*[ko]

The examples above give evidence for disyllabic or bimoraic feet. Evidence for the uneven iamb (LH) from minimal word requirements is difficult to obtain, since both (H) and (LL) are licit feet.

9.4.3   Morphological templates

A final source of evidence for metrical feet comes from templates in prosodic morphology, as found in reduplication, truncation and classical template-based morphology. Further discussion is provided in Ussishkin (Ch.19) and Urbanczyk (Ch.20). McCarthy & Prince (1986) stated the general relation between morphological templates and prosodic categories (including foot) in their *Prosodic Morphology Hypothesis*: "templates are defined in terms of authentic units of prosody (mora, syllable, foot, PrWd, etc.)". They hypothesized that the set of feet required for templatic morphology matches the foot typology for stress systems: syllabic trochee, moraic trochee, and iamb.

Examples of foot-sized templates, including reduplications and truncations, are given in (76–78), for all three foot types:

(76)   *Disyllabic templates* [σσ]

　　　(a) Yidiɲ (Dixon 1977): reduplicant is [σσ]
　　　　　stem　　　　　　　*reduplicated stem*
　　　　　mulari　　　　　　mula-mulari
　　　　　kintalpa　　　　　kintal-kintalpa
　　　(b) French (Tranel 1993): hypocoristic is [σσ]
　　　　　name　　　　　　*hypocoristic*
　　　　　dominik　　　　　domi
　　　　　ameli　　　　　　meli

(77) *Bimoraic templates* [LL], [H]

   (a) Japanese (Poser 1984): hypocoristic is [LL], [H]

name	*hypocoristic*
midori	mido-tjaN, mi:-tjaN
wasaburo:	wasa-tjaN, wa:-tjaN

   (b) Manam (Lichtenberk 1983): reduplicant is [LL], [H]

stem	*reduplicated stem*
salaga	salaga-laga
malaboŋ	malabom-boŋ

(78) *Iambic templates* [H], [LH]

   (a) Arabic (McCarthy & Prince 1993a): broken plural is [LH]

singular	*broken plural*
nafs	nafu:s
ʔasad	ʔusu:d

   (b) Central Alaskan Yup'ik (Woodbury 1987): proximal vocative is [H], [LH]

full noun	*proximal vocative*
qətunɣak	qət~qətun
aŋukaɣnaq	aŋ~aŋuk

The template was translated into an alignment constraint schema by McCarthy & Prince (1993b):

(79) *Constraint schema for classical templates*

MCAT=PCAT
   where Mcat ≡ Morphological Category ≡ Prefix, Suffix,
           RED, Root, Stem, LexWd, etc.
   and Pcat ≡ Prosodic Category ≡ Mora, Syllable (type),
           Foot (type), PrWd (type), etc.

McCarthy & Prince (1994, 1995a, 1999) proposed to eliminate the classical template by interactions of violable constraints. The *Generalized Prosodic Morphology Hypothesis* says that templatic conditions are the reflection of canonical prosodic restrictions on the morphological category that an item (such as a reduplicative morpheme) belongs to, categories like stem and affix. Templatic specification is minimal, consisting only of a statement to the effect that the reduplicant equals an 'affix' or a 'stem', while the reduplicant's shape characteristics are derived from interactions of prosodic well-formedness constraints and constraints on reduplicative identity. This approach can be illustrated with an example from Diyari (80) (Austin 1981, Poser 1989).

(80) Diyari reduplication *(copies initial foot, minus coda of second syllable)*

(a) wiḻa	wiḻa-wiḻa	'woman'
(b) kuḻkuŋa	kuḻku-kuḻkuŋa	'to jump'
(c) tʲilparku	tʲilpa-tʲilparku	'bird species'

Properties of the Diyari stress system underlie the exact disyllabicity of the reduplicant. The language has initial primary stress, and a secondary stress falls on the third syllable of a four-syllable stem.

(81) (a) 'wiḻa   'woman'
      (b) 't̪ilparku   'bird species'
      (c) 'wiḻa͵pina   'old woman'

This trochaic stress pattern is due to the constraint ranking in (82).

(82)   FT-BIN » PARSE-SYL » ALL-FT-LEFT

The disyllabic reduplicant also matches the minimal prosodic word of Diyari: all stems are minimally disyllabic. The claim that the reduplicant is a PrWd is confirmed by stress. The examples in (83) show that a primary stress falls on both the base and the reduplicant:

(83) (a) 'wiḻa   cf.   'wiḻa-'wiḻa   'woman'
      (b) 't̪ilparku   cf.   't̪ilpa-'t̪ilparku   'bird species'
      (c) 'wiḻa͵pina   cf.   'wiḻa-'wiḻa͵pina   'old woman'

Since each primary stress heads one PrWd, the reduplicant must equal a PrWd itself.

According to Generalized Template Theory (McCarthy & Prince 1995a), the shape invariance of reduplicants emerges from interactions of marked-ness constraints and constraints of reduplicative identity. Universally redu-plicants tend to have unmarked prosodic structures, a property which follows from an increased role of prosodic markedness constraints in shaping reduplicants. Template-specific prosodic requirements are thus reduced to a bare minimum, such as 'RED=AFFIX' or 'RED=STEM'.

All that needs to be stated specifically for the Diyari reduplicant is that this equals a stem:

(84)   RED=STEM
       The reduplicant is a stem.

The reduplicant's stem status implies PrWd status, due to undominated STEM=PRWD. Crucially, PrWd must be minimally a foot in size, due to the prosodic hierarchy, in which every PrWd is headed by a foot. This single-foot minimum translates as a *disyllabic minimum*, due to undominated FT-BIN, and the language's overall quantity-insensitivity. What is more, the exact limitation of the reduplicant to a single disyllabic foot follows from metrical constraints that are high-ranked in Diyari.

(85) (a) The reduplicant's foot is disyllabic (by FT-BIN)
      (b) The reduplicant's syllables are exhaustively parsed (by PARSE-SYL)
      (c) The reduplicant's foot is left-aligned, hence single-footed (by ALL-FT-L)

This is a case of the *emergence of the unmarked* in the Diyari reduplicant. Finally, note that strict disyllabicity is imposed on reduplicants, but not on non-reduplicant stems. This is accounted for by having segment faithfulness on the stem domain (IO-correspondence) take precedence over metrical well-formedness, which takes precedence over reduplicative identity (BR-correspondence). This analysis of Diyari shows that 'unmarked' prosody in the reduplicant's shape can be attributed to universal markedness constraints. It takes *violable* constraints to reach this conclusion: the same universal markedness constraints which govern the reduplicant are violated in non-reduplicative forms of the language.

9.5   Conclusion

The metrical theory of word stress captures a range of cross-linguistic generalizations about rhythmic patterns by postulating a mixed rhythmic–constituentized representation, the 'bracketed grid', a small alphabet of metrical feet, together with a small set of metrical constraints. The asymmetrical inventory of feet receives additional support from foot-based segmental processes, as well as from word minima and templates in prosodic morphology. The standard Optimality-Theoretic treatment of stress patterns, based on a gradient interpretation of alignment, which closely mimicked the predictions of earlier rule-based models of directional metrification, has been criticized for giving grid-based rhythmic patterns too small a role in predicting gaps in typologies. Future developments in metrical theory are likely to redress the balance between constituent-based and grid-based principles of explanation.

Note

Many thanks to Paul de Lacy and an anonymous reviewer for comments on an earlier version of this chapter.

10

Tone

Moira Yip

10.1 Introduction

By some estimates as many as 70% of the world's languages are tonal. They include languages spoken by huge numbers of people, and in geographically diverse countries – Mandarin Chinese (885 million speakers), Yoruba (20 million), and Swedish (9 million) are all tonal. There are certain areas of the world where almost all the languages are tonal, such as sub-Saharan Africa, China, and Central America.

A language is a 'tone language' if the pitch of the word can change the meaning of the word – not just its nuances, but its core meaning. In Cantonese, for example, the syllable [jau] can be said with one of six different pitches, and has six different meanings:

(1) *[jau] in Cantonese*

high level	'worry'	high rising	'paint (noun)'
mid level	'thin'	low level	'again'
very low level	'oil'	low rising	'have'

In other languages, the only thing that matters is that the distinctive pitch of a word appear somewhere in that word, but its exact location may change depending on the morphology of the complex word, and the surrounding phonological context. In Chizigula, a language spoken in Tanzania [Bantu][1] (Kenstowicz and Kisseberth 1990), some words have all syllables low-toned, like the various forms of the verb /damaɲ/ 'to do', whereas others have one or more syllables with a high tone, as in the syllables marked with acute accents in the forms of the verb /lombéz/ 'to request'. It is possible to show that the syllables with low tones are not phonologically specified for tone, so they will be called 'toneless' here (2).

(2) *Toneless verbs*   *H-tone verbs*

    ku-damaɲ-a   'to do'   ku-lombéz-a   'to request'
    ku-damaɲ-iz-a   'to do for'   ku-lombez-éz-a   'to request for'
    ku-damaɲ-iz-an-a 'to do for e.o.' ku-lombez-ez-án-a 'to request for e.o.'

The high tones are part of the lexical entry of certain verb roots, like /lombéz/ 'request', but they show up on the penultimate syllable of the complex verb form, and not necessarily on the verb root itself. Nonetheless, the tone is always there somewhere, and distinguishes high-tone verbs from toneless verbs like /damaɲ/ 'do'. This chapter is about languages like Cantonese and Chizigula, which are called 'tone languages', or more precisely 'lexical tone languages', and the phonological representation and analysis of their tonal systems.

Before we continue, we need to distinguish three terms that feature in any discussion of tone: fundamental frequency (F_0), pitch and tone. F_0 is an acoustic term referring to the frequency of the signal measured in Hertz (Hz) where one Hertz is one cycle per second. The next term, pitch, is a perceptual term: is it heard as high or low? Very small F_0 differences may not be enough to result in the perception of pitch differences. Pitch can be a property of non-speech signals too: we talk of a high-pitched scream, birdcall, or squeal of tires. Tone, on the other hand, is a linguistic term. It refers to a phonological category that distinguishes two words or utterances, and is thus a term only relevant for languages in which pitch plays some sort of linguistic role. Hyman (2001c) has proposed the following definition of a tone language (3) (also see Welmers 1973):

(3) *Definition of a tone language*
    A language with tone is one in which an indication of pitch enters into the lexical realization of at least some morphemes.

This definition is designed to include accentual languages like Japanese or Lithuanian (Blevins 1993) as a sub-type of tone language, in which words have one tone (or several) or no tones, and the tone is associated with a particular syllable or mora.

10.1.1   A descriptive summary

Before we look at tonal systems, we need to know how to 'read' them. Unfortunately there is no consensus on how to transcribe tones, and different parts of the world have developed different systems well-suited to their own areas. Africanists have traditionally used a set of accent marks to convey tone, while Asianists have used digits (where 5=high and 1=low), and Meso-americanists have used digits, but where 1=high and 5=low! The following chart may be a useful reference; note that Asianists normally use two digits to show the pitch at each end of the syllable (4).

(4) *Tone symbols*

			Africa	Asia	Central America
High tone	H	acute accent	á	55/5	1
Low tone	L	grave accent	à or unmarked a	11/1	5
Mid tone	M	level accent	ā or unmarked a	33/3	3
Fall from high to low	HL	acute plus grave	â	51	15
Rise from low to high	LH	grave plus acute	ǎ	15	51

Lastly, downstep (a lowered high tone) is traditionally shown by an exclamation point before the downstepped syllable or its vowel, as in [á!ká] for a word with a high followed by a downstepped high. In the IPA, downstep is marked by a superscript down arrow [ꜜ].

With this behind us, what kinds of tonal systems have been discovered so far? There are three questions we can ask: what is the tonal inventory of the language? how do tones change in context? and are the tonal facts influenced in any way by segmental factors such as voicing?

10.1.1.1 Tonal inventories

I start with the range of tonal contrasts that a language may have. First, it is possible to contrast up to four (Mambila – Connell 2000) and probably five (Bencnon – Wedekind 1983) different level tones. The most widespread systems are two-tone languages such as Haya (Hyman and Byarushengo 1984) or Dagaare [Gur] (Anttila and Bodomo 1996) and three-tone languages such as Yoruba [Benue-Congo] (Akinlabi 1985, Pulleyblank 1986). Five-tone ones are very rare. Phonetically, a language may have far more differences as a result of processes like downstep, a common process which lowers high tones after an overt or covert low tone, so that a /H L H/ string is phonetically more like [H L M]. The inverse, upstep, also exists (IPA [ꜛ]). For some proposals on how to handle downstep and the related process of downdrift, see Clements (1979), Huang (1980), and Truckenbrodt (2002, to appear). Nonetheless, such a language only contrasts two tones, H and L.

Apart from level tones, languages may also have contour tones (rising or falling tones), and a language can have at least two and perhaps three tones of one shape (rising or falling). These typically are found only if there is already a level tone contrast. Falls are much more common than rises (Zhang 2000b). Some tones that appear to be non-level may nonetheless be phonologically level. Many Asian languages have a low tone transcribed as 21, but the falling portion is transitional, allowing the voice to descend to the bottom of its range. When a language is reported to have a contour tone, one must also ask where this contour is found. There are three main possibilities. It may be found only on polysyllables, so that each syllable is essentially level, with the first high and the last low, but the word as a whole has a fall. The second possibility is that a contour may occur within a single syllable, but only if that syllable is heavy (a long vowel or closed syllable), and thus contains two moras, each of which may be assumed to bear a level tone. The third possibility is that contours may occur on any syllable, light or heavy, in which case we are dealing with a true contour tone. Note also that contours are quite often restricted as to where in the word the syllable must be located. Language after language allows contours only on the word-final syllable, probably because it is frequently lengthened.

10.1.1.2 Tonal alternations

The second question to be resolved is how to represent tonal changes in context. In some languages, such as Cantonese, underlying tones change little if at all, but in others they may move, delete, or alter. The environments in which changes take place can be divided into two main types.

First, a change may be caused by a specific local tonal context, as in many Bantu languages, Mandarin, Yoruba and Chinantec. The well-known Meeussen's Rule in Bantu is of this sort: if two H tones become adjacent, the second one deletes. In Mandarin, if two L tones become adjacent, the first one changes to a LH rise. Both of these can be seen as caused by the Obligatory Contour Principle (OCP), as we shall see in Section 10.3.3. In Yoruba (Akinlabi and Liberman 2000), a vowel with an underlying L tone surfaces with a HL contour if a H precedes, and a vowel with H surfaces with an LH if L precedes. Chinantec has a rather similar process (Silverman 1997b). In both cases the tone of the first syllable persists on into the start of the next syllable, in a sort of assimilation.

Second, a change may be caused by positional and/or prosodic factors, as in Shanghai, Chizigula, Trique and Min. In Shanghai, tones that are not in the head syllable of the word delete. In Chizigula, H tones migrate to the penultimate syllable, which is probably the word head. In San Juan Copala Trique (Hollenbach 1977), there is an eight-way tone contrast on final syllables, but usually none on non-final syllables. It is clear that the reason the final syllable can carry tone is because it is the head: final syllables are the only ones that support segmental contrasts such as vowel length, nasal vowels, fortis onsets, and laryngeal codas, and are the location of phrasal stress. In Min, every tone has two variants, one of which occurs in head position and the other in non-head position.

10.1.1.3   Segmental influences

The third question was about segmental interference. Pitch differences are primarily achieved by varying the tension in the vocal folds, and adjusting the height of the larynx (Ohala 1978, Hirose 1997). The vocal folds are also responsible for voicing, and as a result there is a connection between voicing and pitch, with voiced obstruents lowering pitch and voiceless obstruents raising it. In some languages voiced obstruents noticeably interfere with tonal changes by lowering the pitch of the adjacent vowel. Such consonants are called depressor consonants. A striking example in which this effect has become phonological is found in Songjiang (5), a Wu dialect of Chinese.

(5)   *Songjiang tones*

ti	53	'low'	di	31	'lift'
ti	44	'bottom'	di	22	'younger brother'
ti	35	'emperor'	di	13	'field'

The words in the right-hand column, which begin with a voiced obstruent, have lowered versions of the pitches of the words in the left-hand column, which begin with a voiceless obstruent. In some languages this difference persists even after the voicing contrast in the obstruents is lost, giving rise to a purely tonal contrast, a process known as tonogenesis. Tone can also interact with other laryngeal properties, such as glottalization and aspiration. In some languages certain tones are associated with particular voice qualities, usually called register. Sometimes the difference is clearly laryngeal, as in Sedang and Chong (Silverman 1996, 1997a, Smith 1968), but sometimes it is pharyngeal, involving the tongue root, as in Cambodian (Gregerson 1976). Finally, there are some instances of correlations between tones and vowel quality (mainly vowel height). See Yip (2002:31) and Dimmendaal and Breedveld (1986) for discussion.

This brief sketch gives us a sense of what a phonology of tone will have to look for and explain. Now we turn to the formal statement of these processes.

10.2   A theoretical framework for tone

10.2.1   Distinctive features of tone

There have been many different attempts to formulate a satisfactory set of features for tonal contrasts. The right system must (i) define four, perhaps five, contrastive levels, (ii) define two (or three) rises and falls, (iii) relate these to laryngeal contrasts, especially voicing, (iv) handle downstep, and (v) simply characterize the observed tonal alternations. There is no consensus at present, but one fairly popular model uses two binary features, [±Upper] for tonal register, which subdivides the pitch range of the voice into two parts, and [±high] for a finer-grained subdivision of each part into two sub-parts. Four levels can thus be captured as shown in (6):

(6)	+Upper	+high	55	extra-high
		−high	44	high
	−Upper	+high	33	mid
		−high	11	low

n-ary systems have also been suggested, such as Tsay (1994), but these have two problems: there is no upper bound to the number of tones, and they define no natural classes. Consider a simple assimilation in Yala (Nigeria – Bao 1999, using data from Armstrong 1968). In Yala, H becomes M after M or L. If M and L are both [−Upper], this is simply explained as the spreading of [−Upper] in a binary Register system, but for Tsay the conditioning environment of M and L must be simply the list [1–2P], where the digits refer to the level and P stands for pitch. In this approach, there is no explanation as to why the output is M, rather than L.

These features may be related to each other and to the laryngeal features that define voicing, aspiration and glottalization in a feature geometry that is still disputed. For various proposals and discussion see Halle and Stevens (1971), Yip (1980), Clements (1983), Yip (1989a), Bao (1990), Duanmu (1990, 1994), Hyman (1993), Snider (1990, 1999), and Hall (Ch.13). In practice, most work on tonal phonology skirts the issue of the features, and represents tones as H, M, L or with digits, and I shall follow this practice in this chapter unless otherwise stated.

In addition to the number of tones that can be expressed by a given feature system, when one is dealing with level tones it is often possible to show that one surface tone is not in fact specified phonologically since it is inert, and does not participate in any active way in alternations. If the feature system contrasts *n* tones, $n+1$ surface contrasts can thus be captured. In a two-tone system, the unspecified tone is usually but not always the low tone, so that the surface high–low opposition is phonologically a H vs. Ø one. Occasionally this is reversed, so that the underlying contrast is L vs. Ø: see Hyman (2001b) for an excellent recent summary.

One issue from early on was whether contour tones should have a feature like [+rise], or whether they were really sequences of level tone targets, LH. Here the evidence is clear: at least some contour tones must be analyzed as sequences of level tones because they can be seen to be derived from that source. In Hausa (Newman 1995, Jagger 2001), some words have two variants, bisyllabic and monosyllabic. If the bisyllabic word is HL, then the monosyllable has a fall. If the fall is analyzed as simply a HL on a single vowel, then we can understand this as vowel deletion, with retention and reassociation of the remaining tone: [mínì] *or* [mîn] 'to me'. In Cantonese there is a widespread phenomenon known as 'changed tone' (Yip 1980). In one sub-type, there are alternations between certain specific morphemes with high tone, such as /jat⁵/, and forms in which the segments delete, but the tone remains behind and attaches to the preceding morpheme. If that morpheme has a low or mid tone, as here, the result is a rise from low or mid to high: jat⁵ t͟i͟u²¹ jat⁵ tiu²¹ ~ jat⁵ t͟i͟u²⁵ tiu²¹ 'one-strip-one-strip (strip by strip)'.

At the same time it must be said that contours sometimes behave as units. Arguments come from both phonetic data and phonological behavior. Xu and Wang (2001) have argued that the phonetic targets in Mandarin are trajectories, not levels. Phonologically, Changzhi (7) has a diminutive suffix /tə(ʔ)/, with no tone of its own. It acquires its tone by the copying or spreading of the entire complex tone of the preceding root (but see Duanmu 1994 for a dissenting view):

(7)   *Changzhi whole tone copying*

     tsə213   tə213   'cart'
     paŋ535   tə535   'board'
     xæ24   təʔ24   'child'
     ɕiaŋ53   təʔ53   'fillings'

This paradox has led to models in which the tonal features form part of a tree-geometric representation, with a tonal node dominating the LH sequence. This node can then spread, giving the unitary contour behavior as shown in (8). (See Section 10.2.2 on the association of tones to syllables.)

(8)   *Contour tone spreading as a unit*

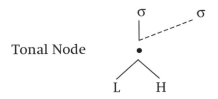

Tonal Node

10.2.2 The autosegmental behavior of tone

As we ask how tone is represented, the second issue relates to how it changes in context. Tone is notorious for its independence from the segments on which it is realized (something that Firth 1948 and Pike 1948 were well aware of), and this fact led Goldsmith (1976a) to propose that it be represented autosegmentally, on a separate tier from the segments but linked to them by association lines. The associations between tone and the Tone-Bearing Units (TBUs) were governed by a set of well-formedness conditions.

(9) *Well-formedness conditions*
  1. Every TBU must have a tone.
  2. Every tone must be associated to some TBU.
  3. Association proceeds one-to-one, left-to-right.
  4. Association lines must not cross.

   The conditions allow tones to spread to more than one segment, and conversely they allow a segment to have more than one tone, forming a contour. It has another consequence: tone can exist in the absence of a segmental host. This can arise in two ways: either the underlying lexical entry contains an unaffiliated tone – a floating tone – or segments may delete, leaving their tone behind either floating, or reassociated to another segment. This last phenomenon is known as 'stability'. A related effect of the separate tiers for segments and tone is found when segments copy, but tones do not. Finally, tones can change affiliations, moving off their host onto another segment: this is called mobility. In the figures below broken lines denote new affiliations, solid lines are underlying ones. Tones are shown associated to the syllable node (see below).

(10) *Tone spreading*   *Contour tones*   *Stability*   *Mobility*

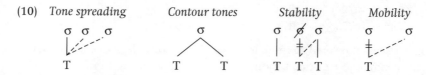

   All of these behaviors are found. In Chilungu [Bantu] (Bickmore 1996), there is unbounded H spread from the infinitival prefix /kú-/ to all except the last syllable of the verb. In Siane nouns [Highlands, Papua New Guinea] (James 1994), contours are formed when excess tones have nowhere else to go. A monomoraic noun with two underlying tones shows up with only one tone on the noun root, and the second tone on any suffix. Only if there is no suffix do the two tones surface on the noun itself, forming a contour. In Cantonese (Yip 1980), as we have seen, there are alternations between morphemes with high tone and forms in which the morpheme deletes, but the tone remains behind and attaches to the preceding morpheme. In Shona (Odden 1984, Downing 2003a) segments reduplicate but tones do not. In Chizigula [Bantu] (Kenstowicz and Kisseberth 1990), H tone migrates from the verb root to the penultimate syllable of the word. It may thus end up three or more syllables away from its source.

   It is not always clear whether tones associate to segments, syllables or moras. In the case of a language with only monomoraic, open CV syllables, where each syllable bears exactly one tone, the TBU could be the vowel, mora or syllable. If the language has syllabic nasals which bear tone, but onset nasals which do not, we can rule out the segment as TBU, since the prosodic affiliation of the segment determines its TBU status. This leaves the mora (or the syllable rhyme) as the possible TBUs: nasals that have moras (or rhymes) will bear tone, but moraless onset nasals will not. If the language has both light monomoraic and heavy bimoraic syllables, and if these differ in the number of tones they can bear, so that monomoraic syllables can have only one tone but bimoraic syllables can have two, then it must be the case that the TBU is the mora, not the syllable. There are languages in which the TBU is not just any mora, but vocalic or sonorant moras only. See Zec (1988) and Steriade (1991) for discussion. Lastly, if the two different syllable weights can bear the *same* number of tones, then the syllable must be the TBU. Since there are cases in which the TBU *must* be the mora or the syllable, and no cases in which it *must* be the segment, it seems that tone always associates to prosodic entities, but languages can differ as to whether the syllable or the mora is the TBU.

The machinery of autosegmental phonology, although originally devised for tone and ideally suited to it, has been co-opted for other phenomena such as harmony (nasal and vowel), and local assimilations. See Archangeli and Pulleyblank (Ch.15) and Baković (Ch.14) for details.

10.2.3   The formal representation of tonal alternations

When tones are placed in context, they may change in a variety of ways. The causes of change are varied. One of the most common is prosodic structure: tones (especially H tones) tend to be attracted to prominent positions, such as stressed syllables and word edges. Conversely, non-head positions such as unstressed syllables may reject tones, resulting in tone deletion or tone lowering (the analogy here is vowel reduction to schwa). A different cause of change is the local tonal context: a tone may spread onto a span of toneless syllables, or onto a neighboring toned syllable to create a contour, or it may assimilate to or dissimilate from an adjacent tone.

In Optimality Theory (Prince and Smolensky 2004, Kager 1999a), the pressures that typically cause tonal change are stated as markedness constraints that dominate faithfulness constraints and thus force changes to take place. These include general markedness constraints relating to tonal features, constraints that deal with associations between tones and the tone-bearing units (roughly Goldsmith's well-formedness conditions, in OT form), constraints that regulate tones in context (such as the OCP), constraints that regulate the mutual influence of tone and prosody, and constraints that assess the positioning of tone within some prosodic or morphological unit. These markedness constraints interact with faithfulness constraints that penalize deletion, insertion, feature change, and movement or spreading (by addition or removal of association lines). As in any other area of phonology, these may apply to input–output relations, base-reduplicant relations, or output–output pairs.

I will illustrate the interaction of some of these constraints with several case studies. Section 10.3.1 shows how basic association patterns in Mende can be explained. Section 10.3.2 looks at tone–prosody interaction, and

Section 10.3.3 shows the way that local tonal changes can be handled. Constraints will be introduced and defined as they are needed.

10.3   Case studies and exemplification

10.3.1   Mende tone association

The West African language Mende, a language first studied theoretically in influential work by Innes (1969) and Leben (1973), is frequently used to exemplify the workings of autosegmental phonology. It has two tones, H and L, and in general they associate one-to-one with syllables from left to right across the word. When there are fewer tones than syllables, the final tone spreads to the remaining syllables to create a plateau. When there are more tones than syllables, the excess tone associates to the final vowel to form a contour. This one-to-one left-to-right mechanism immediately offers an explanation for the very common pattern in which languages only allow contours at the ends of words. However, in a non-derivational theory like OT, we cannot resort to a step-by-step left-to-right procedure (see McCarthy 5.3, de Lacy 1.2.1). Instead, the obvious counterpart is to use left alignment: ALIGN-L-(Tone, PrWd) requires each tone to stay as close to the left edge of the prosodic word as possible. To determine a candidate's violations for this constraint, do the following for every tone: count the number of TBUs between the leftmost TBU to which the tone is attached and the left edge of the PrWd. Sum the results.

While this works fine in the case of fewer tones than TBUs, it fails when there are more tones than TBUs. The following two tableaux (11, 12) illustrate this point. The sad face ⊗ marks the winner as chosen by the grammar, but wrongly so. In the first tableau, candidate (a) wins because H is only one syllable from the left edge, whereas in (b) it is two syllables away.

(11)   *Fewer tones than TBUs*
ALIGN-L correctly chooses (a), with a plateau at the right edge.

/σ σ σ/ L H	ALIGN-L
(a) σ σ σ $\quad$ | V $\quad$ L H	*
(b) σ σ σ $\quad$ V | $\quad$ L H	* *!

In the next tableau, (a) will wrongly win because only one tone fails to attach to the leftmost syllable. Candidate (b) incurs two violations of ALIGN-L: one because the L tone is one syllable away from the left edge, and one because the second H tone is one syllable away from the left edge.

(12) *More tones than TBUs*
      ALIGN-L incorrectly chooses (a), with a contour at the left edge.

/σ σ σ/ H L H	ALIGN-L

☞
☹ (a) σ   σ
   $\diagdown\!\mid\,\mid$
    H L H
	*

(b) σ σ
   $\mid\,\diagdown\!\mid$
    H L H
	* *!

Zoll (1997, 2003) points to an empirical problem with attributing the distribution of contours solely to left-to-right association. In many languages contours can arise from other sources, such as vowel deletion, and even these contours may be disallowed and eliminated non-finally. In Ohuhu Igbo (Clark 1983), falling tones can be created word finally on the subject of an affirmative sentence by the addition of a floating low tone: /ékwé+L/ → [ékwê]. Medially however, spreading rules are not allowed to create contours, and instead the original tone on the target syllable delinks: in this example the H of the first syllable spreads onto the second syllable, but instead of creating a fall the original L delinks: /éwèlàì/ → [éwélàì], *[éwêlàì]. The underlined portions are the affected syllables.

Let us look at Mende (13) again. Consider these basic noun patterns, taken from Zoll's work with slight adaptations in tone and IPA transcriptions. In general, they follow the left-to-right pattern.

(13) *Tone patterns in Mende nouns (Zoll 2003:231)*

	σ		σσ		σσσ	
H	kɔ́	'war'	pélé	'house'	háwámá	'waistline'
L	k͡pà	'debt'	bὲlὲ	'trousers'	k͡pàkàlì	'tripod chair'
HL	mbû	'owl'	ŋgílà	'dog'	félàmà	'junction'
LH	mbǎ	'rice'	nàvó	'money'	lèlèmá	'mantis'
LHL	mb̀â	'companion'	ɲàhâ	'woman'	nìkílì	'groundnut'
HLH	–		ndéwě	'sibling'	jámbùwú	'tree (sp.)'

If the constraint ALIGN-L(Tone,PrWd) fails to handle the facts, what is the alternative? Zoll suggests that the avoidance of non-final contours be attributed to a licensing requirement on contour tones stated as ALIGN-R (Contour), requiring any contours to be final. The motivation for this constraint is drawn from widespread evidence that contours, especially rises, are restricted in many languages to final syllables, perhaps because they are often longer: see Zhang (2001) for discussion.

Provided that ALIGN-R(Contour), MAX-T (which prohibits tone deletion) and *FLOAT (which requires all tones to be associated to some TBU) dominate

ALIGN-L, we will achieve the desired results. The following tableaux illustrate how this works for the words for 'junction' and 'woman'. The circle round the unassociated L tones in some candidates shows that they are now floating. In the case of fewer tones than syllables, ALIGN-L decides the issue, preferring candidate (14a) with a plateau at the end to candidate (14b) with a plateau at the start.

(14) *Fewer tones than TBUs*

/felama/ H L	ALIGN-R (Contour)	MAX-T	*FLOAT	ALIGN-L
☞ (a) fé là mà | V H L				*
(b) fé lá mà V | H L				**!
(c) fé lá má V H (L)			*!	
(d) fé lá má V H		*!		

However, when there are excess tones the high-ranked ALIGN-R(Contour) decides the issue, over-ruling alignment and choosing (15a) over (15d).

(15) *More tones than TBUs*

/ ɲaha / L H L	ALIGN-R (Contour)	MAX-T	*FLOAT	ALIGN-L
☞ (a) ɲà hâ | /\ L H L				* *
(b) ɲà há | | L H (L)			*!	*
(c) ɲà há | | L H		*!		*
(d) ɲǎ hà /\ | L H L	*!			*

Zoll's proposal has the further advantage that unlike left-to-right association it explains the contour shift that happens in cases like (16). Based on other data, Zoll argues that tone association in (16) is cyclic, so that /HL/ must be associated with /mbu/ before the suffix is added. After suffixation, the contour is non-final, in violation of ALIGN-R(Contour), which triggers reassociation.

(16) /mbu -i/   →   [mbu -i]

Lastly, she points out that left-to-right association, and also ALIGN-L, make the wrong prediction for /LH/ on trisyllables. We expect LHH, but actually get LLH. Zoll attributes this to a constraint against adjacent H-toned syllables, *CLASH:

(17) *CLASH
      No adjacent syllables linked to prominent (i.e. H) tone.

Crucially for Zoll, *CLASH does not care whether there are two H tones (one per syllable), or only one shared tone. It is thus much more powerful than the OCP. SPECIFY and DEP-T dominate *CLASH, so a single /H/ survives, and can spread to all syllables. For further details of how *CLASH works, the reader is referred to Zoll (1998).

We can also establish the rankings of *CLASH and ALIGN-L, as well as SPECIFY (which requires every TBU to have a tone) and DEP-T (which prohibits tone insertion), as can be seen from the tableaux for the words for 'mantis' (18) and 'house' (19). The grammar we need is SPECIFY, DEP-T » *CLASH » ALIGN-L. In tableau (18), candidate (18a), with the high tone associated to the final syllable, incurs two violations of ALIGN-L, but still wins out over candidates (18b) and (18d), with only one violation each, showing that SPECIFY and *CLASH must be higher ranked that ALIGN-L.

(18) *Trisyllables with high sequences*

/ le le ma / L H	SPECIFY	DEP-T	*CLASH	ALIGN-L
☞ (a) lè lè má V | L H				* *
(b) lè lé má | V L H			*!	*
(c) lè lé mà | | | L H L		*!		* * *
(d) lè lé ma | | L H	*!			*

In tableau (19), we see that *CLASH may be violated if the underlying representation contains only one tone. Candidate (19a), which violates

*CLASH because two adjacent syllables are both high, wins out over candidate (19b), which has inserted a low tone in violation of DEP-T, showing that DEP-T must be higher ranked than *CLASH.

(19) *Surface violations of *CLASH*

/ pɛ lɛ / H	SPECIFY	DEP-T	*CLASH	ALIGN-L
☞ (a) pé lɛ́ \/ H			*	
(b) pé lɛ̀ | | H L		*!		*
(c) pé lɛ | H	*!			

Zoll's analysis for Mende basic tone association, using alignment and positional markedness in conjunction with SPECIFY and *FLOAT, can be extended to a wide range of languages. I now turn to interactions between tone and prominence.

10.3.2 Tone–stress interaction

It is very common for tone and stress to interact. One of the most widespread phenomena is the loss of all tonal contrasts in unstressed position, in much the same way that unstressed vowels neutralize to schwa in English. In Shanghai (20) (Duanmu 1993), non-initial (i.e. non-head) syllables become toneless, but then the two tones of the initial syllable readjust themselves to cover the first two syllables:

(20) *Shanghai stress–tone interaction*

se52 + pe52	→	55 21	'three cups'
se52 + bø23	→	55 21	'three plates'
sz34 + pe52	→	33 44	'four cups'
sz34 + bø23	→	33 44	'four plates'

Any subsequent syllables also lose their tone, and do not acquire any from the initial syllable. They surface as low, no matter what the tone of the preceding second syllable. Since they are invariantly low, it seems best to assume that they are supplied with a phonological L tone before the phonetics.

Like vowel reduction (Beckman 1997), this can be analyzed as the result of markedness pressures, outranked by positional faithfulness in head position, captured by the constraint HEAD-MAX(T), prohibiting deletion of tones in head position. This must outrank the general markedness constraint *TONE, which in turn must outrank general tonal faithfulness, so the grammar will have HEAD-MAX-T » *TONE » MAX-T. In tableau (21), candidate (21c) deletes even the head tones, in violation of HEAD-MAX-TONE. Candidate (21b) keeps all the tones, incurring massive violations of tonal markedness *TONE. Candidate (21a) wins because it keeps all and only the head tones. Heads are underlined.

(21) *Loss of non-head tones in Shanghai*

	/s<u>z</u>34 + pe52/	HEAD-MAX-T	*TONE	MAX-T
☞	(a) <u>sz</u>3 pe4		* *	* *
	(b) <u>sz</u>34 pe52		* * * *!	
	(c) <u>sz</u> pe	* *!		* * * *

More complex systems like Wenzhou (Yip 1999) reduce the set of contrasts on non-heads, but do not entirely obliterate them.

A second well-known interaction is the attraction of tones to head position in the word or phrase (Goldsmith 1987). In many languages, a word has only one tone or tonal complex on the surface, and it is found on the head no matter where it originates lexically. For example, in Chickasaw the tones of pitch accents are attracted to the head syllable of a phrase (Gordon 2003), and in many Bantu languages (like Chizigula mentioned earlier), they are attracted to the head syllable of the word, the penultimate syllable, which is also lengthened. The position of the head may be predictable, or lexically specified. When tones are sparsely distributed in this way, the language is sometimes called an accentual language rather than a tone language. (See also Kager Ch.9 and de Lacy Ch.12). Formally, we may assume a constraint that attracts tones (usually high ones) to head syllables:

(22) HEAD=H
      Head syllables must bear a H tone.

This will outrank *ASSOCIATE and *DISASSOCIATE, the faithfulness constraints which ban addition and removal of association lines, and result in tonal shift. SPECIFY must be ranked below *ASSOCIATE to ensure that we get shift, not spreading. Head syllables are underlined (23).

(23) *Tonal shift to the head syllable*

/σ σ σ̱ σ/ H	Head=H	*Assoc	*Disassoc	Specify
(a) σ σ σ̱ σ ☞ | H		*	*	* * *
(b) σ σ σ̱ σ ↙↗ H		* *!		*
(c) σ σ σ̱ σ | H	*!			* * *

Candidate (23c), which leaves the tone in place, violates Head=H. Candidate (23b), with spreading, violates *Associate twice, because two new association lines have been added. Candidate (23a) also violates *Associate, but once only, so it prevails over (23b) to win even though it violates both the lowest ranked constraints.

In other languages, there is a preference for stressed syllables to be high. In Mandarin, main stress may be on any tone, including L: mai^L-le 'bought'. However, emphasis placement is subject to avoidance of a L-toned syllable. In the adjective phrases in (24), the usual practice is to emphasize the adjective itself, as in the left-hand example. However, if the adjective is low, emphasis shifts off it onto the modifier. The modifier is also low underlyingly, but undergoes a regular tonal rule of Mandarin which changes it to rising in front of another low syllable. As a result, in the output the emphasis falls on the high rising first syllable (Zhang 1988).

(24) 'very heavy'   'very small'

hen <u>zhong</u>   vs.   <u>hen</u> xiao

L <u>HL</u>   L   L → <u>LH</u> L

A second way to avoid emphasizing a L-toned syllable is to change the phonological phrasing so that it is grouped with another low-toned syllable, and may thus undergo the change to high rising. This happens under contrastive focus (25) (Shih 1997:112). The normal phrasing is shown on the left, and the contrastively focused phrasing on the right. In the normal phrasing, the syllable meaning 'buy' is not phrased with the following syllable, so it does not change to a high rise. When contrastively stressed, the phrasing changes, and it now becomes high rising.

(25)   (a) *Normal phrasing*   (b) *Phrasing under contrastive focus*

	only	buy	stocks		only	[buy	stocks	not	sell	stocks
	zhi	mai	gu-piao		zhi	[mai	gu-piao,	bu	mai	gu-piao
UR:	L	L	L HM		L	[L	L HM	MH	HM	L HM
PR:	(LH	L)	(L HM)		(L)	[(LH	L)(HM)			

Note that if the following syllable is not L, making the tonal change impossible no matter what the phrasing, the focused element becomes the so-called 'full third tone', which is longer and with a final mid rise. See also Shen (1990:51).

Formally, we may propose a constraint *Focus/L, simply a type of *HEAD/L banning L tone on heads, where the head in question is head of a focus phrase. This dominates various constraints on phrasing, including BINARITY. Tableau (26) shows the case of 'only buy stocks', where emphasis changes the preferred phrasing from (26b) to (26a):

(26)   *Change in phrasing under focus*

	/L L L HM/	*Focus/L	BIN
☞	(a) (L) (MH L) (HM)		* *
	(b) (MH L) (L HM)	*!	

Note that *Focus/L doesn't *cause* the tone sandhi rule to apply, otherwise L could become MH even before other tones. Tone sandhi is only triggered by the OCP banning LL sequences within the binary constituent, but *Focus/L selects between two different ways of applying it, by forcing a particular constituent structure.

A much less common but also more interesting type of tone–stress interaction can be found in several dialects of Mixtec, where the placement of stress is dependent on the particular tones of the word, not just on the presence or absence of tone. This case is discussed in some detail elsewhere in this volume (see de Lacy 12.4), but the essential point is that there is a preference for stressed syllables to be H, and for unstressed syllables to be L. In other words, H is intrinsically more prominent than L. De Lacy posits two constraint hierarchies to capture this, restated slightly here.

(27)   *HEAD/L » *HEAD/M » *HEAD/H
       *NON-HEAD/H » *NON-HEAD/M » *NON-HEAD/L

Returning to simpler types of interaction between tone and stress, de Lacy's constraint families can be used for these too. In Shanghai, where all and only head tones survive, we could say that *NONHEAD/H,M,L » MAX-T » *HEAD/L,M,H. And in Bantu languages where H tones are attracted to the head syllable, we could say that *NON-HEAD/H, MAX-T » *DISASSOCIATE, *ASSOCIATE » *HEAD/H.

However, there is a problem in reanalyzing the Shanghai data using de Lacy's positional markedness account as opposed to the positional faithfulness approach offered above in (21). The reason for this is that although the head syllable tones are preserved, they do not actually have to surface on the head syllable. In the last two examples in (20), the rather high tone shown by [4] surfaces on the non-head syllable, in violation of one of the *NONHEAD/T constraints, presumably *NONHEAD/H or *NONHEAD/M. For further discussion of positional faithfulness vs. positional markedness, see Zoll (1998, 2004).

De Lacy's statements are all negative ones, and one might ask whether positive statements such as the HEAD=H constraint used in the Chizigula analysis in (23) are still needed. If low-toned syllables are unspecified for tone, we cannot replace HEAD=H by *HEAD/L and get the same result. However, one could construct an analysis in which *NON-HEAD/H forces the H tones to leave the non-head syllables. Other cases are more recalcitrant. In Mandarin Chinese, contrastive stress avoids L-toned syllables, but is freely allowed on H, MH, and HL syllables. The requirement for a H tone must be stated positively, since HL is acceptable. This issue remains somewhat open, but the close relationship between tone and prominence is clear.

I now turn to tone alternations conditioned by neighbouring tones.

10.3.3   Local tone changes and the OCP in Bantu languages

It is common to find tones changing in particular tonal contexts. There are various possible causes of this, including assimilation and dissimilation. One of the most common is pressure from the Obligatory Contour Principle, or OCP, which bans sequences of adjacent identical elements, such as two H tones. This section shows it in action.

Myers (1997b) gives an elegant overview of the way the OCP influences tonal phonology, and the remainder of this section is taken from his work. Recall that the OCP bans sequences of adjacent identical elements, in this instance H tones. We shall see that the OCP may be observed (Shona), or violated (Kishambaa); the OCP may force a change in the input, a Faithfulness violation (i.e. trigger a rule) or the OCP may block an otherwise expected change (i.e. block a rule). In the languages under discussion, there is a contrast between H tone and the absence of tone, realized on the surface as low pitch.

The first case is one where the underlying form contains a sequence of H tones, and the OCP causes deletion of the second one. This rule, known as Meeussen's Rule, is widespread in Bantu tonology, and these examples come from Shona. Underlining draws attention to underlyingly H-toned vowels, and surface high is shown by an acute accent.

(28)   *OCP-triggered deletion (Shona: Meeussen's Rule)*

báŋgá 'knife'   i̱-ba̱nga 'it is a knife'

The noun 'knife' has one doubly-linked H tone underlyingly, and the copula prefix also has a H tone. Attachment of the copula causes deletion of the H on the noun.

The deletion can be captured by the ranking OCP » Max-T, and the preference for deleting the second of the two tones by invoking Align-L (29).

(29)   *OCP-triggered deletion in Shona*

/i banga/ | V H_1 H_2	OCP	Max-T	Align-L
(a) i banga | V H_1 H_2	*!		*
(b) i banga V H_2		*	*!
☞ (c) i banga | H_1		*	

Our second case shows the OCP blocking the usual spreading from a clitic if doing so would create an OCP violation:

(30)   *Failure to spread H from clitic* (Shona)
       Normal spreading: sadza 'porridge' í-sádza 'it is porridge'
       Spreading blocked: badzá̱ 'hoe'   í-badzá̱ 'it is a hoe' (*í-bádzá̱)

Let us assume that the spreading is caused by pressure from Specify, and that Specify dominates *Associate. The blocking effect will then be caused by the OCP outranking Specify. Lastly, since we do not get spreading followed by deletion (candidate (b)), Max-T must also dominate Specify (31). The ranking OCP » Max-T was justified in tableau (29).

(31)   *OCP » Max-T » Specify-T » *Associate*

/i badza/ | | H_1 H_2	OCP	Max-T	Specify-T	*Associate
(a) i badza V | H_1 H_2	*!			*
(b) i badza V H_1		*!		**
☞ (c) i badza | | H_1 H_2			*	

The final way OCP violations are avoided in Shona is by fusion of two H tones into one, which is limited to applying within the part of the verb Myers calls the macrostem, made up of the root and any suffixes, the object prefix, and subject prefixes in the subjunctive, negative, and participial forms.

(32)   *Fusion (within macrostem only)*

(a) tí-téng-és-é   'we should sell'
    Evidence for fusion
    Whole H sequence deletes by Meeussen's Rule after the H-toned clitic /há/
(b) há-ti-teng-es-e   'let us sell'   (*há-ti-téng-és-é)

In (32a), we see that in this environment two adjacent underlyingly H syllables remain high-toned, in apparent violation of the OCP. However, Myers points out that it can be shown that these two syllables are now associated with a single H tone, because if the word is placed in the environment of Meeussen's rule, as in (32b), both of them lose their high pitch. The two underlying tones of /tí-téng/ have thus fused into one. Fusion is a Faithfulness violation, stated as a constraint we can call NoFusion, so clearly the OCP dominates NoFusion. Since fusion is preferred to deletion, we must also say that Max-T dominates NoFusion. In tableau (33) the subscripts simply allow one to track the tones. In the final candidate, the output tone is a fusion of both input tones.

(33)   *Fusion (Macrostem): OCP » Max-T » NoFusion*

/ti -teng-es-e/ $\mid$ $\mid$ H_1 H_2	OCP	Max-T	NoFusion
(a) ti -teng-es-e $\mid$ $\mid$ H_1 H_2	*!		
(b) ti -teng-es-e $\mid$ H_1		*!	
☞ (c) ti -teng-es-e $H_{1,2}$			*

Note that the difference between the macrostem grammar, where fusion removes OCP violations, and the phonological word grammar, where deletion is used, is only in the relative ranking of NoFusion and Max-T. Before we leave fusion, it is worth noting that one very common tonal process, tonal absorption, can be viewed as a sub-case of OCP-triggered fusion. Hyman and Schuh (1974) note that in many languages, including Bamileke, Mende, Kikuyu, Hausa and Ngizim, sequences of /HL.L/ become [H.L], and sequences of /LH.H/ become /L.H/. They view this as rightward shift, followed by loss of one of the two identical tones on the second syllable, but it could equally well be fusion of the two tones. No matter which, the OCP is clearly at work here too.

We have seen that Shona and many other languages carefully observe the OCP, but not all languages rank it so highly, as noted by Odden in an influential 1986 paper. For example, in Kishambaa, spreading is not blocked by the OCP (Odden 1981, 1986):

(34)   *Surface OCP violations (Kishambaa)*

/ní-ki-chí-kómá/ ⟶ [níkí-!chíkómá]   'I was killing it'

Quite generally in Kishambaa H tones are downstepped after another H tone. Since there is downstep between [kí] and [chí], these must be associated to two different H tones, one spread from /ní/ onto /ki/ and one underlying on /chí/. Since the OCP violation is not fixed up by deletion (35a), fusion (35c), or by the blocking of spreading (35b), the OCP must be ranked below all the constraints discussed earlier. We see then that like any other constraint in OT, the OCP is violable if it is outranked by other conflicting constraints.

(35)   *Kishambaa: Survival of H tone sequences:* MAX-T, SPECIFY-T, NO-FUSION » OCP

/niki-[chikoma]/ H_1 H_2	MAX-T	SPECIFY-T	NOFUSION	OCP
(a) niki-[chikoma] H_1	*!	***		
(b) niki-[chikoma] H_1 H_2		*!		
(c) niki-[chikoma] $H_{1,2}$			*!	
☞ (d) niki-[chikoma] H_1 H_2				*

The case-studies in this section have offered a fairly typical cross-section of the mechanisms needed for tonal phonology in OT, including positional markedness (ALIGN-R(Contour), *HEAD/L) and positional faithfulness (HEAD-MAX-T). These are mechanisms often motivated first in the segmental domain, yet clearly applicable to tonal phonology also, underlining the observation that although tone may seem exotic to an English speaker, it is nonetheless governed by the same mental machinery as vowels, consonants, and stress systems.

10.4   Tone and its surroundings

This brief chapter does not have room to explore the full range of issues related to tonal phonology. For more details see Yip (2002). The following brief remarks are included to emphasize that the full picture is far more complex than the fragments that have been dealt with above.

10.4.1   The interfaces between tone and intonation

This chapter concerns lexical tone, but even languages that lack lexical tone typically use the pitch of the voice to convey sentence level meanings, or intonation. It appears that both uses of tone use the same primitives, and can interact with each other. They also share certain other properties, in particular an attraction to head positions. (See Gussenhoven Ch.11). Languages may use tone for both purposes, although lexical tone languages sometimes use other mechanisms instead of pitch for sentence-level meanings, for example sentence-final particles. Sentence-level perturbations may increase the pitch range, or raise or lower the whole pitch range, or add boundary tones. For further discussion see Gussenhoven (2004), Ladd (1996), and Xu (2006).

10.4.2   Phonetics of tone

A full understanding of tone needs an understanding of how it converts into a precise phonetic implementation. A central question is whether every syllable has a specification for tone at the end of the phonology, or whether some are unspecified and acquire their surface pitch by interpolation from surrounding tonally-specified syllables, which serve as targets. Although languages like Mandarin Chinese (Chen and Xu forthcoming), in which perhaps all syllables have lexical tones, do exist, a considerable body of evidence shows that in many languages only H are targets (Shona: Myers 1999), or that even if both H and L are targets (as in Navajo: deJong and McDonough (1993) and McDonough (1999)) many syllables are unspecified for either (Pierrehumbert and Beckman 1988 on Japanese).

   A second unresolved issue is the location, if any, of the phonetics/phonology boundary. Many tonal changes have clear roots in phonetics. Two phenomena – declination and peak delay – are of interest here because they have been phonologized in many languages. The phonologization of declination is extremely widespread, especially in Africa, where it has given rise to a phonological process called downdrift by which high tones are drastically lowered after low tones. Turning to peak delay, in Yoruba (Akinlabi and Liberman 2000), peak delay has developed into a phonological process that turns a high-low sequence into a high-falling sequence by spreading the high tone.

(36) rárà (H.L)   ⟶   rárâ   (H.HL)   'elegy'

More generally, tone spread or shift to the right is very common, but tone shift or spread to the left is much rarer.

I end this section with a rather obvious point. Just like segmental contrasts, tonal contrasts can be affected by co-articulation effects (Peng 1997, Xu 1994). The laryngeal articulators have their own inertia, and it takes time for change to take place. Hearers seem well able to compensate for these effects, and continue to recognize the tones, but nonetheless caution must be observed in deciding whether some particular tonal effect is phonetic or phonological, and the answer is not always clear (Kuo, Xu, and Yip 2007).

10.4.3 Acquisition of tone

Very little is known about the acquisition of tonal phonology. We do know that infants mimic the pitch contours of the ambient language very early, and this applies to lexical tone as well as intonation, so the inventory of contrastive tones is acquired early. Children successfully master lexical tonal contrasts by around their third year, and even earlier if the language does not have too many alternations. They produce the tones quite accurately at a stage when some adult-like segmental production is still eluding them. See Li and Thompson (1977), Tse (1978), Demuth (1992, 1993, 1995a), So and Dodd (1995). However, we know much less about the acquisition of the phonology proper, including alternations. Li and Thompson's work finds that the third-tone sandhi rule is not fully reliable at age three, when their study stops, but Demuth's work on Sesotho finds good control of some but not all rules by age three. (See Fikkert Ch.23 for some remarks, and also the summary in Yip 2002: Ch.10).

Notes

This chapter has benefited greatly from the advice of too many colleagues and students for me to name, but without whom it would have been much worse! Thanks also to the reviewers and editor for this volume, whose excellent suggestions resulted in improvements of both style and content. All errors are of course my own responsibility.

1 After a language name, square brackets identify the language's affiliation (see http://www.ethnologue.com for further information).

11

Intonation

Carlos Gussenhoven

11.1   Introduction

Intonation refers to the structured variation in pitch which is not deter-mined by lexical distinctions. As will become clear, there is no particular theoretical motivation for this division from a phonological perspective, and the two domains often overlap (see Yip Ch.10). In this chapter, I concentrate on the representation of the melodic aspects of intonation.

Beginning with simple structures in Section 11.2, where the association of tones to the 'text' is discussed, the representations acquire greater complexity in later sections. Over the past decades, phonological ap-proaches to intonation have converged with the theory and description of other aspects of sound structure. This happened both because innovative work in intonation turned out to be applicable to other phenomena and because work on intonation followed phonological models developed for related phenomena. These developments came in the wake of the adoption in intonation research of the autosegmental phonological model (discussed in Section 11.3.1), a framework originally developed for dealing with lexical tone (Leben 1973, Goldsmith 1976a). A contribution by intonation research-ers to the wider field is in elucidating the relation between phonology and phonetics. For example, as illustrated in Section 11.3.3, their work has revealed the context-sensitive and language-specific nature of phonetic implementation (e.g. Pierrehumbert 1990). Another contribution is the insight that the phonological surface representation may remain unspeci-fied for phonological features (Pierrehumbert and Beckman 1988), which was carried over to other phonological features (11.3.2).

Section 11.4 discusses four frequent tendencies in the realization of pitch contours, like declination and peak delay, and discusses their possible effects on phonological representations. The discussion continues in Section 11.5 with a consideration of the fate of unassociated ('floating') intonational tones, and the way in which their location must be accounted for in situations in which they are pronounced. It is argued that association and alignment (in the sense in which it is used in Optimality Theory – Prince & Smolensky 2004) are independent forms of phonological representation, and are both necessary to account for the facts. Finally, Section 11.6 attempts to classify and illustrate the kinds of arguments that have been used for particular phonological analyses.

11.2   Basic structures

A prosodic structure takes the form of a hierarchical set of speech chunks, or prosodic constituents, each one except the lowest of these is made up of one or more prosodic constituents of the rank below (Selkirk 1978; Selkirk 1995b; Nespor and Vogel 1986; Hayes 1989a). As the rank of these prosodic constituents is higher, greater degrees of initial strengthening – measurable as the longer duration and articulatory precision of the first consonant (Fougeron and Keating 1997; Fougeron 2001; Cho and Keating 2001) – and final lengthening – measurable as the duration of the pre-boundary syllable (Wightman et al. 1992; Gussenhoven and Rietveld 1992) – are to be found at their edges.

In addition, one or two higher-ranked prosodic constituents are marked by *boundary tones* at their beginning or end. Such tones often enhance the perceptual salience of the boundaries. The intonational structure of some languages is restricted to just this kind of structure, like the Eastern Aleut language Unangan as reported by Taff (1999). In (1) the outer boundary tones come with the Intonational Phrase, symbolized as ι here, and the inner ones with the Phonological Phrase – ϕ. The latter constituent is equivalent for our purposes to the Accentual Phrase, or α, as used in the analysis of Korean and Japanese (Jun 1993; Kubozono 1993). Every Unangan α begins with a H_α and ends with a L_α, where H(igh) and L(ow) are tone segments, comparable to vowels and consonants, but with just a single feature differentiating them, and the subscript identifies the prosodic constituent the tone comes with. The only variation reported for Unangan is that non-final ι's may have H_ι finally, instead of the L_ι shown in (1), creating a 'continuation rise'. The bold dots in the contour represent idealized pitch targets, and the lines trace idealized pitch levels between them, known as 'interpolations'.

(1)

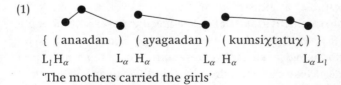

{ (anaadan)   (ayagaadan)   (kumsiχtatuχ) }

$L_\iota H_\alpha$ $L_\alpha\ H_\alpha$ $L_\alpha\ H_\alpha$ $L_\alpha L_\iota$

'The mothers carried the girls'

In addition to the boundary tones, tones may appear inside prosodic constituents. A *pitch accent* is a tone or sequence of tones which are often associated with metrical prominence (Kager Ch.9, Yip 10.3.2), but whose location may also be lexically specified. In either case, that location is referred to as the *accented* syllable. Manado Malay uses an intonational

H* pitch accent on the last α (or φ) for declaratives, and associates it to the word stress in the last word, as shown by the association lines in (2) (Stoel 2005). The superscript star indicates that the tone must associate with the accented syllable. A tone can be associated with the help of an autosegmental association line to a syllable, as shown, and the line formally represents (near-)temporal simultaneity between associated elements.

(2)

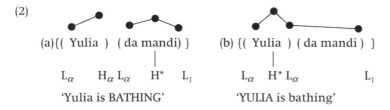

(a){(Yulia) (da mandi) }   (b) {(Yulia) (da mandi) }

L_α $H_\alpha L_\alpha$ H* L_l L_α H* L_α L_l

'Yulia is BATHING'   'YULIA is bathing'

Manado Malay illustrates a frequent use to which intonational tone is put, that of expressing information focus. Expression (2a) can serve as an answer to 'What is Yulia doing?', but if the sentence is a reply to 'Who is bathing?', expression (2b) would be appropriate. After the focus constituent, *Yulia* in (2b), no tones appear with the exception of a possible final boundary tone of the *l* (for details see Stoel 2005).

Pitch accents may be lexical or intonational. In Japanese, they are lexical: words differ as to whether and if so where a bitonal H*L appears in citation forms, where H* associates with the accented syllable, allowing the 'trailing' L to be pronounced after it. An example of a minimal pair for an unaccented word and a word with an accent on the last syllable is [hasi] 'edge' and [hasí] 'bridge', while a minimal pair for two accented words with accent on different syllables is [hási] 'chopsticks' and [hasí] 'bridge'. The pitch of preceding and following syllables is predictable from the location of the pitch accent and the proximity of the phrase boundaries. Example (3) gives the representation of a Japanese utterance containing three accentual phrases the second of which is accented (Pierrehumbert and Beckman 1988; Venditti 2005).

(3)

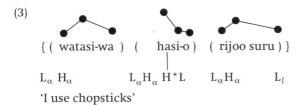

{ (watasi-wa) (hasi-o) (rijoo suru) }

L_α H_α $L_\alpha H_\alpha$ H*L $L_\alpha H_\alpha$ L_l

'I use chopsticks'

In English, pitch accents occur on the word-stressed syllable of words when said in isolation, as shown by *aberDEEN, aLASka, WASHington*. A variety of factors determines which of these accents are maintained in the sentence, most notably the morphology (e.g. the noun *WHITE House* vs. the phrase *a WHITE HOUSE*), rhythm (e.g. *SWEET sixTEEN* vs. *SIXteen SWEETS*), syntax (e.g. *(we) used CHOPsticks* vs. *USED CHOPsticks*, where the predicate status of *used* in the first example is responsible for its lack of accent) and information structure (e.g. *GREEN TEA, please* vs. *GREEN tea, please*, the former in reply to 'What would you like to drink?' and the latter to 'What kind of tea would you like?').

While phonologically comparable, the pitch accents of Japanese and English have very different morphological statuses. In Japanese, they form part of the underlying phonological specification of morphemes, along with the vowels and consonants. Intonational pitch accents are morphemically independent of the words they come with, and are chiefly used to express the information status of the expression. The fact that the English example in (4) seems to have an accentuation similar to the Japanese example in (3) is entirely accidental. In contrast to the α, the domain of pitch accent placement in English has long been recognized as the Intonational Phrase (here *ι*, also called 'tone group' by O'Connor and Arnold 1973, and 'tone unit' by Halliday 1970).

(4)

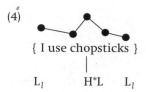

$$\{ \text{ I use chopsticks } \}$$

$$L_\iota \qquad H^*L \quad L_\iota$$

Intonational tone systems, like those of Manado Malay and English, typically consist of more than one pitch accent, conveying different informational meanings. Pierrehumbert (1980) recognized six pitch accents in English and two final boundary tones, leading to 24 contours (in effect 22, as two of these were phonetically identical with two other contours). Thus, it is not only possible to shift the position of the accent, as shown for Manado Malay in (2), but also to replace the 'declarative' contour H*L L*ι in (4) with the 'surprised questioning' contour L*H H*ι, to produce the echo-question in (5). This utterance would be felicitous in a situation in which the hearer had just claimed that the speaker habitually eats with chopsticks. An equivalent prosodic manipulation is impossible in (3).

(5)

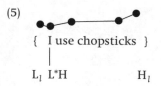

$$\{ \text{ I use chopsticks } \}$$

$$L_\iota \ L^*H \qquad\qquad H_\iota$$

In terms of their intonational structure, languages vary in many ways. They can have different numbers of pitch accents and boundary tones, and thus different numbers of intonational meaning distinctions. They can differ in whether certain boundaries may or must be provided with tones, whether certain phrases may or must have a pitch accent, whether there may be more than one pitch accent in a phrase, and if there are more in how many *different* pitch accents there may be in a phrase. The last pitch accent in an intonational phrase is often referred to as the 'nuclear pitch accent', pre-final ones being 'pre-nuclear'. Many languages, like Bengali (Hayes and Lahiri 1991), have only one pre-nuclear pitch accent in addition to a set of nuclear ones and so the number of *different* pitch accents in an intonational phrase is at most two. Similarly, although English has at least four pre-nuclear pitch accents to choose from, within any given sentence all the pre-nuclear pitch accents tend to be the same (Ladd 1996:210). Languages also differ in where the pitch accents come in the sentence, both in sentences with 'broad' focus and in those with 'narrow' focus or 'corrective/counterassertive' focus (Gussenhoven 1984: Ch.1; Ladd 1996: Ch.5). In some, the choice is different for interrogative and declarative intonation, as in Russian, which accents the last noun in declaratives but the verb in interrogatives (Ladd 1996) or Chickasaw, which places it on the final syllable of the last word in declaratives and on the antepenult in questions (Gordon 2003).

The *phonological* equivalence between lexical and intonational tones is illustrated by Northern Bizkaian Basque. Some words have a lexical pitch accent on one of their non-final syllables, while others do not. However, unlike what is the case in Japanese, unaccented words that happen to end up in pre-verbal or sentence-final position in this SOV language acquire a default pitch accent on the final syllable. This 'default' pitch accent should be seen as intonational, as it is not lexically determined (other than by the unaccented status and the position of the word in question). The point is that there is no phonetic difference between the lexical pitch accents and the default pitch accent, and both come out as a pitch fall, due to H*L (Hualde et al. 2002).

11.3   Representations and phonetic implementation

An autosegmental tonal analysis implies that the phonetic contour is constructed from 'levels', a traditional term for 'pitch points', rather than 'contours', a traditional term for 'pitch movements'. The representations presented so far are in the autosegmental tonal tradition: tone is represented by discrete elements (i.e. H and L) that are interpreted as pitch levels. In this 'levels' approach, a rising pitch contour is represented as a L followed by a H, and a falling contour as a H followed by a L. The pitch between the H's and L's must be filled in by the phonetics.

Many earlier theories developed a 'contours' approach, in which pitch *movements* were the smallest elements. Contour analyses of intonation include the descriptions in the British tradition, which divided the intonational phrase up into (i) a nuclear tune, equivalent to the last pitch accent and the final boundary tones, (ii) a head, equivalent to the stretch from the first pitch accent up until the nuclear syllable, and (iii) a prehead, the initial unaccented syllables (Crystal 1969; Halliday 1970; O'Connor and Arnold 1973; Cruttenden 1997) (for a survey of these units and the terminologies, see Ladd 1980). Each of these three types of constituents came in a number of movements, such as the 'low prehead', the 'stepping head', and the 'nuclear fall-rise', and others.

Similarly, 't Hart, Collier, and Cohen (1990) analyzed the contours of Dutch in terms of a number of rises and falls, smaller elements than those recognized in the British tradition, but still movements rather than 'levels'. Quite apart from the merits of the two kinds of approaches, 'contour' analyses tend to lead to a closer association between phonological representations and the phonetics of the contour. 't Hart, Collier, and Cohen (1990) have quite detailed phonetic descriptions of the movements, which are specified in terms of pitch range and F_0 slope, and also Crystal (1969) contains a large number of detailed contour sections. Since the targets in a 'levels' analysis are independently specifiable for their timing with the segmental string (their 'phonetic alignment') and their F_0 (their 'scaling'), the variation in these phonetic parameters due to various contextual factors has become a particularly prominent area of study in the past years. Early 'levels' analyses employed four levels to represent intonation contours: extra high, high, mid, and low (Pike 1945; Trager and Smith Jr. 1951). Pierrehumbert (1980) introduced an analysis with two levels, H and L. As a result, the relation between the phonology and the phonetics has become less straightforward, but is now also much better defined than before.

Sections 11.3.1 and 11.3.2 are devoted to the association of tones to TBUs, and describe the situation in which there are more tones than TBUs as well as the situation in which tones are located a fair distance apart.

11.3.1 Tone-Bearing Units

The term 'T(one)-B(earing) U(nit)' refers to the phonological element to which tones are associated. Languages tend to employ either the syllable or the mora for this purpose. If the TBU is the mora, two tones HL will co-occur on the same syllable of a disyllabic word if it is long (e.g. [táàtà]), but on different syllables if it is short (e.g. [tátà]). By contrast, if the syllable is the TBU, the H will be on the first syllable and the L on the second, regardless of the quantity of the first syllable (i.e. [táátà] and [tátà]).

In Japanese, the TBU is the mora, as illustrated in (6) (Kubozono 1993). The examples show how the tones distribute themselves over the TBUs in situations in which there are more tones than TBUs. The two tones of the lexical pitch accent H*L associate with the moras [o] and [n] in the rhyme of the first syllable of the disyllabic word in (6a), but to the two moras [i] and [u] in the two syllables in (6b). As a result, [da] in (6a) has low level pitch, but [ru] has falling pitch. In (6a), the mora in the last syllable is available for association to the final declarative boundary tone L_ι. Similarly, the behaviour of this tone structure on a monosyllable depends crucially on whether the syllable is bimoraic, as in [djóo] 'the best', where H* and L can associate and the contour is a sharp fall, or monomoraic, as in [hí] 'fire', where only H* associates, and a high tone results. Strictly speaking, the Japanese TBU is the *sonorant* mora, since tones associate with sonorant segments in the rime. The verb stem [móru] 'leak' would be treated just like [íru]; also, voiceless segments in the rhyme, as occurring in geminates, are exempt from TBU-status, so that [tjótto] 'a little' is treated like (6b), not (6a), causing the final [o] to reveal part of the pitch fall.

(6)

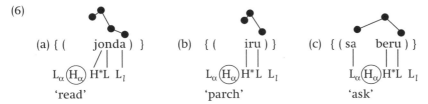

(a) { (jonda) }   (b) { (iru) }   (c) { (sa beru) }

L_α (H$_\alpha$) H*L L$_l$ L_α (H$_\alpha$) H*L L$_l$ L_α (H$_\alpha$) H*L L$_l$

'read'   'parch'   'ask'

Example (6c), which is like (6b), but has a pre-accentual monomoraic syllable, shows that not only the tones of pitch accents but also boundary tones associate with TBUs, in this case L_α. In this way, Pierrehumbert and Beckman (1988) account for the different realizations of L_α in (6a,b) on the one hand and (6c) on the other. When a TBU is available, as in (6c), its pronunciation is fully low, but if the first mora of the α is associated to a H-tone, L_α has at best mid pitch.

The L_l in (6a) and the L_α in (6c) illustrate 'secondary associations', Pierrehumbert and Beckman's (1988) term for a boundary tone with a TBU-association. But now what happens to the floating tones? Instead of the declarative L_l in (6a,b,c), H_l is used in questions, as in (7a,b,c). Better than the floating L_l's and L_α's in (6), the H_l's illustrate that an unassociated tone may be in fact pronounced. In (7a), the interrogative H_l is associated, creating an early rise in [a] after the fall in [on]. In (7b) the H_l is not associated, yet it is pronounced, creating a late rise on the final [u]. Example (7c) shows what happens in a word with a final monomoraic accented syllable. There is no TBU available for the L of the H*L pitch accent, and it leaves no trace in the contour. However, H_l is pronounced as an extra high target. This suggests that in Japanese, phrase-peripheral floating boundary tones are retained in the representation, but internal floating tones are deleted (and have been circled in (6) and (7), by way of reminder of their presence in the underlying representation). Whether floating tones are deleted is a language-specific feature.

(7)

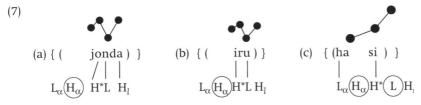

(a) { (jonda) }   (b) { (iru) }   (c) { (ha si) }

L_α (H$_\alpha$) H*L H$_l$ L_α (H$_\alpha$) H*L H$_l$ L_α (H$_\alpha$) H* (L) H$_l$

The association of tones in Optimality Theory has been dealt with by Anttila and Bodomo (2000), de Lacy (2002b), Yip (2002), Gordon (2003), and Gussenhoven (2004:Ch.8), among others. In situations in which there are fewer TBUs than tones, tones must either share the same TBU ('contouring') or remain unassociated. NoCrowd (8) forbids 'contouring', and if it is high-ranked, as in Japanese, priorities must be established to determine which tone associates. T→TBU (9) is a general format where T ranges over the individual tones types. If, as appears to be the case, L_α associates in preference to H_α (cf. (6c), (7c)), then L_α→TBU » H_α→TBU. Also, example (7c) shows that H*→TBU ranks above L→TBU, and (6b,c) and (7b) show that L→TBU ranks above T_l→TBU.

(8) NoCrowd
     A TBU is associated to at most one tone.

(9) T→TBU
     Tones are associated to a TBU.

In intonation languages, the TBU is typically restricted to stressed syllables, or the subclass of stressed syllables that is accented, as was illustrated in (4) and (5). Some languages reveal that unaccented stressed syllables are also TBUs when boundary tones or trailing tones associate with them, which is particularly apparent when those syllables are some distance away from where that tone would normally be expected (see further Section 11.5). Clear cases of moraic associations in non-tonal languages have not been reported. Many of the tonal dialects in the Dutch-German varieties known as 'Franconian', which apart from their lexical tone contrast are structured much like Dutch and English, have the mora in stressed syllables as their TBU (Gussenhoven and van der Vliet 1999; Gussenhoven 2000b; Gussenhoven and Peters 2004). They form an interesting contrast with similar dialects spoken in Belgium, which have the syllable as their TBU. As a result, the mora-based languages make various distinctions between syllables with one TBU and those with two TBUs which have no counterpart in the dialects spoken in Belgium. One of these concerns a distributional restriction in the mora-based varieties, where the lexical tone contrast occurs only on syllables with two sonorant moras; in the Belgian dialects, no such restriction exists (Peters, to appear a). Constraint (10) can serve to account for these differences in the definition of the TBU, if 'TBU' is a variable ranging from the most liberal (presumably every mora) to least liberal (presumably accented syllable). In Section 11.3.2 I will illustrate how it creates multiple associations of tones.

(10) TBU←T
      TBUs are associated to a tone.

11.3.2 Interpolation

A 'levels' description implies that contours arise from interpolations between targets. This is true even in a situation where utterances consist of strings of largely contiguous tone-bearing units each of which is associated to a tone. Describing the shapes of these phonetic interpolations can be a challenging task in languages like Standard Chinese, where a variety of contour shapes can arise as a result of the interaction of adjacent tones (Xu 1999). The main contribution of intonation studies has not lain in a typology of interpolation functions, but in the realization that interpolations can cover long stretches of speech. That is, long strings of syllables may remain without a phonological specification for pitch, and be pronounced at a pitch as determined by the interpolation between two surrounding targets. The case was most clearly made by Pierrehumbert and Beckman (1988). The issue was whether the H_α in the initial boundary sequence $L_\alpha H_\alpha$ of Japanese associated to all the tone-bearing units in an unaccented α or alternatively provided a target from which an interpolation was created to the target of the L_α in the following α.

Assuming that multiple association ('spreading') implies consistent high pitch across the (first) α, due to the repetition of the same high target, the prediction for multiple association is that there is a sharp fall from the last syllable of the first α to the first syllable of the second. By contrast, if inter-polation between high and low targets follows a straight line, an analysis whereby the intervening TBUs are not associated with any tone implies a descending slope from the second syllable of the first α to the first syllable of the second α. Because the non-specification persists in the surface representa-tion (unlike cases of underspecification that receive default phonological specifications on the surface), this type of representation is often referred to as 'phonetic underspecification' (even though the phonetic implementation will be responsible for the creation of appropriate rates of vocal fold vibra-tion!). Moreover, the slope of the late fall predicted by the association analysis must be invariant under variation in the length of the first α, since it always connects the last syllable of the first and the first syllable of the second α. However, in a phonetic underspecification analysis, the slope should become less steep as the first α is longer. They showed that the angle of the slope indeed correlated with the length of the first α, and followed a more or less straight line, as shown graphically in (11) for the stretch -*yanomawarino*. In other cases, interpolations may show drooping or sagging shapes, rather than straight lines (Pierrehumbert 1980; Hayes and Lahiri 1991).

(11)

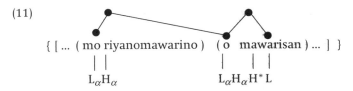

$$\{ \; [\ldots \; (\text{mo riyanomawarino}) \quad (\text{o} \quad \text{mawarisan}) \ldots] \; \}$$

$$L_\alpha H_\alpha \qquad\qquad L_\alpha H_\alpha H^* L$$

'The Forest's guard's policeman'

Optimality Theory bans spreading by NoSpread (12). The requirement that TBUs must have tone, expressed by TBU←T (10), is overridden by ranking NoSpread (12) above it in Japanese.

In Northern Bizkaian Basque, a similar tonal configuration is subject to spreading (Elordieta 1997), for which the opposite ranking must be assumed, as shown in (13). Also, because the final [a] is realized as a sharp fall, Basque ranks T→TBU (9) above NoCrowd (8), allowing contouring on the last syl-lable. In the equivalent configuration in Japanese, e.g. when (7c) is said with declarative intonation, the final accented monomoraic syllable has high pitch, which only falls slightly.

(12) *NOSPREAD*

A tone is associated to at most one TBU.

(13)

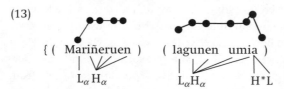

L$_\alpha$ H$_\alpha$ L$_\alpha$H$_\alpha$ H*L

'The fisherman's friend's child'

Tableaux (14) and (15) show the effects of different rankings for a simplified structure as for Northern Bizkaian Basque and Japanese, respectively.

(14)

(H$_\alpha$ H*L, μμμ̈)	TBU←T	NOSPREAD	T→TBU	NOCROWD
☞ (a) μ μ μ̈ V ∧ H$_\alpha$ H*L		*		*
(b) μ μ μ̈ | | H$_\alpha$ H*L	*!		*	
(c) μ μ μ̈ V | H$_\alpha$ H*L		*	*!	
(d) μ μ μ̈ | ∧ H$_\alpha$ H*L	*!			*

(15)

(H$_\alpha$ H*L, μμμ̈)	NOSPREAD	TBU←T	NOCROWD	T→TBU
(a) μ μ μ̈ V ∧ H$_\alpha$ H*L	*!		*	
☞ (b) μ μ μ̈ | | H$_\alpha$ H*L		*		*
(c) μ μ μ̈ V | H$_\alpha$ H*L	*!			*
(d) μ μ μ̈ | ∧ H$_\alpha$ H*L		*	*!	

The idea of underspecification in the surface representation (phonetic underspecification) has been applied to other phonological features. English /h/ is unspecified for oral features, and in a phrase like *See who it is*, the tongue and lip postures during [h] of *who* traverse the path between [iː] and [uː]. Likewise, an oral–nasal cline is created during the vowel in *teen*, while the reverse occurs in *neat* (Keating 1988c).

11.3.3 From representation to implementation

In addition to implementation rules that require a particular phonological representation, the phonetic realization will depend on 'global' paralinguistic factors that affect contours regardless of their phonological composition, like overall register and pitch span (Ladd 1996; Gussenhoven 2004:Ch.5; Chen 2005). Phonetic implementation rules generally abstract away from these paralinguistic effects, and I will ignore them here. To illustrate context-sensitive implementation, consider two implementation rules taken from Janet Pierrehumbert's seminal thesis (1980), Downstep (16), which lowers a H-tone after a bitonal pitch accent, and Upstep (17), which raises an *ι*-final L% to the value of a H-tone and an *ι*-final H% to an extra-high pitch after a H-, a final boundary tone of the Intermediate Phrase (a prosodic constituent below the *ι*). The iterative effect of downstep is illustrated in (18), where the second H* is lower than the first and the third lower than the second.

(16) DOWNSTEP

H → !H / T*T ... ____ ... T% (Implementation)

(17) UPSTEP

T% → raised T% / H- ____ (Implementation)

(18)

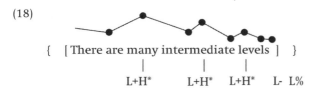

{   [There are many intermediate levels]   }
        | | |
      L+H*   L+H*   L+H*   L- L%

In (19), H- is downstepped and L% is upstepped. In this grammar, a mid tone at the end of an *ι* is therefore obtained by the combined working of DOWN-STEP (lowering H- after L+H*) and UPSTEP (raising L% after H-). In (19b), UPSTEP is responsible for the extra-high H% in (19b). The low pitch at the beginning of (19b) was assumed to be a default realization, but might equally be transcribed as an initial L$_ι$.[1]

(19)

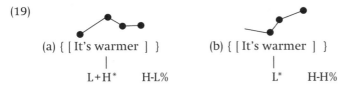

(a) { [It's warmer] }   (b) { [It's warmer] }
          | |
      L+H*   H-L%   L*   H-H%

11.4 Aspects of phonetic implementation

A persistent research problem is posed by the definition of the dividing line between context-sensitive differences in the implementation of a given phonological representation and the existence of different phonological representations. For instance, Face (2001) postulates different pitch accents for Spanish pre-nuclear and nuclear peaks on the grounds that pre-nuclear peaks occur later than nuclear peaks. However, as noted by Face, despite the evidently consistent phonetic differences between the peaks, it is in principle possible to formulate a description with a single pitch accent, with allophonic realizations created by phonetic implementation rules that are sensitive to position.

Intonation contours display tendencies that appear to be shared by many languages. Bearing in mind that it may be hard to decide whether a given phonetic difference is to be accounted for in the phonetics or the phonology, this section discusses four phonetic tendencies, together with some of the ways in which these are reflected in phonological representations. As will become clear, in many cases they have clearly led to reinterpretations of the phonology, and thus language change.

11.4.1   Truncation

Languages and language varieties vary in the extent to which they allow contours to run their full course at the end of an utterance. When they don't, they have a curtailed, or 'truncated' contour finally (Grabe, Post, Nolan, and Farrar 2000); when they do, they may speed up the movement ('compression', Grønnum, 1991) or lengthen the final syllable (e.g. for lexical tones, Zhang 2000a). The truncation may be confined to contexts with final voiceless consonants, as in German, where syllables with a short vowel and a voiceless obstruent (e.g. *Schiff* [ʃɪf] 'ship') have truncated falls, leaving just a level pitch. The same intonation contour in non-final contexts or in final syllables with long vowels or sonorant codas appears as a fall (Grabe 1998b). In Hungarian, the truncation of the interrogative rise–fall contour occurs regardless of the segmental structure of the last syllable, and shows up as a rise on final accented syllables and a rise–fall if the accented syllable is penultimate or earlier (Ladd 1996:132; Varga 2002). The same thing happens in Cologne German (Gussenhoven and Peters 2004:266), while an extreme case of truncation occurs in the Dutch dialect of Tongeren (Belgium) (Gussenhoven 2004:246).

Phonologization of truncation has occurred in German in the sense that speakers avoid using the low-to-high L*H H$_i$ on final accented syllables and use the more level-pitched H* H$_i$, both of which occur in expressions with non-final accented syllables (Ladd 1996:135). As pointed out by Ladd, the case is related to avoidance of H*L H$_i$ on monosyllables noted by Féry (1993:91), which could arguably be interpreted to mean that German allows at most two tones on final accented syllables. Truncation may also give rise to the restructuring of contours. The rising declarative contours of certain varieties of Scandinavian may well have developed from delayed (see below), truncated falls (Bye, to appear).

11.4.2   Peak delay

Pitch movements have a tendency to occur later than the segmental structures they are associated to, which appears to be true for the targets of H-tones, in particular. Language varieties may vary in the extent to which they allow peaks to be aligned late. For instance, Atterer and Ladd (2004) show that Southern German has later alignment of pre-nuclear peaks than Northern German, while in their turn Northern German peaks are later than British English peaks. As Atterer and Ladd make clear, these relatively subtle differences will have to be accounted for in the phonetic implementation. Over time, however, the gradual delay of pitch peaks at varying speeds may lead to phonological differences between language varieties. For instance, Donegal Irish has later peaks than Mayo Irish, to the extent that the former is best analyzed as having a L*H pitch accent and the latter H*L (Dalton and Ní Chasaide 2003), while a similar difference exists between Orkney English and Shetland English, respectively (van Leyden 2004).

A number of phonological factors have been shown to affect peak alignment. Pre-nuclear peaks tend to be later than nuclear peaks, while a larger distance to the phrase-end or the next accent tends to allow for later alignment (for English: Silverman and Pierrehumbert 1990, for Dutch: Lickley, Schepman and Ladd 2005). As mentioned before, this tendency has given rise to the postulation of different pitch accents for pre-nuclear and nuclear rises in Castillian Spanish, L*+H and L+H*, respectively (Face 2001). Second, the segmental composition of the syllable has been shown to affect peak alignment in English (Santen and Hirschberg 1994), Mexican Spanish (Prieto, Santen, and Hirschberg 1995) and Dutch (Rietveld and Gussenhoven 1995), where peak delay shows a positive correlation with the duration of the sonorant portion of the rhyme as well as a negative one with the length of the onset. Since the low target before the peak is more stably timed to occur at the beginning of the syllable (Caspers and van Heuven 1993; Prieto, Santen, and Hirschberg 1995), rises may display different slopes. Rises in Dutch were shown to end a little earlier if the accented syllable contained a short 'tense' high vowel than if it contained a short 'lax' high vowel by Ladd, Mennen, and Schepman (2000), arguably a phonetic left-over from the days when the tense high vowels were long, on the assumption that the rise shortened along with the vowel.

Studies of phonetic alignment of tonal targets have tended to underscore the language-specific nature of phonetic implementation. For instance, while Dutch tends to align rises with the beginning and end of the syllable, equivalent pre-nuclear rises in Greek end in the post-accentual syllable (Arvaniti, Ladd, and Mennen 1998; Ladd, Faulkner, Faulkner, and Schepman 1999; Ladd, Mennen, and Schepman 2000; Atterer and Ladd 2004).

11.4.3 Dipping

The perceptual salience of a tone is greater if the pitch to the left or right of its target is different. HL* is in this sense a better contour than LL*, all else being equal, which is one of the facts underlying the OCP, originally motivated for the phonology of lexical tone (Leben 1975; Goldsmith

1976a). Indeed, one way of perceptually enhancing the low pitch of L-tones is by creating a slight fall towards, or a slight rise away from the low target, a tendency that may lead to the introduction of a H-tone in the representation. For instance, the lexical L-tone (Tone 3) of standard Chinese has a slight fall towards its low target and, in phrase-final position, a rise away from it. The rise in particular is commonly interpreted as a H-tone (cf. Duanmu 2000a:221). Stockholm Swedish Accent 1, which has a L* on the stressed syllable, tends to be preceded by mid or high pitch, which may be analyzed as a H-tone (Bruce 1977; 1990) or be left to the phonetic implementation (Riad 1998). In Northern European Portuguese, the interrogative contour L*HL$_i$ may likewise be preceded by H (Vigário and Frota 2003). Example (20) is from unpublished work by Jörg Peters (Peters, to appear b) and shows a realization of a L*HL$_i$ contour in the dialect of Borgloon (Belgium). While the accented syllable shows a clear fall, perceptually there is a low-pitched target, and the falling movement would appear to bring out the speaker's intention to reach low pitch. (The final fall is truncated.)

(20)

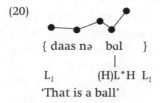

{ daas nə bɑl   }
         |
L$_i$ (H)L*H L$_i$
'That is a ball'

11.4.4 Declination

The natural tendency for fundamental frequency to lower over the course of an utterance is known as 'declination'. Its widespread existence is generally attributed to a gradual decrease in the subglottal air pressure during the slowed down exhalation phase used for the production of the utterance, but, as with most aspects of phonetic implementation, its phonetics is language-specific and under speaker control (Ladd 1984; Strik and Boves 1995; Rialland 2001).

   Downstep is a grammaticalized form of declination: in a given contour, it either does or does not occur. Although in some tone languages L-tones undergo downstep by the side of H-tones, intonational downstep would always appear to target H-tones. Still, the effect will persist in that the pitch range after the downstepped H will be reduced proportionally, while the pitch before it may also be affected if the triggering context occurs in a different phrase. Example (21) compares a non-downstepped and down-stepped H* in English. In (21a), the pitch in the second accented syllable, *tell*, falls from high pitch, while in (21b) it falls from mid pitch. Examples (22a,b), after Pierrehumbert and Beckman 1988, show a contrast between a non-downstepped accentual phrase, which occurs after an unaccented accentual phrase in (22a), and a downstepped accentual phrase, occurring after an accented accentual phrase in (22b).

(21)

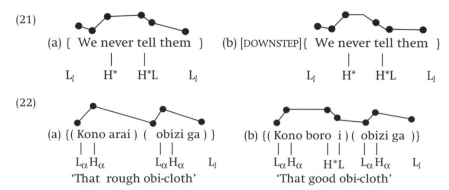

(a) { We never tell them }   (b) [DOWNSTEP]{ We never tell them }

L$_l$ H*   H*L   L$_l$ L$_l$ H*   H*L   L$_l$

(22)

(a) {(Kono arai) (obizi ga) }   (b) {(Kono boro i)(obizi ga)}

L$_\alpha$H$_\alpha$ L$_\alpha$H$_\alpha$ L$_l$ L$_\alpha$H$_\alpha$ H*L   L$_\alpha$H$_\alpha$ L$_l$

'That rough obi-cloth'   'That good obi-cloth'

In a widely adopted view, the phonological discreteness of downstep is given by the conditioning context of the downstepped tone, rather than in the downstepped tone itself (^{l}H), which is an allophone of H in the context concerned, created by a phonetic implementation rule of the type shown in (16).

The view that the F$_0$ lowering due to downstep is effected in the phonetic implementation (as advocated by e.g. Clements 1979 and Pierrehumbert 1980) contrasts with a view in which the downstepped tone is phonologically distinct from a non-downstepped tone, either by means of a feature [±downstep] (Ladd 1983b) or by incorporating phrases or tones in a binary-branching tree, either for lexical tone (Clements 1983; Snider 1999) or intonational tone (Ladd 1990).

On the assumption that downstep is contextually effected in the phonetic implementation, contexts will understandably vary across languages. In all cases, the context includes a specification of the prosodic constituent within which trigger and target must occur, like the *ı*. For instance, Japanese downsteps (the H-tone of) an accentual phrase after a pitch accent H*L within the Intermediate Phrase, though not after the boundary sequence L$_\alpha$H$_\alpha$ (see (22a,b)). English downstep has been analyzed by Beckman and Pierrehumbert (1986) as occurring after a bitonal pitch accent in the same Intermediate Phrase. However, in the ToBI transcription system (*Tone and Break Indices*), downstepped tones are transcribed as such (i.e. as ^{l}H), after a critical evaluation of Pierrehumbert's (1980) original proposal by Ladd (1983b). In (21), a morphological analysis is followed, which claims that any non-downstepped contour with H* can be downstepped, with a concomitant change in meaning, provided a H-tone precedes in the same *ı* (Gussenhoven 2004:Ch.15). In French, downstep is phonological and occurs on H* after any H (39), again within the *ı*, but unlike English, French does not have an equivalent non-downstepped contour for every downstepped one; see also Section 11.6.2.

11.5 Phonological timing relations: association and OT alignment

So far, we have assumed that intonational tones can be associated to a TBU or remain floating. In the case of floating tones, a general problem arises as to how their position in the expression is to be accounted for. If the H-tones in a

H* L H* contour are associated to accented syllables that lie far apart, the position of a floating medial L is in principle undescribed. In addition to association, Optimality Theory offers the concept of 'alignment', henceforth 'OT-alignment' in order to distinguish it from the use of the term 'alignment' for the detailed phonetic timing of a target. OT-alignment goes back to the notion of 'edge-based prosodification' (Selkirk 1986). Often, prosodic domains and morpho-syntactic domains 'co-end' or 'co-begin'. An example of the coincidence of prosodic and morphological boundaries in English is provided by *uneasy*, which is structured [*un* [[*ease*] *y*]]. The left edge of the stem *ease* coincides with the left edge of a phonological word, as shown by the syllable boundary, the diagnostic for a phonological word boundary ([ʌn.iː.zi]). The right edges do not coincide, however, as shown by *[ʌ.niːz.i], *[ʌn.iːz.i]. Generally, OT alignment constraints require that the right or left edge of some element (segment, mora, phrase, morpheme, tone) coincides with the same edge of some other constituent. The notion has been applied to many phenomena (McCarthy and Prince 1993a), and has also been used to locate intonational tones (Gussenhoven 2000a). One prediction here is that the medial L-tone is pronounced closely after the lefthand H* (left-alignment), closely before the right-hand H* (right-alignment), or both (left-alignment and right-alignment), but not half-way between them. True cases of sagging, therefore, must be described in the phonetic implementation under this view. The concept of OT-alignment of floating tones with the edges of adjacent tones was introduced, avant la lettre, by Pierrehumbert (1980), where it was symbolized with the help of the +. An example of an alignment constraint for tone is (23).

(23) ALIGN(H$_ι$,Rt)
     The right edge of H$_ι$ coincides with the right edge of ι.

Knowing with which side a tone OT-aligns does not tell us (a) whether it associates in that location, which may depend on the availability of a TBU, or (b) its phonetic alignment – i.e. its detailed timing with respect to the segmental structure, which is to be described in the phonetic implementation.

   Association and OT-alignment have generally been conflated in descriptions of lexical tone, but there are two reasons why they need to be distinct. The first was noted above, to describe the location of floating intonational tones that are pronounced. The second is that alignment is needed to determine the order of tones from different morphemic sources competing for the same location.

11.5.1   Locating unassociated tones

The phonetic timing of the trailing T in a L*+H or H*+L pitch accent often cannot adequately be described with an association to a TBU. As we have seen, its target may occur some approximate time interval after the target of the preceding T*, when it will end up in the accented syllable if it is ι-final and, depending on their duration, in one of the post-accentual syllables if it is not (Bruce 1987). In this case, the trailing tone left-aligns with its tone on the left. Alternatively, it is pronounced as far to the right as allowed by the next tone's target or the phrase end, where it may end up in an unstressed syllable, or be located in one of the two or three pre-accentual syllables. Right-alignment can be used for the right-shifting trailing tone in pre-nuclear position in (24a), adapted from Gussenhoven (1984:Ch.6). This analysis is to be compared with the leading-tone analysis in (24b), as in Pierrehumbert (1980), Beckman and Pierrehumbert (1986), Silverman et al. (1992), and many other analyses. In Section 11.6, some arguments for (24a) will be presented.

(24)
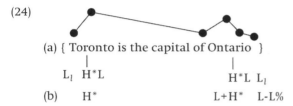

(a) { Toronto is the capital of Ontario }

L_l H*L   H*L L_l

(b)   H*   L+H*   L-L%

In addition to shifting tones either left or right, OT-alignment can be used to create level pitch by simultaneously aligning tones left and right. In OT, this is achieved by ranking a constraint NOTARGET below both left-alignment and right-alignment. The alternative rankings lead to a single alignment (e.g. ALIGNTLEFT » NOTARGET » ALIGNTRIGHT) or the deletion of the floating tone (NOTARGET » ALIGNTLEFT, ALIGNTRIGHT).

(25) *NOTARGET (T)*
T has no target.

For instance, a falling–rising contour that begins on an early accented syllable in English typically has a low level stretch between the accented syllable and the final rise, as shown in (26), where the location of L indicates its left alignment and the arrow its right alignment. Again, the alignment may or may not result in an association (and if it does, the arrow is redundant with the association line). In the case of (26), the left target varies, as explained above, while the location of the right target is underinvestigated.[2] An alternative solution to the problem of creating level stretches is to assume an additional tone, as proposed by (Dilley 2004), who introduces a tone E, for 'equal', for this purpose. In (26), the relevant specification would be +L E+, where E takes on the value of L.[3]

(26)

{ Is Toronto the capital of Ontario }

L_l H*L→ H_l

Roermond Dutch illustrates two-edge alignment plus association of boundary tones to phrase-internal TBUs. Example (27) shows the pronunciation of the interrogative L* H_lL_l in a sentence with an unaccented final word with antepenultimate stress. Right-alignment leads to an association

in the rightmost stressed syllable. The tone thus satisfies T→TBU and
ALIGNTRIGHT as far as it can, there being no TBU further right. In addition
to the secondary association in the right-aligned location, there is left-
alignment of H₁. The left-alignment does not lead to an association, even
though a TBU is available in the syllable *PLOAN*. The reason for this failure is
that the dialect does not allow LH within a syllable, due to the high ranking
of a constraint NoRISE, banning rising tones (Gussenhoven 2000a).

(27)

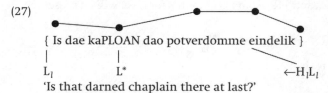

{ Is dae kaPLOAN dao potverdomme eindelik }

L₁   L*   ←H₁L₁
'Is that darned chaplain there at last?'

Two-edge alignment with association in both locations is illustrated by Venlo
Dutch. In (28) a lexical L-tone is right-aligned with the stressed syllable, where
it associates with the second mora of *bein*, and left-aligned so as create a target
in the accented syllable *VOOT*, where it associates with the second mora.

(28)

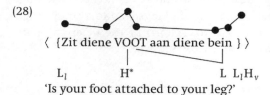

⟨ {Zit diene VOOT aan diene bein } ⟩

L₁   H*   L L₁Hᵥ
'Is your foot attached to your leg?'

Association to a TBU of boundary tones with single-edge alignment occurs in
the Greek interrogative contour L* H-L% (Grice, Ladd, and Arvaniti 2000; Arvaniti and Baltazani 2003). L* associates to the accented syllable and H- to the last
stressed syllable, as is evident when a final unaccented word with non-final
word stress appears in post-nuclear position, as in (30). This case is describable
if H→TBU is ranked above a constraint forbidding associations, NoAssoc
(29), and the stressed syllable is the TBU. The association will be to the *last*
stressed syllable because ALIGN(H-,Rt) is obeyed. Grice et al. referred to a tone
like Greek H- as a 'phrase accent', reinterpreting the earlier meaning 'boundary tone of the Intermediate Phrase' by Beckman and Pierrehumbert (1986).

(29) *NoAssoc(T)*
      T is not associated.

(30)

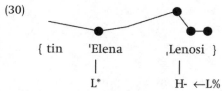

{ tin   'Elena   ‚Lenosi }

          L*   H- ←L%
'[Are you asking about] ELENA Lenosi?'

The various options are shown in tableau (31), with a focus on H₁. The winning
candidate (31a) is the most elaborate structure. This case of two-edge alignment
and association of H₁ in both locations corresponds to (28). Candidate (31b)

is the Roermond case in (27), which is obtainable if NoRise is ranked above H_ι→TBU. Candidate (31c), the Greek case, is obtained if NoTarget(H_ι) ranks above Align(H_ι,Left) but below Align(H_ι,Right), making candidate (31g) worse for having no target at all and (31a) for having two. Candidate (31d), possibly the most usual case, attested in Bengali (Hayes and Lahiri 1991), requires that same ranking as does candidate (31c), but also needs NoAssoc(H_ι) to rank above H_ι→TBU. Candidates (31e) and (31f) are hypothetical; they are like (31c) and (31d) respectively, except that Align(H_ι,Right) and Align(H_ι,Left) are switched round. Candidate (31g) requires NoTarget(H_ι) to rank above both alignment constraints, which amounts to the deletion of the floating tone, as in the case of Japanese i-internal floating tones in (6) and (7).[4]

(31)

{ μμ ... μ ... } L* H_ι L_ι	Align(H_ι, Right)	Align(H_ι, Left)	H_ι→TBU	NoRise	NoTarget(H_ι)	NoAssoc(H_ι)
☞ (a) { μμ ... μ ... } L* $H_\iota L_\iota$				*	**	**
(b) { μμ ... μ ... } L* ←$H_\iota L_\iota$			*!		**	*
(c) { μμ ... μ ... } L* $H_\iota L_\iota$		*!	*		*	*
(d) { μμ ... μ ... } L* $H_\iota L_\iota$		*!	**		*	
(e) { μμ ... μ ... } L* $H_\iota L_\iota$	*!		*		*	*
(f) { μμ ... μ ... } L* ←$H_\iota L_\iota$	*!		**		*	
(g) { μμ ... μ ... } L* $H_\iota L_\iota$	*!	*!	**			

11.5.2   Competing for the same edge

The second reason for separating OT alignment and association is that tones representing different morphemes may compete for the same edge. In Venlo Dutch, as shown in (28), a lexical L-tone on the last mora of the ι *precedes* the final boundary tone(s) (Gussenhoven and van der Vliet 1999). While the Venlo case is entirely as expected, the equivalent lexical tone in Roermond Dutch *follows* the boundary tones, as shown in (32). The $H_\iota L_\iota$ of the interrogative contour is sequenced *before* the lexical H-tone, if it occurs on the last mora of the ι. Unfortunately, in the traditional interpretation, whereby a violation is incurred by any tone which is not associated to the last TBU, both orders would satisfy right-alignment (e.g. Zoll 1997). Since alignment constraints are generally used as the mechanism to determine the order of morphemes, it stands to reason to call upon them to differentiate between (28) and (32).

(32)

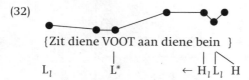

{Zit diene VOOT aan diene bein }

L$_\iota$ L*   ← H$_\iota$ L$_\iota$ H

The choice between (28) and (32) arises because tones are aligned with coinciding, though different, constituent edges. Specifically, the lexical L or H aligns with the right edge of the syllable and T$_\iota$ with the right edge of ι. In ι-final position, these edges are identical, prosodic structure being hierarchical. Right-alignment with σ and right-alignment with ι are in conflict if the right edge of σ coincides with the right edge of ι. The crucial assumption to be made is that the constituent with which the tone is aligned includes all phonological material in it, *including its tones*. In (28), the right edge of lexical L does not in fact coincide with the right edge of the ι, which after all ends in L$_\iota$H$_\upsilon$. This parallels the requirement that a segment that right-aligns in a word must be word-final, and cannot occur before other segments it shares a mora with. It implies that right-alignment can be violated either because an element is not final in its string, or because it is not associated to the last mora or syllable. Thus, in (28), the alignment of the lexical tone with the right edge of the syllable ranks below the alignment of the boundary tones with the right edge of the ι and the υ. In (32), this ranking is reversed (Gussenhoven 2000a,b; 2004: Ch.8).

11.6   Arguments used in tonal analyses

While there needs to be a systematic and natural relation between phonetic implementation and the phonological representation, a given contour in some language is in principle not analyzable as a string of phonological tones unless the set of contrasts in the language is known. In this, intonation is no different from segmental structure. The decision to transcribe English 'cat' as /kæt/ rather than /khæt/ or /kʰæt/ can only be made once further data show that English does not have onset clusters with /h/ and that the language contrasts aspirated plosives with plosives that are interpreted as voiced, as opposed to voiceless unaspirated. Arguments for the presence of a tone, its value (H or L) or its status (starred tone, leading or trailing tone in a pitch accent, boundary tone) can therefore not only be based on phonetic criteria, but also on distributional criteria. In addition, because intonational tones represent morphemes, arguments can also be based on semantic criteria.

11.6.1 Phonetic considerations

Some representative examples of the large body of work relating phonetic findings to phonological representations are briefly considered here. First, Truckenbrodt (2002) shows that in Southern German an *ɩ*-final H-tone may escape downstep, where the H in the pitch accent on *Nonne* reaches the same pitch as that on *Lena*, rather than undergoing a further downstep from *Manu* or reproducing its pitch height. To account for this situation, Truckenbrodt proposes that the *ɩ*-final pitch accent is associated to the *ɩ*-node rather than the accented syllable of the word itself. Metrical strength is taken to ensure that it is realized on the head of the *ɩ*, *Nonne* (33). (In like manner, the pre-nuclear pitch accents associate with lower phrase nodes, rather than the accented syllables, in Truckenbrodt's proposal.)

(33)

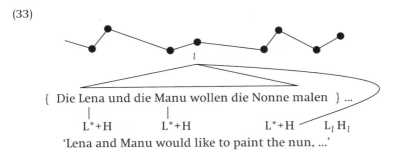

{ Die Lena und die Manu wollen die Nonne malen } ...

L*+H   L*+H   L*+H $L_\iota H_\iota$

'Lena and Manu would like to paint the nun, ...'

The second example concerns an analysis of Catalan pre-nuclear accent peaks as L* followed by a word boundary tone by Estebas-Vilaplana (2003), which in our notation would be given as L* H_ω. Her first finding was that the beginning of the rise was located inside the accented syllable. On the assumption that a tone's association to an accented syllable implies that its target is reasonably accurately aligned with that syllable, this finding suggests that the low target is due to a L*. The second finding was that the peak occurred at the end of the word, regardless of the number of post-stressed syllables in it, motivating an analysis of the high target as a word boundary H-tone.

The third example concerns the bitonal analyses of two pitch accents in European Portuguese by Frota (2002). The 'neutral' pitch accent is realized as a fall starting in the pre-accentual syllable and ending in the accented syllable, while the pitch accent used to express corrective focus is a fall that starts in the accented syllable and ends after the accented syllable. The first question was whether the pitch accents have starred tones. Since the neutral pitch accent consistently had a low target in the accented syllable, it was analyzed as L*, and since the corrective pitch accent typically had its peak in the accented syllable, with only 16% of the tokens being timed just after the accented syllable, it was taken to contain H*. The second question concerned the status of the tone responsible for the target in the adjacent syllable, which together with T* could be part of a bitonal pitch accent or be an independent tone, e.g. a boundary tone. The pre-accentual peak of the neutral fall turned out to be firmly located in the pre-accentual syllable and its timing therefore appears not to be influenced by the distance to a preceding boundary or a pre-nuclear stressed syllable. This suggests it is a leading H in a H+L* pitch accent. Similarly, the timing of the end of the fall is not determined by the distance to the phrase end, suggesting that the 'corrective' pitch accent, too, is bitonal, H*+L. A third and final question was if there was a constant time interval between the two tones in each pitch accent. This appeared to be the case in H*+L, whose slope is steeper as its peak is higher, but not for H+L*, whose H is timed more consistently with the pre-accentual syllable than in terms of a fixed distance from the target for L*. To express this difference in the structure, Frota adopted Grice's proposal for a difference between pitch accents with leading tones, see (34a), and those with trailing tones, see (34b), which proposal goes back to a distinction between tone sequences and tone clusters made by Yip (1989a). The leading tone is high-attached to a Pitch Accent node and entertains a looser bond with the starred tone, but the trailing tone forms a cluster with the starred tone, implying a closer bond between the tones. On the structure of pitch accents and tunes, see also Ladd (1996, p. 218) and Face (2002).

(34)   (a)   PA   (b)   PA

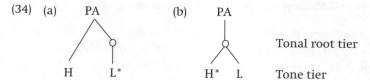

                        Tonal root tier

    H   L*   H* L   Tone tier

Fourthly, Ladd and Schepman (2003) argued against Pierrehumbert's (1980) description of sequences of non-downstepped peaks as sequences of H* pitch accents between which the pitch sagged, like powerlines between pylons. Given that Pierrehumbert's bitonal pitch accents trigger downstep, the absence of downstep needs to be described with the help of monotonal pitch accents. In this analysis, implementation rule (35), which is attested in languages with H* pitch accents (e.g. Bishop 2004), is needed to create a contour like (36).

(35)   ENGLISH SAG

    Low pitch / H* _____ H*

(36)

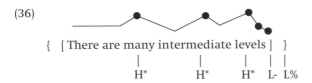

    {   [There are many intermediate levels]   }
          | | | |
         H*   H*   H* L- L%

Ladd and Schepman (2003) show, however, that the low target is reliably located at the start of the upcoming accented syllable, and does not indiscriminately occur between the accents. This suggests that a L-tone is needed in the representation and that (18) should be analyzed as either L, H*L H*L H*L or LH* LH* LH* L, (cf. 24a)), but without a rule downstepping H after a bitonal pitch accent. A similar realization of inter-peak valleys with a fall of variable duration and a rise with a more or less fixed duration was found in Neapolitan Italian declarative sentences, where the two peaks are located on the first and last stressed syllables of longer focus constituents (D'Imperio 2003). For instance, in *Vedrai [la bella mano di Mamma] domani* 'You will see mother's beautiful hand tomorrow', a reply to 'What will you see tomorrow', peaks occur on *bel-* and *Mam-*, while the valley is located on *di*. Again, this suggests that there is a L-tone which is OT-aligned right with the following H, creating a low target just before the peak.[5]

In a follow-up to Ladd and Schepman (2003), Dilley, Ladd, and Schepman (2005) show that the duration between the low target and the target of the following H* does not represent a constant interval. On this ground, they call an analysis of the pitch rise as a L+H* pitch accent (cf. (24b)) into question. This latter argument presupposes that a bitonal accent must always be realized with a constant time interval between the associating tone and the trailing or leading tone, a view ascribed to Pierrehumbert (1980) as well as later work. However, as was apparent from the discussion of structure (34a) and Frota (2002), tones that OT-align with other tones may well be implemented with reference to the segmental string, just as the phonetic alignment of associated tones may be sensitive to segmental conditioning.

Finally, a representation of the Greek pre-nuclear rise as a bitonal LH cluster was argued for by Arvaniti, Ladd, and Mennen (2000) on the grounds that the two targets are equally stably aligned relative to the segmental string: the low target occurs at the end of the preceding syllable and the high target at the beginning of the vowel in the following syllable. A slightly different motivation for postulating a structure of this type was advanced by Face (2001), who showed that both the low and high targets are timed to occur *within* the accented syllable in the case of (final or non-final) narrow-focus peaks in Castillian Spanish. Since a LH-cluster can in principle be provided with a star at the higher node, as shown in (37), it avoids singling out either L or H as the starred tone.

(37)

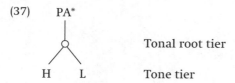

Tonal root tier

Tone tier

11.6.2   Distributional considerations

Distributional criteria have been appealed to in the analysis of final low-pitched accents in French as downstepped !H* (Post 2000, Gussenhoven 2004). Like many other languages, French allows a two-accent phrase like *deux garçons* to be pronounced with a high first and a low final syllable, in addition to a contour with two equally high peaks. While the second contour is described by means of a L, H*L H*L, tone sequence, the first contour might be either L, H* L* L, or L, H* !H* L, (Ladd 1996:127). At first sight, it would appear reasonable to analyze the second pitch accent as L* in view of the fact that it is phonetically low-pitched. Under that view, it would be difficult to explain that a high-pitched realization is always preceded by a valley. That is, it would not be clear why there is no contour of type (38c). An interpretation of the low-pitched final syllable of (38a) as a downstepped H* would explain this gap, and it would imply that H* after H* is downstepped. This requires the downstep rule (39).

(38)

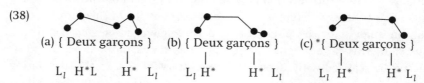

(a) { Deux garçons }   (b) { Deux garçons }   (c) *{ Deux garçons }
     | | | | | | |
   L, H*L   H* L,   L, H*   H* L,   L, H*   H* L,

(39)   FRENCH DOWNSTEP *(implementation)*
       H* → !H* / H ____ ... (L,)

A prediction by (39) is that *ι*'s with more than two pitch accents undergo downstep only in staircase-shaped contours (see (40a)), not in the peak-valley-peak sequences that are familiar from West-African and Germanic languages (see (40b)), which would appear to be correct (40) (cf. Gussenhoven 2004:104).

(40)

    (a)   (b)

A further example of an analytical decision that is made on non-phonetic grounds is the assignment of the L in (39a) to the status of a trailing tone of the H* on its left, rather than that of a leading tone of the H* on its right. As we saw in Section 11.6.1, arguing on phonetic grounds would inescapably lead to the conclusion that the L is a leading tone in L+H*, because the low target occurs at the start of the accented syllable; its distance from the preceding peak is variable and depends on the duration of the stretch of speech between the accented syllables. However, the postulation of L+H* leads to uncomfortable analyses if the pre-nuclear fall is followed by the *cliché mélodique*.[6] This pitch accent creates a high-pitched pre-accentual syllable and a mid-pitched accented syllable. If the preceding L cannot be a trailing tone of the preceding pitch accent, it ends up as a leading tone in a pitch accent that already has a leading H, i.e. as L+H+H*. Such an analysis has not otherwise been contemplated, and would involve a third type of structure by the side of (34a,b), one with two non-head positions to the left of a head position. It seems preferable, therefore, to assume H*L, where L aligns right. In (41), the mid pitch on the nuclear syllable is due to (39); the fact that it is not fully low, as in (38b) is due to the absence of L_i. Such a low-pitched accented syllable due to L_i makes for a well-formed contour, as does one where the syllable rises, due to H_i. This argument transfers to English, where Grice's (1995a) H+H*, realized [H+$^!$H*], may appear after H*L, as in *ToMORRow we're going to the MARket*.

(41)

{ Au CLAIR de la LUNE }

L_i H*L   H+H*

11.6.3 Semantic criteria

Semantic criteria are rarely used in phonological analyses of intonation. Our intuitions about intonational meaning are easily contaminated by the pragmatic meaning on the one hand and the meaning of the words and the syntax on the other. Also, the existence of a semantic difference between two contours is not sufficient evidence for a phonological contrast, since semantic differences, like differences in emphasis, may well be expressed in the phonetic implementation (Ladd and Morton 1997, Gussenhoven 1999). Arguments have been based, however, on the intuitive judgment that certain phonetically different contours are morphologically identical. Gussenhoven (1984:Ch.6) identified a pre-nuclear rise-fall as an *i*-internal version of a H*LH*, 'nuclear tone'. That is, the tone structure of (42b), with its right-aligning H-tone, is morphologically equivalent to that of (42a), with its medial H_i (see also Cruttenden 1997:67). Recall that the same kind of argument was used with respect to the analysis of (24). This analysis implies the 'derived' existence of a pitch accent with two trailing tones in English.

(42)

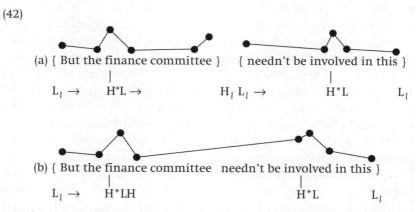

(a) { But the finance committee }   { needn't be involved in this }

$L_I \rightarrow$ $H^*L \rightarrow$ $H_I\, L_I \rightarrow$ H^*L L_I

(b) { But the finance committee   needn't be involved in this }

$L_I \rightarrow$ H^*LH H^*L L_I

To return to (24), a morphological argument for the correctness of (24a) is the apparent semantic identity of the pre-nuclear and nuclear accents. Analysis (24a) expresses this by assigning them the same underlying representation, H*L, and deriving the phonological difference from the context: the left-alignment of the trailing tone occurs ɪ-finally. By contrast, (24b) suggests the pitch accents are not only phonologically different, but also morphologically, and thus semantically.

The results of perception experiments eliciting semantic judgments by native listeners have also been brought to bear on analytical questions. An important theme here is whether phonetically different contours are realizations of the same phonological representation or of different ones. An experimental task underlying the work by 't Hart et al. (1990) is the judgment by native speakers whether two contours can pass as imitations of each other, ignoring differences in pitch range and tempo. The task has only recently been used in a perception experiment by Odé (2005), who wanted to determine whether two nuclear pitch accents in Russian, which come out very differently when used on a penultimate accented syllable, are still distinct on final syllables, where they are truncated and phonetically very similar. On the basis of the results, the answer is affirmative. Second, Gussenhoven and Rietveld (2000) showed that Dutch listeners perceive a higher degree of surprise in a contour that goes from mid pitch in the accented syllable to high pitch at the end of the utterance, if the mid pitch is raised. By contrast, for the same increase in perceived surprise, the low pitch of the low rise, which goes from low pitch in the accented syllable to high pitch at the end of the utterance, must be lowered. On the basis of these results, these contours were represented differently, as H^*H_I and $L^*H\ L_I$, respectively. For perception of intonation, see Vaissière (2005), and for approaches to issues of discreteness, Ladd and Morton (1997), Gussenhoven (1999), and Dilley (2004), among others.

11.6.4 Analytical coherence

In the ideal case, an analysis makes sense in more ways than one, making a number of rather different predictions. For instance, the conclusion that there is no L* in the phonology of French suggests that in contours like (38b), the low-pitched syllable is felicitously pronounced with a fall from mid to low pitch, where the mid pitch is the target predicted by !H*. Or again, the absence of L* forces one to analyze the high rising nuclear contour as H* H,, rather than L* H,, which predicts that the rise on -*çons* in a questioned *Garçons?* need not start from low pitch, and cannot be emphasized by starting from a very low pitch, in the way a low-to-high rise in English can be to express a greater degree of surprise. It also predicts that French does not have the English or Dutch contrast between a low rise, L*H H,, and the high rise, H* H,. If the experiment by Gussenhoven and Rietveld (2000) were to be repeated for French, it should not yield the result that lowering leads to more surprise. None of these predictions have been tested, but they obviously could be.[7]

11.7 Conclusion

Over the last decades, considerable progress has been made in our conception of tonal structures. Future work is likely to see an expansion of the data base, which is to be welcomed, since the number of languages for which comprehensive phonetic and phonological descriptions are available is still limited. The integration of lexical tone and intonational tone in theory and description, begun by Bruce (1977), consolidated by Pierrehumbert and Beckman (1988), and more recently exemplified for an African tone language by Laniran and Clements (2003), will hopefully seal a permanent merger between intonational phonology and the phonology of lexical tone.

Notes

I am grateful to Yiya Chen, José Elías-Ulloa, Martine Grice, Bob Ladd, Jörg Peters and the editor for their comments on an earlier version of this chapter.

1 A synthesis-by-rule program for intonation is embedded in the interactive transcription course for the intonation of Dutch: http://todi.let.ru.nl/. It contains a large number of context-sensitive rules for scaling and aligning targets and adjusting durations in particular tone contexts (Gussenhoven, Terken, and Rietveld 1999; Gussenhoven 2005).

2 For recent work on the influence of post-nuclear stress on the timing of the right-aligned low target in Dutch, see Lickley, Schepman, and Ladd (2005).

3 If association is assumed for all tones, as Dilley (2004) does, spreading would be yet another option.

4 For L_i, I'm assuming right-alignment as in (27), rather than two-edge alignment, as in (30).

5 In Mandarin Chinese, the same pattern of falls with variable durations followed by a relatively short rise occurs across sequences of syllables with 'neutral' tone (Chen and Xu, 2006). The frequent occurrence of this pattern suggests that slow falls are easier to produce than slow rises.

6 There is in fact a variety of such pitch accents (cf. Ladd 1996:139; Gussenhoven 2004:217).

7 French does have a contrast between the 'continuation mineur' and 'continuation majeur' contours (Delattre 1951), or the high rise $H^* H_i$ and the (plain) rise H^* (Post 2000), which equally exists in English and Dutch.

12

The interaction of tone, sonority, and prosodic structure

Paul de Lacy

12.1 Introduction

The aim of this chapter is to link the major aspects of suprasegmental phonology discussed in this part of the *Handbook* (i.e. tone – Yip Ch.10, Gussenhoven Ch.11; sonority – Zec Ch.8; prosodic structure – Zec Ch.8, Kager Ch.9). It shows how sonority and tone can both influence and be influenced by prosodic structure. It argues that there is a unifying theoretical mechanism that accounts for such influences and how this same mechanism accounts for interactions at all prosodic levels, from below the syllable to the Utterance. To illustrate the theoretical points, the initial empirical focus will be on the influence that sonority can have on foot structure, often called 'sonority-driven stress'. Relevant data from the North New Guinea language Takia are provided in (1).

(1) *Takia sonority-driven stress (Ross 2002, 2003)*

    (a) Stress the rightmost syllable with [a]

        [taˈma-n] 'father {3sg}'   [araˈtam]   'you (pl.) bite us'

        [ɲiˈsaŋes] 'hawk'   [ˈŋa-sol]   '1sg-flee'

        [ˈabi]   'garden'   [buguˈgaru] 'twins'

    (b) Otherwise stress the rightmost syllable with [e] or [o]

        [kirˈŋen] 'her/his finger, toe' [ɲiˈemi]   'your (pl.) legs/feet'

        [ifuˈno]   's/he hit you'   [mulˈmol] 'a kind of tree'

    (c) Otherwise stress the rightmost syllable

        [ifiˈni]   's/he hit him'   [tuˈbun]   'her/his grandparent'

As with other stress systems, edge-attraction is evident (Kager Ch.9): in a word where all vowels are the same, stress is attracted to the right edge (e.g. [araˈtam], [ifiˈni], [tuˈbun]). However, the most important factor for Takia is sonority: stress must fall on the most sonorous vowel available, where the part of the sonority scale that is relevant for Takia is | a ⟩ e,o ⟩ i,u | (for details on sonority, see Section 12.2). The sonority requirements also override conditions on foot form: while [(ta'man)] has an iambic (right-headed) foot, [('abi)] has a trochaic one in order to have a higher sonority foot head.

Section 12.2 identifies several competing theories that aim to account for the interaction seen in Takia and others like it. It argues that recent approaches that derive constraints from markedness hierarchies in a restrictive fashion can account for the observed patterns with sonority and stress (Kenstowicz 1997/2004, de Lacy 2004); it contrasts this approach with ones that employ representational devices (e.g. distinctions in mora count, featural impoverishment).

Section 12.3 identifies analogous influences between sonority and unstressed positions, demonstrating the generality of the interaction between prosodic structure and sonority. The constraint-based proposal is extended to tone-prosody interactions in Section 12.4, different prosodic levels in Section 12.5, and Section 12.6 shows that it can also account for tone- and sonority–prosody interactions involving metathesis, deletion, epenthesis, and neutralization.

This chapter links a number of traditionally distinct areas of research. It discusses markedness and its formal expression: sonority- and tone-driven stress are transparently sensitive to markedness hierarchies, unlike many segmental phenomena (Rice 4.6, de Lacy 2006). It is also a crucial complement to metrical stress theory (Kager Ch.9) since it is not possible to fully account for influences on foot form without considering sonority and tone. Non-metrical stress also provides a link to syllable theory. As Zec (Ch.8) shows, sonority plays a crucial role in the formation of syllables, and the same principles are relevant in foot formation. Finally, tone-driven stress provides insight into how tone and prosodic structure interact, relating to research on both tone (Yip Ch.10) and intonation (Gussenhoven Ch.11).

To give a brief overview of the current state of research in this area, some aspects of the interaction of tone and sonority with prosodic structure have a large literature behind them while others do not. While a great deal has been written about the influence of edges and moraic content on foot structure (see Kager Ch.9), work on sonority- and tone-driven stress is extremely limited in comparison (see the overviews for sonority in Section 12.2, and for tone: de Lacy 2002b). Other related phenomena, such as sonority-driven deletion, also do not have a large literature (see Gouskova 2003 and references cited therein). In contrast, there has been a large amount of research into sonority-driven neutralization (also called 'vowel reduction' or 'raising') (see Crosswhite 1999, 2004 and references cited therein). A great deal has also been written about metrical influences on tone, forcing tone shift, deletion, neutralization, and so on (see Goldsmith 1987, Downing 1990, Yip 2002, Sec.3.9, 10.3–4 for overviews). Despite the various approaches and different amounts of research on these topics, it is clear that they are currently converging in a theoretical sense. This chapter aims to illustrate the convergence: the same theoretical devices can be used to provide an account of all these disparate phenomena.[1]

12.2   Sonority and prosodic position

The aim of this section is to provide an analysis of Takia's sonority-driven stress system. In doing so, two major theoretical approaches will be identified: (a) constraint-based and (b) representational. These approaches will be evaluated and their typological predictions examined.

By way of general theoretical background, both of the most recent theories of sonority-driven stress (Kenstowicz 1997/2004, de Lacy 2002a, 2004, 2006) advocate the use of constraint interaction as a means of explanation. The idea that constraint interaction can be used to account for sonority-driven stress is proposed in Kenstowicz (1997/2004), who advocates a fixed hierarchy of foot-head and non-head constraints. Kenstowicz' theory relates directly to Prince & Smolensky's (2004) proposal about fixed ranking and the influence of sonority on syllable structure (see Zec 8.5). Building on this approach, the recent alternative advocated by Prince (1997, 1998, 2000, 2001) and de Lacy (2002a, 2004, 2006) is to rely on constraint form entirely and avoid positing universally fixed rankings. Both of these approaches will be discussed below. Theories that use representational devices will also be examined in Section 12.2.3, including those by Hayes (1995:Ch.7), building on proposals by Everett & Everett (1984), Davis (1988b) and Everett (1988).

12.2.1   Sensitivity through stringent constraint form

This section develops an analysis of Takia's stress system. All the data discussed in this section, and the core analytical insight that Takia vowel quality influences stress, are from Ross (2002, 2003). The following discussion focuses on the assignment of primary stress only; Takia has a number of other interesting phenomena that interact with the phenomena discussed here.

Takia has five vowels [a e o i u] and a syllable structure of (C)V(C), though closed syllables are reportedly rare in non-final position. The default position for stress in Takia is on the rightmost syllable. This is evident in words where all vowels have the same sonority level: [ara'tam] 'you (pl.) bite us', [ifi'ni] 's/he hit him', [tu'bun] 'her/his grandparent'. This pattern is the result of requiring right-headed feet ('iambs') to be aligned with the right edge of the Prosodic Word (PrWd); the relevant constraints are in (2) (after McCarthy & Prince 1993a, see Kager 9.3).

(2)   *ALIGN-R(Ft, PrWd)*

"The right edge of every foot must coincide with the right
edge of a PrWd."

IAMB

"The head of every foot must be rightmost" (i.e. ALIGN-
R(Hd_{Ft},Ft))

Sonority

Takia's stress system is governed by a number of conflicting requirements.
One involves 'sonority', which refers to a hierarchy of segment types;
the vocalic portion is given in (3), adapted from Kenstowicz (1997/2004)
and de Lacy (2006).[2] The exact number of sonority distinctions and their
phonetic basis (if there is any) is a very contentious issue: see Parker (2002)
for a comprehensive overview. The distinctions given here are needed to
account for the range of sonority-driven stress systems identified in
Section 12.2.2.[3] (See Section 12.2.2 for discussion of whether sonority can
be decomposed into sub-hierarchies and which other features can influence prosodic structure.)

(3)   *Vowel Sonority Hierarchy*

low peripheral vowels 'a'	>	mid peripheral vowels 'e•o'	>	high peripheral vowels 'i•u'	>	mid central vowels 'ə'	>	high central vowels 'ɨ'

Representative vowels are given for each category and will be used as
abbreviations for the categories in the rest of this chapter. Of course, many
more vowels belong to the categories than the abbreviations suggest; for
example, 'high peripheral vowels' includes [y ʉ] as well as [i u]. For discussion about whether hierarchies other than or instead of sonority can influence foot placement, see Section 12.2.2.

Optimality Theory provides the means to formally express the sonority
hierarchy in (3) through the form of constraints, as in (4). Because these
constraints are in a subset-relation in terms of their violation marks, they
are in a 'stringency' relation (Prince 1998 et seq.). This general approach to
expressing markedness hierarchies is called 'Stringent Markedness'.[4]

(4)   *Stringent sonority constraints (Prince 1998, de Lacy 2002a, 2004, 2006)*

(a) *$Hd_\alpha/ɨ$ "Incur a violation for every head of constituent α that
                         contains a high central vowel"

(b) *$Hd_\alpha/ɨ,ə$ "Incur a violation for every head of constituent α that
                         contains a high or mid central vowel"

(c) *$Hd_\alpha/ɨ,ə,i•u$ "Incur a violation for every head of constituent α that
                         contains a central or high peripheral vowel"

(d) *Hd$_\alpha$/i,ə,i•u,e•o   "Incur a violation for every head of α that contains either a central or non-low peripheral vowel"

(e) *Hd$_\alpha$/i,ə,i•u,e•o,a   "Incur a violation for every head of α that contains either a central or peripheral (i.e. any) vowel."

There are specific instantiations of the constraints in (4) for each level of the prosodic hierarchy. From the data given above, it is impossible to tell for Takia whether sonority refers to foot heads (i.e. all stressed syllables) or PrWd heads (i.e. just the main-stressed syllable). Either will work for Takia, so reference to foot heads will be arbitrarily assumed here as it makes no difference to the main points of the analysis. (Other types of head and non-head are discussed in Section 12.3.) So, *Hd$_{Ft}$/i,ə,i•u is violated whenever a stressed syllable (i.e. the head of a foot) contains a high central, mid central, or high peripheral vowel. For example, [('pɨka)(ˌtəki)(ˌtipa)] violates it three times, as do [('pika)(ˌtiki)(ˌtipa)] and [('pəka)(ˌtəki)(ˌtəpa)].

The term 'head' is slightly imprecise as it has been used in a variety of different ways. For the cases discussed here, the 'head of α' is the nuclear vowel of α dominated by a series of prosodic heads up to α-level. See Zec's (8.5.1, 2000, 2003) theory of prosodic thresholds and de Lacy's (1999b, 2002a, 2006) Designated Terminal Element theory for more explicit approaches to prosodic reference.

Avoidance of stressed high vowels

The forms in (5) show the influence of the *Hd$_{Ft}$/i,ə,i•u constraint. Stress could fall on the default (i.e. rightmost) syllable, but doing so would result in a stressed high peripheral vowel when there is a more desirable non-high vowel elsewhere in the word. Instead, stress is attracted away from a fixed position on the final syllable to fall on the highest sonority syllable.

(5) *Avoidance of stressed high vowels in Takia*

    (a) Avoidance of ['i]

['abi]	'garden'	[i'lodi]	'their insides'
[ŋi'emi]	'your (pl.) legs/feet'		

    (b) Avoidance of ['u]

['nanun]	'child-3sg.'	[buga'garu]	'twins'
['sobul]	'feast, celebration'	['bemfufu]	'index finger'

Tableau (6) illustrates with the word ['bemfufu]. Candidate (a) fares best in terms of the foot-form and location constraints, but in doing so fatally violates *Hd$_{Ft}$/i,ə,i•u. In contrast, candidate (b) avoids violations of *Hd$_{Ft}$/i,ə,i•u by stressing the initial mid vowel, and in doing so violates both ALIGN-R and IAMB. Even though Takia does not allow central vowels on the surface, the constraint *Hd$_{Ft}$/i,ə,i•u is used here because constraints are universal – i.e. there is no *Hd$_{Ft}$/i•u.

(6)   *Avoidance of stressed high vowels*

/bemfufu/	*Hd$_{Ft}$/i,ə,i•u	ALIGN-R(Ft,PrWd)	IAMB
(a) bem(fu'fu)	*!		
☞ (b) ('bemfu)fu		*	*

Avoidance of stressed mid vowels

Similarly, the forms in (7) show that mid vowels are avoided when there is a higher sonority option. This can be formally expressed by using *Hd$_{Ft}$/i,ə,i•u, e•o, as in tableau (8).

(7)   *Avoidance of stressed mid vowels in Takia*

[ti'manek]	'meeting'	[ɲi'saɲes]	'hawk'
['ŋasol]	'I run away'	[ka'naorig]	'earthquake'
[ka'nagioi]	'name of peak on external rim of Karkar crater'		

(8)   *Avoidance of stressed mid vowels*

/kanaorig/	*Hd$_{Ft}$/i,ə,i•u,e•o	*Hd$_{Ft}$/i,ə,i•u	ALIGN-R(Ft,PrWd)	IAMB
(a) kana(o'rig)	*!	*		
(b) ka(na'o)rig	*!		*	
(c) ('kana)orig			* *	*!
☞ (d) (ka'na)orig			* *	

Candidates (a) and (b) fatally violate *Hd$_{Ft}$/i,ə,i•u,e•o by having a non-low vowel as a foot head. As candidate (d) has a stressed [a], it wins despite its foot being two syllables from the right edge. Candidate (c) also has a stressed [a], but violates the metrical constraints more than (c).[5]

Emergent edge attraction

Despite the fact that the *Hd$_{Ft}$-sonority constraints dominate, the metrical constraints are still active in the system. Their effect emerges whenever there is a 'tie' on constraint violation of the *Hd$_{Ft}$-sonority constraints. This happens most strikingly when there are only high vowels in a word, as illustrated in tableau (9). All the candidates equally violate the *Hd$_{Ft}$-sonority constraints, so ALIGN-R and IAMB are crucial in eliminating the competitors.

(9)   *Emergent effect of metrical constraints*

/ifini/	*Hd$_{Ft}$/i,ə,i•u,e•o	*Hd$_{Ft}$/i,ə,i•u	ALIGN-R(Ft,PrWd)	IAMB
(a) ('ifi)ni	*	*	*!	*
(b) (i'fi)ni	*	*	*!	
(c) i('fini)	*	*		*!
☞ (d) i(fi'ni)	*	*		*

Do feet exist in Takia?

The preceding analysis has assumed that PrWds are parsed into feet. This assumption is based on the hypothesis that all languages employ all prosodic constituents in the Prosodic Hierarchy, including feet. The fact that foot form is blithely ignored in Takia's stress system does not mean that feet do not exist in the language. In fact, there is evidence that they are important. All of the content words cited by Ross (2002, 2003) are minimally disyllabic; none have the form [(C)V(C)]. As Kager (Ch.9) explains, such minimal word restrictions can be accounted for by requirements on the form of feet. Specifically, FtBin-σ "Feet are disyllabic" (based on McCarthy & Prince's 1986 FtBin) must outrank a relevant faithfulness constraint so that underlying /pa/ would surface as [pata] (through epenthesis) or ∅ (through deletion).[6] In any case, the influence of foot structure is evident in many sonority- and tone-driven stress systems, and will be discussed in Section 12.3.

The final main-stress ranking

Some rankings cannot be determined from the available data. For example, there is no way to determine the ranking of $^*\mathrm{Hd}_{Ft}/i,\partial,i{\bullet}u$ and $^*\mathrm{Hd}_{Ft}/i,\partial,i{\bullet}u,e{\bullet}o$ with respect to each other. Even more acutely, the ranking of $^*\mathrm{Hd}_{Ft}/i,\partial,i{\bullet}u,e{\bullet}o,a$ cannot be determined in regard to the constraints discussed above as every winning candidate violates this constraint in Takia. Similarly, the ranking of constraints such as $^*\mathrm{Hd}_{Ft}/i$ cannot be determined as Takia bans [i] on the surface (by means of *Nuc/i – Prince & Smolensky 2004). I add that the ranking of constraints in a stringency relation can be determined in some cases if there is another constraint C which dominates one constraint and is dominated by the other (see de Lacy 2006 Sec.5.3.2 for an example).

Takia's response to the sonority-head conditions is to deviate from the default metrical structure, and not delete the offending elements (/abi/ → ['ab]), epenthesize (/abi/ → [abi'a]), neutralize (/abi/ → [a'ba]), or metathesize (/abi/ → [i'ba]). Faithfulness constraints must therefore outrank the head-sonority constraints; these are discussed further in Section 12.6 but grouped under Faith here (10).

(10)   *Takia's sonority-driven stress ranking*

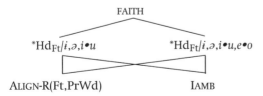

Expressing universality

The constraints make it impossible to produce an 'anti-Takia' system where stress seeks out high vowels, then mid vowels, and only grudgingly falls on [a].

For such a language, there would have to be a freely rankable constraint that assigns a violation to ['a] but not to any less sonorous stressed vowel: i.e. $*Hd_{Ft}/a$. However, there is no such constraint in the set provided in (4).[7] Similarly, to have stress avoid mid vowels and favour high vowels, there would have to be a constraint $*Hd_{Ft}/e•o$ (or $*Hd_{Ft}/a,e•o$). Again, there is no such constraint. In fact, no matter how the $*Hd_{Ft}$-sonority constraints are ranked, stressed low vowels will always be favoured over stressed mid- and high-peripheral vowels, and stressed mid-peripheral over high-peripheral vowels, and so on. This follows from the form of the constraints. Their effect can be seen visually in the quasi-tableau (11). Every stressed vowel incurs a proper subset of violations of all the less sonorous stressed vowels, so no matter how the constraints are ranked, the relative markedness of the vowels will remain the same. In this way, the constraint's form expresses the universal relations in the sonority hierarchy.

(11)   *A stringency relation produces universal markedness implications*

	$*Hd_{Ft}$ /ɨ	$*Hd_{Ft}$ /ɨ•ə	$*Hd_{Ft}$/ /ɨ•ə•i,u	$*Hd_{Ft}$ /ɨ•ə•i,u•e,o	$*Hd_{Ft}$ /ɨ•ə•i,u•e,o•ɛ,ɔ•a
'ɨ	*	*	*	*	*
'ə		*	*	*	*
'i/'u			*	*	*
'e/'o				*	*
'a					*

12.2.2   Typology and fixed ranking

The theory of sonority-driven stress presented above expresses the sonority hierarchy through constraint form. An alternative is to employ a universally fixed ranking, and yet another is to rely less on constraints and more on representation. Both approaches will be discussed below.

Hierarchy through fixed ranking

Kenstowicz (1997/2004) proposes that the sonority-head constraints are in a universally invariant ranking, with the form in (12). The symbol '»»' denotes a 'fixed ranking'.

(12)   *Universally fixed ranking*

   $*Hd_{Ft}/ɨ$ »» $*Hd_{Ft}/ə$ »»$*Hd_{Ft}/i,u$ »»$*Hd_{Ft}/e,o$ »»$*Hd_{Ft}/a$

The Fixed Ranking approach can deal with Takia equally as well as the Stringency approach by the ranking || $*Hd_{Ft}/i,u$ » $*Hd_{Ft}/e,o$ » ALIGN-R(Ft,PrWd), IAMB ||. However, it makes different typological predictions from the stringency theory.

The differences relate to whether sonority categories can be ignored. The Stringent Markedness approach allows for categories to be collapsed (or 'conflated'). For example, a constraint such as *Hd$_{Ft}$/i,ə,i•u assigns the same violations to both stressed central and high peripheral vowels, thereby allowing a situation where central and high peripheral vowels might be treated in the same way for stress purposes. In contrast, the Fixed Ranking approach prevents such conflation.

A relevant example is found in the Uralic language Nganasan (de Lacy 2004; data from Castrén 1854, Helimski 1998). The default position for stress is on the penult: e.g. [a'baʔa] 'older sister, aunt'. However, stress will avoid a penultimate central or high peripheral vowel whenever it can: e.g. ['aniʔə] 'large', ['baruʃi] 'devil', ['neɡyʃa] 'tease', ['ʝembiʔʃi] 'dressing', ['solətu] 'glass' (FTBIN and TROCHEE block options such as *[neɡy('ʃa)], *[ne(ɡy'ʃa)]). Both theories can successfully model this pattern by having constraints against central and high peripheral vowels outrank ALIGN-R(Ft, PrWd). In the Fixed Ranking theory, || *Hd$_{Ft}$/i » *Hd$_{Ft}$/ə » *Hd$_{Ft}$/i,u » ALIGN-R (Ft,PrWd) || would account for the avoidance, as in tableau (13).

(13) *Nganasan with Fixed Ranking produces sonority-driven stress*

/baruʃi/	*Hd$_{Ft}$/i	*Hd$_{Ft}$/ə	*Hd$_{Ft}$/i,u	ALIGN-R(Ft,PrWd)
(a) ba('ruʃi)			*!	
☞ (b) ('baru)ʃi				*

Tableau (13) helps see a strong prediction of the Fixed Ranking theory: it predicts that stress should avoid a penultimate schwa for high vowels. A word like *cintəɟi* 'stoke' should be stressed on the antepenult because [cin('təɟi)] would fatally violate *Hd$_{Ft}$/ə. However, Nganasan does not distinguish between central and high peripheral vowels for stress purposes; stress does not retract off a central vowel onto a high peripheral vowel: e.g. [cin('təɟi)] 'stoke', *[('cintə)ɟi]; [kun('sini)] 'inside', *[('kunsi)ni]. The problem is illustrated in tableau (14). The symbol ☛ indicates that the wrong winner is chosen.

(14) *Nganasan with Fixed Ranking prevents conflation*

/cintəɟi/	*Hd$_{Ft}$/i	*Hd$_{Ft}$/ə	*Hd$_{Ft}$/i,u	ALIGN-R(Ft,PrWd)
(a) cin('təɟi)		*!		
☛ (b) ('cintə)ɟi			*	*

In contrast, the Stringent Markedness theory allows for the collapse of category distinctions. To get stress to favour mid peripheral and low vowels over high peripheral and central vowels, *Hd$_{Ft}$/i,ə,i•u must outrank ALIGN-R(Ft, PrWd). However, no other head-sonority constraint has to, crucially including *Hd$_{Ft}$/i and *Hd$_{Ft}$/i,ə. The effect is that stress treats central and high peripheral vowels equally, as shown in tableau (15). Because *Hd$_{Ft}$/i and *Hd$_{Ft}$/$i,ə$ are ranked below ALIGN-R(Ft,PrWd), they have no effect on the outcome.

(15)   *Nganasan with Stringent constraints*

/cintəɟi/	*Hd$_{Ft}$/$i,ə,i•u$	ALIGN-R(Ft,PrWd)	*Hd$_{Ft}$/$i,ə$	*Hd$_{Ft}$/i
(a) ('cintə)ɟi	*	*!		
☞ (b) cin('təɟi)	*		*	

In short, the Stringent theory is empirically more adequate than the Fixed Ranking theory – Fixed Ranking prevents attested cases where distinctions between sonority categories are ignored for stress purposes.

Typology

The table in (16) summarizes the typological predictions of the Stringency Theory, including cases with conflation. Almost every possible contiguous conflation in stress-sonority interaction is attested. Categories are marked as conflated if they are grouped inside the same oval. For example, the mid and low vowels are conflated in Pichis Asheninca, but the central and high vowels are not.

For ease of presentation the table uses 'i/ə' to stand for any central vowel (e.g. Pichis Asheninca has [ɨ], not schwa); in any case, it is rare to find a language with a contrast between /ə/ and /i/ (Nganasan is one of the few). Similarly 'e o' stands for all mid vowels, including [e o ɛ ɔ] even though [e o] are demonstrably less sonorous than [ɛ ɔ] (see de Lacy 2006:Ch.7).

(16)   *Head-sonority conflation typology*

Categories	Languages
(i/ə) (i/u) e/o (a)	Gujarati (de Lacy 2002a:Ch.3, 2006: Sec.5.3.2)
(i/ə) (i/u) ‹e/o› a	Pichis Asheninca (J.Payne 1990)
(i/ə) ‹i/u› e/o a›	Yil (Martens & Tuominen 1977)
‹i/ə i/u› ‹e/o› (a)	–
‹i/ə i/u› ‹e/o› a›	Nganasan (de Lacy 2004)
‹i/ə i/u› ‹e/o› (a)	Kara (Schlie & Schlie 1993, de Lacy 1997)
‹i/ə i/u e/o a›	All vowels are treated the same

The different systems are generated by different sets of active constraints. The Gujarati system, for example, is due to both *Hd$_{Ft}$/$i,ə,i•u,e•o$ and *Hd$_{Ft}$/$i,ə$ being active, while *Hd$_{Ft}$/ $i,ə,i•u$ is not (to allow conflation of high and mid vowels) (see de Lacy 2006 Sec.5.3.2). The table also shows that almost every imaginable conflation of vowel sonority is attested: any set of contiguous categories can be conflated.

There are two systems missing from the table. One is a language that distinguishes all sonority levels: i.e. ə vs. i/u vs. e/o vs. a. Kobon is reported to have such distinctions (Kenstowicz 1997/2004), but Davies' (1981) data only provide evidence for the distinctions | a ⟩ o ⟩ i, ə ⟩ i | – i.e. high vowels and schwa could be conflated. Given the existence of languages like Takia and Nanti (Crowhurst & Michael 2005) which distinguish every sonority level they have (i.e. *i,u* vs. *e,o* vs. *a*) it is likely that this gap is due to the limited range of data currently available rather than signifying a theoretical issue.

Similarly, I have not found a system that definitely conflates ['ə] and ['i 'u] but distinguishes mid from low vowels. In such a language, stress would first seek out a low vowel and otherwise a mid vowel; if there were only high and central vowels, stress would fall on the default position. Given that there are languages in which stress favors low vowels over mid vowels (e.g. Gujarati) and languages in which high peripheral vowels and schwa are conflated (e.g. Nganasan), I assume that this gap is accidental.

There are a number of languages that have stress systems that are insensitive to sonority, even though they have very low sonority vowels. My own dialect of New Zealand English is one: schwa (which corresponds to [ɪ] in many other dialects) can be stressed and more sonorous vowels do not attract the stress away from it: e.g. [dʒu'dʒətsu] 'jujitsu', *['dʒudʒətsu], /həstɔɹi/ 'history' → ['həstəɹi]/['həstʃɹi], *[hə'stɔri]. Other languages include Iaai (Lynch 2002) which has the vowels [a ɛ ɔ e o i u ə], with consistent word-initial stress and schwa permitted word-initially.

Theoretically significant gaps are those in which stress seeks out lower sonority vowels and disregards higher sonority ones. Such systems are unattested, as predicted by the constraint-based theories.

There is one other systematic and theoretically significant gap: no language conflates non-contiguous categories. An example would be a language which conflates low and high vowels, but not mid vowels: stress would fall on the leftmost [a], [i], or [u], and skip over intervening mid vowels [e] and [o]. The stringent constraints predict that such a language cannot exist. It would require a constraint that favored stressed high vowels over stressed mid vowels (e.g. *Hd_{Ft}/mid vowels) and there is no such constraint in the theory.

Sonority, or something else?
After Kenstowicz (1997/2004), the discussion above has assumed that Takia and systems like it are sensitive to sonority rather than some other hierarchy. In contrast, Crowhurst & Michael (2005:70) propose that such stress systems are instead sensitive to two separate hierarchies: one on vowel height (HEIGHTPK: | high ⟩ mid ⟩ low |), and one on vowel peripherality (PERIPHPK: | central ⟩ peripheral |) (also see Smith 2002 Sec.23.2.2-fn.48).

This proposal essentially splits the sonority hierarchy along its two major dimensions (at least for vowels).

There are two problems with this view. One is that it incorrectly prevents central and peripheral vowels from conflating. To explain why, it is first necessary to point out that the constraints from PERIPHPK (i.e. *Hd$_{Ft}$/high »» *Hd$_{Ft}$/mid »» *Hd$_{Ft}$/low) must be universally outranked by the constraints from HEIGHTPK (i.e. *Hd$_{Ft}$/central (»» *Hd$_{Ft}$/peripheral)). (If the opposite ranking was permitted, it would generate a language where foot heads avoid high peripheral vowels [i u] for the mid central vowel schwa: i.e. *Hd$_{Ft}$/high » *Hd$_{Ft}$/central would favor ['pəki] over [pə'ki] even in a system with default rightmost stress. However, there is no such language. This result holds regardless of whether fixed ranking or stringency is used.) However, if *Hd$_{Ft}$/central universally outranks *Hd$_{Ft}$/high, it is impossible to conflate schwa and high vowels, incorrectly predicting that Nganasan is impossible for the same reason as illustrated in tableau (14). In short, to allow for conflation of central and peripheral vowels, it is crucial for them to be on the same hierarchy, therefore ruling out approaches that appeal to vowel height and peripherality as separate hierarchies.

The other problem with approaches that seek to eschew sonority in favor of sub-hierarchies of features is that stress is never sensitive to features apart from sonority and tone. There is no system in which, for example, stress falls on the leftmost round vowel, or nasal vowel, and so on (de Lacy 2002a). Therefore, no stress system could refer directly to height *features* like [±high] and [±low] (and [±round], and so on). In contrast, sonority is arguably not a subsegmental feature – it behaves like manner features, which McCarthy (1988) proposes inhabit the root node.

12.2.3   Representational approaches

The two approaches discussed so far are both based on the assumption that markedness effects should be expressed through constraint form or ranking; this idea began with Prince & Smolensky (2004[1993]) and Smolensky (1993). An entirely different class of theory employs representational devices. Both Hayes' (1995:Ch.7) 'prominence grid' proposal and the approach of representing distinctions through moraic or featural content will be discussed here.

Prominence grids

Hayes (1995:Ch.7), building on Halle & Vergnaud (1987), Davis (1989b) and Everett & Everett (1984), proposes a device called a 'prominence grid'.[8] A prominence grid is akin to a metrical grid (see Kager 9.2.1), but the grid-marks are assigned to syllables on the basis of certain properties. For example, Takia syllables with [a] would be assigned three grid-marks, syllables with mid vowels would get two, and syllables with high vowels just one. General rules or constraints require that the head syllable have the highest prominence grid-mark (in OT the prominence grid is accessed through the constraint PKPROM – Prince & Smolensky 2004).

While prominence grids are empirically adequate in accounting for sonority-driven stress – and every other type of stress – they are much too powerful when compared with approaches such as Kenstowicz' (1997/2004). Prominence grids are unique devices: as Hayes (1995:274) observes, they are not like true metrical grids as they do not avoid clash or lapse (Kager 9.2.1). In contrast, the constraint formation mechanism that accounts for sonority-driven stress discussed above is not unique to foot–sonority relations; it also applies to tone (12.4) and can motivate deletion, epenthesis, metathesis, and neutralization (12.6). While prominence grids are transitory devices, and are only relevant to one rule or one constraint (i.e. PKPROM), Kenstowicz' proposal refers to an inherent property of segments – sonority – and one that can be accessed by any relevant constraint (or rule). The proposal also made a direct formal relation between sonority-driven stress and syllable construction, a relation that prominence grids obscure.

On the empirical side, Hayes' prominence grid formalism predicts that sonority and tone are irrelevant to foot construction (1995:272). Evidence against this prediction is found in systems where secondary stress (i.e. foot location) is influenced by sonority (see Section 12.3, McGarrity 2003, Crowhurst & Michael 2005). In short, the constraint-based approach avoids employing a transitory rule/constraint-specific device that unnecessarily abstracts away from properties such as sonority and tone.

Moras and featurelessness

An entirely different approach is to rely on the representation of individual segments to account for their behavior with stress. For example, a number of authors have proposed that schwa lacks subsegmental features, or a mora, or both (for recent discussion, see e.g. Oostendorp 1995, Crosswhite 2004). This idea is part of a broader approach to markedness that attempts to derive markedness relations from aspects of representation (e.g. Paradis & Prunet 1991b, Rice 1996, Morén 2003, and many others; cf. de Lacy 2006 Sec.8.4 and references cited therein for critical appraisal).

The 'moraic' approach postulates that all syllable distinctions in stress are due to moraic content. In Gujarati, for example, stress seeks out [a] over [ɛ ɔ e o i u], and avoids [ə] whenever possible. In a moraic approach, Gujarati [ə] could have no moras, [a] two, and the other vowels one; preference for stressed syllables with greater moraic content would produce the observed stress system. In such an approach conflation is a side-effect of mora assignment; it is the fact that high and mid vowels have the same moraic content that results in their conflation.

In effect, the moraic approach to sonority-driven stress outlined above converts moras into little more than a language-specific diacritic device that is almost synonymous with sonority. However, there is a difference between it and the sonority approach. Because moras represent duration, they make undesirable predictions for phonetic realization. In Gujarati, low vowels should be appreciably longer than high and mid vowels, and all should be longer than schwa. This is not so: there is no significant difference between [a]'s duration and the other vowels' in Gujarati (de Lacy 2002a, 2006). The same point can be made for other languages. For example, Takia's high vowels would have to have one mora, mid vowels two, and [a] three; however, Ross does not report any significant length difference between them. Nganasan distinguishes two groups of vowels for stress: [ɨ ə i y u] and [a e o]. The former group cannot have fewer moras than the latter because there is no significant durational difference between the two sets (de Lacy 2004 Sec.2.6.3). Finally, as Nina Topintzi (p.c.) observes, moraic approaches face a significant challenge when a language's stress placement relies on both sonority and a syllable's moraic content (e.g. Nanti – Crowhurst & Michael 2005).

Representational theories also make strong predictions about other processes in the same language. Proposing that low vowels have more moras than other vowels predicts that they can – and perhaps must – be treated differently for other mora-referring processes. This prediction is criticized at length by Gordon (1999).

Another popular representational theory relates specifically to the opposition between schwa and peripheral vowels, and relies on the idea that schwa lacks phonological features (e.g. Oostendorp 1995 and references cited therein). With additional theoretical devices, this fact makes schwas 'weak', and consequently unable to bear stress. This theory is one of a class that considers schwa to be fundamentally phonologically different from all other vowels. In contrast, the approach to stress proposed here denies that schwa is significantly different from other vowels in phonological terms – the only difference is that schwa is lower on the sonority hierarchy than (most) other vowels.

A problem with relating lack of features to stress avoidance arises in languages in which schwa is conflated with other vowels. In Nganasan, [ɨ], [ə], and [i y u] repel stress equally – i.e. they are conflated for stress purposes. If lack of features is the reason that schwa repels stress, then all of [ɨ ə i y u] must be featureless. However, if all these vowels are featureless, then they should be phonologically indistinguishable. At the very least, it is clear that featurelessness is not sufficient on its own to account for stress repulsion.

In the constraint-based approach, there is no need to appeal to lack of features or any other representational devices. Schwa is not fundamentally different from other vowels in terms of its representation. It is simply low on the sonority hierarchy; its behaviour in phonological processes follows from its sonority level, not from its lack of features. In short, attempts to deal with sonority-driven stress by appealing to representational differences among vowels lead to unsupported predictions regarding duration, mora-sensitive phonological processes, or difficulties in accounting for vowel contrasts. For further critiques of representational theories of stress, see Gordon (1999), and de Lacy (2002a Sec.3.3.4, 2004 Sec.2.6.3). For a general critique of representational theories of markedness, see de Lacy (2006 Sec.8.4) and the references cited therein (cf. Rice 1996, to appear).

12.3   Non-heads and other levels

Prince & Smolensky's (2004) proposal about sonority and syllable structure not only draws a relation between syllable heads (i.e. nuclei) and sonority, but also between non-heads (i.e. margins) and sonority (see Zec 8.5.2). If sonority-driven stress is analogous to syllable form, it is therefore expected that there could be constraints on non-heads of feet. In addition, the reverse sonority relation should apply: non-heads should prefer low sonority elements, with the resulting constraints as in (17), adapting a proposal by Kenstowicz (1997/2004), and explored further in de Lacy (2002a,b, 2004).

(17)

    (a) *non-Hd$_\alpha$/a   "Incur a violation for every non-head of constituent α that contains a low vowel"

    (b) *non-Hd$_\alpha$/a,e•o   "Incur a violation for every non-head of α that contains either a low or mid peripheral vowel"

    (c) *non-Hd$_\alpha$/a,e•o,i•u "Incur a violation for every non-head of α that contains either a high, mid, or low peripheral vowel."
                           ...and so on.[9]

The effect of such constraints can be seen in Kiriwina (de Lacy 2004 Sec.4; for other cases, see Kenstowicz 1997/2004, de Lacy 2002a:Ch.4). As shown in (18a), a quantity-sensitive trochaic foot is built at or as near to the right edge of the PrWd as foot binarity will allow (CVV and CVC are heavy) (see Kager 9.2.3.2). However, the foot will appear away from the right edge if doing so will allow it to have a lower sonority non-head (i.e. a high vowel), in (18b).

(18)   *Kiriwina sonority-driven stress (Senft 1986, Lawton 1993)*

(a) Right-aligned trochee
    (i) Final heavy syllable ((C)VC, (C)VV)
        [i.ki('um)]   'he did secretly'   [tau('au)]   'hey, men!'
    (ii) Penultimate heavy syllable
        [('peu)la]   'strong'   [am('bai)sa]   'where?'
    (iii) Penultimate and final light ((C)V) syllables
        ka('wala)   'canoe pole'   bo('nara)   'shelf (in house)'
        igibu('lu.i)   'he is angry at'   [i.koi.('su.vi)] 'he puts in'

(b) Except when foot retraction would result in a low-sonority non-head
        [('migi)la]   'the face'   [('kuli)a]   'cooking pot'
        [('megu)va]   'white magic'   [('lugu)ta]   'yam type'
        [('lami)la]   'outrigger log'   [katusa('wasi)la] 'clear throat'
        [la('siku)la]   'pull canoe'

It is clear that Kiriwina is not concerned with the sonority of its foot *head*. In [('migi)la] the foot is not aligned with the right edge even though its competitor *[mi('gila)] has the *same quality* stressed vowel. Instead, what matters is the sonority of the non-head vowel of the foot: in *[mi('gila)] the foot has a very high sonority non-head vowel [a], whereas in [('migi)la] it has a low sonority one – i.e. [i].

This pattern is generated by ranking *non-Hd$_{Ft}$/a,e•o over the constraints that require right-alignment: i.e. ALIGN-R(Ft,PrWd) (19):

(19) *Kiriwina: Non-head sonority*

/migila/	*non-Hd$_{Ft}$/a,e•o	ALIGN-R(Ft,PrWd)
(a) mi('gila)	*!	
☞ (b) ('migi)la		*

Interaction with metrical structure

It is interesting to note that Kiriwina is far more respectful of metrical restrictions than Takia. In its desire to have a high sonority stressed vowel, Takia will tolerate trochees instead of iambs. In contrast, Kiriwina will only tolerate trochees: i.e. *[mi(gi'la)] is banned, and so is *[vi('la)] (cf. [vi#('vila)] 'woman'); in constraint terms, TROCHEE outranks *non-Hd$_{Ft}$/a,e•o in Kiriwina. Kiriwina will not tolerate degenerate feet, either: ['waga], *[wa('ga)] 'canoe'; *[mi('gi)la]. The contrast can be generalized to the rankings in (20).

(20) *Interaction of sonority conditions with metrical conditions*

"π/son" regulates the interaction of prosodic structure with sonority
             (e.g. *Hd$_{Ft}$/i)
"π-align" regulates the position of prosodic structure (e.g. ALIGN-R(Ft,PrWd))
"π-shape" regulates the shape and size of prosodic structure (e.g. FTBIN)
(a) || π/son » π-align, π-shape ||
             (e.g. Takia; Nanti – Crowhurst & Michael 2005)
             Sonority conditions take precedence over both position
             and shape
(b) || π-shape » π/son » π-align ||
             (e.g. Kiriwina; Gujarati – de Lacy 2006)
             Sonority conditions take precedence over position,
             but not shape
(c) || π-align » π/son » π-shape || (e.g. Harar Oromo – de Lacy 2002a:Ch.4)
             Sonority conditions can force a change in shape,
             but only within a 'window'
(d)|| π-align, π-shape » π/son || (e.g. Iaai)
             Sonority has no effect on stress placement

Further details of the analysis of Kiriwina are given in de Lacy (2004 Sec.4). For a particular striking example of a system in which sonority interacts with metrical conditions, see Crowhurst & Michael (2005).

12.4   Tone

The same constraint mechanism that was used with sonority also applies to the tonal hierarchy | High ⟩ Mid ⟩ Low |. The constraints proposed in de Lacy (2002b) are expressed with stringent form in (21). Precursors to these constraints include Goldsmith's (1987) 'Tone–accent attraction condition', which favors accented syllables with specified tone over accented toneless syllables, and Jiang-King's (1996:99) proposal that there is a tonal hierarchy | +Upper ⟩ –Raised | (see Yip 10.2.1) (also see Hayes 1995 Sec.7.1.3); for further discussion see Yip (2001a; 2002 Sec.3.9; 10.3.2).

(21)   *Tone-head, and -non-head constraints (after de Lacy 2002b)*
    (a) *Hd$_\alpha$/L, *Hd$_\alpha$/L•M, *Hd$_\alpha$/L•M•H
    (b) *non-Hd$_\alpha$/H, *non-Hd$_\alpha$/H•M, *non-Hd$_\alpha$/H•M•L

The effect of both sets of constraints can be seen in Ayutla Mixtec. The foot is attracted to the left edge of a word, as seen in (22a). However, the foot will appear elsewhere if the 'perfect toned foot' can be produced: i.e. where the head has a high tone and the non-head has a low tone.

(22)   *Ayutla Mixtec tone-driven stress (data from Pankratz & Pike 1967)*
    (a) Default = leftmost trochaic foot

        ('HH)H   [('ʃíní)rá]   'he understands'
        ('LL)L   [('ʃàtù)ì]   'my trousers'
        ('MM)M   [('ʃ̩n̄ū)rā]   'his pineapple'

    (b) Deviate from leftmost position in order to:
       (i) Create the tonally perfect foot ('HL)
       H('HL)   [lú('lúrà)]   'he is small'
       LM('HL)   [lùlū('úrà)]   'he is not small'
       (ii) Else create a degenerate foot with a H-toned head
       ML('H)   [kūnù('rá)]   'his tobacco'
       (iii) Else create the next best foot ('ML)
       L('ML)   [tì('kātʃ î?)]   'whirlwind'
       M('ML)   [lā('ʃàrà)]   'his orange'

Attraction of the foot head to a high-toned syllable can be dealt with by having *Hd$_{Ft}$/L•M outrank ALIGN-L(Ft,PrWd) and FTBIN, as in tableau (23). To make candidates easier to read, forms like /kūnùrá/ are schematized as candidates as [ML('H)] and so on.

(23) *Seeking out a H-toned head, regardless of the metrical cost*

/kūnùrá/	*Hd$_{Ft}$/L•M	FtBin	Align-L(Ft,PrWd)
(a) ('ML)H	*!		
(b) M('LH)	*!		*
☞ (c) ML('H)		*	**

*Hd$_{Ft}$/L is also crucial in favoring mid- over low-toned heads (24):

(24) *Seeking out a mid-toned head*

/ʃàkùūrì?/	*Hd$_{Ft}$/L•M	*Hd$_{Ft}$/L	Align-L(Ft,PrWd)
(a) ('LL)ML	*	*!	
☞ (b) LL('ML)	*		**

The importance of non-heads is seen in forms like [lú('lúrà)] 'he is small' (i.e. [H('HL)]). The competitor *[('lúlú)rà] ([('HH)L)]) also has a high-toned foot head; the only difference is in the foot non-head's tone. Having *non-Hd$_{Ft}$/ H•M outrank Align-L(Ft,PrWd) is responsible here (25):

(25) *Seeking out a low-toned non-head*

/lúlúrà/	*non-Hd$_{Ft}$/ H•M	*Hd$_{Ft}$/ L•M	*Hd$_{Ft}$/ L	FtBin	Align-L(Ft,PrWd)
(a) ('HH)L	*!				
(b) ('H)HL				*!	
☞ (c) H('HL)					*

*non-Hd$_{Ft}$/H•M is needed (as opposed to *non-Hd$_{Ft}$/H) to account for [lā('ʃārà)] – i.e. [M('ML)] (not *[('MM)L]).

The tableau also shows that there is a crucial ranking between FtBin and Align-L. Without this ranking, feet would be degenerate in order to be better-toned.

Align-L(Ft,PrWd) is especially crucial in two contexts. One is where all syllables have the same tone, as in [(('ʃíní)rá] (i.e. not *[ʃí('nírá)], *[ʃíní('rá)]). The other is when there are two HL or ML sequences in the same word: e.g. /ʃáàʃî/ 'is not eating' → [('ʃá.à)ʃí.ì], *[ʃá.à('ʃí.ì)].

In summary, the tonal hierarchy acts in a similar fashion to the sonority hierarchy. Tone-driven stress systems are reported in languages as genetically diverse as Chickasaw (Muskogean – Gordon 2003: Sec.4.3), Golin (East New Guinea Highlands – Bunn & Bunn 1970), Serbo-Croatian (Slavic – Inkelas & Zec 1988, Zec 1999), Tibetan (Sino-Tibetan – Meredith 1990), and Vedic Sanskrit (Indo-Aryan – Kiparsky & Halle 1977).

However, there is some disagreement over the form of tone-(non)head constraints. For example, Yip (2001a) argues that they must be formulated positively (cf. de Lacy 2002a: Sec.3.5.1.3).

Yip also emphasizes that positional faithfulness constraints for tone are needed in addition to the Head-tone constraints; see Yip (10.3.2) and Yip (2002) for discussion. There is no problem with having both positional markedness and positional faithfulness constraints. Both types seem necessary for many phenomena.

Tone and sonority?

The only interaction not discussed between tone, sonority, and prosody is between tone and sonority. In some languages, tone can only appear on sonorant coda consonants, but this type of restriction is often seen as an indirect relation between sonority and tone. In these cases, sonorants are assumed to be moraic while obstruents are not, and only moras can bear tone (see Gordon 2001 for recent discussion and references). I know of no other evidence that requires a direct relationship between sonority and tone. For example, there is no language in which low vowels must carry low tone while high vowels must be high-toned (this sort of restriction would make phonetic sense as there seems to be a correlation between low sonority and lower tone (e.g. for Thai, see Abramson 1962)). In constraint terms, there must be no constraint with the general form *$son/tone$, where *son* is a sonority level (e.g. *$\{a,e{\bullet}o\}/Low$, etc.).

12.5 Other prosodic levels

The theoretical proposals outlined above are not limited to feet. Some proposals allow sonority (and tone) to combine with heads and non-heads of *any* prosodic category (de Lacy 2002a, Zec 2003). Evidence for this view is presented here.

Below the foot are the syllable and the mora. The head of the syllable is its nucleus (i.e. the segment dominated by the head mora), and the preference for high sonority elements in nuclei is well documented (Prince & Smolensky 2004, Zec 8.5.1). Similarly, the 'non-head' of the syllable (i.e. its margins) favors low sonority segments; this preference is typically evident in syllabification, but can also exert itself in neutralization and even foot placement (de Lacy 2001, Smith 2002, Topintzi 2006).

The same is true for tone: as discussed in Section 9.4, heads favor higher tone, and non-head moras favor lower tone. This is shown at the moraic level in the northern Min language Fuqing (Jiang-King 1996: Sec.3.3.2): only H and M tone can appear on head moras, and only L tone can appear on non-heads (i.e. monomoraic syllables can only have H or M tone, and bimoraic syllables can only have HL or ML contours).

McGarrity (2003) shows the need for sonority constraints that refer to the foot level. Most languages with sonority-driven stress have no reported secondary stress, so it is often not clear whether the motivating constraints refer to the head of the foot or PrWd. However, secondary stress avoids the least sonorous vowel [ɨ] in Yimas: [(ˈtiŋkɨm)pi(ˌɲawa)] 'wild fowl', *[(ˈtiŋkɨm)(ˌpiɲa)wa]; cf. [(ˈmaman)(ˌtakar)man] 'land crab', *[(ˈmaman)ta(ˌkarman)]; there is clearly need for *Hd_{Ft}/i here as opposed to *Hd_{PrWd}/i. Crowhurst & Michael (2005) show the same for Nanti: sonority conditions can result in trochees instead of iambs even for non-head feet: e.g. [(ˌnabi) (gʒi'ta)ksero] 'it crushed it', *[(ˌnaˌbi)(gʒi'ta)ksero] (cf. [(iˌpi)(riˌni)te] 'he sits'). In addition, for Kiriwina it is crucial that non-heads of *feet* are sensitive to sonority: stress in [('migi)la] does not fall at the right edge because the unstressed vowel in the *foot* (i.e. not unfooted unstressed vowels) ends up with a less sonorous segment. McGarrity's general point is that in terms of sonority, secondary and primary stress are independent. A ranking such as || *Hd$_{Ft}$/x » ALIGN || will affect all stressed syllables, but || ALIGN-R-Hd$_{PrWd}$ » *Hd$_{Ft}$/x » ALIGN-R-Ft || will only affect secondary stressed syllables, while || *Hd$_{PrWd}$/x » ALIGN-R-Ft » *Hd$_{Ft}$/x || will only affect primary stressed syllables; all these types are attested. McGarrity (2003: Sec.4.2) also identifies Chamorro as having sonority-driven neutralization in secondary stressed syllables; this case is discussed in Section 12.6.

Immediately above the foot is the Prosodic Word. The head of the Prosodic Word is its main-stressed syllable (i.e. the segment dominated by the head mora of the head syllable of the head foot). Some languages place sonority and tone restrictions specifically on the head of the PrWd rather than the head of the foot. McGarrity (2003) identifies Axininca Campa as this type for sonority-driven stress (Payne 1990). Masset Haida provides an example for tone (Enrico 1991). As shown in (26), every syllable has either high or low tone, and iambic feet are arrayed from left to right; every syllable is parsed into a foot. As a visual aid, main-stressed syllables are given in bold. Main stress is attracted to the rightmost vowel with high tone. However, secondary stress makes no tone distinction, falling freely on low-toned vowels even when high-toned ones are available. Form (26d) is of special interest. While main stress falls on the rightmost high-toned syllable (i.e. [gwáːŋ], not [áː]), secondary stress falls on the low-toned [dà], ignoring the high-toned [áː]: i.e. *[(gùˌdàŋ)(ˌá-dà) - (t'sà-'gwáːŋ) - (ˌgàn)]. In other words, the position of the head of the PrWd is influenced by tone, but foot heads are not.

(26)   *Masset Haida tone-driven primary stress and tone-insensitive secondary stress*

    (a) [(ˌɡùː)(dà'ŋáː)-(dà-ˌt'sà)-(7wà-ˌgàn)]   'spy.on-causative-into-pl-past'
    (b) [(kìlˌx̣àl)(dàːnhláŋ)-(ˌìd)-(7wà-ˌgàn)]   'caus.-potential.be.slave-inceptive-pl-past'
    (c) [(ˌɡàd)(làˌdàn)(jàn-'dáːl)-(ˌgàŋ)]   'jump.up,iter.-along-pr'
    (d) [(ɡùːˌdàŋ)(áːˌdà)-(t'sà-'gwáːŋ)-(ˌgàn)] 'spy.on-causative-into-around-past'

In de Lacy (2002a, 2004) I argued that 'PrWd non-heads', when restricted by constraints on foot heads, can be used to refer to the informal notion of 'unstressed syllable'; the influence of sonority on unstressed syllables is discussed in Section 12.6.

The same type of influences are seen above the PrWd, though they are clearer for tone than sonority. For example, the head of a Phonological Phrase in Digo attracts high tone (Kisseberth 1984, Goldsmith 1988:85). This is a case of stress-dependent tone, with the constraint *Head$_{PPh}$/L playing a decisive role. For Korean, Kim (1997) argues that every Major Phrase must contain at least one high tone and that no other high tones are permitted.

The constraints *Head$_{MajorP}$/L and *non-Head$_{MajorP}$/H must therefore outrank tone-faithfulness to achieve this result.

At the highest level, Yip (10.3.2) proposes the constraint *FOCUS/L, which bans a low tone on a focused head. Truckenbrodt (1995) argues that the focused syllable is the head of the Utterance Phrase (or some other high prosodic constituent), so the tonal preferences can be seen even at the highest prosodic level.

So, the same sonority and tone attractions are seen at every level in the prosodic hierarchy: heads of moras, syllable, feet, PrWd, Prosodic Phrases, and Utterance Phrases attract and are attracted by higher tone and high sonority segments, while non-heads of all these categories favor lower tone and lower sonority.

12.6   Faithfulness responses

In Optimality Theory, no constraint is phenomenon-specific (see 1.2.2). Constraints with the form *π/p (π is a prosodic category, p is a property like sonority or tone) have many possible resolutions. The previous sections have focused on just one: i.e. moving π, through the general ranking || *π/*son*, FAITH » π-{align,shape} ||. This section focuses on resolutions that involve p – through || *π/*son*, π-{align,shape} » FAITH || which can cause deletion, epenthesis, neutralization, metathesis and coalescence. In a sense, such resolutions are 'stress-driven sonority/tone': they are cases where prosodic structure is kept constant and sonority/tone changes.

12.6.1   Neutralization

The most common response to conditions on heads and sonority is probably neutralization. The most extensive recent work on this topic in OT is Crosswhite (1998 et seq.), who proposes that (non-)head-sonority relations are responsible for a great deal of vowel reduction. In foot heads, vowels can become more sonorous, while in foot non-heads and unstressed syllables they typically become less sonorous. For example, in Chamorro (27) high vowels become mid in stressed syllables:

(27)   *Chamorro sonorization in stressed syllables (Chung 1983, Crosswhite 1998)*

/laːpis/	[ˈlaːpis̩]	'pencil'	[laˈpessu]	'my pencil'
/hugandu/	[huˈgandu̥]	'play'	[ˌhuganˈdoɲɲa]	'his playing'
/læguʔ/	[maˈlæːgu̥ʔ]	'wanting'	[ˌmalæˈgoʔmu]	'your wanting'

Sonorization is obligatory in main-stressed syllables and optional in secondary stressed syllables: e.g. [tiṇˈtaguʔ] 'messenger' c.f. [ˌtentaˈgoʔta]∼ [ˌtintaˈgoʔta] 'our (incl.) messenger'.

Adapting Crosswhite's (1998) analysis, sonorization in Chamorro is caused when *Hd$_{Ft}$/ə,$i•u$ outranks IDENT[high], a constraint that preserves underlying [high] values. It is crucial that metrical constraints (like TROCHEE and ALIGN-R(Ft,PrWd)) outrank IDENT[high] (also see McGarrity 2003) otherwise the system would have sonority-driven stress. All other relevant faithfulness constraints like those against deletion, epenthesis, metathesis, and so on must also outrank IDENT[high] (28).

(28)   *Chamorro vowel sonorization in stressed syllables*

/lapissu/	*Hd$_{Ft}$/ə,i•u	ALIGN-R(Ft,PrWd)	IDENT[high]
(a) la('pissu)	*!		
(b) ('lapis)su		*!	
☞ (c) la('pessu)			*

The fact that main-stressed high vowels always become more sonorous can be accounted for by having *Hd$_{PrWd}$/ə,i•u outrank IDENT[high] in all registers; the optionality of sonorization for secondary stress can be explained by allowing *Hd$_{Ft}$/ə,i•u to vary in its ranking with IDENT[high] (see Anttila Ch.22).

The most common sonority-related neutralization involves vowels in foot non-heads or unstressed syllables becoming less sonorous. Often this involves all such vowels becoming [ə] or [ɨ] (i.e. 'vowel reduction'), but it can also involve raising vowel height, thereby lowering sonority (e.g. in Sri Lankan Portuguese Creole unstressed syllables /æ/→[e], /a/→[ə], and /ɔ/→[o] – Smith 1978, Crosswhite 2000). Such cases can be analyzed using *non-Hd$_{PrWd}$/x or *non-Hd$_{Ft}$/x constraints outranking relevant IDENT constraints (Crosswhite 2000). There are complications with this pattern because unstressed vowels can sometimes become more sonorous; for recent discussion and proposals see Crosswhite (1999, 2004), de Lacy (2006:Ch.7), Harris (2005), and references cited in these works. For discussion of sonority–stress interactions elsewhere (especially with regard to onsets in stressed syllables) see de Lacy (2001) and Smith (2002).

Neutralization also happens for tone and stress. For example, in Lithuanian low tone becomes high in stressed syllables under the influence of *Hd$_{Ft}$/L: e.g. /prànèʃù/ → [('práne)ʃù] 'I announce' (Blevins 1993:244, de Lacy 2002a: Sec.4.1).

12.6.2   Deletion

(Non)head-sonority and -tone constraints can also force deletion. For example, when [a] would appear in the non-head of a foot (or perhaps more generally an unstressed syllable), it deletes in Lushootseed (29) (Urbanczyk 1996, Gouskova 2003 Sec.4.6.1). 'RED' is a reduplicative morpheme. The footing in (29) is mine.

(29) *Lushootseed [a]-deletion in the non-head of a foot (Urbanczyk 1996, Gouskova 2003)*

    (a) Delete [a] if it would appear in the non-head of a foot
        /RED-caq'/ → [('c̲a̲cq')] 'to spear big game on salt water', *[('c̲a̲caq')]
        /RED-walis/ → [('w̲a̲wlis)] 'little frog', *[('w̲a̲wa)lis]
        /RED-laq-il/ → [('l̲a̲ʔlqil)] 'be a little late', *[('l̲a̲ʔla)qil]

    (b) When deletion is blocked by a cluster condition, reduce to [ə]
        /s-RED-ɬagʷid/→[('s-ɬa̲ɬə)gʷid] 'little mat', *[('s-ɬa̲ɬa)gʷid],*[('s-ɬa̲ɬgʷid)]
        /RED-tabəc/ →[('ta̲ʔtə)bəc] 'slowly, softly'

    (c) Other vowels do not delete
        /RED-hiqəb/   → [('h̲i̲hi)ʔəb] 'too, excessively', *[('h̲i̲hʔəb)]
        /RED-wiliqʷid/ → [('w̲i̲wi)liqʷid] 'quiz someone', *[('w̲i̲wli)qʷid]

Following Gouskova (2003 Sec.4.6.2.2), this pattern can be modeled by *non-Hd$_{Ft}$/a outranking the anti-deletion constraint MAX. Constraints on footing (e.g. ALIGN-L(Ft,PrWd)) and other faithfulness resolutions (e.g. IDENT[low]) must also outrank MAX (30).

(30) *Lushootseed non-head [a]-deletion*

/RED-walis/	*non-Hd$_{Ft}$/a	ALIGN-L(Ft,PrWD)	IDENT[low]	MAX
(a) ('w̲a̲wa)lis	*!			
(b) wawa('lis)		*!*		
(c) ('w̲a̲wə)lis			*!	
☞ (d) ('w̲a̲wlis)				*

*non-Hd$_{Ft}$/a outranks IDENT[low] because when deletion is blocked by constraints on consonant clusters (called CLUSTERCOND here), IDENT[low] is violated instead, producing reduction (31).

(31) *Lushootseed non-head [a]-reduction*

/s-RED-ɬagʷid/	CLUSTER COND	*non-Hd$_{Ft}$/a	ALIGN-L (Ft,PrWD)	IDENT[low]	MAX
(a) ('sɬa̲ɬa)ʷid		*!			
(b) sɬa̲ɬa('gʷid)			*!*		
☞ (c) ('sɬa̲ɬə)gʷid				*	
(d) ('sɬa̲ɬgʷid)	*!				*

For a detailed analysis, along with discussion of Lushootseed's sonority-driven stress, see Gouskova (2003:Ch.4).

    Pulleyblank (2004) provides some examples for tone and deletion from a related but slightly different theoretical perspective.

Non-metrical conditions can also force epenthesis. For example, Alderete et al. (1999 Sec.2.3) argue that Lushootseed /RED-gʷədil/ → [('gʷi̱gʷə)dil] 'sit down' involves epenthesis. The base's [ə] cannot be copied because *Hd_Ft/ə bans it; so a default vowel is inserted instead – i.e. ['i]. An example from New Zealand English is given in note 2. For an example where tone–head interaction forces epenthesis, see Yip (10.3.2) on Mandarin focus and Yip (2002 Sec.3.9) on Mandarin Third Tone Sandhi.

12.6.3   Metathesis and coalescence

The final example (32) shows an extremely complex response to non-metrical conditions in Saanich (a Salish language – Montler 1986).[10] Saanich has lexical stress: the surface position of stress often depends on underlying forms. However, when no morphemes have underlying stress, the output surfaces with a right-aligned trochee: e.g. [kʷʼə('sinəs)] 'burn one's chest (drinking something hot)', [('matʃ-ət)] 'aim it'. While penultimate stress is preferred, there is also a desire to avoid stressed schwa, as shown in (32a). When an underlying schwa would receive stress (i.e. appear in the penult), it deletes and the root's vowel (if it is not schwa) moves into the schwa's place. In serial terms: /kʷʼes-ət-əs/ → [kʷʼe('sət-əs)] triggers deletion: [kʷʼe('st-əs)], which triggers metathesis: [('kʷʼset-əs)]. Deletion and metathesis do not occur when a non-schwa appears in penultimate position (32b). A complication is that unstressed vowels reduce to [ə]. This will be discussed below.

(32)   *Saanich (Montler 1986)*

(a) Stress avoids schwa through VC metathesis and schwa deletion
  /qʷiχʷ-ət-əs/→ [('qʷχʷitəs)] 'he missed it' (cf. [('qʷiχʷ-ət)] 'miss it (a shot)')
  /kʷʼes-ət-əs/ → [('kʷʼsetəs)] 'he scalded it' (cf. [('kʷʼes-ət)] 'scald it')
  /tɬʼep'-ət-əŋ/ → [('tɬ͡ʼp'-etəŋ)] 'it was felt' (cf. [('tɬʼep'-ət)] 'feel it')
  /matʃ-ət-əŋ/ → [mə('tʃatəŋ)] 'it was aimed'[11] (cf. [('matʃ-ət)] 'aim it')
(b) Stress does not avoid other vowels
  /kʼʷes-ins/   → [kʷə('sinəs)] 'burn one's chest (drinking something hot)'
                   *[('kʷʼsenəs)]
  /ʔel-i-ŋ-əɬ/   → [ʔə('linəɬ)] 'I saved (money, etc.)' (cf. [('ʔel-ət)]), *[('ʔenəɬ)]
(c) Stress does not avoid schwa when it has no other option
  [('p'əl'p'əɬ)] 'hatch a bunch of eggs'
  [('χɬ-ət-əs)] 'he hurt him'
  [('χʷ tɬ͡ʼəqtnətʃ)] 'cougar'

To rule one avenue of explanation out, the morphemes do have underlying schwas. If, for example, the underlying form for 'aim it' [('matʃət)] is /matʃ-t/ and not /matʃ-ət/, there would be no motivation for inserting [ə] as [tʃt] clusters are permitted on the surface: [qəp'əlitʃt] 'close a box', [tʃtaləs] 'marry', [χələtʃtən] 'twist something'.

While the change in (32a) is complex, it has a straightforward motivation: i.e. *Hd_Ft/i•ə. /kʷʼes-ət-əs/ cannot surface faithfully with penultimate stress as it would violate *Hd$_{Ft}$/*i•ə*: i.e. *[k'^{w}e('sətəs)]. The solutions to *Hd$_{Ft}$/*i•ə* identified in previous sections are blocked in Saanich. The metrical constraint ALIGN-R (Ft,PrWd) requires penultimate stress, so foot retraction *[('k'^{w}esə)təs] is ruled out. Epenthesis is banned by DEP: *[k'^{w}esə('atəs)]. IDENT[F] rules out vowel sonorization: [k'^{w}ə('satəs)]. Finally, deletion is ruled out by MAX: *[('k'^{w}estəs)].

Instead, Saanich responds by coalescence and metathesis. The underlying root vowel and affix /ə/ merge so that: /k'^{w}e$_1$s-ə$_2$t-əs/ → [('k'^{w}se$_{1,2}$təs)]. Coalescence is an essential part of the analysis; if the /ə/ instead deleted, there would be no reason for the root vowel to metathesize with the following consonant (i.e. the outcome should be *[('k'^{w}estəs)]; note that medial [st] is otherwise permitted: e.g. [speṣtən'əɫ] 'American', [qə?jəstetʃəl] 'newcomer').

Tableau (33) illustrates this analysis. LIN(earity) bans metathesis, and UNIF(ormity) bans coalescence.

(33)   *Sonority-driven metathesis in Saanich*

/k'^{w}e$_1$s-ə$_2$t-əs/	*Hd$_{Ft}$/*i•ə*	ALIGN-R (Ft, PrWd)	MAX	DEP	LIN	UNIF
(a) k'^{w}ə('sətəs)	*!					
(b) ('k'^{w}esə)təs		*!				
(c) ('k'^{w}estəs)			*!			
(d) k'^{w}esə('tatəs)				* *!		
☞ (e) ('k'^{w}se$_{1,2}$təs)					*	*

There are other candidates to be ruled out. For example, the candidate *[('k'^{w}e$_{1,2}$stəs)] can be ruled out by preventing morphemes from splitting (in this form the affix's /ə/ is not adjacent to its /t/). In the winner [('k'^{w}se$_{1,2}$təs)] /ə/ effectively takes on [e]'s features, so feature change without metathesis (i.e. *[k'^{w}sə$_1$('setəs)]) must be ruled out (probably by OI-∃IDENT[F], which requires every output segment to have the same features as some input segment – after Struijke 2000a). Finally, *[('k'^{w}estə$_{2,3}$s)]) with coalescence of the two suffix schwas must be ruled out, probably by a restriction on coalescence of segments of different affix classes.

Metathesis (movement of a segment to the metrically prominent position) is a rare response to sonority requirements. However, it is a fairly common response for tone, as discussed by Yip (10.3.2) (also see Goldsmith 1987, Downing 1990, 2003b, Bamba 1991, Bickmore 1995, de Lacy 2002a Sec.3).

12.7 Conclusions

This chapter has focused on a theoretical device that combines markedness hierarchies (i.e. sonority and tone) with prosodic heads and non-heads to form constraints. This approach was compared with representational ones which seek to account for the range of behavior documented above by appealing to either differences in moraic content or sparseness of featural structure; representational approaches were argued to be inadequate.

The theory relates many disparate areas of research, including markedness theory, tone, sonority, and the influences on the form and position of metrical structure (and in fact, all levels of the prosodic hierarchy). In terms of empirical phenomena, it shows that there is a common motivation behind many cases of neutralization (i.e. vowel reduction and raising), deletion, epenthesis, metathesis, and location of prosodic constituents; furthermore, its influence was argued to extend throughout the prosodic hierarchy.

As with any area of research, many questions remain to be answered. At a fundamental level, if a functionalist approach to phonology is assumed (e.g. Gordon Ch.3), what is the motivation for sonority- and tone-driven stress? Is the same functional factor responsible for the similar effects seen in all the different empirical phenomena discussed above? For some recent discussion along these lines, see Gordon (1999, 2002b, 2004) and Ahn (2000). In contrast, if a formalist approach is assumed, one might expect a small number of mechanisms (e.g. constraint schemata) to be able to account for all the patterns identified here (as hinted at here).

The empirical generalizations for many of the phenomena discussed here have emerged only recently. In contrast to areas such as syllable structure, metrical stress, and tone, there is a rather small empirical base to areas like sonority-driven deletion, epenthesis, stress, and metathesis. However, the amount of research in this area is increasing rapidly, as is work on much more well-known areas such as vowel reduction and the influence of prosodic structure on tone.

Notes

My thanks to José (Beto) Elías-Ulloa, Kate Ketner, Michael O'Keefe, and Laura McGarrity for their comments.

1 Structural elements such as onsets and non-moraic codas may also influence prosodic structure, but they will not be discussed here due to lack of space (see Everett & Everett 1984, Davis 1985, 1988b, Halle & Vergnaud 1987, Everett 1988, Goedemans 1993, 1998, Hayes 1995:Ch.7, de Lacy 1997, 2001, Rosenthall & Hulst 1999, Gordon 1999, to appear, Smith 2002, Hajek & Goedemans 2003, McGarrity 2003, Elías-Ulloa 2005, Topintzi 2006 and others cited in these works).

2 There is no particular reason to consider the vocalic and consonantal parts of the sonority hierarchy as separate. The prediction is that stress should avoid consonants with even more vigor than central vowels. For example, in my dialect of New Zealand English, [ə] is allowed in main stressed syllables (e.g. ['pən] 'pin', ['bərə] 'bitter'), but consonants

are not. In fact, stress actively avoids consonants through epenthesis: /ejbl/ 'able' surfaces as ['ej.bɬ], but when main stress would shift onto the [l] in suffixation, a vowel is inserted: /ejbl-əti/ 'ability' → [ə.'bə̰lə.ɾi], *[ə'.bɬ.ə.ɾi]).

3 There is evidence from phenomena such as vowel reduction that mid-high vowels (e.g. [e o]) are distinct from mid-low vowels (e.g. [ɛ ɔ]) in sonority. As there are no known stress systems that make this distinction, I will omit it for convenience.

4 See Gouskova (2003) for the view that there is no constraint against every hierarchy element (or, in Fixed Ranking terms, against the least marked element). For the opposing view, see de Lacy (2006: Sec.8.7.3).

5 The winner could be [ka('na.o)rig] if Align-R(Ft,PrWd) outranks Iamb. As there is no phonetic realization of foot boundaries, there is no way to tell which ranking is correct in Takia. See Section 12.3 for further discussion of the interaction of metrical structure and sonority. Thanks to José Elías-Ulloa and Laura McGarrity for raising this point.

6 As FtBin must outrank a faithfulness constraint which in turn must outrank all foot-locating constraints, no winner can have a degenerate foot in Takia, so candidates like [ifi('ni)] were not considered.

7 The lack of a *Hd_{Ft}/a constraint raises the question of *why* such a constraint cannot exist. The answer is beyond the scope of this chapter; it derives from general theories of markedness and its relation to constraint form (Prince & Smolensky 2004, de Lacy 2002a, 2006).

8 Halle & Vergnaud (1987) also analyze stress systems which refer to features other than weight or edges. In a sense, their proposal is to employ a combination of a metrical and prominence grid: syllables project gridmarks based on their internal properties, both moraic and non-moraic. As with Hayes' (1995) approach, Halle & Vergnaud's theory did not restrict the form of such rules.

9 José Elías-Ulloa raises the issue of whether the non-head constraints refer to consonants as well as vowels. If they did, the most harmonic unstressed nucleus would be one that contains a stop. Similarly, neutralization could force unstressed nuclei to become liquids or nasals. Given the relative rarity of languages that permit non-vocalic nuclei, it is not clear that this prediction is obviously wrong.

10 My thanks to Timothy Montler for discussing the details of Saanich stress with me.

11 The first schwa in [mə̰('tʃatəŋ)] is epenthetic, motivated by a general condition banning word-initial clusters of a sonorant+C.

Part III

Segmental phenomena

13

Segmental features

T. A. Hall

13.1   Introduction

The goal of this chapter is to provide a summary of the current status of segmental features. I discuss below the evidence for these features and summarize controversies involving them. Although the emphasis is on the features themselves, the article also includes discussion of the relationships proposed involving two or more features in Feature Geometry (Clements 1985a, Sagey 1986, Clements and Hume 1995). The chapter presupposes some familiarity with this approach and with Nonlinear Phonology in general.

The chapter is organized in the following way. In Section 13.2 I provide an introduction in which I discuss some general properties of phonological features. In the subsequent sections I present the features in sets: Section 13.3 is devoted to major class features, Section 13.4 to laryngeal features, Section 13.5 to manner features and Section 13.6 to place features. Section 13.7 analyzes featural representations for complex and contour segments. The article concludes with an appendix with feature matrices; a section on further reading is available on the Handbook website: http://handbookofphonology.rutgers.edu.

This chapter is not concerned with properties once considered to be features but which are now captured with nonlinear representations involving prosodic units. For example, length, stress and tone are properties once assumed to require binary features (Chomsky and Halle 1968, henceforth *SPE*). Length and stress are now uncontroversially analyzed in terms of skeletal/moraic and metrical structure respectively (Zec Ch.8 and Kager Ch.9 resp.). Tone requires features linked to the mora (Yip Ch.10), although Yip (2002:60) suggests that there is some evidence for treating tonal features on par with segmental features. See Fox (2000) for an overview of featural approaches to length, stress and tone.

13.2   Phonological features

The segment can be decomposed into a set of smaller units, or *features* (Jakobson, Fant and Halle 1952, *SPE*). Features are psychological entities defined in terms of acoustic and/or articulatory realization which provide the link between cognitive representation of speech and its physical manifestation.

Any given segment is simply an abbreviation for an unordered bundle of features. A sample phonological representation for /n/ is presented in (1).

(1)   *A subset of features for /n/*

$$\begin{bmatrix} +\text{consonantal} \\ +\text{sonorant} \\ -\text{continuant} \\ +\text{nasal} \\ +\text{coronal} \\ \dots \end{bmatrix}$$

There are two arguments for features. First, features are necessary to account for *natural classes*. For example, /d/ is [+voice]. This does not just mean that [d] will be phonetically realized with voicing; it also groups it with the class of sounds that is [+voice] (e.g. /b ɖ ɟ g/). Phonological evidence for natural classes typically takes the form of some rule or constraint that refers to the relevant feature(s). Second, features are necessary to capture *contrasts* in natural languages. For example, since there are many languages in which /p t k/ contrast with /pʰ tʰ kʰ/, the feature [±spread] is required where [+spread] corresponds to the spreading of the glottis characterized by aspirated sounds and [−spread] to no aspiration.

There is a brief period of noise following the release of closure in stops like /p t k/. However, no language contrasts stops with that (burst) noise from stops without it. The standard way of explaining the difference between [±spread] and the presence vs. absence of burst noise is to say that only the former is a *distinctive feature* (or *phonological feature*), whereas the latter is not.

Features can be distinctive in some languages and nondistinctive in others. For example, [±spread] is distinctive in Korean because there are minimal pairs of words which contrast solely in terms of aspiration (e.g. [tal] 'moon' vs. [tʰal] 'mask'), but it is nondistinctive in English since [p t k] and [pʰ tʰ kʰ] do not contrast.

Many recent studies have questioned the idea that distinctiveness is crucial for phonological features (Flemming 1995, Kirchner 1997, Boersma 1998, Steriade 2000, Hamann 2003). Much of this current work is part of the general goal of (re)introducing functional explanations into phonology (Martinet 1964, Stampe 1973, Gordon Ch.3).

In generative phonology each feature is defined in terms of some phonetic property. For example, [+nasal] corresponds to the lowering of the velum (see *SPE*). In general, phonologists have followed the *SPE* tradition by giving features articulatory definitions, although there is a recent trend to allow acoustic or auditory definitions (Flemming 1995, Boersma 1998, Steriade 2000, Hamann 2003).

One common assumption in the Jakobsonian and *SPE* systems is that distinctive features are *binary*, meaning that each feature has two *values*, namely '+' and '−'. An alternative is that some (if not all) features are *privative* − they are either present or absent. Since the latter approach is influential in current theory, it will be discussed below.

It is usually assumed that if a feature is distinctive in a language then only those sounds for which it is distinctive are marked underlyingly for that feature. For example, in a language with a voicing contrast for stops (e.g. /p t k/ vs. /b d g/) but not for nasals (e.g. only /m n ŋ/ are present) only the stops are underlyingly [±voice] and the nasals are *unspecified* for that feature. In some approaches it is assumed that a *default rule* fills in such redundant values in the derivation but more recent treatments reject such default rules and therefore see /m n ŋ/ as being underspecified for [voice] on the surface. See Itô, Mester and Padgett (1995), and Clements (2001, 2003) for discussion on this issue.

A number of approaches to distinctive features will not be dealt with below due to reasons of space, including Dependency Phonology (Anderson and Ewen 1987), Charm and Government Theory (Kaye, Lowenstamm and Vergnaud 1985), and Browman and Goldstein's (1989) Theory of Articulatory Gestures.

The Feature Geometry model referred to in Section 13.1 presupposes that distinctive features are arranged hierarchically in a *feature tree*, in contrast to (1). An example is provided in (2).

(2) *A feature tree*

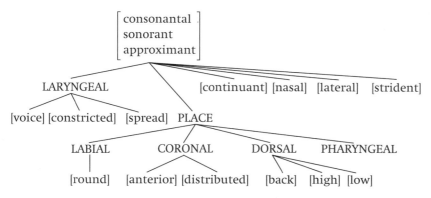

According to (2) the segment consists of a *root node* which dominates two privative *class nodes*, namely LARYNGEAL and PLACE. Here and below class

nodes are in small capitals and features in lower case letters. The distinctive features are located either under the class nodes, under the ROOT, or
they belong to the ROOT node itself. Sections 13.3–13.7 discuss the status of
the features and nodes in (2).

13.3   Major class features

Major class features are necessary to account for large natural classes like
sonorants, obstruents, approximants and consonants. In combination with
manner features (see Section 13.5), major class features define other large
groupings as well (e.g. stops and fricatives). In Section 13.3.1 I discuss
[consonantal] and [sonorant] and in Section 13.3.2 [approximant].

13.3.1   [consonantal] and [sonorant]
Two of the most well-known major class features are [consonantal] and
[sonorant], which are defined according to *SPE* (p.302) as in (3).

(3)   *SPE definitions for [consonantal] and [sonorant]*
    (a) [CONSONANTAL]:   ". . . sounds [are] produced with a radical obstruc-
tion in the midsagittal region of the vocal tract; nonconsonantal
sounds are produced without such an obstruction."
    (b) [SONORANT]:   "Sonorants are sounds produced with a vocal tract
cavity configuration in which spontaneous voicing is possible;
obstruents are produced with a cavity configuration that makes
spontaneous voicing impossible."

The motivation behind [consonantal] is to group together obstruents,
liquids and nasal consonants ([+consonantal]) and vowels, glides and laryngeals ([−consonantal]). Note that (3a) requires that laryngeals like /h ʔ/ be
[−consonantal] because their constriction is in the larynx itself and not in
the midsagittal region, which is above the larynx.

    The feature [sonorant] distinguishes stops (including affricates) and frica-
tives (which are [−sonorant]) from nasals, liquids, glides and vowels
([+sonorant]). Laryngeals (/h ʔ/) are [−sonorant] because they involve a
constriction in the larynx, which is not in the vocal tract. The constriction
involved in [+sonorant] sounds allows the air pressure inside and outside
the mouth to be relatively equal, while this is not true for [−sonorant]
sounds (Halle and Clements 1983:6). Thus, [−sonorant] sounds have either
an oral constriction which causes significant increase in the air pressure
behind it (e.g. stops and fricatives), or there is no constriction in the vocal
tract (i.e. the laryngeals).

    The natural classes captured by the features in (3) are illustrated in (4).
Here and below, the category 'liquid' subsumes lateral approximants like /l/
and 'rhotics', i.e. central approximants like /ɹ/ and trills like /r/.

(4) *Feature specifications for [consonantal] and [sonorant] for seven classes of sounds*

	stops	fricatives	nasals	liquids	glides	vowels	laryngeals
[consonantal]	+	+	+	+	−	−	−
[sonorant]	−	−	+	+	+	+	+

Phonological rules can refer to the natural classes in (4). For example, Final Devoicing in German only affects a [−sonorant] segment (e.g. /taːg/ 'day' → [taːk] vs. /taːl/ 'valley' → [taːl], *[taːl]). Similar processes involving [consonantal] will be discussed below.

McCarthy (1988) and others working within Feature Geometry argue that the ROOT node consists of [consonantal] and [sonorant] because these features do not display autosegmental properties. In particular, these features are assumed not to spread, delink, or display OCP effects. These unique properties of the major class features fall out from the representation in (5a) proposed by McCarthy (1988:97).

(5) (a) *McCarthy's (1988) representation of major class features*

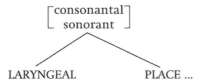

(b) *Kaisse's (1992) representation of major class features*

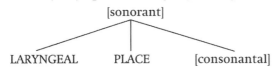

Given (5a) the only way for [consonantal] to spread in an assimilatory process is if the entire ROOT spreads. Thus, only a total assimilation resulting in a geminate should show a change in consonantality.

Kaisse (1992) argues that [consonantal] can spread (in assimilations) or delink (in dissimilations) independent of any other feature. Since Kaisse did not find similar examples for [sonorant], she proposes the structure in (5b). An assimilatory process supporting the model in (5b) is the consonantalization of the glide /j/ to a voiceless palatal or velar stop in the neighborhood of consonants in Cypriot Greek (Kaisse 1992). An example of the dissimilation of [consonantal] is the change from the fricative /ʁ/ to the glide [ɰ] before a consonant in Halland Swedish.

Although there is agreement that the features in (3) are necessary, this view is not unanimous. In particular, Hume and Odden (1996) argue that [consonantal] is superfluous. One argument supporting their view is that there are no clear examples of phonemic contrasts involving [consonantal] alone. For example, the contrast between the [−consonantal] glide /w/ and the [+consonantal] fricative /β/ can be captured using [sonorant] as /w/ is [+sonorant] and /β/ is [−sonorant]. Hume and Odden (1996:352–353) also argue that natural classes do not require [consonantal] because there are ". . . no compelling cases which single out the class of segments characterized solely by [+consonantal], i.e. obstruents, nasals and liquids." Hume and Odden (1996) analyze apparent examples of processes changing consonantality (e.g. the ones discussed by Kaisse 1992) not as ones involving a change in consonantality, but instead as either prosodically-driven changes or ones involving the change in some other feature.

Additional proposals in which [consonantal] (and [sonorant]) are dispensed with include Selkirk (1984a), Dogil and Luschützky (1990) and Hulst and Ewen (1991).

13.3.2   [approximant]

Clements (1990:292–293) proposes the major class feature [approximant]. [+approximant] sounds are those segments which have a constriction in the vocal tract which allows a frictionless escape of air, while this is not the case for [−approximant] sounds.[1] [approximant] groups together vowels, glides and liquids ([+approximant]) from stops, fricatives and nasals ([−approximant]). Clements (1990) argues that [approximant] is necessary because it captures natural classes that cannot be expressed by independent features. For example, in many languages complex onsets are only allowed if the second member is an 'oral sonorant' ([+approximant]) sound. An example of a language in which [−approximant] is active phonologically is Luganda, in which only obstruents and nasals can occur as geminates.

13.4   Laryngeal features

Laryngeal features account for contrasts in voicing (6a), aspiration (6b), and breathy voice (6c). They are also required to capture contrasts between 'plain' sounds vs. the corresponding ejectives and implosives ((6d) and (6e) respectively). The languages cited in table (6) are from Ladefoged & Maddieson (1996:Ch.3). For typological studies of laryngeal contrasts, see Lombardi (1991), Kehrein (2002:66ff.) and Clements (2003).

(6)   *Possible laryngeal contrasts*

	Contrast		*Language*
(a)	/p t̪ ʈ tʃ k/	vs.	/b d̪ ɖ dʒ g/	Hindi
(b)	/p ts tʃ k/	vs.	/pʰ tsʰ tʃʰ kʰ/	Eastern Armenian
(c)	/b d̪ ɖ dʒ g/	vs.	/bʱ d̪ʱ ɖʱ dʒʱ gʱ/	Hindi
(d)	/p t/	vs.	/p' t'/	Uduk
(e)	/b d/	vs.	/ɓ ɗ/	Uduk

Additional articulations captured with laryngeal features include laryngea-lization or 'creaky voice' (e.g. in Guinée), stiff voice (in Korean), slack voice (in Javanese), and preaspiration (in Icelandic).

Laryngeal features are also required for phonological processes which change sounds from one of the categories listed above into another, such as assimilations and dissimilations involving voicing and/or aspiration, devoicing in final position.

Contrasts as in (6) are commonly assumed to require the features [voice], [spread glottis] (henceforth [spread]) and [constricted glottis] (hence-forth [constricted]). The feature [voice] accounts for the presence vs. absence of vocal cord vibration, as in (6a). Hence, voiceless segments are [−voice] and voiced segments are [+voice].[2] According to Halle and Stevens (1971) "spread sounds are produced by a displacement of the arytenoid cartilages creating a wide glottal opening; nonspread sounds are produced without this gesture." [+spread] sounds include both aspirated and breathy voiced segments. Halle and Stevens (1971) state that "constricted sounds are produced by adduction of the arytenoid cartilages causing the vocal cords to be pressed together and preventing normal vocal cord vibration; non-constricted (non-glottalized) sounds are produced without such a gesture." According to this definition, [+constricted] sounds include ejectives and implosives. These three laryngeal features can account for the contrasts between the six sets of sounds in (6) as in (7). The feature values in (7) are usually assumed to hold also for the corresponding fricatives (e.g. /f s x/ are [−voice, −spread, −constricted]); in contrast, Vaux (1998) argues that in their unmarked state voiceless fricatives are [+spread].

(7)   *Feature specifications for the three laryngeal features for six classes of sounds*

	p t k	pʰ tʰ kʰ	p' t' k'	b d g	bʱ dʱ gʱ	ɓ ɗ ɠ
[voice]	−	−	−	+	+	+
[spread]	−	+	−	−	+	−
[constricted]	−	−	+	−	−	+

Implosives and ejectives are both [+constricted] and only differ in terms of voicing. Note that this treatment sees the different airstream mechanisms for ejectives and implosives as being phonologically inert. Presumably this information would be added to the relevant featural representations in phonetic implementation.

Other segments assumed to be [+constricted] are laryngealized sounds and stiff voiced sounds. An implicit claim then is that no language can contrast (voiceless) stiff voice vs. (voiceless) ejectives or (voiced) implosives vs. (voiced) laryngealized sounds.

It is often assumed that the features in (7) are privative and not binary. According to the privative analysis only the '+' value of the features in (7) is present and there is no '−' value (Lombardi 1991:27, Clements and Hume

1995:270, Kehrein 2002:66). This approach seems to be correct for [spread] and [constricted], since it is difficult to find examples in which the negative values of these features are necessary for a phonological analysis. The claim that [voice] is a privative feature is controversial. See in particular Wetzels and Mascaró (2001), who argue that it is binary because [−voice] is sometimes active phonologically.

There is general agreement that the features in (7) are dominated by the class node LARYNGEAL (Clements 1985a, Lombardi 1991, and others), as in (8):

(8)   *The* LARYNGEAL *node and its dependents*

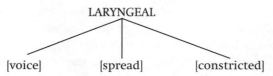

Evidence for LARYNGEAL comes from languages in which more than one laryngeal feature is manipulated simultaneously by a phonological rule; for example, in Thai the three-way contrast between voiced, voiceless and aspirated is neutralized to (plain) voiceless in syllable-final position (Lombardi 1991:107). Given (8), these neutralization facts suggest that in Thai the rule deletes LARYNGEAL in final position.[3] See Lombardi (1991) and Kehrein (2002:171ff.) for similar examples.

Some linguists have argued that the feature for voicing does not form a natural class with the features [spread] and [constricted] (Keyser and Stevens 1994, Avery and Idsardi 2001).

The features in (7) (together with (8)) are often assumed to characterize the laryngeals /h ʔ/; /h/ is [+spread] and /ʔ/ is [+constricted] and neither segment has PLACE (Clements 1985a, Steriade 1987, Lloret 1995). An alternative is that laryngeals in some languages require PLACE rather than laryngeal features (McCarthy 1994); this issue will be discussed in Section 13.6.4.

13.5   Manner features

Manner features are usually assumed to subsume [continuant], [nasal], and [lateral]. [strident] is sometimes included as a manner feature as well, although some linguists have argued that it should be treated as a place feature (see Section 13.6.2). In an early version of Feature Geometry Clements (1985a:248) posited a MANNER node, which dominates [continuant], [nasal] and [strident]. However, most subsequent researchers do not accept a 'manner node' because there is little evidence that these features pattern together as a unit (Keyser and Stevens 1994:208, cf. Hulst & Ewen 1991:22ff, Kehrein 2002). In this section I discuss [continuant], [nasal], [lateral] and [strident] in order.

13.5.1 [continuant]

The feature [continuant] is necessary to distinguish stops from the corresponding fricatives (e.g. /k/ vs. /x/). According to Halle and Clements (1983:7) "Continuants are formed with a vocal tract configuration allowing the airstream to flow through the midsagittal region of the oral tract." According to this definition [+continuant] includes fricatives, rhotics, vowels and glides, while [−continuant] describes stops and nasals and (because of the clause "midsagittal region") lateral approximants like /l/, which are realized in such a way that the air escapes through the side. This definition of [continuant] is illustrated in (9).[4]

(9)   *Feature specifications for [continuant] and [sonorant] for seven classes of sounds*

	stops	fricatives	nasals	laterals	rhotics	glides	vowels
[continuant]	−	+	−	−	+	+	+
[sonorant]	−	−	+	+	+	+	+

I include [sonorant] in (9) to illustrate that the natural classes of stops and fricatives are captured by referring to two feature values: [−continuant, −sonorant] and [+continuant, −sonorant] respectively – both of which can be referred to in rules. Additional features are required to distinguish nasals from laterals. Contrasts between glides and vowels (e.g. /i/ vs. /j/ and /u/ vs. /w/) are captured in terms of moraic and/or syllable structure. Thus, /i/ and /j/ are the same featurally but /i/ is nuclear and /j/ is not (Levin 1985).

Considerable debate has focused on the relationship between [continuant] and other features. The consensus is that there is a close connection between continuancy and PLACE, but individual proposals differ significantly. For example, Clements (1987:39) and Clements and Hume (1995:272) argue that PLACE and [continuant] are sisters dominated by an ORAL CAVITY node. This representation is supported by intrusive stops in English (e.g. the [t] in *sense* [sɛnts]), which require the spreading of ORAL CAVITY (i.e. PLACE and [continuant] together). Van de Weijer (1992, 1993, 1994) argues that PLACE is dominated by [continuant] – an approach supported by rules spreading PLACE and [continuant] together and by those in which only the former feature spreads. In contrast, Padgett (1994) proposes that [continuant] is a dependent of PLACE. Note that van de Weijer's model predicts that [continuant] cannot spread independently of PLACE but Padgett's model allows for such processes.

13.5.2 [nasal]

The feature [nasal] derives support from languages in which this feature (and none other) assimilates. Such processes include local assimilations (e.g. *thin* /θɪn/ → [θĩn] in English), but also nonlocal processes of nasal harmony (Archangeli & Pulleyblank Ch.15). According to Halle and Clements (1983:7): "Nasal sounds are produced by lowering the velum and allowing the air to pass outward through the nose; oral sounds are produced with the velum raised to prevent the passage of air through the nose." [+nasal] therefore includes nasal consonants (/m n ŋ.../) and nasal vowels (/ã ẽ.../). Obstruents, liquids and oral vowels are [−nasal]. Lesser known nasal segments include pre-nasalized stops (e.g. /ⁿd/ – Feinstein 1977, Herbert 1986, Rosenthall 1988, Padgett 1991:Ch.2), nasal glides (e.g. /w̃ j̃/) and nasal fricatives and trills (e.g. /ṽ s̃ z̃ r̃/) (Cohn 1993b). For discussion of these segments in the context of nasal harmony, see Piggott (1992), Rice (1993), Walker (2000b) and Grijzenhout (2001). [nasal] is usually assumed to be a direct dependent of the ROOT as in (2) (McCarthy 1988) (cf. the view that [nasal] is dominated by a SONORANT VOICE node – Rice and Avery 1991, Rice 1993, and Piggott 1992).

There is some discussion in the literature on whether or not [nasal] is binary or privative. Linguists who assume that [nasal] is privative include Rice and Avery (1991:104). Trigo (1993) discusses this question with respect to the nasal segments of Guaraní and concludes that oral vowels in that language are [−nasal]. Cohn (1990) examines the behavior of nasal segments in Sundanese, English and French and argues that some sounds in these languages are [−nasal] and that this feature value persists into the phonetics. Sagey (1986:96–99) maintains that pre-nasalized stops like /ⁿd/ have a [−nasal] component (see Section 13.7). For an alternative proposal for the representation of pre-nasalized stops in which no reference to [−nasal] is made see Steriade (1993) and van de Weijer (1994:147–164).

13.5.3 [lateral]

The feature [lateral] is necessary to distinguish /l/ from /r/, even though these two segments also differ in terms of [continuant] (see Section 13.5.1). Blevins (1994:309–311) notes that one cannot analyze the /l/ vs. /r/ contrast in terms of continuancy (and therefore dispense with [lateral]) because lateral fricatives like /ɬ ɮ/ behave phonologically as [+continuant] (cf. Spencer 1984, Brown 1995, Walsh Dickey 1997:19ff.). Halle and Clements (1983:7) define [lateral] as follows: "Lateral sounds . . . are produced with the tongue placed in such a way as to prevent the airstream from flowing outward through the center of the mouth, while allowing it to pass over one or both sides of the tongue; central sounds do not involve such a constriction."

Within Feature Geometry there is controversy concerning the locus of [lateral]. Some authors have argued that [lateral] is a dependent of CORONAL (McCarthy 1988, Grijzenhout 1995 and especially Blevins 1994). This analysis derives some phonetic support, since laterals are almost always coronal sounds from the phonetic perspective: i.e. dental/alveolar /l/, retroflex /ɭ/ and palatal /ʎ/. The one noticeable exception is the velar lateral /ʟ/, which one would expect to be dorsal and not coronal. Blevins (1994:312ff.) considers the phonological patterning of /ʟ/ in a number of languages including Yagaria and Waghi and concludes that this segment behaves phonologically as coronal.

Blevins proposes that the feature [lateral] is a dependent of CORONAL and that /ʟ/ is represented as a complex segment which is both [CORONAL, +lateral] and [DORSAL, +high, +back]. For an alternative approach to the representation of laterals see Shaw (1991:146ff.), who argues on the basis of sibilant harmony in Tahltan that [lateral] is not a coronal feature, but a direct dependent of the ROOT. See also Rice and Avery (1991) for an alternative proposal.

13.5.4 [strident]

The feature [strident] accounts for the contrast between interdentals and alveolars: i.e. [−strident] /θ ð/ vs. [+strident] /s z/ (Jakobson, Fant, and Halle 1952, *SPE*, Hume 1992, Hall 1997). A commonly assumed definition says that "strident sounds are marked acoustically by greater noisiness than their nonstrident counterparts" (*SPE*:329). Some authors use [strident] to distinguish palatoalveolars from palatals, i.e. [+strident] /ʃ ʒ/ vs. [−strident] /ç ʝ/ (*SPE*:329, Hume 1992:90−91).

    Many writers assume that [strident] is independent of PLACE in the sense that it is attached to the ROOT, as in (2), or to some intermediate node (Clements & Hume 1995:292−293, Kehrein 2002:10). Alternatively, Shaw (1991:130ff.) argues on the basis of sibilant harmony in Tahltan that [strident] is a daughter of CORONAL. See also Clements (2001:109−114) for a similar approach.

    [strident] is often employed to distinguish oral stops from the corresponding affricates: e.g. /t/ vs. /t͡s/ (Jakobson, Fant and Halle 1952, LaCharité 1993, Rubach 1994, Clements 1999, Kehrein 2002). According to this view affricates are 'strident stops': i.e. stops are [−continuant, −strident] and affricates [−continuant, +strident]. It is not clear how nonstrident affricates are represented in this approach, e.g. Tahltan /t͡θ/. See Section 13.7 for earlier approaches.

13.6   Place features

There is general agreement that there is a PLACE node which dominates the class nodes LABIAL, CORONAL and DORSAL, as in (2) (simplified in (10)). These three *articulators* are required for segments pronounced with the lips, the tongue front and the tongue dorsum respectively (Sagey 1986, Clements and Hume 1995). Many authors also see evidence for an additional articulator relevant for pharyngeals. I do not include this node in (10) because its relationship with the other place features is an issue open for debate (see Section 13.6.4).

(10)   *The three articulator nodes*

The PLACE node derives support from assimilation processes that spread all place features as a unit, independently of all other features (e.g. nasal place assimilation) and from debuccalization processes, in which all and only place features delete (e.g. /s/ → [h] in rhymal position in some varieties of Spanish – Harris 1983:45ff.).

The approach to place features in (10) is based on the Articulator Theory, according to which segments are distinguished by the active articulator making the constriction gesture (Sagey 1986). This treatment is very different from the Place of Articulation Theory, which expresses place of articulation primarily in terms of the values of the binary features [coronal] and [anterior] (see *SPE*). I emphasize below proposals in the Articulator Theory, since this has proven to be the most influential view of features. See McCarthy (1988:99ff.) and Cho (1991:160–165) for a more detailed comparison.

In Section 13.6.1 I consider the features relating to the lips (LABIAL and [round]), in Section 13.6.2 the features relating to the tongue front (CORONAL, [anterior], [distributed]) and in Section 13.6.3 the features relating to the dorsum (DORSAL, [back], [high], [low], as well as [ATR]). In Section 13.6.4 I discuss features pertaining to the tongue root (PHARYNGEAL).

13.6.1   Features relating to the lips

The features relating to the lips (LABIAL and [round]) are necessary to account for lip rounding in vowels and consonants. Halle and Clements (1983:6–7) write that ". . . labial sounds are formed with a constriction at the lips, while nonlabial sounds are formed without such a constriction." Labial sounds therefore subsume rounded vowels (/y u. . ./, labialized consonants (/p^w t^w k^w . . ./, and (plain) bilabial and labiodental consonants (/p b m f v. . ./ (Anderson 1971: 106–107, Ladefoged and Vennemann 1973:62–66, Hyman 1975:53–55). According to Sagey (1986:277) [+round] and [−round] refer to "rounded lips" and "spread lips" respectively. This feature is necessary to distinguish plain vs. labialized labials ([−round] /p b/ vs. [+round] / p^w b^w/).

[round] is analyzed as a dependent of LABIAL, as in (11); see Sagey (1986:137–145), McCarthy (1988:103–104), and Lahiri and Evers (1991:87), among others.

(11)   *Feature geometric representation of LABIAL and [round]*

LABIAL

|

[round]

In contrast, Odden (1991) maintains that [round] is not a dependent of LABIAL; on the basis of various vowel harmony processes, he argues that [round] and [back] form a constituent. Halle (1995b:31–36) reanalyzes

Odden's examples for the independence of LABIAL and [round] in terms of the model in (11).

Given the approach in (11) with privative LABIAL and binary [round] the contrast between rounded vs. unrounded vowels is captured with LABIAL (and redundant [round]), as in (12). I have included DORSAL as well, which is present in all vowels in certain approaches (Sagey 1986), although an alternative analysis will be discussed in Section 13.6.3.1. In (12) and below '✓' indicates the presence of a privative feature. In (13) the features for plain labials, plain coronals, labialized labials and labialized coronals is illustrated.

(12)   *Contrast between rounded vs. unrounded vowels*

	i e ɯ	y o u
DORSAL	✓	✓
LABIAL		✓
[round]		+

(13)   *Features for plain labials, plain coronals, labialized labials and labialized coronals*

	p b f v	t d s z	pʷ bʷ fʷ vʷ	tʷ dʷ sʷ zʷ
CORONAL		✓		✓
LABIAL	✓		✓	✓
[round]	–		+	+

The features in (12)–(13) make the correct predictions for the natural classes of (a) rounded vowels and labial consonants and (b) plain labial consonants and labialized consonants (Hyman 1975).

It is not clear what feature distinguishes bilabials vs. labiodentals. In languages with /p/ vs. /f/ this contrast is captured with [continuant], but in languages like Ewe with /Φ/ vs. /f/ it might require a place feature like [labiodental] (see Palmada 1995, who proposes this feature on the basis of data from Catalan).

13.6.2   Features relating to the front of the tongue

The 'front' of the tongue refers here and below to articulations involving the tip, the blade, and the forward part of the body of the tongue, which typically forms a constriction under the hard palate (Clements and Hume 1995: 302). The features relating to the front of the tongue include CORONAL (13.6.2.1), [anterior] (13.6.2.2), and [distributed] (13.6.2.3).

13.6.2.1   CORONAL

The feature CORONAL captures natural classes involving sounds like /t d n l r θ ð s z ʃ ʒ tʃ dʒ/ and is usually defined as those sounds articulated with the front part of the tongue (as defined above; see Paradis and Prunet 1991b, Hume 1992, Hall 1997). The places of articulation considered to be CORONAL are dental, alveolar, retroflex, palatoalveolar (e.g. /ʃ ʒ/), alveolopalatal (e.g. /ɕ ʑ/) and palatal (e.g. /c ɟ ç j/).

The articulatory feature [coronal] (proposed in *SPE*) replaced the acoustic feature [grave] proposed by Jakobson, Fant and Halle (1952: 43).

There is now consensus that palatals are coronal (contra *SPE*) (Hyman 1973, Clements 1976, Vago 1976, Odden 1978, Lahiri and Blumstein 1984, Hume 1992, and Hall 1997). Some linguists see palatal sounds as complex in the sense that they are both CORONAL and DORSAL (Keating 1988b:98, Pulleyblank 1989:391, Robinson 2001:107–108). Hall (1997:10ff.) argues that palatal noncontinuants (i.e. stops, nasals, laterals) and palatal glides are noncomplex CORONAL segments, but that palatal fricatives like /ç j/ are DORSAL and not CORONAL.

In Feature Geometry CORONAL (as well as LABIAL and DORSAL) is considered to be a privative articulator node, as in (2). In this approach the following seven places of articulation are captured featurally in terms of articulators as in (14).[5] For reasons of space alveolopalatals are not included here and below. See Hume (1992) and Hall (1997) for discussion.

(14)   *Seven places of articulation distributed among the three class nodes* LABIAL, CORONAL *and* DORSAL

	labials	dentals	alveolars	retroflexes	palato-alveolars	palatals	velars
CORONAL		✓	✓	✓	✓	✓	
DORSAL							✓
LABIAL	✓						

According to *SPE* and many Feature Geometry treatments CORONAL is a distinctive feature for consonants and not for vowels. Hume (1992) and Clements and Hume (1995) as well as several other authors argue that front vowels are CORONAL (and central and back vowels are DORSAL). This reanalysis of sounds like /i e/ as CORONAL falls out from these linguists' definition of CORONAL (see Section 13.6.2) as those sounds "involving a constriction by the front of the tongue" (Clements and Hume 1995:277). This approach is discussed in Section 13.6.3.1.

13.6.2.2   [anterior]

The feature [anterior] distinguishes sounds in front of the alveolar ridge (/s z. . ./) from sounds produced behind the alveolar ridge (/ʃ ʒ. . ./). In Feature Geometry [anterior] (and [distributed] – see Section 13.6.2.3) are restricted to sounds that are coronal, as in (2) (Sagey 1986:132–137, McCarthy 1988: 103–105, Paradis and Prunet 1991b, Hume 1992, Hall 1997 and Clements 2001). According to Sagey (1986:277–278) [anterior] refers to a constriction formed by the tongue front either in front of the palatoalveolar region ([+anterior]) or behind it ([−anterior]). The matrices in (15) include seven places of articulation with their specifications for CORONAL and [anterior]. This system predicts that [+anterior] dentals and alveolars and [−anterior] retroflexes, palatoalveolars and palatals can pattern as natural classes (see the literature cited above and Gnanadesikan 1993 for discussion).

(15)   *Feature specifications for [anterior]:*

	labials	dentals	alveolars	retroflexes	palato-alveolars	palatals	velars
CORONAL		✓	✓	✓	✓	✓	
[anterior]		+	+	−	−	−	

The treatment of [anterior] in (15) implies that labials and dorsals cannot be marked for these features, contrary to what was assumed in *SPE* (p. 304).

13.6.2.3 [distributed]

The feature [distributed] accounts for the contrast between apical and laminal sounds in languages indigenous to Australia and India: e.g. apical /t/ vs. laminal /t̪/ as well as (apical) retroflex /ʈ/ vs. (laminal) palatal /c/. These contrasts hold not only for stops, but also for fricatives, nasals and laterals. According to Sagey (1986:278) [+distributed] describes a "constriction formed by the tongue front that extends for a considerable distance along the direction of airflow and [−distributed] to a constriction formed by the tongue front that extends only for a short distance along the direction of air flow." Thus, apical sounds are [−distributed] because they have a relatively short length of constriction and laminal ones are [+distributed].[6] [distributed] also accounts for the contrast between the two [CORONAL, +anterior] places of articulation: 'dentals' (e.g. /t̪/) and 'alveolars' (e.g. /t/); the usual assumption is that the former sounds are [+distributed] and the latter ones [−distributed]. The reason for this is that unmarked dentals and alveolars are often said to be laminal and apical respectively (Ladefoged and Maddieson 1996:20−21). These authors note that the West Atlantic language Temne is a rare exception because dentals and alveolars in that language are apical and laminal respectively. This example is important because it shows that there is no inherent correspondence between the values of [distributed] and place of articulation. The traditional view in phonology is that rules of phonetic implementation would specify the exact place of articulation of a coronal segment.

As noted in Section 13.6.2.2 [distributed] is distinctive only for coronal sounds (recall (2)). This treatment is illustrated with the following matrices (16, 17). The feature necessary to distinguish palatoalveolars and palatals is discussed below.

(16) *Feature specifications for [distributed] and [anterior]*

	labials	dentals	alveolars	retroflexes	palato-alveolars	palatals	velars
CORONAL	✓	✓	✓		✓	✓	
[anterior]	+	+	−		−	−	
[distributed]	+	−	−		+	+	

(16) predicts that in languages with a four- or five-way contrast among coronals (e.g. in some Australian languages), [+distributed] dentals, palatoalveolars and palatals should pattern together as a natural class, as should the [−distributed] alveolars and retroflexes. See Gnanadesikan (1993:32ff.) and Hamilton (1993), who document examples of this type.

[anterior] and [distributed], together with [strident], can be used to distinguish fricatives at six places of articulation (see also Keating 1988a:6):

(17) *Feature specifications for coronal fricatives*

	θ ð	ş z̧	s z	ʃ ʒ	ş z̧	ç ʝ
CORONAL	✓	✓	✓	✓	✓	✓
[anterior]	+	+	+	−	−	−
[distributed]	+	+	−	+	−	+
[strident]	−	+	+	+	+	−

The three-way contrast among [−anterior] sounds in (17) holds for fricatives but not for stops, nasals or laterals. Among the latter segments the contrast between palatoalveolar and palatal is notoriously difficult to find (Lahiri and Blumstein 1984, Ladefoged and Maddieson 1996); hence [−sonorant, −continuant, CORONAL, −anterior, +distributed] describes both palatoalveolar and palatal stops. The three-way [+anterior] contrast in (17) is attested in the Dravidian language Toda; such contrasts among (plain) stops, nasals and laterals are predicted to be nonoccurring.

In a number of languages there is a strong affinity between retroflex consonants and back vowels, as in the change from alveolar to a retroflex in back vowel contexts (see Hamann 2003:90ff. for a survey of this phonological evidence). A number of phonologists have used this kind of evidence to argue that retroflex segments are marked for the same feature as back vowels (i.e. DORSAL or [+back] − see Section 13.6.3.1), although the individual proposals differ widely. For example, Gnanadesikan (1993) argues that [anterior] should be replaced with [back], so that sounds like /ʈ ɖ/ are [CORONAL, −distributed, +back]. Lin (1989) argues that [distributed] is replaced with [back], so that /ʈ ɖ/ are [CORONAL, −anterior, +back]. See Rubach (1984), Pulleyblank (1989), and Hall (1997) for similar approaches and Hamann (2003:141−144) for criticisms thereof. For a very different proposal concerning the representations of retroflex sounds see Flemming (2003).

13.6.3 Features relating to the dorsum

The features relating to the tongue dorsum are important for distinguishing vowels (i.e. front vs. back as well as high vs. mid vs. low) and for the velar vs. uvular contrast among consonants. In Section 13.6.3.1 I discuss features referring to the 'horizontal' dimension (DORSAL and [back]) and in Section 13.6.3.2 the 'vertical' dimension ([high], [low] and [ATR]).

13.6.3.1 DORSAL and [back]

Sagey (1986:274) proposes the articulator DORSAL, which is defined as involving the tongue body. According to this definition, all vowels, as well as velar and uvular consonants are DORSAL. The feature DORSAL is argued to dominate the binary features [back], [high] and [low], as in (18):

(18) *A feature tree for DORSAL and its dependents*

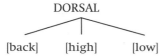

According to Sagey (1986:278), [+back] and [−back] refer to a 'retracted tongue body' and a 'fronted tongue body' respectively. On this view [back] is not distinctive for (plain) dorsal segments (e.g. /x/ vs. /χ/), which are distinguished by [high]; see Section 13.6.3.2. The primary function of [back] in the approach in (18) is to account for the front vs. back dimension in vowels, as in (19):

(19) *Features for front, central and back vowels (Sagey 1986)*

	i	e	ɨ	u	o
DORSAL	✓	✓	✓	✓	✓
[back]	−	−	+	+	+

The back vs. central contrast (e.g. /u/ vs. /ɨ/) is captured with LABIAL. It is not clear how this contrast is captured if both vowels are (un)rounded (e.g. /ɨ/ vs. /ɯ/); see Flemming (2003:340) for discussion.

One unresolved issue is whether or not vowels and consonants have the same set of place features. According to Sagey (1986) in (19), all vowels are DORSAL, while CORONAL is relevant only for consonants. However, the Sageyian system was criticized by a number of linguists for its inability to account for the connection between front vowels and coronal consonants (Pulleyblank 1989, Lahiri and Evers 1991, Hume 1992, van de Weijer 1994:38ff.). An example of a phonological process in which front vowels and coronal consonants pattern together is the commonly occurring change from velar to palatoalveolar in the neighborhood of front vowels (i.e. /k g/ → [tʃ dʒ] / __ [i e]). This type of process is awkward in the Sageyian approach because it involves the shift from DORSAL to CORONAL; this cannot be captured as an assimilatory process because front vowels are not coronal.

The basic intuition of the linguists cited above is that front vowels and coronal consonants form a natural class which can be expressed if front vowels are CORONAL and central and back vowels DORSAL, as in (20). Front vowels are expected to be coronal given the definition of CORONAL as proposed by Clements and Hume (1995:277) (recall Section 13.6.2.1) as those sounds "involving a constriction formed by the front of the tongue."

(20)   *Alternative features for front, central and back vowels*

	i	e	ɨ	u	o
DORSAL			✓	✓	✓
CORONAL	✓	✓			

In the approach in (20) the shift from velar to palatoalveolar (i.e. /k/→ [tʃ]/_[i e]) requires the spreading of CORONAL from /i e/.[7] The natural class of coronal consonants and front vowels cannot be captured by analyzing both sets of sounds as [−back] because not all coronal consonants are pronounced with a fronted tongue body (Hume 1992:52ff.) For criticisms of the approach in (20) see Ní Chiosáin and Padgett (1993) and Flemming (2003).

   Another unresolved question is the correct representation of secondarily palatalized segments, e.g. /pʲ tʲ kʲ/. According to Sagey (1986:216ff.) palatalized segments consist of the articulator node representing the primary place plus [DORSAL, −back], e.g. /pʲ/ is [LABIAL, DORSAL, −back]. For alternative approaches see Hume (1992), Lahiri and Evers (1991) and Ní Chiosáin (1994).

13.6.3.2   Tongue height features

According to Sagey (1986:278) [+high] refers to a 'raised tongue body' while [−high] involves the tongue body which is 'distinctively not raised'. [+low] indicates a 'lowered tongue body', while [−low] describes an articulation involving the tongue body which is 'distinctively not lowered'. Since plain labials and coronals are not DORSAL in (18), these sounds cannot be marked for [high] or [low]. The feature [high] is therefore restricted in its function among vowels to distinguishing between high vs. nonhigh and [low] to mid vs. low (see (21)). Among consonants, [high] distinguishes velars and uvulars and [low] is redundant (see (22)). See section 13.6.4.1 for further discussion of uvulars.

(21)   *Features for high, mid and low vowels (Sagey 1986)*

	ɪ	ɛ	æ	ɯ	ʌ	a
DORSAL	✓	✓	✓	✓	✓	✓
[back]	−	−	−	+	+	+
[high]	+	−	−	+	−	−
[low]	−	−	+	−	−	+

(22)   *Features for velar and uvular consonants (Sagey 1986)*

	k g x ɣ	q ɢ χ ʁ
DORSAL	✓	✓
[high]	+	−
[back]	+	+
[low]	−	−

The feature [ATR] is used to capture the contrast between /i e o/ ([+ATR]) and /ɪ ɛ ɔ/ ([−ATR]) – both in West African languages with [ATR] harmony, as well as Germanic languages like English. ([ATR] replaced the *SPE* feature [tense]). The use of [ATR] is motivated partly because the *SPE* definition of tenseness is vague phonetically, whereas [ATR] is clearly associated with a particular articulator (i.e. the tongue root, or 'radix'). This suggests that [ATR] be situated under the articulator required for pharyngeals; see Section 13.6.4. Ladefoged & Maddieson (1996:302ff.) criticize the usage of [ATR] to distinguish what are in actuality different vowel heights in Germanic languages.

Some linguists have argued (contrary to (18)) that vowel height features should be separated from DORSAL. For example, Odden (1991) proposes a model in which [high] and [ATR] are placed under a HEIGHT node and that [back] and [round] form a separate constituent. Odden tentatively assumes that [low] is also situated under HEIGHT as well. Arguments in support of this approach come from vowel harmony processes in Kimatuumbi and Ewe which spread only [high] and [ATR] but not [back] or [round]. See also Hyman (1988:269–270) and Lahiri and Evers (1991), who also propose models in which [high] and [low] are separate from [back].

Wetzels (1995) and Clements and Hume (1995:282–283) have argued that vowel height should be captured not with [high], but instead with an APERTURE node, which dominates one or more (binary) [open] tiers. These authors argue that the aperture model derives support from 'scalar' processes, e.g. vowel alternations in Brazilian Portuguese, whereby vowels are raised or lowered in steps.

13.6.4   Features relating to the tongue root

Recent research has uncovered evidence that pharyngeals need to be captured directly with an articulator involving the tongue root: i.e. PHARYNGEAL. PHARYNGEAL has been argued to be present on pharyngeals, but also in uvulars and in laryngeals.

In many languages the 'guttural' consonants (i.e. glottals, pharyngeals and uvulars) form a natural class. For example, Classical Arabic has many processes referring to glottals /h ʔ/, pharyngeals /ħ ʕ/ and uvulars /χ ʁ/ (Hayward and Hayward 1989). These sounds have been captured with [guttural] (Hayward and Hayward 1989) or PHARYNGEAL (McCarthy 1994).

Phoneticians sometimes employ the term 'radical' to refer to articulations involving the tongue root (see Ladefoged and Maddieson 1996: 37–38). Radical sounds subsume not only pharyngeals, but also a lesser-known place of articulation, namely epiglottals. In Ladefoged and Maddieson's system uvulars are dorsal and hence it is not clear how they would capture the natural class of the gutturals referred to above. For a useful overview of the features for the pharynx and the larynx see Trigo (1991).

While there is agreement that a feature like PHARYNGEAL is necessary there is controversy concerning the relationship this feature has with other features. In one approach, McCarthy (1994) argues that PHARYNGEAL is linked to PLACE but that the three articulators LABIAL, CORONAL and DORSAL are linked to an ORAL node, as in (23).

(23)   *A partial feature tree representing the* ORAL *and* PHARYNGEAL *class nodes and their dependents (McCarthy 1994)*

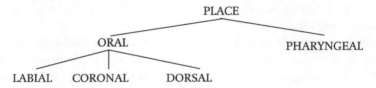

In the model in (23) 'guttural uvulars' in Classical Arabic are [PHARYNGEAL, DORSAL], while pharyngeals and laryngeals are simply [PHARYNGEAL]. For alternative proposals concerning the representations of pharyngeals see Keyser and Stevens (1994), Halle (1995b), and Rose (1996).

Recall from Section 13.3.1 that some linguists have argued that laryngeals are placeless (e.g. Lloret 1995). Rose (1996) argues that laryngeal consonants are specified for PHARYNGEAL only when pharyngeal or uvular continuants are also present in the inventory of the language; otherwise laryngeals are placeless. Her evidence involves processes of vowel lowering in Semitic, Salish and Afroasiatic.

13.7   Complex vs. contour segments

Sagey (1986) draws a distinction between simple, complex and contour segments. In this section I discuss the structure of these segment types.

A simple segment consists of a ROOT dominating at most one articulator (e.g. /k/ is simple because it is DORSAL only). A complex segment is 'a root node characterized by at least two different oral articulator features, representing a segment with two or more simultaneous oral tract constrictions' (Clements and Hume 1995:253). Given the model in (10) we would therefore expect three complex segments, namely labio-coronal, labio-dorsal, and corono-dorsal. In fact, all three articulations are attested: the labio-coronal /p͡t/ occurs in Margi and the labio-dorsal /k͡p/ in Yoruba. The third articulation is attested in Zulu as a corono-dorsal click /||/. Sagey (1986:99ff.) and McCarthy (1988:100) propose that these complex segments have the representations in (24). In contrast, Halle (1995b) has a featural system which represents these three complex segments by means of a single articulator and the feature [+suction].

(24)   *Representations for three complex segments (Sagey 1986, McCarthy 1988)*

/p͡t/	/k͡p/	/‖/
PLACE	PLACE	PLACE
LABIAL CORONAL	LABIAL DORSAL	CORONAL DORSAL

The representations in (24) have a single PLACE (and ROOT) node each. An alternative approach to the representation of complex segments is defended by van de Weijer (1994), who argues that the segments in (24) have two ROOT nodes as opposed to one.

Contour segments contain sequences (or 'contours') of different features. An example of a contour representation is the one for affricates in (25a), which was proposed by Sagey (1986). She proposes the similar representation in (25b) for pre-nasalized stops as well. See also Campbell (1974:60–61), Hualde (1987), Lombardi (1990), van de Weijer (1994), and Schafer (1995) for representations for affricates similar to (25a). These treatments are an alternative to the one in Section 13.5.4, in which affricates are analyzed as strident stops.

(25)   *Representations for contour segments (Sagey 1986)*

(a)	ROOT		(b)	ROOT	
	[–continuant] [+continuant]			[+nasal] [–nasal]	

In the contour segment analysis the two 'contour' features are situated on the same autosegmental tier and they should therefore display 'edge effects'. Edge effects mean that a segment behaves as though it bears the feature [+F] with respect to the segments on one side and [–F] on the other. Thus, if affricates were to display edge effects then they should behave as [–continuant] segments on their left side and as [+continuant] segments on the right.

Research has revealed that affricates in many languages do not display edge effects as predicted (Lombardi 1990); this is one of the reasons why the linguists cited in Section 13.5.4 see affricates as being strident stops, without a [+continuant] component. By contrast edge effects have been demonstrated for pre-nasalized stops.

13.8 Feature value charts

(26) *Features for obstruents*

	p b	t d̪	t d	ʈ ɖ	c ɟ	k g	q ɢ	ts dz	tʃ dʒ	Φ β	f v	θ ð	s̠ z̠	s z	ʂ ʐ	ʃ ʒ	ç ʝ	x ɣ	χ ʁ	ħ ʕ
[consonantal]	+	+	+	+	+	+	+	+	+	+	+	+	+	+	+	+	+	+	+	+
[sonorant]	–	–	–	–	–	–	–	–	–	–	–	–	–	–	–	–	–	–	–	–
[approximant]	–	–	–	–	–	–	–	–	–	–	–	–	–	–	–	–	–	–	–	–
[continuant]	–	–	–	–	–	–	–	–	–	+	+	+	+	+	+	+	+	+	+	+
[strident]	–	–	–	–	–	–	–	+	+	–	–	–	+	+	+	+	–	–	–	–
LARYNGEAL	✓	✓	✓	✓	✓	✓	✓	✓	✓	✓	✓	✓	✓	✓	✓	✓	✓	✓	✓	✓
[voice]	–/+	–/+	–/+	–/+	–/+	–/+	–/+	–/+	–/+	–/+	–/+	–/+	–/+	–/+	–/+	–/+	–/+	–/+	–/+	–/+
PLACE	✓	✓	✓	✓	✓	✓	✓	✓	✓	✓	✓	✓	✓	✓	✓	✓	✓	✓	✓	✓
LABIAL	✓									✓	✓									
[round]	–									–	–									
CORONAL		✓	✓	✓	✓			✓	✓			✓	✓	✓	✓	✓	✓			
[anterior]		+	+	–	–			+	–			+	+	+	–	–	–			
[distributed]		+	–	–	+			+	–			+	+	–	–	+	+			
DORSAL						✓	✓											✓	✓	
[back]						+	+											+	+	
[low]						–	–											–	–	
[high]						+	–											+	–	
PHARYNGEAL																				✓

(27) *Laryngeal features for plain voiceless stops, (voiceless) aspirated stops, ejectives, plain voiced stops, breathy voiced stops, and implosives*

	p t k			pʰ tʰ kʰ			p' t' k'			b d g			bʱ dʱ gʱ			ɓ ɗ ɠ		
LARYNGEAL		✓			✓			✓			✓			✓			✓	
[voice]		–			–			–			+			+			+	
[spread]		–			+			–			–			+			–	
[constricted]		–			–			+			–			–			+	

(28) *Features for sonorant consonants and glides (including laryngeals)*

	m	m̥	n	n̥	ɳ	ɲ	ŋ	N	l	l̪	ɭ	ʎ	ʟ	r	ʀ	ɾ	ɹ	j	w	h	ʔ
[consonantal]	+	+	+	+	+	+	+	+	+	+	+	+	+	+	+	+	+	–	–	–	–
[sonorant]	+	+	+	+	+	+	+	+	+	+	+	+	+	+	+	+	+	+	–	–	
[approximant]	–	–	–	–	–	–	–	–	+	+	+	+	+	+	+	+	+	+	+		
[continuant]	–	–	–	–	–	–	–	–	–	–	–	–	–	+	+	–	+	+	+	+	–
[nasal]	+	+	+	+	+	+	+	–	–	–	–	–	–	–	–	–	–	–	–		
[lateral]	–	–	–	–	–	–	–	–	+	+	+	+	+	–	–	–	–	–	–		
LARYNGEAL																				✓	✓
[spread]																				+	–
[constricted]																				–	+
PLACE	✓	✓	✓	✓	✓	✓	✓	✓	✓	✓	✓	✓	✓	✓	✓	✓	✓	✓	✓		
LABIAL	✓																		✓		
[round]	–																		+		
CORONAL			✓	✓	✓	✓			✓	✓	✓	✓		✓		✓	✓	✓			
[anterior]			+	+	–	–			+	+	–	–		+		+	+	–			
[distributed]			+	–	–	+			+	–	–	+		–		–	–	+			
DORSAL						✓	✓					✓	✓						✓		
[back]						+	+					+	+						+		
[low]						–	–					–	–						–		
[high]						+	–					+	–						+		

(29) *Features for vowels*

	i	ɪ	y	ʏ	ɯ	u	ʊ	e	ɛ	ø	œ	ɤ	o	ɔ	ʌ	æ	a	ɑ	ɒ
DORSAL	✓	✓	✓	✓	✓	✓	✓	✓	✓	✓	✓	✓	✓	✓	✓	✓	✓	✓	✓
[back]	–	–	–	–	+	+	+	–	–	–	–	+	+	+	+	–	+	+	+
[high]	+	+	+	+	+	+	+	–	–	–	–	–	–	–	–	–	–	–	–
[low]	–	–	–	–	–	–	–	–	–	–	–	–	–	–	–	+	+	+	+
[ATR]	+	–	+	–	–	+	–	+	–	+	–	+	–	–	–	–	–	+	+
LABIAL			✓	✓		✓	✓			✓	✓		✓	✓					✓
[round]			+	+		+	+			+	+		+	+					–

Notes

I would like to thank Paul de Lacy, Wolfgang Kehrein, Kate Ketner and Jaye Padgett for comments on an earlier version. All disclaimers apply.

1 This definition differs from the one traditionally assumed in phonetics, according to which only sounds like /j w l ɹ/ but not vowels are approximants (Ladefoged 1993: 64ff.). Clements notes that [+approximant] also includes voiceless sonorants, which are normally produced with audible turbulence (1990: 327). It is unclear whether or not laryngeals (/h ʔ/) are [+approximant] or [–approximant].

2 Halle and Stevens (1971) propose [stiff vocal cords] (=[stiff]) and [slack vocal cords] (=[slack]) instead of [voice]. On this view voiceless obstruents are [+stiff] and voiced obstruents are [+slack]. See also Avery and Idsardi (2001) and Keyser and Stevens (1994). Lombardi (1991: 5–7) argues against [stiff]/[slack] and for [voice]. Halle and Stevens (1971) contend that [stiff] and [slack] can also capture the connection between laryngeal activity and tone, i.e. low tones are [+slack, –stiff], high tones are [–slack, +stiff] and mid tones [–slack, –stiff]. See Yip (2002: 57–58) for criticisms of this use of [stiff] and [slack].

3 Lombardi's treatment relies on a constraint saying that the laryngeal features are licensed by a following tautosyllabic sonorant. Both Lombardi's analysis and the rule-based analysis described above presuppose that the neutralized stops in final position have no LARYNGEAL node at all.

4 Among rhotics it is unclear what feature distinguishes /r/ from /ɾ/. Another controversial question is whether or not flaps like /ɾ/ are plus or minus [continuant]. See Hall (1997:112–124) for some discussion. /l/ behaves phonologically as a [–continuant] sound in many languages, e.g. in Belfast English /t d n l/ (i.e. the coronal noncontinuants) undergo a rule of dentalization (Harris 1989:40–41). The definition of [continuant] is problematic for languages in which laterals behave as [+continuant], e.g. vowel nasalization in Frisian (Gussenhoven and Jacobs 1998:73).

5 (14) predicts that labials and dorsals cannot function as a natural class. Evidence that labials and dorsals can pattern together is discussed by Rice (1994), who proposes that this natural class be captured by positing

that LABIAL and DORSAL be dominated by a PERIPHERAL node, which is a sister of CORONAL.

6 Some authors opt for features like [apical] and [laminal] instead of [distributed] (Hamilton 1993, Flemming 2003:341ff.).

In a detailed phonetic study Dart (1991) shows that [distributed] should not be defined in terms of length of constriction. She found that the real distinction in languages which contrast a [+distributed] and a [−distributed] sound was in the active articulator (i.e. the lamina = [+distributed] vs. the apex = [−distributed]).

7 To account for the fact that the output sounds of /k/→[tʃ] are palatoalveolar and not alveolar, front vowels are sometimes assumed to be redundantly [+anterior, −distributed] (Hume 1992:67). That the output sounds are affricates requires that [+strident] be added by default rule. The spreading of CORONAL described above triggers the deletion of the DORSAL node of the target segments /k g/ (Lahiri and Evers 1991:91).

14

Local assimilation and constraint interaction

Eric Baković

14.1 Introduction

A phonological process is called an *assimilation* if, as a result of its application, two or more segments in a form agree in their value for some phonological feature(s) or feature class(es). Assimilation processes can be roughly divided into two types, *local* and *long-distance*. Local assimilations obtain between strictly adjacent segments, such as between the consonants in a consonant cluster. Long-distance assimilations obtain between segments that are not (necessarily) adjacent, such as between consonants across a vowel. The focus of the present chapter is on local assimilation, and in particular on a set of issues that arise in the formal analysis of processes of local assimilation within Optimality Theory (Prince & Smolensky 2004). See Archangeli and Pulleyblank Ch.15 for discussion of long-distance vowel and consonant assimilation.

Two cases of assimilation in American English are discussed in (1) below. In (1a) are examples of place assimilation, whereby a nasal is made to agree in place of articulation features with a following consonant. In (1b) are examples of voicing assimilation, whereby an obstruent is made to agree in voicing with an adjacent (in this case, preceding) consonant.

(1) *Local assimilations in American English*

    (a) Place assimilation: negative prefix *in-*/ɪn/
        (i) i<u>na</u>pplicable   [næ]
        (ii) i<u>mp</u>ossible   [mp]   i<u>mb</u>alance   [mb]
        (iii) i<u>nt</u>olerable   [nt]   i<u>nd</u>ecent   [nd]
        (iv) i<u>nc</u>onceivable [ŋk]   i<u>ng</u>ratitude   [ŋg]
    (b) Voicing assimilation: past tense suffix *-ed* /d/
        (i) stra<u>ye</u>d   [eɪd]
        (ii) tra<u>pp</u>ed   [pt]   pa<u>ss</u>ed   [st]   pa<u>ck</u>ed   [kt]
        (iii) gra<u>bb</u>ed   [bd]   bu<u>zz</u>ed   [zd]   ba<u>gg</u>ed   [gd]

In each of these sets of examples, the example in (i) shows the relevant consonant in a context where assimilation is not expected; namely, when the consonant is adjacent to a vowel. This reveals the underlying specification of the consonant: a coronal nasal [n] in (1ai) and a voiced obstruent [d] in (1bi). The remaining examples in each set show the same consonant of the same morpheme when it is in an assimilation context. The nasal of the negative prefix in (1a) is realized as labial [m] before labial consonants [p,b], as coronal [n] before coronal consonants [t, d], and as dorsal [ŋ] before dorsal consonants [k,g]. The obstruent of the past tense suffix in (1b) is realized as voiceless [t] after voiceless consonants [p, s, k] and as voiced [d] after voiced consonants [b, z, g].

When there is assimilation, a segment surfaces with the same value(s) for some feature or feature class as an adjacent segment. Assimilation is subject to a variety of restrictions. For example, it can be bounded by morphological and phonological constituents: the place assimilation in (1a) applies between prefixes and stems, but not between words (e.g. 'in principle' [np], *[mp]). It can also be dependent on the features or relative position of the segments involved: to wit, only nasal consonants assimilate place in English ('misplace' [sp], *[fp]), and nasals only assimilate to following consonants ('acne' [kn], *[kŋ]); likewise, the voicing assimilation in (1b) only applies between obstruents in English ('rent' [nt], *[nd]) and only in non-intervocalic clusters ('baseball' [sb], *[zb]/[sp]). Assimilation can also be blocked by other phonological conditions, exemplified in detail in Section 14.2.

In OT, any change from an underlying form (input) to a surface form (output) involves a crucial violation of a faithfulness constraint. This violation must be compelled by some higher-ranked markedness constraint that is satisfied by the surface form but violated by a competing output candidate in which the relevant change is not made. In the case of assimilation in terms of a feature x, the faithfulness constraint is IDENT(x) (McCarthy & Prince 1995a, 1999), which regulates identity in terms of x between input segments and their output correspondents.

(2) IDENT(x)
     Corresponding input and output segments have the same value of the feature x.

As stated, IDENT(x) is violated by any change from one value of x to the other from input to output. For present purposes, I assume that the markedness constraint crucially compelling violation of IDENT(x) in assimilation is AGREE(x) (Lombardi 1999, Baković 2000), which regulates agreement in terms of x between adjacent output segments. (Alternatives are noted in Section 14.4.4.)

(3) AGREE(x)
     Adjacent output segments have the same value of the feature x.

The necessity of ranking AGREE(x) above IDENT(x) in order to guarantee assimilation is shown schematically by the tableau in (4). From an input that contains adjacent segments that disagree in their value of x, an output in which those segments have been changed to agree in terms of x fares better than the input-faithful alternative in which no change has been made. The comparative tableau format (Prince 2002a) is used here to clarify necessary constraint rankings. Each row (after the first) of a comparative tableau is a comparison between the optimal candidate (the 'winner') and a relevant suboptimal competitor (a 'loser'), arranged in that order (*winner* ∼ *loser*), and each cell in a constraint's column indicates whether that constraint prefers the winner ('W'), the loser ('L'), or neither member of the pair being compared in that row. In order for the winner to be optimal under the ranking given, every row must contain at least one W, and all Ls within each row must be preceded by at least one W (that is, for each winner–loser comparison there must be at least one constraint preferring the winner, and all constraints preferring the loser must be dominated by at least one constraint preferring the winner).

(4)   *Agreement trumps faithfulness:* AGREE(x) » IDENT(x)

/ +x −x / → [+x +x]	AGREE(x)	IDENT(x)
[+x +x] ∼ [+x −x]	W	L

Which of the adjacent segments changes to agree with the other is not determined by the AGREE(x) or IDENT(x) constraints. This is shown in (5) with place assimilation in English: the application of place assimilation is captured by the ranking of AGREE(*place*) over IDENT(*place*), but which consonant changes to agree with the other is not, as indicated by the lack of a 'W' in comparison row (b). (The candidates given in the tableaux will be pared down to just the interesting parts. So, instead of /ɪn+pəlaɪt/ 'in+polite', I will consider the input /ɪn+p. . ./, and so on.)

(5)   *English place assimilation:* AGREE(place) » IDENT(place)

/ ɪn + p... / → [ɪmp...]	AGREE(*place*)	IDENT(*place*)
(a) [ɪmp...] ∼ [ɪnp...]	W	L
(b) [ɪmp...] ∼ [ɪnt...]		

In other words, the interaction of these types of constraints does not determine the *direction* of assimilation, only that there *is* assimilation. This leaves directionality to be determined by the relative ranking of other constraints, several types of which are noted in Section 14.4; until then, I simply assume that the directionality of assimilation in particular cases is predetermined, and underdetermined candidate comparisons like the one in (5b) are simply not considered.

Another apparent fact about assimilation that is not captured by the simple interaction of constraints like AGREE(x) and IDENT(x) is the observation that the assimilating feature is not simply repeated on each segment but is rather implemented as a single articulatory gesture, extending across the assimilated segments. This can be formally represented as multiple linking of the assimilatory feature — the *autosegmental* representation of assimilation (Goldsmith 1976a, Cho 1999) — as exemplified in (6) with some cases of English nasal place assimilation.

(6) *Assimilation as multiple linking*

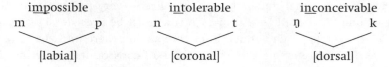

The connection between these types of representations and the uninterrupted phonetic implementation of assimilated features is intuitively appealing, but whether or not the kinds of representations in (6) are *phonologically* more accurate than ones in which each segment in an assimilated sequence of adjacent segments is linked to its own 'copy' of the feature is not a matter that will be discussed here (for some discussion, see Baković 2000). However, it must be remarked here that the types of representations in (6) were central to phonological theory before the advent of OT and have continued to be defended in current work (see Section 14.4). Following much other work — most notably Ní Chiosáin & Padgett (2001) and Padgett (2002) — representations take a back seat in this chapter to the explanatory role of OT constraint interaction.

The remainder of the chapter is organized as follows. The interaction of segmental markedness constraints with assimilation is discussed in Section 14.2. In Section 14.3, I consider possible processes other than assimilation by which AGREE(x) constraints can be satisfied, and examine the implications of different hypotheses concerning these possible alternatives. Some remaining issues about assimilation are briefly discussed in Section 14.4.

14.2   Interaction with segmental markedness

Every gain along one dimension of markedness is a potential loss along another. For example, when an AGREE(x) constraint is satisfied by assimilation in terms of the feature x, the resulting output segment created by the change in x potentially violates some markedness constraint(s) that might otherwise be satisfied. For assimilation to be optimal, then, any such markedness constraints must also be dominated by AGREE(x).

Consider once again nasal place assimilation in American English. When the underlyingly coronal nasal of the negative prefix assimilates to a following dorsal consonant, it incurs a violation of a markedness constraint against dorsal nasals (referred to here as NoDorsNas) that it would not have incurred had the nasal surfaced faithfully. This is shown in (7) below.

(7)   *American English:* Agree(place) » Ident(place), NoDorsNas

/ ɪn + k... / → [ɪŋk...]	Agree(*place*)	Ident(*place*)	NoDorsNas
[ɪŋk...] ~ [ɪnk...]	W	L	L

In some other varieties of English (for example, the Received Pronunciation variety of British English), nasal place assimilation is blocked in exactly these contexts. This indicates that NoDorsNas dominates Agree(*place*), as shown in (8). (Note that in order to allow dorsal nasals to surface faithfully stem-finally (e.g. *sing* [sɪŋ], *walking* [wɔkɪŋ], etc.), NoDorsNas must in turn be dominated by a stem-sensitive faithfulness constraint Stem-Ident(*place*).)

(8)   *RP British English:* NoDorsNas » Agree(place) » Ident(place)

/ ɪn + k... / → [ɪnk...]	NoDorsNas	Agree(*place*)	Ident(*place*)
[ɪnk...] ~ [ɪŋk...]	W	L	W

In the remainder of this section I examine several different variations on this type of situation; the examples discussed are cases of nasal place assimilation drawn from Padgett (1991, 1994, 1995). One of Padgett's concerns in these works is the observed assimilation patterns of nasals when followed by fricatives. Instead of place-markedness, the markedness constraint of particular interest in the examples to be discussed below is the following.

(9)   NoNasFric
      An output consonant specified as [+nasal] must not also be specified as [+continuant].

NoNasFric reflects the articulatory difficulty inherent in producing a nasal fricative (Ohala 1975). Few languages (if any) have contrastive nasal fricatives, which will be reflected through the relative (and possibly universal) ranking of NoNasFric above Ident(*cont*) or Ident(*nas*).[1]

NoNasFric interacts with the constraints responsible for nasal place assimilation because of a dependency relation between place of articulation and stricture features. Padgett (1991, 1994, 1995) accounts for this featural dependency relation representationally, but I pursue an account in terms of constraint interaction here instead (as noted toward the end of Section 14.1). In particular, I assume that place-assimilated output candidates are subject to the following constraint.

(10) STR/PL

Adjacent output segments that have the same place feature value must also have the same value of the stricture feature [±continuant].[2]

Like NoNasFric, STR/PL is also meant to address an articulatory difficulty: that of implementing a single (assimilated and therefore extended) place of articulation with a change in stricture. All else being equal, an articulatory gesture with no change in stricture is better than one with a stricture change. All else is not equal, however, under constraint interaction.

To summarize, the core constraints to be considered in the remainder of this section are the following.

(11) *Constraints*

(a) AGREE(*place*), penalizing adjacent output segments with different place values;

(b) IDENT(*place*), penalizing changes in place values from input to output;

(c) NoNasFric, penalizing nasal fricatives in the output;

(d) STR/PL, penalizing output segments with the same place but different [±cont] values;

(e) IDENT(*cont*), penalizing changes in [±cont] values from input to output.

To simplify matters, I will only be considering rankings in which AGREE(*place*) dominates IDENT(*place*) — that is, rankings under which place assimilation is generally expected — and in which NoNasFric dominates IDENT(*cont*) — that is, rankings under which nasal fricatives are not contrastive. Note that this latter ranking condition is more or less equivalent to simply not considering inputs with nasal fricatives, since these will generally neutralize to nasal stops. In situations where either NoNasFric or IDENT(*cont*) can be held responsible for the choice between competing candidates, I will only refer to NoNasFric since this markedness constraint will make the correct choice regardless of the input [±cont] specification of the nasal.

14.2.1 Blocking of assimilation

In some cases, nasals assimilate to following stops but not to following fricatives. In the latter case, the nasal simply surfaces with its under-lying place value. The English negative prefix *in-* exhibits this behavior: it assimilates to a following labial stop ('impossible') but not to a following labial fricative ('infallible' [nf], *[ɱf], *[f̃f], where [f̃] represents a labiodental nasal fricative).[3] This pattern can be accounted for by ranking NoNasFric and STR/PL above the basic ranking responsible for assimilation in the first place, AGREE(*place*) » IDENT(*place*) (12).

(12) *NoNasFric, Str/Pl » Agree(place) » Ident(place)*

/ n + f / → [nf]	NoNasFric	Str/Pl	Agree(*place*)	Ident(*place*)
(a) [nf] ~ [f̃f]	W		L	W
(b) [nf] ~ [ɱf]		W	L	W

The optimal candidate from input /n + f/ is [nf], without place assimilation. Although it violates Agree(*place*), this candidate is optimal because it avoids violation of NoNasFric, as shown by the comparison with the suboptimal candidate [f̃f] in (12a), and because it avoids violation of Str/Pl, as shown by the comparison with the suboptimal candidate [ɱf] in (12b). [f̃f] could also be ruled out by Ident(*cont*) in this case, under the assumption that the nasal in the input is [−cont]. However, as noted earlier, the input assumption itself is unnecessary: NoNasFric » Ident(*cont*) ensures that any [+cont] input nasal is generally neutralized to [−cont] in the output.

14.2.2 Assimilation, respecting dependency

In other cases, nasals assimilate both to following stops and to following fricatives, and in the latter case, the assimilated nasal violates NoNasFric. This is the pattern found in Castillian Spanish (Honorof 1999) (and perhaps in other varieties, as Padgett suggests for Mexican Spanish – Harris 1969, 1984a, 1984b).[4] Some examples are provided in (13).

(13) *Spanish nasal place assimilation to fricatives*

    (a) / digan # paxa /→ [diɣampaxa] 'say (imp. pl.) 'straw''
    (b) / digan # faxa /→ [diɣaf̃faxa] 'say (imp. pl.) 'sash''

This pattern can be accounted for by ranking Str/Pl and Agree(*place*) above NoNasFric, Ident(*place*), and Ident(*cont*). This is shown by the tableau in (14).

(14) *Agree(place), Str/Pl » NoNasFric, Ident(place), Ident(cont)*

/ n + f / → [f̃f]	Agree(*pl*)	Str/Pl	NoNasFric	Ident(*pl*)	Ident(*cnt*)
(a) [f̃f] ~ [nf]	W		L	L	L
(b) [f̃f] ~ [ɱf]		W	L		L

In this tableau, the optimal candidate from input /n + f/ is [f̃f], with place assimilation and a concomitant nasal fricative. Although it violates NoNasFric, this candidate is optimal because it avoids violation of Agree(*place*), as shown by the comparison with the suboptimal candidate [nf] in (14a), and because it avoids violation of Str/Pl, as shown by the comparison with the suboptimal candidate [ɱf] in (14b). (Note that the assessment of candidate comparisons by Ident(*cont*) here is made under the assumption that the input nasal is [−cont]; again, the ranking NoNasFric » Ident(*cont*) renders the opposite input specification for the nasal inert.)

14.2.3   Assimilation, respecting markedness

In still other cases, nasals assimilate both to following stops and to following fricatives, but in the latter case the nasal remains [−cont] and thus violates STR/PL. I assume that this is the pattern that Padgett (1994, 1995), following Steriade (1993), describes for Venda (15) (Ziervogel et al. 1972): nasal place assimilation to a following fricative neutralizes with a nasal + affricate cluster.

(15)   *Venda nasal place assimilation to fricatives and affricates*

    (a) / n + vulɛdza / → [mɓvulɛdzɔ]   'finishing'
    (b) / n + bvuda / → [mɓvudɔ]   'a leak'

I follow Padgett and Steriade in their interpretation of this neutralization in terms of gestural timing: "the stop portion of the articulation exceeds the nasal portion in duration" (Padgett 1995:53).[5]

This kind of pattern can be accounted for by ranking NoNasFric and AGREE(*place*) above STR/PL and IDENT(*place*). This is shown by the tableau in (16). Note that I use the same candidate transcriptions as in previous tableaux here, glossing over the fact that what I transcribe as [ɱf] is expected to be phonetically implemented as a nasal + affricate cluster [mp͡f] in Venda.

(16)   *AGREE(place), NONASFRIC » STR/PL, IDENT(place)*

/ n + f / → [ɱf]	AGREE(*pl*)	NONASFRIC	STR/PL	IDENT(*pl*)
(a) [ɱf] ~ [nf]	W		L	L
(b) [ɱf] ~ [f̃f]		W	L	

In this tableau, the optimal candidate from input /n + f/ is [ɱf], with place assimilation but no nasal fricative. Although it violates STR/PL, this candidate is optimal because it avoids violation of AGREE(*place*), as shown by the comparison with the suboptimal candidate [nf] in (16a), and because it avoids violation of NoNasFric, as shown by the comparison with the suboptimal candidate [f̃f] in (16b). (Note in this latter case that the ranking between NoNasFric and IDENT(*place*) is technically inconsequential; both candidates violate IDENT(*place*) equally.)

14.2.4   Summary

The preceding subsections have demonstrated how the different interactions between an assimilation ranking (here, AGREE(*place*) » IDENT(*place*)) and segmental markedness constraints (NoNasFric and STR/PL, plus the associated faithfulness constraint IDENT(*cont*)) can account for a typologically-relevant set of assimilation patterns. The three rankings discussed above are summarized with informative Hasse diagrams in (17). (Where IDENT(*cont*) is not shown, its relative ranking is irrelevant except that it is assumed to be dominated by NoNasFric.)

(17)   *Factorial typology*

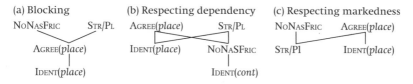

(a) Blocking
NoNasFric   Str/Pl
AGREE(*place*)
IDENT(*place*)

(b) Respecting dependency
AGREE(*place*)   Str/Pl
IDENT(*place*)   NoNasFric
IDENT(*cont*)

(c) Respecting markedness
NoNasFric   AGREE(*place*)
Str/Pl   IDENT(*place*)

Within the confines of the assumptions that AGREE(*place*) » IDENT(*place*) (i.e., that there is assimilation) and that NoNasFric » IDENT(*cont*) (i.e. that nasal fricatives are not constrastive), the three rankings in (17) exhaust the typological possibilities afforded by just these constraints. The description of further types of patterns requires the addition of further competing candidates and constraints to distinguish them, as discussed in the next two sections.

14.3   Heterogeneity of process

One of the more interesting properties of constraint ranking in OT is what McCarthy (2002c:25ff.) calls 'homogeneity of target / heterogeneity of process'. This slogan refers to the ability within OT to relate several different faithfulness constraint violations (processes) to the demands of a single markedness constraint (target), both across languages and within a single language.

Heterogeneity of process is an advantage of OT but it is also argued by some to have an accompanying liability, known as the 'too many solutions' problem: many different processes are logically expected to be associated with certain targets but appear not to be. For example, if assimilation processes are driven by constraints like AGREE(*x*) that penalize sequences of disagreeing adjacent segments, then such sequences should in principle be avoidable either by making the segments agree or by making them nonadjacent. Two ways in which the latter could be accomplished are (i) deletion of one of the disagreeing segments and (ii) epenthesis between the disagreeing segments. Given these possibilities, the question is: are such patterns attested?

Several researchers have recently attempted to make the case that such patterns are *not* attested, and have devised different formal accounts for their absence (Steriade 2001a, 2001b, Pater 2003, Baković & Wilson 2004).[6] A strong case that such patterns are indeed attested is made by de Lacy (2002a, 2006), casting serious doubt on the motivations behind those accounts. In Sections

14.3.1–14.3.2 below I present two cases demonstrating the use of deletion and epenthesis as 'backup' processes in situations where a more general pattern of assimilation is blocked. This is followed in Section 14.3.3 by some discussion of the ramifications for the 'too many solutions' problem.

14.3.1   Deletion as a backup to assimilation

Nasal place assimilation in Lithuanian (Kenstowicz 1972, Padgett 1991, 1994, 1995) occurs before stops (18) but is blocked before fricatives, respecting NoNasFric and Str/Pl. Rather than sacrificing Agree(*place*) as in English, however, an unassimilated nasal before a fricative in Lithuanian is deleted (19) (with compensatory lengthening of the preceding vowel).[7]

(18)   *Lithuanian nasal place assimilation before stops*

       (a) / san + pilas /   →   [sampilas]   'stock, store'
       (b) / san + taka /   →   [santaka]   'confluence'
       (c) / san + kaba /   →   [saŋkaba]   'coupling, clamp'

(19)   *Lithuanian nasal deletion before fricatives*

       (a) / san + voka /   →   [saːvoka]   'idea'
       (b) / san + skambis /   →   [saːskambis]   'harmony'
       (c) / san + ʃlavos /   →   [saːʃlavos]   'sweepings'

In order to account for this pattern, a candidate with deletion of the nasal must favorably compare with the other candidates we have considered thus far. Any constraint disfavoring the candidate with deletion must be ranked below NoNasFric, Str/Pl, and Agree(*place*). Deletion is directly penalized by the faithfulness constraint Max (McCarthy & Prince 1995a, 1999).

(20)   Max
       An input segment must have an output correspondent.

Max must in turn dominate Ident(*place*), or else the expectation is that Agree- (*place*) will generally be satisfied by deletion rather than assimilation, contrary to fact. This is shown in (21).

(21)   Agree(*place*), Max » Ident(*place*)

/ n + p / → [mp]	Agree(*place*)	Max	Ident(*place*)
(a) [mp] ~ [np]	W		L
(b) [mp] ~ [p]		W	L

The crucial ranking of Max below all three markedness constraints is shown in (22).

(22) NoNasFric, Str/Pl, Agree(place) » Max » Ident(place)

/ n + v / → [v]	NoNasFric	Str/Pl	Agree(*pl*)	Max	Ident(*pl*)
(a) [v] ~ [nv̊]			W	L	
(b) [v] ~ [ṽv]	W			L	W
(c) [v] ~ [ŋv]		W		L	W

The crucial difference between Lithuanian and English with regard to nasal place assimilation, then, is that Max is ranked together with NoNasFric and Str/Pl above Agree(place) in English. Assimilation is thus blocked and the unassimilated candidate is tolerated in English, while Lithuanian employs deletion as a backup strategy to the failure of assimilation.[8]

14.3.2 Epenthesis as a backup to assimilation

Another strategy that may in principle be used as a backup to the failure of assimilation is epenthesis — the insertion of material between the unassimilable segments so that they are no longer adjacent. Ponapean exhibits a case of this with respect to nasal place assimilation (Rehg & Sohl 1981, Goodman 1995, de Lacy 2002a); following my own recent work (Baković 2005), I discuss here two such cases with respect to voicing assimilation.

Coincidentally, the two examples are from English and Lithuanian. As was shown in (1b), relevant examples of which are repeated in (23), the English past tense suffix -*ed* (underlyingly voiced /d/) assimilates in voicing to the final obstruent of the stem to which it is attached.

(23) *Voicing assimilation in English: past tense suffix -ed /d/*

(a) *tra<u>pped</u>*	[pt]	*pa<u>ssed</u>*	[st]	*pa<u>cked</u>*	[kt]
(b) *gra<u>bbed</u>*	[bd]	*bu<u>zzed</u>*	[zd]	*ba<u>gged</u>*	[gd]

There is no assimilation to stem-final /t/, however, and there is epenthesis of schwa between the consonants instead: *sea<u>ted</u>* [təd]. As I argue in Baković (2005), assimilation fails here because of the independent avoidance of geminate consonants in English, at least in this word-final context, as evidenced by the fact that there is also epenthesis after stem-final /d/: *ce<u>ded</u>* [dəd].[9] That is, assimilation is blocked by a constraint penalizing geminates (S. Rose 2000):

(24) NoGem
      Geminate consonants are disallowed in the output.

Epenthesis can thus be seen as stepping in as a backup strategy to avoid adjacent obstruents that disagree in voicing. In order to account for this pattern, a candidate with epenthesis of a vowel must favorably compare with two other relevant candidates, one with voicing assimilation and one without. Any constraint disfavoring the candidate with epenthesis must thus be ranked below NoGem and Agree(voice). Epenthesis is directly penalized by the faithfulness constraint Dep.

(25) DEP

An output segment must have an input correspondent.

DEP must in turn dominate IDENT(voice), or else the expectation is that AGREE(voice) will generally be satisfied by epenthesis rather than assimilation, contrary to fact. This is shown in (26).

(26) AGREE(voice), DEP » IDENT(voice)

/ s + d / → [st]	AGREE(voice)	DEP	IDENT(voice)
(a) [st] ~ [sd]	W		L
(b) [st] ~ [səd]		W	L

The crucial ranking of DEP below NoGEM and AGREE(voice) is shown in (27).

(27) NoGEM, AGREE(voice) » DEP » IDENT(voice)

/ t + d / → [təd]	NoGEM	AGREE(voice)	DEP	IDENT(voice)
(a) [təd] ~ [td]		W	L	
(b) [təd] ~ [tt]	W		L	W

The relevant facts in Lithuanian are perfectly parallel to those in English and submit to the same analysis. Final consonants of a pair of verbal prefixes /at/ and /ap/ assimilate in voicing to following stem-initial obstruents; assimilation fails when the following consonant differs from the prefix consonant at most in voicing,[10] and epenthesis of a high front vowel applies instead (28).

(28) *Voicing assimilation (a, b) and epenthesis (c, d) in Lithuanian*[11]

(a) / at + praʃiːti / → [atpraʃiːti]   / ap + ʃaukti /   → [apʃaukti]
(b) / at + bukti / → [adbukti]   / ap + draskiːti / → [abdraskiːti]
(c) / at + deti /   → [atideti]   / ap + berti /   → [apiberti]
(d) / at + teisti / → [atiteisti]   / ap + puti /   → [apiputi]

14.3.3 Discussion

The analyses in the preceding two subsections depend on the assumption that satisfaction of AGREE(x) constraints can be achieved via deletion or epenthesis as well as via assimilation; i.e. that all three processes are possible solutions to an AGREE(x) target. As noted at the outset of this section, this assumption has been the topic of some debate in recent work. Steriade (2001a, 2001b), Pater (2003), and Baković & Wilson (2004) have all claimed that AGREE (x) constraints are *never* optimally satisfied by segmental manipulations such as deletion or epenthesis. Each of these authors offers a different proposal intended to accommodate this empirical claim; I briefly discuss each of them in turn in the context of the analyses above.

Steriade's proposal is that there is a fixed ranking among faithfulness constraints such that, for example, deletion and epenthesis violate universally higher-ranked faithfulness constraints than does assimilation.[12] Note that this proposal is technically consistent with the analyses proposed for Lithuanian and English above, in which MAX and DEP dominate their respective IDENT(x) constraints; the reason that deletion or epenthesis sometimes manages to emerge as optimal against the odds set up by this ranking is due to the blocking of assimilation by other constraints (NoNASFRIC and STR/PL in one case, NoGEM in the other). This is in fact one of the problems with Steriade's proposal as an account of the strong empirical claim that deletion and epenthesis are never recruited as processes for the purposes of AGREE(x) satisfaction: higher-ranked markedness constraints that mimic the activity of lower-ranked faithfulness constraints can partially subvert the intended effect of the proposed fixed ranking among faithfulness constraints (Pater 2003, Baković & Wilson 2004).

Pater (2003) also proposes universally-fixed rankings, but instead of fixing the ranking among faithfulness constraints he stipulates that all "constraints on segmental correspondence" (crucially including MAX and DEP) universally outrank all markedness constraints that "require feature sharing between segments [. . .] or for adjacent segments to have the same value" (Pater 2003:15 – in other words, AGREE(x) constraints). Baković & Wilson's (2004) proposal involves a complete departure from the standard conception of markedness constraints as constraints that penalize certain forms but that fail to distinguish among alternatives. Baković & Wilson's markedness constraints are 'targeted' (Wilson 2000, 2001, 2003a, Baković & Wilson 2000), which essentially means that certain alternatives to penalized forms are directly favored over others.[13] For example, a targeted AGREE(x) constraint would treat deletion and epenthesis on a par with disagreement, favoring only assimilation. The analyses proposed above are, of course, directly incompatible with both of these proposals.

In sum, the analyses in Sections 14.3.1–14.3.2 suggest that the empirical claim made by Steriade, Pater, and Baković & Wilson may only be true to a limited extent. In other words, it may be the case that AGREE(x) constraints generally only enforce assimilation via violations of featural faithfulness constraints like IDENT(x), but that contextual blocking of assimilation due to other constraints can lead to violations of other faithfulness constraints like MAX and DEP. Only Steriade's proposal appears to be compatible with this conclusion without modification. Another possible conclusion, of course, is that the empirical claim itself is simply wrong, and that AGREE(x)-type constraints can and do enforce epenthesis or deletion even in the absence of assimilation. This is the position explicitly taken by de Lacy (2002a, 2006).

14.4   Remaining issues

It goes without saying that patterns of assimilation, both local and long-distance, raise a far wider range of empirical and analytical issues than space allows me to address in this necessarily brief chapter. In this last section I attempt to at least touch on the remaining kinds of issues that are, in my view at least, of particular relevance to the contemporary research community.

14.4.1   Phonetic substance

One popular approach in current phonological research is to argue that constraints are substantively grounded (see Gordon Ch.3). Under this general view, assimilation is motivated by substantive (articulatory and perceptual) considerations, though it is (also) constrained by formal factors such as those defined by constraints on representations and rule parameters (Archangeli & Pulleyblank 1994) or constraint interaction (Jun 1995, 1996a, 1996b, 2004, Gafos 1999, Steriade 1999b, 2001a, Myers 1997a, Boersma 1998). Different types of assimilation may also be motivated by formally distinct types of constraints (Lombardi 2001), and these distinctions may themselves be substantively motivated. An important strand of current research in this area concerns the precise relationship between phono-logical ('categorical') assimilation and phonetic ('gradient') coarticulation — where and even whether to draw a line between the two. As Myers (1997a) makes particularly clear in the case of assimilation, constraint violability as defined in OT makes direct phonetic explanation of phonological patterns possible. (See Hale & Reiss (2000b) for an opposing view; cf. also the discussion in McCarthy (2002c:220ff.).)

The remaining issues mentioned in the subsections below intersect with the issue of phonetic substance in rather obvious ways, but are separated out here to better reflect the types of specific questions that are addressed in current research on assimilation.

14.4.2   Features and segments

I have focused in this chapter exclusively on the assimilation of major places of articulation and voicing, which are by far the most common features to assimilate between adjacent consonants. Minor place of articu-lation (e.g., the distinction among different coronal consonants) is also known to assimilate (English teṇ [n] ~ teṉth [n̪θ]), as are other laryngeal features such as aspiration (Greek [pɛmpoː] ~ [ɛpɛmpʰtʰeːn] 'send', [triːboː] ~ [ɛtriːpʰtʰeːn] 'rub').[14]

Other very common assimilations take place between adjacent conson-ants and vowels. The features of vowels often manifest themselves as secondary articulations on adjacent consonants; for example, front vowels in Lithuanian cause preceding consonants to become *palatalized*, such that the consonants of the verbal prefixes /at/ and /ap/ in (28) further above are realized as [tʲ] and [pʲ], respectively, when [i] is epenthesized. Such interactions between vowels and consonants can also be more dramatic; for example, palatalization can lead to a major place change in the affected consonant (Slovak [vnuk] 'grandson' ~ [vnutʃik] 'grandson, *dim*.').

Languages often impose conditions on assimilation that appear to be independent of the specification of the assimilatory feature on the relevant adjacent segments. For example, voicing assimilation is often limited to clusters of obstruents (Lombardi 1999), place assimilation is often limited to nasal + consonant clusters (Jun 2004), and palatalization is often limited to nonlabial consonants (Bateman in prep.). In the obstruent-cluster voicing case and others like it, these conditions appear to reduce to a general condition of *similarity* between the trigger and the target of assimilation: the more similar two segments are, the more likely they are to assimilate, though this is clearly not what's going on in the case of nasal place assimilation, for example.

In some languages, only segments with some values of a feature or feature class trigger or undergo assimilation for that feature or feature class. For example, only coronals undergo place assimilation in Catalan (Mascaró 1976), dorsals do not trigger place assimilation in RP British English (recall (8) above), only voiced obstruents undergo assimilation in Swedish (Lombardi 1999, Baković 1999), and only voiceless obstruents trigger assimilation in Mekkan Arabic (Abu-Mansour 1996, McCarthy 2003a). There is some debate over whether any set of feature values can assimilate, or whether there are implicational relations between feature values. For example, Jun (1995) proposes that only highly marked elements can avoid assimilation; this view accords to some extent with proposals in autosegmental phonology (Cho 1999). By contrast, de Lacy (2002a, 2006) argues that any set of feature values can fail to assimilate.

14.4.3 Directionality

Assimilation is typically *unidirectional*; for example, nasals typically place-assimilate to following consonants, not to preceding consonants, as in all the examples cited so far in this chapter. Some authors cite substantive motivation behind unidirectionality; for example in the case of place assimilation (Jun 1995, 1996a, 1996b, 2004): distinctive preconsonantal place is more difficult to perceive than prevocalic place. A perceptibility–based account appears better able to explain the often-observed "reversal" of assimilatory direction in word-final clusters: distinctive word-final, postconsonantal place is more difficult to perceive than postvocalic place, and so we have German *ha<u>ben</u>* [bm̩] 'to have', where the nasal place-assimilates to the preceding consonant.

Distinctive voicing is also difficult to perceive preconsonantally, forming the basis of Steriade's (1999b) account of the fact that voicing in an inter-vocalic cluster typically assimilates regressively (from the last consonant in the cluster leftward).[15] The fact that voicing assimilation is progressive (rightward) word-finally in English thus submits to a similar explanation as the one offered for the case of German nasal place assimilation noted in the preceding paragraph.

Another factor that often enters into the determination of directionality, in voicing assimilation at least, is morphological status: affix segments often assimilate to root/stem segments, which can be seen either in terms of the psychological prominence of roots/stems (Beckman 1998 and related work on positional faithfulness) or in terms of cyclic evaluation of forms (Benua 1997 and related work on output–output correspondence). (Note that both the voicing and nasal place assimilation examples in English discussed in this chapter are also consistent with an account in terms of morphological status, since affixes consistently assimilate to roots/stems.)

As expected in OT, whatever constraints are responsible for the preferred directionality of an assimilation process can be overridden by higher-ranked constraints. For example, as noted earlier, Swedish voicing assimi-lation does not create voiced obstruents, and so both voiced + voiceless and voiceless + voiced obstruent clusters surface as voiceless + voiceless, even though voiced obstruents are not otherwise avoided in the language. This suggests that AGREE(voice) and a markedness constraint penalizing voiced obstruents ranks above the constraint responsible for the directionality of voicing assimilation (Lombardi 1999, Baković 1999).

14.4.4 Alternatives to *Agree(x)*

There have been a number of different proposals regarding the formal statement of assimilation constraints in the OT literature, several of which still receive active attention; AGREE(x) is but one of these. Perhaps the earliest type of assimilation-driving constraint is in terms of featural alignment (Kirchner 1993, Akinlabi 1994, Pulleyblank 1996, Walker 1998, 2003b). Thorough critiques of this approach are provided by Beckman (1997, 1998), Wilson (2003a), and McCarthy (2004a). Beckman's alternative, criti-qued by Baković (2000), relies on the autosegmental view that assimilation is the extension of a single feature value; because assimilation reduces the number of feature values in the representation, assimilation can be viewed as markedness reduction: fewer feature values mean fewer markedness violations. Wilson's and McCarthy's alternatives respond to the negative typological consequences of previous proposals; Wilson argues for a strictly local and bounded targeted constraint theory, echoing earlier work on rule iterativity, while McCarthy offers an alternative theory more in line with autosegmental representations.

A different perspective on assimilation is offered by Pulleyblank (2002) and de Lacy (2002a, 2006). Both authors propose to account for assimilation in terms of markedness constraints that are superficially similar to AGREE(*x*) constraints. In Pulleyblank's theory, these constraints are of the form *FG, where F and G are potentially different values of the same feature (driving assimilation), the same values of the same feature (driving dissimilation), or different features entirely. In de Lacy's theory the constraints are also of the form *FG, but in this case F and G are particular subsets of feature or feature class values determined by markedness considerations; these markedness constraints interact with similarly-formulated featural faithfulness constraints to derive attested markedness asymmetries in assimilation.

14.5 Concluding remark

There is much more to be said about assimilation than I have been able to address in this chapter, but my aim has been to at least touch on some of the major empirical, analytical, and theoretical themes that are the subject of current research in phonological theory.

Notes

I would like to thank Colin Wilson for early discussion of some of the content of this chapter, and Paul de Lacy for comments and suggestions that have improved the final product. Remaining deficiencies are my own fault.

1 Nasal fricatives do arise frequently (though noncontrastively) due to nasal harmony; see e.g. Walker (1998).

2 Alternatively, one might follow the program of Padgett (2002) and assume that place and stricture features form a feature class, subject to a gradiently violable AGREE(*x*) constraint where *x* is the feature class. McCarthy (2003b) presents arguments against gradiently violable constraints in general and against Padgett's feature class constraints in particular (2003b: 84–85); I believe that STR/PL effectively addresses both of these authors' concerns.

3 I follow Padgett here in assuming that gestural overlap (Browman & Goldstein 1990) is responsible for the apparent assimilation of *in-* to following fricatives in casual speech.

4 For Castillian Spanish, Honorof experimentally confirms that "[w]hen a nasal assimilates to a following non-coronal segment, the oral tract gesture for the nasal takes on the exact place and stricture characteristics of the non-coronal consonant" (1999: 58). With following coronals, there is "a variable blending of the place and stricture targets of the two coronal gestures" (199: 59), suggesting gestural overlap in these latter

cases (see note 3). Honorof found no significant difference within words vs. across words, contra impressionistic claims to the contrary (Navarro Tomás 1957, Harris 1969, Padgett 1994, 1995:50).

5 By contrast, the stop and nasal gestures in these kinds of clusters coincide in Shona (Doke 1931, Myers 1991), giving the appearance that affricates are 'softened' to fricatives when clustered with nasals.

6 In related work, Lombardi (2001) claims that constraints against laryn-geally-marked coda consonants are likewise only satisfied by featural change and not by deletion or epenthesis. See Baković & Wilson (2004) for a critique.

7 Assimilation is also blocked before sonorants; deletion and compensatory lengthening also apply there.

8 When English *in-* is prefixed to sonorant-initial stems, there is deletion; what is spelled with a doubled consonant is typically only a single surface consonant (*immature* [ɪmətʃɚ], *innumerable* [ɪnuːməɚəbl], *illegal* [ɪliːgl], *irrelevant* [ɹɛləvnt]).

9 In American English, stem-final /t, d/ both undergo flapping in the intervocalic context created by epenthesis.

10 As discussed in Baković (2005), a more accurate statement is "at most in voicing *or palatalization*", due to an independent process of palatali-zation assimilation (see Section 14.2.2). Following Odden's (2005) text-book presentation and analysis of the relevant Lithuanian facts, I simplify things by ignoring palatalization and its assimilation here.

11 Glosses for (28): (a) 'to ask', 'to proclaim'; (b) 'to become blunt', 'to tear'; (c) 'to postpone', 'to strew all over'; (d) 'to adjudicate', 'to grow rotten'.

12 These universally-fixed rankings among faithfulness constraints are, at least in theory, not directly stipulated; Steriade proposes to derive them from independently-motivated perceptual considerations.

13 The definition of targeted constraints in Baković & Wilson (2004) specif-ically follows Wilson (2003a), which addresses some of the criticisms of targeted constraints raised by McCarthy (2002b) and Pater (2003). As in Steriade's proposal (see note 12), the preferences of targeted constraints are in theory not directly stipulated but are meant to be derived from independent perceptual considerations.

14 Note that there is also voicing assimilation evident in these Greek examples. Laryngeal features, like (major) place features, are often as-similated as a class (though not always; see de Lacy 2002a, 2006).

15 Lombardi (1991, 1995b, 1996) has argued that the distribution of contrast-ive voicing is (also) crucially sensitive to syllable structure. Because relevant intervocalic clusters are often limited to two consonants — a coda followed by an onset — the constraint is often simplified to one that references onsets (Beckman 1998, Lombardi 1999).

15

Harmony

Diana Archangeli
Douglas Pulleyblank

15.1   Introduction

Broadly speaking, a harmony system requires that two or more not-neces-sarily-adjacent segments must be similar in some way. Here, we address a range of phenomena fitting this description, considering which features tend to harmonise and in what ways. Our focus is to explore the various parameters along which harmonic patterns vary (such as direction, iter-ation, morphological requirements, etc.).

Two central points become apparent while reviewing harmonic proper-ties. First, the term 'harmony' is a descriptor of a class of similar phenom-ena, rather than a technical term referring to phenomena with a clearly defined set of properties. We may not expect any single formal operation common to all harmony systems. We may not expect any pre-theoretical way of distinguishing between an 'assimilatory' pattern (see Baković Ch.14) and a 'harmonic' one. Second, the necessary formal capabilities are not specific to harmony, but rather are necessary independently of harmonic patterns, to account for other types of phenomena as well. It may be, for example, that both local assimilation and non-local harmony are derived by a single set of constraints or it may be that distinct formal devices are responsible for the two classes of patterns. From these two points, we draw the obvious conclusion: harmony is an effect or epiphenomenon, not a phenomenon with a single unified formal explanation. While this means that non-harmonic phenomena must be understood to gather a full under-standing of harmony, it also means that harmony provides a lens for the examination of phonological patterns in general.

This chapter is organised as follows. We begin with a sketch of the prototypical harmony pattern, used throughout the chapter as a point of departure for discussion. We then explore variations on that canonical theme, considering conditions on harmonic triggers, targets, and both; the various domains of harmonic patterns; and consideration of direction, iteration, and locality. Our review leads us to the conclusion that harmony results from particular constellations of properties, most or all of which are independently necessary to account for other types of phonological patterns: there is no need for theoretical constructs specific to the harmony phenomena.

15.2   Description of harmonic patterns

This section considers what constitutes harmony: we define a canonical harmony system, and consider some of the ways in which attested patterns deviate from the idealised canonical system.

15.2.1   What is '(canonical) harmony'?

Probably the most commonly observed pattern in phonological systems is that two or more segments must resemble each other with respect to some feature(s). When does this count as 'harmony'?

We take as a point of departure for this discussion two variants of the pattern we might think of as canonical. One possibility is that literally all segments within a word show agreement for the harmonic feature; the second possibility is that all vowels within a word show agreement for the harmonic feature.[1]

(1)   *Canonical harmony*
    (a) $[X_F\ X_F\ X_F \ldots X_F]$
    (b) $[V_F \ldots V_F \ldots V_F \ldots V_F]$

An example of a language exhibiting canonical harmony is Degema (Elugbe 1984, Kari 1995, 1997), where ten surface vowels fall into two tongue root categories: (i) advanced tongue root ([+ATR]) {i, e, ə, o, u}, (ii) retracted tongue root ([−ATR]) {ɪ, ɛ, a, ɔ, ʊ}. Within a word, all vowels belong to a single category.[2]

(2)   *Degema*

(a)	*Advanced: [i u e o ə]*		(b)	*Retracted: [ɪ ʊ ɛ ɔ a]*	
[i]	u-bí-ɔ̄	'state of being black'	[ɪ]	á-kɪ̄	'pot'
[u]	u-pú-ɔ̄m	'closing'	[ʊ]	ʊ-fʊ́-ā	'state of being white'
[e]	u-dér-ɔ̄m	'cooking'	[ɛ]	ɔ-ɗɛ́ɗɛ̄	'chief'
[o]	i-sór-ɔ̄	'passing liquid faeces'	[ɔ]	ʊ-bɔ́m-ām	'beating'
[ə]	o-gədəgɔ́	'mighty'	[a]	ɔ-kpakɪraká	'tough'

While the standard analysis of this case is in terms of vowel-to-vowel harmony (1b), an alternative, consistent with Local & Lodge's (2004) analysis of Kalenjin, is that the ATR feature actually affects *all* segments, type (1a).[3] One issue, then, is whether both types in (1) actually exist.

A second and very interesting issue is precisely how the attested systems deviate from the canonical pattern(s). Numerous deviations from (1) show that agreement is curtailed in some way. Just how deviant can a pattern be and still be considered 'harmony'? Is there actually any theoretical content to the notion of 'harmony', or is it simply a useful term for a heterogeneous collection of phenomena involving featural agreement in one way or another?

In the next sections, we consider which sorts of features exhibit harmonic behaviour and then turn to the various ways in which patterns may be non-canonical. Our goal is to present a range of harmonic patterns that must be accounted for, organising our discussion by the different ways in which natural language systems deviate from canonical patterns.

15.3   Harmonic features

Defining what harmony is and deciding which features are harmonic are integrally connected. For example, can voicing exhibit harmonic behaviour? If we define 'harmony' strictly as in (1) then the answer is probably "no": we know of no case where *all* segments within a word necessarily show agreement in voicing – and we assume that the common case where all vowels are voiced is due to vowels typically being voiced, not to some pressure for vowels to agree in voicing. But we commonly find cases where adjacent strings of consonants agree in voicing (Russian, English) and cases where strings of adjacent consonants and vowels agree in voicing (Japanese vowel devoicing; Korean intervocalic voicing of consonants). Should such cases be considered non-harmonic by definition? While less well known, we also find patterns, as in Kera, an East Chadic language, where stops and affricates show agreement for voicing within the word, both root-internally and between roots and affixes, regardless of intervening vowels and sonorant consonants (Hansson 2001b).

The examples in (3) show that the nominal prefix is voiced when the base begins with a voiced obstruent (3a) and voiceless elsewhere (3b); (3c) shows that the voicing affects suffixes too, and can cross sonorant consonants to do so.

(3)   *Kera laryngeal harmony: the nominal prefix /k-/*

(a)	gə-dàarə̀	'friend'
	gə-dàjgá-w	'jug (plur.)'
(b)	kə-màanə̀	'woman'
	kə-taatá-w	'cooking pot (plur.)'
	kə-kámná-w	'chief (plur.)'
(c)	sár-ká	'black (fem.)'
	dʒàr-gá	'colourful (fem.)'

Is the Kera case harmony? Should voicing be considered a harmonic feature? We find no examples of iterative, consecutive agreement in voicing between consonants and vowels (the canonical (1a)); we find a small number of long-distance cases of consonant agreement over vowels; and we find many instances of local agreement in voicing.

There are at least two approaches to answering such a question. One is to define particular types of phenomena as harmonic, and then examine whether voicing exhibits the patterns so defined. An alternative is to define particular theoretical constructs as harmonic (e.g. terminal nodes in a feature geometry, or particular types of rules/constraints), and then examine the effects of those constructs.

Both approaches have been taken and the two approaches are often intertwined. For example, Rose and Walker (2004) consider a large number of cases of the Kera type, explicitly limiting their theoretical proposals (agreement-by-correspondence) to cases of "agreement for an articulatory or acoustic property that holds between consonants separated by at least one segment" (Rose & Walker 2004:476). This definition clearly includes cases of the Kera type, but excludes cases of local harmony (1a) and 'local assimilation' (cases where trigger and target are strictly adjacent). They justify dividing assimilation in this way, suggesting that long-distance consonant-to-consonant cases exhibit effects distinct from cases of assimilation by spreading (e.g. they suggest that *only* long-distance skipping cases require similarity).

Is it useful to provide a list of the 'harmonic' features: rounding, backness, tongue root advancement, nasality, etc.? And if so, should tone be on the list? Though often not thought of as a 'harmonic' feature, tonal behaviour is quintessentially harmonic cross-linguistically. We suggest that while such features should certainly be on any such list, it is unclear both that the 'list' has any formal status and that there are any features that should be *excluded a priori* from consideration. While features like [sonorant] and [consonantal] may not exhibit assimilatory properties, and place features like [labial], [coronal], and [dorsal] may not (often) exhibit harmonic properties of either the local spreading or long-distance varieties (Ní Chiosáin & Padgett 2001, Rose & Walker 2004, and others), we suspect that the phonetic and phonological considerations that make harmony unlikely with such features also play a role in limiting the harmonic behaviour of prototypically harmonic features like rounding and nasality.

In the short survey we present here, our approach is to place harmony in a larger phonological context, to determine what, if anything, might be specific only to harmony. With respect to the class of harmonic features, evidence suggests that there is no *a priori* list, but rather that the differential behaviour of features *vis-à-vis* harmony is an artifact of other properties of those features and their interactions, not specific to harmony itself.

15.4   Conditions on harmonic elements

Deviation from the canonical harmony pattern occurs when either the targeted element or the triggering element is somehow restricted. This section focuses on limits placed specifically on the target and/or trigger.

15.4.1 Conditions on targets
Features as delimiters

In Turkish (Clements & Sezer 1982), there are two harmonic patterns: back harmony (which affects all vowels) and round harmony (restricted to high vowel targets).

(4) *Turkish vowel harmony*

nom.sg.	*gen.sg.*	*nom.pl.*	*Gloss*
ip	ipin	ipler	'rope'
kɨz	kɨzin	kɨzlar	'girl'
jyz	jyzyn	jyzler	'face'
pul	pulun	pullar	'stamp'
eʎ	eʎin	eʎʎer	'hand'
sap	sapin	saplar	'stalk'
cœj	cœjyn	cœjʎer	'village'
son	sonun	sonlar	'end'

There are both high and nonhigh round vowels in Turkish, so harmony must restrict the targets to only those segments that actually undergo the harmony – here, the high vowels. Otherwise, we would expect to find non-high vowels rounding as well in the harmonic environment.[4]

The restriction to high vowel targets is common cross-linguistically. In a survey of round harmony systems, Kaun (1995) notes that imposing conditions on triggers and/or targets of round harmony systems is more common than the absence of such conditions. In addition to requiring that the target be high, common requirements are that the triggering segment be non-high, that the trigger and target agree in height, and that the trigger and target be front.

The condition on targets in Turkish is independent of inventory considerations: were harmony to affect non-high vowels, the resulting nonhigh rounded vowel would be an attested vowel of Turkish. In other cases, the conditions on harmonic targets are precisely the same conditions as hold generally of the language's segment inventory. An example can be seen with ATR harmony in Akan (Archangeli & Pulleyblank 1994 and references therein). The following examples in (5) show that vowels agree in [ATR] both within roots and between roots and affixes:

(5) *Akan tongue root harmony: within morphemes and across morpheme-boundaries*

Advanced		*Retracted*	
[e-bu-o]	'nest'	[ɛ-bʊ-ɔ]	'stone'
[o-kusi-e]	'rat'	[ɔ-kɔdɪ-ɛ]	'eagle'
[e-sĩnĩ]	'piece'	[ɛ-pʊnʊ̃]	'door'
[o-fiti-i]	'he/she pierced (it)'	[ɔ-cɪrɛ-ɪ]	'he/she showed (it)'
[o-susu-i]	'he/she measured (it)'	[ɔ-bɛ-tʊ-ɪ]	'he/she came and throw (it)'
[e-tene]	'it (news) spreads'	[ɔ-fʊrʊ-ɪ]	'he/she went up'

However, low vowels do not participate in the advanced tongue root harmony pattern.[5]

(6) *Akan tongue root harmony does not affect low vowels (roots are /tu/ and /ji/)*

    [wa-tu]   *he has dug it*   *[wə-tu]

    [ba-ji-e]   *witchcraft*   *[bə-ji-e]

This nonparticipation is not surprising in light of the Akan segment inventory: Akan does not have advanced low vowels. Thus, the statement of harmony need not overtly limit targets to non-low vowels. The constraints that govern the vowel inventory must also govern harmony. Such a pattern, typical of many harmony systems, is 'structure preserving' (Kiparsky 1985).

In some cases, harmony is not subject to lexical constraints, resulting in allophonic alternations (Archangeli & Pulleyblank 1994). One such case is Kinande (Archangeli and Pulleyblank 1994, 2002, Mutaka 1995, Gick et al. in press; see (17)). Nonhigh vowels bear [ATR] only as the outcome of harmony; lexically there is no [ATR] contrast on mid or low vowels. Another case is Fula (21): there are no lexical contrasts for [ATR] on any vowel class. The high vowels are necessarily realized as advanced and initiate harmony on mid vowels to their left. In the absence of advanced vowels to their right, mid vowels are realized with retracted tongue root.[6] Thus, mid vowel allophonic harmony can be triggered by a high vowel's noncontrastive tongue root advancement.

A very interesting case of allophonic harmony is found in Nkore-Kiga (Hansson 2001b), where [s, z] and [ʃ, ʒ] are in complementary distribution, with [s, z] preceding [i] and [ʃ, ʒ] occurring elsewhere.

(7) *Nkore-Kiga distribution of [s] vs. [ʃ] and [z] vs. [ʒ]*

  si   ʃu   zi   ʒu
  ʃe   ʃo   ʒe   ʒo
     ʃa   ʒa

This description of the distribution of the sibilants is not surface true, however. Within a word, sibilants agree for place, where {s,z} may not precede {ʃ,ʒ}. In these examples, the root sibilants alternate depending on the suffix vowel following the root-final consonant.

(8) *Nkore-Kiga sibilant harmony*

	UR	Expected	Actual	Gloss
(a)	/-Sa:S-ire/	*-ʃa:sire	-sa:sire	'be in pain (perf.)'
	/-Sa:S-a/		-ʃa:ʃa	'be in pain'
(b)	/-SíS-a/	*síʃa	-ʃíʃa	'compensate'
	/-SíS-ire/		-sísire	'compensate (perf.)'
(c)	/-SinZ-a/	*-sinʒa	-ʃinʒa	'testify against'
	/-SinZ-ire/		-sinzire	'testify against (perf.)'

The place features of the sibilants are allophonic, conditioned by the following vowel. Nonetheless, there is a harmonic pattern involving those features, restricted to sibilants.

As seen, limiting targets by features is possible whether a pattern is structure preserving or allophonic. It is also possible whether a pattern is harmonic or not. These effects, though important, are not special properties of harmonic systems.

Positions as delimiters

Targets can also be limited by positional phonological effects (Beckman 1997, 1998, Barnes 2002). For example, in the Ascrea dialect of Italian, a high vowel raises a stressed mid vowel to its left, shown by (9a,b) (Walker 2005); (9b) also shows that only stressed vowels raise. The forms in (9c) show that the pattern is one of raising, not lowering, since high stressed vowels can occur before non-high vowels.[7]

(9)   *Post-stress triggered height harmony in Ascrea Italian*

(a)	'sorda	'deaf (f sg)'	'surdu	'deaf (m sg)'
	'veʃte	'this (f pl)'	'viʃti	'this (m pl)'
(b)	pre'fonna	'profound (f sg)'	pre'funnu	'profound (m sg)'
(c)	'kupa	'dark, deep (f)'		
	'fume	'smoke'		

A particularly intriguing case of tongue height harmony involving a positional condition on the target is found in C'Lela (Dettweiler 2000, Pulleyblank 2002). As (10) shows, high affix vowels are mid when attached to roots with non-high vowels; cf. the contrast between the alternations in (10a,b) and the lack of alternation when the affix is mid (10c).[8] The high roots used in the data are /buzᵊkᵊ/'chased', /sipkᵊ/'grabbed', /fumtᵊkᵊ/'pulled', and the low roots are /ɛpkᵊ/'bit', /wegaka/'indicated', and /batkᵊ/'released'.

(10)   *C'Lela direct object pronouns*

		High root		Nonhigh root	
(a)	mi/me	buzᵊkᵊ mi	'chased me'	ɛpkᵊ me	'bit me'
		sipkᵊ mi	'grabbed me'	wegaka me	'indicated me'
		fumtᵊkᵊ mi	'pulled me'	batkᵊ me	'released me'
(b)	vu/vo	buzᵊkᵊ vu	'chased you'	ɛpkᵊ vo	'bit you'
		sipkᵊ vu	'grabbed you'	wegaka vo	'indicated you'
		fumtᵊkᵊ vu	'pulled you'	batkᵊ vo	'released you'
(c)	o	sipkᵊ o	'grabbed him'	wegaka o	'indicated him'
	na	sipkᵊ na	'grabbed us'	wegaka na	'indicated us'
	co	buzᵊkᵊ co	'chased us'	batkᵊ co	'released us'
	no	buzᵊkᵊ no	'chased you'	batkᵊ no	'released you'

A striking pattern arises when there are multiple affixes. As the left-hand column in (11) shows, the class marker suffixes *-i/-e* and *-u/-o* alternate depending on the root vowel. However, a further suffix may follow the class marker, such as the adjectival suffix *-ni/-ne*, shown by the right-hand columns in (11). The word-final adjectival marker shows the expected alternation, but the now-medial class marker no longer alternates: it is high regardless of the flanking vowel qualities.

(11)   *C'Lela: medial transparency vs. final visibility (CM = class marker; ADJM = adjectival suffix)*

    (a)   *High root*

i-zis-i	'CM-long-CM'	i-zis-i-ni	'CM-long-CM-ADJM'
u-pus-u	'CM-white-CM'	u-pus-u-ni	'CM-white-CM-ADJM'
u-rim-u	'CM-black-CM'	u-rim-u-ni	'CM-black-CM-ADJM'

    (b)   *Nonhigh root*

i-rek-e	'CM-small-CM'	i-rek-i-ne	'CM-small-CM-ADJM'
i-po-jɨ	'CM-new-CM'	i-po-i-ne	'CM-new-CM-ADJM'
u-gʲɔz-o	'CM-red-CM'	u-gʲɔz-u-ne	'CM-red-CM-ADJM'
u-rek-o	'CM-small-CM'	u-rek-u-ne	'CM-small-CM-ADJM'
u-sʷa-wɨ	'CM-big-CM'	u-sʷa-u-ne	'CM-big-CM-ADJM'

The key point for our current discussion is that the target of height harmony in C'Lela is restricted to word-final vowels, a not uncommon positional restriction. No restrictions on target features are necessary since [−high] is the harmonic feature: only high vowels will show a phonological change since all other vowels are already non-high. C'Lela illustrates a further point, that the trigger and target of harmony need not be in adjacent syllables, a point we return to in Section 15.8.

15.4.2   Conditions on triggers

Just as there can be a feature or positional condition on the target, so too can there be such restrictions on the trigger. Again, there are cases of inherent conditions: [+ATR] harmony is triggered by high vowels in Kinande (17), where lexically only high vowels contrast for [ATR]; [−ATR] harmony is triggered only by non-high vowels in Standard Yoruba, where high vowels are never retracted. There are also cases where the conditions must be overtly stated, because the set of triggers is a subset of the segments carrying the harmonic feature.

Features as delimiters

Perhaps the most common type of condition is to limit the triggers to segments with particular feature combinations. In Menominee, only high vowels trigger [+ATR] harmony despite the presence of both high and non-high [+ATR] vowels in the inventory (Archangeli and Pulleyblank 1994). In Mòbà Yoruba, nasality harmonises from vowels, but not from nasal consonants (see (35), Ajiboye 2002).

Positions as delimiters

Position can also limit triggers. For instance, a variety of languages determine a harmonic trigger by the location of stress. In Servigliano Italian, pretonic vowels agree in height with a stressed high vowel (Walker 2005).

(12)   *Stress triggered height harmony in Servigliano Italian*

(a) verd-'o   'very green (m sg)' vird-'u   'very green (m pl)'
(b) kommonek-'a   'to communicate' kummunik-'imo 'we communicate'
(c) predik-'a   'to preach'

As (12b) shows, this pattern extends to the beginning of the word; (12c) shows the trigger is stressed – the unstressed high vowel does not induce raising to its left.

15.4.3   Conditions on targets and triggers

As is expected, it is possible to find simultaneous restrictions on both trigger and target. It is also possible to find cases where the trigger and target values are interdependent.

In Basque roots, for example, sibilants agree in place features (Hualde 1991). There are three places of articulation for sibilant fricatives and affricates: apico-alveolar (s̄, ts̄), dorso-alveolar (ś, tś), and palatal (ʃ, tʃ). Within morphemes, sibilants must all belong to one of these places; that is, apico-alveolar sibilants may not co-occur with dorso-alveolar or palatal sibilants, and dorso-alveolar and palatal sibilants may also not co-occur.

(13)   *Basque sibilant harmony*

asots	[aśotś]	'noise'	zuzen	[šušen]	'straight,correct'
eltsuntse	[eltśuntśe]	'gadfly'	azazkal	[ašāškal]	'fingernail'
urtxintx	[urtʃintʃ]	'squirrel'	zimitz	[šimitš]	'tick'
samats	[śamatś]	'fertiliser, manure'	sasoin	[śaśoin]	'season'

Comparable cases requiring identity between trigger and target involve other features. Round harmony in Khakass is triggered by and targets only high vowels while in Bashkir it is triggered by and targets only non-high vowels (Hong 1994).[9] A further type of identity between trigger and target is found in the Yokuts language (Newman 1944, Archangeli 1985), where spans of vowels within words typically agree in rounding provided those vowels are of the same height.

(14)   *Yokuts height-dependent round harmony: only vowels of like height affected*

/dub-ʔinˀaj/	[dubʔunˀaj]	'while leading by the hand'	*dubʔinˀaj
/dos-ʔinˀaj/	[dosʔinˀaj]	'while reporting'	*dosʔunˀaj
/dos-hatn-xoo-hin/	[doshotinxoohin]	'was trying to tell'	*doshatinxoohin
/hud-hatn-xoo-ʔ/	[hudhatinxoʔ]	'wants to know about'	*hudhotinxoʔ

Note that complete identity is not required when there are both trigger and target conditions. For example, in Menominee, while both trigger and target must be high vowels, only the target must be a long vowel (Archangeli and Pulleyblank 1994).

15.4.4 Summary

Harmony has the effect of making segments more like each other. In some cases, either the triggering or the targeted set of segments is a subset of the segments which are compatible with the harmonic feature in the language. Interestingly, as the restrictions increase, thereby narrowing the effect of harmony, we find many cases where those restrictions serve to make a somewhat similar trigger and target even more similar. We suspect that this observation is a cross-linguistic tendency, and that greater similarity is needed as trigger and target become more distant from each other.

These apparent tendencies raise the question of whether long-distance effects, which tend to require similarity of some sort, are formally distinct from local effects, which do not necessarily impose similarity between trigger and target (cf. Rose and Walker 2004). It is not clear that this is a clear-cut distinction, and there are certainly near-minimal pairs (such as the two dialects of Italian exemplified in (12) and (9)) which suggest that local and long-distance assimilation are variations on a single theme rather than two discrete phenomena requiring distinct formal accounts. At the same time, the issue of whether the trigger or target of some phenomenon might be a restricted set of potential triggers/targets in the language is by no means solely a characteristic of harmonic systems (see e.g. Barnes 2002). In fact, cases without such limitations are perhaps the anomaly.

15.5 Domain of harmony

Unlike a canonical case such as Degema (2), apparent targets of harmony may be ineligible because the domain of harmony is restricted in some way, whether phonologically or morphologically.

15.5.1 Phonological domain restrictions

The extent of harmony can be restricted by phonological domains. The following example from Yoruba illustrates the syllable as the domain of harmony.[10]

Standard Yoruba exhibits a pattern whereby sonorants within a syllable agree in their value for nasality (Clements & Ṣọnaiya 1990, Pulleyblank in press). The examples in (15a) illustrate the pattern whereby a nasal vowel induces nasalisation on a tautosyllabic sonorant consonant; while (15b) illustrates the flipside of this process where a nasal consonant induces nasalisation of a tautosyllabic vowel. The upshot is a fully nasal syllable. Cases like (15c) show that adjacent syllables are unaffected.

(15) *Standard Yoruba: syllable-bounded nasal harmony*

(a) [r̃ĩ]   *[rĩ]   'to walk'

    [ɟṹ]   *[ɟṹ]   'to dispense'

(b) [nũ̀]   *[nù]   'to feed'

(c) [ìbínũ̀]   *[ìbínù̃]   'anger'

    [r̃ã́tí]   *[r̃ã́tĩ́]   'remember'

    [r̃ĩ́r̃ã́tí]   *[r̃ĩ́r̃ã́tĩ́]   'remembering'

    [ìdáwò]   *[ìdáw̃ò̃]   'examination'

    [ɔ̀mɔ̃̀wé]   *[ɔ̀mɔ̃̀w̃ẽ́]   'educated person'

In Standard Yoruba, there are two options. Whether this phenomenon is called nasal assimilation or nasal harmony, the simplest analysis is to define the domain of nasalisation as the syllable. An alternative is to analyse the nasalisation as two processes, both strictly local, distinguishing left-to-right C-to-V assimilation from right-to-left V-to-C assimilation. The possibility of interpreting this case as syllable-bounded suggests that some cases of apparent noniterativity are due to a small domain.

Mòbà, a dialect of Yoruba described in Ajiboye (2002), provides an interesting contrast (16). The pattern is like Standard Yoruba in that sonorant consonants within the syllable are nasalised. Unlike Standard Yoruba, the domain of nasalisation is larger, namely, the word.

(16) *Mòbà Yoruba: word-bounded nasal harmony*

ũ̀r̃ĩ̀	'walk (n.)'	r̃ĩ̀	'walk (v.)'
ũ̀ɟĩ̀	'praise (n.)'	ɟĩ̀	'praise (v.)'
ũ̀nĩ́	'possession'	nĩ́	'have'
ũ̀w̃ã̀ / ũ̀ã̀	'measurement'	w̃ã̀ / ã̀	'measure'

As (16) shows, the nasal feature of a root harmonises at the word level, affecting prefixes.

15.5.2 Morphological domains

Morphological properties are common domain-limiters. For example, the root may be the primary or sole domain of a harmonic pattern, illustrated by the verb roots in Tiv (Pulleyblank 1988, Archangeli and Pulleyblank 1994). Another possibility is that the harmonic pattern may extend to a larger morphological domain which is nonetheless smaller than the phonological word, as in Kinande. Here, we consider a variety of ways in which morphology limits the size of the harmonic span.

Morphologically-delimited triggers

A pattern known as 'root-controlled harmony' exemplifies the morphologically defined trigger. This class of phenomena is characterised by harmony that is induced primarily by features of the root. Harmony affects affixes, but, crucially, the root's harmonic values never change. An example of root-controlled harmony is found in Akan (5). Akan words share a value for ATR. The one exception is the low vowel [a], which does not have a phonological advanced counterpart. When an [a] occurs in an affix, it does not affect the ATR value of the root: advanced roots remain advanced (6).[11]

Morphologically defined targets

Just as there can be morphological restrictions on the trigger, there can also be morphological conditions on the target, which also serve to delimit the domain of harmony. In such cases, the harmonic domain is restricted to include only certain morphemes, typically the root and certain affixes as in Kinande (Archangeli and Pulleyblank 1994, 2002, Mutaka 1995). In Kinande, tongue root advancement affects prefixes (17a,b); however, the 'augment' prefix (a mid vowel) only optionally harmonises. (The form in (17c) shows that the root -hEk- 'carry' is intrinsically without [+ATR] specification. It is advanced in (17b) due to the agentive suffix –i.)

(17)   *Dominant-recessive harmony in Kinande*

   (a)   /E-rI-lib-A/   èrìlíbà *or* ɛ̀rìlíbà   'to cover'
   (b)   /O-mU-hEk-i/   òmùhékì *or* ɔ̀mùhékì   'porter, carrier'   *ɔ̀mùhɛ́kì
   (c)   /E-rI-hEk-A/   ɛ̀rìhɛ́kà   'to carry'

Another type of morphological restriction is for harmony to induce alternations in affixes, even though stems do not show the harmonic pattern. For example, Clements & Sezer (1982) argue that both round and back harmony in Turkish apply only across morpheme boundaries, from root to affix, and from affix to affix (4). Within morphemes (18), we find that harmony does not always hold: vowels may differ for backness.

(18)   *Turkish vowel harmony: not necessary within morphemes*

   takvim   'calendar'
   adet   'item, piece'
   bobin   'spool'
   peron   'railway platform'
   muzip   'mischievous'
   kubbe   'dome'

Morphologically-delimited trigger and target

As might be expected, there are examples of morphological restrictions on both trigger and target. And, as with the phonological cases, the morphological cases also show a strong preference for similarity.

   A frequent pattern is restricting both trigger and target to roots. (We know of no comparable cases restricting both triggers and targets to affixes.) With this restriction, there are no alternations that show the harmony pattern is phonologically active. Rather, harmony is revealed as a distributional pattern, where root segments are constrained to certain patterns. In Ngbaka, for example, in disyllabic words the vowels are largely identical (e.g. [jèlè] 'stranger', [kamá] 'sibling') or consist of a high vowel and [a] ([títa] 'grandparent', [dúká] 'shoulder'). Where there are two distinct mid vowels, they nonetheless share tongue root position ([sekò] 'chimpanzee'; [kɔndɛ̀] 'heart'). (See Archangeli and Pulleyblank 1994.) Importantly, this pattern does not extend beyond the domain of the root. Affix vowels do not alternate.

The net effect has been called a 'morpheme structure condition'. A further illustration is found with Basque sibilant place harmony (13). The examples in (13) show this effect within roots while (19) shows that harmony does not cross morpheme boundaries: the suffix is invariant, even when the root sibilant differs in place.[12]

(19)   *Basque sibilant harmony: inapplicable across morpheme boundaries*

Absolute indefinite		*Benefactive indefinite*		
lagun	[lagun]	*lagunentzat*	[lagunentšat]	'friend'
baso	[baśo]	*basorentzat*	[baśorentšat]	'forest'
gizon	[gišon]	*gizonentzat*	[gišonentšat]	'man'
etxe	[etʃe]	*etxerentzat*	[etʃerentšat]	'house'

Syntactically-delimited targets

An example of a domain larger than the word is found in Vata (20), where tongue root advancement in the final word of a phrase optionally causes the preceding words to also be advanced (Kaye 1982, Hong 1994).

(20)   *Vata phrasal harmony*

/ǹ lâ jò/	ǹ lâ jò ~ ǹ lÂ jò	'I called a child'	
/ǹ jì àɓà/	ǹ jì àɓà	'I know Aba'	*ǹ jì ʌɓʌ, *ǹ jì àɓà
/ɔ́ká zā pī/	ɔ́ká zā pī ~ ò kʌ́ zʌ̄ pī	'he will cook food'	

15.5.3   Summary

Again we find that either the triggering or the targeted set of segments – or both – can be a subset of those segments which might otherwise participate in harmony. The examples in this section present instances where the restrictions serve to define the eligible triggers and targets simply by their position in the form, whether phonological, morphological, or syntactic.

There is nothing novel or harmony-specific about limits on the domain in which some phenomenon is found. For example, the observation that specific phenomena are only relevant in particular domains is at the core of Lexical Phonology and Morphology (Kiparsky 1982b, Mohanan 1986, and others). Similarly, phrasal and foot-based phonological phenomena are well-attested in the literature.

15.6 Directionality

Just as the extent to which a harmonic feature propagates may depend on trigger and target conditions or domain restrictions, so can the extent of harmony be curtailed by restricting the set of targets to one side or other of the harmonic trigger. For example, Paradis (1986) shows that in the Pulaar dialect of Fula, mid vowels surface as retracted (21a) except when preceding an advanced vowel (21b).

(21) *Fula: mid vowels are advanced only preceding an advanced vowel*

    (a) ɓɛt-dɛ 'to weigh'   (b) ɓet-ir-dɛ 'to weigh with'
          hɛl-dɛ 'to break'   hel-ir-dɛ 'to break with'
          fɛjj-a 'to fell (imperfective)'   fejj-u-dɛ 'to fell'

Of particular importance, root vowels undergo harmony induced by a suffixal high vowel. That is, directionality in such a case cannot be accounted for by reference to morphological structure, with the harmonic direction defined as root-to-affix. In addition, this is not a case where a particular value of the harmonic feature bidirectionally dominates the other value; while tongue root advancement is dominant, causing otherwise retracted vowels to advance, this 'domination' is unidirectional.

An example in the other direction is Sundanese nasalisation (Cohn 1990, Benua 1997). Vowels nasalise when following a nasal consonant as seen in all the examples of (22); examples such as (22b) also show that vowels to the left of a nasal do not nasalise.

(22) *Sundanese nasal assimilation*

    (a) ɲĩãr   'seek'   (b) biɲhãr   'to be rich'
          ɲĩsər   'displace'   omõŋ   'say'
          mãrios 'examine'   nãʔãtkɨn 'dry'
          ɲĩwat   'elope'

Affixes can induce nasalisation on a root, as seen in the examples in (23).

(23) *Normal application of nasal spread after infixation*

gəde	'big'	g-um-ə̃de	'be conceited'
rasa	'feel'	r-um-ãsa	'admit to'
indit	'leave'	paŋ-ĩndit	'reason for leaving'
omõŋ	'say'	paŋ-õmõŋ	'reason for saying'
dɤhɤs	'approach'	d-um-ɤ̃hɤ̃s	'approach a superior'
saŋliŋ	'to polish'	s-in-ãŋliŋ	'to glitter'

As in the Fula example, harmony is not in the direction of affixation; unlike Fula, harmony is left-to-right, not right-to-left.

In many cases, directionality of harmony appears to depend on morphology: root segments serve as triggers and affix segments serve as targets (see Baković 2000). Hence a strictly prefixing language like Yoruba would be expected to exhibit right-to-left harmony (see discussion of (16) and (28)) and a strictly suffixing language like Turkish would be expected to exhibit left-to-right harmony (see discussion of (18)). Hansson (2001b) and Rose & Walker (2004) have both noted an interesting (though probably not absolute) asymmetry in this respect as concerns non-local consonant harmony: directionality in consonant harmony appears to either be consistent with morphological direction, or else be from right to left. Missing or rare are cases where left-to-right directionality is crucial, independently of morphological structure. Such observations, if borne out by further research, may support separating the formal accounts of long-distance harmony from those for strictly adjacent – or 'local' – assimilation (Hansson 2001b, Rose & Walker 2004).

In some instances, it appears that the harmonic trigger is restricted to some particular element within the relevant domain – such as 'within the first syllable' or 'within the stressed syllable'. This is particularly true of patterns of feature distribution, though it is also found in active harmonic systems. The question arises of how this primarily distributional restriction relates to harmonic systems. Two points are significant here. First, the harmonic feature always appears with respect to some edge, only on stressed vowels, etc., and harmonises from that point. The distributional limitation of 'first syllable', 'stressed syllable', and the like, relates directly to this point (Beckman 1997, 1998): the prosodically-defined syllable identifies an edge that is relevant for the process in question. Second, independently of harmony, there are cases where some feature docks to the leftmost or rightmost element in a domain. In short, any analysis must allow for 'edge anchoring' independently of whether harmony exists as a linguistic phenomenon. Thus, it is not surprising to find edge anchoring in the analysis of both distributional and harmonic patterns.

15.7   Iteration

Once trigger conditions, target conditions, domain, and directionality are established, the expectation is that harmony will proceed as far as it can – and it often does. There are cases, however, where harmony seems only to affect the segment closest to the trigger, regardless of direction, conditions and the size of the domain. Compare, for instance, the difference between the tongue root distribution in Akan (5) and Kinande (17) with that in Lango (24). In Akan and Kinande, all appropriate vowels in a sequence agree in their harmonic value; in Lango, only the vowel immediately preceding the triggering vowel is affected (Noonan 1992).[13]

(24) *Lango vowel harmony: affects the nearest vowel only*

| /bɔ̀ŋɔ́ + ní/ | bɔ̀ŋòní | 'your dress'[14] |
| /òkwɛ́'cɛ́ + ní/ | òkwɛ́'cɛní | 'your bitch' |

The difference is whether the harmony pattern iterates across the relevant domain: the Akan case is *iterative* while the Lango case is *noniterative*.[15] These two types of cases are sometimes distinguished in the literature by the terms 'harmony' and 'umlaut' respectively, implying that each is inherently different from the other. Thinking of the two phenomena as varying only in the dimension of iteration implies that there is one type of phenomenon – sharing of features between like elements – which varies along a number of dimensions, one of them being iteration. Distinctions between the two would then be due to other dimensions interacting with iteration specifically.

Domain limitations often mean that it is extremely difficult to determine whether a local effect is iterative or not. For instance, nasal place assimilation in English (*i*[mb]*alance*, **i*[nb]*alance*, etc.) selects a nasal as its target; since we do not have sequences of multiple nasals followed by a potential place assimilation trigger, we cannot determine whether the phenomenon is formally local, or inherently local due to other factors in the language. In the English case, for instance, the locality of the phenomenon may be simply the result of the interaction between restrictions on the target ([+nasal]) and restrictions on syllable margins (no nasal–nasal CC codas, no nasal–obstruent CC onsets).

15.8 Consecutive sequences of harmonic elements: locality issues

As sketched so far, an iterative harmonic process involves a harmonic trigger inducing harmony in some direction within some domain, affecting every consecutive target. If a potential target is encountered that cannot harmonise because of target conditions, then harmonic propagation stops, an effect known as *opacity*. For example, in Maasai (Tucker and Mpaayei 1955, Levergood 1984, Cole and Trigo 1988, Archangeli and Pulleyblank 1994), advanced tongue root harmony generally propagates throughout the word (25a). However, harmony is stopped by a low vowel encountered to the left of a harmonic trigger, such as the past tense suffix /tA/ in (25b). Harmony does not affect the low vowel, shown by (25c). Nor does it skip the low vowel, shown by (25d). Such blocking elements are called *opaque*.

(25)   *Opaque low vowels in Maasai*

  (a) harmony /kI-dot-Un-ie/   [kidotuɲie]   'we shall pull it out
                                                     with s.t.'
  (b) opaque [a] /kI-tA-dot-Un-ie/ [kɪtadotuɲie] 'we pulled it out
                                                     with s.t.'
  (c)   *[kitạdotuɲie]
  (d)   *[kitadotuɲie]

One of the most intriguing issues in the investigation of harmony concerns
cases where instead of opacity we observe *transparency*: the offending
segment is simply skipped and harmony proceeds to other eligible targets
past the transparent segment. Transparency is illustrated by the form in (25d)
(though in this instance, transparent application would be ungrammatical).

Numerous issues arise. Are transparent segments really skipped? What
kinds of segments can be transparent? What are the prosodic and featural
properties of transparent segments? How far apart can a trigger and target
be? What are the formal mechanisms that make transparency possible?

It is impossible to do justice in this short section to the range of proposals that have been made concerning the transparency/opacity distinction. What we hope to make clear is that the issue is both intriguing and
important, involving what appears to be an array of disparate phenomena,
not a single phenomenon, that in some cases transparent segments really
are skipped, and that the relevant issues intersect with core aspects of
phonological theory.

15.8.1 Apparent transparency

In a large number of cases, it appears on the surface that vowels are
harmonising and that consonants are transparent to harmony. A typical
example is Turkish (4), where the frontness or backness of a non-initial
vowel is determined by a preceding vowel, and (most) consonants appear
to be both irrelevant and transparent. It can be argued, however, that
such a case is actually consistent with local harmony, with the harmonic
feature hitting both vowels and any intervening consonants. Ní Chiosáin &
Padgett (2001), for example, discuss the case of Turkish in some detail,
arguing in favour of local harmony and against any representation where
vowel-to-vowel spreading would formally skip intervening consonants. Another relevant case mentioned above is Local & Lodge's (2004) analysis of
Kalenjin.

If we adopt the proposal that featural representations cannot formally
skip any segments at all (Gafos 1999, Ní Chiosáin & Padgett 2001, Rose &
Walker 2004, and others) then many cases of harmony involving apparent
transparency would be reanalysed as involving local harmony (1a) – consecutive sequences of harmonically specified segments.

There are many cases, however, where it appears that harmony skips over some types of segments, and where the segments skipped over ('transparent' segments) do not appear to bear the harmonic feature. These cases range from patterns where the transparent segment is completely incompatible with the harmonic feature to cases where it is fully compatible with it. While such cases merit considerable attention, we restrict ourselves here to giving a sample of the types of patterns with brief remarks about the significance of the individual patterns.

15.8.2   Transparency of impossible targets

Some featural combinations are illicit, either phonetically or within the grammar of a particular language. For example, nasality cannot be realised on a voiceless stop[16]; tongue root retraction cannot co-occur with high vowels in the grammars of numerous languages (Archangeli & Pulleyblank 1994). While in some cases, the presence of an incompatible segment serves to interrupt harmony (an expected 'opaque' pattern), there are instances where the incompatible segment is transparent.

One example of an incompatible segment being transparent to harmony was seen above in Mòbà (Ajiboye 2002). Nasality harmonises within a word, skipping over obstruents, both voiced and voiceless: [ĩsũ̀gbĩ] 'traditional singers'. In this case, the incompatibility appears to be at least close to universal (though Gerfen 1999 provides phonetic evidence for nasalised fricatives in Coatzospan Mixtec). A case of transparency based on language-specific incompatibility is found in Wolof (Ka 1988, Archangeli & Pulleyblank 1994, Pulleyblank 1996). In Wolof, non-high vowels undergo harmony for tongue root retraction. High vowels cannot be retracted in Wolof, and are transparent to harmony. Hence all non-high vowels in (26a) are advanced because the initial low vowel is advanced. (The symbol [ə] is used for the advanced low vowel.) In (26b), all non-high vowels are retracted because the initial low vowel is retracted, with both high vowels transparent to harmony.

(26)   *Wolof: transparent high vowels with the [boobule/bɔɔbulɛ]*

    (a)   [kəriɲəmboobule]   'that coal of his/hers just mentioned'
    (b)   [xaritambɔɔbulɛ]   'that friend of his/hers just mentioned'

In the Wolof case, the incompatibility of high vowels with retraction is a language-specific property, though quite common cross-linguistically.

Cases where incompatibility gives rise to transparency can involve interesting assemblies of patterns. For example, Yaka nasal consonant harmony (Hyman 1995) causes voiced consonants to nasalise even if at quite some distance from the nasal trigger. Vowels in Yaka (27) are incompatible with nasality and are transparent to harmony; voiceless consonants are incompatible with nasality and are similarly transparent.

(27) *Yaka nasal harmony*

(a)	tsúb-idi	'wander'	(b)	tsúm-ini	'sew'
	kúd-idi	'chase s.o. away'		kún-ini	'plant'
	kík-idi	'erase'		hámúk-ini	'break'
	kás-idi	'bind'		míítuk-ini	'sulk'

In contrast, nasal harmony in Mòbà (16) shows a different constellation of effects. Obstruents, both voiced and voiceless, are incompatible with nasality and exhibit transparency (28).

(28) *Mòbà Yoruba: transparency of obstruents*

ĩdũ	'bed bug'	ĩtã	'story'
ĩsĩ	'worship'	ũgũ	'corner (of a house)'
ìká̃	'termite'	ĩsũ̀gbĩ̀	'traditional singers'

Mid vowels are incompatible with nasality but exhibit opacity, not transparency (29a); low vowels are compatible with nasality in general, but are opaque to nasal harmony (29b).

(29) *Mòbà Yoruba opacity of non-high vowels*

(a) ùsègũ̀ 'act of medication'
(b) ìsasũ̀ 'kind of pot'

Cases where transparent segments are incompatible with the harmonic feature are problematic if analysed via local harmony. In Yaka, the vowels intervening between nasal trigger and target are oral, not nasal, suggesting that harmony cannot be achieved by multiply linking a nasal feature throughout the relevant harmonic domain. Similarly, transparent obstruents in Mòbà are oral, not nasal, again inconsistent with a representation where nasality harmonises by spreading to a series of consecutive segments. If we are to maintain the representational notion of local harmony, therefore, such cases require either (i) a harmonic mechanism that can produce local harmony in some instances but skip some segments in others (presumably via the 'twin peaks' representation (Archangeli & Pulleyblank 1994)), for example, as in Pulleyblank (1996), or (ii) two different harmonic mechanisms, one for cases of consecutive harmony and a second one for long-distance cases, for example, as in Gafos (1998b), Hansson (2001b), Rose & Walker (2004), or (iii) a two-stage analysis where local harmony exists at some level of analysis but is repaired to achieve the surface form, e.g. via sympathy theory (McCarthy 1999; Walker 1998 [2000b]).

Three sub-types of incompatibility transparency can be distinguished and all appear to exist. First, the transparent segments may be universally incompatible with the harmonic feature: we have suggested that voiceless obstruent stops in Mòbà are such a case. Second, the transparent segments may be compatible with the harmonic feature in some languages but incompatible in others: retraction on high vowels in Wolof is a case of this type since high retracted vowels are not part of the Wolof vowel inventory but do occur in languages such as Degema. Third, the transparent segments may be compatible with the harmonic feature in a language's inventory, but exhibit incompatibility and transparency with respect to harmony. An example of this can be found in Menominee (Archangeli & Pulleyblank 1994, Archangeli & Suzuki 1998). Low vowels in Menominee may be either retracted ([a], as in [siːpiah] 'river-LOC') or advanced ([a̠], as in [tʊːtʃkinạw] 'he nudges him'; [maskʊːtạːw] 'prairie'). Harmony, however, skips over low vowels, affecting only high vowels:

(30)   *Menominee tongue root harmony: low vowels transparent*

    (a)   [tʃɪːpaːhkʊw]   'he cooks'
    (b)   [nɪtʃiːpaːhkim]   'cook-NOM'

Harmony, triggered by the final advanced high vowel in (30b) only affects long vowels. Of the two potential long vowels, the high vowel undergoes harmony but the low vowel is skipped. In this type of case, general incompatibility of tongue root advancement with low vowels manifests itself, even though the Menominee inventory in general permits such marked vowels.

15.8.3   Irrelevant, or marginally interacting, transparency

In Section 15.8.1, it was suggested that many cases of transparency are really only apparent, that there is no reason not to analyse them as involving the harmonic feature hitting all segments within the harmonic span. The results of Section 15.8.2 are not of this type, exhibiting segments within the harmonic span that are actually skipped. Many issues arise, however, as regards limitations on just what can be legitimate cases of each type. For example, there are many instances in the harmony literature of 'translaryngeal' harmony (Steriade 1987), cases where vowel features are shared across a laryngeal consonant, such as [h], giving a $V_i h V_i$ sequence. The following is an example of this from Arbore (Rose 1996).

(31)   *Translaryngeal harmony in Arbore*

    /ma beh-o/   [ma boho]   'he is not going out'
    /ma beʔ-i/   [ma biʔi]   'he did not go out'

If we assume that consonants with oral occlusion cannot bear vowel features, then harmony affects only vowels and those consonants not specified for supralaryngeal features.

    While work such as Steriade (1987) considered the transparency of laryngeals to be due to such consonants not having place specifications, Rose (1996) argues that placelessness cannot be a satisfactory account because

such harmony takes place over a larger class than just laryngeals; specifically, such harmony can apply over the class of gutturals. Rose (1996:77)
presents the following example from Iraqw.

(32) *Transguttural harmony in Iraqw*

    (a)   /buuʔ-iim/   [buuʔuum]   'harvest pay (durative)'
           /ufaaħ-iim/   [ufaaħaam]   'blow (durative)'
           /waʔalah-iim/   [waʔalahaam]   'exchange (durative)'
    (b)   /tutuuw-iim/   [tutuwiim]   'open a new farm (durative)'
           /hamaatl-iim/   [hamtliim]   'wash (durative)'
           /baal-iim/   [baaliim]   'defeat (durative)'

As seen in these examples, the suffix vowel agrees in features with the root
vowel when the intervening consonant is either laryngeal or pharyngeal
(32a); with any other consonants intervening, agreement is blocked (32b).
While it may be possible to analyse these cases as involving vowel features
actually hitting the transparent guttural consonants, it becomes less clear
whether local harmony is really the appropriate representation for such
cases.

The difficulties in assuming local harmonic representations become even
greater in cases involving full vowel copy over all consonants. For example,
Efik has a class of vowels referred to by Cook (1986) as 'chameleonic'. In
particular morphemes, vowels copy their features from a neighbouring
vowel. For example, the second person singular and third person singular
concord prefixes both harmonise their vowel features with the root to
which they are attached. With non-high vowels, the prefix vowel is identical to the adjacent root vowel (illustrated in (33) with forms described by
Cook as 'Post-Verb-Focus Present Positive'):

(33) *Efik chameleonic vowels*

2nd sg	3rd sg	verb	gloss
è-bèd	é-bèd	/béd/	'wait'
à-kàŋ	á-kàŋ	/káŋ/	'deny'
ɔ̀-wɔ̀k	ɔ́-wɔ̀k	/wɔ́k/	'swim'
ò-dòm	ó-dòm	/dóm/	'bite'
à-twàk	á-twàk	/twàk/	'hit, tug'

The fact that vowels copy even over glides suggests that the source of the
consonantal transparency is not that the harmonic features are irrelevant
to the consonants, or that the harmonic features are intrinsically unable to
interact with the contrastive features of the transparent consonants.

Cases like Arbore, Iraqw and Efik seem to be part of a transparency
continuum based on featural independence. At one end of the continuum,
the harmonic features (supralaryngeal specifications) are phonetically
irrelevant to the transparent segments (laryngeal consonants); in the middle

of the continuum, the harmonic features are largely independent phonetically (features determining tongue dorsum shape and lip position) from
the features of the transparent segments (features determining pharyngeal
and laryngeal constrictions); at the other end of the continuum, the harmonic features appear to be phonologically independent (vowel features)
from the features of the transparent class (consonant features, including
glides) even though the two sets of features clearly interact phonetically.
While the 'phonetically irrelevant' cases seem fully consistent with the
postulation of local harmony, the other end of this continuum seems much
less clearly amenable to such an interpretation. As a result, there are
numerous analyses of harmony that differentiate formally between
'spreading' type cases of the local variety and 'copying' type cases where
segments agree over intervening segments whose features are compatible
with the harmonic value.

15.8.4   Transparent segments are fully compatible with the harmonic feature

A particularly striking class of transparency, the last that we will consider,
involves transparent segments that are fully compatible with the harmonic
feature and yet are transparent.[17]

C'Lela is an example of this type, where harmony causes a high vowel to
become non-high, (11). Transparent vowels are high vowels, and there is no
featural reason why a transparent vowel cannot lower. Indeed, as seen in
(11), a particular high vowel will undergo harmony or act as transparent
depending on its location in the word.

A second example of such transparency can be seen in Menominee. As seen
in (30), high vowels become advanced when there is a following high advanced vowel. Not mentioned above is the additional fact that only long high
vowels are targeted by advancement harmony. If a short high vowel intervenes between a high advanced trigger and a long high target, the short high
vowel is transparent: it remains retracted and fails to interrupt harmony.

(34)   *Menominee: transparency of short high vowels*

    [tuːtʃkɪnᶏw]   'he nudges him'
    [tuːtʃkɪnihᶏw]   'he nudges him in body/belly'

When the suffix −*ih* is introduced, its high advanced vowel induces advancement harmony; harmony skips over the short high vowel of the
syllable [kɪ] affecting the long high vowel of the syllable [tuːtʃ].

These cases are particularly important for the analysis of harmony. Since
the transparent segments are fully compatible with the harmonic feature,
no adequate analysis can invoke local spreading even if only a stage in the
derivation or a candidate to which the optimal output is sympathetic. If a
transparent vowel in C'Lela were to lower, there would be no reason for it

to surface as high; if a transparent vowel in Menominee were to advance, there would be no reason for it not to surface as advanced – as short high vowels routinely do. These cases are not amenable to absolute neutralisation, whatever the rule or constraint producing such an effect. Such cases of *compatible transparency* clearly demonstrate either that more than one harmonic mechanism is required – one for local harmony and one for copy-like transparency – or else that the mechanism inducing harmony must be able to produce both effects.

15.8.5 Local harmony but non-local target–trigger relations

Outside of the realm of harmony, there is a tendency for phonological relations to be local, but there is no absolute requirement to that effect. Dissimilation, for example, can affect segments at some distance from each other – a well-known example is Lyman's Law in Japanese (Itô & Mester 1986). While there is certainly a tendency for phonological interactions to involve segments that are closer together rather than further apart, requiring strict segmental adjacency in general would seem difficult to maintain; see, for example, Suzuki (1998). To wind up our discussion of transparency, therefore, we consider an interesting point with respect to harmonic trigger–target relations.

Adopting strict locality for harmonic representations, that is, disallowing any representation with a skipped segment, may be a move towards a more rigorous theory of locality. It is nevertheless important to note that non-local relations between triggers and targets persist in numerous examples, as seen above. Even in cases where the representations may be consistent with strictly local harmony, relations between trigger and target may not be. This is because in many cases, the consonants in such 'local' systems are irrelevant to the harmonic system, and do not themselves trigger harmony. Consider the case of Mòbà seen above: a nasal *vowel* triggers nasalisation of a vowel to its left (35a) while a nasal *consonant* does not trigger nasalisation of a vowel to its left (35b).

(35)   *Nasalisation of vowels before nasal vowels, not before nasal consonants*

    (a) ĩmṹ 'nose'   (b) ùmoɟi 'name of a village'
         ĩmã̀ 'palm leaf'   ìmèlé 'laziness'
         ĩ̀málè̀ 'light'   ùmórù 'personal name'

Even though (35a) shows that nasal consonants do not interrupt harmony, they simply cannot initiate it (35b). So even if we assume strictly local representations, we must allow for the possibility of harmonic triggers being nonadjacent to harmonic targets.

This, of course, leaves us on one of the many insufficiently investigated questions raised by harmonic phenomena: just how far apart can a harmonic trigger be from a harmonic target? They can clearly be adjacent, in adjacent syllables (Mọ̀bà), in syllables further apart than that (Yaka) – but are there interesting formal constraints on just how far apart they can be?

15.9   Conclusion

In this chapter, we have sketched an array of properties requiring explanation in an account of harmony. These properties, we suggest, constitute a set of interactions with core phonological patterns of nonharmonic types. *Harmony* is the result of particular constellations of properties, most or all of which are crucial for other phonological phenomena as well. We have deliberately steered clear of detailed discussion of how to derive these properties within either a rule-based or a constraint-based grammar. Our aim has been to present the sorts of properties that any model must derive, rather than focus on the formal properties of the grammar *per se*.

Whatever the model, it must be possible to impose a variety of featural restrictions on the triggers and targets of harmony, as well as restrictions of positional and prosodic types. While many restrictions may hold of either the trigger or the target independently, harmony may also require that certain non-harmonic features on the trigger and target agree. The domain of a harmony process may be delimited by phonological, morphological, and syntactic factors, and harmony may apply bidirectionally or unidirectionally, and perhaps also be limited to a single non-iterative application. While harmony may frequently apply to a consecutive string of segments, there are numerous cases where featural agreement skips over segments, whether because the segment is irrelevant for harmony, incompatible with the harmonic feature or because harmony is positionally or prosodically restricted in some way.

Notes

Thanks to José Ignacio Hualde for discussion of the Basque section, to Rachel Walker for discussion of the Ascrea Italian section, and to Fiona McLaughlin, Noriko Yamane-Tanaka, Paul de Lacy and two anonymous reviewers for overall discussion. This research was supported in part by SSHRC Standard Research Grant #410-2002-0041 to Douglas Pulleyblank.

1 Less common are cases where a set of consonants agree for some feature. Some such cases are discussed in Sections 15.3, 15.6 and 15.8.

2 Throughout, we use binary features; while this is undoubtedly a theoretical decision, the validity of the main points do not hinge on this assumption. In addition, we assume that patterns are frequently expressed with regard to a single, dominant feature; for our purposes, the inertness of the recessive feature may be due either to some degree

of underspecification or to the ranking of constraints on the dominant feature above constraints on the recessive one.

3 This position characterises recent phonological proposals which formally require that a harmonic representation be of the 'local spreading' type seen in (1a), disallowing any representations where a feature skips over another segment (Gafos 1999, Ní Chiosáin & Padgett 2001, and others), i.e. disallowing type (1b). Such an analysis of harmony is strictly 'local' in that every segment targeted by harmony is string-adjacent to a segment bearing the triggering harmonic feature. See Section 15.8 for discussion.

4 As noted by Clements & Sezer (1982), it is sometimes suggested that the vowel [o] is not possible in non-initial position in Turkish. If this were true, it would mean that the impossibility of [o] could be explained by that distributional restriction rather than by a restriction on harmony *per se*. Clements & Sezer provide a range of evidence demonstrating that the assertion is false, cases of borrowings, adjective reduplication, vowel assimilation, and so on, all showing instances of non-initial [o].

5 Akan does show a heavy degree of co-articulation so that retracted vowels, including [a], are pronounced with some degree of tongue root advancement when preceding an advanced vowel. See Clements (1981) for discussion.

6 As noted by Paradis (1986), there are three suffixes in Fula that exceptionally exhibit advanced mid vowels without an overt high vowel trigger. Paradis analyses these suffixes as involving a floating high vowel that triggers harmony.

7 We are grateful to Rachel Walker for her assistance in providing the forms in (9c).

8 The raised schwa is an excrescent, nonphonemic vowel. Dettweiler (2000:4) describes it as "a nonphonemic vowel which serves as a short transition between certain occurrences of consonants in clusters" and characterises it as often sounding like "an echo of the full vowel preceding the consonant." As in Pulleyblank (2002), we assume the representation is a featureless mora if, indeed, it has any phonological representation.

9 There are also cases of apparent identity which, on closer inspection, need not be formally expressed by stipulated conditions on both trigger and target. For instance, rightward [+ATR] in Kinande targets high vowels, and there is always a high vowel trigger (Archangeli and Pulleyblank 2002). The fact that high vowels trigger rightward harmony, however, follows from pressure in the language to associate [+ATR] as far to the right in the root as possible. Thus, [+high] is an inherent trigger condition in Kinande rightward [+ATR] harmony.

10 The foot is a potential domain of harmony as well. Recall the Ascrea dialect of Italian (9), in which the target was limited to a stressed vowel: a possible interpretation is that this phenomenon is restricted to a phonological foot. See also Rose and Walker (2004).

11 As an aside, root-controlled systems contrast with 'dominant-recessive' systems. The dominant-recessive pattern might also be called a phonological pattern: the harmonic feature pervades the harmonic domain, regardless of its original morphological affiliation. Nilotic languages provide good examples of dominant-recessive patterns (Archangeli and Pulleyblank 1994, Baković 2000).

12 On the bases of loanword adaptation, Hualde (1991) suggests that sibilant harmony is active in Basque even though restricted to morpheme-internal application.

13 There are numerous complexities to the Lango case; see Noonan (1992). With respect to bounded spreading, Noonan (1992:32) describes harmony as 'ordinarily' affecting a single syllable though in fast speech the domain may increase to two syllables.

14 Orthogonal to harmony, a rule deletes an intervocalic velar nasal and nasalises the flanking vowels, resulting in [bɔ̃ɔ̃ní] as the surface form for such an example.

15 See Archangeli & Pulleyblank (1994) for general discussion of iterativity as well for literature references.

16 Phonologically, it may be possible to have a voiceless nasal stop if this is interpreted as a prenasalised or postnasalised stop.

17 In this chapter, we do not consider cases of morphological transparency, for example, of the Semitic type. Whether the properties of such cases are special or not is an issue warranting more consideration than is available here. One possibility is that they should be accounted for by the same 'copying' type mechanisms as discussed briefly in this section; see Gafos (1998b).

16

Dissimilation in grammar and the lexicon

John D. Alderete
Stefan A. Frisch

16.1   Introduction

Dissimilation is the systematic avoidance of two similar sound structures in relatively close proximity to each other. It is exhibited in static generalizations over the lexicon, where combinations of similar sounds are systematically avoided in lexical items, like the avoidance of two homorganic consonants in Arabic roots (Greenberg 1950; McCarthy 1994). Dissimilation is also observed in phonological processes in which the target and trigger become less alike phonologically. In Tashlhiyt Berber, for example, two primary labial consonants in the same derived stem trigger a process of delabialization: /m-kaddab/ → [n-kaddab] 'consider a liar (reciprocal)' (Elmedlaoui 1992, Jebbour 1985).

   Dissimilation has been an important empirical testing ground for many of the central research paradigms in modern linguistics. For example, dissimilatory phenomena have been crucial to the development of theories of feature geometry and feature specification in autosegmental phonology (McCarthy 1986, 1988, Padgett 1995, Yip 1989b). As the results emerging from this research were incorporated into constraint-based theories of phonology like Optimality Theory (Prince & Smolensky 2004), dissimilation became an important problem in the study of phonological markedness and constraint composition (Alderete 1997, Itô & Mester 2003). In a different line of research, dissimilation has been argued to have its seeds in the phonetics of sound change, restricted by the same vocal tract constraints involved in speech production and perception (Ohala 1981 et seq.). Finally, dissimilation has been shown to be statistically systematic when observed over lexical items, raising a host of questions about the interface between categorical and statistical information in grammatical models (Pierrehumbert 1993b, Frisch et al. 2004). The discussion below summarizes the results emerging from these separate theoretical enterprises, and it also strives to identify problems for future research that may require new models of grammar that mix symbolic, statistical, and phonetic information.

This chapter is structured as follows. Section 16.2 provides a basic tool-box for describing the ways in which dissimilation differs cross-linguistic-ally. Section 16.3 introduces the hypercorrective theory of dissimilatory sound change proposed in Ohala (1981) and uses some of the background from Section 16.2 to assess this theory. In Section 16.4, generative approaches to dissimilation are discussed that make use of the principles of autosegmental phonology and Optimality Theory. Section 16.5 focuses on statistical patterns of dissimilation in the lexicon and lays out the analysis of these statistical patterns based on the scalar and quantitative property of similarity. Finally, the conclusion ties together some of the open issues arising from these discussions and clarifies some questions for future research.

16.2   Parameters of dissimilation

What are the 'parameters' of dissimilation? Which features are typically involved and what types of conditions may be placed on dissimilation rules? Direct answers to these questions are limited by the fact that, to date, there has not been a controlled study of the cross-linguistic variation in dissimilation. On the other hand, the wealth of examples available in the literature set the stage for further empirical investigation and assessment of scientific hypotheses.

One of the main ways dissimilation may differ cross-linguistically is whether it is observed in dynamic alternations or as static generalizations over the lexicon. An example of the former type is illustrated by the data from Tashlhiyt Berber below (Elmedlaoui 1992, Jebbour 1985, Selkirk 1993). Derived stems in Berber may only have one primary labial consonant, that is, one consonant from the set [b f m]. When a derivational prefix, like the reciprocal prefix /m(m)-/, attaches to a root that also contains a primary labial consonant, a process of labial dissimilation is triggered, causing the prefix to change to [n], as shown on the right. The left columns contain the surface forms, and the right columns the roots (marked by a √).

(1)   *Primary labial dissimilation in Tashlhiyt Berber*

(a) m-xazar	√xzr 'scowl'		(b) n-fara	√fra 'disentangle'
m-saggal	√sggl 'look for'		n-ħaʃʃam	√ħʃʃm 'be shy'
m-!ʃawar	√!ʃawr 'ask advice'		n-xalaf	√xalf 'place crosswise'
mm-ʒla	√ʒla 'lose'		n-kaddab	√kddb 'consider a liar'

Dissimilation is also exhibited in static generalizations over the lexicon. That is, statistical analysis of the frequency of segment types in lexical items may reveal significant over- or under-representation of these types. Dissimilation in the lexicon involves significant under-representation of two similar segments in lexical items. A well-known example of this type is

Modern Arabic, where homorganic consonant pairs are significantly under-represented in roots (Greenberg 1950, McCarthy 1994). Table (2), taken from Frisch et al. (2004), illustrates the relative frequencies of adjacent consonants in Arabic verb roots ($n = 2,674$), sorted by place and manner of articulation classes. Each cell gives a measure of over- or under-representation as a value for O/E, or observed/expected (Pierrehumbert 1993b), where observed is the number of occurrences and expected is the number of occurrences that would be expected if the consonants combined at random. A value less than one therefore indicates that there are fewer observed consonant pairs than would be expected if they combined at random, as shown in the shaded portions below.

(2) *Co-occurrence of adjacent consonant pairs in Arabic*

	Lab	Cor Stop	Cor Fric	Dorsal	Uvular	Phar	Cor Son
Labial [b f m]	0.00	1.37	1.31	1.15	1.35	1.17	1.18
Cor Stop [t d tˤ dˤ]		0.14	0.52	0.80	1.43	1.25	1.23
Cor Fric [θ ð s z sˤ zˤ ʃ]			0.04	1.16	1.41	1.26	1.21
Dorsal [k g q]				0.02	0.07	1.04	1.48
Uvular [χ ʁ]					0.00	0.07	1.39
Pharyngeal [ħ ʕ h ʔ]						0.06	1.26
Cor Son [l r n]							0.06

The patterns of over- and under-representation above indicate that there is a systematic avoidance, though not an absolute avoidance, of adjacent homorganic consonants. For example, roots containing two labials (O/E = 0.00) or two dorsals (0.02) in a row are significantly under-represented, contrasting sharply with roots containing one labial and dorsal (1.15). These patterns also show the effect of manner features on coronals, as coronals co-occur with a relatively high frequency if they are not in the same manner classes, stop, fricative, and sonorant, but a sequence of two coronals within one of these classes is under-represented. Avoidance of two similar sounds may thus be observed in the statistical analysis of the frequency of segment co-occurrence in the lexicon.

In terms of the range of features referred to by dissimilation rules, there is no specific typological evidence that any particular feature is not active in dissimilation. However, a review of the commonly cited examples suggests that certain features are more frequent than others. In Suzuki (1998), 53 examples of dissimilation were amassed from some of the principal works on the subject (especially Odden 1994, Ohala 1981, Padgett 1995, Walsh Dickey 1997, and Yip 1989b). The list in (3) organizes these examples, from both alternations and lexical dissimilation, and sorts them by the principal feature or feature class that triggers dissimilation.

(3)   *Examples from Suzuki 1998 (n = 53, of 21 features; 2.5 expected frequency)*

(a) Place, total _____ 15
    [place] (=homorganic)_____ 5
    [labial] _____ 7
    [coronal] _____ 2
    [dorsal] _____ 0
    [pharyngeal] _____ 1

(b) Laryngeal, total _____ 8
    [±voice]_____ 3
    [±constricted glottis] _____ 1
    [±spread glottis]_____ 1
    [tone] (H and L)_____ 3

(c) Liquids, total_____10
    [liquid]_____ 1
    [±lateral]_____ 4
    [rhotic]/[retroflex]_____ 5

(d) Major class, total_____ 0
    [±consonant]_____ 0
    [±sonorant]_____ 0
    [±approximant]_____ 0

(e) Vowel features, total_____ 8
    [±high]_____ 2
    [±low]_____ 4
    [±back]_____ 2

(f) Manner, total_____ 3
    [±continuant]_____ 2
    [±nasal] _____ 1
    [±strident] _____ 0

(g) Other, total_____ 9
    NC cluster _____ 3
    Length_____ 6

As a convenience-based sample, the dataset is not suitable for statistical analysis. However, the patterns in the first column (3a–c) suggest that dissimilation of place features, laryngeals (including tone), and liquids may have a greater than chance occurrence. When compared to the non-existent cases of dissimilation of the major class features, and the small number of cases with manner features, these cases stand out. Furthermore, there seem to be certain types of place restrictions that are more common than others, like those prohibiting a double occurrence of labials or any two homorganic consonants (i.e., identical [place] specifications).

With the exception of tone, the term dissimilation is more often applied to subsegmental attributes of segments, like the features listed above. However, the mode of analysis 'avoid similar elements' has also been applied with some success to prosodic features, such as vowel and conson-ant length, as well as complex phonological structures like pre-nasalized stops and nasal-obstruent clusters. For example, Japanese loans from Eng-lish have geminate stops after lax vowels, as in *rakkii* 'lucky', but double geminate loans with two such lax vowel-stop clusters only allow a single geminate: *ma*[p]*etto* 'Muppet', **ma*[pp]*etto* (Iwai 1989, Itô & Mester 2003). Thus, two similar elements are avoided, though the prohibited structures are not subsegmental features of individual segments.

The validity of the dissimilation analysis for these non-segmental elements, however, is sometimes confounded by the availability of alternative analyses. For example, the resolution of sequences of NC clusters found in many aboriginal languages of Australia (e.g. Yinjibarndi, Gurindji, and Gooniyandi) seems to have a more natural analysis in terms of nasal spreading, because this resolution is blocked by intervening oral stops (see Odden 1994 for relevant examples and discussion). Likewise, the proposal to capture Clash Avoidance effects in stress systems as a consequence of a dissimilatory constraint against two adjacent stressed syllables (Yip 1988) must compete with the plausible alternative in which stress is the realization of the head of a metrical stress foot, which is rhythmically distributed because of robustly supported binarity requirements on stress feet.

Finally, there is a set of conditions on dissimilation that accounts for known cross-linguistic variation, defined and discussed below.

(4) *Conditions on dissimilation*

    (a) <u>Root adjacency</u>: the target and trigger must be adjacent segments, i.e., adjacent root nodes

    (b) <u>Syllable adjacency</u>: the target and trigger must be contained in adjacent syllables

    (c) <u>Domains</u>: the target and trigger must fall within a specified domain, e.g., a morphological domain (root, stem, word, morpheme) or prosodic domain (e.g., syllable, foot, 'rime')

    (d) <u>'No intervener'</u>: for target segment x and trigger y, there must be no segment z, of a specified type, that intervenes between x and y

One class of conditions involves requirements on the locality of the target and trigger of dissimilation, conditions that stem from a long line of research on locality in phonology (Archangeli & Pulleyblank 1987, Steriade 1987, Odden 1994). Root adjacency (4a) requires target and trigger to be adjacent segments, as illustrated by a second dissimilatory pattern in Berber. In the Tiznit variety of Tashlhiyt Berber reported in Jebbour (1985), rounded velar consonants unround when immediately preceded by a primary labial consonant, e.g. [gʷ]rd 'tame (preterit)', cf. am-[g]rad, im-[g]rad 'tame (agentive singular, plural)'; velars thus lose their rounding and become less like the adjacent labial segments. Locality requirements can also be somewhat looser, requiring only that target and trigger appear in adjacent syllables (4b), as exemplified by Dahl's Law in many Bantu languages. This process changes /k/ to [g] when another voiceless obstruent appears in an adjacent syllable, as shown by the following data from Kikuria (Odden 1994): /oko-téma/ → o[g]o-téma 'to hit', cf. o[k]o-bára 'to count' (no voiceless obstruent) and o[k]o-ménénɛkánya 'to make each other shine' (no voiceless obstruent in adjacent syllable).

While locality requirements such as these are rather common, perhaps due in part to their history (see Section 16.3), it is not uncommon for the target and trigger of dissimilation to be limited to some domain that is defined by a coherent linguistic unit. For example, Berber labial dissimilation described above in (1) is limited to the morphological stem, so the target and trigger must fall within this morphological domain. Other morphological domains, e.g., verb roots in Arabic (2), and even prosodic domains like syllables or feet may be placed as domain conditions on the application of dissimilation, as has been argued for syllable-bound glottal stop dissimilation in Seri (Marlett & Stemberger 1983, Yip 1988).

While the patterns of dissimilation in the lexicon in Arabic are limited to the root, there is a second sense in which locality is relevant to these patterns. It has long been known that the dissimilation patterns are stronger for consonant pairs that are adjacent in the root (e.g., forms with coronal stops like *dtC, O/E = 0.14) than for consonant pairs that are non-adjacent in the root (e.g., forms with coronal stops like *dCt, O/E = 0.38) (Greenberg 1950, McCarthy 1994, Pierrehumbert 1993b). In other words, the extent to which similar sounds are avoided in the roots of Arabic depends on their proximity to one another.

Finally, the parameters of dissimilation seem to also require a condition on the material intervening between target and trigger, namely that this intervening material does not contain a segment of a specified type. Latin lateral dissimilation is often described in this way, where a sequence of two laterals triggers dissimilation, /lun-alis/ → *lun-a*[r]*is* 'lunar', but this process is blocked if target and trigger are separated by a rhotic [r], e.g., /flor-alis/→ *flor-a*[l]*is* 'floral' (Walsh Dickey 1997).

In summary, cross-linguistic variation in dissimilation may be described using the distinction between dynamic processes and static lexical dissimilation, the specific features involved, and a set of conditions on the application of dissimilation. These parameters of dissimilation provide useful background for the understanding and assessment of the approaches to dissimilation discussed below.

16.3 Diachronic seeds of dissimilation: hypercorrection

Considerable attention has been paid in recent years to how phonological processes come about historically, often with careful examination of the phonetic structures that give rise to synchronic phonological patterns (Hyman 1976, Ohala 1983a, Blevins 2004). One approach to dissimilation has been developed within this program that attributes dissimilation rules to hypercorrection, a kind of mental inversion of a perceived phonetic co-articulation (Ohala 1981, 1992, 1993). Rich in predictions, this theory clarifies a number of questions for future work, some of which have been taken up in the lines of research discussed below.

Ohala's hypercorrection theory is illustrated below with an example from Slavic (5). In this sound change, the low front vowel [a] is shifted to back [ɑ] after palatal and palatalized consonants, e.g., *stoj + /aː/ → *stoj*[ɑː] 'stand'. This change is a case of dissimilation for the feature

[±back]: palatals are [−back], and so are front vowels, so *ja > jɑ avoids two adjacent segments that are both [−back].

(5) *Scenario for hypercorrective sound change*

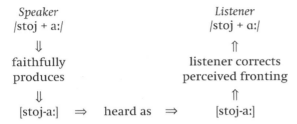

According to the hypercorrection theory, the listener in the scenario above falsely attributes the frontness of [a] to the neighboring palatal, a plausible assumption, given the ubiquity of C-V co-articulation. Believing that [j-a] is co-articulated, the listener posits a mental representation that inverts the [−back] specification, and if the same action is copied by other listeners, a regular sound change may develop.

The attraction of the hypercorrective theory is that it draws on a number of parallels between known patterns of co-articulation in speech production and the observed patterns of dissimilatory sound change. These parallels make for a highly constrained theory of the historical source for dissimilation, as explicated in the list of predictions given below.

(6) *Predictions of hypercorrective theory*
   (a) <u>Locality</u>: since hypercorrective dissimilation is due to perceived co-articulation, the target and trigger must be adjacent segments, unless the relevant phonetic feature is mediated by an intervening segment.
   (b) <u>Which features dissimilate</u>: 'stretched out' features that have longer temporal intervals are more likely to dissimilate than others because they provide better cues that the listener can attribute to a false co-articulation.

Predicted to dissimilate	*Predicted not to dissimilate*
labialization, uvularization, pharyngealization, palatalization, retroflexion, place, glottalization, aspiration, laterals	continuancy (stop/fricative) complex segmenthood voice

   (c) <u>Persistent triggers</u>: because hypercorrection depends on the existence of a triggering element, the triggering segment is never lost at the same time as a dissimilatory sound change; thus, e.g. *bʰandʰ > ban is predicted not to exist as a single sound change
   (d) <u>No new segments</u>: hypercorrective dissimilation involves a normalization, i.e., a reverting back to an assumed input; if the input

is constructed from a common stock of sounds, no new segments can result from dissimilation.

How do these predictions measure up? Beyond Ohala (1981), we know of no works that have investigated these predictions systematically in dissimilatory sound change. However, it seems plausible to test some of them, albeit indirectly, using data from synchronic patterns, under the assumption that the sound changes that fall under the scope of this theory will give rise to lexical and morpho-phonemic patterns of dissimilation, and that many of these patterns inherit the primary characteristics of the original sound changes. These assumptions seem plausible, since lexical dissimilation is quite naturally analyzed as the accumulation of regular sound changes affecting lexical items, and an extension of the resulting lexical patterns is a likely source of synchronic alternations.

It seems fair, therefore, to consider the dataset in (3) in connection with the prediction that only features with long temporal intervals may dissimilate. In this light, the patterns in (3) are in large part consistent with this prediction: dissimilation of place, tone and laryngeal features are quite common, which clearly have a long temporal interval, as does retroflexion in liquid dissimilation. Laterals probably have prominent cues too, because they have long F2 and F3 transitions, which accounts for the large number of cases of dissimilation of [±lateral]. One sticking point is dissimilation of [voice], supported by three examples in (3), though at least one of these, Thurneysen's Law, has been reanalyzed with reference to higher-level prosodic structure (Ohala 1981; see also Ohala 1993).

The locality question is also interesting in connection with the observed conditions on dissimilation from Section 16.2. Since co-articulation has the greatest effect on adjacent segments, the prediction is that hypercorrective inversion of a perceived co-articulation will also be of local elements, relating naturally to patterns of root-adjacent dissimilation. Dissimilation of vowels in adjacent syllables is also a possibility, since it is known that vowels can influence each other across consonants, at least in VCV structures (Öhman 1966). As for dissimilation of consonant attributes across vowels, this too seems to be possible, because of the robust phonetic evidence that consonants may be co-articulated with neighboring vowels. For example, the F2 and F3 formant transitions that constitute the main cues for consonantal place of articulation are known to persist into a significant portion of neighboring vowels. If attested, this C-V co-articulation effectively makes the dissimilation between local segments because the vowel mediates the dissimilating feature (see Ohala 1981 for explicit discussion and examples). This analysis does not seem to work, however, in cases where the target and trigger of dissimilation are separated by more than a consonant or vowel. Labial dissimilation in Berber, for example, occurs over two heterosyllabic vowels and consonants, e.g. /m-kaddab/ → [n-kaddab] 'consider a liar (reciprocal)', making inversion of a phonetic assimilation highly implausible. Such long-distance dissimilations are not uncommon, but they are not predicted by the hypercorrective theory.

Another problem is the apparent asymmetries in the perceptual response to co-articulation. The crux of the hypercorrective theory is that when a surface form contains two neighboring elements that share a feature compatible with co-articulation, the listener may interpret this as the result of co-articulation and correct the structure. Consequently, the theory predicts, as emphasized in (Ohala 1981 et seq.), that there are two plausible responses to these forms: (i) hypercorrection, leading possibly to dissimilation, or (ii) hypocorrection, where the listener does nothing to the heard form and adopts the co-articulated structure at face value. Ohala's work enumerates dozens of very plausible examples of both types, but certain cases seem to favor one type of response over another. For example, co-articulation in nasal-obstruent clusters is extremely common cross-linguistically, and has led to countless examples of phonological nasal-place assimilation, i.e., hypocorrection caused by co-articulation of place features. But we know of no dissimilatory examples of this type, so hypercorrection seems impossible. A similar argument could be made for C-C [voice] assimilation, though this is confounded by the question of whether [voice] dissimilation arises from hypercorrective sound change. Conversely, liquid dissimilation is extremely common, second only to place dissimilation in (3), but liquid assimilations are vanishingly rare (though Palaun liquid assimilation may be a counterexample; see Josephs 1975). Why is hypercorrection favored here? It seems therefore that the conditions on the perceptual responses to co-articulation must be different in these examples, and future hypothesis-testing may profit from linking these conditions to whether or not the listener actively responds to co-articulation with hypercorrection.

While there is a relatively good fit between many of the above predictions and observed dissimilatory sound changes, the limits of this theory suggest that there may be additional causes of dissimilation. One additional cause may follow from the difficulty in producing speech that contains repeated items (Dell et al. 1997). For example, tongue twisters containing repeated similar onset consonants (e.g. *sit zap zoo sip*) are more difficult to produce than those that do not contain repeated onsets (e.g. *sit shop zoo tip*). Tongue twisters containing repetition are analogous to polysyllabic words containing pairs of similar segments, i.e., the input to dissimilation rules. Thus, there may be an additional functional motivation for dissimilation in the difficulty in processing words containing repeated segments during speech production (Berg 1998, Frisch 2004).

Furthermore, though the hypercorrective theory is a predictive theory in terms of the types of dissimilatory patterns that are likely to be found, it is not a theory of the representation of dissimilation in synchronic grammars. Thus, the hypercorrective theory may explain sound changes that result in systematic changes to lexical entries, but when morpho-phonemic alternations are involved, formal mechanisms are needed to model dynamic processes of dissimilation. This limitation applies to any functional explanation of dissimilation. Therefore, we next consider generative approaches to synchronic dissimilation, as considerable progress has been made in modeling dissimilation as a dynamic process.

16.4   Generative approaches to dissimilation

Advancements in autosegmental and prosodic phonology in the 1980s provided many of the leading ideas behind the generative approach to dissimilation, including explicit formalisms for morpho-phonemic alternations and long-distance dissimilation. Indeed, dissimilatory phenomena constituted an important empirical testing ground for proposals concerning tier structure in phonology, feature geometry, and the nature of feature specification. In addition, these investigations of dissimilation clarified a number of problems with autosegmental approaches that were later addressed in constraint-based approaches to dissimilation like OT and probabilistic linguistics.

16.4.1   Tier phonology, the OCP, and feature specification

Generative approaches to dissimilation were born out of investigations of autosegmental tone. In this work (pioneered by Leben 1973 and Goldsmith 1976a), it is argued that many properties of tone systems can be explained with a phonological tier for tone that is distinct from the tier for units sponsoring tone. In addition, the tiers and association of tonal units to their sponsors is governed by a general set of principles and constraints. One set of conditions, dubbed the Association Conventions, constitutes an algorithm for linking up the elements on the two tiers, stipulating essentially that associations are made from left-to-right, one-to-one, until the end of the string has unassociated elements, in which case, the unassociated elements are linked with the rightmost element on the other tier (Goldsmith 1976a). These conventions for linking up structure on distinct tiers led to a parallel between tone and segmental phonology (McCarthy 1979a), illustrated in (7), which in turn engendered the autosegmental analysis of dissimilation.

(7)   *Autosegmental association for tone and segmental features*

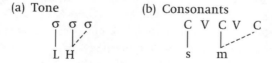

    (a) Tone   (b) Consonants

The shortage of tones in the LH melody in the tone example requires the last tone to link up with both the second and third syllable, which produces a low-high-high tone shape in the surface form. This analysis has the effect of systematically prohibiting words with a low-low-high tone shape, an important fact in tone systems like Mende (Leben 1973), because the Association Conventions do not allow double linking of a non-final L tone. In his study of root-and-pattern morphology in Arabic, McCarthy (1979a) found the same directionality pattern in root consonantism, accounting for Arabic roots like *s-m-m* but excluding non-existent **s-s-m* as a straightforward consequence of left-to-right association to the CV tier.

This analysis, however, depended crucially on the absence of LLH tone melodies, and for example *s-s-m* consonantal roots in Arabic; otherwise, LLH surface forms could be produced with simple one-to-one association. In autosegmental phonology, these structures are ruled out by the Obligatory Contour Principle (OCP).

(8)   Obligatory Contour Principle *(Leben 1973, Goldsmith 1976a, McCarthy 1986)*
      At the melodic level, adjacent identical elements are prohibited.

The OCP rules out LLH and *s-s-m* melodies because they contain two identical elements on the same tier. This insight behind the OCP, that adjacent identical elements are prohibited, has been extended to analyses of a host of dissimilation patterns, observed in both alternations (Itô & Mester 1986, Myers 1987a, Selkirk 1993, Yip 1988) and lexical distributions (Itô & Mester 1986, MacEachern 1999, McCarthy 1988, Mester 1986, Padgett 1995, Yip 1989b). The tier structures in (9) illustrate how the OCP motivates processes like long-distance labial dissimilation in Berber (1), as well as two important assumptions about feature structure and specification necessary to the analysis.

(9)   *Autosegmental analysis of Berber labial dissimilation*

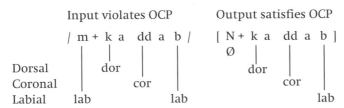

The input contains two primary labial segments, which, because of the separation of tiers, are adjacent on the labial tier. Deletion of the [labial] feature in the output, the representation of delabialization, therefore satisfies the OCP. Crucially, the nasal prefix is not specified for place at the point at which the OCP applies; otherwise, the [coronal] feature would also violate the OCP. In cases like this, it is typically assumed that unspecified segments received a default feature specification, in this case [coronal], at a final step in the phonological derivation. In this way, appeal to the OCP in the analysis of dissimilation is often tied in explicit ways to assumptions about tier structure and feature specification, two points taken up below.

Part of the appeal of the autosegmental analysis of dissimilation is the application of the OCP to both lexical representations and alternations. When these two types of dissimilatory patterns are found in the same language, however, a problem arises, stemming more from the implementation of autosegmental ideas in derivational phonology than the content of the OCP itself. A well-known example is Lyman's Law in Japanese, a restriction against two voiced obstruents in a stem (Itô & Mester 1986; Itô et al. 1995). Lyman's Law applies both as a restriction on a lexical stratum, namely the Yamato stock of the Japanese lexicon, and to the output of phonological rules. In rule-based phonology, the static Lyman's Law amounts to a lexical redundancy rule, perhaps motivated by the OCP, acting on Yamato stems. However, this same restriction must be active in phonological derivations as well, because it blocks the application of Rendaku, a systematic morpho-phonemic process that voices stem-initial obstruents in the second member of a compound. The application and blocking of Rendaku is illustrated in (10).

(10)   *Blocking of Rendaku sequential voicing by Lyman's Law*

(a)	/ori + kami/	$\rightarrow$	[ori-gami]	'folding paper'
	/oo + sumoo/	$\rightarrow$	[oo-zumoo]	*'sumo* tournament'
	/jama + tera/	$\rightarrow$	[jama-dera]	'mountain temple'
	/mizu + hana/	$\rightarrow$	[mizu-bana]	'running nose'
(b)	/kami + kaze/	$\rightarrow$	[kami-kaze]	'divine wind'
	/ʃiro + tabi/	$\rightarrow$	[ʃiro-tabi]	'white tabi'
	/mono + ʃizuka/	$\rightarrow$	[mono-ʃizuka]	'tranquil'
	/maru + hadaka/	$\rightarrow$	[maru-hadaka]	'completely naked'

The realization of the full potential of the autosegmental analysis is thus hampered by a technical problem, namely that restrictions on lexical items and constraints on the output of phonological rules are governed by different mechanisms. Though this issue is complex, and there are reasons to want to separate the analysis of lexical distributions from alternations, there is a consensus in the generative literature that this allocation of resources to two separate domains, dubbed the Duplication Problem, stands in the way of genuine explanation.

The derivational implementation of the autosegmental analysis commonplace in the 1980s, together with the necessary assumptions tied to feature specification, leads to another problem. A fundamental assumption in the autosegmental analysis is that the features that are active in dissimilation are specified, and those that are not active are not specified at the time at which the OCP is applied. It is necessary to assume, for example, [coronal] is unspecified at the derivational instant at which the OCP is applied in the Berber example illustrated above. It turns out that the assumption 'active is specified' leads to serious empirical problems, because dissimilation often requires specificational assumptions that are not consistent with other facts. For example, in the Japanese example above, it is assumed that redundant sonorant voicing is not specified in examples like *ori-gami*; otherwise, voicing in [m] would block Rendaku, just like voiced obstruents do. However, derived voicing in post-nasal obstruents also blocks Rendaku, as exemplified by examples like /ʃirooto-kaŋkae/ → ʃirooto-[k]aŋgae 'layman's idea'. A [voice] specification is therefore necessary prior to the application of Rendaku in order to give a natural analysis of voice assimilation in nasal-obstruent clusters, an assumption that is inconsistent with [voice] specification in *ori-gami* (see Itô et al. 1995 for explicit derivations and discussion, and Alderete 1997 for a parallel example in Berber). This problem, like the Duplication Problem, stems directly from the assumption that phonological generalizations are expressed as rules that are serialized in a phonological derivation.

16.4.2 Cumulative markedness in Optimality Theory

One of the core assumptions of Optimality Theory (OT – Prince & Smolensky 2004) is that phonological activity is driven by markedness (see Smolensky 1995, Rice (Ch.4) for cogent argumentation). The motivation for phonological processes in OT is to satisfy markedness constraints, a family of well-formedness constraints that prohibit cross-linguistically marked structure. Building on this insight, Alderete (1997) and Itô & Mester (2003) construct an account of dissimilatory phenomena that derives from the cumulative effects of markedness constraints. In this approach, complex markedness constraints are generated from simple ones through the operation of local self-conjunction (Smolensky 1995). The effect of this conjunction is a set of OCP-like markedness constraints that specifically ban multiple instances of marked structure. This type of analysis gives a natural account to many types of dissimilation processes, because they specifically prohibit multiple instances of marked structures. Lyman's Law is a case in point. Voiced obstruents are cross-linguistically marked. This is supported by the implicational relation in segment inventories where the presence of a voiced obstruent series requires a voiceless obstruent series, as well as abundant evidence from alternations, like coda devoicing of obstruents. These facts entail a constraint against marked obstruent voicing, *VOICEDOBSTRUENT. In cumulative markedness theory, this constraint can be doubled via local self-conjunction to produce a constraint that specifically prohibits two voiced obstruents (i.e., *VOICEDOBSTR^2, the exact restriction in Lyman's Law). This result is illustrated in a standard OT tableau (11).

(11) *Lexical dissimilation: Lyman's Law in Japanese*

/D … D/	*VOICEDOBSTR^2	FAITHFULNESS	*VOICEDOBSTR
☞ T … D		*	*
D … D	*!		**

Importantly, the same self-conjoined markedness constraint has a role in dynamic alternations, blocking the effects of a regular pattern of sequential voicing, Rendaku, as illustrated in (12).

(12)   *Dynamic effects: blocking of Rendaku sequential voicing*

(a)

	/kami+kaze/	*VoicedObstr^2	Rendaku	Faithfulness
☞	kami-[k]aze		*	
	kami-[g]aze	*!		*

(b)

	/ori+kami/	*VoicedObstr^2	Rendaku	Faithfulness
☞	ori-[g]ami			*
	ori-[k]ami		*!	

The analysis of the inventory limitation on more than one voiced obstruent is unified with the blocking effect in dynamic alternations — they are due to the same constraint, applied consistently to pick the winning output form.

The activity of obstruent voicing is also evident in stems with derived obstruent voicing, the context that leads to the ordering paradox for the derivational analysis discussed above. In the OT analysis, however, the blocking effect is simply a matter of markedness, not the specific instant at which [voice] is specified. With an independently motivated constraint requiring voicing in post-nasal obstruents (Pater 1999) ranked above Rendaku, the blocking effect is explained with the same ranking employed above (13).

(13)   *Phonological activity of derived obstruent voicing in Japanese*

	/ ʃirooto-kaŋkae/	*VoicedObstr^2	*NC̥	Rendaku	Faithfulness
☞	ʃirooto-[k]aŋgae			*	*
	ʃirooto-[g]aŋgae	*!			**
	ʃirooto-[g]aŋkae		*!		*

The solution to both the Duplication Problem and the ordering paradoxes with feature specification therefore draws directly on one of the basic premises of OT, namely that constraints apply in parallel to output forms.

16.5   Probabilistic approaches to dissimilation

The generative approaches to dissimilation have focused on pin-pointing specific features or feature combinations that trigger dissimilation. An alternative approach has also been proposed in which dissimilation is grounded in the scalar and quantitative property of similarity (Pierrehumbert 1993b, Frisch et al. 2004). In this alternative approach, patterns of dissimilation have been analyzed statistically in an attempt to demonstrate that dissimilation is gradient and predictable from probabilistic functions that refer to categorical targets only as endpoints on a continuum. Statistical studies of dissimilation have focused on phonotactic patterns in the lexical items of particular languages. Such patterns have been documented in a wide variety of languages, including Arabic (see Section 16.2), English (Berkley 1994), Russian (Padgett 1995), Italian, and Thai (Frisch et al. 2004); in fact every language that has been studied statistically has revealed such patterns. This section will review the methods and findings that are representative of these studies, and present an argument that theories of grammar must account for gradient phonological patterns like that found in dissimilation.

16.5.1 Probability in the lexicon

It is well documented that speakers of a language are sensitive to the statistical distribution of phonological and morphological forms in the language (e.g., Frisch et al. 2000, Hay et al. 2004, Kessler & Treiman 1997, Zuraw 2000). In other words, speakers can make judgements not just about the possible and impossible forms in a language, but also differentiate degrees of acceptability and wordlikeness within the groups of acceptable and unacceptable forms. In general, more wordlike forms provide a closer match to the statistical patterns of the language than less wordlike forms (though see Crosswhite et al. 2003, Moreton 2002 for potential counter-examples).

So far, two types of statistical pattern in phonotactics have been examined and shown to have been acquired by experiment participants: constituent probabilities and constituent combination probabilities (Frisch et al. 2000). Constituent probabilities refer to the distribution of segments within the phonological constituents of words, such as syllable onsets and rimes. Constituent combination probabilities refer to the probability of the co-occurrence of two constituents, relative to their chance rate of occurrence. The product of constituent probabilities for two (or more) different constituents in a word provides a statistical estimate of the likelihood that these two constituents would be found together at random (or by chance). If the observed constituent combination probability is significantly below the probability of co-occurrence by chance, then there is statistical evidence in the lexicon for a phonotactic constraint between the constituents. This is found in cases of dissimilation in the lexicon. Similar consonant pairs that are subject to a dissimilatory constraint are found together less frequently than would be expected by chance, like lexical dissimilation in Arabic. The fact that knowledge of these statistical constraints has been acquired by native speakers is established by experiments asking for wordlikeness or

acceptability judgments for novel forms containing combinations that
have different frequencies of occurrence (Frisch et al. 2000, Frisch and
Zawaydeh 2001).

16.5.2   Probabilistic dissimilation in the lexicon

Statistical analyses of lexical patterns of dissimilation have revealed that
similarity between consonants along any dimension is avoided. Thus, the
pattern appears to be one of dissimilation in its truest sense, dubbed
'similarity avoidance' by Frisch et al. (2004). Consonants that share place
of articulation only, but differ in manner and voicing (e.g., [t] and [n]) have
the weakest restriction. Consonants that share major place and manner
features (e.g., [t] and [d] or [n] and [r]) are much more strongly restricted.
Figure (14) shows the co-occurrence of adjacent consonant pairs in Arabic,
based on the data in (2), but as a function of similarity. For these data,
similarity was computed using a metric of shared natural classes between
segments (Frisch et al. 2004) and groups of consonants were aggregated
together into similarity intervals of 0.1. In this figure, similarity 0 consonant pairs (non-homorganic) and similarity 1 consonant pairs (identical) are
presented in distinct categories (note also that there happened to be no
consonant pairs with similarity that fell into the range 0.6–0.7 or 0.9–1).
Figure (14) also shows a curve fit to the Arabic data based on a stochastic
model of co-occurrence where rate of occurrence (O/E) is a decreasing
function of similarity.

(14)   *Consonant co-occurrence in Arabic by similarity*

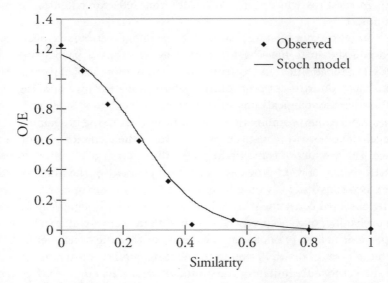

In addition to the quantitative pattern presented above, it can also be
argued that co-occurrence is similarity based by considering co-occurrence

in specific natural classes that share or do not share features. The co-occurrence restrictions in Arabic have been shown to be sensitive to secondary place of articulation features (Frisch et al. 2004), the manner of articulation of the consonants (McCarthy 1994, Padgett 1995), and the voicing of the consonants (Frisch et al. 1997). In short, any co-occurrence of features appears to influence the probabilistic likelihood of co-occurrence. Thus, it has been proposed that the categorical co-occurrence restrictions in the Arabic lexicon are merely the extreme end of a range of statistical co-occurrence restrictions. The effect in Arabic is strongest along the place of articulation dimension, weaker for manner of articulation, and weakest of all for voicing. It has also been argued that the number of segments that intervene between the consonants influences co-occurrence probabilistically (Berkley 1994, Buckley 1997, Pierrehumbert 1993b).

These sorts of statistical observations were addressed by generative models of Arabic consonant co-occurrence. In Padgett (1995), an autosegmental account is proposed in which the OCP is sensitive to features that are subsidiary to place of articulation features in feature geometry, like the manner features [±continuant] and [±sonorant] for Arabic and Russian. While Padgett's account correctly identifies the classes over which co-occurrence constraints are applied, the generative implementation does not address the statistical nature of these patterns. In particular, Frisch et al. (2004) argue that these patterns are best explained probabilistically, because solutions based on categorical rules and exceptions miss significant generalizations. In particular, they argue that an analysis that rules out consonant pairs categorically based on feature classes cannot simultaneously explain exceptions to the rule, and the low rate of occurrence of consonant pairs that do not violate the rule.

The table in (15) presents various feature class analyses, and their implications in terms of lexical statistics. Feature classes based only on very general features have large numbers of exceptions, like the 'Place only' class, which would rule out any word containing a consonant pair sharing place of articulation, such as [t] and [n]. More specific feature classes can reduce the number of exceptions, but combinations outside of these classes should co-occur freely. For example, in the 'Place & [son] & [cont]' class, combinations of [t], [n], and [s] should be found freely. If combinations outside of these classes co-occur freely, then an estimate of the number of combinations that should be found in the lexicon can be made based on the rate of co-occurrence of non-homorganic consonant combinations. Thus, for any particular definition of classes, all under-representation outside of those classes is unexplained. So, for example, while the 'Place & [son] & [cont]' co-occurrence classes have few exceptions (36), they also predict many combinations of consonants that should be found in the lexicon but are not (estimated 430.5).

(15) *Trade-off with the rule plus exceptions approach*

Definition of Classes	Exceptions	Unexplained Under-representation
Place only	816	–
Place & [son]	123	160.8
Place & [son] & [cont]	36	312.7
Enumerated pairs	–	430.5

In summary, it appears that statistical phonotactic dissimilation patterns in the lexicon are grounded in similarity, as the degree to which co-occurrence is avoided is straightforwardly reflected in the degree to which consonants are similar (Pierrehumbert 1993b, Frisch et al. 2004). These differences in degree of co-occurrence suggest that grammar itself includes probabilistic information. Otherwise, the grammar will either contain systematic exceptions, or be unable to explain systematic non-occurrence. The question of how to interface categorical and probabilistic patterns is raised below, but it appears to be one of the real challenges of contemporary linguistics.

16.6   Conclusion and issues for further research

Generative linguistics proposes to restrict the range of possible grammars in several ways by hypothesizing that speakers construct a grammar by selecting rules or constraint rankings from an inventory available in Universal Grammar (e.g., Chomsky & Halle 1968, Prince & Smolensky 2004). Universal Grammar (UG) accounts for parallels in the grammatical patterns of unrelated languages. UG also provides a limited set of possible grammars, and predicts that some linguistic patterns cannot occur because they cannot be described by one of the possible grammars. In the same way, UG can also explain why the same phonological patterns are seen in different domains of grammar. As mentioned in Section 16.4, dissimilation is observed in both segmental and suprasegmental phonology, and exhibited in both static lexical distributions and dynamic alternations. These different types of dissimilation can be unified in the grammar under certain guiding principles, like the OCP and parallel evaluation of markedness constraints.

The unification of facts about lexical distributions and facts about morpho-phonological alternations is desirable when it can be achieved, because the resulting theory of phonological competence is simpler than a theory that proposes distinct mechanisms. This is the analytical reasoning supporting the Duplication Problem. However, their unification rests on the conclusion that the patterns are indeed the same. There is growing evidence that phonotactic constraints, including dissimilation, can be gradient and statistical in nature, and that native speakers have very fine-tuned intuitions about phonotactic distributions. Since statistical dissimilation patterns in the lexicon can be learned and generalized probabilistically, based on lexical data, reference to specifically linguistic constraints or learning mechanisms is not necessary to account for them. (Though specifically linguistic representations of segments or other prosodic constituents are still necessary in any analysis, as these categories are the foundation upon which the statistics are computed.) Morpho-phonological processes, on the other hand, may be more readily captured by a non-statistical constraint-based analysis and may be more naturally encoded in specifically linguistic ways in a grammar. No case studies of dissimilation that we are aware of, however, have actually empirically examined the distribution of similar elements in the lexicon and the occurrence of phonological rules that resolve them in alternations. Thus, it is not clear at this time whether the two types of generalizations should be accounted for using the same mechanisms.

Though outside the domain of dissimilation, one study that shows that these two types of generalization should in fact be due to different mechanisms is Crosswhite et al. (2003). Based on a *wug*-test for stress (Berko 1958), this study showed that native speakers of Russian have a categorical rule assigning default stress to stem-final syllables in novel nouns. Examination of the lexical statistics of Russian noun stress, however, showed that, while stem-final stress is the most common pattern of stem stress, its rate of occurrence far undershoots the rate of stem-final stress in the experimental data: stem-final stress was assigned to 80–90% of all experimental items, but this pattern is observed in only 30–60% of stem-stressed nouns in the Russian lexicon (with a higher percentage for low frequency items). Stress assignment in the novel words, therefore, does not directly match lexical frequencies for stress, but could perhaps be derived from a more intelligent algorithm that works from statistically systematic patterns to derive categorical ones.

If it is indeed the case that the language learner acquires both statistical phonotactic patterns and categorical morpho-phonological patterns, then a significant challenge for this line of linguistic research lies in resolving how these different types of generalization interface with one another. The integration of statistical and symbolic generalizations has been at the core of phonetics–phonology interface research for many years, since at least the departure from the interface model of Pierrehumbert (1990). Within the generative community, considerable attention has been given to producing statistical outputs from variable rankings of categorical constraints in OT (Albright & Hayes 2003, Anttila 1997, Hayes 2000). Outside of the generative community, the approach has been to take the gradient and statistical patterns to be the norm, and to attempt to derive the categorical patterns through some type of abstraction or generalization over the statistical data (Bybee 2001, Pierrehumbert 2001, 2003b, Skousen 1989).

On the other hand, even if the two types of dissimilation might not be formally unified within the grammar, they could still be unified in their functional origin. For example, Ohala's hypercorrection model of dissimilation could be applied to either type of data, and the fact that one is statistical while the other is categorical may be derived from the difference in kind between statistical lexical distributions and symbolic morphophonological processes. The lexicon is a large database of relatively static forms, so statistical generalization over this database is a natural process. Morpho-phonological processes, on the other hand, are symbolically formalized within a limited inventory of phonological structures (e.g. features, segments, etc.), leading more naturally to categorical generalization. The difference in kind between inventory restrictions and phonological processes is not specific to dissimilation, and could be applied to other cases of phonological processes that have a potential functional motivation.

Finally, it is important to note that the probabilistic account crucially depends upon linguistic categories, as these are the categories over which probabilities are determined. In an exemplar model, for example, each instance in which a lexical item is encountered is a distinct item encoded in the model, as no two experiences with a lexical item are physically exactly identical. Without some degree of generalization, there are no groups of patterns over which to encode probabilities. Thus, even the most gradient and statistical model requires some sort of categorical underpinning to account for phonological generalizations.

Note

We thank Paul de Lacy, Scott Myers, Jaye Padgett, and Kie Zuraw for their insightful comments.

Part IV

Internal interfaces

17

The phonetics–phonology interface

John Kingston

17.1   Introduction

Phonetics interfaces with phonology in three ways. First, phonetics defines distinctive features. Second, phonetics explains many phonological patterns. These two interfaces constitute what has come to be called the 'substantive grounding' of phonology (Archangeli & Pulleyblank 1994). Finally, phonetics implements phonological representations.

The number and depth of these interfaces is so great that one is naturally moved to ask how autonomous phonetics and phonology are from one another and whether one can be largely reduced to the other. The answers to these questions in the current literature could not differ more. At one extreme, Ohala (1990b) argues that there is in fact no interface between phonetics and phonology because the latter can largely if not completely be reduced to the former. At the opposite extreme, Hale & Reiss (2000b) argue for excluding phonetics entirely from phonology because the latter is about computation, while the former is about something else. Between these extremes is a large variety of other answers to these questions, ranging from Blevins's (2004) claim that phonetics motivates sound change but does not otherwise regulate synchronic sound patterns to Browman & Goldstein's (1995) assertion that phonological representations are merely an assemblage of phonetic units of a grain coarse enough to be reliably categorized (see also Hayes 1999).

These examples aren't a comprehensive list of current points of view, nor do they represent the principal alternatives from which one might choose. They instead merely show that the field has reached no consensus about what the interface is, nor has it even agreed that one exists at all. The field therefore cannot agree about how distinctive features are defined, phonological patterns explained, or phonological representations implemented by the phonetics. The confident assertions about the three interfaces with which I began this paper are not self-evident truths to everyone, much less any particular phonetic definitions, explanations, or implementations.

These disagreements could be nothing more than the consequences of lacking the evidence needed to choose between competing hypotheses. But I think the disagreements reflect something more than the commonplace struggle between hypotheses. There is a broader and deeper dispute here about how one can reliably separate the phonetic from the phonological.

In this chapter, I lay out some of the difficulties one encounters in trying to answer this question for each of the three ways that phonetics interfaces with phonology: definition, explanation, and implementation. I do so by displaying some of the enormous richness of the interchange between phonetics and phonology. This richness is what forestalls any simple solution to the division of labor between these two components of the grammar. Nonetheless, where it is possible to do so, I show solutions – even incomplete ones – to the problem of dividing labor between phonetics and phonology. I have omitted many technical details in discussing the various cases presented in this chapter when doing so would not impair understanding or when they may be easily found in the sources that I cite.

The problem of defining distinctive features apparently can be solved by starting with the phonetics and working up to the phonology. Solving the problem of explaining phonological patterns is not so simple, because more than one force is at work even in apparently simple cases, these forces are phonological as well as phonetic, and finally they compete with one another. The phonological pattern that results represents the often delicate resolution of this competition. Finally, the problem of implementing phonological representations cannot be solved by simply reversing the solution to defining their constituents and working down from the phonology to a pronunciation or percept. Instead, the phonetic implementation also determines what kind of phonological representation is possible in the first place.

17.2   Definition

17.2.1   Resolving the variability problem

Phoneticians and phonologists have worked hard to define distinctive features phonetically. Landmarks in this effort are the acoustic-auditory definitions in *Preliminaries to Speech Analysis* (Jakobson, Fant, & Halle 1952), the articulatory alternatives in Chapter 7 of the *Sound Pattern of English* (Chomsky & Halle 1968), and most recently, the combined acoustic and articulatory definitions in *The Sounds of the World's Languages* (Ladefoged & Maddieson 1996) and *Acoustic Phonetics* (Stevens 1998). Distinctive features would be easy to define phonetically if some articulatory or acoustic property or properties could be observed every time a distinctive feature has a particular value in an utterance's phonological representation. Unfortunately, this is not the case. Rather than invariant phonetic realizations, distinctive feature values are realized differently in different languages, contexts, speaking styles, and even speakers (Kingston & Diehl 1994; cf. Stevens & Blumstein 1978; Sussman, McCaffrey, & Matthews 1991). How then can distinctive features be defined phonetically?

Some research suggests that distinctive feature values are in fact polymorphous, in that their phonetic realizations bear at best a family resemblance to one another (Kluender 1994; Kingston 2003). However, two recent approaches find invariance by stepping away from the detail of a particular utterance's phonetic realization. The approaches differ in the direction they recommend one should step away to find this invariance: Articulatory Phonology recommends one step back from the utterance's articulatory detail to the speaker's plan for the utterance (Browman & Goldstein 1995), while Auditorism instead recommends one step forward from the utterance's acoustic detail to the acoustic properties' auditory effects (Kingston & Diehl 1994, 1995; Kingston, Diehl, Kirk, & Castleman, in preparation). The two approaches resemble one another in finding invariance by moving to a description of the utterance with many fewer dimensions than are necessary to describe its articulatory or acoustic realization.

17.2.1.1 Articulatory Phonology

In Articulatory Phonology, an utterance is represented as a collection of *gestures*.[1] Gestures specify that the vocal tract be constricted at a particular location to a particular degree for a particular interval of time. As such, a gesture specifies the speaker's goal in the time interval during which the gesture is active, and this specification evokes the coordinated action of the various articulators whose movements achieve that goal. Because the gesture specifies the goal rather than the movements of individual articulators, an articulator can contribute different amounts to achieving that goal in different contexts. For example, the goal in [b], [p], or [m] is to close the lips, and the upper and lower lips and the jaw all move to accomplish this goal, but each moves differently depending on the neighboring vowel because the vowel's gestures are active at the same time as the lip closing gesture and they compete for control over these articulators (Sussman, MacNeilage, & Hanson 1973; Macchi 1988). This competition is resolved by the *task dynamics*, which calculates articulator movements by resolving the demands imposed by all the gestures that are active at any moment in time. The different combinations of upper and low lip and jaw movement that contribute to closing the lips next to different vowels are *motor equivalent*, because they all succeed in achieving that goal. The gesture that specifies that goal in the first place is then the desired step back from the variable realization of that goal by the different combinations of individual articulator movements to the invariant specification of the goal itself.[2]

17.2.1.2 Auditorism

Auditorism finds invariance in the listener's percepts rather than the speaker's goals. Just as the individual articulators' movements vary, so too do their acoustic consequences. Listeners could therefore perceive each token as a different value, yet they don't do so. They don't because different arrays of acoustic properties are perceptually equivalent to one another. For example, a stop with a relatively short delay in voice onset time (VOT) following its release and a relatively high onset frequency for the first formant (F1) of the following vowel is equally likely to be perceived by an English speaker as [+voice] as one with a relatively longer VOT and a relatively lower F1 onset frequency (Lisker 1975; Summerfield & Haggard 1977; Kluender 1991; Benkí 2001). Kingston, et al. (in preparation) argue that acoustic properties can be perceptually equivalent like this when their auditory effects are similar enough that they integrate perceptually with one another (see also Kingston & Diehl 1994, 1995; Kingston & Macmillan 1995; Kingston, Macmillan, Walsh Dickey, Thorburn, & Bartels 1997; Macmillan, Kingston, Thorburn, Walsh Dickey, & Bartels 1999). In the example, a shorter delay in voice onset and a lower F1 onset frequency both create the percept that low frequency energy occurs near the stop release.

Perceptual equivalence could arise from a source other than the auditory similarity of acoustic properties. The properties could be perceptually equivalent simply because listeners have experienced them covarying reliably (see Holt, Lotto, & Kluender 2001): stops with shorter voice onset delays usually have lower F1 onset frequencies, too. However, Kingston, et al. (in preparation, also Kingston & Diehl 1995) obtained the same responses from listeners to non-speech analogues in which acoustic properties are manipulated in the same way as in the speech signals. Because these stimuli aren't recognized as speech, they should not evoke the listeners' experience with the reliable covariation of acoustic properties in the speech signals they mimic. Listeners should only respond in the same way to the non-speech analogues if their acoustic properties are auditorily similar enough to integrate perceptually. Moreover, if speech sounds are to contrast reliably with one another, speakers may be enjoined to produce articulations whose acoustic correlates integrate perceptually with one another.

Perceptual integration thus achieves the same result as the motor equivalence embodied in gestures: a variable, high-dimensional description is reduced to an invariant, low-dimensional one whose units correspond to the contrastive units of which phonological representations are composed. Distinctive features may therefore emerge out of humans' speaking or listening behavior, i.e. either out of the motor equivalence of different combinations of articulations or out of the perceptual integration of different combinations of acoustic properties. If this is correct, then distinctive features can be obtained without the phonological component of the grammar having to impose formal constraints requiring structural symmetry such as those argued for by Hayes (1999). At a gestural or auditory level of description, much of the phonetic particularity that phonological constraints typically ignore has already been lost.

17.2.2   Articulatory or auditory targets?

We are burdened here with an embarrassment of riches, two ways of getting distinctive features to emerge out of the phonetics. Is there any reason to decide that speakers' targets are articulatory or auditory? Speakers' compensation for artificial perturbations of articulations and natural covariation between articulations suggests that their targets are auditory rather than articulatory.

As long as the perturbations of articulations are not too extreme, speakers immediately and successfully compensate for them. For example, when the jaw is prevented from moving by a bite block between the molars, speakers still constrict the vocal tract in the same locations and to the same degree in producing vowels, and the vowels differ very little acoustically from those produced without the bite block (Lindblom, Lubker, & Gay 1979; Fowler & Turvey 1980; Kelso & Tuller 1983).[3] Similarly, if a light load is randomly and infrequently applied to the lower lip at the moment when a bilabial closure is initiated, the speaker exerts more force to lower the upper lip more as well as to overcome the load on the lower lip, and the closure is achieved (Abbs, Gracco, & Cole 1984). Both results demonstrate that different combinations of articulations are motor equivalent, and they suggest that speakers' targets are local constrictions of the vocal tract, as are Articulatory Phonology's gestures.

Other results, however, suggest that speakers' targets are global configurations of the vocal tract. For example, when the upper lip is prevented from protruding in a rounded vowel, speakers compensate by lowering their larynges more (Riordan 1977). As speakers lower their larynges anyway in pronouncing rounded vowels (Lindblom & Sundberg 1971), this additional lowering simply exaggerates an articulatory movement they already make. This finding suggests that the speakers' target is a long resonating cavity rather than a local constriction at the lips. A similar effort to keep resonator length constant can be observed in unperturbed pronunciations of American English [u] and [ʃ], where lip protrusion trades off with tongue backing from token to token (Perkell, Matthies, Svirsky, & Jordan 1993; Perkell, Matthies, & Zandipour 1998).

All these results can also be interpreted as evidence that the speaker is trying to produce a particular acoustic or auditory effect. Variation in lingual articulations of American English [ɹ] provides further evidence that the speaker's target is auditory: speakers use the more efficient bunched articulation after lingual consonants and a retroflexed articulation elsewhere (Guenther, Espy-Wilson, Boyce, Matthies, Zandipour, & Perkell 1999; cf. earlier studies suggesting this is variation between speakers: Delattre & Freeman 1968; Westbury, Hashi, & Lindstrom 1998; Alwan, Narayanan, & Haker 1997). [ɹ] can be pronounced in both ways because they both lower F3 extremely. Bunching produces a long constriction on the palate where F3 has a velocity maximum, and retroflexing creates a large sublingual cavity from which a low F3 arises. Neither the local constriction nor the global configuration of the vocal tract is the same in these two articulations.

The most compelling evidence that speakers' targets are auditory rather than articulatory comes from studies in which auditory feedback about the sound is perturbed rather than its articulation (Houde & Jordan 1998, 2002; Jones & Munhall 2002, 2003). Houde & Jordan (1998, 2002) gradually altered auditory feedback to listeners such that the vowel [ɛ] in *pep* came to sound increasingly like the higher vowel [i]. In response, speakers shifted their articulations of [ɛ] toward the lower vowels [æ] or [a], undoing the alteration. Speakers also compensated by shifting their articulations on trials where the feedback about *pep* was replaced by noise. They did so, too, in pronouncing [ɛ] in words other than *pep*, and for other vowels, even though feedback wasn't altered for [ɛ] other than in *pep* or for other vowels. These other shifts show that speakers have auditory rather than articulatory targets, and that these targets are determined in relation to the auditory targets of other sounds in the same class.

All these results are compatible with the hypothesis that speakers' targets are auditory rather than articulatory, while only some of them are compatible with the opposing hypothesis. They thus suggest that the invariants from which distinctive features emerge are the auditorily similar effects of covarying acoustic properties and not the motor equivalences of different combinations of articulations.

17.3   Explanation

17.3.1   Introduction

Phonetic explanations of phonological patterns are built from physical, physiological, and/or psychological properties of speaking and listening. For example, /g/ is missing in Dutch and Thai but not /b/ or /d/ because it is much harder to keep air flowing up through the glottis when the stop closure is velar rather than bilabial or alveolar (Ohala 1976; Javkin 1977). Stops intrude between nasals or laterals and following fricatives in many American English speakers' pronunciations of words such as *warm[p]th*, *prin[t]ce*, *leng[k]th*, and *el[t]se* because voicing ceases and in the case of the nasal–fricative sequences the soft palate rises before the oral articulators move to the fricative configuration (Ohala 1971, 1974, 1981). The velar stop [k] palatalizes to [kʲ] before [i] because the consonant coarticulates with the vowel, and it eventually affricates to [tʃ] because [kʲ] is auditorily similar to [tʃ] (Plauché, Delogu, & Ohala 1997; Guion 1998; Chang, Plauché, & Ohala 2001).

Although all of these phonological patterns are peculiar to particular speech communities or even individuals (many languages have /g/ as well as /b, d/; stops don't intrude between nasals or laterals and fricatives in South African English (Fourakis & Port 1986), and [k] often remains unpalatalized and unaffricated despite coarticulating with [i]), they recur in unrelated speech communities, and they are phonetically possible in all speech communities. They recur and are always phonetically possible because all humans who aren't suffering from some speech or hearing pathology possess essentially the same apparatus for speaking and listening. Indeed, as Ohala has repeatedly shown, these and many other phonological patterns can be reproduced in the laboratory with speakers and listeners whose languages don't (yet) exhibit them. Explanations of this kind are highly valued because they are built on generalizations of properties that can be observed any time the affected sound or sounds are uttered or heard, and they are in many instances built on generalizations of properties that can be observed in other domains than speaking and listening. This section illustrates how such explanations are constructed for languages' synchronic sound inventories and for the diachronic changes they undergo.

17.3.2   Explaining inventory content
17.3.2.1   Introduction
There is considerable evidence that the contents of segment inventories can be explained phonetically. Languages have the oral, nasal, and reduced vowels they do because vowels must be dispersed perceptually in the vowel space, certain vowel qualities are more salient than others, and a long vowel duration makes it possible for a listener to hear nasalization while a short duration prevents the speaker from reaching a low target. These factors don't completely explain the contents of these inventories, but they will form a part of any eventual complete explanations. The lesson is that the contents of segment inventories, even apparently compact subsets of inventories such as these, are determined by many more than just one factor. These factors may conflict with one another, and a balance must be struck between them when they do.

17.3.2.2   Oral vowels: the facts to be explained
Languages' vowel inventories resemble one another closely. This section begins by describing these resemblances among the oral vowel inventories in the areally and genetically balanced database of 451 languages in the UCLA Phonological Segment Inventory Database (UPSID, Maddieson & Precoda 1992). Liljencrantz & Lindblom (1972) and subsequent work by Lindblom (1986) established that two factors contribute to these resemblances: the vowel space is limited[4] and vowels mutually repel one another within that space. Following up proposals in Stevens (1989), Schwartz, Boë, Vallée, & Abry (1997a,1997b) added a third factor: languages prefer vowels that are made salient by the close proximity of two of their formants, an effect called 'focalization'. These forces successfully predict that inventories of certain sizes are preferred over both smaller and larger ones but fall short in predicting which vowels are most likely to occur in an inventory of a given size.[5]

The short and long oral vowels were extracted from each of the 451 languages in UPSID. All secondary articulations were stripped off, and the

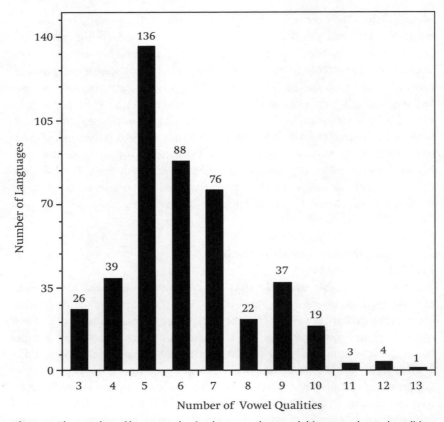

Figure 1: The number of languages having between three and thirteen oral vowel qualities, based on the short and long oral vowel inventories in UPSID.

distinct short and long vowel qualities were counted. If a language's long vowels distinguished more qualities, their number was used to represent how many vowels that language had; otherwise, the number of distinct short vowel qualities was used.[6]

The smallest number of distinct vowel qualities was three and the largest number thirteen. The histogram in Figure 1 shows how many languages have each number of vowels within these two extremes.

There is a very clear mode at five vowels, which are found in 136 languages. Even though many languages have either six or seven vowels, only about 65% as many have six vowels as have five vowels and only about 56% as many have seven.

Fully two-thirds of the languages in the sample (300/451) have the three most common numbers of vowels: five, six, and seven. The strength of this preference is emphasized by how few languages have four or eight vowels: in each instance just under 29% as many languages as have five or seven vowels, respectively. A surprisingly large number of languages have nine, substantially more than have eight.

17.3.2.3 Peripheral vs. central vowels

Aside from these preferences for a certain number of vowels, the remaining facts to be explained are the preferred arrangements of vowels in the vowel space for inventories of different sizes. The 45 oral vowel qualities distinguished in UPSID were divided into 15 *peripheral* vowels and 29 *central* qualities: [i u ɪ ʊ e̞ o̞ e o ɛ ɔ æ a̠ a ɑ ɒ] vs. [y ɯ ʏ ɰ ø̞ ɤ̞ ø̞> ɤ< e̞> o̞< ø ɤ e> o< œ ʌ Œ ɨ ʉ ɨ ʉ ə̞ ə̞ ə ɘ ɜ ɞ ɐ ɐ>]. The symbols < and > indicate advanced and retracted pronunciations, respectively.

At the top of the vowel space, only [i] and [u] are peripheral. For non-low peripheral vowels, the tongue body is either as far forward or backward as possible, and the lips are unrounded if the tongue is front, but rounded if the tongue is back. In low peripheral vowels, the tongue is as low as it can get. This cluster of properties shows that peripheral vowels are actually defined acoustically rather than articulatorily: if non-low, they have the highest or lowest F2 and F3 frequency values for their tongue height, or if low, they have the highest F1 frequency values. Central vowels include those articulated with the tongue body in a central position as well as vowels in which the tongue body is fully front or back, but the lips are rounded when the tongue is front or unrounded when it's back. This definition is also acoustic rather than articulatory in that F2 and F3 frequencies are neither lowered nor raised particularly when the tongue body is central or when the lips are rounded in front vowels or unrounded in back ones. Thus, peripheral vowels are acoustically farther apart from one another in the vowel space than central vowels.[7]

Following Schwartz, et al. (1997a), the vowel inventories for each of the languages with from three to ten vowels were then classified into patterns by how many peripheral and central vowels they have – the 8 languages with more than 10 vowels are ignored in the rest of this discussion. A pattern is identified by a 'P(eripheral)+C(entral)' formula. The results are shown in Figure 2, where each panel corresponds to a number of vowels, and the bar heights indicate the proportion of languages with that many vowels which have a particular pattern.[8]

In the vast majority of five-vowel languages, all five vowels are peripheral (Figure 2c). In all but three of the 127 languages with this 5+0 pattern, front unrounded and back rounded high and mid vowels contrast and there is one low vowel. The remaining 9 languages have four peripheral vowels and one central vowel, the 4+1 pattern.

Figure 2d shows that the most common pattern among six-vowel languages is 5+1, which occurs in 64 languages. It is distantly followed by 6+0, at just a third of the 5+1's pattern's frequency, in 22 languages.

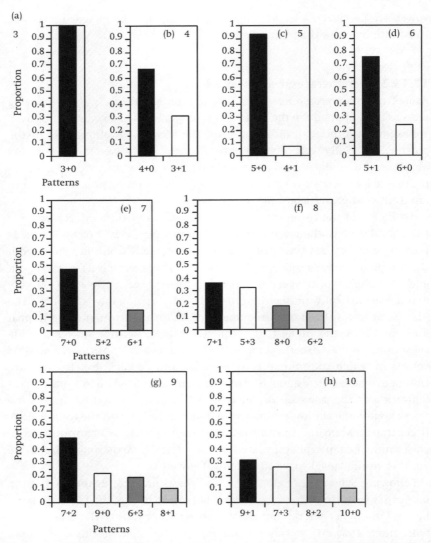

Figure 2: Proportions of languages with from three to ten vowels that exhibit particular common patterns of peripheral and central vowels for languages. Some proportions don't add up to 1 because patterns aren't shown that appear in only a very few languages or that can't be classified as one of these patterns.

Two patterns are common among the seven-vowel languages (Figure 2e), 7+0 in 36 languages and 5+2 in 28. The most common 7+0 inventory adds a height distinction between mid vowels to the 5+0 pattern, distinguishing /i, ẹ, ɛ, a, ɔ, ọ, u/. Languages with five peripheral vowels and two central vowels are much less common than those with five peripheral vowels and just one central vowel, 28 vs. 64. A dozen languages have the third most common pattern among the seven-vowel languages, 6+1.

The large proportion of languages with the 5+1 and 5+2 patterns shows that many languages with six or seven vowels have 'added' central vowels to the very popular 5+0 peripheral vowel inventory.[9] The heights and other properties of the central vowels in these languages are unpredictable from what peripheral vowels they have, which suggests that central and peripheral inventories are independent of one another.

The other way to increase inventory size is to add one or two peripheral vowels. Adding central vowels doesn't change the distribution of peripheral vowels, but adding one peripheral mid vowel, in either the front or the back, usually entails adding the other at the same height, as well as shifting the existing mid vowel's height to equalize the intervals between vowels of different heights.

All 26 languages with just three vowels have the 3+0 pattern (Figure 2a).[10] 22 of them are missing the two mid vowels that occur in the 5+0 pattern, while just 4 are missing one or both high vowels. The 39 languages with four vowels divide unevenly into 24 with four peripheral qualities and 14 with three peripheral qualities and one central quality – the remaining four-vowel inventory /i, ɜ, a, ɒ/ is unclassifiable (Figure 2b).

Turning now to the languages with more than seven vowels, Figures 2f–h show that the most common patterns have odd numbers of peripheral vowels: five, seven, or even nine. An odd number of peripheral vowels occurs in 13 of the 22 languages with eight vowels (8 with 7+1, 5 with 5+3), in 28 of the 37 languages with nine vowels (19 with 7+2, 9 with 9+0), and 11 of the 19 languages with ten vowels (6 with 9+1 and 5 with 7+3). More often than not, the peripheral vowels in larger inventories also symmetrically contrast front unrounded with back rounded vowels at all non-low heights.

In summary, the most common vowel patterns contrast front unrounded with back rounded peripheral vowels at all but the lowest height, where only a single vowel is found. Larger vowel inventories differ from smaller ones in two ways: they may have central vowels that are absent in the smaller inventories and/or they may have more contrasts between the high and low peripheral extremes. The most common inventory by far is the 5+0 pattern. The next smallest inventory is more likely to have lost one of the mid vowels, producing the 4+0 pattern in 24 languages, than to lose both and add one central vowel, producing the 3+1 pattern in only 14 languages. It's far more likely that a language will add one central vowel than one peripheral vowel (64 languages with 5+1 vs. just 22 with 6+0). However, when two or more vowels are added to 5+0, it is far more likely that a single front:back pair will be added before any other vowels: 7+0 > 5+2, 7+1 > 5+3, 7+2 > 9+0, and the 7+3 occurs in nearly as many languages as 9+1. Once this additional pair of peripheral vowels is added, any more vowels are likely to be central.

17.3.2.4 The explanation

Why are certain total numbers of vowels and particular patterns within each total number preferred over others? Liljencrantz & Lindblom (1972) and Lindblom (1986) showed that five to seven vowels are preferred over fewer or more vowels because these numbers of vowels divide the vowel space efficiently. Fewer vowels than five are dispreferred because the space can be divided more finely without crowding the vowels so close together that they're likely to be confused, while more vowels than seven are dispreferred because above that number the vowels *are* crowded too closely together. This outcome would be obtained if vowels are required to contrast or disperse sufficiently but not maximally within the limits of the vowel space. Up to a point, height contrasts can multiply among the peripheral vowels without the vowels coming too close together, but central vowels are resorted to when a vowel inventory gets so large that a yet finer division of the height continuum among the peripheral vowels pulls adjacent vowels below the threshold for sufficient contrast.

These are all functional explanations. On the one hand, if a vowel inventory is too small, more consonants or longer strings of segments will have to be used to create distinct messages (see also Flemming 2001, 2004). On the other hand, if an inventory is too large or its members are acoustically too close to one another, then distinct messages will be confused with one another.

Other kinds of explanations can also be imagined. For example, a language may prefer to have a back rounded vowel for every front unrounded non-low vowel it has because languages prefer symmetry. This alternative is not implausible because symmetry is not in this instance an abstract, geometric property of a vowel inventory but instead a requirement that a language efficiently use all the possible combinations of distinctive feature values (Ohala 1980; Clements 2003). If a language has a front unrounded vowel of height *n* and it also has a back rounded vowel at that height, then it combines height *n* with both [−back] and [+back] rather than with just one value of this feature. This, too, is plainly a kind of functional explanation, but one concerned with making maximal use of the available resources for contrast between messages rather than with the distinctness of messages.

Sufficient contrast or dispersion is a property of an entire vowel inventory. The sum of the auditory distances between all pairs of vowels is calculated, and then the reciprocal is taken of this sum. The resulting value is larger when the vowels are crowded together in an inventory, so it reflects the energy with which the vowels mutually repel one another, the 'dispersion energy'.

Some vowel qualities, e.g. /i/, occur so often, in inventories of different sizes and compositions, that they appear to be favored *intrinsically* and not just for their auditory distance from other vowels. These vowels may be special because two of their formants are so close in frequency that they merge auditorily into a single, relatively narrow yet intense spectral prominence. Formant frequencies converge when an articulatory change switches the resonating cavities adjacent formants come from (Stevens 1989). The

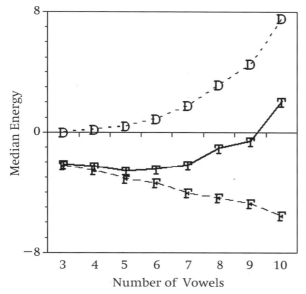

Figure 3: Median focalization energy (F), dispersion energy (D), and total energy (T) for languages with from three to ten vowels.

resulting 'focalization' of acoustic energy makes these vowels more salient than acoustically similar vowels whose formants are farther apart (Schwartz, et al. 1997b). Focalization values are calculated for each vowel as a function of how close adjacent formants are to one another, these values are then summed, and the reciprocal of this sum is taken. The resulting 'focalization energy' is larger for languages with fewer focal vowels. (See Schwartz, et al. 1997b, for the algorithms for calculating these energies.)

The hypothesis tested here is that both dispersion and focalization energies and their sum 'total energy' are larger for less favored inventories. Figure 3 shows median focalization, dispersion, and total energy (F, D, and T) for vowel inventories with from three to ten vowels.[11]

Unsurprisingly, dispersion energy grows with the number of vowels. Inventories with more vowels also include more in which two formants are close together, and focalization energy drops steadily as the number of vowels increases. Up to seven vowels, this steady drop in focalization energy offsets the growth in dispersion energy, and total energy remains relatively unchanged. Indeed, focalization energy drops more than dispersion energy grows between four and five vowels, and total energy is thus somewhat lower in a typical five- than four-vowel inventory, which may contribute to five vowels being more popular than four. Total energy then grows only modestly from five to seven vowels. However, as the number of vowels in an inventory increases beyond seven, dispersion energy grows much faster than focalization energy drops, and total energy climbs with increasing steepness. This jump in crowdedness probably explains the markedly lower frequency of languages with eight or more vowels compared to seven or fewer. Total energy also grows less steeply between eight and nine vowels than between seven and eight or nine and ten vowels, which may partly explain why nine-vowel inventories are surprisingly popular: they contain more vowels which are made salient by the closeness in frequency of adjacent formants but which are not crowded excessively closely together. (Languages with fewer than five vowels are probably less frequent for a very different reason: they under-use the capacity of the vowel space to distinguish messages reliably from one another.)

The minima and maxima for focalization (F), dispersion (D), and total energy (T) are shown together with the medians in Figure 4 for inventories of different sizes and compositions.

For inventories of four to seven vowels (Figures 4a–e), the more popular patterns aren't noticeably less energetic. The maximum dispersion and total energies are smaller for the more popular 5+1 pattern than the less popular 6+0 pattern (Figure 4d). However, the median for the 6+0 pattern also lies very close to the minimum, which shows that very few languages with the less popular pattern have the higher energy versions of this pattern. Moreover, energy values differ very little between the wildly popular 5+0 pattern and the decidedly unpopular 4+1 pattern (Figure 4c), and they differ equally little between the 4+0 vs. 3+1 and 7+0 or 5+2 vs. 6+1 patterns, despite their marked differences in popularity (Figures 4b,e). Energies are also not uniformly lower for the more popular patterns in languages with from eight to ten vowels (Figures 4f–h).

To see if some relationship might nonetheless be hidden in the data, the proportions with which each pattern occurred were correlated with the median focalization, dispersion, and total energies for vowel inventories containing four to ten vowels. If the more popular inventories have lower energies, then all these correlations should be negative. The correlations were significantly negative for dispersion and total energies (dispersion $r(21) = -0.472, p = 0.031$; total $r(18) = -0.447, p = 0.042$; two-tailed), but, curiously, significantly positive for focalization energy ($r(21) = 0.455, p = 0.038$). This correlation turns out positive because focalization energy drops as inventory size increases, and larger inventories are divided into more patterns, each making up a smaller proportion of the total than do the fewer divisions of smaller inventories. The correlations with dispersion or total energy are also influenced by this artifact, but it's hidden in their case because it works in the same direction as the prediction. Accordingly, the correlations were recalculated using only the proportions of the most popular pattern for each inventory size. The results are quite similar: the most popular patterns' proportions correlate negatively with dispersion and total energies (dispersion $r(7) = -0.741, p = 0.056$; total $r(7) = -0.752$, $p = 0.051$) and positively with focalization energy ($r(7) = 0.777, p = 0.040$), except that the correlations with dispersion and total energy are now only

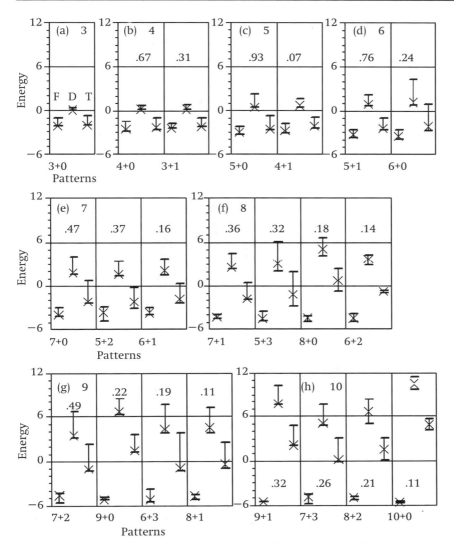

Figure 4: Minimum (bottom whisker), median (X), and maximum (top whisker) values of focalization (F, left), dispersion (D, middle), and total energies (T, right) for inventories of three to ten vowels, broken down by pattern. The arrangement matches that in Figure 2. The numbers in each division of a panel are the proportions of languages with that inventory pattern; they correspond to the values that are displayed graphically in Figure 2.

marginally significant. These correlations show that the more popular patterns are less energetic but also that the energy differences between them and the less popular inventories aren't enormous.

In summary, the popularity of five to seven vowels is well explained by the combined effects of dispersion and focalization energy, but energy differences explain little about why certain patterns are preferred within inventories of a given size.

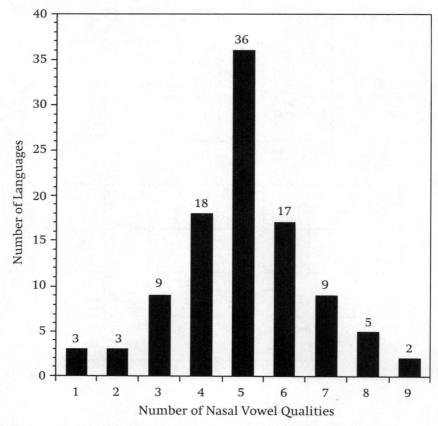

Figure 5: Number of languages with between one and nine nasal vowels.

17.3.2.5   Nasal vowels

Nasalization is the only property other than length that distinguishes vowels of the same quality in more than a very few languages. 102 nasal vowel inventories were extracted from UPSID in exactly the same way as the oral inventories. Nasal inventories are structured much like oral inventories, except they're often smaller. Figure 5 shows that languages have fewer nasal than oral vowels: one more language has three or four nasal vowels than has six or seven, 6 languages have fewer than three nasal vowels, and no languages have more than nine (cf. Figure 1).

Nasal vowels never occur in an inventory without oral vowels. Though their presence unequivocally implies the presence of oral vowels, is the size and composition of a language's nasal inventory otherwise related to its oral inventory?

Taking up size first, a little over half the languages with nasal vowels, 53 of 102, have fewer nasal than oral vowels in their inventories, and none have more nasal than oral vowels. The languages with fewer nasal than oral vowels have on average 2–3 fewer,[12] and some as many as 6 fewer.

What vowels are missing in the nasal inventories that are found in the corresponding oral inventories? In two languages, Zoque and Cherokee, all the oral vowel qualities are missing from the nasal inventories, which each consist of a single central nasal vowel. Otherwise, one or more mid nasal vowels are missing in 41 languages ("gutless" inventories), one or more high nasal vowels are missing in 20 languages ("headless"), and one or more low nasal vowels are missing in just 6 languages ("footless").[13] Senadi exemplifies the gutless type, with oral /i e̞ ɛ a ɔ o̞ u/ vs. nasal /ĩ ɛ̃ ã ɔ̃ ũ/, Amuzgo is headless, with oral /i e æ a ɒ o u/ vs. nasal /ẽ æ̃ ã ɒ̃ õ/, and Chatino shows what the rare footless type is like, with oral /i e a o u/ vs. nasal /ĩ ẽ õ ũ/. Some languages lack nasal counterparts to their oral vowels at more than one these three height divisions: of the 6 footless languages, 2 are also headless, 1 is also gutless, and 1 is also headless and gutless, while 12 of the 20 headless languages are also gutless. In short, nasalization reduces height contrasts, and it does so most often by eliminating mid vowels.

Why should it do so? The answer lies in the perceptual consequences of acoustically coupling the nasal to the oral cavity. Coupling adds pairs of poles and zeroes to the poles produced in the oral cavity. The lowest nasal pole (N1) and zero (Z1) occur close to the lowest oral pole (F1) and change both the center of gravity and the bandwidth of this lowest spectral prominence.

N1 is below F1 when the F1 is high and lowers the prominence's center of gravity, but N1 is above F1 when F1 is low, and raises the prominence's center of gravity. Z1 is just above N1. When N1 is below F1, Z1 is likely to coincide with F1 and attenuate it. This attenuation also lowers the center of gravity of the lowest spectral prominence. When both N1 and Z1 are above F1, the center of gravity is instead likely to be raised. Lowering the center of gravity makes the vowel sound higher, raising it makes the vowel sound lower. Headless inventories such as Amuzgo's may be more common than footless inventories such as Chatino's because adding N1 and Z1 more often raises than lowers the lowest spectral prominence's center of gravity.

N1 and Z1 also increase the bandwidth of this lowest spectral prominence, which may make the vowel sound lower. What's probably more important perceptually is that a broader bandwidth makes it harder to detect this prominence's center of gravity and thus to determine the vowel's height. Gutless nasal inventories such as Senadi's may be most common simply because fine distinctions in height between mid vowels or between mid and high or low vowels are made very hard to detect by this bandwidth increase. The perceived centers of gravity differ enough between the remaining high and low vowels that they're preserved. (See also Wright 1986 where it's shown that nasal vowels are perceptually closer to one another than their oral counterparts.)

Perceptual results reported in Kingston (1991), Kingston & Macmillan (1995), and Macmillan, et al. (1999) add to the explanation of gutless inventories' greater frequency. Listeners in these studies identified and discriminated vowels in which vowel height and nasalization were manipulated independently. They were more likely to identify a vowel as high when it was more nasalized, and more likely to identify a vowel as oral when it was lower. Listeners were also consistently better at discriminating a higher, more nasalized vowel from a lower, less nasalized one than at discriminating a higher, less nasalized vowel from a lower, more nasalized one.[14] Both results show that height and nasalization integrate perceptually, and their integration disfavors intermediate percepts for both height and nasalization.

The perceptual integration of nasalization and height predicts incorrectly that low nasal vowels should often denasalize because a lower vowel is more likely to be identified as oral. Two factors keep low vowels nasalized. First, the soft palate is actually permitted to lower more in lower nasalized vowels (Clumeck 1976; Bell-Berti, Baer, Harris, & Niimi 1979; Al-Bamerni 1983; Henderson 1984) and is actively kept high in higher vowels by contracting the levator palatini and relaxing the palatoglossus (Moll & Shriner 1967; Lubker 1968; Fritzell 1969; Lubker, Fritzell, & Lindqvist 1970; Bell-Berti 1976; Kuehn, Folkins, & Cutting 1982; Henderson 1984). Second, low vowels are longer than higher vowels, apparently because the jaw must lower more (Lehiste 1970; Westbury & Keating 1980), and even light nasalization is easier to detect when the vowel lasts longer (Whalen & Beddor 1989; Hajek 1997). Indeed, nasal vowels of a given height are often longer than the corresponding oral vowels (Whalen & Beddor 1989). Whether a low vowel lasts longer merely because the jaw moves slowly or it is also deliberately prolonged, its greater duration compensates for its height's reducing the perceptibility of nasalization.

Once again, competing factors trade off, delicately: the broadening of the lowest spectral prominence's bandwidth obscures its center of gravity, the integration of vowel height with nasalization discourages mid percepts, while the lower soft palate and greater duration of low vowels ensures they remain nasalized. The next section portrays the consequences for the contents of reduced vowel inventories of having to shorten a vowel. Rather than dispersing vowels in terms of height, shortening compresses them upward.

17.3.2.6 Vowel reduction

In many languages, fewer vowels contrast in unstressed than stressed syllables. The proper characterization of unstressed vowel reduction has raised fundamental questions about how the phonetics influences phonology. At least three proposals can be distinguished in the recent literature, Crosswhite's (2001, 2004), Barnes's (2002), and Flemming's (2001, 2004, submitted). The proposals agree that vowel contrasts are reduced in unstressed syllables because these syllables are shorter than stressed syllables, but they disagree as to how.

Crosswhite distinguishes contrast-enhancing reduction, in Italian (1a) and immediately pre-tonic syllables in Standard Russian (1b), from prominence-reducing reduction, in (Eastern)[15] Bulgarian (1c) and all other unstressed syllables in Standard Russian (1d). Each chart shows the vowels in stressed syllables (except see note in (1d)) and the arrows indicate what they reduce to when they are unstressed (1a,c), or in Russian immediately pretonic (1b) vs. all other positions (1d).

(1)

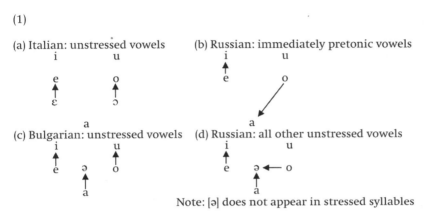

(a) Italian: unstressed vowels   (b) Russian: immediately pretonic vowels

(c) Bulgarian: unstressed vowels (d) Russian: all other unstressed vowels

Note: [ə] does not appear in stressed syllables

Contrasts are enhanced by reduction in Italian and in immediately pretonic syllables in Standard Russian because the neutralization of height contrasts involving mid vowels leaves the remaining contrasting vowels farther apart. Contrasts are enhanced in unstressed syllables because their short duration makes it hard to maintain small differences in vowel height, particularly for vowels that aren't at the corners of the vowel space. Crosswhite formalizes this result as a phonological constraint licensing short vowels only at extreme heights.

Prominence is reduced in Bulgarian and in all other unstressed syllables in Standard Russian because the low vowel is raised, in both cases to a mid central unrounded vowel with the quality of [ə]. Raising lowers the vowel's F1 and shortens it – higher vowels are shorter than lower ones (Lehiste 1970). Both these changes reduce the vowel's overall intensity and presumably its prominence; in doing so, they make the vowel more compatible with its prosodically weak position. The shorter duration of unstressed syllables is the effect of reduction when prominence is reduced rather than its cause, as when contrasts are enhanced. Crosswhite formalizes this compatibility requirement in a scale that values higher vowels in unstressed syllables more than lower ones.

Because the high vowels remain unchanged and mid vowels rise in both kinds of reduction, they are distinguished by whether the low vowel remains low – contrast-enhancing – or is raised – prominence-reducing.

Crosswhite's analyses of both kinds are explicitly functional: contrast-enhancing reduction maintains only the vowel height contrasts whose members can be reliably distinguished in the short span of an unstressed syllable, and prominence-reducing reduction ensures that unstressed syllables aren't so prominent that they're mistaken for stressed ones. This functionalism is, moreover, built explicitly into the phonological formalizations.

Neither Barnes (2002) nor Flemming (2001, 2004, submitted) distinguishes between two kinds of reduction, and both treat the shortening of unstressed vowels as reduction's *primum mobile*. Both rely on Lindblom's (1963) finding that the F1 frequencies of Swedish non-high vowels decrease with vowel duration, because speakers undershoot the non-high vowel height targets when there's too little time to reach them. Shortening causes undershoot because speakers don't speed up articulatory movements, particularly of the massive jaw,[16] to reach those targets in the time available. The result is that all the non-high vowels are raised, compressing the vowel space upward from bottom. This outcome resembles Crosswhite's prominence-reducing reduction but both reverses its *explicanda* and *explicandum* and loses its functional motivation. Instead of speakers raising a vowel to lower its F1's frequency, shorten it, and thereby reduce its intensity and prominence, the vowel is raised, more or less automatically, because it's shortened.

Both Barnes and Flemming also argue that there may be no contrast-enhancing reduction. They cite instrumental studies of Italian (Farnetani & Vayra 1991; Albano Leoni, Caputo, Cerrato, Cutugno, Maturi, & Savy 1995) which show that in unstressed syllables the low vowel [a] is realized with a considerably lower F1 frequency, i.e. as a higher vowel, perhaps [ɐ]. For Standard Russian, Barnes shows that the low vowel produced by reduction in immediately pre-tonic syllables does not have a categorically different quality from that produced in other unstressed syllables. Instead, that vowel remains long enough that speakers have the time needed to lower the jaw and tongue and raise F1's frequency to a value that sounds like [a]. Reduced low vowels in other unstressed syllables are usually shorter and this target is often undershot as a result. Thus, in both Italian and Standard Russian, the phonetic evidence indicates that the low vowel is raised when reduced, as in so-called prominence-reducing reduction, rather than remaining low as would be expected if reduction were contrast-enhancing.

Here, Barnes and Flemming part ways. Barnes argues that the undershooting that occurs when a vowel is shortened in an unstressed syllable can be phonologized, as categorical alternations between the vowel qualities in stressed syllables and the higher vowel qualities heard in unstressed ones. Once phonologization occurs, reduction is no longer governed by the phonetic constraints that originally motivated it, and the vowels that participate in the alternation may freely undergo further sound changes (see the end of Section 17.3.3.2 below for discussion of this claim).

Unlike Barnes, Flemming does build the phonetic motivation for vowel reduction into his phonological account. He uses constraints on what contrasts may occur in a language in place of Crosswhite's licensing or markedness constraints limiting the circumstances in which individual segments may occur. Two kinds of constraints regulate contrasts: the first requires that contrasting sounds be some minimal distance apart within the phonetic space occupied by the sounds (MINDIST=n) and the second requires that the number of contrasts be maximized (MAXCON). These constraints obviously conflict with one another, as requiring that contrasting sounds be far apart limits the number of possible contrasts, while requiring a large number of contrasts forces contrasting sounds close together. This conflict is resolved by ranking the contrast maximization constraint relative to the minimal distance constraints.

Imagine the range of vowel heights is divided into seven, equally spaced heights: (1) high [i u], (2) lowered high [ɪ ʊ], (3) raised mid [e̝ o̝], (4) mid [e o], (5) lowered mid [ɛ ɔ], (6) raised low [æ ɐ ɒ>], and (7) low [a, a, ɑ]. In a language with the seven vowels /i, u, e̝, o̝, ɛ, ɔ, a/ found in Italian stressed syllables, the constraint requiring that contrasting vowels differ by at least two steps (MINDIST=2) is ranked immediately above the constraint requiring that the number of contrasts be maximized. MAXCON is a positive requirement rather than a prohibition, and a ✓ is listed in tableau (2) for each contrasting category:

(2)

	MINDIST=1	MINDIST=2	MAXCON	MINDIST=3	MINDIST=4
(a) i:a			✓✓!		
(b) i:e:a			✓✓✓!		*(i:e)*(e:a)
☞(c) i:e̝:ɛ:a			✓✓✓	*(i:e̝)*(e̝:ɛ) *(ɛ:a)	*(i:e̝)*(e̝:ɛ) *(ɛ:a)
(d) i:ɪ:e:ɛ:a		*(i:ɪ)!*(e:ɛ)	✓✓✓✓	*(i:ɪ)*(ɪ:e) *(e:ɛ)*(ɛ:a)	*(i:ɪ)*(ɪ:e) *(e:ɛ)*(ɛ:a)

To reduce this inventory to the five vowels found in Italian's unstressed syllables, /i u e̝ o̝ ɐ/, Flemming (2004) adds a constraint prohibiting short low vowels (*SHORTLOW) and ranks it above MINDIST=2 (see (3)):

(3)

	SHORT LOW	MINDIST=2	MAXCON	MINDIST=3
☞ (a) i:e̝:ɐ			✓✓✓	
(b) i:e̝:ɛ:a	*(a)!		✓✓✓	*(i:e̝)*(e̝:ɛ)*(ɛ:a)
(c) i:e̝:ɛ:ɐ		*(ɛ:ɐ)!	✓✓✓	*(i:e̝)*(e̝:ɛ)*(ɛ:ɐ)

This new constraint rules out the candidate with [a] (3b), while MINDIST=2 rules out the candidate which retains [ɛ] (3c), because the raised low vowel [ɐ] is only one step away from it. What's left as the optimal candidate has only three heights and a raised low vowel [ɐ] (3a).

Flemming (submitted) lays out a more explicitly quantitative account of vowel reduction. Rather than requiring that all contrasting vowels be at least some minimum distance apart, the minimum distance between any pair of vowels now must be maximized. This approach closely resembles that in Section 17.3.2.3, except here an inventory's dispersion energy and goodness is measured by the distance between its closest pair of vowels. Unstressed and stressed vowels remain subject to the same distance requirements, so the minimum distance is the smallest distance found in either inventory. The new account also retains the requirement that the number of contrasts be maximized.

Following Lindblom (1963), the actual formant frequencies of the vowels in the full and reduced inventories are predicted with functions that undershoot their target frequencies as declining exponential functions of the vowel's duration. Since unstressed vowels are shorter than stressed ones, these functions correctly predict that height contrasts neutralize in unstressed vowels and that the unstressed low vowel is raised relative to its stressed counterpart, so long as the functions' other parameters are appropriately set. The parameter settings also ensure that F2 is undershot less than F1, which coincides with observed patterns of vowel reduction. Shortening doesn't affect the extent to which vowels coarticulate with consonants with respect to the articulations that implement the vowels' front–back or rounding contrasts, but it does affect the vowels' height because a consonant's constriction is usually just as close in an unstressed syllable as a stressed syllable, and coarticulated vowels are raised as a consequence.

Flemming's new account invokes the phonetic motivation for and mechanisms of vowel reduction far more directly than his earlier one did. The Minimum Distance and Maximize Contrast constraints are now implemented with continuous rather than discrete mathematics, and their ranking or priority is expressed by varying their relative weights. The only explicitly phonological aspect of this account is its outcome: fewer vowels contrast in the reduced inventories. That's an emergent property, not one that's in any way preordained by obedience to some phonological constraint.

17.3.2.7 The phonological consequences of vowel reduction vs. nasalization

Vowel reduction raises vowels by compressing them upward, while nasalization either disperses vowels toward the top and bottom of the vowel space or more rarely lowers them. Their effects differ because the speaker's goals are different.

The goal in pronouncing an unstressed vowel is to produce one that's shorter than a stressed vowel, which leads to the vowel's target being undershot. Shortening is not the goal in a nasal vowel, quite the reverse. Conveying the vowel's height and nasalization instead demands that the vowel last long enough for the spectral modification caused by nasalization to be detected and may even demand that the vowel be prolonged (Whalen & Beddor 1989). Nasalization's need for a longer vowel can even have phonological consequences: contrastive nasalization may only develop on long or stressed vowels, as in Guaraní (Gregores & Suárez 1967), Copala Trique (Hollenbach 1977), Teke (Hombert 1987), and northern Italian dialects (Hajek 1997), and it may inhibit extreme vowel reduction, as in Brazilian Portuguese (Major 1985).

Mid vowels are eliminated from nasal vowel inventories because nasalization alters and obscures the center of gravity of the vowel's lowest spectral prominence, effects which are exacerbated by the perceptual integration of vowel height and nasalization, which disfavors percepts of intermediate height and nasalization. Low nasal vowels, which integration would otherwise denasalize, remain nasal because they last long enough for listeners to detect whatever nasalization may be present and because speakers actually lower the soft palate more.

17.3.3 Explaining sound change
17.3.3.1 Introduction
Many, perhaps most of the sound changes languages undergo are phonetically motivated. What does this mean? It means that something about how the speaker pronounces the sound that changes, how that sound is transmitted to the listener, or how the listener perceives that sound makes it possible for that sound to be phonologically different at some later time in its history than it was at some earlier time.

In the next section, I describe tonogenesis in Athabaskan as an example of a phonetically motivated sound change. Discussing this sound change is an occasion to evaluate Steriade's (1999b) 'licensing by cue' proposal that contrasts are maintained in those contexts where their phonetic cues are easy to detect and neutralized in contexts where their cues are hard to detect – as discussed in Section 17.3.2.5 above, Crosswhite used such a licensing constraint to explain the loss of mid vowels in contrast-enhancing reduction. This example is also evidence that the phonetic motivation for a sound change persists after it's been phonologized, contrary to the claims of Barnes (2002) and Blevins (2004).

17.3.3.2 The phonetics of Athabaskan tonogenesis
In Proto-Athabaskan, glottalic and non-glottalic stops, affricates, nasals, and glides contrasted at the ends as well as the beginnings of stems (Krauss 2005), but in many present-day members of this family, the stem-final contrast has been replaced by tone in stems ending in stops and affricates (henceforth just 'stops').

The development of tone from an earlier contrast in laryngeal articulations of an adjacent consonant is an extremely common sound change (Hombert, Ohala, & Ewan 1979), particularly in the language families of East and Southeast Asia. It can occur because one of the phonetic correlates of a laryngeal contrast in consonants is differences in the fundamental frequency (F0) of adjacent vowels. These F0 differences become tone contrasts in the vowels and replace the original laryngeal contrast between the consonants when they lose the other phonetic correlates of the contrast.

Explaining tonogenesis in Athabaskan is complicated by three factors. First, nearly all the tonal Athabaskan languages maintain the contrast between stem-final glottalic and non-glottalic sonorants and between stems ending in a glottal stop vs. a vowel. Even so, the same tone appears in stems ending in glottalic sonorants and glottal stop as in stems that once ended in glottalic stops, and the other tone in stems ending in non-glottalic sonorants or a vowel. In these stems, the F0 differences remain synchronically predictable from other properties of the stem-final consonant, and tone doesn't convey the contrast alone.

The second complication is that the tone which developed in stems that ended in glottalic stops only did so when the stem vowel was short. When the vowel was long, the tone appears that otherwise developed in stems that ended in non-glottalic stops. In certain morphological constructions, however, the stem-final stop was spirantized, and the same tone then developed on long vowels as on short ones. This tone also develops on long as well as short vowels in stems ending in glottalic sonorants. Short and long vowels don't contrast before a stem-final glottal stop; their modern reflexes uniformly indicate that the vowel is long. Nonetheless, the same tone appears in these stems as in those in which a short vowel preceded a glottalic stop in the protolanguage or those ending in a glottalic sonorant. In short, vowel length doesn't matter if the stem-final consonant was not an oral stop.

Both complications can be accounted for by a difference in the relative timing of laryngeal and oral articulations in stops vs. other manners of articulation (Kingston 1985, 2005). Their relative timing differs because a stop closure's release differs acoustically from its onset. The brief but intense noise burst that occurs when the stop is released is apparently salient enough that the stop's laryngeal articulation is timed to coincide with it. This timing ensures that different laryngeal articulations modify the burst in characteristic ways that convey their nature to the listener. No comparably salient acoustic event occurs at the closure's onset, or at either the onsets or releases of fricatives and sonorants.[17] Because no similarly salient acoustic event occurs at either the onset or release of the oral constriction in fricatives or sonorants, the timing of laryngeal articulations relative to oral ones is freer. In many languages, however, the laryngeal articulation is timed to coincide with the onset of the oral constriction in these manners of articulation (Kingston 1985, 1990).

Because the laryngeal articulation coincides with the release of the oral constriction in a stop, it is farther from and coarticulates less with a preceding vowel than it would in a fricative or sonorant, at least when the laryngeal articulation coincides with the onset of the constriction in those manners of articulation. Tonogenesis indicates that coarticulation with a stop was still extensive enough to alter a short vowel's pronunciation if not a long one's. Enough of the vowel would be altered by coarticulating with the nearer laryngeal articulation in a sonorant or fricative to change a long as well as a short vowel.

The timing difference also explains why tone replaced the glottalic:non-glottalic contrast in stem-final stops but merely supplements it in stem-final sonorants. If the stop were not released in some contexts or the release were inaudible, the principal cue to the consonant's identity would become the acoustic effects of its coarticulation with the preceding vowel and not any properties heard during the consonant itself. The absence or inaudibility of the release in a sonorant would be of little consequence for conveying its laryngeal articulation, particularly if that articulation coincides with the onset of the oral constriction. The principal cues to that articulation are already its coarticulatory effects on the preceding vowel, so there's little reason to expect them to change or shift off the consonant.

For the contrast to shift to the vowel from the consonant, the listener has to misinterpret the coarticulatory effects of the consonant's laryngeal articulation as the speaker intending to alter the vowel (Ohala 1981). The listener may be inclined to do so if other evidence that these effects are properties of the consonant is frequently weak or missing.

The third complication is perhaps the most intriguing: some of the present-day daughter languages have high tones in stems that ended in a glottalic consonant and low tones elsewhere, while others have low tones in such stems and high tones elsewhere. One of these developments could be original and the other a reversal, but in Kingston (2005) I show that it's actually possible to get both high and low tone directly from different pronunciations of the glottalic consonants.[18] Glottalic consonants are distinguished from non-glottalic ones by a constriction of the glottis that is tight enough to curtail or even cut off air flow through the glottis. The glottis is closed by contracting the interarytenoid and lateral cricoarytenoid muscles while relaxing the posterior cricoarytenoid muscles, and the constriction is tightened by the forceful contraction of the thyroarytenoid muscles, which stiffens the inner bodies of the vocal folds and causes the folds to press firmly against one another. If this is all the speaker does, the voice quality of adjacent vowels is creaky and its F0 is low because the vibrating outer covers of the folds remain slack. However, if the speaker also contracts the cricothyroid muscle at the same time, the folds' outer covers are stretched and the voice quality in the adjacent vowel is tense and its F0 high instead. The available evidence suggests that speakers choose to contract the cricothyroid as well as the thyroarytenoid muscles independently of other choices they make about how to pronounce glottalic consonants (Kingston 1982, 1985; Bird 2002; Wright, Hargus, & Davis 2002).

In this account, speakers choose (1) whether to contract the cricothyroid as well as the thyroarytenoid muscles in pronouncing glottalic consonants, a choice which determines whether high or low tone eventually develops on preceding vowels, (2) not to release stem-final stops or to release them inaudibly such that only the F0 and voice quality of the preceding vowel are reliable cues to the stops' laryngeal articulations, and (3) to time the laryngeal articulations of sonorants and fricatives so that they coincide with the onset of the oral constriction, and thus noticeably alter the F0 and voice quality in long as well as short preceding vowels. None of these choices are obligatory, even if they are more typical than alternatives. Crucially, listeners also mistakenly interpret the coarticulatory effects of the consonant's laryngeal articulation on the preceding vowel's F0 and voice quality as intentional. This mistake is encouraged if speakers fail to release stops or do so inaudibly and if laryngeal articulations are timed to coincide with the onset of the oral constriction in fricatives and sonorants.

17.3.3.3   Licensing by cue

Laryngeal contrasts are kept and lost from consonants in other languages in similar circumstances to Athabaskan. For example, in Lithuanian and Klamath laryngeal contrasts in obstruents are maintained before sonorants and lost elsewhere. Steriade (1999b) proposes that contrasts are maintained in contexts where the cues to their identity are robust and neutralized where those cues are reduced, obscured, or absent. Laryngeal contrasts are maintained before sonorants because cues to those articulations in the consonant's release and in the transition to the following sonorant are robust in that context. They are neutralized before obstruents and word-finally because the release cues are frequently absent in these contexts, and the cues in the transitions from preceding vowels are less robust. The Athabaskan case is quite similar: the glottalic:non-glottalic contrast is kept in stem-initial stops because they reliably precede vowels, and lost stem-finally, where they do not. Stem-final stops may even have been unreleased when the contrast was lost from them, inducing listeners at that time to think the consonants themselves weren't different. Moreover, laryngeal contrasts are probably maintained to this day in stem-final sonorants because the cues are timed to occur early enough that they are robustly signaled during the transition from the preceding vowel.

The licensing by cue account of Athabaskan tonogenesis is, however, incomplete: the glottalic:non-glottalic contrast didn't in fact neutralize in stem-final stops, but instead shifted to a tonal contrast on preceding vowels. How were speakers of Athabaskan languages able to keep morphemes distinct whose stem-final consonants once contrasted in their laryngeal articulations while speakers of Lithuanian or Klamath failed to do so? If the phonetic correlates *available* to act as cues to a particular laryngeal contrast are the same in all languages where that contrast is found, then Lithuanian and Klamath speakers and listeners had at their disposal more or less the same materials to convey these contrasts, among them differences in F0 and voice quality on preceding vowels, as Athabaskan speakers. Yet they failed to use them. The solution to this conundrum lies in the idea that speakers choose how they are going to pronounce a contrast, and therefore which of the available phonetic materials they're going to use.

Licensing by cue falls short because it conceives the phonetics as something that happens to speakers, rather than also conceiving the speakers as actively manipulating the phonetics to meet their communicative needs. Contrasts are certainly more robustly signaled in some contexts than others, but phonetic materials are available for speakers to use to increase the robustness with which they're signaled in other, ostensibly less favorable contexts. The unanswered question then becomes: why do speakers choose to do so in some languages but not others? The answer to this question will probably turn out to be that speakers make this choice when the contrast is lexically or morphologically informative and not otherwise. (For further criticism of licensing by cue see Gerfen 2001; Kingston 2002.)

17.3.3.4 Evolutionary phonology

Tonogenesis in Athabaskan also clearly shows that a sound change's phonetic motivation remains active even after the sound change has been phonologized, contrary to the claims of Barnes (2002) and Blevins (2004). In the tonal Athabaskan languages, the tones that appear in stems ending in glottalic sonorants and glottal stop are always the same as those appearing in stems that ended in glottalic stops in the protolanguage, modulo the effects of vowel length. If it were once possible to constrict the glottis in such a way as to either lower or raise F0, then it should still be possible to do either one, and therefore it should have been possible in the subsequent history of a tonal Athabaskan language for its speakers to adopt the pronunciation of glottal constriction that has the opposite effect on F0 and tone in the preceding vowel. The result would be that stems which originally ended in glottalic stops in the protolanguage would have one tone, while those that end today in glottalic sonorants or glottal stop would have the opposite tone. This has never happened. It hasn't because when the sound change was phonologized, the phonetics of the pronunciation of glottal constriction were, too.[19] Doing so has constrained glottalic sonorants and glottal stop to be pronounced in the same way throughout the subsequent history of each tonal Athabaskan language as its own glottalic stops were when the sound change was actuated.

17.4   Implementation

17.4.1   Introduction

In this concluding section, I discuss two examples of how the phonetics implements phonological representations. In the first example, I take up the question of what it means phonetically for a sound to be phonologically marked vs. unmarked. The discussion shows that the pronunciation of the unmarked member of the contrast is more variable and hypo-articulated than that of the marked member(s). Listeners apparently expect this variability and adjust for it. The adjustments they make suggest that the unmarked sound is phonologically unspecified.

It is often proposed that phonetics manipulates gradients, while phonology instead manipulates categories. This distinction is the central issue in the second example where it is extended to differences in how phonetic and phonological constraints are prioritized. One phonetic constraint isn't categorically ranked above or below another in the way phonological constraints are, but the phonetic constraint with higher priority is weighted more heavily in evaluating a possible output's well-formedness. Weight is inherently gradient rather than categorical.

17.4.2   The phonetics of place and markedness

In heterosyllabic sequences of a coronal stop followed by a non-coronal stop in English, e.g. [t.k] or [d.g], the coronal articulation is typically briefer, it may be substantially reduced, even to the point where the tongue tip and blade don't reach the alveolar ridge, and it is often fully overlapped by the following non-coronal articulation (Nolan 1992; Byrd 1996). For some speakers, coronal stops in this context assimilate completely to the following non-coronal, in some or all tokens (Ellis & Hardcastle 2002). When the order of the places of articulation is reversed, the non-coronal isn't shortened, reduced, or overlapped nearly as much, nor does it assimilate to the coronal.

This articulatory asymmetry is matched by a corresponding perceptual one. Gaskell & Marslen-Wilson (1996) report the results of a cross-modal priming task, in which, relative to a control stimulus, an assimilated pronunciation of a coronal consonant, e.g. *lea[m] bacon*, sped up recognition that a simultaneous visual probe *lean* was a word just as much as did the unassimilated pronunciation, *lea[n] bacon* (Gaskell & Marslen-Wilson 1996). Gow (2002) reports similar results for heavily overlapped but not fully assimilated coronals. However, an assimilated pronunciation of a non-coronal consonant, e.g. *la[ŋ]e goat*, slowed recognition that the visual probe *lame* was a word significantly compared to the unassimilated pronunciation, *la[m]e goat* (Gaskell & Marslen-Wilson 1996). Monitoring for the phoneme beginning the second word, e.g. the /b/ in *lean bacon*, was also facilitated by an assimilated pronunciation of the preceding coronal, whether the coronal was assimilated (Gaskell & Marslen-Wilson 1998) or only heavily overlapped (Gow 2003). These phoneme monitoring results suggest that the listener parses the non-coronal place information off the assimilated consonant and attributes it to the following non-coronal.

Both Gaskell & Marslen-Wilson and Gow argue that listeners parse the place information like this because they know that coronal stops are extensively overlapped by and even assimilate to following non-coronals. Their results show that when listeners hear, for example, the non-word *lea[m]* before *bacon*, and this non-word would become the word *lea[n]* if its final non-coronal were replaced by a coronal, they infer that the non-coronal place information belongs to the following consonant and that the intended consonant is coronal. They don't infer another non-coronal when they hear the non-word *la[ŋ]e* before *goat* because they have no comparable experience of non-coronals being extensively overlapped by or assimilating to the place of articulation of the following consonant. This interpretation is supported by Gaskell & Marslen-Wilson's (1996, 1998) findings that an assimilated coronal that isn't homorganic with a following non-coronal, e.g. *lea[m] goat*, neither primes recognition of the visual probe *lean* nor facilitates detection of the initial /g/ in the following word. The inferences are blocked in this 'non-viable' assimilation because the non-coronal place of the [m] cannot be parsed onto the following [g].

Coenen, Zwitserlood, & Bölte (2001) report cross-modal priming experiments run with German listeners in which the procedures and results closely resemble those reported by Gaskell & Marslen-Wilson (1996). Lahiri & Reetz (2002) also report the results of cross-modal priming experiments with German listeners, but they presented the primes in isolation, without any following word whose initial consonant might be an assimilation trigger. In the first experiment, the auditory primes were words ending in either a coronal or non-coronal, e.g. *Bahn* 'railway' or *Lärm* 'noise', and non-words made by replacing the final coronal with a non-coronal or vice versa, *Bahm* vs. *Lärn*. Both *Bahn* and *Bahm* primed recognition of the related visual probe *Zug* 'train' but only *Lärm* primed *Krach* 'bang, racket'. Although this result can't be attributed to the listeners' actually parsing the non-coronal place information at the end of *Bahm* onto a following homorganic consonant, they may still separate the labial place information from *Bahm* because *Bahn* is sometimes pronounced *Bahm* in front of a word beginning with a bilabial consonant. This alternative is ruled out by the second experiment, where the manipulated consonants were inter-vocalic rather than final, and therefore in a context where there's never a following consonant to assimilate to. Auditory primes were words with medial coronal or non-coronal consonants, e.g. *Düne* 'dune' or *Schramme* 'a scratch', and corresponding non-words, *Düme* or *Schranne*. Both *Düne* and *Düme* primed recognition of the related visual probe *Sand* 'sand' but only *Schramme* primed *Kratzer* 'a scratch'. These results definitively rule out the inferential parsing account proposed by Gaskell & Marslen-Wilson or Gow.

Lahiri & Reetz interpret their results as evidence that coronal place is not specified phonologically, while the labial and dorsal places are specified. When there is phonetic evidence in the signal for a non-coronal place, as in *Bahm* or *Düme*, this evidence doesn't mismatch the stored forms of the words *Bahn* or *Düne*, because the /n/ in these words isn't specified for place, and these words are activated. Because *Bahm* and *Düme* aren't words, this evidence for non-coronal place also doesn't activate any competing words. Phonetic evidence of coronal place, as in *Lärn* or *Schranne*, however, does mismatch the phonological specification for labial place in the words *Lärm* or *Schramme*, which inhibits their activation.

This interpretation doesn't easily handle the failure of the non-viable assimilation in *lea[m] goat* to prime *lean*. The phonetic evidence for the labial place in the [m] wouldn't mismatch the missing place specification of the /n/ in this string any more than in an isolated word. However, in an earlier cross-modal priming study with German listeners where the auditory primes were followed by another word whose initial consonant could be an assimilation trigger (1995), Lahiri obtained priming for non-viably- as well as viably-assimilated coronals, i.e. *Bahm* primed *Zug* even when the following word didn't begin with a labial consonant. This result indicates that viability needs to be re-examined.

The articulatory data show that the unmarked member of a contrast may vary substantially more in its pronunciation than the marked member(s). The perceptual data indicate that listeners can readily tolerate the phonetic effects of the unmarked member's variation, either because they've had long experience of it or because the unmarked member is actually not specified phonologically, and the variation creates no mismatch between the phonetic evidence and the phonological specification.

17.4.3   Categories and gradients

Phonology is commonly thought to deal in categories, while phonetics deals instead in gradients. Keating (1988c), Pierrehumbert (1990), Cohn (1993a), Zsiga (1995), Holst & Nolan (1995), and Nolan, Holst, & Kühnert (1996) explicitly use the distinction between categories and gradients to *define* phenomena as phonological vs. phonetic.

Recently, Zsiga (2000) has extended this use of the distinction between gradients and categories to separate phonetic from phonological constraints. Using acoustic evidence, she shows that in English the end of the coronal gesture in an [s] is overlapped by the palatal gesture of a following [j] across word boundaries. This evidence agrees with palatographic evidence reported in Zsiga (1995), which showed a shift from coronal to palatal contact at the end of an [s] preceding [j]. Starting after the middle of the fricative, the [s]'s coronal articulation gradually blends with the following [j]'s palatal articulation and produces an articulation midway between these two articulations by the end of the fricative. The acoustics of Russian speakers' pronunciations, however, show that the two articulations don't overlap in [s# #j] sequences, and that in palatalized [s^j], they overlap completely. Even though the coronal and palatal articulations are simultaneous in the Russian speakers' palatalized [s^j], they aren't blended: both coronal and palatal articulations are produced, not an articulation midway between them.

Zsiga proposes that English and Russian differ in the relative priorities of faithfulness-like phonetic constraints requiring the speaker to achieve particular articulatory targets specified in the phonological representation. For English speakers, the requirement to maintain the coronal constriction specified by /s/ gradually gives way over the last half of the fricative to the requirement to reach the following palatal constriction. The two constrictions blend progressively until a constriction is produced midway between the alveolar ridge and the palate by the end of the fricative. For Russian speakers, however, the requirement to maintain the coronal constriction remains a higher priority all the way to the end of the fricative constriction in [s# #j] sequences, as well as in palatalized [s^j], where the coronal articulation is maintained despite complete overlap with the palatal articulation.[20] Because the coronal constraint's priority doesn't change in Russian even when the coronal articulation is completely overlapped by the palatal articulation, while its priority diminishes gradually as a result of overlap in English, Zsiga argues that these phonetic constraints are weighted continuously with respect to one another and not ranked categorically. Because the priority conflict between phonetic constraints is resolved by continuous weighting and not strict ranking, she also argues that phonetic constraint evaluation is autonomous from and follows phonological constraint evaluation.

This sequential model is quite different from that advocated by Steriade (1999b) or Flemming (2004, submitted) in which phonetic constraints are integrated among and even supplant phonological constraints, and where the phonetic constraints are also strictly, i.e. categorically, ranked. Their models do not, as far as I know, try to account for phonetic detail to the extent that Zsiga's proposal does, but there is no formal barrier to their doing so. Future research will determine whether phonological and phonetic constraint evaluation are a single, integrated process, as advocated by Steriade and Flemming or instead sequential, as advocated by Zsiga.

17.5 Summary and concluding remarks

I have tried to show here how distinctive features might be defined, how phonological patterns might be explained, and how phonological representations might be implemented.

The essential problem that has to be solved in defining distinctive features is that their articulations and acoustics vary so enormously that it's impossible to identify any articulatory or acoustic property that's essential to defining a feature. This variability can be largely eliminated by moving away from the details of particular phonetic realizations, either toward the articulatory plan for the utterance embodied in Articulatory Phonology's gestures or toward the auditory effects of the signal's acoustic properties. Evidence was reviewed that taken together pointed to the second move as the right one.

Explaining phonological patterns is difficult because they are typically determined by more than one phonetic constraint, as well as by phonological constraints, and these constraints may conflict with one another. The eventual explanation is a description of the resolution of this conflict. It is largely because phonetic explanations are complex in this way that I think no bright line can be drawn between the phonetic and phonological components of a grammar. It is interesting in this connection that many of those who advocate such bright lines (e.g. Hale & Reiss 2000b; Blevins 2004) also reject phonological models in which the surface phonological representation corresponding to a particular underlying representation is selected by applying well-formedness constraints in parallel to all possible surface representations, as in Optimality Theory. Replacing serial derivation by parallel evaluation removes the barrier to phonetic constraints being interspersed among and interacting with phonological constraints. (Zsiga's 2000, proposal, as described in Section 17.4.3, is an obvious exception to this generalization.)

The problem in trying to understand phonetic implementation is actually very similar to that arising in attempts to explain phonological patterns in phonetic terms: phonetic constraints not only regulate how a phonological representation can be realized but also determine at least some of its properties. These properties of the phonological representation emerge out of its implementation in much the same way that the distinctive features emerge out of the solution to the variability problem.

Notes

I could not have written this chapter without the feedback and stimulation I received from the students in the seminar I taught on the phonetics–phonology interface at the University of Massachusetts, Amherst in the fall of 2004: Timothy Beechey, Kathryn Flack, Shigeto Kawahara, Anne-Michelle Tessier, and Matthew Wolf. Finally, I must thank Paul de Lacy for inviting me to write this chapter in the first place; his doing so forced me to take up a task that I had been putting off for some time: working out just what I think the interface is (and isn't) between phonetics and phonology. His reactions to earlier versions were also very helpful in getting the chapter into its final form. In short, I owe many of the virtues of the present chapter, such as they are, to others, particularly to my students. As is customary, I keep the faults, of which there are many, for myself.

1 In Articulatory Phonology, this collection of gestures is actually the phonological representation of the utterance. Browman & Goldstein make this move because it is very difficult to translate an utterance's linguistic representation as a sequence of discrete cognitive categories into its physical realization as continuous and overlapping actions having spatial and temporal extents (Fowler, Rubin, Remez, & Turvey 1980). If the phonological and phonetic representations differ to this extent, it's also hard to see how either could constrain the other, yet they do (Browman & Goldstein 1995).

2 Keating's (1990b, 1996) window model of coarticulation achieves a similar result by specifying spatial and temporal ranges for particular articulators' movements. These ranges' limits ensure that the speaker reaches the goal, but their width permits individual articulators' movements to vary in extent depending on context.

3 Lindblom et al.'s (1979) data show that the vocal tract's configuration does differ substantially elsewhere than at the point of constriction when the bite block prevents jaw movement.

4 The vowel space has a fixed acoustic volume because when the articulators move past certain limits, they impede air flow enough that what was a vowel becomes a fricative.

5 A very different and apparently more successful approach to predicting the contents of vowel inventories of particular sizes is presented by de Boer (2000).

6 51 languages in the sample contrast long with short vowels: 23 distinguish more short than long vowel qualities, 14 distinguish more long than short vowel qualities, and 14 distinguish the same number of qualities in long as short vowels.

7 An otherwise central vowel, e.g. /ɯ/ or /ɐ/, was counted as peripheral if a language lacked a more peripheral vowel at that height or backness. A vowel quality is only central if it contrasts with a minimally different peripheral vowel.

8 These patterns and their frequencies closely resemble those in Table I in Schwartz et al. (1997a), who analyzed an earlier, smaller version of UPSID consisting of 317 languages (Maddieson 1984).

9 Vowels were not literally added to an earlier 5+0 inventory at some time in these languages' histories. This is instead a description of how vowel patterns differ or remain the same when additional vowels are present in an inventory.

10 This generalization holds if /ə/ is treated as a front vowel in the Qawasqar inventory /ə, a, o/. It is at least more front than /o/.

11 Because half the values in the range are below the median and half are above, all the values are on average closer to the median than to any other value, and it is less affected by extreme values than the mean.

12 The average deficit in nasal vowels is 2.45, but a language cannot have a fraction of a vowel.

13 Here 'mid' encompasses the range from lower to higher mid, 'high' includes high and lowered high, and 'low' includes low and raised low.

14 Other studies also report that a higher vowel sounds more nasalized than a lower one for a given degree of nasal–oral cavity coupling (House & Stevens 1956; Lubker 1968; Ohala 1975; Abramson, Nye, Henderson, & Marshall 1981; Benguerel & Lafargue 1981; Stevens, Fant, & Hawkins 1987; Maeda 1993, cf. Lintz & Sherman 1961; Massengill & Bryson 1967; Bream 1968; Ali, Gallagher, Goldstein, & Daniloff 1971).

15 Barnes (2002) restricts the reduction pattern shown in (1c) to Eastern Bulgarian; Crosswhite does not.

16 Pettersson & Wood's (1987a,1987b) cineradiographic study of Bulgarian vowels shows that the jaw but not the tongue undershoots its target in unstressed syllables. The tongue remains lower for the non-high vowels [e o a] than for [i u ə], but the jaw is higher, close to its position in [i u ə], apparently enough to lower F1 and make unstressed [e o a] sound like the vowels just above them.

17 Steriade (1993) discusses other phonological consequences of the acoustic difference between a stop's onset and release.

18 In Kingston (2004, see also Kingston & Solnit 1989; Solnit & Kingston 1988), I show that apparent tone reversals of this kind are widespread and also occur when the historical sources of the tones are an earlier contrast between voiced and voiceless obstruents or between aspirated and unaspirated consonants – the latter include sonorants as well as obstruents. In these cases, too, it may be possible to pronounce the consonants such that they either raise or lower F0.

19 Blevins might appeal to structural analogy as the source of this uniformity. Its influence would be exerted through alternations in the verbs, but it's hard to see how it could be extended to the nouns where few if any helpful alternations occur. This is not to say that analogy has played no role in Athabaskan tonogenesis, but its role is limited to the extension of tonogenesis to morphemes other than stems (Kingston 2005).

20 Zsiga notes that Russian speakers may wish to avoid any blending in [s# #j] because they must keep /s/, /ʃ/, and /sʲ/ distinct.

18

The syntax–phonology interface

Hubert Truckenbrodt

18.1 Introduction

Phonological structure is sensitive to syntactic phrase structure. This chapter discusses central aspects of this relation: What elements of the phonological representation are influenced by phrase structure? How are they influenced? How does focus affect prosody? What role does the distinction between lexical and functional elements play? A recurring theme will be the role of syntactic XPs in shaping the important layer of p-phrases in different ways.

Section 18.2 identifies prosodic structure above the word level, including the p-phrase. Section 18.3 reviews evidence for edge-alignment of the p-phrase with syntactic XPs. Section 18.4 discusses the further requirement that XPs be fully contained inside p-phrases. Sections 18.5 and 18.6 seek to connect the literature on prosodic phonology of the preceding sections with the literature on phrasal stress: Section 18.5 identifies the main influence of focus on stress, and Section 18.6 tries to show that the additional influence of syntax on stress is also defined in terms of XPs. Section 18.7 addresses the distinction between lexical and functional projections in the syntax–phonology interface. Section 18.8 discusses eurhythmic influences on prosodic structure. Section 18.9 addresses the dependency of intonation phrases on root clauses. Section 18.10 sums up the results.

18.2 The prosodic representation

Syntactic structure influences prosodic structure above the word level. This section identifies the most relevant prosodic constituents involved and introduces important assumptions about their representation.

Since Selkirk's (1980b) modifications of Liberman and Prince (1977) there is a broad consensus that syllables are grouped into *feet* (see Kager Ch.9), which are in turn grouped into *prosodic words* (or *p-words*). Feet and p-words serve as metrical domains in which stress is assigned at or near an edge. In English, feet are left-prominent ('moraic trochees') and prosodic words are right-prominent, as shown for the words 'Beverly' and 'Alabama' in the boxed parts of the representation in (1). In the bracketed grid representation in (1), the strongest element in each prosodic constituent is marked by an *x* on the same line as that constituent (Hayes 1995; see Halle & Vergnaud 1987 for the original and minimally different suggestion for a bracketed grid representation).

```
(1)  (                                 x              )    i-phrase
     ( x            )  (                x              )    p-phrases
     ( x          )  (x) (              x              )    p-words
     ( x      )        (x) (x      )(  x  )                 feet
       μ   μ    μ      μμ    μ    μ   μμ    μ               moras
     Be  ver <ly>    likes  A   la   ba  <ma>
```

Of interest in this chapter is the prosodic organization above the p-word. There is a greater diversity of views as to the extension of this representation upward.[1] The synthesis of ideas discussed in this article adopts the view that higher prosodic structure is organized by the same principles as lower prosodic structure: there is a small number of higher prosodic levels, and their prosodic constituents are also metrical constituents in which stress is assigned at or near an edge (Nespor and Vogel 1986, 1989, Hayes and Lahiri 1991). Relevant here are the most well-established of these levels. *Phonological phrases* (or *p-phrases*) relate to syntactic phrases (XPs) such as Noun Phrases (NPs), Verb Phrases (VPs), and Adjective Phrases (AP) (see Truckenbrodt 1999 on this terminology). *Intonation phrase* (or *i-phrase*) refers to prosodic constituents related to syntactic clauses. The hierarchy of levels is often called the *prosodic hierarchy*.

The organization of the prosodic constituents is taken to obey a number of restrictions (Selkirk 1984b, Nespor and Vogel 1986). In Optimality Theory (Prince and Smolensky 2004), some of these have been argued to be violable (Selkirk 1995a). Two important ones are given in (2):

(2) EXHAUST(IVITY)   Every constituent of level *l* is contained in a constituent of level *l+1*. (Example: every syllable is contained in a foot.)

NONREC(URSIVITY)   No constituent of level *l* is contained in another constituent of level *l*. (Example: no foot is contained in another foot.)

Thus, an ideal of the organization is that all syllables be parsed into feet, but this constraint is violated by the syllable *ly* and by the syllable *ma* in (1). Across levels, this violable condition is called EXHAUST(IVITY). Another restriction relates to recursive structure. In syntax, a DP may contain another

DP, as in [DP [DP John]'s book]. In the prosodic representation, a constraint NONREC(URSIVITY) has been argued to punish such recursive representations: a foot that contains another foot is in violation of NONRECURSIVITY. This constraint has also been argued to be violable in the prosodic representation.[2]

18.3   Edge-alignment of XPs

This section shows how phonological phrases are shaped by edge-alignment with syntactic XPs, illustrating with Xiamen Chinese.

Xiamen tone groups (here: p-phrases) are diagnosed by a phenomenon of tone sandhi that transforms, in a good approximation, all but the last tone in a tone group: (T′ T′ T′ T), where T is an underlying tone surfacing unchanged and T′ is the sandhi version of an underlying tone.[3]

Chen (1987) has argued that the *tone groups* (here: p-phrases) of Xiamen Chinese are formed by right-alignment of syntactic XPs with tone group boundaries.[4] As an example, a topic XP may precede the subject. Subject and topic are followed by tone group boundaries, as shown in (3).

(3) [   ]XP   [   ]XP   [   ]XP ...
   (hai-kih)TG   (tsin tsue lang)TG   (leq san-po)TG
   beach   very many people·   ASP walk
   'Many people are taking a walk on the beach.'

As shown in (4), the verb is not separated from an object by a tone group boundary. This shows that the left edge of the object XP and the right edge of the verbal head V do not introduce a p-phrase boundary. However, the first object XP is followed by a tone group boundary and thus separated from a second object as shown in (5).

(4) [V   [   ]XP]VP
   (pang   hong-ts'e)TG
   fly   kite
   'fly a kite'

(5) [[   ]XP   [   ]XP]VP
   (hoo yin sio-ti)TG   (tsit pun ts'eq)TG
   give his brother   one CL book
   'give his brother a book'

So p-phrases in Xiamen Chinese are shaped by right-edge alignment with syntactic XPs. The right edge of syntactic heads (X) and the left edge of syntactic XPs do not trigger boundaries. I return to Xiamen Chinese below.

Selkirk (1986, 1995a) has convincingly generalized Chen's proposal to a cross-linguistic theory of edge-alignment. The right edge of XP has also been argued to be aligned with phonologically detectable prosodic domains in Chi Mwi:ni (Kisseberth and Abasheikh 1974, Selkirk 1986) and

Tohono O'odham (with modifications noted below – Hale and Selkirk 1987). The left edge of XP aligns with prosodic domains in Shanghai Chinese (Selkirk and Shen 1990), Japanese (Selkirk and Tateishi 1991) and Northern Kyungsang Korean (Kenstowicz and Sohn 1997). The constraints are here called ALIGN-XP,R and ALIGN-XP,L.

(6) (a) ALIGN-XP,R = ALIGN(XP, R; p-phrase, R)
         "The right edge of each syntactic XP is aligned with the right edge of a p-phrase."

     (b) ALIGN-XP,L = ALIGN(XP, L; p-phrase, L)
         "The left edge of each syntactic XP is aligned with the left edge of a p-phrase."

Selkirk's theory of edge alignment was later generalized to the influential format of Generalized Alignment in McCarthy and Prince (1993a) in Optimality Theory (Prince and Smolensky 2004). Selkirk (1995a) formulated the syntax–prosody alignment constraints as ranked and violable constraints in this format. Both left-alignment and right-alignment are universal in this theory. They are active if they are ranked above the constraint *P-PHRASE, which in effect minimizes the number of p-phrases (Truckenbrodt 1999); they are inactive if ranked below *P-PHRASE. An argument for this conception of the alignment requirements is provided by de Lacy (2003a): in parametric accounts a choice has to be made between left- or right-alignment. Māori, however, shows simultaneous alignment of left and right edges of XPs. This can be accounted for by ranking both left- and right-alignment above *P-PHRASE, but it could not be accounted for by parametric theories of alignment.

18.4   Wrapping of XPs

Although Alignment is necessary to account for the interaction of syntax and prosodic structure, it is not enough. This section reviews evidence for a further constraint that seeks to prevent XPs from being split up into multiple p-phrases.

In the Native-American language Tohono O'odham (Hale and Selkirk 1987), *tonal phrases* (here: p-phrases) are bounded on the right by a L(ow) tone. H(igh) tones are found on vowels with word stress and between the first and the last of these word-stresses in the tonal phrase. Remaining vowels at the edges of the tonal phrase carry L tone.

A clause-initial XP such as *wakial* in (7a) is followed by a finite auxiliary. If the initial XP contains lexical material, its right edge regularly coincides with a tonal phrase boundary as in (7a). The language also has a productive process of extraposition. The right edges of XPs are regularly separated from the extraposed constituent by a tonal phrase boundary. In (7b), such a tonal phrase boundary coincides with the right edge of the lower VP node, preceding the extraposed object.

(7)

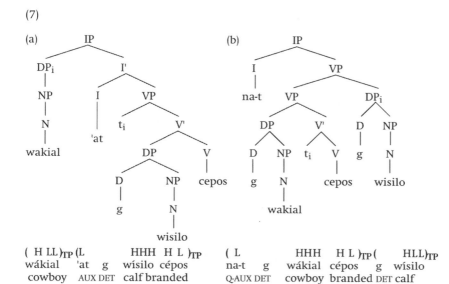

(a)

(H LL)$_{TP}$ (L   HHH H L)$_{TP}$
wákial   'at g wísilo cépos
cowboy AUX DET calf branded
'The cowboy branded the calf.'

(b)

(L   HHH   H L)$_{TP}$(HLL)$_{TP}$
na-t   g   wákial cépos   g wísilo
Q-AUX DET cowboy branded DET calf
'Did the cowboy brand the calf?'

However, right-alignment of XPs with p-phrases is not found with arguments of lexical categories in situ. In (7a), there is no tonal phrase boundary following the object, and in (7b), there is no tonal phrase boundary following the subject. Structures like . . . *([Subject Object V]$_{VP}$)$_{TP}$* and *([Possessor N]$_{NP}$)$_{TP}$* also form a single tonal phrase. Hale and Selkirk (1987) suggest a parameter: in some languages such as Tohono O'odham, lexically governed elements like the object in (7a) and the subject in (7b) are systematically exempt from triggering prosodic boundaries at their right edges.

Building on Hale & Selkirk's proposal, Truckenbrodt (1999) argues that right-alignment of the verb's arguments in (7a,b) is suppressed by another constraint relating to the syntax–phonology mapping, WRAP-XP.

(8) WRAP-XP
    For each XP there must be a p-phrase that contains the XP.

In (7a,b), the effect of WRAP-XP on the VP is decisive: if the object in (7a) or the subject in (7b) were right-aligned with a p-phrase boundary, the VP would not be contained in a single p-phrase. Following Selkirk (1995a), the constraints mapping between syntax and phonology are taken to be universal constraints of Optimality Theory. In Tohono O'odham, WRAP-XP suppresses ALIGN-XP,R within lexical projections, as shown in (9) for example (7a). Here candidate (9c), with a boundary after the direct object, is crucially ruled out by WRAP-XP. ALIGN-XP,R still chooses between candidates (9a) and (9b), deriving the boundary after the initial XP. (On the application of WRAP-XP to lexical projections such as VP, but not functional projections such as IP in (7a,b), see Section 18.7.)

(9)   *Tohono O'odham:* WRAP-XP » ALIGN-XP,R

[wakial]$_{NP1}$ 'at [g [wisilo]$_{NP2}$ cepos]$_{VP}$ cowboy AUX DET calf branded	WRAP-XP	ALIGN-XP, R
(a) (H HH H HHH H L)$_P$ wákial 'at g wísilo cépos		*NP2, *NP1!
☞ (b) (H HL)$_P$ (L HHH H L)$_P$ wáki a l 'at g wísilo cépos		*NP2
(c) (HHL)$_P$ (L HLL)$_P$ (H L)$_P$ wákial 'at g wísilo cépos	*VP!	

Not all languages show the suppression of boundaries internal to lexical projections. Languages in which Hale and Selkirk's parameter would be set the other way around are analyzed by the opposite ranking of ALIGN-XP and WRAP-XP. Example (5) shows that Xiamen Chinese is such a language. (10) shows how this is derived by ALIGN-XP,R, unimpeded here by the lower-ranked WRAP-XP.

(10)   *Xiamen Chinese:* ALIGN-XP,R » WRAP-XP

[hoo [yin sio-ti]$_{XP1}$ [tsit pun ts'eq]$_{XP}$]$_{VP}$ give his brother one CL book	ALIGN-XP,R	WRAP-XP
(a) (hoo yin sio-ti tsit pun ts'eq)$_P$	*XP$_1$!	
☞ (b) (hoo yin sio-ti)$_P$ (tsit pun ts'eq)$_P$		*VP

Two arguments for the constraint WRAP-XP are given in Truckenbrodt (1999). One of them is outlined here.

In the Bantu language Chicheŵa (Kanerva 1989, 1990), the penultimate vowel of a p-phrase is lengthened (vowels are otherwise short) and a number of tonal rules are sensitive to the end of a p-phrase (not detailed here for reasons of space). Constituents preceding the VP such as the subject (and initial topics) are bounded at their right edge by a p-phrase boundary as in (11). The VP is also separated by a following p-phrase boundary from constituents moved to the right. A head and its complement are in the same p-phrase as in (12). As in Tohono O'odham, the right edge of a VP-internal object XP does not trigger a p-phrase-boundary, as shown in (13). This is derived by ranking WRAP-XP above ALIGN-XP, as in Tohono O'odham. ALIGN-XP,R thus inserts a boundary after the initial subject in (11) (and after initial topics, and after the VP before constituents moved to the right). Yet its effect is blocked within VP by WRAP-XP in (13).

(11) [XP₁ XP₂]ᴵᴾ/ᶜᴾ   [NP   VP   ]ᴵᴾ
      (   )ₚ(   )ₚ   (kagaálu)ₚ (kanáafa)ₚ
                                 (small) dog died
                                 'The (small) dog died.'

(12) [X₁ XP₂]ₓₚ₁   [V   NP   ]ᵥₚ
      (   )ₚ   (tinabá káluúlu)ₚ
                                 we-stole hare
                                 'We stole the hare.'

(13) [X₁ XP₂ XP₃]ₓₚ₁   [V   NP   [P   NP]ₚₚ]ᵥₚ
      (   )ₚ   (anaményá nyuᵐbá ⁿdí mwáála)ₚ
                                 he-hit   house   with rock
                                 'He hit the house with a rock.'

In Chicheŵa, the interaction with an effect of focus on phrasing leads
to additional evidence for this analysis. Focused constituents are followed
by a p-phrase boundary, as shown in (14) and (15). As these examples show,
the effect of focus overrides Wʀᴀᴘ-XP as the effect of focus forces a p-phrase-
boundary to the right of the focus even within a VP. The effect of focus is
captured in a constraint Aʟɪɢɴ-F,R, ranked above Wʀᴀᴘ-XP.

(14)   [What did they do in Mavuto's house?]
      [Vꜰ   NP]ᵥₚ   (anagóona)ₚ (mnyuᵐbá yá mávúuto)ₚ
      (   )ₚ(   )ₚ   'They *slept* in Mavuto's house.'

(15)   [What did he hit with the rock?]
      [V NPꜰ   PP]ᵥₚ   (anaményá nyuúᵐba)ₚ (ⁿdí mwáála)ₚ
      (   )ₚ(   )ₚ   'He hit   the *house*   with a rock.'

The crucial case, then, involves focus on a verb that has two objects, as in
(16). With the parametric account of Hale and Selkirk, the unfocused case
in (13) requires setting the parameter in such a way that lexically governed
XPs (such as the first object) do not trigger p-phrase boundaries at their
right edges. Consequently, one does not expect a p-phrase boundary at the
right edge of the first object when focus is on the verb. Unexpectedly,
however, such a p-phrase boundary occurs in this case.

(16)   [What did he do to the house with the rock?]
      [Vꜰ   NP   PP]ᵥₚ   (anaméenya)ₚ (nyuúᵐba)ₚ (ⁿdí mwáála)ₚ
      (   )ₚ(   )ₚ(   )ₚ   'He *hit*   the house   with a rock.'

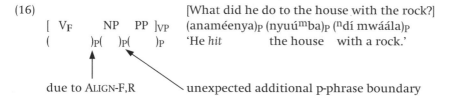

      due to Aʟɪɢɴ-F,R   unexpected additional p-phrase boundary

The constraint-based account predicts the presence of this additional
boundary as shown in (17). The p-phrase around the VP in (a), preferred by
Wʀᴀᴘ-XP, is ruled out by Aʟɪɢɴ-F,R which insists on a p-phrase boundary

after the focused verb, as in (b) and (c). Both (b) and (c) violate WRAP-XP. With the possibility of wrapping the VP thus eliminated by the focus effect, the subordinated ALIGN-XP,R makes its effect felt even within the VP. It eliminates (b) and enforces the additional p-phrase boundary after the first object in (c).

(17)   *Chicheŵa: subordinate* ALIGN-XP,R *shows an effect where* WRAP-XP *is ineffective*

	[anaményá$_F$ [nyu^{m}bá]$_{XP}$ [^{n}dí mwáála]$_{XP}$]$_{VP}$	ALIGN-F,R	WRAP-XP	ALIGN-XP,R
(a)	(anaményá$_F$ nyu^{m}bá ^{n}dí mwáála)$_P$	*!		*NP
(b)	(anaméenya$_F$)$_P$ (nyu^{m}bá ^{n}dí mwáála)$_P$		*VP	*NP!
☞ (c)	(anaméenya$_F$)$_P$ (nyuú^{m}ba)$_P$ (^{n}dí mwáála)$_P$		*VP	

This case supports the analysis in which the effect of ALIGN-XP,R is suppressed within lexical projections, but not turned off once and for all in a given language. Where its suppression by WRAP-XP is ineffective, as in the case at hand, the subordinate effect of ALIGN-XP,R can still be seen inside of VP. The reader is referred to Truckenbrodt (1999) for further details of the analysis, and for a further argument for WRAP-XP, in which ALIGN-XP,R and WRAP-XP jointly force recursive p-phrasing in the Bantu language Kimatuumbi.

18.5   Stress and focus

In English, Dutch, and German, prosodic structure above the word also shows relations to focus and to syntactic structure. This prosodic structure is manifested in (a) intuitions about stress, be it the strongest stress of a sentence or phrasal stress; (b) providing the anchors for the assignment of tones in intonational analyses in the framework of Pierrehumbert (1980), Beckman and Pierrehumbert (1986) (see Ladd 1996, Gussenhoven 2004, Ch.11); (c) judgments about stress shift which seems to be conditioned by prosodic domains (Hayes 1989b; see also Nespor and Vogel 1989 for Italian); and (d) articulatory phonetic consequences of stressed positions and peripheral positions of prosodic domains (see Fougeron and Keating 1997, Cho 2004 and references there for English, see Cho 2003 for Dutch). I here concentrate on (a), on the assumption that the same prosodic system, or an extension of it, will be able to account for the prosodic structure observed in connection with criteria (b) – (d). This section introduces the main effect of focus on stress; the following section turns to the effect of syntax on stress.

The same sentence can be stressed as [$_F$ *John*] *likes blueberries* or *John likes* [$_F$ *blueberries*]. The former may be an answer to the question *Who likes blueberries?*, the latter an answer to the question *What does John like?*. Since

Jackendoff (1972), the meaning difference between such cases is connected to their stress difference by a feature F, assigned to syntactic constituents. Due to its meaning[5], F is here assigned to the part of an answer that gives the requested information: the subject *[F John]* in the first case, the object *[F blueberries]* in the second. If F is a syntactic feature, then its consequences for stress are part of the syntax-phonology mapping. Jackendoff (1972) made a suggestion that is here formulated in two parts. The first part is the mapping constraint (18).

(18)   The strongest stress of the sentence falls inside of the constituent marked F.

Thus the strongest stress of the sentence will correctly fall on *[F John]* in the first example used here, and on *[F blueberries]* in the second example.

In Truckenbrodt (1995) the perspective is developed that (18) (or a refinement of it) may be the only constraint relating focus to prosodic structure. That perspective excludes the existence of constraints like ALIGN-F,R, employed in connection with Chicheŵa above. Truckenbrodt (1995) shows how this effect can be indirectly derived from (18). (The argument made in connection with (17) is not affected by the difference.) This perspective is explored in Kenstowicz and Sohn (1997), Büring (2001), Selkirk (2002, 2004), and Sugahara (2005).

18.6   Stress and XPs

In the examples in (19) F-marking of the information sought for by the question applies to a larger constituent. (18) correctly requires the strongest stress to be within this larger constituent F. Where is stress assigned within this larger constituent? The second part of the suggestion of Jackendoff (1972) is that within the focus, 'the regular stress rules' determine the position of the strongest stress of the sentence.

(19)   (a) Who likes blueberries?   *[F Mary's <u>brother</u>]* likes blueberries.
                               # *[F <u>Mary's</u> brother]* likes blueberries
        (b) Who likes blueberries?   *[F The brother of <u>Mary</u>]* likes blueberries.
                               # *[F The <u>brother</u> of Mary]* likes blueberries.
        (c) What did you learn?   *[F Everyone likes <u>blueberries</u>]*

A famous proposal that works well for English is the *Nuclear Stress Rule* (NSR) of Chomsky and Halle (1968). This rule assigns phrasal stress to the rightmost word in a syntactic constituent, and thus correctly to the rightmost words inside of the focus in the examples in (19).

Comparison with German and Dutch showed that the NSR does not work for all languages, and suggested that rules of assigning phrasal stress are sensitive to the syntactic head–argument relation. It is not easy to distinguish this sensitivity from rightmost stress in English because the complement is regularly the rightmost element in the XP: in (19b) *[brother of Mary]* and (19c) *[. . . likes blueberries]* phrasal stress is in each case rightmost, but it is also on the *complement* of the preceding (nominal or verbal) head. In contrast, in Dutch and German VPs the object precedes the verb and systematically receives the phrasal stress in a larger focus, as in the German examples in (20a). A few postpositions exist in German, and show the same stress-pattern, as in (20b). In NPs (21a) and with prepositions (21b) the head precedes the complement, and stress is again on the complement.

(20)

(a) [What does Hans want to do?]   [What did you do?]
   [Bücher ausleihen]_F   [Ich habe einen Mechaniker angerufen]_F
   books   borrow   I   have a   mechanic   called
   'to borrow books'   'I have called a mechanic.'

(b) [Where did you walk?]   [Why did you do it?]
   [den Fluss entlang]_F   [Anna-s   wegen]_F
   the river along   Anna-GEN because-of
   'along the river'   'because of Anna'

(21)

(a) [What did they mourn?]   [Who did you meet?]
   [die Zerstörung (von) der Stadt]_F [die Schwester von Peter]_F
   the destruction of   the city   the sister   of   Peter
   'the destruction of the city'   'the sister of Peter'

(b) [Where did you walk?]   [Why did you do it?]
   [neben dem Fluss]_F   [wegen   Anna]_F
   next-to the river   because-of Anna
   'next to the river'   'because of Anna'

This led to new proposals by Gussenhoven (1983a, 1992) and Selkirk (1984b, 1995b), in which reference was made to argument structure in the account of stress. Both Gussenhoven and Selkirk cast their suggestions in terms of the assignment of accents (tones on stressed syllables), rather than in terms of the assignment of stress. Sentences can, and often will, have multiple accents, and so these suggestions introduced a perspective that moved away from the concentration on the strongest stress to an account of all positions of prominence. Consider the German example in (22) from an experiment reported in Truckenbrodt (2002, 2004, to appear). Seven speakers regularly assigned measurable pitch accents in the underlined words in this example and in many other examples like it.

(22) [Die <u>Nonne</u>] will   [der <u>Lola</u>] [in <u>Murnau</u>] [[eine <u>Warnung</u>] geben]
       subject   *verb*   *indir.obj.*   *adjunct*   *direct object*   *verb*
       the nun   wants the Lola   in Murnau   a   warning   give
       'The <u>nun</u> wants to give <u>Lola</u> a <u>warning</u> in <u>Murnau</u>.'

Here the subject, the indirect and the direct object, as well as the adjunct each carry accent. The element that is shared with (20) and (21), as well as with (19b,c) is that a head (*geben* in (22)) that stands next to an accented argument (*eine <u>Warnung</u>* in (22)) does not carry accent. All this is correctly predicted by the accounts of Selkirk and of Gussenhoven.

The proposal of Selkirk (1984b, 1995b) departs from Jackendoff's perspective, in which the effect of focus and the effect of syntax can be stated independently. Selkirk suggests a mechanism of focus feature percolation that connects the position of accent to the assignment of F. The head–argument structure is given a privileged status in the percolation mechanism, in such a way that a head next to an accented argument need not be accented itself. Other elements, such as heads without accented arguments, adjuncts, and specifiers are not attributed the same percolation privileges and, in all-new sentences, end up having to carry accent. The suggestion of Gussenhoven (1983a, 1992), on the other hand, is in keeping with Jackendoff's perspective, and states the special status of heads next to accented (stressed) arguments directly:

(23) *Sentence Accent Assignment Rule (SAAR; Gussenhoven 1992)*
      If focused, every predicate, argument, and modifier must be accented, with the exception of a predicate that, discounting unfocused constituents, is adjacent to an argument.

I believe these accounts successfully showed that a complete explanation of stress-assignment (strongest stress and other positions of stress/accents) is most straightforward if two levels are separated: first, the level at which accents are assigned, and at which the SAAR (or the focus percolation mechanism) require accent. Second, the strongest stress of the sentence is simply the last one of these, strengthened by an additional provision as suggested by Uhmann (1991) for German, Hayes and Lahiri (1991) for Bengali, and Selkirk (1995b) for English.[6]

An important prediction of these accounts concerns the difference between arguments and adjuncts, and is illustrated in the English and German examples in (24) and (25) (see also Jacobs 1993, 1999). In all four examples, the object or the adjunct next to the verb is accented by the SAAR. The verb (predicate), however, does not receive phrasal stress next to the accented *arguments* in (24), but does receive accent next to the accented *adjunct* in (25). The resulting argument/adjunct distinction in German is dramatic: while the verb without accent after the argument in (24b) does not qualify for strengthening on the level of the intonation phrase, the verb with accent after the adjunct in (25b) constitutes the last accent of the intonation phrase, and thus attracts the overall strongest stress. The consequence for English is more subtle, but has been shown to be real in a perception experiment (Gussenhoven 1983b): while there is no obligatory accent on the verb in (24a), there is accent on the verb in (25a), in addition to the accent on the adjunct.

(24)   (a)   [What does he do?]   He [teaches <u>linguistics</u>]$_F$
        (b)   [What does he do?]   Er soll   [<u>Linguistik</u> unterrichten]$_F$
                                        he MODAL linguistics teach
                                        'He is said to teach linguistics.'

(25)   (a)   [What does he do?]   He [teaches in <u>Ghana</u>]$_F$
        (b)   [What does he do?]   Er soll   [in <u>Ghana</u> <u>unterrichten</u>]$_F$
                                        he MODAL in Ghana teach
                                        'He is said to teach in Ghana.'

The core cases of Gussenhoven's SAAR and Selkirk's sensitivity of focus percolation to the head–argument relation can be subsumed under a much simpler formulation. I offer the constraint in (26).[7]

(26)   STRESS-XP
       Each XP must contain a beat of stress on the level of the p-phrase.

In (22), for example, the arguments and the adjunct are each XPs, and thus receive a beat of phrasal stress to satisfy STRESS-XP. (26) works in conjunction with the suggestion of Pierrehumbert 1980 that pitch accents (tones on stressed syllables) in English are assigned to a representation of stress that is independently determined. The strongest stress is then assigned as in (27), similar to the suggestions of Uhmann (1991), Hayes and Lahiri (1991), and Selkirk (1995b).

(27)   On the level of the intonation phrase, the rightmost stress of the level
       of the p-phrase is strengthened.

Like the account of Xiamen Chinese in terms of ALIGN-XP,R, (26) makes use of syntactic XPs and does not make reference to the relation among nodes (such as whether they are arguments, adjuncts or predicates). Rather, the effect of these relations on the assignment of phrasal stress falls out from the standard syntactic representation of these syntactic relations. To see how, consider the two structures in (28). Arguments of V as in (28a) are standardly represented as syntactic sisters to the V head and daughter to the verb phrase. They are genuinely inside of VP. STRESS-XP requires that the argument contains phrasal stress, since it is an XP (NP in (28a)). STRESS-XP makes no demands on V, which is not an XP. STRESS-XP does require that VP contains phrasal stress. If VP contains a stressed argument, as in (28a), this requirement on VP is fulfilled: the VP contains phrasal stress, located in the argument. There is therefore no need for stressing the verb. On the other hand, if there is no stressed argument inside of VP, then the requirement of phrasal stress within VP must be satisfied by stressing the verb. Such cases include VPs with no object, such as *Maria* hat [*geniest*]$_{VP}$, *Mary has [sneezed]*$_{VP}$, or with an unstressable object (see also below), as in *Maria* hat [*etwas gesehen*]$_{VP}$, *Mary* has [*seen something*]$_{VP}$. A further case of this kind is (28b). In this standard syntactic representation of adjuncts, the adjunct is not inside of the VP in the same way as the argument. The adjunct is outside of the lower VP node. STRESS-XP requires stress on the adjunct XP, which is assigned. However, this cannot now serve to also satisfy STRESS-XP for the VP, since the adjunct (unlike the argument) is outside of VP, i.e. outside of the lower VP-node in (28b). STRESS-XP requires independent stress in this VP, which can only be assigned on the verb. In other words, the verb needs to be stressed in (28b) because it is itself a syntactic phrase there (i.e. a VP), but it need not be stressed in (28a), because it is not itself a syntactic phrase there.[8]

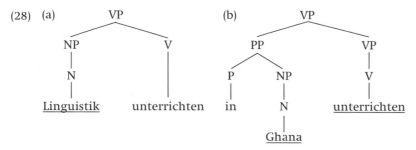

(28) (a) [tree: VP → NP (N: Linguistik), V (unterrichten)] (b) [tree: VP → PP (P: in, NP (N: Ghana)), VP (V: unterrichten)]

We have, then, STRESS-XP in (26) and rightmost strengthening in (27) as a good approximation to the English, Dutch and German facts on the location of phrasal stress.

STRESS-XP and ALIGN-XP show considerable overlap in the results they derive. For example, stress on the arguments and adjuncts XPs in (22) could also be derived by (a) right-aligning these XPs with p-phrase boundaries and (b) assigning rightmost stress within the domains thus derived. However, distinctions also exist. ALIGN-XP,R would (on its own) derive identical prosodic structures for (28a) and (28b) (wrongly: *(Linguistik)(unterrichten)* and correctly: *(in Ghana)(unterrichten)*). Inversely, STRESS-XP could predict the p-phrase final position of non-sandhi tone in Xiamen Chinese in a variety of cases, including (3), (4) and (5). In Xiamen Chinese, however, a complement that precedes a head is phrased separately from the head *(complement-XP)(head)* (see Chen 1987:131). Here ALIGN-XP,R makes the correct prediction, while STRESS-XP would not work without further ado. Other cases in which a replacement of ALIGN-XP with STRESS-XP raises serious questions can be found in the detailed discussion of Shanghai Chinese in Selkirk and Shen (1990). It is still possible that one of ALIGN-XP and STRESS-XP can take on the work of both when interactions with other constraints (such as WRAP-XP or p-phrase-final stress-assignment) are taken into account. The issue is left open here. What seems to be plausible, however, is that across languages, there is a level of prosodic structure (p-phrases) that is related to syntactic XPs, as captured by the constraints ALIGN-XP, WRAP-XP and STRESS-XP.

18.7   The distinction between lexical and functional projections

There is strong evidence that the syntax-phonology interface distinguishes lexical words/lexical projections from function words/functional projections. An important proposal for this difference is due to Selkirk (1995a): it is a general fact, or principle, about the syntax–phonology mapping that the constraints of the mapping, such as ALIGN-XP,R, only apply to lexical categories (here: lexical XPs such as NP and VP) but not to functional categories (here: functionally headed XPs such as DP and CP). The proposal also predicts that STRESS-XP and WRAP-XP apply to lexical XPs but not to functional XPs. The proposal is adopted in Truckenbrodt (1999), where the name *Lexical Category Condition* (LCC) is suggested for a particular formulation of it.

For example, Chen (1987) notes that functional elements such as pronouns do not trigger right-alignment. While a full subject is followed by a tone group boundary (p-phrase boundary) in (3), the pronominal subject is not in (29). Similarly, the first object triggers such a boundary at its right edge in (5), but a pronominal first object does not, as in (30).

(29) [   ]$_{DP}$
      yi/lang   sia   k'a   kin
      (he/someone   write more fast)$_{TG}$ (no internal tone-group boundary)
      'He/someone   writes faster.'

(30) [[   ]$_{DP}$]$_{VP}$
      (sang gua/lang   nng opun ts'eq)$_{TG}$ (no internal tone-group boundary)
      give I/someone two CL   book
      'give me/someone two books'

In the syntactic analysis that has become standard since Abney (1987), pronouns and determiners are both of category D, heading a DP. Pronouns (like intransitive verbs) do not normally have a complement, thus [she$_D$]$_{DP}$. Determiners (like transitive verbs) normally have a complement, an NP, thus [the$_D$ [student$_N$]$_{NP}$]$_{DP}$. In this analysis, pronouns like the ones in (29) and (30) are DPs, and thus functionally headed projections. The fact that they do not invoke ALIGN-XP follows from the LCC: Functional projections (such as DP) do not invoke mapping constraints (such as ALIGN-XP).

Selkirk and Shen (1990) argue that prosodic words in Shanghai Chinese are derived by left-alignment with lexical words (X⁰s) while functional words do not trigger prosodic word boundaries. They further argue that p-phrases are derived by left-alignment with lexically-headed syntactic phrases (XPs), while functional XP projections do not trigger p-phrase boundaries. The phenomenon is found in many other languages as well, and I am not aware of systematic counterexamples.

Pronouns are similarly unstressed by default in English, Dutch, and German. (31) contrasts with (32) and (33): the pronominal subject and object do not receive phrasal stress by default.

(31) [the [mayor]$_{NP}$]$_{DP}$ won their support.

(32) [he]$_{DP}$ won their support

(33) [the [mayor]$_{NP}$]$_{DP}$ won [something]$_{DP}$

The LCC correctly predicts that functional XPs do not receive phrasal stress: functional XPs (here: DP) do not invoke the mapping constraints (here: STRESS-XP).

Functional XPs also do not need wrapping (Truckenbrodt 1999). If IP/CP would need wrapping in (7a,b) and (11), this demand would wrongly suppress the p-phrase boundary after the initial XP in these examples, due to the high ranking of WRAP-XP over ALIGN-XP,R in Tohono O'odham and Chicheŵa. Here the LCC correctly predicts that Wrap-XP does not apply to the functional projections IP and CP.

On the account that makes use of the LCC, we have to refine what constituents exactly trigger alignment and stressing in the earlier examples. In (31), for example, the DP constituent that is the subject argument does not literally invoke STRESS-XP: like the subject DP in (32), it is exempt in principle from invoking STRESS-XP. In (31), it is then the lexical NP inside of DP that correctly invokes STRESS-XP. Similar refinements apply to most earlier examples: arguments and adjuncts in these examples attract stress by STRESS-XP and trigger alignment by ALIGN-XP not at the DP-level, but because the NP inside of DP invokes these constraints. Where the DP is present without the NP inside, as with pronouns, STRESS-XP and ALIGN-XP are correctly not applied.

The LCC is not the only approach to the difference between lexical and functional projections. A different proposal comes from the literature on focus. Ladd (1980, 1983a) made the argument that final constituents are *deaccented* if contextually given. Ladd argues that deaccenting does not require the contrastive effect of focus on the element that receives the main stress. This is the 'givenness effect': being contextually given alone is enough for deaccenting. In (34), for example, there is no contextual contrast on *like*, yet stress retracts to *like* (relative to the predictions of the NSR or, in the perspective developed here, STRESS-XP) since the final element *Fred* is contextually given.

(34) A: What about Fred?
      B: I don't like Fred.

Interesting examples for deaccenting in non-final positions are discussed in van Deemter (1994). Observations like those of Ladd and van Deemter have led to refined theories of focus in Selkirk (1995b) and Schwarzschild (1999). In Selkirk (1995b) the focus percolation mechanism mentioned above is integrated with an account of both the givenness effect and the attraction of stress by focus in the more traditional sense of Rooth (1992). (In an account using STRESS-XP in (26), this would have to be replaced by an overriding constraint that prevents the stressing of contextually given elements, in addition to (18).) For discussion of different kinds of givenness, see Baumann and Grice (to appear).

The consequences of the givenness effect for the stressing and phrasing of functional elements have not yet been systematically explored, to the best of the author's knowledge, but they turn out to be remarkable. The cases that are often taken for granted involve definite pronouns as in (32), which have an independent lexical requirement of being contextually given. Satisfaction of this requirement will, in normal cases, lead to their destressing. Indefinite pronouns, as in (33), do not carry such a lexical requirement, yet they can be construed as trivially given in a different sense: *something* can be construed as given in any context that contains anything at all (see the discussion in Schwarzschild 1999:154).

The two accounts, Lexical Category Condition (LCC) and the givenness effect, have a good deal of overlap. For example, both account for the initial intuition that the subject is unaccented in (32). Yet it seems that neither of the two proposals can cover all the territory on its own. An obvious shortcoming of the LCC is that it does not extend to contextually given lexical categories, such as the destressed NP inside of the object in (34) (or, avoiding a proper name, in the similar example *What about the mayor?* I don't *like* the [mayor]$_{NP}$). The LCC alone will also not suffice for pronouns in English. Consider (35). The LCC may explain why the functional DP subject does not require accent here but it cannot account for the stresslessness of the objects on its own: the LCC has only the weak consequence that the functional objects do not require phrasal stress. STRESS-XP still requires stress in the VP, but it is now left open whether this falls on the verb or on the functional object. Since, empirically, stress must fall on the verb (unless the object is narrowly focused), a stronger requirement than the LCC seems to be at work, forcing stress away from the object. Here we must invoke the givenness effect.

(35) (x   )   (x   )
     He [likes her]$_{VP}$ Someone [likes someone]$_{VP}$

However, it seems that givenness cannot replace the LCC in all cases. There is a robust generalization in many languages that lexical words form prosodic words while function words do not (Selkirk 1995a). This plays out in an interesting way in interaction with focus in the phrasal phonology of Xiamen Chinese/Taiwanese as shown in Hsiao (2002). Further, it seems that the application of WRAP-XP to lexical projections like VP in (7a,b) but not functional projections like IP in (7a,b) cannot be reduced to a givenness effect. A further interesting case has been suggested to me by Lisa Selkirk in a review of the present chapter: in the sequence *V NP PP* in English, where NP is given but V and PP are not, a likely phrasing seems to be (V̲ NP)(P̲P̲).[9] It seems that the phrase-boundary after the NP must here come from right-alignment with a given constituent, suggesting that givenness does not exempt one from invoking the mapping constraints.

In conclusion, there seems to be evidence for two overlapping but independent factors that may affect functional and lexical elements differently. As proposed by Selkirk, mapping constraints are invoked by lexical syntactic constituents but not by functional syntactic constituents (LCC). Further, as argued by Ladd and others, contextually given elements show an effect of rejecting accent. The latter is not inherently tied to the lexical/functional distinction. However, the anaphoric nature and/or the small content of functional elements will often allow them to be taken as given, in which case deaccenting results.

Interesting issues in connection with the correct account of the behavior of function words and their projection in the mapping are also raised by the detailed studies by Soh (2001) of Shanghai Chinese and Hokkien/Taiwanese and by Zec (2005) of Standard Serbian.

18.8 Eurythmic effects on phrasing

The constraints that relate phonological phrases to syntax are not the only ones that influence the shape of p-phrases. They can interact with constraints on preferred size of prosodic constituents and constraints against stress-clash that give rise to eurhythmic preferences. Similar constraints on binarity of feet and even spacing of stress play a crucial role in shaping the stress patterns within words in many languages (see Kager Ch.9).

At the level of the p-phrase they have been found and studied in Romance languages. An early important step in this was the phrasing algorithm of Nespor & Vogel (1986) for Italian. (In Italian, p-phrases and the rightmost stress assigned in them are diagnosed by a number of phonological and phonetic rules sensitive to them.) I begin by relating Nespor and Vogel's algorithm to the discussion in this chapter, since Nespor and Vogel's suggestions approach the issue from a different angle, and have also formed a basis of further insightful work on phrasing in Romance languages (see for example Frascarelli 2000 and Frota 2000). Applied to Italian, the algorithm works as follows. First, general statements of *Φ domain/Φ construction* build small p-phrases by grouping a noun together with preceding numerals, determiners and prepositions, an adjective with preceding degree expressions, and a verb with preceding negation and auxiliaries. A phrasing as resulting from this first step is shown in (36). Second, a rule of Φ *restructuring* allows two small p-phrases to merge into a larger one if the second is the syntactic complement of the first and is not branching. Restructuring of the AP in (36) (taken as a complement of the noun) with the noun *cittá* is blocked, since the AP is branching. In the otherwise similar structure in (37), however, the separate phrasing of the first step *(le cittá)ₚ(nordiche)ₚ* allows restructuring into a larger p-phrase in the second step. The result is as shown in (37). (The accent on *cittá* is orthographic.)

(36)   [[|ᴀᴘ|ɴᴘ ···
            (Le cittá)ₚ (molto nordiche)ₚ   (non mi piacciono)ₚ
            the cities   very Nordic   not me please
            'I don't like very Nordic cities.'

(37)   [[|ᴀᴘ|ɴᴘ   ···
            (Le cittá nordiche)ₚ   (non mi piacciono)ₚ
            the cities Nordic   not me please
            'I don't like Nordic cities.'

Ghini (1993) developed a reanalysis of Italian phrasing in terms of Aʟɪɢɴ-XP,R and additional eurhythmic conditions. As his work brings out, the boundaries that would be assigned by Aʟɪɢɴ-XP,R are always also predicted by Nespor and Vogel's algorithm. An example is the p-phrase boundary following the subject in (36) and (37). However, Nespor and Vogel's algorithm assigns additional boundaries between heads and complements, such as the subject-internal boundary in (36), which would not be assigned by Aʟɪɢɴ-XP,R. Ghini (1993) argues that eurhythmic constraints are responsible for these additional divisions. In his account, the branchingness condition of Nespor and Vogel's Φ restructuring goes back to a binarity requirement 'Uniformity and Average Weight'. In Optimality Theory, the idea that the prosodic representation is simultaneously subject to constraints of the interface and to eurhythmic constraints has been developed by Selkirk (2000). Selkirk suggests that in English, Aʟɪɢɴ-XP,R and Wʀᴀᴘ-XP are tied in a particular way, and that they interact with a subordinate constraint BɪɴMɪɴ, which requires a minimally binary prosodic length of the Major phrase (here: p-phrase). Selkirk also formulates a constraint BɪɴMᴀx, which may be employed to capture the main effects of Ghini's 'Uniformity and Average Weight'. I use the formulation in (38) in terms of prosodic words, in parallel to Ghini's formulation. For the simple case in (36) the interaction of the constraints may be as shown in (39), following the analysis of a similar case in Brazilian Portuguese in Sandalo and Truckenbrodt (2002). Here the constraint Wʀᴀᴘ-XP in subordinate ranking can be seen as an implementation of a further factor of Ghini's analysis, 'Increasing Units'.

(38) BINMAX

P-phrases consist of maximally two prosodic words.

(39)

Le [cittá [molto nordiche]$_{AP}$]$_{NP}$	ALIGN-XP,R	BIN-MAX	WRAP-XP
(a) (Le cittá molto nordiche)$_p$		*!	
☞ (b) (Le cittá)$_p$ (molto nordiche)$_p$			*NP
(c) (Le cittá molto)$_p$ (nordiche)$_p$			*NP, *AP!

Notice that BINMAX does not lead to the insertion of a similar p-phrase boundary in the subject in (37), since the subject here is no longer than two prosodic words.

Ghini's perspective, thus implemented in Optimality Theory, has recently been pursued for other Romance languages. Prieto (2005) shows that an impressive range of Catalan patterns of phrasing can be accounted for by an interleaving of ALIGN-XP,R and WRAP-XP with four eurhythmic constraints. While in Italian ALIGN-XP,R seems to be undominated, in Catalan eurhythmic constraints also dominate and override the syntax–phonology mapping constraints. In the interaction of all constraints, ALIGN-XP,R and WRAP-XP still play a crucial role.

Elordieta, Frota and Vigário (2005) investigate differences in the formation of intonation phrases between Spanish and European Portuguese (also see the following section). They argue that syntax–phonology mapping constraints of alignment and wrapping interact with eurhythmic constraints, with interesting differences between Spanish (preference for *(S)(VO)*) and European Portuguese (preference for *(SVO)*).

An issue that remains in a reanalysis of Nespor and Vogel's algorithm as discussed here is that, in terms of their algorithm, *Φ* restructuring is never obligatory. In other words, a lexical head and its lexical complement, even if they can be, or are preferred to be, phrased together, can also be phrased separately in many languages. In English, for example, though we can have *(He teaches linguistics)*, we can also have *(He teaches) (linguistics)*. It is not clear that mapping constraints are responsible for such optionality. Selkirk (2005) suggests to account for some variability on the level of the intonation phrase (see following section) by allowing the promotion of a lower prosodic constituent (her major phrase) to an intonation phrase. It seems similarly possible that we are here dealing with optional gratuitous promotion of a postlexical prosodic word, such as *he teaches*, to a phonological phrase. Note that such gratuitous promotion is empirically not possible in head-final structures like (20) or (24b), where it would wrongly lead to a shift in the strongest stress to the final head. Thus, gratuitous promotion would be limited either to prenuclear position, or to cases in which it does not reverse relative prominence relations.

18.9   Intonation phrases

The position of intonation phrase boundaries shows a good amount of variability. These have been studied in English on the basis of positions of possible pauses within clauses (Selkirk 1984b, Taglicht 1998 and references there) and positions of obligatory pauses (Downing 1970). The detailed and extensive study of Downing (1970) is still relevant today. The core result is that *root clauses, and only these, are bounded by obligatory intonation phrase breaks.* (Root clauses are clauses (CPs) not embedded inside of a higher clause that has a subject and a predicate.) Downing 1970 argues that obligatory pauses separate coordinate root clauses as in (40). Where the coordinate clauses are together embedded as in (41), there is an optional pause as indicated, but not the obligatory pause of interest for the generalization at issue. He also makes this point in regard to (42): in a coherent reading, coordination is at the root level, entailing obligatory pause. If the pause is instead omitted, embedded coordination, and hence a contradictory reading results.

(40)   Mary will sing / and Bob will play his banjo.

(41)   I hope that Mary will sing (/) and Bob will play his banjo.

(42)   Bill believes his father was older than his mother, / and his mother
        was older than his father.

Downing also argues that certain left-peripheral constituents as in (43) as well as certain right-peripheral elements are separated by obligatory pause (see also Bing 1979). In Downing's analysis, these elements are moved to, or generated in, a position external to the root clause.

(43)   John, / he never does anything right.
        In the afternoon / everyone went swimming.
        In fact / you seem to have put on some weight.

The formation of separate intonation phrases for left- and right-peripheral topics has been established in Italian by Frascarelli (2000). In Italian dialects, the intonation phrase can be diagnosed separately from the p-phrase by different phonological rules.

   Downing also analyzes different classes of parentheticals (44), as well as appositive relative clauses and other appositive elements (45), and argues that they are separated by obligatory pauses. In Downing's analysis, they are elements outside of the root clause at an abstract relevant stage of the derivation. Nespor and Vogel (1986) have shown that the intonation phrase boundaries around parentheticals can be demonstrated with the help of the phonological diagnostics for intonation phrase boundaries in Italian.

(44)   The operation, / I'm sure, / won't take very long.

(45)   The library, / which is a large stone and glass building, / is on the east side of the campus.
       The library, / a large stone and glass building, / is on the east side of the campus.

Ladd (1986) has suggested that structures of this kind involve recursive intonation phrases. Frota (2000) has been able to establish this for a case of appositive relative clauses in European Portuguese on the basis of phonological diagnostics.

A recent suggestion for a comprehensive treatment of the interacting factors that govern intonation phrasing can be found in Selkirk (2005). Downing's root clauses are there reanalyzed in terms of the feature [+comma] by Potts (2005), for which Potts provides a semantic/pragmatic interpretation. A different approach to intonation phrases is pursued in Gussenhoven (2004:287ff.) in terms of output-to-output faithfulness. Recent psycholinguistic literature – often working experimentally with intonational cues of intonation phrase boundaries – has investigated the linguistic and contextual conditions under which intonation phrase boundaries are employed and useful for syntactic disambiguation; see Clifton, Carlson and Frazier (2002), Fodor (2002), Kraljic and Brennan (2005), Watson and Gibson (2005) and references therein.

18.10   Summary

This chapter has reviewed and presented arguments that (i) prosodic structure – particularly at the p-phrase level – is influenced by syntactic structure; (ii) syntactic XPs play a crucial role in shaping p-phrases; (iii) the forming of p-phrases can be forced by the constraints ALIGN-XP,L/R; (iv) the forming of p-phrases can be blocked by the constraint WRAP-XP; (v) an additional constraint STRESS-XP allows us to understand the assignment of phrasal stress in related terms; (vi) focus affects prosodic structure by attracting stress and in other ways; (vii) the mapping constraints are invoked by lexical XPs but not by functional XPs; (viii) they may interact with eurhythmic constraints; and (ix) root clauses determine positions of obligatory intonation phrase boundaries.

Notes

Many thanks to Paul de Lacy, Jessica Rett, and Lisa Selkirk for lots of useful comments that helped improve this chapter.

1 Some prominent examples of the diversity of views in this area: Halle and Vergnaud (1987) and Cinque (1993) assume an arbitrary number of levels in the metrical representation; syntax-oriented accounts of

metrical structure like Cinque (1993) and Zubizarreta (1998) are interested in syntax-related stress-generalizations rather than edgemost
placement of stress; Odden (1987b) develops accounts of phrase-level
phonology that refer to syntactic structure, without invoking phrasal
prosodic constituents; Beckman and Pierrehumbert (1986) name constituents across languages with reference to the phenomena sensitive to
them (rather than, as done here, with reference to the syntactic elements
that they derive from); many authors who postulate higher prosodic
constituents are uncommitted as to whether these also serve as metrical
domains.

2 See Peperkamp (1997) and Vigário (2003) for prosodic words, Truckenbrodt (1999) and Gussenhoven (2004) for phonological phrases, and Ladd
(1986) and Frota (2000) for intonation phrases.

3 See Chen (2000) for discussion of the system of tone sandhi that affects
the five long tones and the two short tones of this language. Hsiao (2002)
has convincingly argued that the Xiamen tone domains are domains of
abstract prominence.

4 An exception is a class of adjuncts that do not show p-phrase boundaries.
Soh (2001) has later argued convincingly for a syntactic analysis of these
adjuncts in which they are not exceptions to the general mechanism of
right-alignment. Soh however adds a class of exceptions of her own,
certain indefinite elements.

5 See Rooth (1992) and Schwarzschild (1999) for influential theories of the
meaning of focus.

6 Some later proposals about sentence stress such as Cinque (1993) and
Zubizarreta (1998) do not employ this separation of two levels and
concentrate on the position of main stress. See Truckenbrodt (2006) for
some more discussion.

7 This constraint was originally proposed in Truckenbrodt (1995). In Truckenbrodt (2006), an introduction to phrasal stress, this analysis is motivated in some more detail.

8 For a more refined development of the application of mapping-
constraints to adjunction structures, see Truckenbrodt (1999); the effect
is the same for the case at hand.

9 This can be diagnosed in the presence of a H* pitch accent on V, which is
followed by a fall and low valley to the end of the NP, characteristic of the
L- phrase accent/edge tone of Beckman and Pierrehumbert (1986).

19

Morpheme position

Adam Ussishkin

19.1   Introduction

Affixes are commonly classified as prefixes or suffixes. Prefixes appear at the left edge of a stem, like American English [ɪn] 'in-' (e.g. [ɪnseɪn] 'insane'); suffixes appear at the right edge of a stem, like [ɪɾi] '-ity' (e.g. [sænɪɾi] 'sanity'). However, affixes can appear in other positions as well. For instance, they can appear 'infixed' inside a morpheme like the Tagalog morpheme [-um-] in [s-um-ulat] 'write'.

   Morpheme position can vary by a range of parameters. The following three parameters are relevant here:

  (i)   whether an affix is default-prefixing or default-suffixing (i.e. whether it is oriented toward the left or the right edge of the word)
 (ii)   whether or not an affix is influenced by phonological pressures (i.e. whether an affix always occurs at an edge, or whether phonological well-formedness overrides edge placement)
(iii)   whether or not an affix is contiguous (i.e. whether an affix is concatenative or not)

Despite the wide array of positions affixes can appear in, this chapter will argue, following McCarthy and Prince (1986 et seq.), that there are only two basic types of affix: prefixes and suffixes. When affixes occur anywhere other than the edge of a word, phonological pressures are always responsible.

   Because of the interesting behavior of nonconcatenative morphology, special attention is paid in this chapter to the properties and analysis of interfixes, affixes that tend to be segmentally discontiguous and that typically replace material in the content morpheme they combine with. The core of the discussion concerns the extent to which phonology has an influence on morpheme position; as we will see, the influence can be quite important, to the extent that phonological well-formedness can determine morpheme position.[1]

19.2   The theory of edge orientation

19.2.1   Generalized Alignment

Current models of phonology tend to view concatenative affixation as an edge-oriented phenomenon. Within Optimality Theory, Generalized Alignment (GA; McCarthy and Prince 1993a) provides a framework for analyzing morpheme position. The overarching schema of GA holds that edges of both Phonological Categories (PCat) and Morphological or Grammatical Categories (GCat) should coincide. In particular, GA constraints are typically of the form given in (1):

(1)   *Generalized Alignment* (McCarthy and Prince 1993a)

ALIGN (Cat1, Edge1, Cat2, Edge2) $=_{\text{def}}$
     $\forall$ Cat1 $\exists$ Cat2 such that Edge1 of Cat1 and Edge2 of Cat2 coincide.
Where Cat1, Cat2 $\in$ PCat $\cup$ GCat
     Edge1, Edge2 $\in$ {Right, Left}

Deconstructing (1), the basic thrust of GA is that there are output-oriented constraints that state "align some edge of every element *x* with some edge of an element *y*."

19.2.2   Cases

The type of demand made by alignment constraints is most easily understood in a simple case. To begin, consider the case of English *in-* prefixation. Prefixes attach to the left edge of a word, as seen in the following examples (2) from American English, which prefixes *in-* to an adjective to convey the meaning 'not {adjective}'. The phonological exponence of the prefix's nasal consonant varies in place of articulation depending on the first segment of the stem to which it attaches.

(2)   *Prefixes: American English in- 'not' prefixation*

	Adjective		in-*adjective*	
Orthography	*IPA*		*Orthography*	*IPA*
audible	[ɔrəbl̩]		inaudible	[ɪnɔrəbl̩]
sane	[seɪn]		insane	[ɪnseɪn]
competent	[kɑmpərn̩ʔ]		incompetent	[ɪŋkɑmpərn̩ʔ]
congruent	[kəŋgɹun̩ʔ]		incongruent	[ɪŋkəŋgɹun̩ʔ]
possible	[pɑsəbl̩]		impossible	[ɪmpɑsəbl̩]
movable	[muvəbl̩]		immovable	[ɪmuvəbl̩]

Under GA, no prefixal status need be granted to *in*. Its location at the left edge of forms is the result of a high-ranking constraint aligning *in* to the left edge of a stem. The formal constraint is provided in (3):

(3)   ALIGN-L (*in*, Stem)

Effectively, (3) states "the left edge of every instance of the morpheme *in* coincides with the left edge of some stem." This constraint will be referred to as ALIGN-*in* below, for convenience. The constraint, as an undominated constraint in English, is always satisfied; that is, *in-* never appears anywhere but at the left edge – thus its uniform status as a prefix. Thus, in OT, the prefixhood of *in-* is achieved through a constraint on output well-formedness, rather than being specified lexically. Suffixes are treated in a similar fashion under this approach, with the simple parametric modification that alignment is to the right edge rather than the left. A simple example to illustrate suffixation comes from the verbal paradigm of Modern Hebrew (4), where the suffix [-ɛt] is used to mark feminine gender in the present tense (these examples all involve the same prefix as well):

(4) *Suffixes:* Modern Hebrew 'feminine' [-ɛt] suffixation

Verb (masculine)	*Verb-et (feminine)*	*Gloss*
medaber	medaberɛt	'speak'
megadel	megadelɛt	'raise'
mefakses	mefaksesɛt	'send a fax'
metaʔer	metaʔerɛt	'describe'
metajek	metajekɛt	'file'
medamem	medamemɛt	'bleed'

In the interesting case of circumfixes, alignment to *both* edges is crucial. That is, an affix appears to simultaneously exhibit properties of both prefixes and suffixes. Representative data come from German verbal past participles (5); regular verbs have the circumfix *ge- -t*:

(5) *Circumfixes:* German past participles

Verbal root		*Past participle*		*Gloss*
spiel	[ʃpiːl]	gespielt	[ɡəʃpiːlt]	'play'
such	[zuːx]	gesucht	[ɡəzuːxt]	'search'
koch	[kɔx]	gekocht	[ɡəkɔxt]	'cook'
hör	[høːʁ]	gehört	[ɡəhøːʁt]	'hear'
blick	[blɪk]	geblickt	[ɡəblɪkt]	'look'

Analysis of such forms within GA involves alignment constraints that reference both the left and right edges; in undominated position, such constraints result in circumfixion.

19.2.3 Alternative approaches

In the GA approach to morpheme position, distance from the left (or right) edge is assessed gradiently. That is, for morphemes whose position does not fall at an edge, they are nonetheless edge-oriented in that the same morpheme consistently occurs *close* to an edge (see the case of Tagalog, presented below). Recent work by McCarthy (2003b) presents an alternative view whereby all constraints are categorical, and develops this idea even for cases where gradient constraint evaluation seems crucial. Another

alternative is presented by Horwood (2002), where the analysis of morpheme position depends on faithfulness, rather than on markedness (more
specifically, on the preservation of precedence relations).

19.3   Phonological demands on well-formedness may override alignment

The main idea behind the GA approach is that all affixes are essentially
prefixes or suffixes, and that deviations from edgemost position are due to
phonological requirements. In more theoretical terms, every affix is
affected by the demand to appear at either the left or the right edge of a
stem; this is expressed via an alignment constraint. Deviations from the
edge are caused by higher-ranking markedness constraints on phonological
well-formedness. Two types of phonologically induced edge-deviation exist:
cases where the affix cannot occur within the stem (variable-direction
affixes), and cases where the affix can appear inside the stem (infixes).

19.3.1   Variable-direction affixes

As discussed by Fulmer (1997), based on data from Bliese (1981), the Cush-
itic language Afar presents an interesting case of variable-direction affixes.
These occur in the verbal system, where the affix-expressing person
marking on verbs varies in its location due to phonological requirements.
For instance, in the second-person form of verbs, the person marker [-t-]
occurs stem-finally if the stem begins with a consonant (6a), and stem-
initially if the stem begins with a vowel (6b):[2]

(6)   *Afar variable-direction person marking (data from Fulmer 1997)*

		Verb	*Gloss*
	(a)	nak-t-eː	'drink milk'
		haj-t-eː	'put'
		sug-t-eː	'had'
		kal-t-eː	'prevent'
	(b)	t-eḥ-eː	'give'
		t-ibbiḍ-eː	'seize'
		t-okm-eː	'eat'
		t-usuul-eː	'laugh'

Variability in the position of the second-person marker [-t-] can be viewed
as phonologically based: the affix occurs to the right of the stem (i.e. as
a suffix), except when the stem is vowel-initial, in which case the
affix surfaces as a prefix. Abstracting away from complexities involving the
position of the person marker relevant to the affix marker, a GA-based
account of this variability is easily available: a right edge-oriented alignment

constraint on the person marker (capturing its suffixal nature) is dominated by ONSET, a constraint requiring syllables to have onsets. Since consonant-initial stems have an onset, the alignment constraint exerts its
effect on the position of the person marker. However, vowel-initial stems
surface with the person marker at the left edge, resulting in a more
harmonic output from the point of view of syllable structure, to which
alignment is subordinated.

19.3.2 Phonologically driven infixation

Phonological restrictions can force morphemes to appear away from stem
edges. In these situations, the affected morpheme is called an 'infix'.
Although typically edge-oriented, infixes appear *within* a form, rather than
at the absolute edge of a form. A well-known example comes from English
expletive infixation (7), where the expletive prefixes to a stressed syllable.

(7) *American English expletive infixation* (McCarthy 1982, Hammond 1999)
     (examples appear orthographically)

Base	*With expletive infix*
Arizóna	Àri-fùckin-zóna
Càlifórnia	Càli-fùckin-fórnia
Àlamagórdo	Àlama-fùckin-górdo
Àppalàchicóla	Àppa-fùckin-làchicóla, Àppalàchi-fùckin-cóla
Mìnnesóta	Mìnne-fùckin-sóta

Tagalog presents another well-known case of infixation. In Tagalog, the
agentive focus marker [-um-] may occur either at the left edge of a form or
within a form. As we will see, this distribution is not random. Relevant data
appear in (8).

(8) *Tagalog [-um-] agentive focus* (French 1988, McCarthy 2003b)

Root	*root + -um-*	*Gloss*
aral	um-aral	'teach'
abot	um-abot	'reach for'
sulat	s-um-ulat	'write'
gradwet	gr-um-adwet	'graduate'
preno	pr-um-eno	'to brake'

The basic analysis of Tagalog presented in Prince and Smolensky (2004) and
McCarthy and Prince (1993a) involves an alignment constraint that is
morpheme-specific, requiring [-um-] to occur at the left edge of the stem:

(9) ALIGN-L(*um*, STEM)   (abbreviated to ALIGN-*um* below)

This constraint on its own has the effect of placing the affix [-um-] at the left
edge of a form, resulting in the prefixal nature of the affix. In other words, as

explained in Prince and Smolensky (2004) and McCarthy and Prince (1993a), [-um-] is basically a prefix and when possible surfaces as such: [um-aral]. However, the data from Tagalog show that the affix is not consistently realized at the left edge of every form: consonant-initial forms, when combined with [-um-], surface with the initial consonant (or consonant cluster) at the left edge. This is due to the overriding effect of high-ranking NoCODA, as tableau (10) from McCarthy and Prince (1993a) shows. For the sake of clarity, violations of ALIGN-*um* are marked using the segments that cause the violation.

(10)   *gradwet-um*

/gradwet-um/	NoCODA	ALIGN-*um*
(a) um.grad.wet	***!	
(b) gum.rad.wet	***!	g
(c) gra.dum.wet	**	grad!
☞ (d) gru.mad.wet	**	gr

Violations of the alignment constraint are assessed by counting the number of segments separating the left edge of [-um-] from the left edge of each candidate form. Candidate (10a) achieves perfect alignment of [-um-] to the left edge, while candidates (10b-d) exemplify varying distances from the left edge of the word. Since the well-aligned candidate (10a) is not the actual output, some other constraint must be responsible for the surface position of [-um-] in (10d), the optimal form. It is clear that avoidance of syllable codas (formalized by the constraint NoCODA) is more important than edge-realization of [-um-] in Tagalog. The alignment-based analysis, then, has as a consequence that infixation is viewed as an edge-oriented phenomenon: an affix prefers to be realized at an edge, *modulo* demands made by phonological markedness like syllable structure constraints (such as NoCODA). Although the Tagalog case is not as cut and dried as presented here, the basic message of the analysis holds: that infixation, like prefixation or suffixation, is an edge-oriented phenomenon. For more on Tagalog, see Zuraw (1996), Orgun and Sprouse (1999), McCarthy (2003b), Yu (2003), and Klein (2005) on the variability of the locus of infixation. An alternative to the Generalized Alignment approach is presented in McCarthy (2003b), who argues for a categorical interpretation of all constraints in OT. Another alternative analysis is the Exogenesis Theory of Infixation of Yu (2003), who argues for true infixes – morphemes that always appear inside a stem.

19.3.3   Infixation to a prosodic category

Earlier treatments of prosodically driven infixation were proposed in McCarthy and Prince (1986 et seq., McCarthy 2000a) using the notion of *prosodic circumscription*. Under this notion, a stem is divided into two parts, and an affix is attached to one of these. For instance, in Ulwa, a Nicaraguan language, the possessive marker [-ka-] 'his' always occurs after the head foot of the word it attaches to. If the word only contains one foot, [-ka-] is a suffix (11a); otherwise, it is an infix (11b), as illustrated in the following data from McCarthy and Prince (1993a):

(11)   *Infixes: Ulwa possessive* [-ka-]

	Unaffixed	*Possessive*	*Gloss*
(a)	'bas	('bas)–ka	'hair'
	'kiː	('kiː)–ka	'stone'
	a'mak	(a'mak)–ka	'bee'
	sa'paː	(sa'paː)–ka	'forehead'
(b)	'suːlu	('suː)–ka–lu	'dog'
	ku'luluk	(ku'lu)–ka–luk	'woodpecker'
	a'naːlaːka	(a'naː)–ka–laːka	'chin'
	ka'rasmak	(ka'ras)–ka–mak	'knee'

Under the prosodic circumscription account, the head foot of the unaffixed form is circumscribed from the word, followed by suffixation of the possessive affix to this foot. Under an OT alignment-based account, the position of the possessive affix is determined by the constraint ALIGN-TO-FOOT (McCarthy and Prince 1993a), which requires that the left edge of the possessive affix coincide with the right edge of the head foot of the word. For words containing only one foot (11a) the result is that the possessive surfaces at the end of the word – that is, as a suffix. When the word contains more material than fits into a single foot (11b), the affix is essentially suffixed to the head foot, but surfaces as an infix.

19.4   Phonology beats both alignment and morpheme contiguity

In addition to forcing a morpheme to surface as an infix, phonological constraints can also force a morpheme to split apart. The result is a type of morphology known as *nonconcatenative* morphology, where the segmental content of an affix may be distributed within a stem (thus, they are sometimes referred to as *interfixes*). A classic case of nonconcatenative morphology is exemplified by Modern Hebrew (henceforth referred to as Hebrew) and other Semitic languages. The most influential study of nonconcatenative morphology can be found in McCarthy (1979a, 1981), where important notions of morpheme position and compositionality are formalized. More recent work within current models can be found in Bat-El (1989, 1994, 2003) and Ussishkin (2000, 2005), where nonconcatenative behavior emerges through the interaction of constraints in OT.

Along with the discontiguous character of Semitic affixes, another note-worthy property of nonconcatenative morphology is the templatic effects so widely observed in these languages. These effects demonstrate the exist-ence of strong preferences in these languages for words to conform to a very limited set of prosodic structures. Hebrew affixation shows that tem-platic effects are the result of two subcategories of constraints: ones on syllable structure, and ones on prosodic word size. Together, these two types of structural constraints impose a set of restrictions on the optimal phonological shape of words that results in interfixational phenomena, without explicit recourse to interfixes as a special class of morpheme. In this way, interfixes behave similarly to the GA view of infixes: namely, that they are emergent elements and not a special category of affix.

Here, two types of affixation are considered: 'non-hybrid' affixation (affixation of a prefix alone to a form, or of an interfix alone to a form) and 'hybrid' affixation (affixation of a prefix and an interfix to the same form).[3] For the non-hybrid cases in Hebrew the affixes in question are composed of two vowels. For instance, consider the case of the puʕal binyan[4], which is in a clear relationship with the piʕel binyan: a puʕal verb is always a passive version of a corresponding active piʕel counterpart. A verb in the puʕal binyan is formed by affixing the vowels /u a/ to an existing piʕel form – the problem to be solved concerns how a form such as *dubar* 'it was spoken' results from affixing this vocalic pattern to the form *diber* 'he spoke' (12).

(12) *Non-hybrid affixation:* Interfix only – piʕel vs. puʕal

Piʕel	Gloss	Puʕal	Gloss
gidel	'he raised'	gudal	'he was raised'
ʔikel	'he consumed'	ʔukal	'it was consumed'
kibel	'he received'	kubal	'it was received'
diber	'he spoke'	dubar	'it was spoken'

In the following non-hybrid examples (13), a prefix *ni-* is added to a paʕal verb, resulting in a verb in the nifʕal binyan. In addition to prefixing *ni-*, the nifʕal forms all involve deletion of one of the vowels with the result that the forms are all bisyllabic, like the paʕal forms. An incidental process of spirantization causes [k] and [b] to become [x] and [v] respectively.

(13) *Non-hybrid affixation:* Prefix only – paʕal vs. nifʕal

Paʕal	Gloss	Nifʕal	Gloss
katav	'he wrote'	nixtav	'it was written'
badak	'he checked'	nivdak	'it was checked'
ganav	'he stole'	nignav	'it was stolen'
raʔa	'he saw'	nirʔa	'it seemed'

The next examples illustrate hybrid affixation, where both a prefix and an interfix occur. In (14), a causative hifʕil form results from prefixing *hi-* and interfixing *–i–* to a paʕal verb.

(14) *Hybrid affixation:* Prefix and interfix – paʕal vs. hifʕil

Paʕal	Gloss	Hifʕil	Gloss
katav	'he wrote'	hixtiv	'he dictated'
paxad	'he was scared'	hifxid	'he frightened'
gadal	'he grew up'	higdil	'he enlarged'

And in (15), a reflexive or reciprocal verb results from prefixing *hit-* and interfixing *a e* to a paʕal verb:

(15) *Hybrid affixation:* Prefix and interfix – paʕal vs. hitpaʕel

Paʕal	Gloss	Hitpaʕel	Gloss
katav	'he wrote'	hitkatev	'he corresponded'
raxat͡s	'he washed'	hitraxet͡s	'he washed himself'
lavaʃ	'he wore'	hitlabeʃ	'he dressed himself'

Other examples of interfixation are widely found in Semitic. For instance, Modern Standard Arabic differentiates its active vs. passive voice marking via this strategy, as seen in (16):

(16) *Arabic active and passive voice*

Active	Gloss	Passive	Gloss
kataba	'he wrote'	kutiba	'it was written'
kattaba	'he caused to write'	kuttiba	'it was dictated'
faʕala	'he did'	fuʕila	'it was done'
dafana	'he buried'	dufina	'he was buried'

Also found in Semitic languages is an interfixational pattern marked by a prosodic change. Maltese verbs exemplify this type of pattern, as seen when comparing binyan 1 verbs (with a $C_1VC_2VC_3$ structure) to binyan 2 verbs (with a $C_1VC_2C_2VC_3$ structure) (17). Binyan 2 in Maltese typically denotes valency change, resulting in causative and intensive verbs.

(17) *Maltese Binyan 1 vs. Binyan 2* (Borg and Azzopardi-Alexander 1997, Aquilina 1999)

Binyan 1	Gloss	Binyan 2	Gloss
bidel	'to change (opinion)'	biddel	'to change'
dahal	'to enter'	dahhal	'to admit'
ferah	'to rejoice'	ferrah	'to make happy'
gideb	'to lie'	giddeb	'to say that someone lied'
libes	'to dress'	libbes	'to dress someone'
ʔasam	'to split'	ʔassam	'to distribute'
ʔatar	'to fall by drops'	ʔattar	'to drip'

The unifying phonological pattern among the pairs of binyan 1 and binyan 2 verbs is the doubling (or gemination) of the second consonant in binyan 2. Other than this geminate, the two verbal binyanim are identical. The analysis of such forms involves affixation of a mora, or unit of phonological weight, to binyan 1 forms in order to arrive at the binyan 2 forms (see McCarthy 1993 and Ussishkin 2000 for an analysis of how this works in Arabic).

Returning to the Hebrew data provided above, it is clear that the majority of verbal classes contain only bisyllabic forms. This restriction follows from constraints on word size that limit an output Prosodic Word to two syllables in length. Constraints on maximal word size are found in a number of other languages as well. Occasionally they are restricted to a particular morphological environment as in Japanese (Itô et al. 1996) and Southern Tepehuan (Black 1996). Such constraints may also apply to most or all words in the language, as in Hebrew (Ussishkin 2000, 2005) and Māori (de Lacy 2003c).

To begin the analysis of Hebrew, (18) introduces a bisyllabic upper limit on prosodic words, effectively limiting words to two syllables as a maximal size:

(18) *Syllable-PrWdAlignment (abbreviated as σ-Align)*

$\forall\sigma\exists$PrWd [PrWd $\supset$ σ and ALIGN (σ, PrWd)]
($\equiv$Every syllable must be aligned to the edge
of some prosodic word containing it.)

The constraint in (18), called σ-Align, is based on the concept of Hierarchical Alignment as developed by Itô et al. (1996), with further refinements developed by Ussishkin (2000, 2005). Essentially, the constraint demands that every syllable within a prosodic word share some edge with the same edge of the prosodic word. Alternative constraints achieve similar results, but the σ-Align approach will be taken here, as this is the most successful approach for maximal word size effects in Hebrew (Ussishkin 2005). The result is a situation where any non-edge syllable within a prosodic word violates this demand, as illustrated schematically in (19):

(19) *σ-Align: scalar illustration*[5]

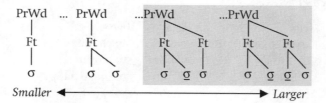

The shaded structures in (19) are larger than two syllables and as a result violate σ-Align; the violation-incurring syllables are underlined. The main effect of the constraint then is that when a Hebrew verb is derived by affixing a bivocalic pattern to an existing form, melodic overwriting is forced as the only way to both realize the affix and maintain the bisyllabic maximal size restriction. Effectively, the vowels of the base are deleted in order to express the affix, as figure (20) illustrates:

(20) *Schematic illustration of melodic overwriting*

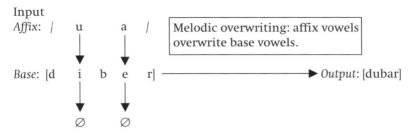

Note that the contiguous character of the affix is lost in the output: essentially the segments of the affix are split among the segments of the stem. Also, it is clear that the affix takes precedence over the stem, to the point where the affix in fact overwrites material in the stem. This points to the need for a high-ranking constraint forcing the realization of affix material, known as FAITH-AFFIX. This constraint must crucially outrank FAITH-STEM, which demands that all stem material surface in the output. Tableau (21) shows the effect of this high-ranking constraint in deriving the form *dubar* 'it was spoken' from *diber* 'he spoke'.

(21) *Deriving* dubar *from* diber

	[diber]-u a	σ-ALIGN	FAITH-AFFIX	FAITH-STEM
	(a) di.ber		u! a	
	(b) di.bar		u!	e
	(c) du.ber		a!	i
	(d) di.be.rua	*!		
☞	(e) du.bar			i e

A candidate such as (21d), which faithfully realizes all input material, loses due to its violation of the two-syllable size limit imposed by σ-ALIGN. Violations of faithfulness constraints are shown by including unparsed segmental material in the relevant cells. As seen in the tableau, high-ranking AFFIX-FAITH is indeed necessary; without it, it is impossible to predict the optimal form, as seen in tableau (22), where the relative position of the two faithfulness constraints in the hierarchy are switched:

(22) *Deriving* dubar *from* diber

	[diber]-u a	σ-ALIGN	FAITH-STEM	FAITH-AFFIX
☞	(a) diber			u a
	(b) dibar		e!	u
	(c) duber		i!	a
	(d) diberua	*!		
☞	(e) dubar		i! e	

Once again, a candidate such as (22d), which faithfully realizes all input material, loses due to its violation of the two-syllable size limit. Meanwhile, the pointing hand signals the actual output, while the imminently exploding bomb signals the output that this ranking predicts as optimal. This demonstrates the need for FAITH-AFFIX and its high-ranking status. For further arguments in favor of FAITH-AFFIX (as opposed to a constraint such as REALIZE-MORPHEME), see Ussishkin (2005).

This account correctly predicts all cases of affixation in the Hebrew verbal system that involve an interfix. Two further cases remain to be accounted for: non-hybrid cases involving a prefix, and hybrid cases involving the combination of a prefix and an interfix. For non-hybrid cases that involve just a prefix, recall the nifʕal binyan, which involves prefixation of *ni-* to a paʕal form. Such cases require the prefix to align to the left edge of the prosodic word, as formalized by constraint (23):

(23)   ALIGN-L (*ni*, PrWd)
       The left edge of *ni-* is aligned to the left edge of a prosodic word.

Given that no nifʕal forms ever violate this constraint in Hebrew, it is taken to be undominated. Such cases are now almost trivial, given the maximal bisyllabic restriction imposed on Hebrew verbs. σ-ALIGN rules out any candidates longer than two syllables (24):

(24)   *nixtav* 'it was written' from *katav* 'he wrote': derivation of nifʕal forms

[ka_1ta_2v]-ni	σ-ALIGN	FAITH-AFFIX	FAITH-STEM
(a) $nixa_1ta_2v$	*!		
☞ (b) $nixta_2v$			a_1

Although forms longer than two syllables are clearly excluded from consideration under the analysis, there remains a potential bisyllabic output still in need of rejection. Such an output chooses to parse the first stem vowel while deleting the second, resulting in a complex coda. Here is our first evidence, therefore, of syllable structure constraints at work in the affixational system; in this case a constraint barring complex syllable codas prevents the wrong vowel from being deleted (25).

(25)   *nixtav* 'it was written' from *katav* 'he wrote': derivation of nifʕal forms

[ka_1ta_2v]-ni	*COMPLEXCODA
(a) $nixa_1tv$	*!
☞ (b) $nixta_2v$	

The ban on complex codas is observed throughout the native vocabulary in the language, with the exception of an inflectional suffix marking second person, past tense, feminine forms. Elsewhere, the constraint is satisfied, including within the verbal paradigm of binyan relations.

Consider our hybrid cases: Hebrew verbs involving a base form combined with a prefix and an interfix. As an example, take the hifʕil form *hixtiv* 'he dictated', based on the paʕal form *katav* 'he wrote'. Here, we have a prefix *hi-*, in addition to a second component, the vowel *i*. *Hi-* receives its prefixational status via an alignment constraint, similar to the constraint for *ni-*:

(26) ALIGN-L (*hi-*, PrWd)
    The left edge of *hi-* is aligned to the left edge of a prosodic word.

Given the prefix/interfix combination in such cases, the only way to realize all of the affixal material (at the behest of high-ranking FAITH-AFFIX) is to both delete a vowel from the stem and overwrite a vowel from the stem, as illustrated in (27):

(27) *hixtiv* 'he dictated' from *katav* 'he wrote'

[ka$_1$ta$_2$v]-hi i	σ-ALIGN	FAITH-AFFIX	FAITH-STEM
(a) hixa$_1$ta$_2$v	*	i!	
(b) hixa$_1$tiv	*!		a$_2$
(c) hixita$_2$v	*	i!	a$_1$
☞ (d) hixtiv			a$_1$ a$_2$

In the hifʕil binyan a CV- prefix plus an additional vowel are affixed to the base form. Interestingly, such cases force a .CVC.CVC. output in order to satisfy σ-ALIGN. In other words, the *x* and *t* are adjacent to each other in the hifʕil, as opposed to in the paʕal (e.g. *katav*). The same result obtained in the nifʕal.

Finally, consider the case of the hitpaʕel binyan, which appears to be the only verbal class in Hebrew that violates the bisyllabic size restriction. The analysis of these forms is fairly straightforward; once again, an alignment constraint forces realization of *hit-* as a prefix:

(28) ALIGN-L (*hit-*, PrWd)
    The left edge of *hit-* is aligned to the left edge of a prosodic word.

Such forms, like the hifʕil, involve a prefix/interfix combination, though the additional vowel in the hitpaʕel forces a trisyllabic output as seen in tableau (29):

(29) *hitraxets* 'he washed himself' from *raxats* 'he washed': derivation of hitpaʕel forms

[raxafs]-hit a e	FAITH-AFFIX	σ-ALIGN	FAITH-STEM
(a) hitraxafs	e!	*	
(b) raxefs	h! i t		
☞ (c) hitraxefs		*	a a

The optimal form violates σ-ALIGN, justifying the ranking FAITH-AFFIX » σ-ALIGN. Interestingly, since σ-ALIGN must outrank FAITH-STEM, then by transitivity the ranking FAITH-AFFIX » FAITH-STEM also results. This consequence has implications for phonological theory in the context of contrast preservation, especially under the well-known observation that cross-linguistically, affixes tend to be weaker than stems when the two compete for phonological exponence.

This analysis of Hebrew morpheme position is heavily word-based, meaning that the affixes in question always combine with existing words, in the spirit of Benua's (1995) model of output-output correspondence. An alternative analysis based on affixation to the consonantal root is also possible, and will be briefly discussed here. Such an approach relies on earlier treatments of Semitic morphology whereby affixes combine not with an existing word, but rather with a consonantal root (McCarthy 1979a, 1981). For instance, in a root-based account, the form *dubar* 'it was spoken' is derived not from *diber* 'he spoke', but from the root /d b r/. Under this view, how do the vowels of the affix /u a/ surface in the correct position?

Once again, phonological considerations motivate morpheme position. The relevant considerations here are syllable structure constraints (also see Zec sec. 8.3.2):

(30) *Hebrew syllable structure constraints*[6]
    ONSET   "Syllables must have onsets."
    NOCODA   "Syllables must not have codas."
    *COMPLEXCODA   "Syllables must not have more than one coda consonant."
    *COMPLEXONSET "Syllables must not have more than one onset consonant."

The analysis also assumes undominated faithfulness constraints, forcing all input-specified material to be present in the output. Given an input of /d b r/ + /u a/, the most harmonic output is *dubar*, according to the ranking in tableau (31):

(31) *Deriving* dubar *from* diber ('.' indicates a syllable boundary)

/d b r/+/u a/	ONSET	*COMPLEXCODA	*COMPLEXONSET	NOCODA
(a) .dbrua.			*!	
(b) .du.abr.	*!	*		*
(c) .dbu.ra.			*!	
(d) .ud.bar.	*!			*
☞ (e) .du.bar.				*

The best syllabification happens to also be the optimal form, *dubar*. Under this view, Hebrew morpheme position can be viewed as a result of phonological well-formedness exerting a strong influence on the morphology, consistent with the overall theme of this chapter. Interestingly the issue of templatic effects – the rampant bisyllabicity of the verbal system – becomes secondary in the root-based approach because the lexical specification of the input in the root-based approach happens to contain exactly two syllables' worth of material.

19.5   Conclusion

In conclusion, this chapter has presented data that illustrate the different ways in which morpheme positions are manifested, and how morpheme position may be phonologically influenced. The essential claim of the chapter, after McCarthy & Prince (1986 et seq.), is that affixes come in two main flavors: prefixes and suffixes, and any deviation from position at the left or right edge is phonologically based. Aside from the interesting case of infixes, the chapter examined interfixes, as exemplified by the nonconcatenative systems typified by Semitic languages.

Questions regarding morpheme position remain. For instance, a strict interpretation of the prosodic morphology hypothesis holds that alignment to only prosodic categories can influence the position of an affix, but recent work (e.g. Yu 2003) provides compelling evidence for a broader view whereby sub-prosodic constituents (such as single consonants) must be referred to. Yu also discusses the historical basis for many cases of infixation, though this approach remains difficult to implement in a purely synchronic theory of morpheme position.

Notes

Thanks to Samira Farwaneh, Dafna Graf, and Alina Twist for help with some of the data in this chapter. Thanks as well to Paul de Lacy, Kate Ketner, and an anonymous reviewer for very helpful comments, suggestions, and corrections. Any errors remain my own responsibility. Except where noted, all data are provided in IPA.

1 Subsegmental/featural morphemes are not addressed here; readers are referred to the work of Lieber (1987), Akinlabi (1996), Rose (1997), Kurisu (2001), and Zoll (2001).

2 The [eː] suffix in the Afar verbal forms is an aspect marker. The transcription of tone in these examples has been suppressed, as it is not relevant to the discussion here.

3 See recent work by Graf (2005) for more on the distinction between hybrid and non-hybrid affixation in Semitic.

4 'Binyan' (plural='binyanim') here refers to the verbal class, and is the traditional term used in Semitic linguistics to describe classes of verbs that share phonological, morphosyntactic, and semantic features.

Binyan is equivalent to Classical Arabic 'measure', and to Maltese 'theme', and refers to the phonological structure, the morphosyntactic structure, and the semantic content of verbs.

5 The prosodic categories PrWd (prosodic word), Ft (metrical foot), and σ (syllable) are represented in these hierarchical structures, following work in prosodic phonology and morphology (Selkirk 1980a, b, among many others).

6 See the recent work of Bat-El (2003) and Graf (2005) motivating these and other constraints on syllable structure in Hebrew.

20

Reduplication

Suzanne Urbanczyk

20.1   Introduction

Reduplication refers to a word formation process that repeats all or part of a word or phrase. The range of what can be copied, how reduplication interacts with other morphemes and phonological processes, and the sorts of meanings that can be expressed via reduplication all factor into making the study of reduplication a vast and rich area of linguistic investigation. This chapter provides an overview of the range of patterns found and introduces current approaches to analyzing the phonological aspects of reduplication, such as issues of segmental identity and prosody. There is necessarily some interaction with morphology, but the discussion here is confined to issues of deriving the shape of reduplicative morphemes and determining the base of reduplication. Before starting it is useful to have some terms to refer to the component parts of reduplicated words. 'Reduplicant' refers to the exponent of the reduplicative morpheme, while 'base' is the portion of the word that supplies the copied portion (these terms will be defined more precisely as the chapter progresses).

A range of phonological activity can be found when examining the segmental quality of the reduplicant with respect to its base. While reduplicant segments are typically identical to their corresponding segments in the base, regular or exceptional phonological processes can interfere with perfect copying. Sometimes the lack of segmental identity is due to the neutralization of a contrast in the reduplicant, but not the base. Sometimes the reduplicant contains marked affix-like segments as well. For example, in English *schm-* (/ʃm/) reduplication, like "Tolstoy-Schmolstoy! Space Mutants II is what I call the work of a genius" (Bart Simpson), the fixed segments are not even part of the language's phonotactic patterns (though they are possible and pronounceable).

When examining the shape of reduplicants, it turns out that there is also a great deal of diversity. Languages exhibit total reduplication of a root, and sometimes even an entire idiom or phonological phrase, as in the English contrastive reduplication: *Do you LIKE-HIM like-him?* (Ghomeshi et al. 2004). Languages also exhibit partial reduplication in which the reduplicant can be a bisyllabic foot, a heavy syllable, a light syllable, and even just a single consonant.

An emerging area of investigation is how to define the base of reduplication. For the most part reduplicant and base are adjacent, as in the Lushootseed (Central Salish) word with a CVC- prefix [ʔib-ʔibəʃ] meaning 'walk all about' (Bates, Hess, and Hilbert 1994). However, patterns in which affixes are skipped show a preference to copy root material. Other factors that affect what is copied include making sure that both edges of a fixed-shape reduplicant match those of the root or stem. For example, in the Tsimshian language Nisgha, the plural reduplicant is CVC shaped, and the word [ɬúːtʼuxʷ] 'to value, treasure, cherish s.t./s.o.' is pluralized as [ɬúxʷɬúːtʼuxʷ] (Tarpent 1987, Shaw 1987, 2005). Because the base contains segments that are eligible to be copied in the reduplicant, how it is defined plays a role in predicting the range of what can be copied.

Within this diversity, recurring patterns emerge and generalizations can be made, leading researchers to work towards developing a restrictive theory of reduplication. This chapter will discuss three issues that such a restrictive theory should account for: segmental identity (or lack thereof) between reduplicant and base (20.2), more or less invariant shape (20.3), and identifying the base of reduplication (20.4). Because the research on reduplication is nearly as vast as the patterns themselves, the discussion will be restricted to current approaches and models aimed at developing a restrictive theory of reduplication. The framework of much of this work is Optimality Theory (Prince and Smolensky 2004), in which constraints interact to derive output forms.

20.2   Segmental identity

20.2.1   Overview

Reduplication can result in an identical copy of the base, or not. A variety of patterns of segmental identity have been identified. In the most unremarkable case, phonological alternations produce a reduplicated word that is entirely consistent with the regular phonological patterns of the language. In these cases, nothing extra is needed to account for the surface pattern. However, there are numerous cases in which an alternation unexpectedly applies (or not). The exceptional application of a phonological process falls into two basic categories. In one situation, the result is identity between base and reduplicant. Wilbur (1973) has termed this over-application – when the process applies without its triggering context – and under-application – when the process fails to apply, given the correct context. In a second situation, the reduplicant illustrates a neutralization of a contrast, resulting in a less marked structure in the reduplicant than the base.[1] McCarthy and Prince (1994) have termed this 'emergence of the unmarked'.

An extreme case of neutralization results in a default segment, typically an epenthetic consonant or vowel of the language, appearing as part of the exponent of the reduplicant. This results in a fixed segment in the reduplicant, giving the appearance of not copying a segment from the base; it has been termed 'default segmentism' (Alderete et al. 1999). The counterpart to this is when a marked segment occurs in the reduplicant, displacing segments from the base, as in the *schm-* reduplication (*table-schmable*). McCarthy and Prince (1986, 1990) term this 'melodic overwriting', and it has been analyzed as affixation because the segments are typically peripheral and not derivable by the application of phonological processes. Together these two phenomena are referred to as 'fixed segmentism' because, while most of the segments in the reduplicant vary with those of the base, the reduplicant contains fixed segments that are not copies of base segments.

This section outlines Correspondence Theory (McCarthy and Prince 1995a, 1999), an OT model to account for the range of these segmental alternations (20.2.2), and illustrates how to derive these patterns of segmental identity (20.2.3–2.4). The phenomenon of fixed segmentism is discussed next (20.2.5). There is a final discussion of alternative approaches and extensions to Correspondence Theory (20.2.6).

20.2.2 Correspondence Theory

The most direct way to ensure identity between two segments is to have a link between them in the output form. This is the insight behind Wilbur's (1973) Mate Relation and McCarthy and Prince's (1995a, 1999) Correspondence Theory. McCarthy and Prince propose that Correspondence is a relation that holds between two strings; it encompasses the pairing of input to output as well as the pairing between a reduplicant (the segmental string that comprises the reduplicative morpheme's exponence) and its base. For example, the hypothetical reduplicated word in (1) has a Correspondence relation between input and output (IO-Correspondence) as well as between base and reduplicant (BR-Correspondence).

(1)   *Basic Correspondence Model of Reduplication (McCarthy and Prince 1995a, 1999)*

```
input      / RED – badupi/
                  | | | | | |
output     bad-   badupi
           reduplicant-base
```

Segments that are linked via this relation are called 'correspondents'. Other work has extended the Correspondence model to inter-word relations (Benua 1997, see McCarthy Ch.5) as well as intra-word relations (Rose and Walker 2004; Zuraw 2003).

In Optimality Theory, candidate output forms are generated with their accompanying Correspondence relations. Faithfulness constraints evaluate the identity of strings that stand in correspondence. For reduplication, there are both I(nput)O(utput)-FAITH and B(ase)R(eduplicant)-FAITH constraints. These faithfulness constraints interact with Markedness constraints, which evaluate each candidate output for its relative markedness. McCarthy and Prince have shown that by freely permuting IO- and BR-FAITH constraints with Markedness they are able to successfully derive the range of segmental identity conditions found in reduplication (this is known as a factorial typology). The rest of this section illustrates their results.

20.2.3   Normal and over-/under-application

If the phonological patterns found in a reduplicated word are the same as those found in the language as a whole, then phonological alternations apply without exception; this has been referred to as normal application. The examples below from Texistepec Popoluca (a Zoquean language spoken in Mexico) illustrate this pattern (Reilly to appear). There are two inflectional markers in Texistepec Popoluca that are floating features. One is a front vowel feature, symbolized as /j/ here; the other is a nasal feature, symbolized as /^{N}/. The [j] feature attempts to be realized on the leftmost vowel (2a); the nasal feature docks on to the leftmost consonant (2b). √ marks the root morpheme.

(2)   *Texistepec Popoluca: Normal Application (Zoquean; Reilly to appear)*

    (a)   /j-RED-√hiʔn-deʔ/   →   [hiʔn-hiʔn-deʔ]   'he slithers all about'
    (b)   /^{N}-RED-√das-hoʔj/   →   [nas-das-hoʔj]   'I go all over town'

Interestingly, speakers differ as to whether or not they over-apply these processes, as you can see in the examples below. In the following words, both reduplicant and base have the front vowel (3a) or the nasal (3b), even though the trigger or context for vowel fronting and nasalization is only present in the prefix.

(3)   *Texistepec Popoluca: Over-application (Zoquean; Reilly to appear)*

    (a)   /j-RED-√hiʔn-deʔ/   →   [hiʔn-hiʔn-deʔ]   'he slithers all about'
    (b)   /^{N}-RED-√das-hoʔj/   →   [nas-nas-hoʔj]   'I go all over town'

So, while some speakers apply the processes as expected, others over-apply them. This section illustrates how these effects are achieved in Correspondence Theory, simply by re-ranking constraints. The three types of constraints needed to account for this are IO-FAITH, BR-FAITH and a Markedness constraint.

When determining what the precise Faithfulness constraints are, it is important to consider the nature of the alternation. Because the vowel quality changes, the Faithfulness constraints are those that ensure identity of vowel features between corresponding segments.[2] There are analogous IO-IDENT[VFEAT(URE)] and BR-IDENT[VFEAT] constraints; for the alternation in nasalization, IDENT[NASAL] would be relevant. I will abstract away from the precise markedness constraint that compels violation in this case, referring to it as a phonotactic constraint against falling sonority onsets.

(4) IO-IDENT[VFEAT]   Correspondent input and output vowels are identical.
     BR-IDENT[VFEAT]   Correspondent base and reduplicant vowels are identical.
     *FALLSONONSET   Falling sonority onsets are not permitted

Because the language as a whole allows this alternation to occur, it must be the case that the markedness constraint dominates IO-FAITH. This ranking will hold regardless of the pattern of segmentism found in reduplicated words. In normal application, reduplicant and base are not identical, illustrating that BR-FAITH can be violated and is therefore low-ranking. Tableau (5) illustrates that the actual output (a) violates BR-IDENT[VFEAT], because base and reduplicant have different vowel qualities. The remaining candidates maintain identity between base and reduplicant. However, candidate (b) is ruled out because the vowels in the input and output differ (violating IO-IDENT[VFEAT]), while candidate (c) is ruled out because it violates the undominated markedness constraint.

(5) *Normal application in Texistepec Popoluca*

/j-RED-hiʔn-deʔ/	*FALLSONONSET	IO-IDENT [VFEAT]	BR-IDENT [VFEAT]
☞ (a) hiʔn-hiʔn-deʔ			*
(b) hiʔn-hiʔn-deʔ		*!	
(c) j-hiʔn-hiʔn-deʔ	*!		

Recall that there is speaker variation in Texistepec Popoluca, where some speakers over-apply vowel fronting. Reilly (to appear) analyzes this as constraint re-ranking, wherein some speakers have higher ranked BR-FAITH. Tableau (6) illustrates this. Notice that the constraints and candidates are identical to those in (5) above. The only difference is that BR-IDENT[VFEAT] is high-ranking. As a result, candidate (6b) is selected as optimal.

(6) *Over-application in Texistepec Popoluca*

/j-RED-hiʔn-deʔ/	*FALLSONONSET	BR-IDENT [VFEAT]	IO-IDENT [VFEAT]
(a) hiʔn-hiʔn-deʔ		*!	
☞ (b) hiʔn-hiʔn-deʔ			*
(c) j-hiʔn-hiʔn-deʔ	*!		

Consistent with the phonology of the language as a whole, the markedness constraint still dominates IO-Faith. The precise ranking of Markedness and BR-FAITH cannot be determined, hence the dotted line.

This section has illustrated that normal application and over-application can be derived straightforwardly, illustrating a fundamental principle of OT: variation (between speakers and languages) is the result of constraint re-ranking.

(7)   NORMAL APPLICATION: Markedness » IO-FAITH » BR-FAITH
       OVER-APPLICATION: Markedness, BR-FAITH » IO-FAITH

Because over-application and under-application are functionally similar – both exhibit identity between base and reduplicant – they are analyzed analogously within the Correspondence model of reduplication. Identity between the reduplicant and base is enforced by having high-ranking BR-FAITH. See McCarthy and Prince (1995a, 1999), who propose that under-application is over-application that is blocked by a high-ranking Markedness constraint.

20.2.4   Emergence of the unmarked

The exceptional application of a phonological process can also result in a lack of identity between base and reduplicant. This is observed in the neutralization of a contrast in the reduplicant that is retained in the base. The reduplicant actually eliminates marked structure, and the phenomenon has been referred to as the emergence of the unmarked (TETU) by McCarthy and Prince (1994). An example of this can be seen in Sliammon Comox (Central Salish) plural reduplication, as illustrated in (8). The language as a whole permits glottalized sonorants in onset and coda position. However, they are eliminated in reduplication.

(8)   *Sliammon Comox plural reduplication (Watanabe 2003:373)*

Stem	Plural	Gloss
'hum'hum	'həm-hum'hum	'bluegrouse'
'qin'qin	'qən-qin'qin	'duck'
't'əm'xʷ	't'əm-t'əm'xʷ	'gooseberry'

The neutralization has no phonological trigger: it cannot be an example of neutralization in coda position because, as illustrated in the non-reduplicated words, glottalized sonorants occur in codas elsewhere in the language. Furthermore, there are no reported cases of the neutralization occurring in the base, but not the reduplicant. This phonological alternation is limited to the context of being in a reduplicant. The Correspondence model of reduplication has a straightforward and predicted analysis of this pattern: IO-FAITH, BR-FAITH, and Markedness constraints are ranked differently than for normal and over-application.

In order to account for this, the following constraints are required ([c.g.] refers to constricted glottis – see Hall (13.4)).

(9)   IO-IDENT[+c.g.]   Correspondent input and output segments are [+c.g.].
       BR-IDENT[+c.g.]   Correspondent base and reduplicant segments are [+c.g.]
       *R[+c.g.]   Glottalized sonorants are not permitted.

Because the language as a whole permits glottalized sonorants, IO-FAITH must be ranked above the markedness constraint. This ensures that input and output segments are identical in the winning candidate. However, because glottalized sonorants are eliminated in the reduplicant, the markedness constraint must be ranked above BR-FAITH. The low-ranking of BR-FAITH also permits base and reduplicant to differ. Unmarked structure emerges because the markedness constraint intervenes between IO-FAITH and BR-FAITH, as illustrated in tableau (10).

(10)   IO-IDENT[+c.g.] » *R[+c.g.] » BR-IDENT[+c.g.]

/RED-t'əm'x^w/	IO-IDENT [+c.g.]	*R[+c.g.]	BR-IDENT[+c.g.]
☞ (a) t'əm-t'əm'x^w		*	*
(b) t'əm'-t'əm'x^w		**!	
(c) t'əm-t'əmx^w	*!		

The candidate that is optimal satisfies IO-FAITH, has one fewer violation of the markedness constraint than candidate (b) (which obeys BR-Faith), but violates BR-FAITH. This general pattern is derivable via the ranking schema in (11).

(11)   *The Emergence of the Unmarked*
      IO-FAITH » Markedness » BR-FAITH

As will be illustrated in the following section, an extreme case of the neutralization of a segmental contrast in the reduplicant results in a fixed default segment.

20.2.5 Fixed segmentism

In addition to being composed of segments from the base, reduplicants can also contain fixed segments (see Yip 1992 for a survey). Following the work of McCarthy and Prince (1986, 1994, 1999), Alderete et al. (1999) argue that there are two types of fixed segmentism: default segmentism and melodic overwriting. As mentioned previously, default segmentism is an extreme case of the neutralization of a segmental contrast in the reduplicant. The result is a default segment, generally the least marked segment of a language, which is also frequently the epenthetic segment of a language. An example of this can be seen in the Mainland Comox plural words in (8) above; the vowel of the reduplicant is consistently schwa, the default epenthetic vowel of the language. On the other hand, melodic overwriting refers to relatively marked segments that replace segments from the base, as with the *schm-* reduplication pattern in English. This section illustrates how default segmentism is derived in Correspondence Theory, and discusses how melodic over-writing has been analyzed.

In Mainland Comox, the vowel of the reduplicant is consistently schwa. This can be analyzed as an extreme case of the neutralization of a contrast in reduplication, making use of the TETU ranking introduced above. The motivation behind analyzing default segmentism as TETU is that defaults, by their very nature, are the least marked segments in the language (within a particular context). Schwa itself is analyzed as lacking any vocalic target or place features (Oostendorp 1995; Urbanczyk 1996). Violation of BR-FAITH is compelled by Markedness. In this case the constraint would be something like *VFEAT, a constraint against all vocalic place features. In tableau (12) each non-schwa vowel incurs a violation of *VFEAT. So, candidate (12a) violates this Markedness constraint twice, while candidate (12b) violates it three times. This extra violation proves fatal. On the other hand, candidate (12c) only violates it once. However, it does so at a cost; it violates the even higher ranked constraint IO-FAITH-V because the input /i/ is realized as schwa in the output. So, even though candidates (12b) and (12c) illustrate identity, they are not optimal.

(12)   IO-FAITH-V » *VFEAT » *BR-FAITH-V

/RED_{plural}-qin'qin/	IO-FAITH-V	*VFEAT	BR-FAITH-V
☞ (a) 'qən-qin'qin		**	*
(b) 'qin-qin'qin		***!	
(c) 'qən-qən'qin	*!	*	

In terms of identifying the precise Faithfulness constraints, there are two different approaches one can take. One option is to analyze the segment as truly epenthetic, violating constraints on insertion of segments into the reduplicant (BR-DEP) and deletion of the base vowels (BR-MAX), under pressure from the higher ranking Markedness. In some languages, there is clear evidence to support this.[3] However, in others there is no clear evidence that the default is truly epenthetic, and one can simply treat it as the neutralization of a contrast. This second approach analyzes the default as a correspondent of the base, but a very poor copy violating constraints on featural identity (BR-IDENT-FEAT).

Melodic overwriting refers to fixed segments associated with reduplicative morphemes that are affixal in nature (McCarthy and Prince 1986, 1990). They tend to be more marked and occur in a peripheral position in the reduplicated word, much like affixes. The English *schm*-reduplication is a classic example. The input would contain /ʃm-/ as a prefix. Constraints on affix placement ensure that the affix is located in a peripheral position (see Ussishkin Ch.19). High ranking IO-FAITH ensures that the affix is present in the output, and BR-FAITH is violated in cases in which the affix overwrites segments of the base. Many cases of melodic overwriting also show dissimilatory effects. For example, in Telugu the overwriting morpheme is *gi-*, but if the word begins with this sequence, *pi-* is selected instead (*gilaka-pilaka* 'rattle, etc.'). Any comprehensive analysis should take this dissimilatory effect into account. Finally, evidence that the segments overwrite those in the base comes from the fact that the vowel often inherits the length of the base vowel too, as in the Estonian *pi-* game (*saːda, sapiːda* 'send' 2SG IMPER; Lehiste 1985).

20.2.6 Alternatives and extensions to Correspondence Theory

As one can see, Correspondence Theory can account for a full range of the segmental phonology of reduplication. It incorporates the insights of Wilbur (1973), who proposed that identity effects found in reduplication are due to a formal 'mate' relation between the segments of the base and the reduplicant. By employing the OT principle of constraint re-ranking, Correspondence Theory can account for TETU effects as well. However, there are a number of alternatives to this model. This section provides an overview of these various proposals, by categorizing them into a few general approaches. The strength of some of these proposals comes from the availability of an intermediate level of representation, in which processes can be ordered either before or after reduplication. While reference to an intermediate level of representation is not available in standard OT, an extension to the basic Correspondence model has been proposed that can account for some opacity in reduplication (Spaelti 1997; Struijke 2002a), and this will be discussed at the end of the section.

There are three basic approaches to deriving the segmental phonology of reduplication. One is to directly encode the link between reduplicant and base (Wilbur 1973; McCarthy and Prince 1994, 1995a, 1999). In Wilbur's derivational framework, phonological rules are formulated to target one or both members of the linked relation. We have already seen the OT instantiation of this insight in Correspondence Theory.

A second approach is to have one component of the grammar responsible for copying the base, while phonological rules are ordered and can target either base or reduplicant, depending on the nature of the segmental identity (Marantz 1982, Kiparsky 1986, Steriade 1988b, Inkelas and Zoll 2005). Identity is accounted for when the process applies before reduplication.

A third approach can be termed parafixation; it involves a stage where the representation of the reduplicated form is not a linear sequence of segments (Clements 1985b, Mester 1986, Raimy 2000; Frampton 2003). A hypothetical example (which utilizes CV skeleta) is presented to illustrate this (13). While the formal means of parafixation and linearization differ between earlier models and more current approaches, crucially there is some stage in which the segments that comprise the reduplicant and base are one and the same.

(13) Input: /CV + banupi/→
                 C V
                 | |
                 b ã n u p i
                 | | | | | |
      Output: C V C V C V
                 [bã-bãnupi]

Segmental identity between reduplicant and base (such as over-application of anticipatory nasalization) is achieved because a phonological process applies prior to linearization; a subsequent stage of linearization occurs, and the segments are separated into base and reduplicant, with both being identical. Different identity patterns are achieved because phonological rules can also be ordered after the linearization process. In this approach, there is an abstract intermediate representation that never occurs in natural languages.

The preceding two general approaches can account for the different phonological patterns because they all involve some intermediate stage.[4] This leads to a potential problem facing the standard Correspondence approach to reduplication: there are cases in which the reduplicant contains material from the input that is not present in the base. The Lushootseed diminutive forms in (14) illustrate this pattern. Syncope of the post-tonic vowel results in words in which the diminutive reduplicant contains an input vowel that is not present in the base.

(14) *Lushootseed diminutive (Bates, Hess, and Hilbert 1994; Urbanczyk 1996; Struijke 2000b)*

pús	púps	'kitten'
dúkʷibəɬ	dúdkʷibəɬ	'strange'
skʷatatʃ	skʷakʷtatʃ	'mountain'

If the base is only present in the output, how can one determine the correct vowel quality for the reduplicant? This is a puzzle, because in OT there is no recourse to an intermediate stage in the derivation in which the reduplicant can access or copy the base vowel. Patterns like this illustrate an opacity effect, an issue of ongoing consideration for OT in general (McCarthy Ch.5).

One compelling solution to this puzzle is what can be referred to as Broad-IO Faithfulness (see Spaelti 1997, Struijke 2000a,b, Kalmar 2003). In this approach, input segments have more than one output correspondent: one in the base and one in the reduplicant. Struijke (2000b:614) proposes that Broad-IO ". . .Faithfulness constraints are satisfied if an input element is recoverable from the output." Thus, in the examples above, MAX$_{\text{BROAD-IO}}$ is satisfied because the vowel from the input is present in the output, in this case the reduplicant, rather than the base. As Struijke points out, the Broad-IO Faithfulness model derives the correct pattern and also makes the (true) prediction that in Lushootseed syncope occurs almost exclusively with reduplication.

20.3 Shape

20.3.1 Overview

A great deal of research has addressed the issue of how to derive the shape of reduplicative morphemes. If reduplication is total, one might say that reduplication involves tautologous compounding: the root or stem is literally compounded with itself (Inkelas and Zoll 2005; McCarthy and Prince 1988; Pulleyblank in press; Steriade 1988b; Yip 2001b).[5] However, because reduplicative morphemes are frequently only partial copies, it is necessary to specify the morpheme shape. The meaning of the word is identifiable by the more or less fixed shape of the reduplicant (like in Lushootseed: CVC- is 'distributive', CV- is 'diminutive').

One of the earliest and most striking observations about reduplication comes from Moravscik (1978) whose typological investigation into the form and meaning of reduplication revealed that the shape of reduplicative morphemes is always a target of some sort: total copy or a fixed shape, like CV or CVC. The observations about partial reduplication are particularly striking because Moravscik found that there are no languages that have authentic syllable copying. Such a system would have a CV-reduplicant if the base begins with an open syllable and CVC- if it begins with a closed syllable. For example, there should be languages in which the same meaning is expressed variously with CV-, CVC- and CVCC-, depending on the syllable structure of the base: *ba-ba.du.pi, bar-bar.du.pi, bard-bard.su.pi.* Patterns like "copy the first syllable" are simply not found. Instead, reduplicants generally have a fixed syllable shape that does not necessarily mirror the syllable structure of the base. This observation has led researchers to propose that reduplicative morphemes are empty templates to be filled with segments from some base.

Early research proposed that reduplication is the affixation of a segmentally empty template, defined in terms of empty C and V slots (McCarthy 1979a, 1981; Marantz 1982), or authentic units of prosody (McCarthy and Prince 1986 et seq.). Others have proposed stem doubling accompanied by truncation (Steriade 1988a, Inkelas and Zoll 2005). Recently, Generalized Template Theory has been proposed to account for shape by assuming that reduplicative morphemes illustrate the unmarked morpheme shapes of the language emerging in reduplication (McCarthy and Prince 1994, 1999; Urbanczyk 1996), and is a version of what is also referred to as atemplatic reduplication (Crowhurst 2004; Downing 2006; Gafos 1998a,c; Hendricks 1999; Urbanczyk 1999a). The remainder of this section examines template theory and generalized templates more closely.

20.3.2 Prosodic templates

Marantz (1982) presented the first fully developed template model of reduplication. In this approach, reduplication is the affixation of a template: segmentally empty morphemes specified with C and V skeletal positions.[6] The base is copied to supply phonological content, and the segments are associated to the template via a number of conventions. Unassociated segments are erased. Subsequent work by McCarthy and Prince (1986 et seq.) presented a striking finding about the possible shapes: they are restricted to independently motivated prosodic categories like syllable, foot, and prosodic word. There are no "three-syllable" patterns. This is explained because there are no trisyllabic metrical feet; such a pattern is predicted if templates are merely sequences of C and V slots.

Many variations in the shape of reduplicative morphemes, like Manam CVCV, VCV, and CVC are derivable from reference to prosodic categories.

(15) *Manam (Austronesian; Lichtenberk 1983)*

    (a) sa'laga   salaga-'<u>laga</u>   'long'
           mo'ita   moita-'<u>ita</u>   'knife'

    (b) mala'boŋ   malabom-'<u>boŋ</u> 'flying fox'
           ʔu'lan   ʔulan-'<u>laŋ</u>   'desire'

In this case the target shape is a moraic trochee (a foot with two moras – see Kager (Ch.9)). Furthermore, McCarthy and Prince (1986) observed that skeletal templates tended to mirror the prosody of the language. For example, if a language allowed complex onsets, one might find a reduplicant with CCVC templates. Their proposal was the Prosodic Morphology Hypothesis.

(16) *Prosodic Morphology Hypothesis (McCarthy and Prince 1990:209)*
    Templates are defined in terms of the fundamental units of prosody: mora (μ), syllable (σ), foot (Ft), prosodic word (PrWd), and so on.

If reduplicative morphemes are defined as units of prosody, then there is also the issue of how to fill those templates, by being as large a syllable or foot as possible. This is achieved by the Template Satisfaction Condition (TSC).

(17) *Template Satisfaction Condition (McCarthy and Prince 1990:209)*
    Satisfaction of templatic constraints is obligatory and determined by the principles of prosody, both universal and language-specific.

The TSC ensures that reduplicants have complex onsets if the base has complex onsets, and that the maximal foot is copied, among other effects.

In OT, the concept of template has been incorporated in two forms. One is to straightforwardly adopt the PMH, by having the input to the reduplicated word include empty prosodic units such as syllable or Ft (Pulleyblank in press). The other is to derive the shape via templatic constraints like RED=σ or RED=Ft (Downing 1998a). However, templatic constraints have been shown to exhibit problems in interpretation, such as how to evaluate whether the reduplicant is a syllable (Blevins 1996). For example, with the Lushootseed syncopated word [púps] 'kitten', the reduplicant is not a CV (light) syllable. It is part of a syllable, but it is actually not a syllable on its own, so evaluating whether the constraint is obeyed or violated presents difficulties.[7] A growing body of work in OT has been able to successfully account for a large range of reduplicant shapes without templates (Crowhurst 2004; Downing 1999; Fitzgerald 2000; Hendricks 1999; Gafos 1998a,c; McCarthy and Prince 1995a, 1999; Urbanczyk 1996). The following section illustrates how Generalized Template Theory accounts for shape properties of partial reduplication without reference to templates *per se*.

20.3.3 Generalized templates

McCarthy and Prince (1994, 1995a, 1999) propose that the shape of reduplicative morphemes can be derived from independently motivated constraints on the prosody–morphology interface. For example, stems tend to be prosodic words and prosodic words are minimally a foot in size. This derives foot-shaped reduplication as a TETU effect. This idea is formalized as Generalized Template Theory, and eschews templates, assuming instead that the same constraints that are active in determining the shape of words and morphemes in general (constraints on well-formed syllables, words, stems, roots, affixes, etc.) are also active in determining the shape of reduplicative morphemes.

For example, in Diyari the reduplicant is a prosodic word. There are two pieces of evidence that the reduplicant is a prosodic word and not a foot (Austin 1981; Poser 1989). First, the reduplicant and base both have primary stress, the domain of which is assumed to be a prosodic word. Second, prosodic words are vowel-final, and the reduplicant is also vowel-final, as you can see from example (18c); if the reduplicant were specified as a foot, but not a prosodic word, we would expect it to copy the coda /r/ from the base.

(18)   *Diyari reduplication (Austin 1981; Poser 1989; McCarthy & Prince 1994)*

(a)	ˈwiḷa	ˈwiḷa-ˈwiḷa	'woman'
(b)	ˈkanku	ˈkanku-ˈkanku	'boy'
(c)	ˈt̪ilparku	ˈt̪ilpa-ˈt̪ilparku	'bird species'
(d)	ˈŋankaṇt̪i	ˈŋanka-ˈŋankaṇt̪i	'catfish'

The basic approach is that reduplicative morphemes illustrate TETU effects: the unmarked morpheme shape is emerging in reduplication. In terms of the relevant Faithfulness constraints, partial reduplication always involves a violation of BR-MAX. In terms of the relevant Markedness constraint, these would be those on well-formed prosodic structure or the prosody–morphology interface.[8] In the case of Diyari, the unmarked prosodic word is one in which there is a single foot, aligned at each edge of the stem. It is also marked for syllables to not be parsed into feet. So, in this case there are two Markedness constraints. The relevant constraints are provided in (19). See McCarthy and Prince (1999) for more details on this analysis.

(19) IO-MAX   Every segment of the input is in the output.
      BR-MAX   Every segment of the base is in the reduplicant.
      ALL-FEET-L   Every foot is aligned with the beginning of a prosodic word.
      PARSE-SYLL   All syllables are parsed into metrical feet.

Tableau (20) illustrates that the TETU ranking will derive the correct shape of reduplicant. As a consequence both portions of the reduplicated words are subject to ALL-FEET-L and PARSE-SYLL, because both portions are stems, and hence prosodic words. In order to illustrate these effects most clearly, all the candidates are vowel-final, because all prosodic words are vowel-final in the language as a whole (and so the constraint that ensures vowel-finality is undominated).

(20)

/RED$_{stem}$-tʲilparku/	IO-MAX	ALL-FEET-L	PARSE-SYLL	BR-MAX
☞ (a) (tʲilpa)-(tʲilpar)ku			*	***
(b) (tʲilpar)ku-(tʲilpar)ku			**!	
(c) (tʲilpa)-(tʲilpa)	***!			

The optimal candidate (a) incurs one violation of PARSE-SYLL, because there is a syllable in the base that is not parsed into a foot. Candidate (b), which illustrates total reduplication, incurs an extra (and fatal) violation of PARSE-SYLL. The final candidate has segments from the input that are not present in the output, and so is also ruled out. This last candidate also illustrates that IO-MAX must dominate the constraints on prosodic structure, because the language as a whole allows words to have unparsed syllables and to exceed a foot in size.

Thus, GTT is able to derive the shape of reduplicative morphemes by reference to morphological category alone; the constraints that derive the shape of morphemes in the language as a whole are also active in determining the shape of reduplicants.[9]

Further evidence to support GTT comes from examining Lushootseed reduplication in which the shape and segmental quality of reduplicative morphemes parallels the shape and segmental quality of morphemes in the language as a whole. A correlation has been found that links shape and segmentism together, which is only derivable within Correspondence Theory (Urbanczyk 1996, 2006). In terms of the shape, canonical roots are CVC;

canonical suffixes are -VC. In terms of segmentism, roots permit stressed schwa, while affixes do not. Urbanczyk (1996) proposes that CVC- 'distributive' is a root, while CV- 'diminutive' and -VC 'out-of-control' are both affixes.

A striking result is obtained in GTT because both the shape and segmental properties of the reduplicative morphemes are derivable by having correspondence relations refer to reduplicative roots (BR-FAITH-ROOT) separately from affixes. The 'diminutive' does not permit stressed schwa, a property of affixes in general (21a). This is also true of 'out-of-control' reduplication (21b). However, as can be seen in (21c), 'distributive' does permit stressed schwa, just like other roots in the language.

(21) *Lushootseed (Bates, Hess, and Hilbert 1994; Urbanczyk 1996)*

(a) 'diminutive'
(i)   təˈdᶻil   'lie in bed'   ˈti̲-tədᶻil   'lie down for a little while'
(ii) ˈbətʃ   'fall down'   ˈbi̲-bətʃ   'drop in from time to time'
(iii) ˈs-kʷəbʃəd   'animal hide'   s-ˈk̲ʷi̲-kʷəbʃəd   'small hide'

(b) 'out of control'
(i)   ʔəˈχid   'what happened'   ʔəˈχ-i̲χ̲-əd   'what's he done?'
(ii) ˈkʷʼəq   'fall backwards' s-kʷʼəˈq-i̲q̲   'robin (tilts head back)'

(c) 'distributive'
(i)   ˈdʒəsəd   'foot'   ˈd̲ʒ̲ə̲s̲-dʒəsəd   'feet'
(ii) ˈdᶻəχ   'move'   ˈd̲ᶻ̲ə̲χ̲-dᶻəχ   'move household'
(iii) s-ˈtʃətxʷəd   'bear'   s-ˈt̲ʃ̲ə̲t̲-tʃəχʷəd   'bears'

Approaches in which shape is determined by templates while segmentism is determined separately do not predict any correlation between shape and segmentism. A template derives the shape, and the rules of segmental phonology derive the segmentism. If shape and segmentism are decoupled, there are many more languages predicted to occur, but which seem unattested. For example, one might expect to find a language with the reversal of the Lushootseed pattern: root shape with the phonology of affixes as well as the affix shape having the segmentism of roots (this would be stressed schwa with CV-, but the default with CVC-).

20.4 The base of reduplication

20.4.1 Overview

Bauer (2004:21) provides the following general definition of *base*: "The base of a word is that part of it to which any **affix** is added or upon which any morphological process acts." This definition turns out to have a fairly good match with the base of reduplication: that part of the word that is eligible to supply segmental content to the reduplicant. This section presents the proposal by McCarthy and Prince (1993b, 1995a, 1999) that the base of reduplication is the string following a reduplicative prefix and preceding a reduplicative suffix.[10] Because this definition is fairly simple, there are numerous patterns that appear to contradict or provide evidence against it. Given the framework of OT, in which there are Markedness and Faithfulness constraints that can be violated, these patterns can be derived by constraint ranking.

In terms of delineating what is copied, there seem to be two clear preferences: for reduplicant and base to be adjacent and for the reduplicant to be composed of root material. These two demands are derivable by constraint interaction. Adjacency obeys a Faithfulness constraint (like ANCHOR), demanding that the initial segments of the base and reduplicant coincide. Preference to copy root material seems to obey Markedness constraints on what the best segments are for the reduplicant (like R≤ROOT: "Every segment of the reduplicant corresponds to a root segment in the base"). However, reduplicative morphemes have their own demands (in terms of shape and location), and frequently the base cannot meet these demands (because of its own shape properties). It is these cases of mismatch or conflict that have led researchers to investigate how to delineate and define the base of reduplication.

While research on the base of reduplication is not as extensive as that on segmental identity and shape, there is a growing body of research that tackles this issue. Early research has proposed to account for the variety of base-effects by ordering different rules (Broselow 1983; Marantz 1987; Odden and Odden 1985) or clarifying how the reduplicating or copy mechanism works (Aronoff 1988; Broselow and McCarthy 1983; McCarthy and Prince 1986, 1990; Mutaka and Hyman 1990). However, as mentioned above, in OT one can take a different approach. Because there are clear preferences, these can be cast as violable constraints (which require adjacency and copying root material). This section outlines how recent research has pointed to the importance of adjacency and root preference in determining which segments are eligible to be copied (Downing 1998b; Inkelas and Zoll 2005; McCarthy and Prince 1993b, 1995a; Nelson 2003; Shaw 2005; Urbanczyk 1996, 2000).[11]

20.4.2 Adjacency

In the unmarked situation, reduplicant and base are adjacent to each other. As illustrated in the Lillooet Salish words in (22), regardless of where the reduplicant is in the word, it is adjacent to those segments that supply content to the reduplicant. In many Interior Salish languages, the diminutive morpheme is an infix located adjacent to the stressed syllable (Broselow 1983; Urbanczyk 2000; Shaw 2005). In the examples below, the stressed syllable is underlined, and you will notice that the initial consonant is identical to the one immediately after it. Regardless of where stress falls, the copy is adjacent to it.

(22) *Lillooet consonant reduplication (Salishan; Eijk 1997)*

(a)	s-'qaχaʔ	'dog'	s-'qəqχaʔ	'puppy'
(b)	s-'muɫats	'woman'	s-'m'əm'ɫats	'girl'
(c)	'ɫapən	'to forget s.t.'	ɫəpɫəp'nun'ɫ	'forgetful'
(d)	tɬ'əqʷənwa'l'uz'	'to wrestle, playfight'	tɬ'əqʷəntwa'lulzaʔ	'to wrestle, playfight'

The location of the reduplicant is determined by it being an infix to the stressed syllable (so this is a separate issue from defining the base), and it is clear that non-root material can be copied.

As mentioned above, McCarthy and Prince (1993b, 1995a, 1999) have proposed that the base is a string in the output: it immediately follows the reduplicant if it is a prefix, it immediately precedes it if the reduplicant is a suffix. The following illustrates the bases for the Lillooet words above, under the assumption that the reduplicant is a prefix (23a). Crucially, prefixes and preceding material are not included. To illustrate the full proposal, the Manam suffixal reduplicants are presented in (23b).

(23) *Base as an adjacent string*

(a) Lillooet infix

base	*reduplicant*	
qχaʔ	ˈqə	'puppy'
m'lats	ˈm'ə	'girl'
n'ɬ	ˈnu	'forgetful'
lzaʔ	ˈlu	'to wrestle, playfight'

(b) Manam suffix[12]

base	*reduplicant*	
salaga	laga	'long'
malabom	boŋ	'flying fox'

Typological examination of reduplicative systems reveals that there are many examples in which morphological structure can intervene so that the reduplicant is not adjacent to its correspondents in the base. For example, in many Interior Salish languages, the diminutive reduplicant can intervene with plural reduplication (Broselow 1983; Urbanczyk 2000; Shaw 2005). Lillooet also illustrates this.

(24) *Lillooet plural diminutives (Salishan; Eijk 1997)*

	Stem	*gloss*	*plural-diminutives*	*gloss*
(a)	s-ˈqaχaʔ	'dog'	s-qəχ-ˈqəqχaʔ	'puppies'
(b)	s-ˈqajxʷ	'man'	s-qəj-ˈqəqj'əxʷ	'boys'
(c)	s-ˈqawts	'potato'	s-qəw-ˈqəqw'əts	'little potatoes'

The plural is a $C_1 \partial C_2$- prefix (Eijk 1997, 1998; it is underlined and separated by hyphens) and skips intervening diminutive material to copy the second consonant of the root. Urbanczyk (2000) has proposed that the base for the plural is still the string immediately following the plural (including the diminutive), but that reduplicant and base are not anchored at the left edge. Skipping material violates the Faithfulness constraint ANCHOR-L which requires the initial segment of the base to be the initial segment of the reduplicant. This is compelled by a constraint that requires that reduplicants be composed of root material (like R≤Root).[13] The Lillooet pattern is interesting because it shows that the diminutive prefers adjacency (obeying ANCHOR-L) over copying root material, while the plural prefers copying root material over adjacency (violating ANCHOR-L).[14]

In this OT approach, the preference for correspondents of the base and reduplicant to be adjacent is derived because the base is always the adjacent string (McCarthy and Prince 1993b, 1995a, 1999; Nelson 2003; Urbanczyk 2000). When segmental material intervenes, this violates a constraint requiring the initial segment of the base and reduplicant to correspond (ANCHOR-L). Other approaches assume that the base is defined by violable constraints (Downing 1998ab, 2000, 2001, 2004; Shaw 2005) and that there is a separate constraint on ADJACENCY.

20.4.3   Root preference

A second recurring pattern is that there is a preference to copy root material. McCarthy and Prince (1993b) propose the constraint R≤Root, to account for this. This constraint has the properties of a Markedness constraint. There are languages that only copy root material, those that copy root and affix material, but there are no languages which only copy affix material. This section outlines the evidence for this constraint, as well as pointing out other root-sensitive effects that emerge in reduplication.

In Axininca Campa there is a disyllabic minimality requirement on the reduplicant (Spring 1990; McCarthy and Prince 1993b). If the root is disyllabic or greater, prefix material is not copied (25a). However, if the root is monosyllabic then prefix material can be copied (25b), illustrating that, while the reduplicant prefers to be composed of root material, it can also be composed of affix material. Violation of R≤Root is compelled by the shape requirement of the reduplicant (that it be disyllabic).[15]

(25)   *Axininca Campa (McCarthy & Prince 1993b; Spring 1990)*

(a) Disyllabic or greater

root	reduplicated word	gloss
√kawosi	*noŋ*-kawosi-<u>kawosi</u>-wai-*t*-aki	'bathe'
√tʰaaŋki	*noŋ*-tʰaaŋki-<u>tʰaaŋki</u>-wai-*t*-aki	'hurry'
√kintʰa	*noŋ*-kintʰa-<u>kintʰa</u>-wai-*t*-aki	'tell'

(b) Monosyllabic root

root	reduplicated word	gloss
√naa	*no*-naa-<u>no-naa</u>-wai-*t*-aki	'chew'
√na	*no*-na-<u>no-na</u>-wai-*t*-aki	'carry'
√tʰo	*non*-tʰo-<u>non-tʰo</u>-wai-*t*-aki	'kiss, suck'

R≤Root is obeyed when the root is large enough; however, when it is not large enough to produce a disyllabic reduplicant, affix material is copied violating this Markedness constraint.

Further root-effects occur when the reduplicant shape is smaller than the root. In the Tsimshianic language Nisgha (spoken in British Columbia), 'plural' is expressed by CVC reduplication, as in (26a) (V is a predictable default). If the base exceeds the target shape of the reduplicant then material is skipped to ensure that the reduplicant is anchored with the rightmost segment of the root (26b). If the base begins with a cluster (26c) or has stress on the second syllable (26d), then there is no right anchoring.

(26) *Nisgha CVC 'plural' (Tsimshian; Tarpent 1987; Shaw 1987, 2005)*

(a)	(i)	qaːp	q̲ap̲-'qaːp	'to scratch'
	(ii)	t'ak	t'ix̲-'t'ak	'to forget'
	(iii)	'ʔaq-ɬ-k	ʔax̲-'ʔaq-ɬ-k	'to finally reach the goal'

| (b) | (i) | 'loʔp | li̲p̲-'loʔp | 'stone, rock' |
| | (ii) | 'ɬuːt'uxʷ | ɬux̲ʷ-'ɬuːt'uxʷ | 'to value, treasure, cherish s.t./s.o.' |

| (c) | (i) | | sax̲-sqikskʷ | 'to be injured' |
| | (ii) | | ɬi̲x̲-ɬkiːkʷ-s | 'sister' |

| (d) | (i) | wi'laːx | wi̲l̲-wi'laːx | 'to know someone' |

Nelson (2003) has proposed a constraint EDGE-ANCHOR to account for effects like this.[16]

Finally, if the root is larger than the reduplicant target shape, failure to copy can also occur. In the following Kinande examples (27), the target reduplicant shape is to be disyllabic and vowel-final; one can see that copying may not occur at all, if the base is greater than two syllables. This is known as a morpheme integrity effect (Mutaka and Hyman 1990; Downing 1998b), with the insight that entire morphemes must be copied.

(27) *Kinande (Mutaka and Hyman 1990)*

(a) Disyllabic stems

| o.ku-gulu | 'leg' | o.ku-gulu.gulu | 'a real leg' |
| o.mu-góngò | 'back' | o.mu-góngo-góngò | 'a real back' |

(b) Polysyllabic stems

| o.tu-gotseri | 'sleepiness' | (no reduplication) |
| e.bí-nyurúgúnzù | 'butterflies' | (no reduplication) |

With these observations in mind, it appears that there are two central components that are active in defining the base of reduplication: adjacency and root preference; prosodic requirements like reduplicant shape and prosody–morphology mismatches also influence what is copied, but play a more indirect role in delimiting what is copied.

20.5   Summary

Research on understanding the nature of reduplication has focused on three core areas of investigation: segmental identity, determining the shape of reduplicants, and identifying the base of reduplication. While research has been extensive in all of these areas, there is still much more work to be done. One current approach that seems to be able to account for the widest array of facts, without requiring a great deal of reduplication-specific mechanisms, is Correspondence Theory. In this model, the principle of constraint re-ranking has been able to derive a range of facts. In particular, TETU effects can be found in a variety of reduplicative patterns (from segmentism to shape), and this is a natural and predicted pattern in Correspondence Theory. By examining languages in detail, we can learn a great deal about the typological range of patterns, thus leading to a more comprehensive understanding of the nature of reduplication within the architecture of the grammar.

Notes

Many many thanks to John McCarthy, Joe Pater, and Paul de Lacy for very helpful feedback, comments, and discussion.

1 See also Yip (1998) for cases in which reduplicant and base are not identical due to dissimilation (typically of vowels).
2 See McCarthy and Prince (1995a, 1999) for precise definitions of the various Faithfulness constraints.
3 See Urbanczyk (1996) and Alderete et al. (1999) for arguments that in Lushootseed (Salish) diminutive Cí- reduplication, the vowel is truly epenthetic.
4 However, see McCarthy and Prince (1995a, 1999) for examples of reduplicative phonology that cannot be accounted for by the interleaving of phonological processes with reduplication.
5 This approach to total reduplication has also been proposed for Correspondence-based accounts of reduplication (Pulleyblank, in press); if compounding is only subject to IO-Faith constraints, then this accounts for the observation that TETU effects tend to be found with partial reduplication. Because a base compounds with itself, there is no BR-Correspondence relation, so no TETU effects are expected.
6 Fixed segmentism is accounted for in this model by preassociation of segmental material. See McCarthy and Prince (1986, 1990) for a critique of this.

7 For another problem associated with templatic constraints in OT, see McCarthy and Prince (1999) who discuss the problem of 'over-applying' templatic constraints (known as the Kager–Hamilton effect). Basically, the prediction is that there can be reduplicated words where the base deletes, so *badupi* could reduplicate as *bad-bad* by over-applying the templatic constraint.

8 See also Gafos (1998a), who proposes for single segment reduplication that the Markedness constraints are those against segments and vowels in general.

9 See Downing (2006) for a modification to GTT in which the relative markedness of root and stem reduplicants vs. affixal ones follows from a structural asymmetry between heads and dependents, adopting proposals by Dresher and Hulst (1998). Because roots are morphological heads, they require some complexity manifest in branching structure (i.e. CVC shape branches in the rhyme of the syllable).

10 This assumption about where the base is located with respect to the reduplicant encodes Marantz's (1982) insight about the 'default direction of association' for different reduplicative affixes: Left-to-Right for prefixes, and Right-to-Left for suffixes.

11 See in particular Nelson (2003:Ch.2) for a detailed discussion of how the base is defined in Correspondence Theory, comparing a number of competing approaches. Her central finding is that there is a preference for the base to contain root material, but that the base can be extended to include non-root material under pressure from prosodic constraints like a requirement for onsets (she terms this approach Minimal Base Adjustment).

12 However, see Nelson (2003) for arguments that all reduplication is prefixing. Under her approach, the Manam reduplicant would be a prefix to the stressed foot.

13 See Shaw (2005) for an approach in which the base is determined by Alignment constraints.

14 Broselow (1983) accounts for this by proposing that the plural attaches to a morphological constituent, while the diminutive attaches to a prosodic constituent (in that order).

15 Other cases in which affix material can be recruited for copying include cases in which a vowel-initial root has syllabified with segments from the prefix, resulting in a mismatch between morphological and prosodic structure. See Downing (1999) for an OT approach to effects of this sort, in which she proposes that the base is the morpho-prosodic unit P-Stem.

16 Nelson analyzes this as a Faithfulness constraint. However, if it were, there is the expectation that truncations of this sort would be quite common.

Part V

External interfaces

21

Diachronic phonology

Ricardo Bermúdez-Otero

21.1   Introduction

As the title of this part of the volume indicates, the study of *sound change*[1] compels us to think hard about the relationship between phonological structure and what lies beyond: the physics of sound, the physiology of speech, the social and cultural context of communication. Yet, for that very reason, diachrony lies at the heart of current phonological debates. In particular, historical questions are crucial to the renewed controversy between formalist and functionalist approaches to phonology, which respond in different ways to a fundamental fact: phonological structure is moulded by external forces through change, but also imposes constraints on the possible courses of change (see Gordon Ch.3 and Kingston Ch.17).

One of the basic challenges for diachronic phonology is the problem of *innovation*: how does a phonological variant that has never existed previously in a speech community first come into being? Here, it is commonly agreed that the potential for innovation leading to sound change arises whenever speaker and listener fail to solve the *coordination problem*[2] posed by speech: the speaker must produce a phonetic stimulus that enables the listener to recover the intended phonological representation; the listener must decide which properties of the incoming stimulus are intended by the speaker as signal, and which properties are accidental noise; neither participant can read the other's mind. The innovation mechanisms proposed by Ohala, *hypocorrection* and *hypercorrection*, both involve failures of coordination: the listener does not parse the stimulus in the way that the speaker intended (see e.g. Ohala 1989, Alderete & Frisch 16.3, Kingston 17.3.3). Beyond this point, however, disagreement rages over important questions:

(i)   What are the relative rôles of the speaker and the listener in bringing about a coordination failure?

(ii)   Do the crucial coordination failures that lead to innovation happen when the listener is a child acquiring language or when the listener is an adult?

(iii) To what extent are innovations driven and controlled by *bottom-up* factors (e.g. phonetic effects) and *top-down* biases (e.g. phonological knowledge)?

Question (iii), in particular, has figured prominently in the debate concerning the nature and origins of phonological markedness (see Gordon 3.5, Rice Ch.4): some phonologists argue that markedness is a mere epiphenomenon of sound changes actuated by bottom-up factors; others claim that knowledge of markedness imposes top-down constraints on innovation (Bermúdez-Otero & Börjars 2006; Bermúdez-Otero 2006).

This chapter will largely focus on another challenge: describing and explaining the time course of sound change. Is sound change implemented gradually or abruptly, and why? As we shall see, this question too has profound implications for the nature of phonological representations and the architecture of phonological grammar.

21.2   The implementation problem: how gradual is phonological change?

In a pretheoretical sense, all phonological change is gradual: developments such as the raising of /ɑː/ to /ɔː/ in southern dialects of Middle English – and, *a fortiori*, large-scale upheavals like the Great Vowel Shift – do not take place overnight. However, this obvious fact does not imply that phonological change advances gradually in all dimensions.

One must first distinguish between graduality in *implementation* and graduality in *propagation*. For example, Prehistoric Latin is reconstructed as having left-dominant word stress: the first syllable of the word was the most prominent. Later, Classical Latin developed a right-dominant pattern whereby primary stress was assigned to the penultimate syllable if heavy, otherwise to the antepenult: e.g. prehistoric *má.le.fi.ci.um* > classical *mà.le.fí.cĭ.um* 'bad deed' (Allen 1973: 189–190). Imagine that, while Latin was undergoing this change, every individual speaker fell into just one of two groups: one pronouncing all words invariably with a left-strong contour, the other pronouncing all words invariably with a right-strong contour. Had that been the case, the shift from left to right dominance would have been implemented abruptly: there would have been graduality only in its propagation, as the proportion of speakers with right-dominant stress increased in the community over time. As we shall see presently, however, implementation is never completely abrupt; rather, every phonological change is implemented gradually in one or more of the following dimensions: sociolinguistic, phonetic, and lexical.

Sociolinguistic research indicates that all phonological changes involve a transitional phase of variation (Anttila Ch.22). Therefore, one
can confidently assume that, while Latin was undergoing its shift from
left to right dominance, an individual speaker might pronounce the
same word sometimes with primary stress on the initial syllable, sometimes with primary stress on the penult or antepenult: e.g. *má.le.fi.ci.um*
~ *mà.le.fí.ci.um*. The relative frequency with which speakers used left-
strong or right-strong stress probably reflected external factors such as
sex, age, social status, and so forth. In this sociolinguistic dimension,
phonological change typically advances through generational incre-
ments: successive generations of speakers use the innovative variant
with increasing frequency (Labov 1994:84; 2001:Part D). The omnipres-
ence of variation during change in progress is one of the reasons why
quantitative techniques are indispensable in research into the problem
of implementation.

A change is said to be phonetically gradual – or *gradient* – if it involves a
continuous shift along one or more dimensions in phonetic space, such as
the frequency of the first formant of a vowel as measured in hertz. In
contrast, a change is phonetically abrupt – or *categorical* – if it involves
the substitution of one discrete phonological category for another: e.g.
replacing the feature [−high] with [+high] (see Harris 6.2.1). Deciding
whether the pattern created by a change is gradient or categorical often
requires careful instrumental analysis, as well as a global understanding of
the phonology–phonetics interface in the language in question (Myers
2000). Indeed, laboratory research has in recent times redressed the balance
between gradient and categorical rules in phonology (21.3.1). Languages
have been shown to vary with respect to the phonetic realization of phonological categories down to the finest detail: for example, contrary to the
assumptions of *SPE* (Chomsky & Halle 1968: 295), patterns of coarticulation
are not mechanical and universal, but cognitive and acquired (Keating
1988c:287–288; Pierrehumbert *et al.* 2000: 285–286). In addition, many
phenomena previously thought to be categorical have proved to be gradient (Myers 2000: 257).

The ongoing lengthening and raising of the reflexes of Middle English
short /a/ in contemporary American English (henceforth 'æ-tensing') provides a striking illustration of the contrast between gradient and categorical implementation (Labov 1981, 1994). In the northern dialect area
comprising cities such as Albany, Rochester, Buffalo, Detroit, and Chicago,
æ-tensing is phonetically gradual: the allophones of /æ/ form an unbroken
phonetic continuum from the highest and most peripheral (e.g. in *aunt*) to
the lowest and less peripheral (e.g. in *black*); the degree of tensing displayed
by each allophone is exquisitely sensitive to a broad range of properties of
its phonetic environment (Labov 1994:456–459; see also Matthew J. Gordon
2001:124–140). In Mid-Atlantic cities such as New York, Philadelphia, and
Baltimore, in contrast, æ-tensing is phonetically abrupt: lax /æ/ and tense

/æː/ have widely separated phonetic targets, namely low [æ] vs. mid-high [eːˀ], and their tokens occupy discrete, largely nonoverlapping regions in phonetic space (see e.g. Labov 1989: 7–11).

As a first approximation, lexically abrupt – or *regular* – implementation can be defined as follows: a change is regular if it applies at the same time to all words that are identical with respect to the relevant phonological, morphological, and syntactic conditions. In contrast, a change is lexically gradual – or *diffusing* – if it affects certain words earlier than others with an equivalent phonological and morphosyntactic makeup, i.e. if lexical identity plays an irreducible rôle in controlling the advance of the change. When applying this definition in practice, one must take account of sociolinguistic variation: lexical diffusion can manifest itself through a difference in the relative frequency with which two words display the innovative variant, as long as this difference is not determined by phonological, morphological, or syntactic conditions, or by sociolinguistic factors (e.g. sex, age, social status, style, register, etc.). Accordingly, establishing whether a particular change is regular or diffusing often requires large data-sets and powerful statistical methods (e.g. Labov 1994:Ch.16).

In this connection, a particularly effective way of controlling for unknown phonological factors is to focus on the behaviour of homophones: e.g. the English words /tuː/ 'two' and /tuː/ 'too'. When two initially homophonous words cease to be phonologically identical by undergoing different processes of change, we have strong evidence for lexical diffusion (Chen 1972: Sec. 6). The Chao-zhou dialect of Chinese provides a notable instance of this phenomenon, known as a *homonym split*: in Chao-zhou, twelve pairs of homophonous Middle Chinese words with tone III have become split between the modern tones 2b and 3b (Cheng & Wang 1973; but see Section 21.4.2 below). In contrast, Labov (1994: 460–465) shows that, in Philadelphia English, homophones such as *two* and *too* undergo the fronting of /uː/ to [ʉːᵘ] at exactly the same rate, and on this basis he argues that the change is regular.

Interestingly, Labov also shows that æ-tensing is lexically abrupt in the northern cities of the United States, but lexically gradual in the Mid-Atlantic region. In Philadelphia, for example, there is incipient tensing of æ before /d/: in particular, æ has become tense in the affective adjectives *mad*, *bad*, and *glad*. This is an innovation with respect to the tensing pattern found in Early Modern English: cf. British Received Pronunciation, which has /mæd/, /bæd/, and /glæd/, rather than */mɑːd/, */bɑːd/, or */glɑːd/. Nonetheless, the tensing of æ before /d/ in Philadelphia remains lexically idiosyncratic: most noticeably, the vowel remains lax in the affective adjective *sad* (Labov 1994: 429–437). The contrast between gl[eːˀ]d and s[æ]d is particularly striking, as elsewhere tensing is strongly disfavoured after an obstruent+liquid cluster (Labov 1994: 433, 458–459).

In the 1980s and 1990s, the work of William Labov and Paul Kiparsky brought about a convergence of empirical results and theoretical perspectives on the implementation problem. Labov's (1981, 1994) empirical findings confirmed the existence of two long-recognized mechanisms of phonological change: *Neogrammarian change* (Osthoff & Brugmann 1878) and *classical lexical diffusion* (Wang 1969). The former (exemplified by æ-tensing in the northern cities) is regular but gradient; the latter (instantiated by æ-tensing in the Mid-Atlantic states) is categorical but diffusing (1).

(1)   *The implementation of phonological change: the received view*

		Dimensions	
		Phonetic	*Lexical*
Modes	*Neogrammarian sound change*	gradual	abrupt
	Classical lexical diffusion	abrupt	gradual

Kiparsky (1988, 1995) then showed how the existence of these two modes of implementation follows from the architecture of grammar in generative theory, particularly in Lexical Phonology. Lately, however, the received view has come under challenge, as the claim that all phonological change is both lexically and phonetically gradual (Bybee 2000, 2001) gains increasing currency. The ensuing debate bears directly on a central issue in phonological theory: whether or not lexical representations contain gradient phonetic detail.

21.3   The view from generative phonology

21.3.1   Modular feedforward models: phonological rules vs. phonetic rules

Structuralist and generative theories of phonology assume a fundamental distinction between phonological and phonetic rules,[3] where the term *rule* is to be understood in its widest sense as meaning 'symbolic generalization'. Such symbolic generalizations may be instantiated by various devices, including the input-driven transformations of *SPE* and the output-oriented constraints of OT; but in the discussion that follows I will in general not be concerned with choosing among them. The distinction between phonological and phonetic rules is typically embedded in the general grammatical architecture shown in (2); see Kingston (17.4.3). Following Pierrehumbert (2002), I shall describe all versions of (2) as 'modular feedforward models'.[4] This grammatical architecture is equally compatible with the view that modules are innate (e.g. Fodor 1985) and with the idea that modularity emerges during the child's cognitive development (e.g. Karmiloff-Smith 1994).

(2)   *The classical modular feedforward architecture of phonology*

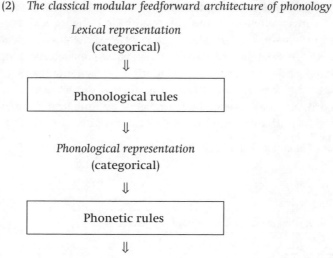

Lexical representation
(categorical)

⇓

| Phonological rules |

⇓

Phonological representation
(categorical)

⇓

| Phonetic rules |

⇓

Phonetic representation
(gradient)

Modular feedforward models of phonology rest on two key assumptions (see the discussion in Pierrehumbert 2002:101–102):

(3)   a.   *Lexical and phonological discreteness*
        In lexical and phonological representations, attributes have discrete values.
    b.   *Modularity*
        Phonetic rules cannot refer directly to lexical representations.

An example of (3a) is the common postulate that, in the phonological module, distinctive feature specifications are maximally ternary: e.g. a segment can at most be [+voice], [−voice], or underspecified for voicing. Here, however, the term *attribute* is intended in a wide sense as including any relevant phonological property: e.g. the presence or absence of an association line between two nodes. Thus, principle (3a) prevents lexical and phonological representations from encoding fine phonetic detail, which would require gradient attribute values. Note, however, that (3a) makes no claim as to whether lexical representations should be minimal (cf. Bybee 2001: Sec.3.4.2–3.4.3). Some versions of the modular feedforward architecture assume that lexical representations do not contain any predictable information (e.g. Kiparsky 1982b, 1995; Archangeli 1984), but others reject this claim (e.g. Prince & Smolensky 2004, Steriade 1995, Bermúdez-Otero & McMahon 2006). Principle (3a) allows allophonic information to be stored in lexical representations as long as this information is categorical rather than gradient.

The principles in (3) give expression to fundamental phonological assumptions. One is the idea that, on the phonological no less than on the syntactic side, linguistic expressions arise from the combination of a small inventory of elements: see Martinet's (1964) notion of the double articulation of language. Given (3a), phonological representations cannot behave as holistic articulatory or auditory patterns because they do not contain continuous phonetic information, but are rather composed of discrete units. Phonologists have also adduced various types of empirical evidence in support of (3). Of particular relevance here are the arguments from diachrony.[5] In line with the received view of implementation outlined in (1), the principles in (3) account for the regularity of gradient changes (Neogrammarian change) and the categorical nature of diffusing changes (classical lexical diffusion):

(i) By (3a), phonetically gradual change can take place only through the alteration of the phonetic rules that assign realizations to phonological categories. But, by (3b), any such alteration must be free of lexical conditioning. This is the key insight behind Bloomfield's (1933:351) slogan 'Phonemes change'.

(ii) Diffusing change involves the alteration of the lexical representations where lexical information is stored. By (3a), however, such alterations must be categorical.

In fact, given all the logically possible interactions between the phonetic and lexical dimensions, the architecture in (2) predicts the existence of not two but three modes of implementation for phonological change (4):

(4) *Modes of implementation predicted by the classical architecture*

Mode of implementation		Possible?	Innovation in what component of grammar?
phonetic dimension	*lexical dimension*		
abrupt	gradual	Yes	lexical representations
abrupt	abrupt	Yes	phonological rules
gradual	abrupt	Yes	phonetic rules
gradual	gradual	No	

To my knowledge, the prediction that regular categorical change exists has rarely, if ever, been explicitly discussed in the literature. As we shall see in Section 21.3.2, however, there are powerful arguments in its favour.

21.3.2 The life cycle of sound patterns, stabilization, and secondary split

At least since Baudouin de Courtenay (1895), phonologists have acknowledged that sound patterns evolve historically according to a characteristic *life cycle*. Modular feedforward models – especially Lexical Phonology and

Stratal OT – provide a perspicuous interpretation of this observation (Kiparsky 1988; McMahon 2000b; Bermúdez-Otero 2006, forthcoming):

Phase I

The life cycle starts with *phonologization* (Hyman 1976), which occurs when some physical or physiological phenomenon gives rise to a new cognitively controlled pattern of phonetic implementation through a coordination failure (see Section 21.1). This development involves the addition of a new phonetic rule to the grammar and manifests itself as Neogrammarian sound change (i.e. regular gradient change: see (1) above).

Phase II

Subsequently, the new gradient sound pattern may become categorical. In the modular feedforward architecture in (2), such a change would involve the *restructuring* of the phonological representations that provide the input to phonetic implementation, with the concomitant development of a new phonological counterpart for the original phonetic rule. As we shall see below, this step in the life cycle corresponds to the process of 'stabilization' discussed in Hayes & Steriade (2004: Sec. 5.6), and is implicated in the rise of so-called 'quasi-phonemes' that precedes secondary split (Janda 1999).

Phase III

Reanalysis can also cause categorical patterns to change. Over time, phonological rules typically become sensitive to morphosyntactic structure, often with a reduction in their domain of application (Dressler 1985:149). In models such as Lexical Phonology and Stratal OT, these changes involve the ascent of phonological rules from the phrase level through the word level into the stem level: see Bermúdez-Otero & Hogg (2003) and Bermúdez-Otero (2006, forthcoming) for discussion. Phonological rules may also develop lexical exceptions: cf. the lexical split of short /a/ in southern British English (Section 21.4.2 below).

Phase IV

At the end of their life cycle, sound patterns may cease to be phonologically controlled. Thus, a phonological rule may be replaced by a morphological operation (*morphologization*), or may disappear altogether, leaving an idiosyncratic residue in lexical representations (*lexicalization*). See Anderson (1988) for examples and discussion.

Let us now focus on Phase II: the emergence of a phonological rule from a phonetic one. By definition, changes of this sort are phonetically abrupt since they have the effect of creating a new distribution of discrete categories in the output of the phonological module. However, the new phonological rule may remain free of lexical idiosyncrasies, for restructuring may fall short of altering the content of lexical representations (cf. Phase III above); in that case, the change whereby the new rule is introduced will be lexically abrupt too. In this sense, the extra mode of implementation predicted in figure (4), viz. regular categorical change, finds a natural niche in our account of the life cycle of sound patterns. Empirically, however, developments of this type may be difficult to detect: as we saw in Section 21.2, the distinction between categorical and gradient rules cannot be reliably drawn on the basis of impressionistic data and, indeed, the change may be largely covert. Of relevance here is Karmiloff-Smith's (1994:700) distinction between behavioural change and representational change during the child's cognitive development: 'The same performance (say, correctly producing a particular linguistic form, or managing to balance blocks on a narrow support) can be generated at various ages by very different representations.' In terms of Karmiloff-Smith's cognitive science metatheory, sound patterns reach Phase II in their life cycle by a process of *representational redescription*.

Regular categorical changes involving the rise of a new phonological generalization out of an existing phonetic rule have the effect of *stabilizing* patterns of allophonic variation (cf. Hayes & Steriade 2004: Sec. 5.6). As noted in Myers (2000: Sec. 6.3), phonetic rules are gradient in respect not only of their effects, but also of the factors that condition them: for example, Sproat & Fujimura (1993) showed that, in the pronunciation of dark [ɫ] in American English, the delay of the coronal C-gesture relative to the dorsal V-gesture increases continuously in proportion to the duration of the syllable rhyme.[6] The modular feedforward architecture in (2) predicts that, in contrast, phonological rules will not be sensitive to quantitative properties of the phonetic environment, since information about such properties is absent at the phonological level. In Modern Japanese, for example, the phonemic opposition between /t/ and /tɕ/ is neutralized before /i/, where only [tɕ] occurs: see (5a,b). This rule probably arose historically through the phonologization of a coarticulation effect in [ti] sequences: anticipating the gesture of tongue front raising for [i] narrows the channel for the release of [t], causing the stop burst to become relatively noisy. In present-day Japanese, however, reducing the amount of CV coarticulation fails to restore the contrast between /t/ and /tɕ/ in the neutralization environment: even in the most careful *hyperspeech* (Lindblom 1990a), the realization of /t/ before /i/ remains [tɕ] (Mitsuhiko Ota, personal communication). The modular feedforward architecture correctly predicts this state of affairs: affrication cannot be blocked by gradient adjustments to gestural timing because it is a categorical rule. This is independently shown by the fact that it has lexical exceptions among loanwords, and so has already progressed to Phase III in its life cycle: see (5c) and cf. Bybee (2001:53).

(5)   *Japanese /t/-affrication (Itô & Mester 1995: 827–828)*

   (a)   /ta/   /t͡ɕa/
          [ta]   [t͡ɕa]
          'field'   'tea'

   (b)   /kat-i/   /kat-e/
          [kat͡ɕi]   [kate]
          'win-INF'   'win-IMP'

   (c)   [t͡ɕimɯ]   'team   but   [tiːN]   'teenager'
          [t͡ɕiketːo] 'ticket'   [paːtiː]   'party'

Interestingly, the innovative phonological rules created by stabilization do not replace the phonetic rules from which they emerge, but typically coexist with them. English palatalization provides a well-studied example of this coexistence: categorical palatalization in stem-level domains, e.g. *confess* [kənˈfɛs] ∼ *confession* [kənˈfɛʃn], coexists with gradient palatalization by gestural overlap across word boundaries, e.g. *press you* [ˈpɹɛʃuː] (Zsiga 1995, discussed in Kingston 17.4.3). For a diachronic illustration, see the discussion of the Scottish Vowel Length Rule and low-level lengthening in McMahon (2000b:Ch.4, especially Sec. 4.5.2).

   In sum, stabilization is a process of regular categorical change that creates a new phonological counterpart for an existing phonetic rule. Understood in this sense, stabilization is a prerequisite for *secondary split*. This structuralist term designates a historical development whereby the destruction of the conditioning environment of an allo-phonic rule gives rise to a new phonemic opposition (see Fox 1995: Sec.3.2). The Sanskrit Law of Palatals (6) provides a justly celebrated example (see Fox 1995:27–29):

(6)   *The Law of Palatals*

   (a)   *Proto-Indo-Iranian*   *-ki-   *-ke-   *-ka-   *-ko-   *-ku-
   (b)   *Palatalization*   *-**ci**-   *-**ce**-   *-ka-   *-ko-   *-ku-
   (c)   *Lowering of /e, o/ to [a]*   *-ci-   *-**ca**-   *-ka-   *-**ka**-   *-ku-
   (d)   *Sanskrit distribution*

          *-ci-   -$\left\{ \begin{matrix} k \\ c \end{matrix} \right\}$a-   -ku-

At the synchronic stage represented by (6b), [k] and [c] are in complemen-tary distribution: the language has a single phoneme /k/, allophonically realized as [c] before nonlow front vowels. At a later point, /e/ and /o/ undergo lowering to [a]. This development removes the trigger of palatal-ization in the reflexes of Proto-Indo-Iranian *-ke-. In consequence, the dis-tinction between [k] and [c] becomes phonemic in Sanskrit, as the two phones are in contrastive distribution before [a].

It is crucial for this development that, at the synchronic stage represented by (6c), the rule of lowering should *counterbleed* the rule of palatalization: i.e. lowering must apply to the output of palatalization, removing the cause of palatalization without reversing its effect; see (7a). This synchronic interaction between the two rules is an instance of *opacity* in the sense defined by Kiparsky (1971) (see McCarthy Ch.5). The counterbleeding relationship between palatalization and lowering caused the restructuring of lexical representations, with the opaque string [-ca-] being reanalysed as underlying; see (7b).

(7)

(a) *Opaque derivation*

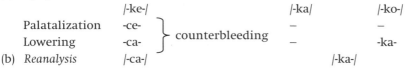

If, upon entering the grammar, lowering had interacted transparently with palatalization, [k] and [c] would have remained in complementary distribution:

(8) *No secondary split without synchronic opacity*

This raises an obvious question: why was the interaction opaque rather than transparent? Assuming the ordinary life cycle of sound patterns as implemented in the classical modular feedforward architecture provides a straightforward solution. Presumably, both palatalization and lowering first came into being as phonetic rules. However, when lowering entered the phonetic implementation module as a gradient pattern, palatalization had already undergone stabilization and become a categorical phonological rule (9).

(9) *Stabilization precedes secondary split*

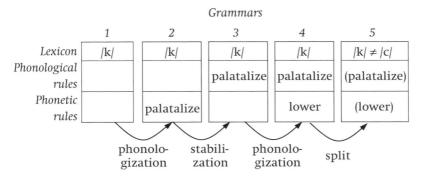

If this analysis is on the right track, the original phoneme /k/ could split only after its allophones [k] and [c] had become discrete phonological categories through the restructuring of the input to the phonetic module. This proposal provides a formal interpretation of the claim that only *quasi-phonemes* can become phonemicized through the loss of their conditioning context (see Kiparsky 1995:657; Janda 1999; and references therein): discrete allophones generated by categorical phonological rules are quasi-phonemes in the intended sense; nondiscrete allophones created by gradient phonetic rules are not.

In nonmodular theories of the phonology–phonetics interface, in contrast, a predictable allophone can remain after the loss of its conditioning environment only if it is already present in lexical representation (Bybee 2001: Sec.3.6). However, this approach misses the crucial rôle of opacity in triggering lexical restructuring: see (7). Modular feedforward models capture the right sequence of cause and effect: in the Sanskrit case, the stabilization of palatalization enabled it to interact opaquely with lowering; this opacity, in turn, prompted lexical restructuring, with the attendant phonemic split.

Note, in addition, that an allophonic pattern may undergo stabilization without necessarily becoming word-bound (i.e. 'lexical' in the sense of Lexical Phonology). The distinction between word-bound rules and phrasal rules does not coincide with the distinction between categorical and gradient processes, for a rule may apply across word boundaries without being gradient. In the case of English palatalization (Zsiga 1995), for example, the categorical neutralizing version of the process happens to apply only in stem-level domains, whereas palatalization across word boundaries is the result of gradient coarticulation (see above). In Sardinian, however, assimilatory external sandhi is categorical (Ladd & Scobbie 2003).

21.3.3   The mechanism of classical lexical diffusion

In modular feedforward models of phonology, classical lexical diffusion is implemented through category substitution in lexical representations: see (4). Consider, for example, the incipient tensing of æ before /d/ in Philadelphia English (21.2). The surface contrast between [sæd, dæd, læd] and [meːˀd, beːˀd, gleːˀd] shows that there is a lexical opposition between /æ/ and /æː/.[7] Thus, the tensing of æ in *mad*, *bad*, and *glad* involved the replacement of /æ/ with /æː/ in the lexical representation of each of the affected items (10):

(10)   *Lexical diffusion by category substitution in lexical representations*

		'mad'	'bad'	'glad'	'sad'	'dad'	'lad'
(a)	(Early) Modern English	/mæd/	/bæd/	/glæd/	/sæd/	/dæd/	/læd/
(b)	Present-day Philadelphia	/mæːd/	/bæːd/	/glæːd/	/sæd/	/dæd/	/læd/

In this section we shall see that, in addition to providing an implementation mechanism for classical lexical diffusion, modular theories of phonology can also make a partial contribution to our understanding of the causes of diffusing innovations. Kiparsky (1988, 1995) states the key ideas. Classical lexical diffusion is driven by a combination of top-down and bottom-up effects (see Section 21.1). Phonological rules introduce a language-specific top-down bias in the learner's expectations regarding the distribution of contrastive features in the lexicon: in particular, the rules designate certain feature values as marked in certain contexts. Under pressure from performance (bottom-up) factors, feature values designated as marked become particularly vulnerable to misperception and therefore misacquisition.

Several observations suggest that, despite their lexical irregularity, diffusing changes are under some sort of phonological control. First, feature substitution in lexical representations is not random, but takes place under fairly well-defined phonological and morphological conditions: in Philadelphia English, for example, æ is prone to tensing when followed tautosyllabically within a stem-level domain by an anterior nasal, a voiceless anterior fricative, or (incipiently) /d/.[8] Second, the conditioning factors of diffusing changes are specific to particular languages or dialects: in New York City, for example, the set of consonants that trigger æ-tensing is much larger than in Philadelphia (11) (Labov 1994: 430, 520).

(11) *Triggers of lexically gradual æ-tensing in the Mid-Atlantic states*

	New York City				Philadelphia		
(a) voiced stops	b	d	ʤ	g			(d)
(b) voiceless fricatives	f	θ	s	ʃ	f	θ	s
(c) nasals	m	n			m	n	

Third, diffusing changes appear in general not to be phonetically unnatural: indeed, in the case of æ-tensing we see the same phenomenon advancing by categorical diffusion in the Mid-Atlantic states and operating as a gradient phonetic rule in the Northern Cities Shift (21.2). All these arguments indicate that, except for its diffusing character, Philadelphia æ-tensing produces similar effects to an obligatory phonological rule that, having emerged through the stabilization of a gradient phonetic pattern, had ascended to the stem level, with a concomitant reduction in its domain of application (Phase III in the life cycle outlined in Section 21.3.2). Kiparsky's crucial insight was to realize that, if Philadelphia æ-tensing behaved so much like a stem-level phonological rule, it was because such a rule was indeed involved. In Kiparsky (1988, 1995), he used Radical Underspecification Theory to formalize his approach; but, as observed in Goldsmith (1995a:17), this particular technology is not essential. Bermúdez-Otero (1998: Sec.3.4) indicates how the same idea can be expressed in terms of OT.

Consider, for example, the phonemic opposition between /æ/ and /æ:/ before a tautosyllabic /f/ in Philadelphia English: e.g. *Afghan* [ǽf.gən][9] vs *after* [eːˀf.təɹ] (Labov 1994:507). Maintaining this contrast requires that the faithfulness constraint IDENT-length should outrank both the context-sensitive markedness constraint *ǽf_σ] and the context-free markedness constraint *ǽ (12).[10]

(12)

Philadelphia		IDENT-length	*ǽf_σ]	*ǽ
/æfgən/	[æːf.gən]	*!		*
	☞ [æf.gən]		*	
/æːftəɹ/	☞ [æːf.təɹ]			*
	[æf.təɹ]	*!	*	

In addition, assume that in this dialect *ǽf_σ], though dominated by IDENT-length, is ranked higher than *ǽ. The effect of this ordering of the constraints will be to designate the input string /-æfC-/ as marked: although [æf.gən] is the optimal output for input /æfgən/, lexical representations containing long /æː/ in the same environment nonetheless allow for input–output mappings with a better constraint profile (13).

(13) *Input /-æfC-/ is marked relative to /-æːfC-/ in Philadelphia English*

input	optimal output	IDENT-length	*ǽf_σ]	*ǽ
/æfgən/	[æf.gən]		*	
/æːftəɹ/	[æː.f.təɹ]			*

By the same token, the following rankings capture the fact that /f/ is a trigger of lexically gradual tensing in both New York City and Philadelphia, whereas /g/ is a trigger only in New York City; see (11).

(14)   (a) Philadelphia   IDENT-length » *ǽf_σ] » *ǽ » *ǽg_σ]
       (b) New York City   IDENT-length » *ǽf_σ], *ǽg_σ] » *ǽ

I suggest that a learner who has acquired the constraint hierarchy in (14a) will be biased to expect input /æː/ in the environment /__fC/, but input /æ/ in the environment /__gC/. Given this bias, any phonetic effect impinging on the realization of the contrast between /æ/ and /æː/ may cause learners to fail to acquire input /-æfC-/ for particular lexical items, substituting unmarked /-æːfC-/ instead. Similarly, a learner who has mistakenly acquired a lexical representation with /-æːfC-/ for a lexical item x will tend not to recover from this error, except upon massive exposure to tokens of x with /æ/. Labov (1994:518–526) provides empirical evidence that the lexical incidence of /æ/ and /æː/ in Philadelphia English is indeed difficult to acquire: children born in Philadelphia to out-of-state parents typically fail to learn the native Philadelphian distribution, presumably because they initially acquire non-Philadelphian lexical entries from their parents and then fail to recover from the error.

As it stands, this account of the top-down factors driving classical lexical diffusion remains incomplete (Goldsmith 1995b). The basic idea is that markedness constraints, even when crucially dominated and therefore unable to cause unfaithfulness, nonetheless exert an indirect pressure on learners to switch features to their unmarked value in input representations. As Goldsmith points out, however, this incorrectly predicts that all lexical contrasts should be vulnerable to loss by diffusion, insofar as every feature has an unmarked value in every context. Goldsmith suggests that, in fact, the pressure towards category substitution in lexical representations is only felt in cases of *marginal contrast*. In the case of Philadelphia æ-tensing, Labov's (1989:45) data strongly corroborate this insight. Labov defines two word classes:

(i)   The 'normally tense' class consists of words containing environments where æ is nearly predictably tense. Only 2.9% of word tokens in this class show /æ/.

(ii) The 'normally lax' class consists of words containing environments where æ is nearly predictably lax. Only 1.2% of word tokens in this class show /æː/.

Strikingly, the 'normally tense' and 'normally lax' classes together account for 91.8% of Labov's data: only 443 out of 5,373 word tokens belong to the residual category, where the tenseness or laxness of æ cannot be predicted with more than 97% accuracy. In this light, it seems desirable to build Goldsmith's notion of marginal contrast into our account of classical lexical diffusion: one should probably say that learners are biased to replace a marked category with an unmarked one in lexical representations when the two categories are only marginally contrastive. Further research should determine the basis of this effect by ascertaining how marginal contrastivity impacts on lexical representation.

Pace Phillips (1998), this approach to the causes of classical lexical diffusion enables one to make correct predictions regarding the impact of token frequency on the progress of diffusing changes. These predictions depend crucially on the recognition that classical lexical diffusion is actuated by a combination of top-down and bottom-up factors:

(i)   In the case of the Mid-Atlantic dialects of American English, for example, I have suggested that phonetic factors tending to compromise the realization of the contrast between /æ/ and /æː/ will cause learners to fail to acquire /æ/ in /æː/-favouring environments. We know, however, that gradient phonetic effects such as coarticulation and gesture reduction are more pronounced in items with high token frequency.[11] From this it follows that the probability of substitution of /æ:/ for /æ/, insofar as it depends on phonetic effects, will be greater for high-frequency words.

(ii) On the other hand, I have suggested that, because of the bias introduced by the constraint hierarchy (in circumstances of marginal contrastivity), children will tend not to recover from overgeneralizations in the distribution of /æ:/, unless assisted by massive exposure to /æ/ in tokens of the relevant words. This predicts that the words with the very highest token frequency may exceptionally withstand the change.

These predictions exactly match Labov's findings about Philadelphia æ-tensing. He reports that, 'In the two cases of change in progress, more frequent words are more frequently selected. [. . .] Yet frequency exhibits only a general correlation with tensing and fails to account for the fact that the most common words [. . .] show the least tendency to shift to the tense class' (Labov 1989:44).

21.4   The view from functionalist phonology

21.4.1   Exemplar clouds

As I pointed out in the conclusion of Section 21.2, there has lately been a vigorous reaction against the classical modular approach to the phonology–phonetics interface (2) and, with it, against the received view of the implementation of phonological change (1). There is of course a wide range of opinion among the dissenters, but one can nonetheless identify a coherent research paradigm coalescing around a few programmatic drives: usage-based functionalism, phonetic reductionism, and connectionism. Bybee (2001) provides a synthetic statement of this research programme, which for convenience I shall call 'functionalism' *tout court*.

Essential to current functionalist thinking is the idea that the lexicon consists of a vast repository of highly-detailed memory traces of phonetic episodes experienced by the speaker: so-called 'exemplars' (Johnson 1997). Exemplars are linked to one another by a network of connections based on similarity in a high-dimensional phonetic space. Crucially, phonological categories do not exist independently of the exemplars. This idea comes in several versions. In the strongest version, categories exist implicitly in the patterns of connection between exemplars: a category, in this sense, is no more than a cloud of similar exemplars connected in some dimension. In a more conciliatory reading, categories exist explicitly as labels attached to the exemplars, and could even be accessed by rules referring to typed variables (see Section 21.4.3).[12] In either case, association with exemplar clouds endows categories with prototype structure: tokens of the category may be more or less central, and categorial boundaries are fuzzy. Finally, lexical representation is continuously updated in performance, as new exemplars are stored in long-term memory and old exemplars decay.

From this position, Bybee (2001:40–41) suggests that many – if not all – sound changes are simultaneously *gradient and diffusing*. This assertion roundly contradicts the predictions of the classical modular architecture, where gradient diffusion is precisely the only mode of implementation ruled out in principle: see (4).

Conceptually, Bybee's assertion rests on the assumption that every lexical item is associated with its own exemplar cloud. The phonetic properties of each lexical item shift as new exemplars are added to its cloud during language use. Accordingly, sound change must be phonetically gradual, insofar as it involves a continuous shift in the aggregated phonetic properties of the cloud. It must also be lexically gradual, since each lexical item has its own pattern of use, recorded in its own exemplar cloud.

Empirically, Bybee draws support from the observation that lexical items with high token frequency display greater amounts of coarticulation and gestural overlap than low frequency items. In a well-known example (15), the average duration of the medial [ə] in a high-frequency word such as *nursery* ['nɜːsəɹi] turns out to be shorter than in a low-frequency word such as *cursory* ['kɜːsəɹi] (Bybee 2000: 68).

(15)   *Effect of token frequency on gradient phonetic patterns*

Token frequency	Amount of coarticulation and reduction	Example
high	high	shorter [ə] in *nursery*
low	low	longer [ə] in *cursory*

Bybee infers that, as predicted by the exemplar model, the lexical representations of *nursery* and *cursory* must contain detailed quantitative information about degrees of gestural reduction and overlap.

21.4.2   The problem of phonetic residue

According to Bybee, all changes are lexically gradual, including those actuated by phonetic factors, whether articulatory or perceptual. However, diffusing changes often become arrested before completion, leaving behind a residue of unaltered words (Wang 1969). Accordingly, Bybee's claim leads to some surprising predictions. For example, endogenous lexical splits should be commonplace: an instance of a lexical split is the unpredictable evolution of Middle English short /a/ in the Mid-Atlantic region of the United States (see Section 21.2 and Section 21.3.3); this split would be described as 'endogenous' if it had not been actuated by contact (cf. below). Moreover, gradient diffusion predicts that, over time, the lexicon will preserve remnants of old phonemes and exceptions to new allophonic patterns, all left behind by arrested changes. Indeed, if holistic phonetic targets were kept in long-term memory in quite the same way as lexicalized morphological constructs, then phonetic relics should be as unremarkable as stored morphological irregularities like *children*, *oxen*, *feet*, or *wolves*.[13]

In fact, lexical splits are rare and typically arise in contact situations. For example, contact appears to have played an important rôle in triggering the lexical split of short /a/ in southern British English during the Early Modern period (Labov 1989: Sec.2). At this point in the history of the language, native Middle English /aː/ had already started on its way to /eɪ/ by the Great Vowel Shift. However, native short /a/ developed a lengthened allophone before coda /f, θ, s/; cf. (11). When this new allophonic [aː] merged with the long vowel present in some French loans such as *France* and *dance*, its distribution became marginally contrastive, and so the conditions arose for the diffusing spread of a new /aː/ phoneme. The Mid-Atlantic version of æ-tensing discussed in Section 21.2 and Section 21.3.3 ultimately descends from this southern British split (see Labov 1994:529ff.). Similarly, *pace* Chen (1972), Wang and Lien (1993) concede that the remarkable lexical split of Middle Chinese tone III in Chao-zhou (21.2) was actuated by prolonged contact between an implanted literary dialect and an indigenous colloquial dialect; see further Labov (1994:451-454).

In response to these problems, Bybee (2000:72; 2001:54) cursorily suggests that speakers are driven by efficiency requirements to constantly reuse a finite set of highly practised neuromotor programmes in speech. The pervasive redeployment of these articulatory plans prevents left-over junk from accumulating in phonological systems. This proposal is eminently reasonable: indeed, the modular feedforward architecture diagrammed in (2) is one of the possible instantiations of this idea. However, Bybee does not fill in the detail. What sizes do these reusable units come in? How exactly do they relate to the episodic memory traces in the lexicon? Do they exist, for example, as labelled pieces of the exemplars themselves? If so, how exhaustively is each exemplar labelled at each level of granularity? Given certain plausible answers to these questions, Bybee's proposal becomes very similar to the hybrid grammatical model proposed by Pierrehumbert (2002), in which each lexical item is associated both with a categorical phonological parse and with a phonetic exemplar cloud (see Section 21.4.3). This type of hybrid model avoids the problem of phonetic residue much more effectively.

21.4.3 Dealing with frequency effects

One of Bybee's key empirical arguments in favour of gradient diffusion is the sensitivity of coarticulation and gestural reduction to the token frequency of lexical items: see (15). How serious a problem is this for modular feedforward models of phonology? Significantly, both Pierrehumbert (2002: Sec.3) and Coleman (2003: Sec.5.4), though sympathetic to Bybee's position, concede that the classical modular architecture can be readily modified to accommodate such effects. Functionally, the correlation shown in (15) makes perfect sense: in order to facilitate the task of lexical recognition for the listener, speakers shift towards hyperspeech, with less coarticulation and reduction, when uttering words that are hard to access. Low-frequency words, with their low resting activation, fall into this group, as do words with low contextual predictability (Jurafsky *et al.* 2001) and words with high neighbourhood density (Wright 2003).[14] Models like (2) could therefore deal with frequency effects by enriching phonological representations with information about lexical accessibility, which would thus be made available to the phonetic module. For example, Pierrehumbert (2002:107) suggests that, when a morph is inserted into a phonological expression, the prosodic-word node that hosts the morph could be annotated with a numerical index of lexical accessibility; in the phonetic module, coarticulation and reduction rules would lower the expenditure of articulatory effort on elements with a high accessibility index. Under this proposal, the lexicon remains free of phonetic detail.[15]

Nonetheless, Pierrehumbert (2002) advocates a more evenly balanced compromise between modular and exemplar-based models (see Harris 6.2.1). In line with traditional approaches, she proposes that, for each linguistic expression, a phonological processor operating symbolic rules constructs a phonological representation consisting of discrete categories. Each of these discrete phonological categories, however, is associated with an exemplar cloud: in production, a phonological category is assigned a phonetic realization target by making a random selection from its cloud. In an utterance of the word *nursery*, for example, a duration target for the medial /ə/ is set by randomly selecting exemplars of /ə/ and calculating their average duration. Crucially, the relative contribution of each selected exemplar to the production target is weighted: e.g. in the production of *nursery*, exemplars of /ə/ located in memory traces of the word *nursery* count for more than exemplars of /ə/ located in memory traces of other words (such as *cursory*). In this proposal, therefore, the highly detailed word-specific phonetic information contained in episodic memory does not supply holistic production targets for lexical items, but rather introduces subtle biases in the phonetic implementation of discrete phonological representations. Thus, "word-specific phonetic effects are second-order effects" (Pierrehumbert 2002:134); that is, "the influence of particular words on phonetic outcomes is secondary, with the actual phonological makeup of the words providing the primary influence" (Pierrehumbert 2002:129).

This integrative approach strikes me as worth pursuing. On a general note, Pierrehumbert's (2002) proposals may find a natural home in a cognitive paradigm like Karmiloff-Smith's (1994) modified constructivism: in Pierrehumbert's model, the acquisition of phonology must involve, *inter alia*, a process of categorical labelling of episodic memory traces, which can easily be conceptualized as representational redescription in Karmiloff-Smith's sense (see Section 21.3.2 above). Also relevant here is Pinker's

(1999:279) assertion that rules and exemplars coexist in human cognition as 'two ways of knowing'. Pursuing these links, one realizes that diachronic phonology provides us with a unique window on the nature of the mind.

Notes

I am grateful to Paul de Lacy, Paula Fikkert, Randall Gess, Larry Hyman, Donka Minkova, and James Scobbie for their comments and suggestions.

1 Phonological change is traditionally divided into *sound change*, initiated by phonetic causes, and *analogy*, driven by morphological factors. This chapter concentrates on the former. Bermúdez-Otero (2006) addresses the study of analogy in Optimality Theory (OT, Prince & Smolensky 2004); Bermúdez-Otero & Hogg (2003: Sec.3) provide an illustrative case study. In 21.3.2 below I discuss the rôle of sound change and analogy in the life cycle of sound patterns.

2 For general discussion of the coordination problem in linguistic communication, see Croft (2000:95ff.).

3 Phonetic rules are often known as 'rules of phonetic implementation'. In the current discussion, therefore, the word *implementation* will occur in two separate senses: 'historical implementation of phonological changes', and 'phonetic implementation of phonological categories'.

4 The currently prevalent version of OT is a modular feedforward model, since it assumes that phonological constraints generate the input to phonetic implementation. Parallelism is stipulated to hold within the phonological module, but not in the relationship between the phonological and phonetic modules.

5 There is also, for example, a long tradition of psycholinguistic research that relies on the classical modular feedforward architecture for the explanation of speech errors (e.g. Fromkin 1971).

6 *Pace* Sproat & Fujimura (1993), however, gradient variation in the phonetic realization of dark [ɫ] is not incompatible with a categorical distinction between light [l] and dark [ɫ]; in fact, the modular feedforward architecture predicts the existence of such a distinction, for in American English dialects the distribution of the light and dark allophones of /l/ is sensitive to morphosyntactic structure (Phase III above; see Hayes 2000: 93). As we shall see below, phonological generalizations typically coexist in the same grammar with the gradient phonetic rules from which they emerge historically.

7 The diffusing substitution of /æː/ for /æ/ in lexical representations should not be conflated with the raising of lexical /æː/ to phonetic [eːˤ]. Labov (1994: Sec.16.5) shows that the raising of /æː/ to [eːˤ] is a regular gradient process of phonetic implementation.

8 Assigning æ-tensing to the stem level accounts for its overapplication in words like *glassy* [gleːˤ.si]. The root vowel and the following fricative are

tautosyllabic at the stem level, before the addition of the suffix *-y* triggers resyllabification: [Word Level [Stem Level glæːs] i]. See Kiparsky (1988: 400).

9 Labov (1989, 1994) provides no information on the Philadelphian pronunciation of the second syllable of *Afghan*. Donka Minkova (personal communication) informs me that the second vowel is rarely reduced in American English. This point is not essential to the discussion below.

10 I do not claim theoretical validity for these markedness constraints, but use them here merely for the purposes of illustration. Further phonetic, phonological, and typological investigation would be needed to ascertain the precise nature of the constraints involved. In the labels, I replace the IPA length symbol (ː) with the classical macron (¯) and breve (˘) just to remind the reader that *ǽf$_\sigma$] specifically bans *short* [æ] before a tautosyllabic [f].

11 The reasons for this phenomenon, and its implications for diachronic phonology and for the phonology–phonetics interface, are discussed in 21.4.3 below.

12 On the need for typed variables in linguistic rules, see Marcus (2001) and Jackendoff (2002).

13 See Kiparsky (1988:366) for discussion of Bloomfield's (1933) formulation of this argument.

14 The phonological neighbourhood density of a word *x* is said to be high if the lexicon contains many words that are phonologically similar to *x*.

15 The lexical accessibility index would be an attribute with gradient values (cf. (3a) above), but, crucially, it would not directly encode phonetic properties.

22

Variation and optionality

Arto Anttila

22.1 Preliminaries

The terms 'variation' and 'optionality' in phonology describe a situation where one phonological input has more than one output. Consider the following examples from American English and South-Eastern Finnish (1). In both cases, variation results from the optional application of one or more phonological processes.

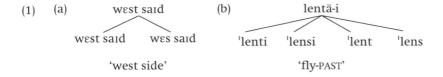

(1)   (a)   wɛst saɪd   (b)   lentä-i

     wɛst saɪd   wɛs saɪd   'lenti   'lensi   'lent   'lens

         'west side'   'fly-PAST'

In (1a), a coronal stop is variably deleted at the edge of a complex coda (*t/d*-deletion) (Labov 1997). In (1b), we have two variable processes working together: /t/ becomes [s] before [i] (assibilation) and /i/ is deleted in an unstressed syllable (apocope). This yields four logically possible outcomes, all attested (Laalo 1988).

Before embarking upon the discussion, it will be useful to draw some pretheoretical distinctions. First, variation may occur *within* an individual (the same individual uses different forms at different times) or *across* individuals (different individuals use different forms). Second, variation may be *free* or contextually *conditioned*. Contextual conditions are usually divided into *internal* and *external* factors. Internal factors may be phonological, such as stress, syllable structure, foot structure, or segment quality, or they may be morphosyntactic, such as part of speech, morpheme type, or morphosyntactic domain. External factors include age, gender, style, register, identity, ethnicity, social class, and target audience. Third, contextual conditioning may be *categorical* or *quantitative*. In the first case, the occurrence of a variant is completely predictable from the context – i.e. we have a 'rule'. In the second case, the occurrence of a variant is not completely predictable, but there is a systematic quantitative pattern – i.e. we have a 'tendency'.

Variation and optionality are pervasive in the phonologies of natural languages and for this reason optional rules have always been part of the generative phonologist's descriptive toolbox (Chomsky and Halle 1968). It is much less clear how to go beyond pure optionality. One view holds that quantitative regularities have no place in the theory of linguistic competence, but belong to the theory of performance (see e.g. Newmeyer 2003) and in practice quantitative aspects of phonological variation have been studied mainly by sociolinguists and phoneticians. There are two observations that are in a deep conflict with this view. First, categorical and quantitative regularities are often conditioned by the same grammatical factors. If the phonological grammar simply delivers the phonologically possible forms, it follows that any quantitative regularities must be explained by external factors, but in reality such regularities often refer to the grammar. Second, phonological variation may involve morphological and lexical conditioning and phonologically conditioned allomorph selection. This means that variation and quantitative regularities are potentially present at every level of phonology and cannot be reduced to 'low-level' phonology or phonetics. We conclude that a satisfactory theory of phonology must be able to provide an explicit theoretical interpretation of variable and quantitative regularities and show how such regularities relate to the more familiar invariant and categorical ones.

The main goal of this chapter is to give a brief overview of three current approaches to phonological variation. All these approaches assume some version of Optimality Theory (Prince and Smolensky 2004, henceforth P&S 2004).[1] For other brief overviews that complement the picture given here, see especially Sankoff (1988) and Pierrehumbert (2003b). The examples have been kept simple in the interest of conceptual clarity. For more detailed analyses, including several examples of quantitative modelling of phonological variation in large naturalistic corpora, the reader is referred to the work listed in the bibliography.

22.2   What should a phonological theory of variation explain?

Whenever we encounter a case of phonological variation, the following questions arise:

(2) (a) Why does variation occur in this environment as opposed to others?
    (b) What determines the phonological shapes of the variants?
    (c) What determines the quantitative preferences among the variants?
    (d) What is universal and what is language-particular about this pattern?

Why does variation occur in certain environments, but not in others? English *t/d*-deletion is variable in complex codas (*lost* ~ *los, lift* ~ *lif*), but blocked in complex onsets (*train* ~ **rain, star* ~ **sar*). In Standard Finnish, assibilation is variable in the past tenses of verbs if the preceding syllable is both stressed and bimoraic ('*vuo.ti* ~ '*vuo.si* 'leak-PAST'), but blocked if the preceding syllable is monomoraic ('*ve.ti* / **'ve.si* 'pull-PAST') and obligatory if the preceding syllable is trimoraic or unstressed (**'kaar.ti* / '*kaar.si* 'veer-PAST', **'ha.lu.ti/'ha.lu.si* 'want-PAST') (Anttila 2003). In both cases, the locus of variation can be defined in phonological terms. Thus, one would expect phonological theory to explain why variation arises in just these particular environments as opposed to others.

What determines the phonological shapes of the variants? Suppose English *t/d*-deletion occurs in coda clusters because both codas and clusters are universally marked. However, this does not yet explain why the repair is stop deletion. Why do we not have fricative deletion (*lost* → *lot*) or schwa-epenthesis (*lost* → *lost*[ə], *los*[ə]*t*) instead? In the case of Finnish assibilation, why does /t/ become [s] (*vuoti* ~ *vuosi*) instead of getting deleted (**vuoi*), or geminated (**vuotti*). Again, one would expect phonological theory to explain why the variants take the particular shapes they do.

What determines the quantitative preferences among the variants? English *t/d*-deletion is systematically more common before consonants than vowels (Guy 1980, Labov 1997) and systematically more common after [s] than after [f] (Guy and Boberg 1997). In regional dialects of Finnish, assibilation and apocope are quantitatively related: apocope is systematically more common if assibilation has applied, e.g. *vuosi* → *vuos* (common) vs. *vuoti* → *vuot* (rare). This pattern holds true across dialects, although the absolute frequencies vary greatly. Such systematic quantitative asymmetries call for a phonological explanation.

Finally, some aspects of variation remain invariant across dialects and some are perhaps universal, whereas other aspects vary from dialect to dialect. For example, English *t/d*-deletion is preferred before a consonant (*cost me* ~ *cos me*) and dispreferred before a vowel (*cost again* ~ *cos again*). This quantitative generalization seems to hold true in all dialects for which sufficient data are available. In contrast, there are dialects where *t/d*-deletion is more common before pauses than before vowels, and there are dialects where we find the opposite pattern. A phonological theory of variation should explain why certain aspects of variation are invariant across dialects, but other aspects may vary from dialect to dialect.

22.3   Three theories of variation

22.3.1   Multiple Grammars

The Multiple Grammars Theory (Kroch 1989, Kiparsky 1993, Anttila 2002b) proposes that variation arises from competing invariant grammars within an individual. The simplest argument for multiple grammars is the phenomenon of multilingualism. It seems uncontroversial that we need two separate grammars to account for an individual's competence in two unrelated languages. The situation is less clear when we are faced with two dialects of the same language, variation among styles and registers, and free variation with little or no semiotic value. Do all these cases involve multiple grammars? The answer is not obvious and it is far from clear how we could even begin to answer this question at this level of generality. One way to make progress is to adopt a particular theory of grammar, combine it with the Multiple Grammars Theory, work out the predictions in special cases, and see whether they are empirically supported.

A multiple grammars analysis involves the following questions:

(3) *Three questions involved in a multiple grammars analysis*
    (a) What are the possible grammars?
    (b) What types of variation can be derived by combining possible grammars?
    (c) How well do the predicted types of variation match the observed types?

As a concrete example, we consider Kiparsky's (1993) analysis of *t*/*d*-deletion in American English. The analysis is based on Optimality Theory (see Reynolds 1994, Côté 2000, and Coetzee 2004 for alternative analyses). We will adopt the following terminological convention: the term 'grammar' (in regular font) will be used to refer to a total ranking of constraints, and the term 'GRAMMAR' (in small caps) will refer to an individual's collection of grammars. Under the Multiple Grammars Theory, an individual's GRAMMAR may contain several different grammars.

To keep things simple, we only consider three possible contexts: prevocalic (_V), preconsonantal (_C) and prepausal (_##):

(4) *cost me ~ cos me* $t, d \;\; \rightarrow \; \varnothing \; / \; \_\, C$
    cost ~ cos $t, d \;\; \rightarrow \; \varnothing \; / \; \_\, \#\#$
    cost again ~ cos again $t, d \;\; \rightarrow \; \varnothing \; / \; \_\, V$

Kiparsky proposes that *t*/*d*-deletion is driven by syllable structure: *t*/*d* is deleted if it ends up being extrasyllabic.[2] The analysis assumes the following five constraints:

(5) *COMPLEX   No tautosyllabic clusters (P&S 2004: Sec. 6.2.1)
    ONSET   Onsets required (P&S 2004: Sec. 2.2)
    PARSE   Segments belong to syllables. (P&S 2004: Sec. 6.1)
    ALIGN-LEFT-WORD No resyllabification across word boundaries. (McCarthy and Prince 1993a: Sec. 5)
    ALIGN-RIGHT-PHRASE Phrase-final consonants are also syllable-final. (McCarthy and Prince 1993a: Sec. 3)

The resulting constraint violations are shown in (6). Brackets ([,]) mark syllable and phrase boundaries. We consider three candidates: (a) the faithful candidate; (b) the deletion candidate; (c) the resyllabification candidate. No rankings are assumed.

(6) *The violation pattern*

		*COM-PLEX	ONSET	ALIGN-L-W	ALIGN-R-P	PARSE
1 /kastəgɛn/	(a) kast][əgɛn	*	*			
	(b) kas]t[əgɛn		*			*
	(c) kas][təgɛn			*		
2 /kast mi/	(a) kast][mi	*				
	(b) kas]t[mi					*
	(c) kas][tmi	*		*		
3 /kast/	(a) kast]]	*				
	(b) kas]]t				*	*

We can now begin to answer the questions in (3). First, what are the possible grammars? The answer: the possible grammars are the 5! = 120 possible ways of ranking the five constraints. Second, what kinds of *t/d*-deletion patterns do these 120 grammars yield? The answer is easy to work out using the OTSoft software package (Hayes, Tesar, and Zuraw 2003). We only get the six distinct patterns shown in (7).

(7) *The factorial typology*

		cost again	cost	cost me
	(a)	faithful	faithful	faithful
	(b)	**deletion**	faithful	**deletion**
	(c)	**deletion**	**deletion**	**deletion**
	(d)	resyllab	faithful	faithful
	(e)	resyllab	faithful	**deletion**
	(f)	resyllab	**deletion**	**deletion**

Table (7) reveals an important general prediction: if *t/d*-deletion occurs before a pause ((7c), (7f)) or before a vowel ((7b), (7c)) it also occurs before a consonant. In contrast, if *t/d*-deletion occurs before a vowel ((7b), (7c)), it may or may not occur before a pause, and if *t/d*-deletion occurs before a pause ((7c), (7f)), it may or may not occur before a vowel.

More generally, the constraints induce a partial ordering on the inputs in terms of their deletion potential. We call this the AISSEN ORDERING (Aissen 2003). An Aissen ordering can be represented as a Hasse diagram (8): if *t/d*-deletion is possible for a lower input (*cost again, cost*), it will be possible for a higher input (*cost me*).

(8) *The Aissen ordering for t/d-deletion*

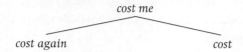

cost again   cost

In its simplest form, the Multiple Grammars Theory says that any combination of possible grammars is a possible GRAMMAR. While this may sound
unrestrictive and raise fears that anything will be possible, recall that the
factorial typology limits us to the six possible patterns in (7). Since all the
possible grammars conform to the ordering in (8), so will all the possible
GRAMMARS. For example, assume a GRAMMAR with three rankings: one that
derives the output pattern (9a), another that derives (9b), and yet another
that derives (9e). The GRAMMAR {a, b, e} predicts that there can be a speaker
with variable deletion before vowels and consonants, but no deletion
before pauses. This is consistent with the Aissen ordering.

(9) *The GRAMMAR {a, b, e}*

	cost again	cost	cost me
(a)	faithful	faithful	faithful
(b)	**deletion**	faithful	**deletion**
(e)	resyllab	faithful	**deletion**

In contrast, there can be no speaker with variable deletion before vowels,
but no deletion before consonants. In such a dialect, *t/d*-deletion would be
possible in *cost again*, but not in *cost me*, contradicting the Aissen ordering.
    The Multiple Grammars Theory has a straightforward quantitative
interpretation:

(10) *A quantitative interpretation of multiple grammars (Anttila 1997)*
    (i) A candidate is predicted if it wins by some grammar;
    (ii) If a candidate wins by n grammars and t is the total number of
          grammars, then the candidate's probability of occurrence is n/t.

If we assume the quantitative interpretation in (10), it follows that *t/d*-
deletion rate should decrease from top to bottom in the Aissen ordering:
any higher input should undergo deletion at least at the same rate as any
lower input. For example, the GRAMMAR {a, b, e} predicts the quantitative
pattern in (11):

(11) *GRAMMAR {a, b, e} and the probability of deletion for each input*

	cost again	cost	cost me
(a)	faithful	faithful	faithful
(b)	**deletion**	faithful	**deletion**
(e)	resyllab	faithful	**deletion**
	1/3	0	2/3

Different deletion probabilities can be derived by varying the number of grammars that predict each output pattern. This is possible because there are several distinct rankings that predict the same output pattern: we have 120 grammars, but only 6 distinct output patterns. Thus, the GRAMMAR {a, b, b, e, e} would predict the deletion probabilities 2/5, 0, and 4/5 for *cost again*, *cost*, and *cost me*, respectively. Crucially, there is no way to construct a grammar that would subvert the Aissen ordering which is thus universal and independent of rankings.[3]

We can now address the last question in (3): how well do the predictions match the observations? The summary in (12) comes from Coetzee (2004:218). The observed quantitative patterns are consistent with the Aissen ordering: in all dialects, *t/d*-deletion is most frequent before consonants; in five dialects, *t/d*-deletion is more common before pauses than vowels; in one dialect, *t/d*-deletion is more common before vowels than pauses.

(12) *The influence of following context on t/d-deletion (Coetzee 2004: 218)*

		_C	_V	_##
Chicano English (Los Angeles)	n	3,693	1,574	1,024
(Santa Ana 1991:76, 1996:66)	% deleted	62	45	37
Tejano English (San Antonio)	n	1,738	974	564
(Bayley 1995:310)	% deleted	62	25	46
African American English	n	143	202	37
(Washington, DC)				
(Fasold 1972:76)	% deleted	76	29	73
Jamaican mesolect (Kingston)	n	1,252	793	252
(Patrick 1991:181)	% deleted	85	63	71
Trinidadian acrolect	n	22	43	16
(Kang 1994:157)	% deleted	81	21	31
Neu data	n	814	495	–
(Neu 1980:45)	% deleted	36	16	–

The Multiple Grammars Theory is a very simple theory of variation: it only assumes that an individual may possess multiple grammars, something that is independently necessary. It is in no way wedded to Optimality Theory or to any particular quantitative interpretation: it can be easily combined with different grammatical theories as well as different quantitative interpretations. However, despite its simplicity and versatility, the Multiple Grammars Theory does not trivialize the study of variation: it makes falsifiable empirical predictions when combined with particular theories and analyses. In this section, we have used Optimality Theory and the Multiple Grammars Theory to draw a distinction between two kinds of quantitative variation patterns: those that are independent of constraint rankings and therefore universal (Aissen orderings), and those that depend on constraint rankings and can be expected to vary from language to language.

22.3.2 Partially Ordered Grammars

We now turn to a theory that derives variation from a single grammar: the theory of Partially Ordered Grammars (Anttila 1997, 2002a, Anttila and Cho 1998; see Reynolds 1994 and Nagy and Reynolds 1997 for a closely related approach). This theory is empirically more restrictive than the Multiple Grammars Theory: we will see that it excludes certain quantitative patterns predicted to be possible under the Multiple Grammars Theory. Based on evidence from Finnish, we will show how the two theories differ and how Partially Ordered Grammars are empirically superior to Multiple Grammars, at least in this particular case.

The empirical data come from a variable process of Vowel Coalescence found in many dialects of Finnish (Paunonen 1995, Anttila in press). Vowel Coalescence applies to sequences of unstressed short vowels, both derived and nonderived, where the second vowel is [+low].

(13) (a) /suome-a/ 'suomea ~ 'suomee   'Finnish-PAR(TITIVE)'
      (b) /ruotsi-a/ 'ruotsia ~ 'ruotsii   'Swedish-PAR(TITIVE)'

The process is variable within an individual. In a corpus of Colloquial Helsinki Finnish (Paunonen 1995), we find several examples of variation within a single noun phrase and even within a single word. The input /usea-mp-i-a/ 'many-COMPARATIVE-PL-PAR' has four logically possible surface variants, all attested.

(14) 'useampia ~ 'useempia ~ 'useampii ~ 'useempii

The central phonological generalization is that coalescence is more common in sequences of mid and low vowels, e.g. *ea* ~ *ee*, than in sequences of high and low vowels, e.g. *ia* ~ *ii* (Paunonen 1995:110). This asymmetry is found across regional dialects: coalescence in *ea* is much more widespread than coalescence in *ia* (15) (Paunonen 1995:106–114).

(15) *Vowel Coalescence patterns in some Finnish dialects (Paunonen 1995:109–111)*

/ea/	/ia/	
ea	ia	Literary Finnish
ee	ia	General Häme
ea ~ ee	ia	Töölö (Helsinki), old upper middle class females
ee	ia ~ ii	Western Uusimaa
ea ~ ee	ia ~ ii	Colloquial Helsinki Finnish

To get the analysis off the ground, we posit the optimality-theoretic constraints in (16). The constraint violations are illustrated in (17).

(16) *Constraints*
      *EA   Avoid /ea, oa, öä/ hiatus.
      *IA   Avoid /ia, ua, yä/ hiatus.
      FAITH   No coalescence.

(17)   *The constraint violation pattern*

			FAITH	*EA	*IA
1	/suome-a/	(a) suomea		*	
	'Finnish-PAR'	(b) suomee	*		
2	/ruotsi-a/	(a) ruotsia			*
	'Swedish-PAR'	(b) ruotsii	*		

The vowel height asymmetry can be captured by positing the fixed ranking *EA » *IA that holds across all dialects of Finnish. This ranking produces the desired typological pattern:

(18)   *The factorial typology*

		suome-a	*ruotsi-a*
(a)	FAITH » *EA » *IA	faithful	faithful
(b)	*EA » FAITH » *IA	**coalesce**	faithful
(c)	*EA » *IA » FAITH	**coalesce**	**coalesce**

How about the variable dialects? Instead of adopting Multiple Grammars, we adopt a slightly more relaxed notion of grammar: we define a grammar as a partial order in a set of constraints. A partial order is a binary relation (i.e. a set of ordered pairs) that is irreflexive, asymmetric, and transitive.[4] By this new definition, {*EA » *IA} qualifies as a grammar, so does {*EA » *IA, *EA » FAITH}. We call such generalized optimality-theoretic grammars Partially Ordered Grammars. A classical optimality-theoretic grammar is a Partially Ordered Grammar where all the pairs are ordered, e.g. {*EA » *IA, *EA » FAITH, *FAITH » *IA}. Any Partially Ordered Grammar can be translated into a set of totally ranked grammars; examples are provided in (19). The reverse does not hold, a fact that will become empirically relevant in a moment.

(19)   *Partially Ordered Grammars translated into total rankings*

	GRAMMAR	TOTAL RANKINGS (TABLEAUX)		
(a)	*EA » *IA	*EA	*IA	FAITH
		*EA	FAITH	*IA
		FAITH	*EA	*IA
(b)	*EA » *IA	*EA	*IA	FAITH
	*EA » FAITH	*EA	FAITH	*IA
(c)	*EA » *IA	*EA	FAITH	*IA
	*EA » FAITH			
	FAITH » *IA			

Since grammars are sets of ordered pairs, a grammar may include other grammars. Figure (20) spells out the Finnish system in terms of the subset relation. Each node is a grammar and each mother grammar is the intersection of its daughter grammars. We call the resulting structure a 'grammar lattice'. Each grammar is annotated with the predicted output pattern.

(20)   *A grammar lattice*

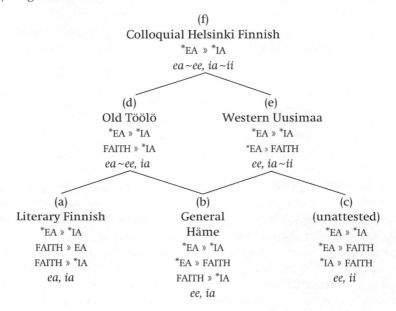

Grammars (20a), (20b), and (20c) are the totally ranked grammars that describe invariant dialects: (20a) is Literary Finnish (*ea, ia*); (20b) is General Häme (*ee, ia*); (20c) is a hypothetical dialect that shows categorical coalescence everywhere. Grammars (20d) and (20e) contain two ranked pairs each: (20d) is the dialect of old upper middle class female residents of Töölö, a traditional upper-class neighborhood of Helsinki, who allow coalescence in *ea*-sequences, but never in *ia*-sequences (*ea~ee, ia*) (Paunonen 1995:111); (20e) is the dialect of Western Uusimaa (*ee, ia~ii*). Grammar (20f) contains only one ranked pair. This grammar translates into three total rankings and predicts variation in both vowel sequences (*ea~ee, ia~ii*), a pattern typical of Colloquial Helsinki Finnish.

   If we continue to assume the quantitative interpretation of Multiple Grammars in (10), we derive the predictions in (21). The most important prediction is that *ea* should coalesce at a higher rate than *ia* in all variable dialects. In other words, the analysis derives Paunonen's quantitative generalization.

(21) *A quantitative typology of Vowel Coalescence*

	ea → ee	*ia → ii*
(a)	0	0
(b)	1	0
(c)	1	1
(d)	1/2	0
(e)	1	1/2
(f)	2/3	1/3

Interestingly, the Multiple Grammars Theory fails to derive Paunonen's generalization. Under this theory, any combination of grammars is a possible GRAMMAR. Now, consider the GRAMMAR {a, c} (22).

(22) GRAMMAR *{a, c} and the probability of deletion for each input*

		suome-a	*ruotsi-a*
(a)	FAITH »*EA »*IA	faithful	faithful
(c)	*EA »*IA » FAITH	**coalesce**	**coalesce**
		1/2	1/2

This combination of two total rankings predicts a variable dialect where both *ea* and *ia* coalesce at exactly the same rate, contradicting Paunonen's generalization. This dialect is correctly excluded by Partially Ordered Grammars because it is not a partial order: there is no set of ordered pairs that would pick out exactly these two total rankings. The most specific grammar that is a subset of both (a) and (c) is *EA » *IA, but this grammar also contains (b) which predicts the familiar vowel height asymmetry. The systematic absence of variation patterns like (22) constitutes empirical evidence for Partially Ordered Grammars against Multiple Grammars. The fact that arguments like this are possible in principle underlines the importance of quantitative evidence for phonological theory.

   If we delve deeper into the data, more quantitative generalizations emerge. Two of them are morphological:

(23) *Morphological conditions on Vowel Coalescence (Anttila in press)*

(A) THE ROOT FAITHFULNESS EFFECT:	Vowel Coalescence is more common across morphemes than within roots.
(B) THE PART-OF-SPEECH EFFECT:	Vowel Coalescence is more common in adjectives than in nouns.

The root faithfulness effect reflects the cross-linguistic generalization that roots are more resilient under markedness pressure than affixes (McCarthy and Prince 1995a). In Finnish, this generalization emerges quantitatively in *ea*-sequences and categorically in *ia*-sequences: *ea*-roots coalesce at a lower rate than derived *ea*-sequences (e.g. *hopea* ~ *hopee* 'silver' vs. *suome-a* ~ *suome-e* 'Finnish-PAR') whereas *ia*-roots never coalesce in any dialect (*lattia/ lattii* 'floor' vs. *ruotsi-a* ~ *ruotsi-i* 'Swedish-PAR'). In order to derive this asymmetry, we adopt the constraint IDENT(Root) which strives to preserve the identity of root segments (McCarthy and Prince 1995a, Beckman 1998, Alderete 2001a). The special pattern of *ia*-roots can be captured by the fixed ranking FAITH$_{root}$ » *IA which holds in all dialects of Finnish. The updated typology is given in (25).

(24) *An analysis of the root faithfulness effect*

    (A) FAITH$_{root}$ Avoid coalescence in roots.

    (B) FAITH$_{root}$ » *IA   No coalescence in *ia*-roots.

(25) *The updated typology*

		suome-a	hopea	ruotsi-a	lattia
(a)	FAITH » *EA » FAITH$_{root}$ » *IA	faithful	faithful	faithful	faithful
(b)	FAITH » FAITH$_{root}$ » *EA » *IA	faithful	faithful	faithful	faithful
(c)	FAITH$_{root}$ » FAITH » *EA » *IA	faithful	faithful	faithful	faithful
(d)	FAITH$_{root}$ » *EA » FAITH » *IA	coalesce	faithful	faithful	faithful
(e)	FAITH$_{root}$ » *EA » *IA » FAITH	coalesce	faithful	coalesce	faithful
(f)	*EA » FAITH » FAITH$_{root}$ » *IA	coalesce	coalesce	faithful	faithful
(g)	*EA » FAITH$_{root}$ » FAITH » *IA	coalesce	coalesce	faithful	faithful
(h)	*EA » FAITH$_{root}$ » *IA » FAITH	coalesce	coalesce	coalesce	faithful

We now draw the Aissen ordering for Vowel Coalescence based on the typology in (25): See (26). The prediction is that a higher input should undergo Vowel Coalescence at least at the same rate as any lower input.

(26) *The Aissen ordering for Vowel Coalescence*

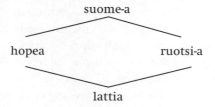

The part-of-speech effect is more problematic. There are at least two kinds of nouns: recently borrowed nouns that never coalesce, e.g. *idea/*idee* 'idea' and a handful of native nouns that coalesce to some extent, e.g. *hopea* ~ *hopee* 'silver'. This means that adding a constraint like IDENT(Noun) (Smith 1997) will not suffice because it cannot distinguish between the two noun classes. An alternative solution is to assume that recently borrowed nouns and adjectives subscribe to slightly different COPHONOLOGIES (Orgun 1996, Inkelas 1998, Anttila 2002b). The cophonologies needed to capture the part-of-speech effect are given in (27).

(27) *A cophonology analysis of the part-of-speech effect*

    (a) FAITH$_{root}$ » *EA (*idea*-nouns only)   No coalescence in *idea*-nouns

    (b) *EA » FAITH$_{root}$ (adjectives only)   Coalescence in *ea*-adjectives

We have used Finnish Vowel Coalescence as an example to illustrate two common phenomena: (i) phonological variation involves both phonological and morphological conditions; (ii) both kinds of conditions yield both categorical and quantitative surface patterns. How well does the present analysis succeed in capturing these patterns? Table (28) summarizes the observations and predictions. The numbers are based on Paunonen's corpus of Colloquial Helsinki Finnish that represents the output of 126 individual speakers (Paunonen 1995, Anttila in press). The counts include all stems ending in the vowel sequences *ea, eä, ia, iä*.

(28)   *Observations and predictions*

	OBS%	PRED%	EXAMPLE	GLOSS	n
/e-a/, ADJ	–	75.0	–		–
/e-a/, NOUN	41.0	50.0	suome-a	'Finnish-PAR'	714
/ea/, ADJ	72.4	75.0	makea	'sweet'	1,745
/ea/, NOUN (native)	18.8	37.5	hopea	'silver'	48
/ea/, NOUN (recent)	0.0	0.0	idea	'idea'	12
/i-a/, ADJ	30.2	25.0	uus-i-a	'new-PL-PAR'	4,264
/i-a/, NOUN	20.0	25.0	ruotsi-a	'Swedish-PAR'	5,059
/ia/, ADJ	0.0	0.0	kauhia	'terrible'	261
/ia/, NOUN	0.0	0.0	lattia	'floor'	847

22.3.3   Stochastic Optimality Theory

In classical Optimality Theory (Prince & Smolensky 2004), ranking is an ordering relation. For example, the ranking PARSE » ALIGN-LEFT-WORD » *COMPLEX can be described as a set of ordered pairs of constraints. In Stochastic Optimality Theory (Boersma 1998, Boersma and Hayes 2001), we encounter a richer notion of ranking. Each constraint is associated with a fixed real-number value called the RANKING VALUE, marked as a • in the figures below. For example, assume two grammars, G_1 and G_2, with the constraints PARSE (= P), ALIGN-LEFT-WORD (= A), and *COMPLEX (*C). The exact real-number values used are arbitrary; only the degree of ranking difference is important.

(29)   *Two grammars (G_1, G_2) with different ranking values*

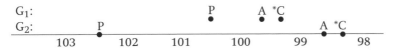

In both grammars, the constraints appear in the same order. However, in grammar G_1 the constraints PARSE and ALIGN-LEFT-WORD are relatively close to each other, whereas in grammar G_2 they are far apart. In both grammars, the constraints ALIGN-LEFT-WORD and *COMPLEX are ranked about equally close to each other. This notion of a *continuous ranking scale* forms the basis for an alternative approach to variation and quantitative patterns.

The central idea in Stochastic Optimality Theory is *stochastic candidate evaluation*. This means that a random positive or negative value ('noise') is temporarily added to the ranking value of each constraint at the moment of evaluation, i.e. a particular speaking event. The resulting value is called the 'selection point' and it is this selection point that determines the ranking in actual evaluation. Selection points are assumed to be normally distributed around the ranking value and each constraint has the same standard deviation ('breadth'). An example will make this more concrete. Assume ranking values as in Grammar G_2. If we test this grammar a large number of times, the selection points will oscillate around the fixed ranking values from evaluation to evaluation. The result might look like (30):

(30)   *Testing grammar G_2*

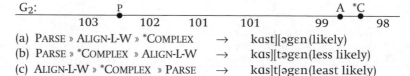

G_2:

	P			A *C	
103	102	101	101	99	98

   (a) PARSE » ALIGN-L-W » *COMPLEX   →   kɑst][əgɛn (likely)
   (b) PARSE » *COMPLEX » ALIGN-L-W   →   kɑs][təgɛn (less likely)
   (c) ALIGN-L-W » *COMPLEX » PARSE   →   kɑs]t[əgɛn (least likely)

Ranking (a) arises when the selection points fall near the center of each constraint and the actual ranking is identical to the ranking in the grammar. Ranking (b) reverses the close neighbors ALIGN-L-W and *COMPLEX, which is not very surprising since their ranking values are so close to each other. Ranking (c) puts the highest-ranked PARSE at the bottom, a selection that is possible, but highly unlikely. It is now clear how variation arises from stochastic candidate evaluation: selection points vary from evaluation to evaluation, which results in different rankings, which in turn results in different outputs. However, the fixed ranking values guarantee that some rankings will have a higher probability than others and the output will quantitatively reflect this.

Stochastic Optimality Theory comes with a learnability algorithm called the 'Gradual Learning Algorithm' (GLA, Boersma and Hayes 2001, Tesar Ch.24). Given a set of constraints and variable learning data, GLA attempts to find the ranking values responsible for the learning data. The input to GLA consists of a set of arbitrarily ranked constraints (e.g. all ranked at 100) and some </input/, [output]> pairs that constitute the learning data. The algorithm first checks whether the current ranking correctly generates the current learning datum. If the answer is no, some learning must take place. This is done by adjusting the ranking values as follows: for every constraint violated by the learning datum (= desired winner), its ranking value is decreased by a small step, and for every constraint violated by the current winner (= wrong winner), its ranking value is increased by a small step. GLA is able to cope with free variation because the individual adjustments to the ranking values are very small: two constraints can be pushed slightly closer to each other while maintaining their relative ranking.[5] Empirical tests of GLA have shown that the algorithm can approximate the relative frequencies in the learning data very well, given a reasonable set of constraints.

We now illustrate how GLA works using Finnish Vowel Coalescence data. To simplify things, we abstract away from the part-of-speech effect and only consider nouns, ignoring the four exceptional roots that coalesce to some extent (*häpeä* 'shame', *hopea* 'silver', *aukea* 'opening', *lipeä* 'lye'). Tableau (31) was given as input to the version of GLA implemented in OTSoft.

(31)   *Vowel Coalescence in Colloquial Helsinki Finnish: regular nouns*

			FREQUENCY	*EA	*IA	FAITHroot	FAITH
(a)	/suome-a/	suomea	421	*			
	'Finnish-PAR	suomee	293				*
(b)	/idea/	idea	12	*			
	'idea'	idee	0			*	*
(c)	/ruotsi-a/	ruotsia	4045		*		
	'Swedish-PAR	ruotsii	1014				*
(d)	/lattia/	lattia	847		*		
	'floor'	lattii	0			*	*

In a representative test run where the algorithm was allowed 50,000 learning trials and the grammar 2,000 test cycles, the ranking values in (32) emerged:

(32)

$\text{FAITH}_{\text{root}} = 106.240$, FAITH = 101.306, *EA = 100.568, *IA = 98.126

	F_{root}					FAITH	*EA			*IA
107	106	105	104	103	102	101	100	99		98

(33)   *Observations and predictions*

	obs%	pred%	Example	Gloss	n
/e-a/, NOUN	0.410	0.420	suome-a	'Finnish-PAR'	714
/ea/, NOUN (recent)	0.000	0.016	idea	'idea'	12
/i-a/, NOUN	0.200	0.130	ruotsi-a	'Swedish-PAR'	5,059
/ia/, NOUN	0.000	0.001	lattia	'floor'	847

As shown in (33), GLA performed quite well, with an average error of 2.414 percent per candidate. In general, one would expect Stochastic Optimality Theory to match quantitative patterns much better than its ordinal competitors because of the increased descriptive power drawn from real numbers. Note that the categorical patterns are not quite categorical: the grammar predicts marginal variation even in roots (*idee*, *rasii*). If we increase the number of exposures to learning data, these ungrammatical forms will eventually disappear: in a run with 100,000,000 learning trials and 50,000 test cycles, $\text{FAITH}_{\text{root}}$ reached the ranking value 114.000 resulting in a virtually categorical pattern. Somewhat surprisingly, the average error per candidate simultaneously increased to 4.050 percent.

Despite its great numerical power, there are variation patterns that are hard for Stochastic Optimality Theory, but easy for Multiple Grammars and Partially Ordered Grammars. For example, consider a pattern that requires a single constraint to range over a set of fixed constraints. In the hypothetical example (34), the ranking A » B is fixed whereas the constraint C is unranked. In Reynolds' (1994) terminology, C is a "floating constraint".

(34)   C » A » B
       A » C » B
       A » B » C

A grammar of this type is not possible under Stochastic Optimality Theory if we want to maintain the assumption that each constraint has the same standard deviation (Boersma and Hayes 2001). Faced with cases like this, one would either have to reanalyze the data using different constraints or complicate the theory by allowing different constraints to have different standard deviations.

22.4   External factors

So far, we have only discussed cases where variation is conditioned by internal (phonological, morphological) factors. There remains the important question how external factors such as age, gender, style, register, identity, ethnicity, social class, and target audience fit into the picture. Vowel Coalescence in Colloquial Helsinki Finnish provides an example of external conditioning that is just as systematic as the cases of internal conditioning discussed above. Of the several external factors discussed by Paunonen, we only consider age: the younger the speaker, the higher the coalescence rate (35) (Paunonen 1995, Anttila in press).

(35)   *The age effect*

	OLD (65-)		MIDDLE-AGED (40-45)		YOUNG (15-20)	
/ea/, NOUN	3.3%	(1/30)	18.2%	(4/22)	50%	(4/8)
/ia/, NOUN	0%	(0/337)	0%	(0/263)	0%	(0/247)
/e-a/, NOUN	24.3%	(65/267)	30.5%	(60/197)	67.2%	(168/250)
/i-a/, NOUN	7.8%	(147/1,886)	11.4%	(182/1,597)	43.5%	(685/1,576)
/ea/, ADJ	49.3%	(242/491)	64.9%	(334/515)	93.0%	(687/739)
/ia/, ADJ	0%	(0/80)	0%	(0/100)	0%	(0/81)
/e-a/, ADJ	–		–		–	
/i-a/, ADJ	9.6%	(146/1,519)	16.8%	(220/1,308)	64.2%	(923/1,437)

The age effect has a natural synchronic interpretation in all three models: young speakers, middle-aged speakers, and old speakers have internalized different GRAMMARS (Multiple Grammars), different partial orders (Partially Ordered Grammars), or different ranking values (Stochastic Optimality Theory).[6] More generally, it is tempting to identify internal factors with grammatical constraints and external factors with choices among grammars, rankings, or ranking values. This view has the advantage of being consistent with a modular view of language: internal factors are about grammars, external factors are about how the grammars are used. This has the perhaps unintuitive consequence that the part-of-speech effect in Colloquial Helsinki Finnish becomes an external factor since it is described in terms of distinct rankings (cophonologies) as opposed to being hard-wired in the constraints. Such analytical ambiguities are to be expected since the distinction between grammar and usage is not given in nature, but remains a central topic of foundational debate in linguistics (Newmeyer 2003, Bybee 2005).

22.5   A methodological note

We conclude with a methodological remark. The typical way of obtaining data in linguistics is to use well-formedness judgments elicited from native speakers or reported in dictionaries and descriptive grammars. The study of variation usually requires more effort. In particular, the quantitative preferences that accompany variation are not easily accessible to intuition, neither are they commonly reported in descriptive grammars. In order to study phonological variation, especially its quantitative aspects, one will typically need large amounts of usage data, such as naturally occurring text or speech corpora, databases compiled by field linguists, dialectologists, and sociolinguists, or acoustic and articulatory databases. While general-purpose data resources are usually not designed to answer one's specific research questions, they can often be converted into a more useful form with a reasonable amount of work. For example, raw text and speech corpora may not be very useful in themselves, but their usefulness can be significantly enhanced by annotating them phonetically, phonologically, morphologically, and syntactically. This can be done either manually or (semi-)automatically with the help of computational parsers. Annotated corpora are extremely useful for hypothesis testing and they often reveal unobvious typological and quantitative generalizations that would be difficult or impossible to establish based on other types of data. Developing such resources for the purposes of phonological research is an important task for the future.

Notes

I thank Andries Coetzee, Paul de Lacy, and Kate Ketner for helpful comments. All errors are mine.

1 For general surveys of Optimality Theory, see de Lacy (Ch.1), Kager (1999a), and McCarthy (2002c).

2 Kiparsky's analysis dates from 1993 and assumes the then-current Containment Theory of Faithfulness (Prince & Smolensky 2004): *t/d* is not literally deleted, but simply left unparsed. While Containment Theory is no longer generally accepted, we have retained Kiparsky's original formulation here.

3 If we further allow for the possibility that a speaker may have multiple copies of the *same* grammar, we can model arbitrarily fine quantitative distinctions, but crucially, still only within the limits of the Aissen ordering.

4 Let C be the set of constraints and R a binary ranking relation in C. R is:

   (i)   irreflexive iff for every x in C, R contains no ordered pair $<x, x>$ with identical first and second members.

   (ii)   asymmetric iff for any ordered pair $<x, y>$ in R, the pair $<y, x>$ is not in R.

   (iii)   transitive iff for all ordered pairs $<x, y>$ and $<y, z>$ in R, the pair $<x, z>$ is also in R.

5 Boersma and Hayes (2001) speculate that the size of these adjustment steps (called the PLASTICITY value) may decrease in the course of learning. The hypothesis is that a mature learner will be more reluctant to change her grammar in the face of unexpected data than an immature learner.

6 Andries Coetzee (p.c.) points out that there is another way in which stochastic grammars can account for the influence of extragrammatical factors: the standard deviation of the normal distribution of the ranking values can be increased or decreased. Increasing the standard deviation will lead to more variation, decreasing it will lead to less variation. Such changes could be correlated with the formality of the speech situation: in more relaxed speech situations a speaker might be more lenient with her grammar in the sense of increasing the standard deviation of constraint rankings.

23

Acquiring phonology

Paula Fikkert

23.1   Introduction

Child language data have usually been considered as external evidence for
linguistic theory, but they have never had much influence on phonological theory. Yet, the central goal of linguistics is to understand what
knowledge of language entails and *how it is acquired*. Recently, Chomsky
(2004) stressed that in order to understand what constitutes syntactic
knowledge it is important to gain insight into how a lexicon is built up
during acquisition, and what lexical representations look like. This also
holds for phonology: insight into the development of both phonological
representations and the phonological system should be of immanent
importance to understanding phonological knowledge, at least on the
assumption that there is 'continuity' between child phonology and adult
phonology. Continuity supposes that child and adult languages can only
vary in limited ways. Under the strong continuity hypothesis child language can only differ from adult language in ways that adult languages
can differ from each other (Pinker 1984). In a weaker definition, continuity refers to the systematicity with which children gradually build up a
phonological system (Jakobson 1941/1968). Most present-day theories
assume continuity. In the nativist view of Optimality Theory, for example,
child phonology has the same substance as adult phonology: a set of
universal markedness constraints on outputs and computational principles to determine optimal input–output mappings (faithfulness constraints and correspondence relations) (Prince & Smolensky 2004, Tesar
& Smolensky 1998). As continuity implies a direct relationship between
adult and child language, the study of child phonology is important for
understanding phonology.

   Over the years many studies have provided insight into the acquisition of
phonology. Why then has the study of phonological acquisition not been
more central to phonological theory? In my view this is due to a number of

factors. First, phonological theories have changed every decade, changing with them the focus of acquisition studies. In the seventies, children were supposed to acquire morpheme structure conditions and the active phonological rules that relate underlying forms to surface forms. In the eighties, the focus was on phonological representations that children had to acquire. In the nineties, child phonology was about defining the (ordering of the) constraints that characterize children's productions (for an overview see Fikkert 2000; Kager et al. 2004).[1]

The lack of sophisticated and thorough analyses of longitudinal databases and complementary experiments where databases do not provide enough information is another factor that has prevented child language data from speaking to a larger audience. Moreover, most studies investigate only one particular phenomenon in a set of child language data, such as cluster reduction (e.g. Ohala 1996, Jongstra 2003) or consonant harmony (e.g. Vihman 1978, Goad 1997, Pater & Werle 2003). Rarely do studies view such phenomena in the light of the whole developing phonological system.[2] A more complete picture of how language acquisition proceeds requires a strong foundation of databases, along with in-depth studies of them. Presently, these are few in number. However, times may be changing, as currently a lot of effort is being put into making phonetically transcribed data publicly available through *Phon*, a new database format in *Childes* (http://childes.psy.cmu.edu/phon/) (Rose 2003, Rose & MacWhinney 2004).

In this chapter I will present an overview of what I regard as the main themes in phonological acquisition. In Section 23.2, I present a brief overview of the short history of the field. Section 23.3 discusses how phonological acquisition is viewed in Optimality Theory. The focus of these analyses is production data (but see e.g. Jusczyk et al. 2002, Davidson et al. 2004, Pater 2004). Section 23.4 focuses on developments in the field of child speech perception. Patterns in infant perception often show great similarity to patterns in production; they just appear much earlier. As developmental patterns in infant speech perception demonstrate acquisition of knowledge about the sound system of the mother language, the implicit assumption often is that when similar developmental patterns show up in production data they merely reflect performance factors, rather than the acquisition of phonology.

Speech perception has not played a dominant role in formal theories of phonology and phonological acquisition, but this is currently changing (e.g. Broe & Pierrehumbert 2000, Hume & Johnson 2001). The growing interest in the role of phonology in perception comes from at least two tendencies. One is the current tendency to relate markedness to phonetic grounding both in perception and production (Hayes, Kirchner & Steriade 2004, Davis, McNeilage & Matyear 2002). The second tendency is the renewed focus on phonological representations – which mediate between perception and production – where the central question is how much detail is stored. This is discussed in Section 23.5.

Interestingly, the main findings from the fields of production and perception seem largely incompatible and differ with respect to the answer to questions concerning continuity, like 'When does the acquisition of phonology start?' and 'Can acquisition of phonology proceed without a lexicon?' Section 23.6 will conclude with the suggestion that we should aim at reconciling the findings for perception and production in a coalition model in which both abstract and detailed representations play a role. It is hypothesized that the nature of acquisition changes in the course of development, particularly when a lexicon is installed and lexical representations appear. The focus may shift from auditory-driven sound classification to lexicon-driven abstract phonology.

Let me end this introduction by remarking that despite the surge of new research on acquisition of phonology, it is striking that an internet search for 'acquisition of phonology' delivers more hits that refer to learnability than to data-driven acquisition studies. There is still regrettably little collaboration across the two domains. In this chapter I will not refer to formal learnability issues, as these are dealt with by Tesar (Ch.24). The reader is invited to help bridge the gap between the two domains.

23.2   Child phonology research: production

Child phonology traditionally studies patterns in child language production data. These data have revealed three simple facts that have to be accounted for. First, children do not speak like adults. Second, children's speech often differs in a systematic fashion from that of adults. Third, child language develops gradually towards the target language.[3] It has proven difficult to explain these simple facts.

Markedness has always played a key role in accounting for acquisition patterns. Researchers usually find that children start out producing relatively simple and unmarked phonological patterns, which become more marked in the course of development. Traditionally, markedness has been related to typology: what is common in languages of the world is unmarked and acquired early. In this view, typology relates to acquisition in much the same way as phylogeny to ontogeny (Jakobson 1941/1968).

However, markedness constraints seem to come in different flavors. Some researchers assume innate and universal markedness constraints; others argue that markedness constraints are grounded in perception and articulation (though grounded constraints could be universal). Yet others view markedness constraints as generalizations over a lexicon (Beckman & Edwards 2000, Pierrehumbert 2003a, Fikkert & Levelt 2004). Thus, much of the diversity in the field of acquisition of phonology today stems from different opinions on the origin of markedness constraints. The study of acquisition of phonology promises to offer a great deal of insight into this issue.

This is of course only true on the assumption that children's productions reflect phonological competence rather than limited performance abilities. It is often assumed that children store the correct form of words on the basis of so-called *fish*-phenomena (Berko & Brown 1960), where the child pronounces the word *fish* as [fis] instead of [fɪʃ], but at the same time rejects his own pronunciation when uttered by an adult (see Smith 1973, for an elaborate discussion). An alternative view is that representations are acquired as part of the grammar; hence, knowledge of representations may not be presupposed (Dresher 2004b, Fikkert & Levelt 2004).

If performance limitations are reflected in the phonology, for instance as constraints on perception and articulation, the distinction between competence and performance is meaningless. This is an area of much controversy in the field: to what extent does production reflect linguistic competence rather than mere performance limitations? Linguists have usually assumed that production reflects competence, whereas psycholinguists often assume that perception reflects competence, while in production competence is obscured by performance limitations. In this section we assume that production data reflect the child's phonological competence.

Relatively theory-independently, one could say that in order to acquire a language's phonology children need to acquire (a) the segmental inventory of that language, (b) phonological processes, (c) restrictions on phonotactics, word prosodic structure and larger prosodic units that define the adult grammar. In addition, children need to build a lexicon in which phonological representations of words are stored. The following sections focus on the first three aspects of phonological acquisition. Section 23.5 discusses phonological representations in the mental lexicon.

23.2.1 Acquiring phonological contrasts

The study of acquiring an abstract phonology is often claimed to have started with Jakobson (1941/1968), who argued that children gradually build up a (universal) system of contrast. Contrasts that are typologically frequent are high up in the hierarchy and acquired early, and vice versa. In this view, acquisition is the unfolding of a pre-existing feature hierarchy, presumably based on positive evidence in the input (see Dresher 2004a for an excellent overview and a modern reinterpretation). This view has been widely criticized because child language shows more variation than expected based on a universal feature hierarchy (Kiparsky & Menn 1977, Macken & Ferguson 1983);[4] it has turned out to be impossible to find such a hierarchy. Children acquiring different languages have different systems of contrasts, and differences sometimes even exist among children acquiring the same language. However, researchers have not refrained from exploring the acquisition of contrasts.

There have essentially been two methods for investigating the construction of a system of contrast by children. The first one (Rice & Avery 1995, Brown & Matthews 1997) focused on contrasts and processes appearing in *child* language. These researchers assumed that processes in child language should largely follow from children's feature representations. Brown & Matthews (1997) argue that building up a system of contrast coincides with the acquisition of lexical representations. Early words are underrepresented (or un(der)specified), as not all contrasts have been acquired.[5]

The second way of viewing the acquisition of contrasts assumed that features that play a role in *adult* phonological processes are acquired early, as the phonological activity of features is a cue for children to pay attention to those features (Dresher 2004a,b, Fikkert & Freitas 2004a). Dresher (2004a) proposes the 'Continuous Dichotomy Hypothesis' (Dresher 2004a, Dresher, Piggott & Rice 1994, Jakobson & Halle 1956). Under this hypothesis, all sounds are assumed to be variants of a single phoneme at the initial stage of acquisition. An initial binary distinction (dichotomy) is made using one of the universal distinctive features (see also Fikkert 1994). This process continues until all distinctive sounds have been differentiated. The crucial question is how to determine what is contrastive, because an initial failure in setting up the system of contrast has far-reaching consequences. Dresher proposes that phonological processes play a key role. He furthermore assumes that only contrastive features can be represented, and hence, be phonologically active. Redundant features are not specified. If the system of contrast is built on the basis of active phonological features, redundancy follows immediately. In this view, children must use systematic variation in the input to build up their system. A current theme in the (child) phonology literature is how the child determines which segments are contrastive in his or her language. Views vary from one extreme where a lot of innate phonological structure is assumed to the other extreme position assuming that all contrasts fall out from statistical learning based on input speech (e.g. Maye *et al.* 2002).

In the views summarized above, child language differs from adult language in the sense that a child's phonological system is immature, and does not allow all contrasts that the adult language exhibits, but it is not fundamentally different.

23.2.2 Processes in child phonology

The majority of studies in acquisition of phonology have focused on processes in child language (Ingram 1974). Let us take the well-known and frequently discussed case of consonant harmony (1) (The numbers x;y refer to age: x years; y months.)

(1)   *Examples of consonant harmony*

    (a) English (data from Pater 1997)

dog	[gɔg]	Trevor	1;4.19~2;3.17
big	[gɪg]	Trevor	1;9.21~1;10.9

    (b) Dutch (data from Levelt 1994)

sop	'suds'	/sɔp/	[fɔp]	Robin	1;10.7
tafel	'table'	/ˈtafəl/	[ˈpafɔ]	Robin	1;10.7

    (c) French (data from Y. Rose 2000)

chapeau	'hat'	/ʃɑˈpo/	[pæˈpo]	Clara
gâteau	'cake'	/gɑˈto/	[tæˈto]	Clara

Most child-language phonologists have explained the differences between adult targets and children's produced forms in terms of different
phonological systems for adults and children. This is true for early generative studies on phonological acquisition (Smith 1973), as well as current
studies on acquisition in Optimality Theory (see papers in Kager et al. 2004).
Consider for instance Smith's analysis of the phonological system of his son
Amahl. On the assumption that input representations are essentially adult-
like, Smith was able to describe the complete data set with fewer than
thirty ordered 'realization' rules. Smith described consonant harmony
forms with a single rule: "Alveolar and palato-alveolar consonants harmonize to the point of articulation of a following consonant; obligatorily if that
consonant is velar, optionally if it is labial". As a result Amahl produces
'duck' as [gʌk]. Later in development, he produces the word as [dʌk]: the rule is
cast out. In general, development is taken to involve rule reordering, rule
simplification or rule loss. Ultimately, however, all rules should be disposed of
to ensure that all words are produced in an adult-like fashion. In other words,
the system of realization rules, so carefully constructed during acquisition,
has to be unlearned at later stages of development. This raises the question
'Where is (adult) phonology?'. In fact, the whole system of realization rules
is child-specific, despite the fact that they were argued to reflect universal
tendencies.

    Kiparsky & Menn (1977) argued that the acquisition process is more
complex and must have at least two types of rules. One set of rules, 'invented'
rules, exists to simplify adult target forms in such a way that they can be
produced by children. Although many of these rules are common in child
phonology, they may also be specific to individual children. These rules are
similar in nature to Smith's realization rules. The second set of rules is the
set that also exists in the adult phonology. These rules need to be learned on
the basis of positive input data. Children start out assuming that inputs they
hear correspond to underlying representations. As input forms are often too
'difficult' to produce, either due to articulatory limitations or to processing

problems, children invent – sometimes quite idiosyncratic – strategies to
deal with these words. As children become more competent language users,
they can do without the simplification rules. As a result the invented, child-
specific, rules gradually disappear. However, as children learn more words,
and also more related words, they may discover (morpho)-phonological
processes that account for alternations: the adult phonological rule
system. This may lead children to restructure the underlying forms to more
abstract representations.

In other words, there are two types of largely unrelated developments.
First, the invented rules appear and gradually disappear. They do not affect
phonological representations or the final-state phonological system.
Second, adult phonological rules appear and cause restructuring of phonological representations. To my knowledge there are very few acquisition
studies that have investigated the acquisition of adult phonological rules
and their effects on phonological representations (a point already made ten
years ago by Macken 1995, see also Bernhardt & Stemberger 1998). The
general assumption seems to be that alternating forms are acquired late,
when children are, phonology-wise, fairly competent speakers (Hayes
2004b, Kerkhoff 2004).

The importance of phonological representations was emphasized in the
eighties, when non-linear phonology dominated the field. Child language
data formed additional evidence for the new linguistic tools of non-linear
representations, which could elegantly account for processes typical for
acquisition like consonant harmony. In consonant harmony, coronals –
considered unspecified for place of articulation – are often targets of
feature spreading (Stemberger & Stoel-Gammon 1991). The process can be
depicted as in (2):

(2) *Consonant harmony: a non-linear account*

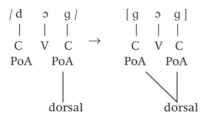

Yet, despite the elegant descriptions, the non-linear rules too ultimately
had to be abandoned by children in order to master adult-like phonological
competence. In this sense, child phonology was still concerned with child-
specific rules, bearing little on the question of phonological knowledge.
However, there is one important difference between this and earlier rule-
based approaches: the option that children could have underdeveloped

phonological representations was considered, as argued by for instance
Menn (1983). We will return to this issue in Section 23.5.

23.2.3   The acquisition of prosodic structure: syllable structure and stress

Prosodic structure is principally different from segmental structure:
whereas the latter largely consists of arbitrary segmental information that
needs to be stored, prosodic structure, particularly syllable structure, is
usually predictable from the string of segments and not used contrastively.
In this sense, prosodic structure is not part of lexical representations, but is
generated by grammatical 'rules'.[6]

The earliest work on prosodic structure stems from the seventies, and
was mainly concerned with the question of what the basic unit of acquisition was (Ferguson & Farwell 1975, Menn 1978). It became clear that
segments are not acquired in isolation, but need a word to surface. Moreover, the position in the word mattered: some contrasts appeared in onset
position earlier than in coda position, and vice versa. According to Moskowitz (1973) the first unit acquired in English is the syllable, but others
argued for a larger unit, i.e. the word (Menn 1971, Ferguson & Farwell
1975). This line of research led to the establishment of more or less fixed
word templates (see for instance Waterson 1971, Macken 1979 and Vihman
1996). These word templates constrained word forms that children produced and formed the basis of children's phonological representations.
A well-known case is the [labial-dental] template described by Macken
(1979), which her Spanish subject Si strictly adhered to by deleting syllables
that do not conform to this pattern, as in (3a,d), and by applying a kind of
'consonant harmony' prior to the deletion of the initial unstressed syllable
in (3b,c):

(3)   *Si's labial-dental word templates*

(a)	*zapato*	'shoe'	[pwatːo]	1;8.7
(b)	*manzana*	'apple'	[manːa]	1;9
(c)	*Fernando*	name	[mano]	1;9
(d)	*elefante*	'elephant'	[batə], [pantɪ]	1;9

With regard to the development of syllable structure, Moskowitz observed that early words in English child language all consisted of CV
syllables, but stated that beyond the primary acquisition of the CV, there
was no unique and specific pattern, or predictable order of acquisition of
syllable types. For example, Hildegard expanded her syllable repertoire
with a CVC syllable (Leopold 1939–49), whereas Joan first had CV and
VC syllables before producing CVC syllables (Velten 1943). The first pattern
is widely attested (Fikkert 1994, Levelt et al. 1999/2000). The second

pattern is reported for German child language (Grijzenhout & Joppen-Hellwig 2002): See (4).

(4) *Syllable structure of children's first words*

    (a) CV > CVC (data from the Dutch child Jarmo)

klaar	'ready'	/klar/	[ka], [kɑ]	1;4.18
poes	'cat'	/pus/	[pu]	1;5.2
poes	'cat'	/pus/	[pus]	1;7.29

    (b) CV > VC (data from the German child Naomi)

Bal	'ball'	/bal/	[ba]	1;2~1;5.01
Milch	'milk'	/mɪlç/	[mi]	1;2
ab	'off'	/apʰ/	[apʰ]	1;4.26

For a long time the study of acquisition of syllable structure kept repeating the following findings: children (i) start with CV syllables, (ii) reduce consonant clusters, and (iii) often delete final consonants. Fikkert's (1994) extensive longitudinal analysis of syllable structure based on data of twelve children also found these same facts for the initial stages. She showed furthermore that the developmental patterns showed relatively little variation among the children.

The developments could be nicely captured in a principles and parameters framework, in which marked parameter-settings have to be acquired. Dutch has a fairly complex syllable structure, allowing for both initial and final clusters, as well as vowel length contrasts; in other words, all syllable parameters have the marked setting. In this respect, Dutch is a good test case for investigating learning paths in acquisition. Variation in learning paths is essentially limited to the following cases. First, whereas most Dutch children have onset clusters consisting of an obstruent followed by a sonorant first, some children acquire /s/-obstruent clusters earlier. Children who correctly produce /s/-obstruent clusters also have final consonant clusters (Fikkert & Freitas 2004b). Second, while some children produce final clusters before they produce initial (obstruent-sonorant) clusters, others have the reverse order (Levelt et al. 1999/2000, Levelt & van de Vijver 2004). As the patterns in acquisition show less variation than expected on the basis of typology, Levelt & van de Vijver (2004) hypothesized that development is guided by the frequency of syllable types in the target language. In terms of decreasing frequency, stressed syllable types in Dutch have the following rank order: CV > CVC > V > CCVC/CVCC. Where frequencies are similar, children's choice of syllable type expansion varies.

However, frequency is not all that matters. The choice for /s/-obstruent vs. obstruent-sonorant clusters cannot be explained on the basis of frequency.[7] The former type of cluster is far less frequent in Dutch than the latter. Yet, some Dutch children start with the least frequent pattern. The same distribution is found in adult European Portuguese. Strikingly, /s/-obstruent clusters are produced months before obstruent-liquid clusters by the Portuguese children studied by Freitas (1997). Fikkert & Freitas (2004b) claim that other factors may interact with local phenomena, such as the acquisition of extraprosodic positions elsewhere and the saliency of morphological marking.

Kirk & Demuth (2003) claim that English children acquire coda clusters before onset clusters; in other words, they do not show the same variation as Dutch children. The time has come for thorough cross-linguistic investigations, combining the knowledge about the acquisition of syllable structure in various languages, such as English, Hungarian (Fee 1996), European Portuguese (Freitas 1997, Vigário et al. 2003), Spanish (Kehoe & Lleó 2003), German (Grijzenhout & Joppen-Hellwig 2002, Kehoe & Lleó 2003), Japanese (Ota 2003), French (Wauquier-Gravelines & Suet-Bouret 2004), and Greek (Kappa 2002) to discover which factors are involved in explaining development.

Cross-linguistic investigation shows that it is not always easy to compare languages. For their study, Levelt et al. (1999/2000) examined all stressed syllables produced by children, which were mostly word-initial, as this is the predominant stress pattern in Dutch. However, in French, stressed syllables are invariably final, and in Portuguese stressed syllables occur either in final or prefinal position (Fikkert et al. 2004). Since position in the word influences the structure of syllables, this introduces an extra variable in the investigation of cross-linguistic syllabic development. It is clear that factors other than universal syllable markedness and frequency must be considered.

Similar issues arise when looking at word prosodic patterns. Prosodic word forms in child language have been studied in a variety of languages. At first, these forms were described as more or less fixed templates, which in English, for instance, is a trochaic template. Subsequent work provided a more formal account of these templates, in terms of parameter settings (Fikkert 1994). Moreover, development was formalized as the change of one or more parameter settings from the default to the marked value, thereby assuming continuity from children's early grammars to the final state grammar. Markedness played a key role in the principles and parameter framework: in the initial state all parameters have the default or unmarked value. In the course of development, parameters are changed to their marked setting if the input data provide positive evidence for that setting. Prosodic templates defined by parameter settings constrain possible output patterns.

A robust finding in the literature is that children acquiring Germanic languages predominantly produce words that are monosyllabic or disyllabic trochees, whereas children acquiring Romance languages seem to produce very few monosyllabic words. Moreover, children acquiring Germanic languages produce disyllabic words with a trochaic foot, truncating target 'iambic' words. Some typical examples from English are given in (5): strings of segments, each dominated by a σ node:

(5)   *Typical early word truncations in English (from Pater 1997)*

banana	[nænə]	Trevor 0;11.10~1;6.8
gorilla	[goːwæ]	Trevor 1;11.12
spaghetti	[gɛdi]	Trevor 1;4.7~1;9.2
guitar	[ga]	Trevor 1;1.19~1;6.17

Children acquiring Romance languages, on the other hand, produce both trochaic and iambic word patterns (Hochberg 1988a, b, Santos 2001, 2003, Vigário et al. 2003). In those languages word stress seems not as reliable a cue for metrical structure as in Germanic languages, as stress can vary depending on morphology. Cross-linguistic research into factors that determine the prosodic shape of early words is very important for our understanding of phonological acquisition. Optimality Theory offers the possibility to investigate the interaction of different grammatical constraints, making it possible to integrate segmental, prosodic and morphological preferences.

23.3 Phonological acquisition in Optimality Theory

Formal phonological approaches to acquisition are currently captured in constraint-based theories. Constraint-based theories like Optimality Theory, henceforth OT (Prince & Smolensky 2004, papers in Kager et al. 2004), are fundamentally different in nature from rule-based theories, as, for example, proposed in Chomsky & Halle's (1968) *Sound Pattern of English* (*SPE*) (see McCarthy Ch.5). In *SPE*, the output is constructed by step-by-step application of rules; in OT, the output is chosen from a range of options by means of output constraints and constraints on input–output relations. The focus on *output* is in sharp contrast to earlier theories, particularly to non-linear phonology, which aimed at providing the most elegant and economic descriptions of *input* representations. A great deal of explanatory power was assumed to come from restrictions on input representations, especially through underspecification of predictable and non-contrastive information (e.g. Jakobson & Halle 1956, Chomsky & Halle 1968, Lahiri & Marslen-Wilson 1991, Steriade 1995; see Dresher 2004a for an implementation of abstract underspecified phonological representations in OT). In contrast, OT places no restrictions on inputs – all explanation is due to constraints on output form and the input–output relation. It is (often tacitly) assumed that input forms to children and adults are identical. However, as noted above, children's output forms differ from adult output forms.

Another assumption is that child and adult phonology are made up of the same ingredients. In the 'classical' view of OT, a grammar consists of a set of ordered innate constraints. There are two sets of constraints: Markedness constraints, which aim at minimizing the degree of markedness in output forms and Faithfulness constraints, which aim at faithfully producing the input structure.[8] Markedness and Faithfulness constraints are often in conflict, and hence constraints are violated, although the grammar keeps violations to the minimum number needed. As inputs and constraints are assumed to be the same for children and adults, output differences must be due to differences in the ranking of the constraints.

At the onset of acquisition Markedness constraints outrank Faithfulness constraints (M » F) (Smolensky 1996, Gnanadesikan 2004, and others, but see Hale & Reiss 1998, Bernhardt & Stemberger Ch.25). Consequently, children's phonological grammars usually deliver more 'unmarked' outputs than adult grammars. Development entails constraint re-ranking, i.e. the demotion of some markedness constraints, which results in output forms that are more marked and at the same time often more faithful to the adult target forms. Learning is error-driven: the detection of mismatches between children's own productions and target forms will trigger changes in the grammar. Once low-ranked, the influence of formerly high-ranked constraints is reduced to a minimum, but their presence can still be felt in cases of 'The Emergence of The Unmarked' (TETU) phenomena (McCarthy & Prince 1994, Pater 1997, Gnanadesikan 2004, Fikkert et al. 2005b). Another consequence of this view is that each phonological system that occurs during the course of acquisition is a possible phonological system of a natural human language (cf. Levelt & Vijver 2004).

However, the innateness of constraints is not an essential property of OT; constraints could also emerge in the course of acquisition. For example, in Boersma (1998), Hayes (1999) and Hayes et al. (2004) constraints are constructed by mechanisms that refer to articulatory and acoustic factors. That is, phonological constraints are grounded in either acoustics or articulation. What is easy to produce or perceive is likely to show up earlier in child language than what is more difficult to produce or perceive (see also Waterson 1971). Boersma, Escudero and Hayes (2003) propose an acquisition model which starts with non-lexically driven distributional learning of phonological categories, based on acoustic properties. Once phonological categories have emerged, faithfulness to phonological categories starts playing a role and interacts with articulatory constraints that are created when the child learns the gestures to produce the phonological categories. In other words, they assume a perception grammar that links the acoustic signal to phonological categories and ultimately to stored phonological representations, and a production grammar that mediates between stored phonological representations and output forms. In such a view markedness is driven by phonetics rather than phonology. How the linking between the different levels of representation takes place remains to be investigated.

Constraints can also emerge as generalizations over the lexicon (Beckman & Edwards 2000, Pierrehumbert 2003a, Fikkert & Levelt 2004).

According to Beckman & Edwards (2000) and Pierrehumbert (2003a) acquisition is guided by frequencies in the target lexicon. In general, it seems hard to distinguish between frequency and 'universal' markedness as often both conspire towards the same patterns (Zamuner 2003, Zamuner et al. 2004). Fikkert & Levelt (2004), however, argue that constraints are generalizations over children's own lexicons. The relation between the make-up of a child's lexicon and frequency in the target language is not 1:1, even though frequent items are more likely to appear in children's lexicons early.

Fikkert & Levelt (2004) investigated the acquisition of place of articulation features in detail. They found that at early stages of acquisition, words consisted of consonants and vowels that shared place of articulation features, where the vowel features are dominant (following Lahiri & Evers 1991, Levelt 1994; for a similar, although not identical view see MacNeilage & Davis 2000, Davis et al. 2002, Vihman 1992). At subsequent stages, first the vowel could be specified independently from the consonants, and later, the consonants in a word could also have different places of articulation. At this stage, a pattern emerged in which specific places of articulation were preferred in specific prosodic positions. That is, Dutch children preferred labials in word-initial position, while they tended to avoid words beginning with dorsals, which is reminiscent of the word templates in (3). At this stage, dorsal-initial words like *koek* [kuk] 'cookie' were produced with an initial coronal, i.e. as [tuk], even if they were produced correctly at an earlier stage.

Another important finding was that children were initially very faithful to the place of articulation make-up of target words (see also Vihman et al. 1994), and that 'incorrect' renditions only occurred at a later stage. The unfaithfully produced words often resulted in labial-initial child's productions, where the adult target was labial-final, as for instance in *zeep* /zep/ 'soap' produced as [fep] (Levelt 1994). In addition, unfaithfulness often affected dorsal-initial target words, such as the *koek* example mentioned above. For those reasons Fikkert & Levelt (2004) argue that children's early lexicons give rise to emerging markedness constraints in the children's grammars: children make generalizations over their own production lexicons. If a child's lexicon contains many labial-initial words, the child may generalize that labial is designated to word-initial position, leading to emerging constraints in the grammar. Because coronals can freely appear in all positions, it is assumed that coronal is underspecified, i.e. the default place of articulation in Dutch. In this view, then, development takes place both in the grammar and in the underlying representations: features first have scope over the whole word, but become part of segments in the course of development.

Future work will undoubtedly focus more on the nature of Markedness constraints and where they come from, as they play a dominant role in (the acquisition of) phonology. Another issue that deserves more attention is

how children manage to construct phonological categories and phonological representations from the continuous speech stream, because the
nature of the input representation is of consequence for the interpretation
of Faithfulness constraints.

23.4   Child speech perception and word recognition

In the seventies and eighties researchers assumed that children pick up
salient parts of the input first (e.g. Ferguson & Garnica 1975, Waterson
1971, 1981, 1987) and initially have global representations of words that
become more detailed under pressure from the increasing lexicon.
Changes in the lexical representations served an efficient organization
of the lexicon. Today, most researchers of infant and child language
perception assume that children have fairly detailed phonetic representations from a very early stage. By simply listening to language, infants
acquire sophisticated information about what sounds and sound patterns
occur in the language and which of those patterns are frequent (e.g. Maye
et al. 2002).

   Current research in child language perception has contributed two insights that have consequences for the understanding of phonological acquisition. First, children already know a lot about the sound patterns of
their language before they speak their first word. Ever since the ground-
breaking work of Eimas et al. (1971) we know that infants are good in
speech perception and the categorization of sounds. Second, there was
the important discovery that, while speech perception may start out as
'universal', it becomes language-specific in the course of the first year of
life (Werker & Tees 1984), when infants are able to distinguish between
sounds, prosodic and phonotactic structures that are specific to their
native language from those that are foreign (for overviews see Jusczyk
1997, 1998, Kuhl 2000, Gerken 2002). Children must be able to deduce this
knowledge on the basis of distributional properties of the input, as they do
not yet have a lexicon.

   When at around 7.5 months of age word learning begins, children prefer
to listen to 'words' that they have been familiarized with over 'words' that
are minimally different (e.g. *feet* vs. *zeet*) suggesting that they have stored
detailed representations of the 'words' they hear (Jusczyk & Aslin 1995).
This study did show that 7.5-month-old infants are able to recognize word
forms – a prerequisite for word learning – but not that they have learned
words, i.e. sound–meaning combinations.

   There is also evidence from early word perception showing that children
do not always use phonetic detail (Werker et al. 2002). Werker and colleagues showed that 14-month old English children could not distinguish
newly learned (non)words that contrast minimally, such as *bin* and *din*.
However, they are able to distinguish the pair in a pure discrimination

task. These results are accounted for by assuming that discrimination of newly learned words is such a demanding task that phonetic detail is temporarily not accessible. In a subsequent study Fennell & Werker (2004) showed that the pair *ball-doll*, i.e. words known to the children, could be distinguished in the same task. However, an alternative view is that phonological representations of stored words contain less detail than the phonetic representation of unanalyzed words of the prelexical child (Pater et al. 2004).

Fikkert *et al.* (2005a) investigated this possibility, replicating the experimental set-up of Werker and colleagues with Dutch 14-month-old infants. Based on the results that children's early words only have one place of articulation, determined by the vowel (see Section 23.3), and assuming coronal underspecification, different responses were predicted for items containing front unrounded, i.e. underspecified vowels, such as [ɪ] in *bin-din*, and specified back rounded vowels, such as [ɔ] in *bon-don*. This prediction was borne out. The pair *bin-din* could not be distinguished, replicating the findings of Werker and colleagues. However, the Dutch children had no problems distinguishing the pair *bon-don*. Both sets of (non)words contrast 'b' and 'd', the difference being that in *bin-din* the vowel is underspecified, while in *bon-don* the vowel has a place feature specification. The presence of a specified feature in children's phonological representations is crucial for detecting mispronunciations: a perceived coronal sound [d], in *don* for *bon*, mismatches with a labial/dorsal place of articulation in the phonological representation of *bon*. On the other hand, mismatches are not detected if the phonological representation is not specified for that feature: whatever place feature is perceived, it will never form a mismatch. This study thus suggests that the same stored phonological representations are used for both perception and production.

Research investigating the relation of perception and production is important in order to gain insight into the nature of phonological representations in the mental lexicon. Although input representations are not the focus in OT, it remains puzzling how they are acquired and what they look like exactly in different stages of the acquisition process.

23.5 Phonological representations in the mental lexicon

Menn (1978) has argued for a two-lexicon model: one for perception, and another for production, which contains "just the information required to keep the child's output words distinct from one another" (Menn & Matthei 1992: 218). For a variety of reasons researchers have assumed that early (stored) words are holistic or un(der)specified. Children may have a preference for certain fixed word templates (e.g. Menn 1978, Waterson 1987, Macken 1979, Vihman *et al.* 1994, MacNeilage & Davis 2000, Davis *et al.* 2002). Another reason is that children's early vocabularies are so small that there is no need to specify all phonological detail in the lexicon (e.g. Ferguson & Garnica 1975, Fischer et al. 2004). Yet another reason is that certain processes could be readily accounted for by assuming underspecification, as we saw in (2). Finally, contrasts that are not yet produced by children are considered absent in children's phonological representations. If children's phonological representations are not adult-like, the continuity hypothesis can in principle still be maintained, but the burden of explanation for how children arrive at an adult-like competence is now not only put onto children's developing phonologies, but also onto developing phonological representations in the mental lexicon.

Of course, child phonology is not only about developing representations. Often children's perception clearly indicates that they perceive differences between words which nevertheless can be mapped onto the same output form (e.g. Jongstra 2003 for the perception and production of clusters). The fact that children's mapping of inputs to outputs is systematic strongly suggests that they have an abstract phonological system. Moreover, different children may use different mappings for the same targets, suggesting that it is not a matter of ease of articulation alone. It is a challenge to distinguish cases in which children systematically alter input forms that they have stored in an adult-like way from cases where children's representations arguably differ from adult representations.

In 'classical' OT there are no restrictions on input forms or underlying representations, *only* output forms may be constrained. The question how phonological representations of words are stored in the mental lexicon is underresearched in OT. Acquisition studies in 'classical' OT tacitly assume that during the whole acquisition process the underlying phonological representation of words is essentially 'adult-like'. Hence, the reason why children do not produce words like adults do is solely due to differences in the child's phonology. This is a direct consequence of the principle of 'Richness of the Base' (McCarthy & Prince 1994, Dinnsen et al. 2001) and 'Lexicon Optimization', stating respectively that, in principle, any input is possible, but input forms that match the output form are preferred and will be the ones stored in the lexicon. In the OT literature on acquisition one finds however very little discussion on the exact shape of stored phonological development, nor on their development (but see Pater 2004).[9]

Incidentally, although there are many differences between current approaches that focus on production and those focusing on perception, what they share is the assumption that stored representations are fairly detailed. If the (developing) lexicon is indeed relevant to, or even crucial for understanding phonological acquisition, then lexical phonological representations should be reassessed. By careful investigation of the evidence from both child language perception and production, we may come closer to an understanding of early phonological representations.

23.6   Summary and directions for future research

Why do children produce words differently from adults? There are several possible explanations. Children may have perceived them differently from adults, they may have stored them differently, they may have a different phonological system which causes divergent patterns, they may lack sufficient processing skills to remember and encode a phonological string in such a way that the output mimics the target, or children may simply lack the articulatory skills necessary to produce the words in an adult-like fashion. Child-language phonologists have mostly been concerned with two of these explanations: child-specific phonological systems or child-specific storage of phonological representations, where the first has been most prominent. I believe, however, that a phonological system and a (phonological) lexicon develop in tandem.

One challenge is to understand the relationship between perception and production. The evidence from both fields seems contradictory. Infant speech perception research suggests that segmental inventories and knowledge about phonotactic and prosodic structures are largely acquired in the absence of a lexicon. In fact, they need to be acquired before lexical learning can even start, as they guide word segmentation. Research into child production has argued that children gradually build up a system of phonological contrasts, phonotactics and prosodic structure. One way to solve this conflict is to assume that children construct phonetic categories that play a role in the target language on the basis of statistical and distributional properties in the input. For storage of words in the mental lexicon, these phonetic categories receive a phonological interpretation, in terms of active or contrastive phonological features.

Another important question that is discussed in this chapter is in what ways children's phonological systems and phonological representations differ from those of adults. Do children follow patterns of (universal) markedness, starting out with unmarked structures that become more marked (and more faithful) on the basis of simple positive evidence? Or do markedness constraints emerge from generalizations based on the 'analysis' of either the input lexicon or children's own lexicons, which, in turn, may affect their output forms? Within phonology an important research question is where markedness constraints come from and it is likely that answers will be found in the study of phonological acquisition. Careful analysis of both perception and production data may help us understand how children manage the complex task of acquiring phonology.

Notes

Many thanks to Susan van der Feest, René Kager, Annemarie Kerkhoff, Paul de Lacy, Bruce Morén, Joe Pater, Jessica Rett, Tania Zamuner, and especially

Claartje Levelt for very useful comments. This research is part of the project 'Changing Lexical Representations in the Mental Lexicon' supported by NWO.

1 Today, another challenge for child language researchers is to link results from child production and perception. Although it has long been an issue whether children use the same representation for perception and production (Menn & Matthei 1992, Boersma 1998), perception and production studies have typically been studied in isolation.

2 Smith (1973) is one of the remarkable exceptions.

3 U-shaped patterns of development have been reported. Yet, these patterns often indicate a change or reorganization of a system, rather than loss or regression of it (Werker, Hall & Fais 2004).

4 Moreover, the theory also seemed hard to falsify (see Kiparsky & Menn 1977).

5 Brown & Matthews (1997) argue that development in perception involves the reduction of the number of contrasts (via 'pruning'), whereas in production, it must expand.

6 The term 'rules' is used loosely here to refer to either syllabification and stress rules, prosodic parameters, or prosodic constraints – i.e. the grammatical rules posit prosodic structure that is not part of the underlying phonological representation, but is part of the output structure.

7 Levelt et al. (1999/2000) and Levelt & van de Vijver (2004) left syllables with /s/-obstruent clusters out of consideration.

8 There are also other types of constraints that play a role when morphology is at stake, such as Output–Output constraints, which aim at paradigm uniformity (Benua 1997). We will not discuss these here, as this has hardly ever been a topic of investigation in the acquisition of phonology.

9 The assumption of fixed input forms is important for learnability models of acquisition. A change in underlying representations in the course of development can have dramatic consequences for the constraint ranking, particularly for the interpretation of faithfulness constraints.

24

Learnability

Bruce Tesar

24.1 Learnability in phonology

A fundamental tenet of cognitive science is that human mental processes, including those involved in language, are computational processes. On this view, for a child to learn their native language, there must exist a learning *algorithm* capable of determining the grammar of that language from a reasonable amount of data, and with a reasonable amount of computational effort. Language learnability is the study of the computational dimensions of language learning. Learnability works in tandem with the study of child language data, commonly known as language acquisition, to constitute the overall study of how children learn their native language.

While it is difficult to quantify how much data a child *needs* in order to reliably learn a grammar, it is not too difficult to impose a generous upper bound on the amount of data a child could possibly have by estimating the number of utterances a child could hear during the waking hours of the first few years of their life. Even such generous overestimates prove to have real consequences for learnability; it is remarkably easy to define learning algorithms which demonstrably require decades' worth of data to work for even rather simple classes of grammars.[1]

Quantifying a 'reasonable' amount of computational effort is a far more murky matter, due in no small part to science's current vast ignorance of the computational properties of the human brain. But some fairly rudimentary assumptions turn out to have non-trivial implications for language learning. The very nature of computation requires that the learning algorithm use only a *finite* amount of computational effort. That requirement turns out to be sufficient to rule out certain simple learning proposals. In practice, researchers use gross measures of evaluation, based upon basic plausibility. If a proposed learning algorithm, implemented on the world's fastest supercomputer, would require several centuries to complete, then it is generally regarded as requiring an implausible amount of computation.

Learnability is a class phenomenon: it is a property of classes of grammars. A class is learnable if an algorithm exists which can determine, based on example data, the target grammar (the one generating that data), and do so for data from every grammar in the class. What makes learning easy or difficult is the amount of data and effort necessary to reliably identify the target grammar out of the class of allowable grammars. The challenge arises from the need to distinguish between different possible grammars, rather than from the individual grammars themselves. Learning Japanese is trivial if you need not consider any alternatives; you just build Japanese into the system. Human language learning is challenging because the class of allowable languages must include all possible human languages.

Linguistic theory is central to language learnability. A linguistic theory proposes a class of possible human languages, which is effectively the class of allowable languages for the learning problem. It is a reasonable and uncontroversial assumption that the formal relationships among the allowable grammars that make language learnable are intimately related to the formal properties of the linguistic theory defining the class of allowable grammars.

In this chapter, I will assume that the class of allowable languages is defined by an Optimality Theoretic system (Prince & Smolensky 2004). Each language is generated by a grammar consisting of a total ranking of the universal constraints and a lexicon of phonological underlying forms for morphemes. The learner's job is to identify, for a given set of data, the *target* grammar that gave rise to that data. The learner attempts to do this by searching for the grammar that best captures the patterns in the data. This involves finding a grammar which generates all of the observed data (it is consistent with the data), but as little as possible of the unattested data (the most restrictive such grammar). If the observed data include no examples of voiced obstruents, a grammar that does not generate any voiced obstruents is more restrictive and more likely to be correct than a grammar that does.

(1) *Goals of the learner*
     (a) to find a ranking and a set of underlying forms that successfully reproduce the observed data.
     (b) to find the most restrictive ranking consistent with the data.

A complete and satisfactory solution to this problem will not be found in this chapter, or anywhere else. Simple exhaustive search of the possible grammars isn't an option for the simple reason that there is an infinite number of possible lexica (plural of 'lexicon'), given that there is in principle no bound on the size of an underlying form. One could derive some formal limits on how long an underlying form could need to be, given some maximal observed morpheme length, but the resulting space of possible grammars would be finite but too large to plausibly search exhaustively. This is due to combinatorial explosion: the number of total rankings of a set of constraints of size C is C! (i.e. the factorial C!: the number of permutations of the constraints). If segments are described with F binary features, there are 2^F possible underlying forms for a segment, and a word with at most S segments in its underlying form has $2^F + (2^F)^2 + (2^F)^3 + \cdots + (2^F)^S$ possible underlying forms, which is on the order of 2^{FS}. Modest assumptions still yield a huge number of grammars. 50 constraints yields 3×10^{64} possible rankings. 10 binary features and an average limit of 4 segments for an underlying form yields $2^{40} \approx 1 \times 10^{12}$ possible underlying forms for a morpheme; for a lexicon of 1000 morphemes, that yields $2^{40 \times 1000} \approx 10^{12041}$ possible lexica. The number of grammars itself is of course the product of the number of possible rankings and the number of possible lexica.

Most of the results in this chapter focus on the learning of constraint rankings, reflecting a majority of the work done to date. These results support algorithms that exploit the formal structure of Optimality Theory to efficiently learn the correct constraint ranking. Relatively little work has been done on learning phonological lexica, but see 24.7 for discussion of current work on this topic.

24.2   Learning with soft constraints: Constraint Demotion

The fundamental unit of information about constraint rankings is the elementary ranking condition. In learning (as in linguistic argumentation), elementary ranking conditions are normally constructed from pairwise comparisons between candidates, with one candidate presumed to be grammatical in the target language, labeled the *winner*, and the other candidate a competitor for the same input, labeled the *loser*. Such comparisons are commonly called winner–loser pairs.

I will illustrate several properties of learning algorithms with a very simple linguistic system allowing grammars with different consonant inventories. The constraints are given in (2).

(2)   *The Consonant Inventory Constraints*

*+VOICE (*VOI)	'Consonants should not be voiced' (Lombardi 1999)
*+NASAL (*NAS)	'Consonants should not be nasal'
{−VOICE&+NASAL} (−VOI/NAS):	'Consonants should not be both nasal and voiceless'
IDENT[voice] (ID[VOI]):	'Correspondents should have the same value for voicing' (McCarthy & Prince 1995a)
IDENT[nasal] (ID[nas]):	'Correspondents should have the same value for nasality' (McCarthy & Prince 1995a)

(3)   *An example winner–loser pair*

input	win ~ lose	*VOI	*NAS	*–VOI/NAS	ID[voi]	ID[nas]
/ni/	ni ~ ti	L	L	e	W	W

A winner–loser pair has a particular logical structure: at least one of the constraints preferring the winner must dominate all of the constraints preferring the loser. In the example in (3), at least one of ID[voi] and ID[nas] must dominate both *VOI and *NAS.

The key to learning a ranking from a set of winner–loser pairs is to find a way of combining the information in each of the pairs. An algorithm which does this is Recursive Constraint Demotion (Tesar 1995, Tesar & Smolensky 1998), referred to here as RCD. RCD constructs a constraint ranking consistent with a set of winner–loser pairs. It does so top-down, determining the highest-ranked constraints first, then the next-highest, and so forth. The key observation is that a constraint can be ranked at the top if it does not prefer the loser for any of the pairs. The discussion will be illustrated using Comparative Tableaux (Prince 2002a).

(4)   *The winner–loser pairs before the first pass of RCD*

input	win ~ lose	*VOI	*NAS	*–VOI/NAS	ID[voi]	ID[nas]
/ni/	ni ~ ti	L	L	e	W	W
/di/	ti ~ di	W	e	e	L	e

In the set of pairs in (4), *–VOI/NAS and ID[nas] do not prefer any losers. RCD places them together at the top of the ranking, as it lacks any basis for determining a ranking relation between them. The top stratum is {*–VOI/NAS, ID[nas]}. RCD then checks for pairs in which one of the constraints just ranked prefers the winner. Such pairs are now fully accounted for. In the example, the first pair is such a case, as ID[nas] prefers the winner. By definition of the algorithm, none of the constraints preferring the loser can have been ranked yet, so the ranking of ID[nas] insures that a constraint preferring the winner dominates all of the constraints preferring the loser. RCD removes all such pairs from the list, as well as the constraints just ranked. In the example, this results in the table in (5).

(5)   *The winner–loser pairs after the first pass of RCD*

input	win ~ lose	*VOI	*NAS	ID[voi]
/di/	ti ~ di	W	e	L

RCD now performs a second pass through the list, using identical logic. For the constraints not yet ranked, the ones that can be ranked highest are those that do not prefer any (remaining) losers. In the example, *VOI and *NAS qualify, and are placed by RCD into the ranking. The top two strata are now {*–VOI/NAS, ID[nas]} » {*VOI, *NAS}. RCD now observes that in the remaining winner–loser pair, *Voɪ prefers the winner, so the pair may be removed. This leaves an empty list; there are no losers remaining, so all remaining constraints are now free to be placed in the ranking. In the example, the only remaining constraint is ID[voi], which is ranked at the bottom. RCD is now complete. The constructed ranking is {*–Voɪ/Nᴀs, ID[nas]} » {*Voɪ, *Nᴀs} » ID[voi].

Given a consistent set of winner–loser pairs, RCD is guaranteed to construct a constraint hierarchy consistent with all of them. In fact, it always constructs a specific hierarchy relative to the winner–loser pairs: it constructs the hierarchy in which each constraint is ranked as high as possible, consistent with the data. This follows from the fact that the algorithm places constraints into the hierarchy as soon as they are 'free' (they do not prefer the loser for any remaining winner–loser pair). Choosing the hierarchy with each constraint ranked as high as possible is very convenient computationally. However, that is not quite the right bias for learning, and that motivates the modifications to the RCD algorithm discussed in the section on phonotactic learning below.

RCD is computationally efficient. Given consistent data, it is guaranteed to place at least one constraint into the hierarchy on each pass through the list of winner–loser pairs, so the number of passes is at most the number of constraints.

One important property of RCD is that it automatically detects inconsistencies in the list of winner–loser pairs, as a side effect of trying to find a ranking. An example of a list of inconsistent winner–loser pairs is given in (6).

(6)   *An inconsistent set of winner–loser pairs ('ŋ̊' denotes a voiceless nasal)*

input	win ~ lose	*Voɪ	*Nᴀs	*–Voɪ/Nᴀs	ID[voi]	ID[nas]
/n̊i/	n̊i ~ ti	e	L	L	e	W
/ni/	di ~ ni	e	W	e	e	L

The first pass of RCD places *Voɪ and ID[voi] into the top stratum of the hierarchy. However, neither constraint prefers a winner, so no pairs are removed from the list. Once those two constraints are removed, the remaining winner–loser pair list is as shown in (7).

(7)   *After the first pass, all remaining constraints prefer a loser*

input	win ~ lose	*Nᴀs	*–Voɪ/Nᴀs	ID[nas]
/n̊i/	n̊i ~ ti	L	L	W
/ni/	di ~ ni	W	e	L

RCD is unable to continue constructing the hierarchy at this point, because all of the remaining constraints prefer a loser. No matter which constraint is placed into the hierarchy next, at least one of the designated optimal candidates (a winner) will lose to a competitor. This is the key indicator that the list is inconsistent. RCD can halt immediately and return an indication to the learner that inconsistency has been detected.

Inconsistency detection is powerful because it allows the learner to test the compatibility of different hypotheses about the grammar. The use of inconsistency detection in learning will be discussed further in the section on structural ambiguity.

24.3   Selecting competitors and the role of parsing

RCD will find a ranking compatible with a list of winner–loser pairs, but does not construct the list itself. One issue in the construction of such a list is the selection of appropriate competitors (the losers). Assuming (for the moment) that a winner can be determined from observed data, there are typically many losing candidates that the winner must beat. Constructing a separate winner–loser pair for each competitor is very computationally expensive and, in cases where the number of competitors is infinite, completely untenable. It is also unnecessary; normally many winner–loser comparisons are redundant in the information they supply about the ranking. What is needed is a way to efficiently select a set of informative competitors.

Informative competitors can be selected using error-driven learning (Tesar 1998). Given a grammatical form, the learner tests the input (i.e. phonological underlying form) for that form with their current hypothesized constraint ranking, to see what candidate is assigned as optimal. If the candidate chosen by the learner's current ranking is identical to the grammatical form, then the grammatical form will not motivate any changes to the ranking; all possible winner–loser pairs for that form are already satisfied. If, on the other hand, a candidate other than the grammatical form is chosen by the learner's current ranking, then the ranking needs to be changed; an *error* has occurred in the sense that the learner's current grammar does not generate the independently observed grammatical form.

In the most general sense of error-driven learning, the error indicates that the learner's grammar must be changed somehow, but doesn't necessarily indicate how. In Optimality Theory, the error gives a concrete indication of how to change the ranking. This is because the learner's parsing mechanism has produced a different candidate as optimal for the learner's current ranking. This means that the comparison between the grammatical candidate and the one generated by parsing is guaranteed to provide information not reflected in the learner's current ranking. In other words, the candidate generated by parsing is informative. Thus the learner can use the parsing mechanism, which is independently necessary in any event, to select informative competitors.

One consequence of using error-driven learning to select competitors is that the learner must have a hypothesis ranking in order to select a competitor. RCD constructs rankings based upon winner–loser pairs. The two can be productively combined in the form of an algorithm known as Multi-Recursive Constraint Demotion, or MRCD (Tesar 1997). MRCD maintains a list of winner–loser pairs at all times. Whenever presented with data in the form of a grammatical candidate, the learner can use RCD to generate a ranking from the list of winner–loser pairs. The learner can then parse the input for the grammatical candidate. If an error occurs, the learner constructs a new winner–loser pair, using the data-presented grammatical candidate as the winner, and the candidate generated by the parser as the loser. This new winner–loser pair is then added to the learner's list. The learner thus accumulates winner–loser pairs over time, with each new pair guaranteed to provide information not found in the previous pairs.

This can be illustrated with data generated by the target grammar in (8).

(8)   *–Voi/Nas » ID[nas] » *Voi » *Nas » ID[voi]

The possible CV-form outputs for the ranking are [ti] and [ni], restricting consonants to coronals and vowels to [i].

The learner starts out with an empty list of winner–loser pairs. When presented with data, the learner needs a hierarchy to parse with. RCD, when applied to an empty list, ranks all of the constraints in the top stratum of the hierarchy (there are no losers to be preferred by any of the constraints).

(9)   *Initial Hierarchy:* {*–Voi/Nas, *Nas, *Voi, ID[nas], ID[voi]}

Suppose the learner first receives (via observed data) the grammatical candidate /ni/↔[ni], with both input and output as [ni]. The evaluation of the four relevant candidates is shown in (10):

(10)   *Evaluation of the four candidates for /ni/*

input: /ni/	*Voi	*Nas	*–Voi/Nas	ID[voi]	ID[nas]
ti				*	*
di	*				*
n̥i		*	*	*	
ni	*	*			

Using the initial hierarchy, the parser will return the outputs [ti], [di], and [ni] as tied for optimal (assuming that evaluation is performed based upon 'pooling the marks' – i.e. taking all the violations of all the constraints of a stratum together). Not all of these candidates match the grammatical output [ni]. The learner (arbitrarily) chooses [ti] as a loser, forms a new winner–loser pair, and adds it to the list, resulting in the list in (11).

(11)   *The list with the first winner–loser pair*

input	win ~ lose	*Voi	*Nas	*–Voi/Nas	ID[voi]	ID[nas]
/ni/	ni ~ ti	L	L	e	W	W

The learner then applies RCD to this list, resulting in the hierarchy in (12).

(12)   {*–Voi/Nas, ID[nas], ID[voi]} » {*Nas, *Voi}

Using that hierarchy, the learner then reparses the input /ni/, and observes that [ni] is now generated. The learner no longer gets a learning error on the form.

Next the learner considers the grammatical candidate /ti/↔[ti]. Using the hierarchy in (12), the learner parses the input /ti/ and generates [ti]. No learning error occurs, so no winner–loser pairs are created.

Next, the learner considers the grammatical candidate /di/↔[ti]. Using the hierarchy in (12), the learner parses the input /di/ and generates [di]. This is a learning error, so the learner constructs a new winner–loser pair for input /di/, with output [ti] as the winner and output [di] as the loser. This results in the list in (13).

(13)   *The list after the second learning error*

input	win ~ lose	*Voi	*Nas	*–Voi/Nas	ID[voi]	ID[nas]
/ni/	ni ~ ti	L	L	e	W	W
/di/	ti ~ di	W	e	e	L	e

The learner then applies RCD to that list, constructing the hierarchy in (14).

(14)   {*–Voi/Nas, ID[nas]} » {*Voi, *Nas} » {ID[voi]}

The learner then parses /di/ with the new hierarchy, and generates [ti]. No more learning errors occur, and in fact the learner now has a constraint hierarchy that is compatible with the entire language, so no more learning errors will occur. Learning has succeeded.

MRCD has efficient data complexity. There is a formally proven upper bound on the number of learning errors that can occur prior to the construction of a compatible constraint hierarchy: $N(N-1)/2$, where N is the number of constraints. This is less than N^2. Each learning error adds a winner–loser pair to the list, so this is also a bound on the number of pairs accumulated during learning with MRCD. In the most extreme case, each pair comes from a distinct data form, so the number of mutually informative pieces of data required by the algorithm is less than the square of the number of constraints. In practice, this upper bound is a gross overestimate, but it makes the point that the data demands of MRCD are not wildly large relative to the number of constraints.

24.4   Robustness to data errors

MRCD is vulnerable to data errors. For present purposes, a data error is a form which is ungrammatical in the target language, but appears in the learner's data. An ungrammatical form will commonly have one of two effects on MRCD: it will detect inconsistency if there is no ranking consistent with all of the data, or it will incorrectly select a less restrictive ranking permitting the ungrammatical form as well as all of the grammatical data.

A learning algorithm that demonstrates some robustness to data errors is the Gradual Learning Algorithm, or GLA (Boersma 1998, Boersma & Hayes 2001). The GLA uses a familiar strategy for error robustness: sensitivity to frequency. It is designed so that patterns which occur more frequently in the data are likely to have a greater impact on the choice of grammar; if errors occur infrequently enough, they probably will not have enough impact to affect the learner's choice of grammar.

The GLA realizes frequency sensitivity in part by adopting a different formal theory of phonology than MRCD does. The GLA presumes a stochastic variation of Optimality Theory (StOT). In this theory, a grammar assigns a *ranking value* to each constraint, where a ranking value is a real number. The absolute values of the ranking values are irrelevant; what matters for the model is the distances between the ranking values assigned different constraints. Whenever the grammar is used to evaluate a form, the ranking values of the constraints are used to determine an 'evaluation ranking' of the constraints. That ranking is then treated exactly as a normal Optimality Theoretic ranking for that evaluation.

The stochastic element of StOT lies in the method for constructing an evaluation ranking from the ranking values. For each constraint, a number called a *selection point* is generated randomly using a normal distribution with a mean equal to the constraint's ranking value. The standard deviation of the distribution is an independent and arbitrary value, called the *evaluation noise*. The selection point will be within one standard deviation of the ranking value approximately 66% of the time (this follows from the definitions of normal distribution and standard deviation). At evaluation time, a selection point is generated for each constraint, and then the constraints are ranked by their selection points, with the highest selection point deciding the highest-ranked constraint, and so forth. New selection points are generated for each evaluation, so it is possible for the same set of ranking values to give rise to different rankings on different evaluations. If constraint C1 has a higher ranking value than C2, we expect C1 to dominate C2 at evaluation time more than half of the time. The probability that C2 dominates C1 on an evaluation is determined by the distance between their ranking values, measured in terms of the evaluation noise. Again, the absolute magnitudes of the differences between ranking values are not key in and of themselves, what matters is the distance between ranking values relative to the size of the evaluation noise.

A StOT grammar really defines a probability distribution over the possible total orderings of the constraints. It is not difficult to define a StOT grammar that is equivalent for practical purposes to a traditional OT ranking: simply assign the constraints ranking values that are several standard deviations apart, ordered according to the desired ranking, and the probability of any ranking other than the ranking value order being used at evaluation time will be extremely small.

In StOT, then, learning a grammar means learning a set of ranking values for the constraints that will generate the target language. That is the task of the GLA. The GLA shares several components with MRCD. It uses error-driven learning, and when a learning error occurs it constructs a winner–loser pair just as MRCD does. Instead of storing the winner–loser pair, however, the GLA uses it to make small changes to the ranking values of the constraints. The algorithm learns 'gradually', through the accumulated effects of many errors upon the ranking values.

The GLA responds to an error-induced winner–loser pair by increasing the ranking values of the constraints preferring the winner, and decreasing the ranking values of the constraints preferring the loser. The amount by which a ranking value is increased or decreased, a value called *plasticity*, is an independent parameter of the learning algorithm. One might normally imagine the size of plasticity to be small relative to the size of evaluation noise. However, versions of the GLA often employ schedules that change the size of plasticity during learning.

The GLA will eventually learn a consistent ranking for consistent data by accumulation of adjustments to the ranking values. The highest-ranked constraint will never prefer any losers. It can have its ranking value increased, but never decreased, and its ranking value will grow until it is enough higher than the ranking values of the relevant other constraints that it never is ranked below them at evaluation time. Given a relatively small plasticity value, constraint ranking values cannot be pushed far apart on the basis of one or a few learning errors; many over time will be needed. This is where the robustness comes from: a data error will only cause a minor change to the learner's grammar; the ranking values will change by at most the plasticity value. To have a long-term impact on learning, data errors would have to occur with some substantive frequency in the data.

The GLA has a couple of parameters that must be set to define a specific algorithm. A set of initial ranking values must be specified, so that error-driven learning can get started. A schedule of values for plasticity must also be provided. Needless to say, the performance of the algorithm can vary depending upon the values chosen for these parameters.

A fundamental difference between the GLA and MRCD lies in the response to inconsistent data. Recall the data in (6), repeated here as (15).

(15)   *An inconsistent set of winner–loser pairs*

input	win ~ lose	*Voi	*Nas	*–Voi/Nas	ID[voi]	ID[nas]
/n̥i/	n̥i ~ ti	e	L	L	e	W
/ni/	di ~ ni	e	W	e	e	L

The GLA treats the winner–loser pairs in succession. The first pair causes the ranking value of ID[nas] to be increased, and the ranking values of *Nas and *–Voi/Nas to be decreased. The second pair then causes the ranking value of *Nas to be increased, and the ranking value of ID[nas] to be decreased. The GLA learner is completely unaware of the fact that these two pairs are contradictory; it just alters ranking values in response to each error. MRCD, on the other hand, is acutely aware of the contradiction, and is so preoccupied that it stops constructing a grammar. If one of the pairs is the result of a data error, then the obliviousness of the GLA pays off, giving it an intrinsic robustness to data errors that MRCD lacks. On the other hand, Section 24.6 below, on structural ambiguity, will argue that the ability to detect inconsistency can be quite valuable in dealing with certain challenges in learning. Constructing a learner that can do both in a satisfying way remains a significant challenge.

24.5   The subset problem and phonotactic learning

Language learning is done largely on the basis of positive evidence; the learner is provided with grammatical data, but not with explicitly labeled ungrammatical data. This can pose a challenge to purely error-driven learners when the linguistic theory defines languages with subset relations. If the grammatical forms of one language are a subset of the grammatical forms of another, then the data from the subset language will be fully consistent with the grammars for both languages. To correctly capture the generalizations of the language, the learner must be able to recognize that the grammar generating the more restrictive (subset) language better captures the learning data than the grammar generating the less restrictive (superset) language. This problem, known as the *subset problem*, requires the learner to attend to more than the ability of a grammar to generate the observed forms. The learner must (directly or indirectly) compare the relationships between multiple grammars and the observed data.

The subset problem relates to the Richness of the Base in Optimality Theory. All languages have the same possible inputs, so differences in restrictiveness between languages must be consequences of differences in constraint rankings. If language A is a proper subset of language B, then each input mapped by the ranking of B to an output not contained in A must be mapped by the ranking of A to some other output, an output in A. If the learner had access to all possible input–output pairs, this would not be a problem. But the learner isn't actually provided with input–output pairs in the data (as was assumed above). The learner is provided with grammatical outputs; the inputs must be inferred. Phonological alternations can provide some information about some non-faithful mappings, but not all, and properly analyzing alternations requires interaction with the determination of the ranking.

This problem of determining inputs can be finessed early in learning by assuming that the phonological input for each word matches the surface form. This is only tenable if the learner either ignores or is not yet aware of morphological relationships between the words. Such a stage has been labeled the phonotactic learning stage (Prince & Tesar 2004). The learner can gain partial information about the constraint ranking by looking for the most restrictive ranking that maps each observed form 'to itself'. The most restrictive ranking will map the most inputs corresponding to unobserved forms not to themselves but to other forms.

One proposal for dealing with restrictiveness relations between grammars builds on the observation that active markedness constraints tend to increase restrictiveness, while active faithfulness constraints tend to decrease restrictiveness. This leads to an intuitive expectation that rankings with lots of markedness constraints dominating lots of faithfulness constraints will be more restrictive than rankings showing the opposite pattern. This suggests an approach to the subset problem: given several rankings capable of producing the observed data, choose the one having the largest degree of markedness dominating faithfulness.

The restrictiveness effects of markedness dominating faithfulness are illustrated in (16) and (17). The rankings differ in the location of the faithfulness constraint ID[nas]: it is dominated by all markedness constraints in (16), but dominates two markedness constraints in (17).

(16)   Ranking: *–VOI/NAS » ID[voi] » {*VOI, *NAS} » ID[nas]
         Mapping: /ta/→[ta]   /da/→[da]   /n̥a/→[ta]   /na/→[da]
         Inventory: {[ta], [da]}

(17)   Ranking: *–VOI/NAS » {ID[voi], ID[nas]} » {*VOI, *NAS}
         Mapping: /ta/→[ta]   /da/→[da]   /n̥a/→[ta]   /na/→[na]
         Inventory: {[ta], [da], [na]}

The language in (16) is a subset of the language in (17); both contain [ta] and [da], but (17) also contains [na]. The more restrictive subset language has ID[nas] dominated by more markedness constraints, and maps /na/→[da].

Of course, it may not be entirely obvious just precisely what a 'degree of markedness dominating faithfulness' is, let alone how to compute the ranking with the greatest amount of it. A formalization of this notion is the *r-measure* (Prince & Tesar 2004). The r-measure assesses a constraint ranking by adding up the number of faithfulness constraints dominated by each markedness constraint, thus expressing 'degree of markedness dominating faithfulness' as a number. Rankings can be compared with respect to their r-measures, with higher r-measures suggesting (but not guaranteeing) greater restrictiveness. The ranking in (16) has r-measure 4, while the ranking in (17) has r-measure 2.

Recall that RCD ranks each constraint as high as possible, consistent with the data provided it. With respect to restrictiveness, this is the right thing to do for markedness constraints, but the wrong thing to do for faithfulness constraints. This is rectified by the Biased Constraint Demotion algorithm (BCD). BCD differs from RCD in that it introduces a bias against placing faithfulness constraints into the ranking. When constructing a stratum of a hierarchy, if both markedness and faithfulness constraints are available to be placed into the ranking, BCD will place the markedness constraints into the ranking but not the faithfulness constraints, with the effect that the faithfulness constraints will end up lower in the hierarchy (and thus be dominated by more markedness constraints).

BCD can be combined with MRCD in the same way the RCD can. Such a learner would construct its initial constraint hierarchy by applying BCD to an empty list of winner–loser pairs, like the one in (18).

(18)   *An empty list of winner–loser pairs*

input	win ~ lose	*VOI	*NAS	*–VOI/NAS	ID[voi]	ID[nas]

BCD observes that none of the constraints prefer any losers, so all are available. Some of them, however, are markedness constraints. BCD places the markedness constraints into the top stratum, but not the faithfulness constraints. Then, on the next pass, it observes that all remaining constraints are available, but all of them are faithfulness constraints, so they are placed into the next stratum, giving the constraint ranking in (19).

(19)   {*–VOI/NAS, *VOI, *NAS} » {ID[voi], ID[nas]}

This hierarchy has all markedness constraints dominating all faithfulness constraints. In this way, BCD derives as a consequence the initial ranking that has been proposed elsewhere (Demuth 1995b, Gnanadesikan 2004, Smolensky 1996, Hale & Reiss 1998).

Suppose that the target language is the one given in (16), with inventory {ti, ni}. The learner will observe [ni], assign it the input /ni/, parse /ni/ with the ranking in (19), and generate [ti]. This provokes the construction of the first winner–loser pair, shown in (20).

(20)   *First winner–loser pair for /ni/*

input	win ~ lose	*Voi	*Nas	*–Voi/Nas	ID[voi]	ID[nas]
/ni/	ni ~ ti	L	L	e	W	W

BCD now applies, and a complication arises. After *–Voi/Nas is ranked, a faithfulness constraint must be placed into the hierarchy. But which one? Either one will account for the winner–loser pair. If the learner chooses ID [nas], the correct one, they will end up with the correct ranking. But what if the learner mistakenly chooses ID[voi]? This would result in the hierarchy in (21).

(21)   *–Voi/Nas » ID[voi] » {*Voi, *Nas} » ID[nas]

The learner at this point will parse /ni/ with the new hierarchy, and generate [di], triggering construction of another winner–loser pair, which is then added to the list as shown in (22).

(22)   *The complete winner–loser pair list*

input	win ~ lose	*Voi	*Nas	*–Voi/Nas	ID[voi]	ID[nas]
/ni/	ni ~ ti	L	L	e	W	W
/ni/	ni ~ di	e	L	e	e	W

BCD now applies to this list, and the complication arises again: which faithfulness constraint to rank? This time, there is a basis for choosing. If the learner places ID[voi] into the ranking first, it will eliminate the first pair only, freeing up *Voi. The learner can then place *Voi into the hierarchy next, but must then rank ID[nas] before ranking *Nas. The resulting hierarchy would be (23), with an r-measure of 3.

(23)   Ranking: *–Voi/Nas » ID[voi] » *Voi » ID[nas] » *Nas
       Mapping: /ta/→[ta]   /da/→[da]   /n̥a/→[ta]   /na/→[na]
       Inventory: {[ta], [da], [na]}

BCD chooses, instead, to maximize the r-measure by choosing the faithfulness constraint that frees up the most markedness constraints. Here that is ID[nas], which accounts for both winner–loser pairs and thus frees up two markedness constraints. The resulting hierarchy, (24), has an r-measure of 4.

(24)   Ranking: *–Voi/Nas » ID[nas] » {*Voi, *Nas} » ID[voi]
       Mapping: /ta/→[ta]   /da/→[ta]   /n̥a/→[na]   /na/→[na]
       Inventory: {[ta], [na]}

By seeking to maximize the r-measure, the learner succeeds in finding the most restrictive grammar consistent with the observed data, solving the subset problem.

Neither BCD, nor the r-measure itself, are perfect. It is possible to construct cases where the hierarchy with the highest r-measure is not the most restrictive grammar, as well as cases where BCD fails to construct the hierarchy with the highest r-measure. For discussion and examples of such cases, see Prince & Tesar (2004).

24.6   Structural ambiguity

An *overt form* is the phonetically audible portion of an utterance. An *interpretation* of an overt form is a full structural description that is phonetically realized as the overt form. The problem of structural ambiguity arises when more than one interpretation may be assigned to the same overt form. Constraints evaluate entire structural descriptions, so the choice of interpretation for an overt form affects the relationship of that form to the grammar.

I will illustrate this problem with stress data from Polish (Rubach & Booij 1985). The word *spo'kojny* has three syllables and medial main stress. Assume for present purposes that GEN permits two interpretations of this overt form: a right-aligned trochaic foot, *spo('kojny)*, and a left-aligned iambic foot, *(spo'koj)ny*. The only way for the learner to choose between these interpretations is to appeal to other data from the language, data which may also be structurally ambiguous. Structural ambiguity is not idiosyncratic to foot structure; the problem arises with other levels of prosodic structure, such as syllable structure, as well as in many aspects of language outside of phonology.

This problem can be approached using an algorithm called the *Inconsistency Detection Learner*, or IDL (Tesar 2004). IDL works by considering different combinations of interpretations of overt forms, and determining which combinations are consistent, that is, which combinations of interpretations can be simultaneously optimal under some ranking. Given sufficient data, the correct combination of interpretations will be the only consistent one.

The illustration continues with a highly idealized linguistic system in which all feet are bisyllabic, and syllables are parsed into feet to the extent allowed by the bisyllabicity restriction. The constraints, which follow the basic pattern of generalized alignment (McCarthy & Prince 1993a), are given in (25).

(25)   *The Stress System Constraints*

   MAINL: the head foot should be aligned with the left edge of the word.

   MAINR: the head foot should be aligned with the right edge of the word.

TROCH: a head syllable should be aligned with the left edge of a foot.
IAMB: a head syllable should be aligned with the right edge of a foot.
FEETL: a foot should be aligned with the left edge of the word.
FEETR: a foot should be aligned with the right edge of the word.

Consider the overt forms given in (26) and (27). Each is structurally ambiguous, and the possible interpretations are indicated for each.

(26) OvertA: *spo'kojny*
      Interpretation A1: *spo('kojny)*
      Interpretation A2: *(spo'koj)ny*

(27) OvertB: *‚saksofo'nista*
      Interpretation B1: *(‚sakso)fo('nista)*
      Interpretation B2: *(‚sakso)(fo'ni)sta*

Suppose IDL processes OvertA first. IDL will observe that OvertA is structurally ambiguous, and separately pursue each interpretation by applying MRCD, building up a separate list of winner–loser pairs for each. The winner–loser pairs for interpretation A1 are shown in the first two rows of (28), while the winner–loser pairs for interpretation A2 are shown in the first two rows of (29).

The learner then processes OvertB, which also has two interpretations. The learner responds to this by creating and testing the four possible combinations of interpretations: A1+B1, A1+B2, A2+B1, and A2+B2. The learner tests a combination like A1+B1 by starting with the winner–loser pairs and the associated ranking for A1, and applying MRCD to B1, adding any new winner–loser pairs to the list for A1. This testing process results in either a hierarchy which makes both A1 and B1 optimal, or an inconsistency, indicating that at least one of the interpretations is wrong.

The correct combination of interpretations, A1+B1, results in a consistent set of winner–loser pairs, defining a ranking, as shown in (28). The incorrect combinations all result in inconsistency. For instance, the winner–loser pairs for A2+B1, shown in (29), are inconsistent, as is apparent from the fact that every constraint prefers at least one loser.

(28) *Winner–loser pairs for interpretations A1+B1*

win ~ lose	MAIN-L	MAIN-R	TROCH	IAMB	FEET-L	FEET-R
spo('kojny) ~ ('spokoj)ny	L	W			L	W
spo('kojny) ~ spo(koj'ny)			W	L		
(‚sakso)fo('nista) ~ sak(‚sofo)('nista)					W	L

(29) *Winner–loser pairs for interpretations A2+B1; they are inconsistent*

win ~ lose	MAIN- L	MAIN- R	TROCH	IAMB	FEET- L	FEET- R
(spoˈkoj)ny ~ spo(kojˈny)	W	L			W	L
(spoˈkoj)ny ~ (ˈspokoj)ny			L	W		
(ˌsakso)fo(ˈnista) ~ (sakˈso)(foˌni)sta	L	W	W	L	L	W

OvertA and OvertB are *mutually constraining*. OvertA constrains the inter-pretations of OvertB: interpretation B2 is not consistent with any interpret-ation of OvertA, so OvertA constrains the interpretation of OvertB to B1. Likewise, OvertB constrains the interpretation of OvertA to A1.

Once IDL has tested the combinations, it discards any inconsistent com-binations. The consistent combinations are retained as active hypotheses, just as the hypotheses for interpretations A1 and A2 were retained after processing OvertA above. It then proceeds on to process further data, combining their interpretations with each of the active hypotheses. Once enough data have been processed, IDL will have determined both the correct interpretations of the data and the correct grammar. In this fashion, IDL uses MRCD to simultaneously eliminate incorrect interpretations via in-consistency detection and construct a ranking based on the correct inter-pretations.

Given data that are all consistent with a single grammar, IDL is guar-anteed to find the correct combination of interpretations and a grammar consistent with them. The efficiency of IDL depends upon the linguistic system. One danger is forms with a very high degree of structural ambi-guity: if the learner needs to learn from the form, it will have to separ-ately consider each of the possible interpretations of the form. A second danger is growth in the combinations of interpretations, which can happen if forms are only weakly mutually constraining. If the learner processes three forms, each two-ways ambiguous, and the forms are not by themselves constraining enough to eliminate any of the combinations of interpretations, the learner will have 8 active hypotheses as a result. The number of combinations of interpretations, unchecked by mutual constraint, grows exponentially in the number of ambiguous overt forms.

IDL will require less work when overt forms have low degrees of ambiguity, and when overt forms are strongly mutually constraining. IDL can benefit from a bias towards processing forms with a low degree of ambiguity earlier. This is because the ranking information obtained from low ambiguity forms can collectively constrain a form with greater ambiguity, eliminating most or all of the latter form's incorrect inter-pretations.

24.7 Learning underlying forms

Learning the content of underlying forms is less well understood than the other issues addressed in this chapter, and it is the subject of current research. The problem is challenging in part because of the strong mutual dependence between the lexicon and the constraint ranking. In general, an underlying form for a morpheme cannot be confidently chosen independently of knowledge about the ranking. At the same time, all of the algorithms for constructing rankings presented in this chapter require underlying forms in order to function. The two need to be learned in tandem.

BCD, for phonotactic learning, can make progress by assuming underlying forms identical to surface forms, but that is not sufficient to determine the entire ranking. In fact, it is possible to have multiple languages with identical surface forms but different mappings: the underlying forms not identical to grammatical surface forms are mapped to different surface forms in different languages, and the different mappings are the result of different constraint rankings. Only information from morphemic alternations can distinguish from among such languages.

Two ideas for learning underlying forms have been proposed that build on the work already presented in this chapter. One proposal is to use the ranking that results from phonotactic learning to test different hypothesized underlying forms (Pater 2000a, Tesar & Prince to appear). This could involve using BCD during the phonotactic learning stage to construct a phonotactic ranking. Then, once the learner is able to segment the words into constituent morphemes, the learner could test different possible underlying forms for the morphemes using the phonotactic ranking, keeping those underlying forms that surface correctly in all attested contexts. When none of the possible underlying forms surfaces correctly in all contexts, it indicates to the learner a shortcoming of the phonotactic ranking, and the learner can explore further changes to ranking, testing them on that morpheme.

Another proposal is to use inconsistency detection to help choose underlying forms (Tesar et al. 2003).[2] The surgery learning algorithm uses MRCD combined with BCD as described in Section 24.5. The algorithm starts with an initial lexicon constructed by comparing the surface realizations of each morpheme to determine which features alternate (have different values in different contexts) and which features do not. The non-alternating features are set underlyingly to match their (unchanging) surface value, while the alternating features are initially set to a default unmarked value. The algorithm accumulates winner–loser pairs until an inconsistency is reached. This is the signal to the learner that something must change in their lexical hypothesis, because no change to the ranking alone can solve the problem. The learner then tries different changes to the lexicon, altering 'surgically' the winner–loser pairs that include the morpheme with the underlying form being altered. If a lexical change is found that resolves the inconsistency, the learner keeps the change to the lexicon.

24.8 Discussion

The learning challenges discussed here arise from the role of non-overt elements (both structural and lexical) in linguistic analyses, the need to relate the different and possibly non-identical surface realizations of a morpheme, and the reliance on positive evidence in learning. Non-overt elements pose a challenge when linguistic theory allows ambiguity, so that different languages assign different interpretations to the same overt forms. This is because of mutual dependence. The constraint ranking and the non-overt elements are mutually dependent, and neither is known in advance by the learner, so they must be learned together. In order to overcome that mutual dependence, the learner must relate different forms of the language to each other, via the grammar. Structural ambiguities must be addressed by relating the full structural descriptions of different forms to each other; underlying forms must be learned by relating the surface realizations of morphemes in different contexts to each other.

The proposed approaches to these challenges draw on the structure of linguistic theory in several ways. Structuring the space of possible grammars via possible rankings of violable constraints leads to an efficient algorithm for constructing rankings from structural descriptions, MRCD. The fact that MRCD detects inconsistency with equal efficiency makes it plausible to approach the problems of structural ambiguity and underlying forms with an inconsistency detection strategy. The fundamental organization of constraints into markedness constraints and faithfulness constraints provides the basis for BCD's approach to dealing with the lack of reliable negative evidence. The learner can be biased towards grammars with more markedness constraints dominating more faithfulness constraints.

Many learning challenges remain. The GLA is robust in the face of errors, but lacks the capacity for inconsistency detection, while BCD is capable of detecting inconsistency but lacks robustness. Clearly, it would be an accomplishment to capture both in a single approach. There is a great deal that is not yet understood about how underlying forms can be efficiently learned. And there are challenges beyond those discussed here, such as the matter of morpheme discovery itself, which has mutual dependencies with phonological learning: you need to know the morphological structure of words in order to identify morphemes that alternate across contexts and from that learn the phonology, but you need some grasp on the phonology in order to identify non-identical surface strings across words that plausibly represent the same morpheme. It remains to be seen if the strategies already developed for learning can be extended to these larger problems.

Notes

Valuable comments on early drafts of this chapter were provided by Paul de Lacy and Nazarré Merchant. Any errors are solely the responsibility of the author.

1 For an example involving parametric grammars, see the discussion by Sakas and Fodor (2001) of the Triggering Learning Algorithm (Gibson & Wexler 1994).

2 An idea of a similar spirit was proposed by Kager (1999a). His proposal used a learning algorithm that could not definitively detect inconsistencies in the way RCD can, and instead looked for patterns in the behavior of the learning algorithm to suggest inconsistency.

25

Phonological impairment in children and adults

Barbara Bernhardt
Joseph Paul Stemberger

25.1 Introduction

Phonological theories are developed primarily to account for synchronic
patterns in the spoken production of language by neurologically intact
adults. However, other sources of data also have the potential to inform
theory about the limits of human language. Jakobson (1941) took into
account language change, typical language development, aphasia, and statistical properties of phonology within and across languages. Bermúdez-Otero
(Ch.21) discusses language change, and Fikkert (Ch.23) deals with typical language development. We address atypical language function in this chapter.
Where phenomena in atypical phonological systems mirror those of normally functioning systems, claims about universality of the phenomena
may be strengthened. Where phenomena differ, theories may need to be
altered to account for the differences. The present chapter brings data from
children and adults with atypical phonological systems to bear on selected
phonological issues. Topics and definitions for the chapter are outlined below.

Atypical systems in child phonological development differ from atypical
adult systems in many ways that are beyond the scope of this paper. When
a mature system suffers damage, it does not become identical to an immature system that has strayed from the path of normal development; and
mature systems can be damaged in many different ways. Nonetheless,
there are many similarities between the two types of atypical systems
(emphasized by Jakobson and many others). In this paper, we will present
a discussion of similar properties presented in a parallel fashion, without
emphasizing the differences between the child and adult systems.

25.1.1 Topics and definitions of phonological terms

Three topics in phonological theory are addressed in this chapter: (1)
markedness, (2) phonological representations, and (3) phonology–morphology

interactions. The first two topics are core to phonology, concerning what is understood about universality and underlying (or input) forms and surface (or output) forms. (For details, see Rice (Ch.4) for markedness and Harris (Ch.6) for representation.) The third topic has been addressed frequently in recent years, especially with the advent of Optimality Theory (OT), where phonology–morphology interactions are often highlighted.

A reasonably standard instantiation of *markedness* is assumed here. In OT, in most cases, the relative markedness of one output with respect to another output is expressed via constraint ranking: the constraints against the more marked output are ranked higher than the constraints against the less marked or unmarked output (Prince & Smolensky 2004). (Less commonly, there may be a constraint against the marked output, but no constraint against the unmarked output.) As Jakobson (1941) noted, marked elements are usually less frequent than unmarked elements, and may be more complex in terms of articulation or the cognitive resources required. The least marked element in a contrasting set of possible outputs is the *default*; the default often appears in the output when some element must be present, if there is no reason to produce a more marked element. For example, for each binary feature, there is a marked (nondefault) value and an unmarked (default) value; for privative features (such as for place), one feature is generally taken to be the unmarked default (e.g. [Coronal]), while the others ([Labial, Dorsal]) are marked nondefaults. Most phonologists have assumed that markedness relations are universal, but at least some markedness relations may differ across languages (see Archangeli and Pulleyblank 1994) and across individuals during language acquisition (Bernhardt and Stemberger 1998). In the present chapter, syllabic and segmental data from atypical phonological systems are brought to bear on the topics of universal and individual markedness; phenomena are also included that show the effects of markedness on output.

In this chapter, the term *phonological representation* encompasses the basic phonological elements (such as features or gestures), their definitions and properties, and how they are coordinated to create larger structures. Aspects of representations that are taken for granted in some theories (e.g. that there is syllable structure) may differ on the details (e.g. whether or not there is an onset node) and have not been a part of all theories (e.g. the lack of syllable structure in Chomsky and Halle 1968). In this chapter the focus is on consonant–vowel representations, and on evidence suggesting that syllable structure has an effect on atypical acquisition and in aphasic speech.

The third topic concerns phonology–morphology interactions, with a focus on reduplication, epenthesis and zero-marking. Phonological constraints can affect the phonological shape of an affix and even whether the affix is (overtly) present, a phenomenon often referred to as *zero-marking* in the child language and psycholinguistics literatures.

In this chapter, we take an approach that has some differences from the most common approaches within OT. Bernhardt and Stemberger (1998) argue that, in order to make communication with related disciplines possible, certain presentational aspects of OT must be altered. They develop a more transparent system for constraint names that are more explicit and systematic in form and that always suggest their meaning. They avoid abbreviation (including use of the asterisk in place of English 'not', and also the shortening of names in constraint tables). Since this chapter especially is intended to cut across disciplines, we adopt here this system that is designed for greater clarity.

25.1.2 Definitions of non-phonological terms

A number of terms have been used to indicate difficulty in speech production. For children, common terms include: articulation or phonological delay, disorder, deviance or impairment; childhood apraxia of speech; and dysarthria. For adults, common terms include: neurogenic language or speech disorder or impairment; aphasia (with subtypes such as Broca's, Wernicke's, conduction, global, and others, and with a common division into fluent and non-fluent aphasias); apraxia of speech; dysarthria; speech sound disturbance; among others. Labels that include the term *phonological* generally focus on the representational (cognitive) aspect of speech/language production, whereas those that utilize the term *speech sound*, *articulation*, *apraxia/dyspraxia*, and *dysarthria* focus on motor aspects of speech production. Such labels imply a strong division between phonology and phonetics, which is controversial but commonly assumed in both competence (e.g. Chomsky and Halle 1968) and performance models of human language (Garrett 1975; Levelt 1989).

In this chapter, the term *atypical phonological system* is used. The word *phonological* is broadly defined and denotes the representation, processing and execution of speech sounds. The term *atypical* implies a difference from typical phonology, a difference which is often one of degree. A child with an atypical phonological system may show phenomena similar to those of typically developing children, but develops more slowly and may show patterns that are uncommon across children (e.g. Beers 1995; Bernhardt and Stemberger 1998; Grunwell 1987; Ingram 1980; Ingram and Terselic 1983). Atypical patterns may be unusual because of *chronological mismatches* (where the child's system combines phenomena usually found in younger systems with phenomena usually found in older systems) or because some aspect of the adult language is realized in a fashion that is rare for typically developing children. It should be noted that the boundary between typical and atypical development is unclear; we do not know how delayed something must be, or how unusual an idiosyncratic pattern must be, before the system is truly atypical, rather than simply near the edge of the distribution of typical systems. Adults with neurogenic language impairments may show phenomena similar to the much less frequent speech errors or slips of the tongue of neurologically intact adults (albeit at a much higher error rate), with some types of errors exacerbated more than others, and with some added qualitative differences. Most adults with neurogenic language impairments who make sound errors (or at least, those whose outputs still contain recognizable and more-or-less appropriately used words) do not entirely lose any particular phonological target type (codas, complex onsets, particular phonemes, etc.), but show variability between correct and incorrect outputs. Finally, the term *system* implies organization and coherence. While some children and adults with atypical phonological systems show more variability than typically developing children and neurologically intact adults, even the most atypical phonological system nonetheless has a systematic aspect.

25.2   Children with atypical phonological systems

The following sections about children's atypical phonological systems address, in turn, syllable and segmental markedness, phonological representation, and phonology–morphology interactions.

25.2.1   Syllable markedness in children with atypical phonological systems

A general observation about phonological development is that marked structures *tend* to emerge later than unmarked structures (e.g. Jakobson 1941; Bernhardt and Stemberger 1998; Levelt, Schiller and Levelt 1999/ 2000). The data from children with atypical phonological development are generally congruent with this observation. Even where the data appear exceptional, markedness continues to be relevant, with children showing a less common option for overcoming multiple markedness constraints. The following section outlines trends in syllable structure development, indicating where children with atypical development follow the trend and where some may diverge. The most common divergences concern the relative order of coda versus onset elaboration, and the relative order of onset clusters versus codas.

What are the common trends in syllable structure development? The CV syllable is considered the least marked syllable type cross-linguistically (e.g. Jakobson, 1941; Blevins 1995), and thus would be predicted to be the earliest acquired syllable type. This does appear to be true for most children (Bernhardt and Stemberger 1998; Levelt et al. 1999/2000). Although singleton codas can occur in children's early words (Bernhardt and Stoel-Gammon 1996; Lleo, El Mogharbel and Prinz 1994), codas typically appear only later in the second year, and consonant clusters only in the third year (Stoel-Gammon and Dunn 1985). Levelt et al. (1999/2000) observed the following progression in syllable type acquisition for 12 typically develop-ing Dutch children: (1) CV only, (2) CV plus CVC, (3) CV and CVC plus V and

VC, and finally, (4) all syllable types, including those with clusters; they note, however, that individual children could skip stages in the course of development. Whether or not all CV(C) syllables started with a consonant (which is unclear, because a glottal stop was apparently used as a diacritic before vowels in initial position to facilitate automatic counts in this study, regardless of whether one was present phonetically), the observed progression is generally consistent with data from many typically developing English-speaking children.

Many English-speaking children with atypical phonological systems follow the same order of acquisition of syllable types as indicated above (i.e. CV > CVC > CCV/CVCC), with some children showing very protracted development of the more marked codas and clusters (Stoel-Gammon and Dunn 1985). However, there are children who diverge from the common path. Some children show *initial consonant deletion* (Yavaş 1998), with initial stages of V and VC that were unattested in the Levelt et al. (1999/2000) study. Other children acquire CCV before CVC (Bernhardt and Stoel-Gammon 1996), diverging from the Levelt at al. study (1999/2000) at stage 2. We address the ramifications of these two divergences in turn.

The emergence of vowel-initial syllables (via initial consonant deletion) before CV syllables does not follow from predictions of markedness. Whether or not the initial consonant is actually deleted (or is in fact an untranscribed glottal onset, as observed in Bernhardt 1990), it is uncommon for children to develop a much larger inventory of features in codas than in onsets in early phonological development. To illustrate, one 3-year-old with atypical development used only [ʔ] and [h] as word-initial onsets, but produced a variety of codas: labial and coronal stops and nasals, and coronal fricatives (Dan – Major and Bernhardt 1998). How can this uncommon profile be reconciled with the notion of markedness as a relevant factor in order of acquisition?

The high-ranked constraint requiring onsets (for the least marked form, CV) can perhaps be satisfied with any onset. As faithfulness increases for both codas and features, the features could appear in the (new) coda position or in onset. Although onset elaboration may be more common for feature development, coda elaboration is presumably another option. In either case, the general developmental process is the same: faithfulness constraints gradually overcome markedness constraints. There may be an additional explanation. Because a coda in utterance-final position is followed by silence, it is more salient in some ways than the onset. The presence of segments after the onset can distract attention, while the silence after an utterance-final coda allows the immediate processing of the segment; a *recency effect* for final elements is common in tasks involving memory, including learning tasks. The high saliency of utterance-final position has been argued to facilitate the learning of verbs (Naigles and Hoff-Ginsberg 1998) and pronouns (Stemberger 2003), as well as to make reduction less likely in historical sound changes (e.g. Guy 1991b). This may be true for codas for some children, especially given that utterance-final position facilitates the learning of words, despite the fact that codas in non-utterance-final position are less salient than onsets (e.g. Steriade 1999a). Many questions remain regarding the pattern of early coda elaboration.

The second infrequent pattern concerns emergence of CCV before CVC. If a language does not have both codas and complex onsets, the language is more likely to have codas than complex onsets, although a few languages have complex onsets but no codas (Blevins 1995). Codas could therefore be considered less marked than complex onsets. Two of the 22 English-speaking children with atypical development in Bernhardt and Stoel-Gammon's (1996) study acquired CCV (stop-glide clusters) before CVC. Acquisition of CCV before CVC is perhaps just one option for development when there are several marked structures to acquire. A child may develop the marked settings for onsets or codas in either order (even though, for whatever reason, most children develop codas before complex onsets). This divergent pattern suggests that there is no single hierarchy of markedness encompassing all syllable structures, but rather separate hierarchies for each syllable position.

The data regarding codas and onsets from children with atypical development confirm the relevance of markedness in development. Marked structures generally emerge later than unmarked structures. Even in the case of apparent exceptions, children can be seen as following a less common option when overcoming multiple markedness constraints.

25.2.2   Segmental markedness in children's atypical phonological systems

In child speech, unmarked features tend to be highly frequent, to substitute for other features, and to be targets of consonant harmony (Bernhardt and Stemberger 1998; Stoel-Gammon and Stemberger 1994). The unmarked (or default) features are *generally* the same as those of the adult language, but may diverge, in children with typical or atypical phonological systems. Children with atypical development appear to follow the general trends of typically developing children in acquisition of manner and voicing features, which show development of marked elements later than unmarked elements. In the clinical literature, it has been suggested that children with atypical phonological systems may be more likely to show divergence in terms of place feature defaults; more children with atypical systems may show [Dorsal] defaults than typically developing children, who are more likely to have the more expected [Coronal] place default (Yavaş 1998). This section discusses patterns for manner, laryngeal and place features in turn, outlining common and uncommon developmental paths and their relationship to theories of markedness.

Children with atypical development generally follow the patterns of typically developing children in acquisition of manner features. The less marked stops, glides and nasals are generally acquired earlier than the more marked fricatives and liquids (with the earlier segments substituting for the later, more marked segments). It has been reported that some children with atypical development substitute later-developing (more marked) categories for earlier ones: e.g. fricatives for stops or [l] for fricatives (Yavaş 1998). Typically developing children can also show such patterns, however: e.g. use of [l] for coronal fricatives in early words (Bernhardt and Stemberger 1998). The variability across children (with typical or atypical development) in terms of which marked categories develop first suggests that there is not a single markedness scale that encompasses all features. Rather, each feature has a marked and an unmarked value, and the unmarked value generally develops first. While there are some strong statistical tendencies about which marked feature values develop first, a child's system can develop the marked values of different features (e.g. [+continuant] versus [+lateral]) in many different orders.

As noted, some children (with typical or atypical phonological systems) have been reported to show earlier development of the apparently marked value of a feature than of the unmarked value, for example, substituting fricatives for oral stops. There are several ways to account for this uncommon pattern. First, for such children, the unmarked default value of the feature may be opposite to what is expected, so that fricatives appear first or develop more quickly than stops: [+continuant] rather than [−continuant]. However, there is another way to think about markedness, based on the entire phonological system. The feature [−continuant] is the unmarked value only for consonants, whereas the unmarked value for vowels is [+continuant]. Within OT, it is reasonable to assume that there is a single ranking of markedness constraints such that [+continuant] is the *global default* for that feature; because of the frequency of vowels, glides, fricatives, and /h/ in English, [+continuant] is the more frequent value of this feature (occurring in 68.2% of all segments in the Denes (1963) English phoneme frequency count). For [−continuant] to *behave* as if it were a default for consonants, it is necessary to make use of constraints on feature co-occurrence, such that obstruents prefer the global nondefault value [−continuant]; while this can be accomplished via constraints against the co-occurrence of two features in the same segment (in our system, **NotCo-occurring(−sonorant,+continuant)**), Bernhardt and Stemberger (1998) argue for constraints in which the presence of one feature implies the presence of another, such as **Co-occurring(−sonorant→−continuant)**. For most children, this co-occurrence constraint will be high-ranked from an early age; for some atypically developing children, it may be low-ranked. A third explanation is to assume that fricatives are more developed than stops for reasons other than markedness: the feature [+continuant] is assimilated from the vowel. If constraints prevent consonants from having an independent value of the feature [continuant], the only choices are to delete consonants, convert them into vowels/glides, or assimilate

[+continuant] from vowels. It is unusual for consonants to assimilate features from vowels to this degree (Ní Chiosáin and Padgett 1993), but this is an uncommon phenomenon. Both alternative analyses are interesting, but it is unclear which is more likely to be correct (and both may be correct, for different children). We are unaware of any reports in which a child replaced all oral stops with fricatives, but markedness does not predict any such reversals, at least word initially. To illustrate, Charles (5 years 11 months old: Bernhardt and Stemberger 1998) replaced all sibilants with [θ] (a not uncommon pattern), but also substituted [θ] for most word-initial /t/'s. It is perhaps relevant that the only substitution of a fricative for a stop was for /t/, which generally is considered to have only default features in English.

In terms of voicing features, developmental patterns often reflect context: short lag stops (i.e. with no voicing during closure and with voicing starting soon after release) generally emerge earlier prevocalically, and voiceless obstruents postvocalically. However, occasional children have initial prevoiced stops (true voiced stops with voicing during closure) and no short-lag stops (Bernhardt and Stemberger 1998). Children with atypical phonological systems do not tend to differ from typically developing children regarding voicing. The same two alternative analyses presented above are relevant: either [+voiced] is the global default (and **Co-occurring (−sonorant→−voiced)** is too low-ranked for [−voiced] to behave like a default for obstruents), or [+voiced] is assimilating from the following vowel (Stoel-Gammon and Dunn 1985).

In terms of place features, [Coronal] ([+anterior]) is often considered the default feature (Paradis and Prunet 1991a) for adult phonology (although Lombardi (2002) argues that this is merely the least marked *oral* place feature, and that only glottals are truly unmarked for place). Most children appear to have default use of [Coronal]: coronals are frequent, substitute for other places of articulation and are the target of consonant harmony (Stoel-Gammon and Stemberger 1994) (e.g. [gag] for 'dog'). Bernhardt and Stemberger (1998) report that occasional children may even epenthesize coronal stops when the target syllable has no onset: e.g. 'lion' [laɪdən]. However, some children (typically or atypically developing) may show [Labial] or [Dorsal] place defaults. In the clinical literature, it has been suggested that children with atypical phonological systems are more likely to show 'backing' of alveolars (i.e. a [Dorsal] default) than typically developing children (Yavaş 1998). If [Labial] or [Dorsal] is the default, labials or dorsals should show patterns typical of coronal defaults – i.e. be highly frequent, appear as substitutions for other place features, and be the target of place harmony. We are unaware of any reports in the literature that have examined data from all of these perspectives. Based on frequency and substitution patterns, Colin (Bernhardt and Stemberger 1998) showed a possible [Dorsal] default. He used a large number of velar stops, which substituted for many other consonants (stops, fricatives, nasals, and liquids). Labial targets sometimes surfaced as labials, but [Labial] never replaced other articulator features, suggesting [Labial] was a nondefault. Coronals did not substitute for other segments and were infrequent in the system, being limited to a very few imitated words with initial [n] (and the spontaneously produced <u>no</u>) or final [s]. The high frequency of [Dorsal] and its prevalence in substitution patterns suggests that [Dorsal] was the default. Velars were not the target of place harmony, however, making velar's status as a default less clear. Furthermore, since the child's vowels were almost invariably [a], it is possible that [Dorsal,+back] assimilated from the vowel; his most common word was [gak]. The same two alternatives thus exist for the place features as for the fricative manner features discussed above: an unusual (global) default for consonants deriving from the unmarked value ([Dorsal,+back]) for vowels, or (velar) assimilation from a vowel.

Some children with atypical systems may show no or very few oral place features, replacing all or many segments with glottal stops or [h]. 'Glottal replacement' has been noted to occur more in the speech of children with atypical phonological systems (e.g. Stoel-Gammon and Dunn, 1985; Yavaş 1998). Depending on the assumed analysis of place features, there are two alternative explanations for this phenomenon. First, if glottals are assumed to have no place features, then they are a reasonable substitution if consonants do not allow place features. Glottals allow a well-formed output without assimilating any place features, even from the vowel. Alternatively, if glottals have a non-oral place feature such as [+glottal], then this is the unmarked place feature for consonants (as Lombardi (2002) has argued universally, on the basis of the commonness of epenthetic [ʔ] contrasted with the rareness of epenthetic coronals). However, the majority of children do not show pervasive use of glottal stop; it appears to emerge as a true default in only a small minority of children with atypical phonological systems. It is possible to argue that 'glottals-only' systems simply have no consonantal place features and that the epenthesis of [ʔ] is common because the lack of place features leads to fewer violations of markedness constraints against the appearance of features, such as **Not(Coronal)**.

There is a question about the stability of defaults throughout development (typical or atypical). Lotte, a German-speaking 3-year-old child with an atypical phonological system (Ullrich 2004) initially replaced velars with coronals. After a 4-month period (before speech therapy), the opposite pattern was observed: when velars entered the system, they frequently replaced coronals in non-assimilatory contexts. The over-generalization of [Dorsal] suggests a possible change in default status. Showing the opposite pattern, Colin (see above) showed a preponderance of alveolars after speech therapy, which replaced many other segments. From a system-wide Place default ([Dorsal,+back] for both consonants and vowels), [Coronal, +anterior] possibly became the C-Place default, in line with adult English.

25.2.3   Summary: markedness and children with atypical phonological systems

In summary, there is a general tendency for atypical phonological development to conform to the predictions of universal markedness, although
some children may show patterns that appear to contradict universal
markedness. Where there are options in language development, the universally unmarked option is likely to be developmentally earlier. But the
apparently more marked option may develop earlier for a variety of
reasons: utterance-final salience (coda elaboration before onsets), articulatory skill (use of 'marked' feature values from consonants, which come
from the default values for vowels via assimilation), randomness in the
initial state (Bernhardt and Stemberger 1998; but cf. the assumption of
Tesar and Smolensky 1998 that all children have the same initial state),
randomness in the resolution of multiple constraints (clusters acquired
before codas), or input frequency. In terms of input frequency, Pye, Ingram
and List (1987) posit a 'functional load' hypothesis for order of acquisition:
they observed the early acquisition of affricates in Quiche Mayan, attributing
the early emergence to their relative high frequency in that language.
Whatever variation there might be in developmental order or patterns,
phonological development (typical and atypical) entails ever-increasing
faithfulness to the ambient language targets and overcoming of markedness constraints in some order that reflects the various interactions of
individual child and language variables.

25.2.4   Phonological representation in children with atypical phonological systems

This section addresses consonant and vowel representation in children
with atypical phonological systems. Harmony and metathesis patterns in
children's phonology are relevant to this discussion. In both the phonology
and phonetics literature, the relative independence of consonants and
vowels has been debated. One proposal places consonants and vowels on
different planes (e.g. McCarthy 1989). McCarthy (1995) has since argued that
CV separation is not needed to account for the facts that motivated his 1989
proposal. However, earlier, Öhman (1966) proposed CV separation in order
to account for vowel-to-vowel coarticulation and Fowler (1980) suggested
that CV separation accounted for phonetic shortening effects of consonants
on vowels. Even if phonological phenomena rarely argue strongly for CV
separation, one can argue that Cs and Vs are on different planes on
phonetic and performance grounds.

In child phonological development, distant consonant harmony and
metathesis are not uncommon (e.g. *dig* as [ɡɪɡ]). Some children with atypical
phonological systems show pervasive harmony and metathesis patterns
(e.g. Harry: Stemberger and Bernhardt 1997). If harmony and metathesis

can skip intervening vowels, consonants and vowels must in some way be independent of one another in representation.

However, a child may show *both* interaction of consonants and vowels (assimilation or dissimilation), *and* distant consonant harmony or metathesis (e.g. Livia: Bernhardt and Stemberger 2000). Although Livia produced labials, coronals and dorsals, there were contextual restrictions. Comparing /t/ and /k/, she usually produced [t] onsets only around high vowels, and [k] onsets only before non-high vowels. This pattern showed a possible CV interaction of a dissimilatory nature: the back of the tongue is relatively low for /t/, and thus contrasts with the high back tongue position of high vowels; for velars, the tongue dorsum is high, and thus contrasts with the lower dorsum position for non-high vowels (1).

(1)

	Pronunciation	
	Adult	*Child*
shoe	[ʃuː]	[tuː]
key	[kʰiː]	[t̪iː]
doll	[dɑːɫ]	[gɑː]

This same child also showed consonant harmony across vowels. She did not produce labials in codas unless there was a preceding labial consonant in the syllable (double linking of [Labial] across vowels). When there was no preceding labial, two options were available for labials: replacement with [Coronal], or progressive assimilation of [Dorsal] (across vowels) (2).

(2)

	Pronunciation		
	Adult	*Child*	
plum	[plʌ̃m]	[pʌ̃m]	Double-linked [Labial]
cup	[kʰʌp]	[kʰʌk]/[kʰʌt]	Double-linked [Dorsal] or [Coronal] default insertion for [p]
soap	[soʊp]	[kot]	[Coronal] default insertion for /p/

The place harmony and double linking of labial place suggest independence of C-Place and V-Place. However, the height dissimilation suggests sequential CV interaction. The divergence of place and height patterns with respect to interaction and independence of consonants and vowels is intriguing and a topic for further investigation.

25.2.5 Phonology–morphology interactions in children with atypical phonological systems

Phonology and morphology may show independence or interaction in development in children with typical or atypical phonological systems. English-learning children with SLI (Specific Language Impairment) have been noted to have difficulty with grammatical morphemes, which may in some cases reflect phonological difficulty: i.e. with coda cluster production, or production of unstressed elements (e.g. Leonard and MacGregor 1992); however, very little is known about the relationship of phonology and morphology in children with atypical phonological systems.

In terms of interaction, high-ranked phonological constraints can either prohibit or facilitate expression of morphological affixes (Bernhardt and Stemberger 1998). For example, if high-ranked constraints prohibit complex codas and lead to greater faithfulness to stops than to fricatives, the child will reduce 'fox' /faks/ to [fak] and *rocks* to [wak] (with apparent zero-marking of plurality); but the same faithfulness to stops will lead to reduction of 'ask' /æsk/ to [æk] and 'laughed' /læft/ to [læt], with past tense expressed overtly. Similarly, if high-ranked constraints lead to greater faithfulness to fricatives than to stops, the child will retain the /s/ of /ks/: Emma (Baker 2000) reduced 'box' /bɔks/ to [bɔs] and 'blocks' /blɔks/ to [bɔs]; because constraint rankings favoured the output of the /s/, plurality could be overtly expressed. The same level of faithfulness to fricatives leads to nonexpression of past tense in some forms, however: 'laughed' /læft/ to [læf], cf. 'ask' /æsk/ to [æs]. If the constraint against complex clusters is ranked above the constraints promoting expression of the morphology, no affix is overtly marked after a consonant-final base (Bernhardt and Stemberger 1998); if faithfulness is greater to fricatives, we find 'fox' reduced to [fas] but 'rocks' produced as [wak], with no expression of plurality. If faithfulness to the base morpheme is additionally ranked higher than the markedness constraint prohibiting clusters, the word 'fox' /faks/ will surface as [faks], even though the similar consonant cluster in 'rocks' (surfacing as [rak], with no plural marking) is avoided. Bernhardt and Stemberger (1998) argue that the apparent difficulty with inflectional morphology in SLI may in fact be due to phonological problems: phonologically marked codas and coda clusters are avoided, especially in inflected forms, but to a lesser extent even in monomorphemic forms in the speech of SLI children.

25.3   Adults with atypical phonological systems arising on an acquired neurogenic basis

The following sections address markedness, phonological representation and phonology–morphology interactions in the speech of adults with atypical phonological systems that arise on an acquired neurogenic basis.

25.3.1   Structural (and segmental) markedness and adult neurogenic disorders

Nickels and Howard (2004) note that large effects have been reported for structural markedness in the speech of adults with acquired neurogenic impairments, especially for syllable structures: more marked structures are subject to greater error rates than less marked structures. They note, however, that there is a confound between the markedness of a syllable and the number of phonemes: unmarked CV syllables have fewer phonemes than marked CCV and CVC syllables, which have fewer than highly marked CCCV and CVCC syllables. Is this truly an effect of markedness, or merely a quantitative effect, showing that words with more phonemes are more difficult? Nickels and Howard investigated this issue with nine English-speaking adults with aphasia (both fluent and nonfluent, including some with apraxia of speech). When they controlled for number of phonemes (contrasting e.g. CVCV words with CCVC words), effects of syllable markedness largely disappeared. Some participants did show syllable markedness effects, in that CVCV words, with simple CV syllables, were more accurate than CCVC and CVCC syllables, with more marked structures.

Romani and Galluzzi (2005) argue that markedness plays a much greater role. They develop a numerical measure of the overall markedness of a word, with specific numerical contributions for specific types of markedness. For example, benchmarking unmarked CV as zero, a complex onset or a simple coda adds 1, and absence of an onset in word-initial position adds 0.5. The measure also includes segmental markedness in the form of position-specific sonority effects: low sonority yields low markedness scores in onsets, but high markedness scores in codas; and the greater the difference in sonority in a cluster, the lower the markedness. They examined this issue with 13 Italian-speaking adults with aphasia (7 fluent and 6 nonfluent) using the repetition of single presented words. They found an effect of phoneme length, but also found an independent effect of markedness. One crucial finding was that consonant deletion is common in CCV, but rare in CV syllables, as predicted by markedness but not by phoneme length. Interestingly, only the nonfluent participants showed an effect of markedness, a finding that the authors could not explain.

While demonstrating the relevance of markedness for the production of words in the speech of adults with neurogenic impairments, there are limitations to such studies. For normal language production, Stemberger and Treiman (1986) proposed *the Addition Bias*: when there is interference between two words being produced in the same utterance (and possibly, by extension, between two syllables within the same word), there is a tendency to add phonemes rather than to delete them. For example, in a nonsense word pair under experimental conditions such as 'type troll', the error 'tripe troll' (with an added phoneme) is far more common than the error 'type toll' (with a deleted phoneme). Stemberger and Treiman interpret this as a faithfulness effect: when interference leads to competition in the output between /t/ vs. /tr/, faithfulness biases the system towards /tr/, in both the target word and the interfering word. Stemberger (1990) argues that the Addition Bias holds only for errors involving interference between two competing words or syllables; if the error occurs as a part of planning the word or syllable in the absence of interference from nearby sounds, then there is a bias towards losing phonemes (a bias towards higher frequency or less marked syllables or sequences). Most research on aphasia does not partition errors out into those that involve interference versus those that do not (though terms such as *syntagmatic* versus *paradigmatic* phonological paraphasias are used by some researchers – e.g. Lecours and Lhermitte 1969). Romani and Galluzzi show that the different sensitivity to syllable markedness for nonfluent versus fluent patients does not derive from differences in the proportion of errors involving interference between nearby phonemes and syllables (where faithfulness leads to the retention of phonemes and so to more marked structures) versus the proportion of non-interference planning errors (where markedness leads to unfaithfulness and less marked structures). Indeed, their nonfluent patients did not show an addition bias in contextual errors, while the fluent patients did. However, further research is needed to pull apart the effects of markedness versus faithfulness in the speech of these aphasic patients (and whether the Addition Bias, which is observed for normals when there is interference between words, is also observed where there is interference between sounds within a single word).

25.3.2   Segmental markedness and adult neurogenic disorders

Effects of segmental markedness have also been investigated for adults with atypical phonological systems arising on an acquired neurogenic basis. Jakobson (1941) suggested that more errors occur on marked than on unmarked features for persons with aphasia. The markedness of place features has been addressed several times; Béland, Paradis and Bois (1993) provide an extensive and intriguing investigation of the effects of the default status of [Coronal] versus the nondefault status of [Labial] and [Dorsal]. In their study, 23 French-speaking adults with aphasias of various types (Broca's aphasia, Wernicke's aphasia, conduction aphasia, mixed aphasia, and progressive aphasia) repeated words and nonwords of various lengths, containing a critical consonant cluster or singleton consonant; the clusters contained consonants with two different places of articulation, either two marked places of articulation (labial, velar, or nonanterior coronal) or one marked place of articulation combined with an anterior coronal place of articulation. They examined errors in which the number of marked place features did not change, versus errors resulting in one fewer marked place feature. Errors that did not change the number of marked place features were equally common on both types of clusters, showing no inherent difference in error rates between the different cluster types. For errors that resulted in one less marked place feature, there was a significant effect of the number of marked place features: 10% of all trials for two-marked-feature clusters, versus only 2% of trials for clusters with only one marked feature. Clusters involving two marked place features were clearly more difficult for the patients than clusters involving one marked and one unmarked place feature.

In OT, there are constraints against sequences of non-identical elements. Bernhardt and Stemberger (1998: ch. 7) emphasize the role of such constraints in the development of consonant clusters and of the sequencing of place and manner features across the word, and the role of default vs. nondefault features in those constraints (see Section 25.3.1 above). Béland et al. show that sequences of nondefault features are especially difficult. Within OT, the constraint **NoSequence (Labial ... Dorsal)** (which prohibits the sequence of a labial consonant followed by a dorsal consonant, if the two consonants are adjacent) is ranked higher than **NoSequence (Labial ... Coronal)** and **NoSequence (Dorsal ... Coronal)**. In adult French, all three must be low-ranked, in order for speakers to produce words with such sequences. In aphasic impairments, we can posit that the rankings are more variable, such that markedness constraints are sometimes ranked higher than faithfulness constraints, leading to elevated rates of errors (unfaithfulness). It should be noted that it is also possible to argue that the observed effects actually reflect the frequency of the features: the lower type and token frequency of nondefault features make them more vulnerable to error, *especially* in combination with other low-frequency elements. However, Bernhardt and Stemberger (1998) argued that constraint rankings are correlated with frequency, and that these are in fact not different explanations, but merely different ways of stating the same effects.

25.3.3   Phonological representation and adult neurogenic disorders

The issue of consonant and vowel representation has recently been addressed by some researchers using data from adults with neurogenic speech impairments. Caramazza, Chialant, Capasso, and Miceli (2000) address the representation of consonants versus vowels using data from two fluent Italian-speaking adults with aphasia. Within neuropsychological studies, it is commonly argued that the best evidence that two things are stored in different parts of the brain or controlled by different processing mechanisms is a *double dissociation*: some patients show a far greater impairment with A than with B, while others show a greater impairment with B than with A. Double dissociations rule out a simple explanation that A or B is inherently more difficult and so is affected more by brain damage. Caramazza et al. demonstrate a double dissociation between consonants and vowels. The two participants in their study repeated words spoken by the experimenter; previous tests demonstrated that these two patients rarely misperceived auditorily presented words, so almost all errors in this task could be attributed to difficulties with production. One participant showed the most common pattern in aphasia, a high error rate on consonants (28.2%) versus a low error rate on vowels (5.3%). The other patient showed the opposite pattern, a low error rate on consonants (9.3%) versus a high error rate on vowels (26.9%). Caramazza et al. addressed whether the differences could be accounted for in terms of features, by examining the effects of features found in both consonants and vowels. Higher-sonority consonants share more manner features with vowels than low-sonority consonants, but sonority was uncorrelated with the rate of errors on different consonants. Consonants with back tongue constrictions (velars and liquids) were no more or less affected than other consonants. The deficits did not simply arise from differential damage to vowel versus consonant manner or place features.

Caramazza et al. argue that consonants and vowels are stored in separate locations in the brain (i.e. in separate channels – Öhman 1966 – or on separate planes – McCarthy 1989), but there are other explanations. Monaghan and Shilcock (2003) have argued that vowels and consonants can be learned in a dissociated fashion in a connectionist model that does not inherently distinguish between consonants and vowels, in such a way that consonants and vowels can be differentially affected by brain damage. More generally, if we assume that syllable structure includes the notions of 'head' and 'nonhead' as part of the representation, then the results here could come from differential damage to the head versus nonhead position in the syllable, leading to greater error rates in the damaged position(s) than in relatively undamaged positions. Caramazza et al.'s results throw important light on phonology, and suggest that consonants and vowels are more independent of each other than generally recognized in recent phonological theories, but further research is needed to determine the exact nature of that independence.

25.3.4 Phonology–morphology interactions and adult neurogenic disorders

It is a standard assumption of modern phonological theory that the realization of inflectional morphemes is strongly affected by phonological markedness constraints (see Section 25.2.4 above). One resulting phenomenon is *morphological haplology* (Stemberger, 1981) or *the repeated morph constraint* (Menn and MacWhinney 1984): an expected affix is apparently absent if it is identical to an adjacent affix or to the adjacent portion of the stem. In the English possessive plural *dogs'*, there is only one token of an *–s* affix where two tokens are expected (cf. simple plural *dog-s* and possessive singular *dog's*). This is common in adult grammars, and occurs as an error for the majority of English-learning children and in adult language production. Berko (1958) originally showed the past-tense suffix *–ed* (pronounced [t] after most voiceless phonemes, [d] after most voiced phonemes, but [əd] after stems ending in /t/ or /d/) is not overtly added after stems that end in /t/ or /d/: *want* or *need* in contexts that require the marking of past tense. Berko argued that verbs ending in /t/ and /d/ are more prone to these *zero-marking errors* in the past tense than verbs ending in other phonemes because verbs like *need* already appear to end in the *−ed* suffix; see also Bybee and Slobin (1982), and Stemberger and MacWhinney (1986) for adult speech.

Morphological haplology has been addressed in OT by Bernhardt and Stemberger (1998), Plag (1998), and de Lacy (1999a). Bernhardt and Stemberger argue that it derives from the interaction of markedness constraints against the presence of elements in the output (**Not(C)**, **Not(V)**, or **Not(σ)**), with the faithfulness constraint **Distinct** (also known as UNIFORMITY or NoMultipleCorrespondence), that prevents the merger of two distinct elements in the input into a single element in the output. If **Distinct** is ranked high, then two tokens of /d/ or /z/ are produced: **dogs's, needed*. This is shown in constraint table (3), which follows the format of Bernhardt and Stemberger (1998), in which constraint names head rows (so that names never need to be abbreviated in large constraint tables) and candidates consequently head columns, and in which cells containing winning candidates and fatal violations receive special borders.

(3)

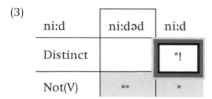

In contrast, if one or more **Not** constraints are ranked higher, then a single token is produced that corresponds to *both* input elements and functions to realize both morphemes: *dogs'*, **need* (4).

(4)

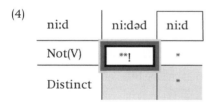

Penke and colleagues have addressed this issue for German and Dutch aphasia. In German, perfect forms do not show morphological haplology (with addition of *−t* in *mal-t* 'painted', and additional schwa-insertion in *gerett-et* 'saved'), while Dutch shows morphological haplology (with no overt addition of *−t* in *gered* 'saved'). Hegenscheidt, Janssen, and Penke (2002) show that some analyses of morphological haplology are not compatible with the hypothesis, discussed above, that in aphasia, markedness constraints are variably ranked higher than corresponding faithfulness constraints and so prevent the faithful realization of some elements.

A traditional analysis of forms such as *needed* and *gerettet* assumes vowel epenthesis. When the affix is added to the base (*need-d*, *gerett-t*), the form ends in a sequence of two identical consonants; this is prevented by a high-ranked markedness constraint (the OCP) in all West Germanic languages. This ill-formedness is eliminated either via insertion of a vowel to separate the two consonants (English, German) or via deletion of one of the two consonants (Dutch). In German, MAX (faithfulness) is ranked higher than DEP (faithfulness), leading to two tokens of /t/ plus vowel epenthesis. In Dutch, DEP (faithfulness) is ranked higher than MAX (faithfulness), leading instead to one token of /t/. If aphasia involves the variable ranking of markedness over faithfulness, and the OCP is already ranked higher than faithfulness, then one possibility is that German and Dutch subjects with aphasia should be as accurate in their perfect forms as normal adults are. If perfect forms *are* affected, however, it implies that the relative ranking of two faithfulness constraints is also affected in aphasia; in that case, both German and Dutch subjects should make errors: German subjects should produce morphological haplology (*gerett), while Dutch speakers should show vowel epenthesis (*gereddet; Penke and colleagues note that vowel epenthesis is attested in other aspects of Dutch phonology). Hegenscheidt et al. examined this question with a production task involving 11 German-speaking and 12 Dutch-speaking clients with Broca's aphasia; they were given a written card with a sentence containing the verb in the present plural, and a sentence fragment requiring the patient to transform the verb into the perfect. In both languages, verb stems that do not end in /t/ or /d/ showed a zero-marking error rate of 5%, which is thus the expected baseline for verbs that end in /t/ or /d/. German subjects with aphasia showed a strongly elevated error rate in verbs that ended in /t/ or /d/ (39.5% of trials), while the Dutch speakers did not (5% of trials). Hegenscheidt et al. argue that the results are not compatible with the standard analysis.

Grijzenhout and Penke (2004) consider a different analysis, in which the faithfulness constraint MAX interacts with an *ad-hoc* markedness constraint against a sequence of two identical consonants separated by a schwa: $^{*}C_1 \vartheta C_1$. In Dutch, $^{*}C_1 \vartheta C_1$ (markedness) is ranked higher than MAX (FAITHFULNESS), and this is predicted not to be affected in aphasia. In German, where MAX (faithfulness) is ranked above $^{*}C_1 \vartheta C_1$ (markedness), aphasia is predicted to cause re-ranking, with a strong increase in errors. However, this analysis cannot be extended easily to morphological haplology in other languages, which can involve VC and CVC and even larger repeating units. The morphological haplology analysis of Bernhardt and Stemberger, where **Not** (markedness) is ranked above **Distinct** (faithfulness), also makes the correct predictions, and can also account for the full range of phenomena across adult languages.

Bernhardt and Stemberger note that the faithfulness constraint DEP-IO is partly redundant in function with the simple markedness constraint **Not(V)**. **Not(V)** prevents any vowel in the output, whether present in the input or epenthetic, unless some constraint (faithfulness or markedness) forces it to be present. DEP-IO is more specific, preventing only epenthetic vowels. Using **Not(V)** to prevent epenthesis makes the right predictions about

Dutch and German aphasic speech, while Dᴇᴘ-IO makes the wrong predictions. This could be taken as evidence that Dᴇᴘ-IO does not exist. Bernhardt and Stemberger note that they know of no certain examples of epenthesis from adult or child language that cannot be solved with **Not(V)**. To argue for Dᴇᴘ-IO, it is necessary to demonstrate that **Not(V)** is too low-ranked (on the basis of independent evidence) to account for the facts, *and* that no conjoined constraint is sufficient. The data of Penke and her colleagues suggest that Dᴇᴘ-IO is not the optimal way to account for epenthesis.

25.4   Discussion and conclusion

A complete model of human phonological behaviour must account for both typical and atypical phonological systems. In this chapter, data from atypical systems were used to reflect on markedness, phonological representation, and phonology–morphology interactions. The same factors that mold typical systems have effects in atypical systems. Certain data from atypical systems also can provide evidence to choose between competing analyses that have been proposed for typical (adult) systems. The phonological systems of atypically developing children show many of the same effects found in those of typically developing children: effects of segmental and syllable markedness, evidence for the independence of consonants and vowels, and phonological constraints on morphological production. The data from atypical development require a particular implementation of markedness: constraints involve the pair-wise markedness of particular properties (simple versus complex onsets; absence versus presence of a coda; [+F] versus [−F]), rather than a single markedness ranking for all contrasts. Children develop the different markedness contrasts in different orders. Some children with atypical systems appear to show advanced development of marked consonant features. This can arise if children have different markedness relations, or from the overgeneralization of vowel markedness values to consonants (a possibility predicted by OT), or via assimilation of vowel features to consonants in a way that some phonological theories rule out. Atypical systems arising from neurogenic impairments also show effects of segmental and syllable markedness, independence of consonants and vowels, and interactions of morphology with phonological constraints. Morphological interactions may indicate that epenthesis is best prevented via **Not** constraints, and that Dᴇᴘ-IO should perhaps be eliminated from OT. Atypical systems provide a useful supplement to typical adult systems for the development and testing of phonological theories.

References

The following abbreviations are for publication information that recurs frequently throughout the text.

Journal, book series, and on-line archive abbreviations

CJL   *Canadian Journal of Linguistics*
IJAL *International Journal of American Linguistics*
JASA *Journal of the Acoustical Society of America*
JCL   *Journal of Child Language*
JIPA *Journal of the International Phonetic Association*
JL   *Journal of Linguistics*
JPh   *Journal of Phonetics*
Lg   *Language*
LI   *Linguistic Inquiry*
Ln   *Lingua*
NLLT *Natural Language and Linguistic Theory*
Ph   *Phonology*
ROA   *Rutgers Optimality Archive* (http://roa.rutgers.edu)
SLS   *Studies in the Linguistic Sciences*

Conference proceedings and working papers

BLS   Berkeley Linguistics Society
CLS   Chicago Linguistics Society
ESCOL East Coast Conference on Formal Linguistics
ICPhS International Congress of Phonetic Sciences
MITWPL MIT Working Papers in Linguistics
NELS   North-Eastern Linguistics Society

TWPL   Toronto Working Papers in Linguistics
UMOP   University of Massachusetts Occasional Papers in Linguistics
WCCFL   West Coast Conference on Formal Linguistics

- e.g. "CLS 18" abbreviates "Proceedings of the 18th meeting of the Chicago Linguistics Society"

Publisher abbreviations

CUP   Cambridge University Press
GLSA   Graduate Linguistics Students Association of the University of Massachusetts Amherst
IULC   Indiana University Linguistics Club
OUP   Oxford University Press
SIL   Summer Institute of Linguistics

Academic institution abbreviations

CUNY   City University of New York
MIT   Massachusetts Institute of Technology
UCLA   University of California at Los Angeles
UCB   University of California at Berkeley
UCSC   University of California at Santa Cruz
UMass   University of Massachusetts Amherst

Abbs, J. H., V. L. Gracco and K. J. Cole (1984). Control of multi-movement coordination: Sensory motor mechanisms in speech motor programming. *Journal of Motor Behavior* 16: 195–231.

Abney, Steven (1987). *The English noun phrase in its sentential aspect.* Doctoral dissertation, MIT.

Abramson, Arthur (1962). *The vowels and tones of Standard Thai: Acoustical measurements and experiments.* Bloomington, Indiana University Press.

Abramson, Arthur, P. W. Nye, J. B. Henderson and C. W. Marshall (1981). Vowel height and the perception of consonantal nasality. *JASA* 70: 329–339.

Abu-Mansour, Mahasen (1996). Voice as a privative feature: Assimilation in Arabic. In Mahasen Abu-Mansour (ed.) *Perspectives on Arabic linguistics VIII.* Amsterdam, Netherlands, John Benjamins, pp.201–231.

Ahn, Mee-Jin (2000). *Phonetic and functional bases of syllable weight for stress assignment.* Doctoral dissertation, University of Illinois.

Aissen, Judith (2003). Differential object marking: iconicity vs. economy. *NLLT* 21.3: 435–483.

Ajiboye, Oladiipo (2002). *Mòbà nasal harmony.* Manuscript, University of British Columbia.

Akinlabi, Akinbiyi (1985). *Tonal underspecification and Yoruba tone.* Doctoral dissertation, University of Ibadan.

Akinlabi, Akinbiyi (1994). Alignment constraints in ATR harmony. *SLS* 24.1/2: 1–18.

Akinlabi, Akinbiyi (1996). Featural alignment. *JL* 32: 239–289.

Akinlabi, Akinbiyi and Mark Liberman (2000). The tonal phonology of Yoruba Clitics. In Birgit Gerlach and Janet Grijzenhout (eds.) *Clitics in Phonology, Morphology and Syntax*, John Benjamins, pp.31–62.

Akinlabi, Akinbiyi and Mark Liberman (2001). Tonal complexes and tonal alignment. In Min-Joo Kim and Uri Strauss (eds.) *NELS 31*, Amherst, GLSA, pp.1–20.

Al-Bamerni, A. (1983). *Oral, Velic and Laryngeal Coarticulation Across Languages.* Doctoral dissertation, Oxford University.

Albano Leoni, F., M. R. Caputo, L. Cerrato, F. Cutugno, P. Maturi and R. Savy (1995). Il vocalismo dell'Italiano: Analisi di un campione televisivo. *Studi Italiani di Linguistica Teorica e Applicata* 24: 405–411.

Alber, Birgit (1997). Quantity sensitivity as the result of constraint interaction. In Geert Booij and Jeroen van de Weijer (eds.) *Phonology in progress: progress in phonology.* HIL Phonology Papers III. The Hague, Holland Academic Graphics, pp.1–45.

Alber, Birgit (2000). *The right stress comes from the left.* Handout, International Conference on stress and rhythm, Hyderabad.

Alber, Birgit (2001). Right-alignment as avoidance of stress lapse and stress clash. *ROA* 515.

Alber, Birgit (2002). Clash, lapse and directionality. *ROA* 568.

Albright, Adam (2002). *The identification of bases in morphological paradigms.* Doctoral dissertation, UCLA.

Albright, Adam and Bruce Hayes (2003). Rules vs. analogy in English past tenses: A computational/experimental study. *Cognition* 90: 119–161.

Alderete, John (1997). Dissimilation as local conjunction. In Kiyomi Kusumoto (ed.) *NELS 27.* Amherst, MA, GLSA, pp.17–32.

Alderete, John (1999a). Faithfulness to prosodic heads. In Ben Hermans and Marc van Oostendorp (eds.) *The derivational residue in phonological Optimality Theory.* Amsterdam, John Benjamins, pp.29–50.

Alderete, John (1999b). *Morphologically governed accent in Optimality Theory.* Doctoral dissertation, University of Massachusetts, Amherst.

Alderete, John (2001a). Root-controlled accent in Cupeño. *NLLT* 19.3: 455–502.

Alderete, John (2001b). Dominance effects as transderivational anti-faithfulness. *Ph* 18: 201–253.

Alderete, John, Jill Beckman, Laura Benua, Amalia Gnanadesikan, John McCarthy and Suzanne Urbanczyk (1999). Reduplication and fixed segmentism *LI* 30.3: 327–364.

Ali, L. H., T. Gallagher, H. Goldstein and R. Daniloff (1971). Perception of coarticulated nasality. *JASA* 49: 538–540.

Allen, William Sydney (1973). *Accent and rhythm*. Cambridge, CUP.

Allison, E. (1979). The phonology of Sibutu Sama: a language of the Southern Philippines. In C. Edrial-Luzares and A. Hale (eds.) *Studies in Philippine Languages*. Vol.3:2, Linguistic Society of the Philippines and the SIL, pp.63–104.

Al-Mozainy, Hamza Q. (1981). *Vowel alternations in a Bedouin Hijazi Arabic dialect: abstractness and stress*. Doctoral dissertation, University of Texas.

Alwan, A., S. Narayanan and K. Haker (1997). Toward articulatory-acoustic models for liquid approximants based on MRI and EPG data. Part II. The rhotics. *JASA* 101: 1078–1089.

Anceaux, J. C. (1965). *The Nimboran language: Phonology and morphology*. Gravenhage, Martinus Nijhoff.

Anderson, John M. and Colin J. Ewen (1987). *Principles of Dependency Phonology*. Cambridge, CUP.

Anderson, Stephen R. (1971). On the description of 'apicalized' consonants. *LI* 2: 103–107.

Anderson, Stephen R. (1974). *The organization of phonology*. New York, Academic Press.

Anderson, Stephen R. (1985). *Phonology in the Twentieth Century: Theories of rules and theories of representations*. Chicago, University of Chicago Press.

Anderson, Stephen R. (1988). Morphological change. In F. Newmeyer (ed.) *Linguistics: The Cambridge Survey*. Cambridge, CUP, pp.324–362.

Anderson, Stephen R. (1992). *A-morphous morphology*. Cambridge, UK, CUP.

Anttila, Arto (1997). Deriving variation from grammar. In Frans Hinskins, Roeland van Hout and W. Leo Wetzels (eds.) *Variation, change and phonological theory*. Amsterdam and Philadelphia, PA, John Benjamins, pp.35–68.

Anttila, Arto (2002a). Morphologically conditioned phonological alternations. *NLLT* 20.1: 1–42.

Anttila, Arto (2002b). Variation and phonological theory. In Jack Chambers, Peter Trudgill and Natalie Schilling-Estes (eds.) *Handbook of language variation and change*. Malden, MA and Oxford, UK, Blackwell, pp.206–243.

Anttila, Arto (2003). Finnish Assimilation. In Makoto Kadowaki and Shigeto Kawahara (eds.) *NELS 33*. Amherst, MA, GLSA, pp.13–24.

Anttila, Arto (in press). Derived environment effects in Colloquial Helsinki Finnish. In Kristin Hanson and Sharon Inkelas (eds.) *The nature of the word: essays in honor of Paul Kiparsky*. Cambridge, MA, MIT Press.

Anttila, Arto and Adams Bodomo (1996). Stress and tone in Dagaare. *ROA* 169.

Anttila, Arto and Adams Bodomo (2000). Tonal polarity in Dagaare. In Vicki Carstens and Frederick Parkinson (eds.) *Trends in African linguistics 4: Advances in African linguistics*. Trenton, NJ, African World Press, pp.119–134.

Anttila, Arto and Anthi Revithiadou (2000). Variation in allomorph selection. In Masako Hirotani, Andries Coetzee, Nancy Hall and Ji-Yung Kim (eds.) *NELS 30*, Vol.1. Amherst, MA., GLSA, pp.29–42.

Anttila, Arto and Young-mee Yu Cho (1998). Variation and change in Optimality Theory. *Ln* 104: 31–56.

Aquilina, Joseph (1999). *Maltese-English dictionary*. Malta, Midsea Publishing.

Archangeli, Diana (1984). *Underspecification in Yawelmani phonology and morphology*. Doctoral dissertation, MIT.

Archangeli, Diana (1985). Yokuts harmony: evidence for coplanar representation in nonlinear phonology. *LI* 16: 335–372.

Archangeli, Diana and Douglas Pulleyblank (1986). *The content and structure of phonological representations*. Manuscript, University of Arizona & University of British Columbia.

Archangeli, Diana, and Douglas Pulleyblank (1987). Minimal and maximal rules: Effects of tier scansion. In Joyce McDonough and B. Plunkett. *NELS 17*, Amherst, GLSA, pp.16–35.

Archangeli, Diana and Douglas Pulleyblank (1994). *Grounded Phonology*. Cambridge, MA, MIT Press.

Archangeli, Diana and Douglas Pulleyblank (2002). Kinande vowel harmony: domains, grounded conditions, and one-sided alignment. *Ph* 19: 139–188.

Archangeli, Diana and Keiichiro Suzuki (1998). Menomini vowel harmony: O(pacity) and T(ransparency) in OT. In K. Suzuki and D. Elzinga (eds.) *Proceedings of the Southwest Optimality Workshop I: Features in Optimality Theory*. Coyote Working Papers, University of Arizona, pp.1–17.

Armstrong, R. G. (1968). Yala (Ikom): a terraced-level language with three tones. *Journal of West African Languages* 5: 41–50.

Aronoff, Mark (1988). Head operations and strata in reduplication: A linear treatment. *Yearbook of Morphology* 1: 1–15.

Arrow, K. (1951). *Social choice and individual values*. New Haven and London, Yale University Press.

Artstein, Ron (1998). The incompatibility of Underspecification and markedness in Optimality Theory. In Ron Artstein and Madeleine Holler (eds.) *RuLing: Rutgers Occasional Papers in Linguistics*. Vol.1. New Brunswick, NJ, Rutgers Graduate Student Association, pp.7–13.

Arvaniti, Amalia and Mary Baltazani (2003). Intonational analysis and prosodic annotation of Greek spoken corpora. In Sun-Ah Jun (ed.) *Prosodic typology: The phonology of intonation and phrasing*. Oxford, UK, OUP.

Arvaniti, Amalia, D. Robert Ladd and I. Mennen (1998). Stability of tonal alignment: The case of Greek prenuclear accents. *JPh* 26: 3–25.

Arvaniti, Amalia, D. Robert Ladd and I. Mennen (2000). What is a starred tone? In Michael Broe and Janet Pierrehumbert (eds.) *Papers in Laboratory Phonology V: Acquisition and the Lexicon*. Cambridge, CUP, pp.119–131.

Ashton, E. O. (1944). *Swahili Grammar*. London, Longman.

Atterer, M. and D. R. Ladd (2004). On the phonetics and phonology of 'segmental anchoring' of F0: evidence from German. *JPh* 32: 177–197.

Auger, Julie (2001). Phonological variation and Optimality Theory: evidence from word-initial vowel epenthesis in Picard. *Language Variation and Change* 13.3: 253–303.

Austin, Peter (1981). *A grammar of Diyari, South Australia*. Cambridge, CUP.

Avery, Peter and William Idsardi (2001). Laryngeal dimensions, completion and enhancement. In T. Alan Hall (ed.) *Distinctive Feature Theory*. Berlin, Mouton de Gruyter, pp.41–70.

Avery, Peter and Keren Rice (1989). Segmental structure and coronal under-specification. *Ph* 6: 179–200.

Bach, Emmon, (1965). On some recurrent types of transformations. *Georgetown University Monograph Series on Languages and Linguistics* 18: 3–18.

Baertsch, Karen, (2002). *An Optimality Theoretic approach to syllable structure: The split margin hierarchy*. Doctoral dissertation, Indiana University.

Baertsch, Karen and Stuart Davis (2001). Turkic C+/l/(uster) Phonology. *CLS* 37: 29–43.

Bagemihl, Bruce (1991). Syllable structure in Bella Coola. *LI* 22: 589–646.

Bagemihl, Bruce (1995). Language games and related areas. In John A. Goldsmith (ed.) *The handbook of phonological theory*. Oxford, Blackwell, pp.697–712.

Baker, Elise (2000). *Changing nail to snail: A treatment efficacy study of phonological impairment in children*. Doctoral dissertation, The University of Sydney.

Baković, Eric (1998). Unbounded stress and factorial typology. In Ron Artstein and Madeline Holler (eds.) *RuLing: Rutgers Occasional Papers in Linguistics*. Vol.1, New Brunswick, NJ, pp.15–28. *ROA* 244.

Baković, Eric (1999). Assimilation to the unmarked. *ROA* 340.

Baković, Eric (2000). *Harmony, dominance and control*. Doctoral dissertation, Rutgers University. *ROA* 360.

Baković, Eric (2005). Antigemination and the determination of identity. *Ph* 22.3: 279–315.

Baković, Eric and Colin Wilson (2000). Transparency, strict locality, and targeted constraints. In Roger Billerey and Brook Danielle Lillehaugen (eds.) *WCCFL* 19. Somerville, MA, Cascadilla Press, pp.43–56. *ROA* 430.

Baković, Eric and Colin Wilson (2004). Laryngeal markedness and the typology of repair. *Talk presented at the 78th Annual Meeting of the Linguistic Society of America*.

Bamba, M. (1991). *De l'interaction entre tons et accent*. Doctoral dissertation, Université du Quebec à Montréal.

Bannert, R. and A.-C. Bredvad-Jensen (1975). Temporal organization of Swedish tonal accent: The effect of vowel duration. *Working Papers 10*, Phonetics Laboratory, Department of General Linguistics, Lund University, pp.1–36.

Bannert, R. and A.-C. Bredvad-Jensen (1977). Temporal organization of Swedish tonal accents: the effect of vowel duration in the Gotland dialect. *Working Papers 15*, Phonetics Laboratory, Department of General Linguistics, Lund University, pp.122–138.

Bao, Zhi Ming (1990). *On the nature of tone*. Doctoral dissertation, MIT.

Bao, Zhi Ming (1999). *The structure of tone*. Oxford, UK, OUP.

Barker, M. A. R. (1964). *Klamath Grammar*. Publications in Linguistics. Berkeley, CA, University of California Press.

Barnes, Jonathan (2002). *Positional neutralization: a phonologization approach to typological patterns*. Doctoral dissertation, UCB.

Bat-El, Outi (1989) *Phonology and word structure in Modern Hebrew*. Doctoral Dissertation, UCLA.

Bat-El, Outi (1994) Stem modification and cluster transfer in Modern Hebrew. *NLLT* 12: 571–596.

Bat-El, Outi (2003) Semitic verb structure within a universal perspective. In J. Shimron (ed.) *Language Processing and Acquisition in Languages of Semitic, Root-Based, Morphology*. Amsterdam & Philadelphia, John Benjamins Publishing Company, pp.29–59.

Bateman, Nicoleta (in prep.). *Full and Secondary Palatalization: A Typological Investigation*. Doctoral dissertation, University of California, San Diego.

Bates, Dawn (1986). An analysis of Lushootseed diminutive reduplication. In V. Nikiforidou, M. VanClay and M. Niepokuj (eds.) *BLS* 12: 1–12.

Bates, Dawn and Barry F. Carlson (1992). Simple syllables in Spokane Salish. *LI* 23: 653–659.

Bates, Dawn, Thom Hess and Vi Hilbert (1994). *Lushootseed dictionary*. Seattle, University of Washington Press.

Battistella, Edwin (1990). *Markedness: the evaluative superstructure of language*. Albany, SUNY Press.

Baudouin de Courtenay, Jan (1895). An attempt at a theory of phonetic alternations. In Edward Stankiewicz (ed.) *A Baudouin de Courtenay anthology*. Bloomington, Indiana University Press, pp.144–212.

Bauer, Laurie (2004). *A glossary of morphology*. Washington, DC, Georgetown University Press.

Bauer, Winifred (1993). *Māori*. London and New York, Routledge.

Baumann, Stefan and Martine Grice (in press). The intonation of accessibility. *Journal of Pragmatics, Special issue on Intonation and Pragmatics*.

Bayley, Robert (1995). Consonant cluster reduction in Tejano English. *Language variation and change* 6.3: 303–326.

Beckman, Jill (1997). Positional faithfulness, positional neutralization, and Shona vowel harmony. *Ph* 14: 1–46.

Beckman, Jill (1998). *Positional faithfulness*. Doctoral dissertation, UMass. ROA 234.

Beckman, Mary E. (1986). *Stress and Non-Stress Accent*. Netherlands Phonetic Archives No. 7. Dordrecht, Foris.

Beckman, Mary E. and Jan Edwards (2000). The ontogeny of phonological categories and the primacy of lexical learning in linguistic development. *Child Development* 71: 240–249.

Beckman, Mary E. and Janet Pierrehumbert (1986). Intonational structure in English and Japanese. *Phonology Yearbook* 3: 255–309.

Beers, Mieke (1995). *The phonology of normally developing and language-impaired children*. Doctoral dissertation, University of Amsterdam. IFOTT Amsterdam.

Béland, R., Carole Paradis and M. Bois (1993). Constraints and repairs in aphasic speech: A group study. *CJL* 38: 279–302.

Bell, Sarah (1983). Internal C reduplication in Shuswap. *LI* 14: 332–338.

Bell-Berti, F. (1976). An electromyographic study of velopharyngeal function in speech. *Journal of Speech and Hearing Research* 19: 225–240.

Bell-Berti, F., T. Baer, K. Harris and S. Niimi (1979). Coarticulatory effects of vowel quality on velar function. *Phonetica* 36: 187–193.

Benguerel, A.-P. and A. Lafargue (1981). Perception of vowel nasalization in French. *JPh* 9: 309–321.

Benjamin, G. (1976). An outline of Temiar grammar. In P. N. Jenner, L. C. Thompson and S. Starosta (eds.) *Austroasiatic Studies*. Oceanic Linguistics Special Publications. Honolulu, University of Hawaii Press, pp.129–188.

Benkí, J. R. (2001). Place of articulation and first formant transition pattern both affect perception of voicing in English. *JPh* 29: 1–22.

Benua, Laura (1995). Identity effects in morphological truncation. In Jill Beckman, Laura Walsh Dickey and Suzanne Urbanczyk (eds.) *UMOP 18: Papers in Optimality Theory*. Amherst, MA, GLSA, pp.77–136.

Benua, Laura (1997). *Transderivational identity: phonological relations between words*. Doctoral dissertation, UMass.

Benua, Laura (2000). *Phonological relations between words*. New York, Garland.

Benua, Laura (2003). Transderivational Identity: Phonological relations between words (excerpt of Benua 1997/2000). In John McCarthy (ed.) *Optimality Theory in phonology: a reader*. Malden, MA and Oxford, UK, Blackwell, pp.419–437.

Berg, Thomas (1998). *Linguistic structure and change: An explanation from language processing*. Oxford, Clarendon Press.

Berkley, Deborah Milam (1994). Variability in Obligatory Contour Principle effects. *CLS 30: Vol.2*. Vol.1–12. Chicago, IL, University of Chicago Press.

Berko, Jean (1958). The child's learning of English morphology. *Word* 14: 150–177.

Berko, Jean and Roger Brown (1960). Psycholinguistic research methods. In P. Mussen (ed.) *Handbook of research methods in child development*. New York, Wiley, pp.517–557.

Bermúdez-Otero, Ricardo (1998). Prosodic optimization: the Middle English length adjustment. *English Language and Linguistics* 2: 169–197.

Bermúdez-Otero, Ricardo (2006). Phonological change in Optimality Theory. In Keith Brown (ed.) *Encyclopedia of language and linguistics*. Oxford, Elsevier, 2nd ed., vol. 9, pp.497–505.

Bermúdez-Otero, Ricardo (forthcoming). *Stratal Optimality Theory*. Oxford, OUP.

Bermúdez-Otero, Ricardo and Kersti Börjars (2006). Markedness in phonology and in syntax: the problem of grounding. In Patrick Honeybone and Ricardo Bermúdez-Otero (eds.) *Linguistic Knowledge: Perspectives from phonology and syntax*. Special Issue. *Lingua* 116.5: 710–756.

Bermúdez-Otero, Ricardo and Richard M. Hogg (2003). The actuation problem in Optimality Theory: phonologization, rule inversion, and rule loss. In D. Eric Holt (ed.) *Optimality Theory and language change*. Dordrecht, Kluwer, pp.91–119.

Bermúdez-Otero, Ricardo and April McMahon (2006). English phonology and morphology. In Bas Aarts and April McMahon (eds.) *The handbook of English linguistics*. Oxford, Blackwell, pp.382–410.

Bernhardt, Barbara (1990). *Application of nonlinear phonological theory to intervention with six phonologically disordered children*. Doctoral dissertation, University of British Columbia.

Bernhardt, Barbara and Joseph P. Stemberger (1998). *Handbook of phonological development: From the perspective of constraint-based nonlinear phonology*. San Diego, Academic Press.

Bernhardt, Barbara and Joseph P. Stemberger (2000). *Workbook in nonlinear phonology for clinical application*. Austin, TX, Pro-Ed.

Bernhardt, Barbara and Carol Stoel-Gammon (1996). Underspecification and markedness in normal and disordered phonological development. In C. Johnson and J. H. V. Gilbert (eds.) *Children's language*. Vol.9. Mahwah, NJ, Laurence Erlbaum, pp.206–244.

Bhat, D. N. S. and M. S. Ningomba (1997). *Manipuri grammar*. Lincom Studies in Asian Linguistics. München, Lincom Europa.

Bickmore, Lee (1995). Tone and stress in Lamba. *Ph* 12: 307–342.

Bickmore, Lee (1996). Bantu tone spreading and displacement as alignment and minimal misalignment. *ROA* 161.

Bing, Janet (1979). *Aspects of English prosody*. Doctoral dissertation, UMass.

Bird, S. (2002). *Dakelh ejectives: evidence for new ways of classifying sounds*. Handout, 76th Annual Meeting of the Linguistic Society of America. San Francisco, CA.

Biró, Tamás (2004). Weak interactions. In Dicky Gilbers, Maartje Schreuder and Nienke Knevel (eds.) *On the boundaries of phonology and phonetics*, CLCG Klankleer, pp.123–146.

Bishop, J. (2004). *'Stress accent' without phonetic stress: Accent type and distribution in Bininj Gun-Wok*. Manuscript, University of Melbourne, Australia.

Blevins, Juliette (1993). A tonal analysis of Lithuanian nominal accent. *Lg* 69.2: 237–273.

Blevins, Juliette (1994). A place for lateral in the feature geometry. *JL* 30: 301–348.

Blevins, Juliette (1995). The syllable in phonological theory. In John Goldsmith (ed.) *The handbook of phonological theory*. Oxford, Blackwell, pp.206–244.

Blevins, Juliette (1996). Mokilese reduplication. *LI* 27: 523–530.

Blevins, Juliette (2003). The independent nature of phonotactic constraints: An alternative to syllable-based approaches. In Caroline Féry and Ruben van de Vijver (eds.) *The syllable in Optimality Theory*. Cambridge, CUP, pp.375–403.

Blevins, Juliette (2004). *Evolutionary Phonology: the emergence of sound patterns*. Cambridge, CUP.

Blevins, Juliette and Andrew Garrett (2004). The evolution of metathesis. In Bruce Hayes, Donca Steriade and Robert Kirchner (eds.) *Phonetically based phonology*. Cambridge, CUP, pp.117–156.

Bliese, Loren (1981). *A generative grammar of Afar*. SIL publications in linguistics. Dallas, SIL/Arlington, Texas: University of Texas at Arlington.

Bloomfield, Leonard (1933). *Language*. New York, Holt.

Blumenfeld, Lev (2005). *Too many solutions: how prosody and segments interact*, Handout from *CLS* 41. http://www.stanford.edu/~lblum/CLS.pdf.

Boas, F. (1947). Kwakiutl Grammar with a glossary of the suffixes. *Transactions of the American Philosophical Society* 37, Part 3.

Boersma, Paul (1998). *Functional Phonology: Formalizing the interactions between articulatory and perceptual drives*. Doctoral dissertation, University of Amsterdam. [Also published by Holland Academic Graphics, The Hague].

Boersma, Paul (2001). Review of Arto Antilla (1997): Variation in Finnish phonology and morphology. *GLOT International* 4: 33–40.

Boersma, Paul (2003). Nasal harmony in functional phonology In J. van de Weijer, V. van Heuven, and H. van der Hulst (eds.), *The phonological spectrum, vol. 1: Segmental structure*. Philadelphia: John Benjamins Publishing Company, pp. 3–36.

Boersma, Paul, Paola Escudero and Rachel Hayes (2003). Learning abstract phonological from auditory phonetic categories: An integrated model for the acquisition of language-specific sound categories. *ICPhS* (Barcelona): 1013–1016. [Also ROA 585].

Boersma, Paul and Bruce Hayes (2001). Empirical tests of the Gradual Learning Algorithm. *LI* 32: 45–86. [Also ROA 348].

Boersma, Paul and Clara Levelt (2004). Optimality Theory and phonological acquisition. *Annual Review of Language Acquisition* 3: 1–50.

Bogoras, W. (1922). Chukchee. In F. Boas (ed.) *Handbook of American Indian languages*. Washington, Bureau of American Ethnology, pp.631–903.

Borg, Albert and Marie Azzopardi-Alexander (1997). *Maltese*. London and New York, Routledge.

Borowsky, Toni (1989). Syllable codas in English and structure preservation. *NLLT* 7: 146–166.

Borowsky, Toni (1993). On the Word-level. In Sharon Hargus and Ellen M. Kaisse (eds.) *Studies in Lexical Phonology*. San Diego, Academic Press, pp.199–234.

Borowsky, Toni and Barbara Horvath (1997). L-vocalization in Australian English. In Frans Hinskins, Roeland van Hout and W. Leo Wetzels (eds.) *Variation, change and phonological theory*. Amsterdam, John Benjamins, pp.101–123.

Boxwell, Helen and Maurice Boxwell (1966). Weri phonemes. In Stephen A. Wurm (ed.) *Papers in New Guinea linguistics*. Vol.5. Linguistic Circle of

Canberra Publications, Series A, No. 7. Canberra, Australian National University, pp.77–93.

Bradley, Travis G. (2001). A typology of rhotic duration contrast and neutralization. In Minjoo Kim and Uri Strauss (eds.) *NELS 31*. Amherst, MA, GLSA, pp.79–97.

Bream, C. (1968). La nasalisation des voyelles orales suivies de consonnes nasales dans le français et l'anglais parlés au Canada. In P. R. Léon (ed.) *Recherches sur la structure phonétique du français canadien*. Montreal, Marcel Didier, pp.100–118.

Breen, Gavan and Rob Pensalfini (1999). Arrernte: A language with no syllable onsets. *LI* 30.1: 1–25.

Brentari, Diane K. (1995). Sign Language Phonology: ASL. In John Goldsmith (ed.) *The handbook of phonological theory*. Cambridge, MA., Blackwell, pp.615–639.

Brockhaus, Wiebke G. (1995). Skeleton and suprasegmental structure within Government Phonology. In Jacques Durand and Francis Katamba (eds.) *New frontiers in phonology*. Harlow, Essex, Longman, pp.180–221.

Broe, Michael and Janet Pierrehumbert (eds.) (2000). *Acquisition and the lexicon. Proceedings of the Conference on Laboratory Phonology 5*. Cambridge, UK, CUP.

Bromberger, Sylvain and Morris Halle (1989). Why phonology is different. *LI* 20: 51–70.

Bromberger, Sylvain and Morris Halle (1997). The contents of phonological signs: a comparison between their use in derivational theories and in optimality theories. In Iggy Roca (ed.) *Derivations and constraints in phonology*. Oxford, OUP, pp.93–124.

Broselow, Ellen (1983). Subjacency in morphology: Salish double reduplications. *NLLT* 1: 317–346.

Broselow, Ellen (1995). Skeletal positions and moras. In John Goldsmith (ed.) *The handbook of phonological theory*. Cambridge, MA., Blackwell, pp.175–205.

Broselow, Ellen, Su-I Chen and Marie Huffman (1997). Syllable weight: convergence of phonology and phonetics. *Ph* 14.1: 47–82.

Broselow, Ellen and John McCarthy (1983). A theory of internal reduplication. *The Linguistic Review* 3: 25–88.

Browman, Catherine P. and Louis Goldstein (1989). Articulatory gestures as phonological units. *Ph* 6: 201–251.

Browman, Catherine P. and L. M. Goldstein (1995). Dynamics and articulatory phonology. In R. F. Port and T. van Gelder (eds.) *Mind as Motion: Explorations in the Dynamics of Cognition*. Cambridge, MA, MIT Press, pp.175–193.

Browman, Catherine P. and Louis Goldstein (1990). Tiers in Articulatory Phonology, with some implications for casual speech. In John Kingston and Mary Beckman (eds.) *Papers in laboratory phonology I: Between the grammar and physics of speech*. Cambridge, CUP, pp.341–397.

Browman, Catherine P. and Louis Goldstein (1992). Articulatory Phonology: an overview. *Phonetica* 49: 155–180.

Brown, Cynthia (1995). The feature geometry of lateral approximants and lateral fricatives. In Harry van der Hulst and J. van de Wiejer (eds.) *Leiden in Last. HIL Phonology Papers*. Vol.1. The Hague, Holland Academic Press, pp.41–88.

Brown, Cynthia and John Matthews (1997). The role of features geometry in the development of phonological contrasts. In S. J. Hannahs and Martha Young-Scholten (eds.) *Focus on phonological acquisition*. Amsterdam, John Benjamins, pp.67–112.

Bruce, G. (1977). *Swedish word accents in sentence perspective*. Lund, Gleerup.

Bruce, G. (1987). How floating is focal accent. In K. Gregersen and H. Basbøll (eds.) *Nordic Prosody IV*. Odense, Odense University Press, pp.41–49.

Bruce, G. (1990). Alignment and composition of tonal accents: Comments on Silverman and Pierrehumbert's paper. In John Kingston and Mary E. Beckman (eds.) *Papers in laboratory phonology I: Between the grammar and physics of speech*. Cambridge, CUP, pp.107–114.

Buckley, Eugene (1997). Tigrinya root consonants and the OCP. *Penn Working Papers in Linguistics* 4: 19–51.

Bunn, Gordon and Ruth Bunn (1970). Golin phonology. *Papers in New Guinea linguistics No.11. Pacific linguistics A23*. Canberra, Australia, SIL Publications, pp.1–7.

Büring, Daniel (2001). What do definites do that indefinites definitively don't? In Caroline Féry and Wolfgang Sternefeld (eds.) *Audiatur vox sapientiae. A Festschrift for Arnim von Stechow*. Berlin, Akademie Verlag, pp.70–100.

Burton-Roberts, Noel, Philip Carr and Gerard Docherty (eds.) (2000). *Phonological knowledge: Conceptual and empirical issues*. Oxford, OUP.

Burzio, Luigi (1994). *Principles of English stress*. Cambridge, CUP.

Burzio, Luigi (2002). Surface-to-surface morphology: When your representations turn into constraints. In P. Boucher (ed.) *Many morphologies*. Somerville, MA, Cascadilla Press, pp.142–177. [Also ROA 341].

Bybee, Joan (2000). The phonology of the lexicon: Evidence from lexical diffusion. In Michael Barlow and Suzanne Kemmer (eds.) *Usage-based models of language*. Stanford, CSLI Publications, pp.65–85.

Bybee, Joan (2001). *Phonology and language use*. Cambridge, CUP.

Bybee, Joan (2002). Word frequency and context of use in the lexical diffusion of phonetically conditioned sound change. *Language Variation and Change* 14.3: 261–290.

Bybee, Joan (2005). *The impact of use on representation: Grammar is usage and usage is grammar*. LSA Presidential Address 2005, http://www.unm.edu/~jbybee/recent.htm.

Bybee, Joan and D. I. Slobin (1982). Rules and schemas in the development and use of the English past tense. *Lg* 58: 265–289.

Bye, Patrik (1996). *Correspondence in the prosodic hierarchy and the grid: Case studies in overlength and level stress*. MPhil Thesis, University of Tromsø.

Bye, Patrik (2001). *Virtual phonology: Rule sandwiching and multiple opacity in North Saami.* Doctoral dissertation, University of Tromsø. [Also ROA 498].

Bye, Patrik (2003). Opacity, transparency, and unification in the phonology of Tiberian Hebrew. In Makoto Kadowaki and Shigeto Kawahara (eds.) *NELS 33.* Amherst, MA, GLSA, pp.475–495.

Bye, Patrik (to appear). Evolutionary typology and the Scandinavian pitch accent. *Diachronica.*

Byrd, Dani (1996). Influences on articulatory timing in consonant sequences. *JPh* 24.2: 209–244.

Calabrese, Andrea (1995). A constraint-based theory of phonological markedness and simplification procedures. *LI* 26.2: 373–463.

Campbell, Lyle (1974). Phonological features: problems and proposals. *Lg* 50.1: 52–65.

Caramazza, A., D. Chialant, R. Capasso and G. Miceli (2000). Separable processing of consonants and vowels. *Nature* 403: 428–430.

Cardona, George (1965). *A Gujarati reference grammar.* Philadelphia, University of Pennsylvania Press.

Cardoso, Walcir (2001). Variation patterns in across-word regressive assimilation in Picard: an Optimality Theoretic account. *Language Variation and Change* 13.3: 305–341.

Carlson, Lauri (1978). *Word stress in Finnish.* Manuscript, MIT.

Casali, Roderic F. (1996). *Resolving hiatus.* Doctoral dissertation, UCLA. [Also ROA 215].

Caspers, J. and Vincent J. van Heuven (1993). Effects of time pressure on the realisation of the Dutch accent lending pitch rise and fall. *Phonetica* 50: 161–171.

Castrén, M. A. (1854). *Grammatik de samojedischen Sprachen.* St. Petersburg, Buchdruckerei der Kaiserlichen Akademie der Wissenschaften.

Causley, Trisha (1999). *Complexity and markedness in Optimality Theory.* Doctoral dissertation, University of Toronto.

Cedergren, Henrietta J. and David Sankoff (1974). Variable rules: performance as a statistical reflection of competence. *Lg* 50: 333–355.

Chang, S. S., M. C. Plauché and J. J. Ohala (2001). Markedness and consonant confusion asymmetries. In E. Hume and K. Johnson (eds.) *The role of speech perception in phonology.* San Diego, Academic Press, pp.79–101.

Chao, Yuen-Ren (1930). A system of tone letters. *Le Maitre Phonetique* 45: 24–27.

Charette, Monik (1991). *Conditions on phonological government.* Cambridge, CUP.

Chen, A. (2005). *Universal and language-specific perception of paralinguistic intonational meaning.* Utrecht, LOT (Netherlands Graduate School of Linguistics).

Chen, Matthew (1972). The time dimension: Contribution toward a theory of sound change. *Foundations of Language* 8: 457–498.

Chen, Matthew (1987). The syntax of Xiamen tone sandhi. *Phonology Yearbook* 4: 109–149.

Chen, Matthew (2000). *Tone sandhi: Patterns across Chinese dialects*. Cambridge, UK, CUP.

Chen, Y. and Y. Xu (2006). Production of weak elements in speech: Evidence from F0 patterns of neutral tone in Standard Chinese. *Phonetica* 63: 47–75.

Cheng, Chin-Chuan and William S-Y. Wang (1973). Tone change in Chaozhou Chinese: A study in lexical diffusion. In Braj B. Kachru, Robert B. Lees, Yakov Malkiel, Angelina Pietrangeli and Sol Saporta (eds.) *Issues in linguistics: Papers in honor of Henry and Renée Kahane*. Urbana, University of Illinois Press, pp.99–113.

Cho, Taehong (2003). Lexical stress, phrasal accent and prosodic boundaries in the realization of domain-initial stops in Dutch. *ICPhS 15 (Barcelona)*: 2657–2660.

Cho, Taehong (2004). Prosodically conditioned strengthening and vowel-to-vowel coarticulation in English. *JPh* 32.2: 141–176.

Cho, Taehong and Patricia Keating (2001). Articulatory and acoustic studies on domain-initial strengthening in Korean. *JPh* 29.2: 155–190.

Cho, Young-mee Yu (1991). On the universality of the coronal articulator. In Carole Paradis and Jean-Francois Prunet (eds.) *The special status of coronals: Internal and external evidence*. San Diego, Academic Press, pp.159–179.

Cho, Young-mee Yu (1999). *Parameters of consonantal assimilation*. Lincom studies in theoretical linguistics 15. Munich, Lincom Europa.

Cho, Young-mee Yu and T. H. King (2003). Semisyllables and Universal Syllabification. In Caroline Féry and Ruben van de Vijver (eds.) *The syllable in Optimality Theory*. Cambridge, CUP, pp.183–212.

Chomsky, Noam (1965). *Aspects of the theory of syntax*. Cambridge, MA, MIT Press.

Chomsky, Noam (1966). *Topics in the theory of Generative Grammar*. The Hague, Mouton.

Chomsky, Noam (2004). *Key note lecture*, GLOW 2004, Thessaloniki, Greece.

Chomsky, Noam and Morris Halle (1968). *The sound pattern of English*. New York, Harper & Row.

Chomsky, Noam and Howard Lasnik (1977). Filters and control. *LI* 8: 425–504.

Chung, S. (1983). Transderivational relationships in Chamorro phonology. *Lg* 59: 35–66.

Churchward, C. Maxwell (1953). *Tongan grammar*. London, UK, OUP.

Cinque, Guglielmo (1993). A null theory of phrase and compound stress. *LI* 24.2: 239–297.

Clark, Mary (1983). On the distribution of contour tones. *WCCFL 2*, Somerville, MA.: Cascadilla Press, pp.44–55.

Clements, G. N. (1976). Palatalization: Linking or assimilation? *CLS* 12: 96–109.

Clements, G. N. (1979). The description of terraced-level tone languages. *Lg* 55.3: 536–558.

Clements, G. N. (1981). Akan vowel harmony: a nonlinear analysis. In G. N. Clements (ed.) *Harvard Studies in Phonology 2.* Cambridge, MA, Department of Linguistics, Harvard University, pp.108–177.

Clements, G. N. (1983). The hierarchical representation of tone features. In I. R. Dihoff (ed.) *Current approaches to African linguistics*, Vol. 1, Dordrecht: Foris, pp.145–176.

Clements, G. N. (1985a). The geometry of phonological features. *Phonology Yearbook* 2: 225–252.

Clements, G. N. (1985b). The problem of transfer in nonlinear morphology. *Cornell Working Papers in Linguistics* 7: 38–73.

Clements, G. N. (1987). Phonological feature representation and the description of intrusive stops. *CLS* 23: 29–50.

Clements, G. N. (1990). The role of the sonority cycle in core syllabification. In J. Kingston and Mary E. Beckman (eds.) *Papers in Laboratory Phonology I: Between the grammar and physics of speech.* Cambridge, CUP, 283–333.

Clements, G. N. (1999). Affricates as noncontoured stops. In O. Fujimura, B. D. Joseph and B. Palek (eds.) *Item order in language and speech.* Prague, Charles University Press, pp.271–299.

Clements, G. N. (2001). Representational economy in constraint-based phonology. In T. Alan Hall (ed.) *Distinctive Feature Theory.* Berlin, Mouton de Gruyter, pp.71–146.

Clements, G. N. (2003). Feature economy in sound systems. *Ph* 20.3: 287–333.

Clements, G. N. and John Goldsmith (1984). *Autosegmental studies in Bantu tone.* Dordrecht, Foris.

Clements, G. N. and Elizabeth V. Hume (1995). The internal organization of speech sounds. In John Goldsmith (ed.) *The handbook of phonological theory.* Oxford, Blackwell, pp.245–306.

Clements, G. N. and Samuel J. Keyser (1983). *CV Phonology. A generative theory of the syllable.* Cambridge, MA, MIT Press.

Clements, G. N. and Engin Sezer (1982). Vowel and consonant disharmony in Turkish. In Harry van der Hulst and Norval Smith (eds.) *The structure of phonological representations II.* Dordrecht, Foris, pp.213–255.

Clements, G. N. and Reomi Sonaiya (1990). Underlying feature specification in Yoruba. *SLS* 20: 89–103.

Clifton, Charles Jr., Katy Carlson and Lyn Frazier (2002). Informative prosodic boundaries. *Language and Speech* 45: 87–114.

Clumeck, H. (1976). Patterns of soft palate movement in six languages. *JPh* 4: 337–351.

Coenen, E., P. Zwitserlood and J. Bölte (2001). Variation and assimilation in German: Consequences for lexical access and representation. *Language and Cognitive Processes* 16: 535–564.

Coetzee, Andries (2004). *What it means to be a loser: Non-optimal candidates in Optimality Theory.* Doctoral dissertation, UMass.

Coetzee, Andries (2005). The OCP in the perception of English. In Sónia Frota, Marina Vigário and Maria João Freitas (eds.) *Prosodies: Selected Papers from the Phonetics and Phonology in Iberia Conference*. Berlin, Mouton de Gruyter, pp.223–245.

Cohn, Abigail (1989). Stress in Indonesian and bracketing paradoxes. *NLLT* 7.2: 167–216.

Cohn, Abigail (1990). Phonetic and phonological rues of nasalization. *UCLA Working Papers in Phonetics* 76: 167–216.

Cohn, Abigail (1993a). Nasalisation in English: Phonology or phonetics. *Ph* 10: 43–81.

Cohn, Abigail (1993b). The status of nasalized continuants. In M. K. Huffman and R. A. Krakow (eds.) *Nasals, Nasalization and the Velum*. Vol.5. Phonetics and Phonology. San Diego, Academic Press, pp.329–367.

Cohn, Abigail and John McCarthy (1994). Alignment and parallelism in Indonesian phonology. *ROA* 25.

Cole, Jennifer and C. W. Kisseberth (1994). An Optimal Domains theory of harmony. *SLS* 24.2: 101–114.

Cole, Jennifer & R.L. Trigo (1988). Parasitic Harmony. In Harry van der Hulst and Norval Smith (eds.) *Features, segmental structure, and harmony processes II*, Foris, Dordrecht, pp. 19–38.

Coleman, John (1995). Declarative Lexical Phonology. In Jacques Durand and Francis Katamba (eds.) *Frontiers of Phonology: Primitives, Architectures and Derivations*. London, Longman, pp.333–382.

Coleman, John (1998). *Phonological representations: Their names, forms and powers*. Cambridge, UK, CUP.

Coleman, John (2003). Commentary: Probability, detail and experience. In John Local, Richard Ogden and Rosalind Temple (eds.) *Phonetic interpretation: Papers in Laboratory Phonology VI*. Cambridge, CUP, pp.88–100.

Connell, Bruce (2000). The perception of lexical tone in Mambila. *Language and Speech* 43.2: 163–182.

Cook, T.L. (1986). The chameleonic vowel in the harmonizing prefixes of Efik. In K. Bogers, Harry van der Hulst and M. Mous (eds.) *The phonological representation of suprasegmentals*. Dordrecht, Foris, pp.209–232.

Côté, Marie-Hélène (2000). *Consonant cluster phonotactics: A perceptual approach*. Doctoral dissertation, MIT.

Côté, Marie-Hélène (2004). Syntagmatic distinctness in consonant deletion. *Ph* 21: 1–42.

Croft, William (2000). *Explaining language change: An evolutionary approach*. Harlow: Pearson Education.

Crosswhite, Katherine M. (1998). Segmental vs. prosodic correspondence in Chamorro. *Ph* 15.3: 281–316.

Crosswhite, Katherine M. (1999). *Vowel reduction in Optimality Theory*. Doctoral dissertation, UCLA.

Crosswhite, Katherine M. (2000). *Sonority-Driven reduction*. In Lisa Conathan, Jeff Good, Darya Kavitskaya, Alyssa Wulf, and Alan Yu (eds.) *BLS 26*, pp.77–78.

Crosswhite, Katherine M. (2001). *Vowel Reduction in Optimality Theory*. New York, Routledge. [Also Crosswhite (1999)].

Crosswhite, Katherine M. (2004). Vowel reduction. In B. Hayes, R. Kirchner and D. Steriade (eds.) *Phonetically-based phonology*. Cambridge, CUP, pp.191–231.

Crosswhite, Katherine M., John Alderete, Tim Beasley and Vita Markman (2003). Morphological effects on default stress placement in novel Russian words. In Gina Garding and Mimu Tsujimura (eds.) *WCCFL 22*. Somerville, MA, Cascadilla Press, pp.151–164.

Crowhurst, Megan (1994). Foot extrametricality and template mapping in Cupeño. *NLLT* 12: 177–201.

Crowhurst, Megan (1996). An optimal alternative to conflation. *Ph* 13: 409–424.

Crowhurst, Megan (2004). Mora alignment. *NLLT* 22: 127–177.

Crowhurst, Megan and Mark Hewitt (1995). Prosodic overlay and headless feet in Yidiɲ. *Ph* 12.1: 39–84.

Crowhurst, Megan and Lev Michael (2005). Iterative footing and prominence-driven stress in Nanti (Kampa). *Lg* 81.1: 47–95.

Cruttenden, A. (1997). *Intonation*. Cambridge, CUP.

Crystal, David (1969). *Prosodic systems and intonation in English*. Cambridge, UK, CUP.

Crystal, David (ed.) (2003). *A dictionary of linguistics and phonetics*. Oxford, Blackwell.

Cutler, A., J. Mehler, D. Norris and J. Segui (1986). The syllable's differing role in the segmentation of French and English. *Journal of Memory and Language* 25: 385–400.

Czaykowska-Higgins, Ewa (1993). Placelessness, markedness, and Polish nasals. *LI* 23.1: 139–146.

D'Imperio, M. (2003). Tonal structure and pitch targets in Italian focus constituents. *Catalan Journal of Linguistics* 2: 55–65.

Dalton, Martha and Ailbhe Ní Chasaide (2003). Modelling intonation in three Irish dialects. *ICPhS 15*, Vol.1, pp.1073–1076.

Daniels, Peter T. and William Bright (1996) *The World's writing systems*, Oxford: Oxford University Press.

Dart, Sarah N. (1991). Articulatory and acoustic properties of apical and laminal articulations. *UCLA Working Papers in Phonetics* 79: 1–155.

Davidson, L., P. Jusczyk and P. Smolensky (2004). The initial and final states: Theoretical implications and experimental explorations of Richness of the Base. In R. Kager, J. Pater and W. Zonneveld (eds.) *Constraints in phonological acquisition*. Cambridge, CUP, pp.321–368.

Davies, John (1981). *Kobon*. Amsterdam, North-Holland.

Davis, Barbara, Peter MacNeilage and Christine Matyear (2002). Acquisition of serial complexity in speech production: A comparison of phonetic and phonological approaches to first word production. *Phonetica: International Journal of Speech Science* 59: 75–109.

Davis, Stuart (1985). *Topics in syllable geometry*. Doctoral dissertation, University of Arizona.

Davis, Stuart (1988a). On the nature of internal reduplication. In Michael Hammond and M. Noonan (eds.) *Theoretical morphology: Approaches in modern linguistics*. San Diego, Academic Press, pp.305–323.

Davis, Stuart (1988b). Syllable onsets as a factor in stress rules. *Ph* 5: 1–19.

Davis, Stuart (1989a). On a non-argument for the rhyme. *JL* 25: 211–217.

Davis, Stuart (1989b). Stress, syllable weight hierarchies, and moraic phonology. *ESCOL* 6: 84–92.

Davis, Stuart (1995). Emphasis spread in Arabic and Grounded Phonology. *LI* 26: 465–498.

Davis, Stuart (1998). Syllable contact in Optimality Theory. *Journal of Korean Linguistics* 23: 181–211.

de Boer, B. (2000). Self-organization in vowel systems. *JPh* 28: 441–465.

de Lacy, Paul (1997). *Prosodic categorisation*. MA Thesis, University of Auckland. [Also ROA 236].

de Lacy, Paul (1999a). Haplology and correspondence. In Paul de Lacy and Anita Nowak (eds.) *UMOP 24: Papers from the 25th Anniversary*. Amherst, GLSA Publications, pp.51–88. [Also ROA 298].

de Lacy, Paul (1999b). Tone and Prominence. *ROA* 333.

de Lacy, Paul (2001). Markedness in prominent positions. In Ora Matushansky, Albert Costa, Javier Martin-Gonzalez, Lance Nathan and Adam Szczegielniak (eds.) *MITWPL 40: HUMIT 2000*. Cambridge, MA., pp.53–66. [Also ROA 432].

de Lacy, Paul (2002a). *The formal expression of markedness*. Doctoral dissertation, UMass. [Also ROA 542].

de Lacy, Paul (2002b). The interaction of tone and stress in Optimality Theory. *Ph* 19.1: 1–32.

de Lacy, Paul (2003a). Constraint universality and prosodic phrasing in Māori. In Andries Coetzee, Angela Carpenter and Paul de Lacy (eds.) *UMOP 26: Papers in Optimality Theory II*. Amherst, MA., GLSA, pp.59–79. [Also ROA 561].

de Lacy, Paul (2003b). *Fixed ranking and the 'Too Many Solutions' problem*, Handout from the CASTL Kick-Off Conference (Tromsø, Norway).

de Lacy, Paul (2003c). Maximal words and the Māori passive. In John McCarthy (ed.) *Optimality Theory in phonology: A reader*. Oxford, Blackwell, pp.495–512.

de Lacy, Paul (2004). Markedness conflation in Optimality Theory. *Ph* 21: 145–199.

de Lacy, Paul (2006). *Markedness: Reduction and preservation in phonology*. Cambridge, CUP.

Deemter, Kees van (1994). What's new? A semantic perspective on sentence accent. *Journal of Semantics* 11.1: 1–31.

Dehaene-Lambertz, G., E. Dupoux and A. Gout (2000). Electrophysiological correlates of phonological processing: A cross-linguistic study. *Journal of Cognitive Neuroscience* 12: 635–647.

deJong, Kenneth and Joyce McDonough (1993). Tone in Navajo. In Kenneth deJong and Joyce McDonough (eds.) *UCLA Working Papers in Phonetics.* UCLA, pp.165–182.

Delattre, P. C. (1951). *Principes de fonétique française: á l'usage des étudiants anglo-américains.* Middlebury, VT, Middlebury College.

Delattre, P. C. and D. C. Freeman (1968). A dialect study of American r's by x-ray motion picture. *Linguistics* 44: 29–68.

Dell, F. and M. Elmedlaoui (1984). Syllabic consonants and syllabification in Imdlawn Tashlhiyt Berber. *Journal of African Languages and Linguistics* 7: 105–130.

Dell, Gary (1986). A spreading activation theory of retrieval in sentence production. *Psychological Review* 93: 283–321.

Dell, Gary S., Lisa K. Burger and William R. Svec (1997). Language production and serial order: A functional analysis and a model. *Psychological Review* 104: 123–147.

Demuth, Katherine (1992). The acquisition of Sesotho. In D. I. Slobin (ed.) *The cross-linguistic study of language acquisition.* Vol.3. Hillsdale, NJ, Lawrence Erlbaum Associates, pp.557–638.

Demuth, Katherine (1993). Issues in the acquisition of the Sesotho tonal system. *JCL* 20: 275–301.

Demuth, Katherine (1995a). The acquisition of tonal systems. In J. Archibald (ed.) *Phonological acquisition and phonological theory.* Hillsdale, NJ, Lawrence Erlbaum, pp.111–134.

Demuth, Katherine (1995b). Markedness and the development of prosodic structure. In Jill Beckman (ed.) *NELS 25.* Amherst, MA, GLSA, pp.13–25. [Also ROA 50].

Demuth, Katherine (1997). Multiple optimal outputs in acquisition. In Viola Miglio and Bruce Morén (eds.) *University of Maryland Working Papers in Linguistics 5.* College Park, MD, University of Maryland, pp.53–71.

Denes, P. B. (1963). On the statistics of spoken English. *JASA* 35: 892–904.

Derbyshire, Desmond C. (1979). *Hixkaryana.* Lingua Descriptive Studies 1. Amsterdam, North-Holland.

Dettweiler, Stephen H. (2000). Vowel harmony and neutral vowels in C'Lela. *The Journal of West African Languages* 28: 3–18.

Dilley, L. C. (2004). *The phonetics and phonology of tonal systems.* Doctoral dissertation, MIT.

Dilley, L. C., D. R. Ladd and A. Schepman (2005). Alignment of L and H in bitonal pitch accents: Testing two hypotheses. *JPh* 33: 115–119.

Dimmendaal, G. J. and S. A. Breedveld (1986). Tonal influence on vocalic quality. In K. Bogers, Harry van der Hulst and M. Mous (eds.) *The phonological representation of suprasegmentals*. Dordrecht, Foris, pp.1–34.

Dinnsen, Daniel A., Kathleen O'Connor and Judith Gierut (2001). The puzzle-puddle-pickle problem and the Duke-of-York gambit in acquisition. *JL* 37: 503–525.

Dixon, R. M. W. (1977). *A grammar of Yidiɲ*. Cambridge, CUP.

Dixon, R. M. W. (1981). Wargamay. In Robert Malcolm Ward Dixon and Barry J. Blake (eds.) *Handbook of Australian languages*. Vol.2. Amsterdam, John Benjamins, pp.1–144.

Dixon, R. M. W. (1988). *A grammar of Boumaa Fijian*. Chicago, University of Chicago Press.

Dogil, Grzegorz and Hans Christian Luschützky (1990). Notes on sonority and segmental strength. *Rivista di Linguistica* 2.2: 3–54.

Doke, C. M. (1931). *The southern Bantu languages*. London, Dawsons of Pall Mall.

Donegan, Patricia J. and David Stampe (1979). The study of natural phonology. In Daniel A. Dinnsen (ed.) *Current approaches to phonological theory*. Bloomington, IN, Indiana University Press, pp.126–173.

Downing, Bruce (1970). *Syntactic structure and phonological phrasing in English*. Doctoral dissertation, University of Texas.

Downing, Laura J. (1990). Local and metrical tone shift in Nguni. *Studies in African Linguistics* 21: 261–317.

Downing, Laura J. (1998a). On the prosodic misalignment of onsetless syllables. *NLLT* 16: 1–52.

Downing, Laura J. (1998b). Prosodic misalignment and reduplication. In Geert Booij and Jaap van Marle (eds.) *Yearbook of Morphology 1997*. Netherlands, Kluwer, pp.83–120.

Downing, Laura J. (1999). Verbal reduplication in three Bantu languages. In Rene Kager, Harry van der Hulst and Wim Zonneveld (eds.) *The prosody-morphology interface*. Cambridge, CUP, pp.62–89.

Downing, Laura J. (2000). Morphological and prosodic constraints on Kinande verbal reduplication. *Ph* 17: 1–38.

Downing, Laura J. (2001). Ungeneralizable minimality in Ndebele. *Studies in African Linguistics* 30: 33–58.

Downing, Laura J. (2003a). Compounding and tonal non-transfer in Bantu languages. *Ph* 20.1: 1–42.

Downing, Laura J. (2003b). Stress, tone and focus in Chicheŵa and Xhosa. In Rose-Juliet Anyanwu (ed.) *Stress and tone: The African Experience*. Vol.15. Frankfurter Afrikanistische Blätter. Köln, Rüdiger Köppe Verlag, pp.59–82.

Downing, Laura J. (2004). Bukusu reduplication. In C. Githiora, H. Littlefield and V. Manfredi (eds.) *Trends in African Linguistics 5*. Lawrenceville, NJ, Africa World Press, pp.73–84.

Downing, Laura J. (2006). *Canonical forms in Prosodic Morphology*. Oxford, OUP.

Downing, Laura J., T. Alan Hall and Renate Raffelsiefen (eds.) (2005). *Paradigms in phonological theory*. Oxford, OUP.

Dresher, B. Elan (1999). Charting the learning path: cues to parameter setting. *LI* 30: 27–67.

Dresher, B. Elan (2004a). On the acquisition of phonological contrasts. In Jacqueline van Kampen and Sergio Baauw (eds.) *Proceedings of GALA 2003*. Vol.1. Utrecht, LOT Occasional Series, pp.27–46.

Dresher, B. Elan (2004b). On the acquisition of phonological representations. In William Sakas (ed.) *Proceedings of the first workshop on psychocomputational models of human language acquisition*. http://www.colag.cs.hunter.cuny.edu/psychocomp [1 April 2006], pp.41–48.

Dresher, B. Elan and Harry van der Hulst (1998). Head-dependent asymmetries in prosodic phonology: Visibility and complexity. *Ph* 15: 317–352.

Dresher, B. Elan and Jonathan Kaye (1990). A computational learning model for metrical phonology. *Cognition* 34.2: 137–195.

Dresher, B. Elan and Aditi Lahiri (1991). The Germanic foot: Metrical coherence in Old English. *LI* 22.2: 251–286.

Dresher, B. Elan, Glyne Piggott and Keren Rice (1994). Contrast in phonology: Overview. In Carrie Dyck (ed.) *TWPL 13:1*. Toronto, Department of Linguistics, pp.ii–xvii.

Dressler, Wolfgang (1985). *Morphonology: The dynamics of derivation*. Ann Arbor, Karoma.

Duanmu, San (1990). *A formal study of syllable, tone, stress and domain in Chinese languages*. Doctoral dissertation, MIT.

Duanmu, San (1992). An autosegmental analysis of tone in four Tibetan languages. *Linguistics of the Tibeto-Burman Area* 15.1: 65–91.

Duanmu, San (1993). Rime length, stress and association domains. *Journal of East Asian linguistics* 2.1: 1–44.

Duanmu, Sam (1994). Against contour tone units. *LI* 25.4: 555–608.

Duanmu, San (2000a). *The phonology of Standard Chinese*. Oxford, OUP.

Duanmu, San (2000b). Tone: An overview. In Lisa Cheng and R. Sybesma (eds.) *The first GLOT International State-of-the-article book: The latest in linguistics. Studies in Generative Grammar 48*. Berlin, Mouton de Gruyter, pp.251–286.

Dubert, Raymond and Marjorie Dubert (1973). Biangai phonemes. In Alan Healey (ed.) *Phonologies of three languages of Papua New Guinea*. Workpapers in Papua New Guinea Languages 2. Ukarumpa, SIL, pp.5–35.

Dupoux, E., K. Kakehi, Y. Hirose, C. Pallier and J. Mehler (1999). Epenthetic vowels in Japanese: A perceptual illusion? *Journal of Experimental Psychology: Human Perception and Performance* 25: 1568–1578.

Dupoux, E., C. Pallier, K. Kakehi and J. Mehler (2001). New evidence for prelexical phonological processing in word recognition. *Language and Cognitive Processes* 16: 491–505.

Durie, Mark (1985). *A grammar of Acehnese on the basis of a dialect of North Aceh*. Dordrecht, Foris.

Dyck, Carrie (1995). *Constraining the phonetics-phonology interface*. Doctoral dissertation, University of Toronto.

Echeverría, Max S. and Heles Contreras (1965). Araucanian Phonemics. *IJAL* 31: 132–135.

Eijk, Jan van (1997). *The Lillooet language: Phonology, morphology, syntax*. Vancouver, University of British Columbia Press.

Eijk, Jan van (1998). CVC reduplication in Salish. In Ewa Czaykowska-Higgins and M. Dale Kinkade (eds.) *Salish languages and linguistics: Theoretical and descriptive perspectives*. Berlin, Mouton de Gruyter, pp.453–476.

Eimas, P. D., E. R. Siqueland, Peter Jusczyk and J. Vigorito (1971). Speech perception in infants. *Science* 171: 303–306.

Eisner, Jason (2000). Easy and hard constraint ranking in Optimality Theory: Algorithms and complexity. In Jason Eisner, Lauri Karttunen and Alain Theriault (eds.) *Finite-state phonology: Proceedings of the 5th Workshop of the ACL Special Interest Group in Computational Phonology*. Luxembourg, SIGPHON, pp.22–33.

Ekeland, Ivar (1988). *Mathematics and the unexpected*. Chicago and London, The University of Chicago Press.

Elbert, Samuel and Mary Kawena Pukui (1979). *Hawaiian grammar*. Honolulu, University of Hawai'i Press.

Elenbaas, Nine (1996). Ternary rhythm in Sentani. In Crit Cremers and Marcel den Dikken (eds.) *Linguistics in the Netherlands 1996*. Amsterdam, John Benjamins, pp.61–72.

Elenbaas, Nine (1999). *A unified account of binary and ternary stress*. Doctoral dissertation, Utrecht University. [Also ROA 397].

Elenbaas, Nine and René Kager (1999). Ternary rhythm and the *LAPSE constraint. *Ph* 16.3: 273–330.

Elfenbein, Josef (1997). Balochi phonology. In Alan S. Kaye (ed.) *Phonologies of Asia and Africa*. Vol.2. Winona Lake, Indiana, Eisenbrauns, pp.761–776.

Elías-Ulloa, José Alberto (2005). *Theoretical aspects of Panoan metrical phonology: Disyllabic footing and contextual syllable weight*. Doctoral dissertation, Rutgers University.

Ellis, L. and W. J. Hardcastle (2002). Categorical and gradient properties of assimilation in alveolar to velar sequences: Evidence from EPG and EMA data. *JPh* 30: 373–396.

Elmedlaoui, Mohamed (1992). *Aspects des representations phonologiques dans certaines langues chamito-semitiques*. Thèse de doctorat d'état, Université Mohamed V, Rabat.

Elordieta, Gorka (1997). Accent, tone and intonation in Lekeitio Basque. In Fernando Martinez-Gil and Alfonso Morales-Front (eds.) *Issues in the phonology and morphology of the Major Iberian languages*. Washington, DC, Georgetown University Press, pp.4–78.

Elordieta, Gorka, Sónia Frota and Marina Vigário (2005). Subjects, objects and intonational phrasing in Spanish and Portuguese. In Merle Horne and Marc van Oostendorp (eds.) *Boundaries in intonational phonology*. Special Issue. Studia Linguistica 59.2/3: 110–143.

Elugbe, Ben O. (1984). Morphology of the gerund in Degema and its reconstruction in Proto-Edoid. *Studies in African Linguistics* 15: 77–89.

Enrico, John (1991). *The lexical phonology of Masset Haida*. Fairbanks, Alaska, Alaska Native Language Center, University of Alaska, Fairbanks.

Erikson, Y. and M. Alstermark (1972). Fundamental frequency correlates of the grave word accent in Swedish: The effect of vowel duration. *Quarterly Progress and Status Report (KTH, Speech Transmission Laboratory)* 2–3.

Ernout, Alfred and Antoine Meillet (1967). *Dictionnaire étymologique de la langue latine*. Paris, Klincksieck.

Estebas-Vilaplana, E. (2003). The modelling of prenuclear accents in Central Catalan declaratives. *Catalan Journal of Linguistics* 2: 97–114.

Everett, Daniel and K. Everett (1984). On the relevance of syllable onsets to stress placement. *LI* 15: 705–711.

Everett, Daniel (1988). On metrical constituent structure in Pirahã. *NLLT* 6: 207–246.

Everett, Daniel (2003). *Postlexical structure preservation in Suya (Ge)*. Handout, Manchester Phonology Conference 2003. http://lings.ln.man.ac.uk/info/staff/DE/DEHome.html.

Ewen, Colin J. (1995). Dependency relations in phonology. In John Goldsmith (ed.) *Handbook of phonology*. Oxford, Blackwell, pp.570–585.

Ewen, Colin J. and Harry van der Hulst (2001). *The phonological structure of words*. Cambridge, CUP.

Fabb, Nigel (1997). *Linguistics and literature*. Oxford, Blackwell.

Face, T. L. (2001). Focus and early peak alignment in Spanish intonation. *Probus* 13: 223–246.

Face, T. L. (2002). Spanish evidence for pitch accent structure. *Linguistics* 40, 319–345.

Fallon, Paul D. (2002). *The synchronic and diachronic phonology of ejectives*. London, Routledge.

Farnetani, E. and M. Vayra (1991). Word- and phrase-level aspects of vowel reduction in Italian. *ICPhS 12*, Vol.2, Aix-en-Provence, Université de Provence Service des Publications, pp.14–17.

Fasold, Ralph (1972). *Tense marking in Black English*. Arlington, TX, Center for Applied Linguistics.

Fee, E. Jane (1996). Syllable structure and minimal words. In Barbara Bernhardt, John Gilbert and David Ingram (eds.) *Proceedings of the UBC International Conference on Phonological Acquisition*. Somerville, MA, Cascadilla Press, pp.85–98.

Feinstein, Mark (1977). *The linguistic nature of prenasalization*. Doctoral dissertation, City University of New York.

Fennell, Christopher & Janet F. Werker (2004). Early word learners' ability to access phonetic detail in well-known words. *Language and Speech* 46: 245–264.

Ferguson, Charles A. and Carol Farwell (1975). Words and sounds in early language acquisition. *Lg* 51.2: 419–439.

Ferguson, Charles A. and Olga Garnica (1975). Theories of phonological development. In E. H. Lenneberg and E. Lenneberg (eds.) *Foundations of language development: Volume 1*. New York, NY, Academic Press, pp.153–180.

Ferguson, Charles A., Lisa Menn and Carol Stoel-Gammon (eds.) (1992). *Phonological development: models, research, implications*. Timonium, MA, York Press.

Féry, Caroline (1993). *German intonational patterns*. Tübingen, Germany, Niemeyer.

Féry, Caroline (2003). Onsets and nonmoraic syllables in German. In Caroline Féry and Ruben van de Vijver (eds.) *The syllable in Optimality Theory*. Cambridge, CUP, pp.213–237.

Fienberg, S. E. (1980). *The analysis of cross-classified categorical data*. Cambridge, MA, MIT Press.

Fikkert, Paula (1994). *On the acquisition of prosodic structure*. Doctoral dissertation, Holland Institute of Generative Linguistics (HIL): Leiden University.

Fikkert, Paula (2000). Acquisition of phonology. In Lisa Cheng and Rint Sybesma (eds.) *The first GLOT International state-of-the-article book: the latest in linguistics*. The Hague, Netherlands, Holland Academic Graphics, pp.221–250.

Fikkert, Paula and Maria João Freitas (2004a). *Allophony and allomorphy cue phonological development: Evidence from the European Portuguese vowel system*. Manuscript, Radboud University of Nijmegen and University of Lisbon.

Fikkert, Paula and Maria João Freitas (2004b). The role of language-specific phonotactics in the acquisition of onset clusters. In Leonie Cornips and Jenny Doetjes (eds.) *Linguistics in the Netherlands 2004*. Amsterdam, John Benjamins, pp.58–68.

Fikkert, Paula, Maria João Freitas, Janet Grijzenhout, Clara Levelt and Sophie Wauquier-Gravelines (2004). Syllabic markedness, segmental markedness, rhythm and acquisition, Talk presented at GLOW 2004, Thessaloniki, Greece.

Fikkert, Paula, Marieke van Heugten, Philo Offermans and Tania Zamuner (2005b). Rhymes as a window into grammar. In Alejna Brugos, Ranvella Clark-Cottan and Seunguran Ha (eds.) *BUCLD 29: Proceedings of the 27th Annual Boston University Conference on Language Development*. Somerville, MA, Cascadilla Press, pp.204–215.

Fikkert, Paula and Clara Levelt (2004). *How does place fall into place? The lexicon and emergent constraints in the developing phonological grammar*. Manuscript, Radboud University of Nijmegen and Leiden University.

Fikkert, Paula, Clara Levelt and Tania Zamuner (2005a). *Perception through production?* Manuscript, Radboud University of Nijmegen and Leiden University.

Firth, J. R. (1948). Sounds and prosodies. *Transactions of the Philological Society*: 127–152.

Fischer, Cynthia, Barbara A. Church and Kyle Chambers (2004). Learning to identify spoken words. In D. Geoffrey Hall and Sandra R. Waxman (eds.) *Weaving a lexicon*. Cambridge, MA, MIT Press, pp.3–40.

Fischer, R. M. and R. N. Ohde (1990). Spectral and duration properties of front vowels as cues to final stop-consonant voicing. *JASA* 88: 1250–1259.

Fitzgerald, Colleen (2000). Vowel hiatus and faithfulness in Tohono O'odham reduplication. *LI* 31: 713–722.

Flemming, Edward S. (1995). *Auditory representations in phonology*. Doctoral dissertation, UCLA.

Flemming, Edward S. (2001). Scalar and categorical phenomena in a unified model of phonetics and phonology. *Ph* 18: 7–44.

Flemming, Edward S. (2002). *Auditory representations in phonology*. New York and London, Routledge.

Flemming, Edward S. (2003). The relationship between coronal place and vowel backness. *Ph* 20.3: 335–373.

Flemming, Edward S. (2004). Contrast and perceptual distinctiveness. In Bruce Hayes, Donca Steriade and Robert Kirchner (eds.) *Phonetically-based phonology*. Cambridge, CUP, pp.232–276.

Flemming, Edward S. (submitted). A phonetically-based model of phonological vowel reduction.

Flemming, Edward S. and Stephanie Johnson (2004). *Rosa's roses: Reduced vowels in American English*. Manuscript.

Fodor, Janet Dean (2002). Prosodic disambiguation and silent reading. In Masako Hirotani (ed.) *NELS 32*. UMass, GLSA, pp.113–132.

Fodor, Jerry A. and commentators (1985). Précis and open peer commentary of The modularity of mind. *Behavioral and Brain Sciences* 8: 1–42.

Fodor, Jerry A., Thomas G. Bever and Merrill Garrett (1974). *The psychology of language*. New York, McGraw Hill.

Fougeron, Cecile (2001). Articulatory properties of initial segments in several prosodic constituents in French. *JPh* 29.2: 109–136.

Fougeron, Cecile and Patricia Keating (1997). Articulatory strengthening at edges of prosodic domains. *JASA* 101.6: 3728–3740.

Fourakis, M. and R. Port (1986). Stop epenthesis in English. *JPh* 14: 197–221.

Fowler, Carol A. (1980). Coarticulation and theories of extrinsic timing. *JPh* 8: 113–133.

Fowler, Carol A. (1986). An event approach to the study of speech perception from a direct-realist perspective. *JPh* 14: 3–28.

Fowler, Carol A., P. E. Rubin, R. E. Remez and M. T. Turvey (1980). Implications for speech production of a general theory of action. In B. Butterworth (ed.) *Language Production, Vol. I: Speech and Talk*. New York, Academic Press, pp.373–420.

Fowler, Carol A. and M. T. Turvey (1980). Immediate compensation in bite-block speech. *Phonetica* 37: 306–326.

Fox, Anthony (1995). *Linguistic reconstruction: An introduction to theory and method*. Oxford, OUP.

Fox, Anthony (2000). *Prosodic features and prosodic structure*. Oxford, OUP.

Frampton, John (2003). *Distributed reduplication*. Manuscript, Northeastern University (http://www.math.neu.edu/ling/dr/dr.html).

Frascarelli, Mara (2000). *The syntax-phonology interface in focus and topic constructions in Italian*. Dordrecht, Germany, Kluwer.

Freitas, Maria João (1997). *Aquisição da estrutura silábica do Português Europeu*. Doctoral dissertation, University of Lisbon.

French, Koleen Matsuda (1988). *Insights into Tagalog reduplication, infixation and stress from non-linear phonology*. MA thesis, University of Texas, Arlington.

Frisch, Stefan (2004). Language processing and segmental OCP effects. In Bruce Hayes, Donca Steriade and Robert Kirchner (eds.) *Phonetically based phonology*. Cambridge, CUP, pp.346–371.

Frisch, Stefan, Michael Broe and Janet Pierrehumbert (1997). *Similarity and phonotactics in Arabic*, Northwestern University, Evanston, Illinois.

Frisch, Stefan A., Nathan R. Large and David S. Pisoni (2000). Perception of wordlikeness: Effects of segment probability and length on the processing of nonwords. *Journal of Memory and Language* 42: 481–496.

Frisch, Stefan, Janet Pierrehumbert and Michael Broe (2004). Similarity avoidance and the OCP. *NLLT* 22: 179–228.

Frisch, Stefan and Bushra Zawaydeh (2001). The psychological reality of OCP-Place in Arabic. *Lg* 77: 91–106.

Fritzell, B. (1969). A combined electromyographic and cineradiographic study: Activity of the levator and palatoglossus muscles in relation to velar movements. *Acta Oto-Laryngologica* Supplement 250.

Fromkin, Victoria A. (1971). The nonanomalous nature of anomalous utterances. *Lg* 47: 27–52.

Fromkin, Victoria A. (ed.) (1978). *Tone: A linguistic survey*. New York, Academic Press.

Fromkin, Victoria (1988). Grammatical aspects of speech errors. In Frederick Newmeyer (ed.) *Linguistics: The Cambridge Survey*. Vol.2. Cambridge, CUP, pp.117–138.

Frota, Sonia (2000). *Prosody and focus in European Portuguese*. New York, NY, Garland.

Frota, Sonia (2002). Tonal association and target alignment in European Portuguese nuclear falls. In Carlos Gussenhoven and Natasha Warner (eds.) *Laboratory Phonology 7*. Berlin/New York, Mouton de Gruyter, pp.387–418.

Fudge, E. C. (1969). Syllables. *JL* 5: 253–286.

Fudge, E. C. (1987). Branching structure within the syllable. *JL* 23: 359–377.

Fudge, E. C. (1989) "Syllable structure: a reply to Davis." *JL* 25: 219–220.

Fulmer, Sandra Lee (1997). *Parallelism and planes in Optimality Theory: Evidence from Afar*. Doctoral dissertation, University of Arizona.

Furby, Christine (1974). Garawa phonology. *Pacific Linguistics* Series A. 37: 1–11.

Gafos, Adamantios (1998a). A-templatic reduplication. *LI* 29: 515–527.

Gafos, Adamantios (1998b). Eliminating long-distance spreading. *NLLT* 16: 223–278.

Gafos, Adamantios (1998c). On the proper characterization of "nonconcatenative" languages. *ROA* 106.

Gafos, Adamantios (1999). *The articulatory basis of locality in phonology*. New York: Garland.

Gafos, Adamantios (2002). A grammar of gestural coordination. *NLLT* 20: 269–337.

Garrett, Merrill (1975). The analysis of sentence production. In G. Bower (ed.) *Psychology of learning and motivation*. Vol.9. New York, Academic Press, pp.133–177.

Gaskell, M. G. and W. D. Marslen-Wilson (1996). Phonological variation and inference in lexical access. *Journal of Experimental Psychology: Human Perception and Performance* 22: 144–158.

Gaskell, M. G. and W. D. Marslen-Wilson (1998). Mechanisms of phonological inference in speech perception. *Journal of Experimental Psychology: Human Perception and Performance* 24: 380–396.

Gerfen, C. (1999). *Phonology and phonetics in Coatzospan Mixtec*. Studies in natural language and linguistic theory. Dordrecht: Kluwer.

Gerfen, C. (2001). A critical view of licensing by cue: The case of Andalusian Spanish. In Linda Lombardi (ed.) *Segmental phonology in Optimality Theory*. Cambridge, CUP, pp.183–205.

Gerken, LouAnn (2002). Early sensitivity to linguistic form. *Annual Review of Language Acquisition* 2: 1–36.

Ghini, Mirco (1993). X-formation in Italian: a new proposal. In Carrie Dyck (ed.) *TWPL* 12.2, Department of Linguistics, University of Toronto, pp.41–78.

Ghomeshi, Jila, Ray Jackendoff, Nicole Rosen and Kevin Russell (2004). Contrastive focus reduplication in English (The salad-salad paper). *NLLT* 22: 307–257.

Gibson, Edward and Ken Wexler (1994). Triggers. *LI* 25.3: 407–454.

Gick, Bryan, Douglas Pulleyblank, Ngessimo M. Mutaka and Fiona Campbell (in press). *Low vowels and transparency in Kinande vowel harmony. Phonolgy* 23.1: 1–20.

Gnanadesikan, Amalia (1993). The feature geometry of coronal subplaces. In T. Sherer (ed.) *UMOP 16: Phonological Representations*. Amherst, MA, GLSA, pp.27–67.

Gnanadesikan, Amalia (1997). *Phonology with ternary scales*. Doctoral dissertation, University of Massachusetts, Amherst.

Gnanadesikan, Amalia (2004). Markedness and faithfulness constraints in child phonology. In René Kager, Joe Pater and Wim Zonneveld (eds.) *Constraints on phonological acquisition*. Cambridge, UK, CUP, pp.73–108. [Also ROA 67].

Goad, Heather (1997). Consonant harmony in child language: An optimality theoretic account. In S. J. Hannahs and Martha Young-Scholten (eds.) *Focus on phonological acquisition*. Amsterdam, Benjamins, pp.113–142.

Goedemans, Rob (1993). An Optimality account of onset sensitivity in QI Languages. *ROA* 26.

Goedemans, Rob (1998). *Weightless Segments: A phonetic and phonological study concerning the metrical irrelevance of syllable onsets.* LOT Dissertations 9. The Hague, Holland Academic Graphics.

Goedemans, Rob, Harry van der Hulst & Ellis Visch (1996). *Stress patterns of the world.* HIL Publications II. The Hague: Holland Academic Graphics.

Goldinger, S. D. (1996). Words and voices: Episodic traces in spoken word identification and recognition memory. *Journal of Experimental Psychology: Learning, Memory, and Cognition* 22: 1166–1182.

Goldrick, Matthew (2000). Turbid output representations and the unity of opacity. In M. Hirotani (ed.) *NELS 30.* Amherst, MA, GLSA, pp.231–246.

Goldsmith, John (1976a). *Autosegmental Phonology.* Doctoral dissertation, MIT.

Goldsmith, John (1976b). An overview of autosegmental phonology. *Linguistic Analysis* 2.1: 23–68.

Goldsmith, John (1984). Meussens' rule. In Mark Aronoff and Richard T. Oerhle (eds.) *Language sound structure.* Cambridge, MA, MIT Press, pp.245–249.

Goldsmith, John (1987). Tone and accent: getting the two together. *BLS* 13: 88–104.

Goldsmith, John (1988). Prosodic trends in the Bantu languages. In Harry van der Hulst and Norval Smith (eds.) *Autosegmental studies on pitch accent.* Dordrecht, Foris, pp.81–93.

Goldsmith, John (1990). *Autosegmental and metrical phonology.* Cambridge, MA, Basil Blackwell.

Goldsmith, John (1993a). Harmonic phonology. In John Goldsmith (ed.) *The last phonological rule: Reflections on constraints and derivations.* Chicago, University of Chicago Press, pp.21–60.

Goldsmith, John (1993b). Introduction. In John Goldsmith (ed.) *The last phonological rule: Reflections on constraints and derivations.* Chicago, Chicago University Press, pp.1–20.

Goldsmith, John (1994). A dynamic computational theory of accent systems. In J. Cole and C. W. Kisseberth (eds.) *Perspectives in phonology.* Stanford, Center for the Study of Language and Information, pp.1–28.

Goldsmith, John (ed.) (1995a). *The handbook of phonological theory.* Oxford, Blackwell.

Goldsmith, John (1995b). Phonological theory. In John A. Goldsmith (ed.) *The handbook of phonological theory.* Oxford, Blackwell, pp.1–23.

Goldsmith, John (1999a). An overview of autosegmental phonology. In John Goldsmith (ed.) *Phonological Theory: The essential readings.* Vol.137–161. Oxford, Blackwell.

Goldsmith, John (1999b). Tone. In R. A. Wilson and K. C. Keil (eds.) *MIT Encyclopaedia of the Cognitive Sciences.* Cambridge, MA, MIT Press, pp.837–839.

Goldsmith, John and G. Larson (1990). Local modeling and syllabification. In M. Ziolkowski, K. Deaton and M. Noske (eds). *CLS 26: The Parasession on the Syllable in Phonetics and Phonology*. vol. 2, Chicago, Chicago Linguistics Society, pp.129–142.

Golston, Chris (1995). Direct OT: Representation as pure markedness. *ROA* 71.

Goodman, Beverley D. (1995). *Features in Ponapean Phonology*. Doctoral dissertation, Cornell University.

Gordon, Matthew J. (2001). *Small-town values and big-city vowels: A study of the Northern Cities Shift in Michigan*. Publications of the American Dialect Society. Durham, NC, Duke University Press.

Gordon, Matthew K. (1999). *Syllable weight: Phonetics, phonology, and typology*. Doctoral dissertation, UCLA.

Gordon, Matthew K. (2001). A typology of contour tone restrictions. *Studies in Language* 25: 405–444.

Gordon, Matthew K. (2002a). A factorial typology of quantity-insensitive stress. *NLLT* 20.3: 491–552.

Gordon, Matthew K. (2002b). A phonetically driven account of syllable weight. *Lg* 78: 51–80.

Gordon, Matthew K. (2003). The phonology of pitch accents in Chickasaw. *Ph* 20.2: 173–218.

Gordon, Matthew K. (2004). Syllable weight. In B. Hayes, R. Kirchner and D. Steriade (eds.) *Phonetically based phonology*. Cambridge, CUP, pp.277–312.

Gordon, Matthew K. (to appear) A perceptually-driven account of onset-sensitive stress. Ms. University of California, Santa Barbara.

Gouskova, Maria (2001). Falling sonority onsets, loanwords, and syllable contact. *CLS* 37: 175–185.

Gouskova, Maria (2003). *Deriving economy: Syncope in Optimality Theory*. Doctoral dissertation, UMass. [Also ROA 610].

Gouskova, Maria (2004). Relational hierarchies in Optimality Theory: The case of syllable contact. *Ph* 21: 201–250.

Gow, David W., Jr. (2001). Assimilation and anticipation in continuous spoken word recognition. *Journal of Memory and Language* 45: 133–159.

Gow, David W. Jr. (2002). Does English coronal place assimilation create lexical ambiguity? *Journal of Experimental Psychology: Human Perception & Performance* 28: 163–179.

Gow, David W. Jr. (2003). Feature parsing: Feature cue mapping in spoken word recognition. *Perception & Psychophysics* 65: 575–590.

Grabe, Esther (1998a). *Comparative intonational phonology: English and German*. Doctoral dissertation, Max-Planck-Institut for Psycholinguistics and University of Nijmegen. http://www.phon.ox.ac.uk/~esther/thesis.html.

Grabe, Esther (1998b). Pitch accent realisation in English and German. *JPh* 26: 129–144.

Grabe, Esther, Brechtje Post, Francis Nolan and K. Farrar (2000). Pitch accent realization in four varieties of British English. *JPh* 28: 161–185.

Graf, Dafna (2005). *Alignment properties of affixes and their role in Hebrew morphology*. Handout, WECOL 2004, http://www.ulcl.leidenuniv.nl/index.php3?c=52.

Green, Thomas (1994). The stress window in Pirahã: A reanalysis of rhythm in Optimality Theory. *ROA* 45.

Green, Thomas and Michael Kenstowicz (1996). The lapse constraint. *Proceedings of the 6th Annual Meeting of the Formal Linguistics Society of the Midwest*, pp.1–16.

Greenberg, Joseph H. (1950). The patterning of root morphemes in Semitic. *Word* 6: 162–181.

Greenberg, Joseph H. (1966). Language universals. In Thomas Sebeok (ed.) *Current Trends in Linguistics*. Vol.3. The Hague, Mouton, pp.61–111.

Gregerson, K. J. (1976). Tongue-root and register in Mon Khmer. In P. Jenner, L. Thompson and S. Starosta (eds.) *Austroasiatic Studies*. Vol.1. Honolulu, University of Hawai'i Press, pp.323–369.

Gregores, E. and J. Suárez (1967). *A Description of Colloquial Guaraní*. The Hague, Mouton.

Grice, Martine (1995a). Leading tones and downstep in English. *Ph* 12.2: 183–233.

Grice, Martine (1995b). *The Intonation of interrogation in Palermo Italian: Implications for intonation theory*. Tübingen, Niemeyer.

Grice, Martine, D. Robert Ladd and Amalia Arvaniti (2000). On the place of phrase accents in intonational phonology. *Ph* 17.2: 143–185.

Grijzenhout, Janet (1995). Feature geometry and coronal transparency. In Harry van der Hulst and J. van der Weijer (eds.) *Leiden in Last: HIL Phonology Papers*. Vol.1. The Hague, Holland Academic Press, pp.165–185.

Grijzenhout, Janet (2001). Representing nasality in consonants. In T. Alan Hall (ed.) *Distinctive feature theory*. Berlin, Mouton de Gruyter, pp.177–210.

Grijzenhout, Janet and Sandra Joppen-Hellwig (2002). The lack of onsets in German child phonology. In Ingeborg Lasser (ed.) *The process of language acquisition (Proceedings of GALA 1999)*. Frankfurt am Main, Peter Lang Verlag, pp.319–339.

Grijzenhout, Janet and Martina Penke (2004). *On the interaction of phonology and morphology in German and Dutch first language acquisition and Broca's aphasia: The case of inflected verbs*. Paper presented at the 11th International Morphology Meeting, Vienna, February 2004.

Grimshaw, Jane (1997). Projection, heads, and Optimality. *LI* 28.3: 373–422.

Grønnum, N. (1989). Stress group patterns, sentence accents and sentence intonation in Southern Jutland (Sønderborg and Tønder) – with a view to German. *Annual Report of the Institute of Phonetics, University of Copenhagen* 23: 1–85.

Grønnum, N. (1991). Prosodic parameters in a variety of regional Danish standard languages. *Phonetica* 47: 188–214.

Grubb, D. M. (1977). *A practical writing system and short dictionary of Kwak'wala (Kwakiutl)*. Ottawa, National Museums of Canada.

Grunwell, P. (1987). *Clinical phonology*. London, Croom Helm.

Guenther, F. H., C. Y. Espy-Wilson, S. E. Boyce, M. L. Matthies, M. Zandipour and J. S. Perkell (1999). Articulatory tradeoffs reduce acoustic variability during American English /r/ production. *JASA* 105: 2854–2865.

Guerssel, M. (1986). Glides in Berber and syllabicity. *LI* 17: 1–12.

Guion, S. G. (1998). The role of perception in the sound change of velar palatalization. *Phonetica* 55: 18–52.

Gussenhoven, Carlos (1983a). Focus, mode and the nucleus. *JL* 19.2.

Gussenhoven, Carlos (1983b). Testing the reality of focus domains. *Language and Speech* 26.1: 61–80.

Gussenhoven, Carlos (1984). *On the grammar and semantics of sentence accents*. Dordrecht, Foris.

Gussenhoven, Carlos (1991). The English rhythm rule as an accent deletion rule. *Ph* 8: 1–35.

Gussenhoven, Carlos (1992). Sentence accents and argument structure. In Iggy Roca (ed.) *Thematic structure: Its role in grammar*. Berlin and New York, NY, Foris, pp.79–106.

Gussenhoven, Carlos (1999). Discreteness and gradience in intonational contrasts. *Language and Speech* 42: 281–305.

Gussenhoven, Carlos (2000a). The boundary tones are coming. In Michael Broe and Janet Pierrehumbert (eds.) *Papers in laboratory phonology V: Acquisition and the lexicon*. Cambridge, UK, CUP, pp.132–151.

Gussenhoven, Carlos (2000b). The lexical tone contrast of Roermond Dutch in Optimality Theory. In M. Horne (ed.) *Prosody: Theory and experiment. Studies presented to Gosta Bruce*. Dordrecht/Boston/London, Kluwer, pp.129–167. [Also ROA 382].

Gussenhoven, Carlos (2004). *The phonology of tone and intonation*. Cambridge, CUP.

Gussenhoven, Carlos (2005). Transcription of Dutch intonation. In Sun-Ah Jun (ed.) *Prosodic typology: The phonology of intonation and phrasing*. Oxford, UK, Oxford University Press, pp.118–145.

Gussenhoven, Carlos and Haike Jacobs (1998). *Understanding phonology*. London, Arnold.

Gussenhoven, Carlos and René Kager (eds.) (2001). *Phonetics in Phonology. Ph* 18.1.

Gussenhoven, Carlos and J. Peters (2004). A tonal analysis of Cologne schärfung. *Ph* 22: 251–285.

Gussenhoven, Carlos and Toni Rietveld (1992). Intonation contours, prosodic structure and preboundary lengthening. *JPh* 20: 283–303.

Gussenhoven, Carlos, J. Terken, and Toni Rietveld (1999). Transcription of Dutch intonation: courseware. http://lands.let.kunn.nl/todi [1 April 2006]

Gussenhoven, Carlos and Toni Rietveld (2000). The behavior of H* and L* under variations in pitch range in Dutch rising contours. *Language and Speech* 43.2: 183–203.

Gussenhoven, Carlos and Peter van der Vliet (1999). The phonology of tone and intonation in the Dutch dialect of Venlo. *JL* 35: 99–135.

Gussenhoven, Carlos and Natasha Warner (eds.) (2002). *Laboratory phonology 7*. Berlin and New York, Mouton de Gruyter.

Gussmann, Edmund (2002). *Phonology: Analysis and theory*. Cambridge, CUP.

Guy, Gregory (1980). Variation in the group and the individual: The case of final stop deletion. In William Labov (ed.) *Locating language in time and space*. New York, NY, Academic Press, pp.1–36.

Guy, Gregory (1991a). Contextual conditioning in variable lexical phonology. *Language variation and change* 3.2: 223–239.

Guy, Gregory (1991b). Explanation in variable phonology: An exponential model of morphological constraints. *Language Variation and Language Change* 3: 1–22.

Guy, Gregory (1994). The phonology of variation. *CLS 30, Vol.2: Parasession on variation in linguistic theory*. Chicago, IL, CLS, pp.133–149.

Guy, Gregory (1997a). Competence, performance and the generative grammar of variation. In Frans Hinskins, Roeland van Hout and Leo Wetzels (eds.) *Variation, change and phonological theory*. Amsterdam, John Benjamins, pp.125–143.

Guy, Gregory (1997b). Violable is variable: Optimality Theory and linguistic variation. *Language Variation and Change* 9.3: 333–347.

Guy, Gregory and Charles Boberg (1997). Inherent variability and the Obligatory Contour Principle. *Language variation and change* 9.2: 149–164.

Haas, Mary (1941). Tunica. In F. Boas (ed.) *Handbook of American Indian languages*. Vol.4. New York, Augustin Publishers, pp.430–530.

Haas, Mary (1946). A grammatical sketch of Tunica. In C. Osgood (ed.) *Linguistic structures of native North America*. Vol.6. Viking Fund Publications in Anthropology. New York, Viking Fund, pp.337–366.

Haas, Mary (1968). Notes on a Chipewyan dialect. *IJAL* 34: 165–175.

Haas, Mary (1977). Tonal Accent in Creek. In Larry Hyman (ed.) *Studies in Stress and Accent*. Southern California Occasional Papers in Linguistics 4: 195–208. Reprinted in William C. Sturtevant (ed.) (1987). *A Creek Source Book*. New York, Garland Press.

Haas, Wim de (1988). *A formal theory of vowel coalescence: A case study of Ancient Greek*. Publications in Language Sciences. Dordrecht, Foris.

Haiman, J. (1980). *Hua: a Papuan language of the Eastern Highlands of New Guinea*. Amsterdam, John Benjamins.

Hajek, John (1997). *Universals of sound change in nasalization*. Oxford, Blackwell.

Hajek, John and Rob Goedemans (2003). Word-initial geminates and stress in Pattani Malay. *The Linguistic Review* 20: 79–94.

Hale, Kenneth and Elisabeth Selkirk (1987). Government and tonal phrasing in Papago. *Phonology Yearbook* 4: 151–183.

Hale, Mark and Charles Reiss (1998). Formal and empirical arguments concerning phonological acquisition. *LI* 29.4: 656–683.

Hale, Mark and Charles Reiss (2000a). Language as cognition. In N. Burton-Roberts, P. Carr and G. Docherty (eds.) *Phonological knowledge: Conceptual and empirical issues*. Oxford, OUP, pp.161–184.

Hale, Mark and Charles Reiss (2000b). 'Substance abuse' and 'dysfunctionalism': Current trends in phonology. *LI* 31: 157–169.

Hall, T. A. (1997). *The Phonology of Coronals*. Amsterdam: Benjamins.

Halle, Morris (1959). *The sound pattern of Russian*. The Hague, Mouton.

Halle, Morris (1983). On distinctive features and their articulatory implementation. *NLLT* 1: 91–105.

Halle, Morris (1990). Respecting metrical structure. *NLLT* 8.2: 149–176.

Halle, Morris (1995a). Comments on Luigi Burzio's 'The rise of optimality theory'. *GLOT* 1(9/10): 27–28.

Halle, Morris (1995b). Feature geometry and feature spreading. *LI* 26: 1–46.

Halle, Morris and G. N. Clements (1983). *Problem book in phonology*. Cambridge, MA, MIT Press.

Halle, Morris and William Idsardi (1995). General properties of stress and metrical structure. In John Goldsmith (ed.) *A handbook of phonological theory*. Oxford, Basil Blackwell, pp.403–443.

Halle, Morris and J.-R. Vergnaud (1980). Three dimensional phonology. *Journal of Linguistic Research* 1: 83–105.

Halle, Morris and Jean-Roger Vergnaud (1982). On the framework of autosegmental phonology. In Harry van der Hulst and Norval Smith (eds.) *The structure of phonological representations*. Vol.1. Dordrecht, Foris, pp.65–82.

Halle, Morris and Jean-Roger Vergnaud (1987). *An essay on stress*. Cambridge, MA, MIT Press.

Halle, Morris and Michael Kenstowicz (1991). The Free Element Condition and Cyclic versus Noncyclic Stress. LI 22:457–501.

Halle, Morris and Kenneth Stevens (1971). A note on laryngeal features. *Quarterly Progress Report 101. MIT.*

Halle, Morris and Kenneth Stevens (1979). Some reflections on the theoretical bases of phonetics. In B. Lindblom and S. Öhman (eds.) *Frontiers of speech communication*. London, Academic Press, pp.335–349.

Hallé, P. A., C. T. Best and A. Bachrach (2003). Perception of /dl/ and /tl/ clusters: A cross-linguistic perceptual study with French and Israeli listeners. *ICPhS 15 (Barcelona)*: 2893–2896.

Hallé, P. A., J. Segui, U. Frauenfelder and C. Meunier (1998). Processing of illegal consonant clusters: A case of perceptual assimilation? *Journal of Experimental Psychology: Human Perception and Performance* 24: 592–608.

Halliday, Michael A. K. (1970). *A course in spoken English: Intonation*. London, UK, OUP.

Hamann, Silke R. (2003). *The phonetics and phonology of retroflexes*. Doctoral dissertation, Utrecht University.

Hamid, A.-H. (1984). *A descriptive analysis of Sudanese colloquial Arabic*. Doctoral dissertation, University of Illinois, Urbana.

Hamilton, Philip (1993). Intrinsic markedness relations in segment structure. *TWPL* 12.2: 79–95.

Hamilton, Philip (1996). *Phonetic constraints and markedness in the phonotactics of Australian Aboriginal languages*. Doctoral dissertation, University of Toronto.

Hammond, Michael (1984). *Constraining metrical theory: A modular theory of rhythm and destressing*. Doctoral dissertation, UCLA.

Hammond, Michael (1990). Deriving ternarity. In Colleen M. Fitzgerald and Andrea Heiberg (eds.) *Coyote Papers: Working Papers in Linguistics*. Vol.9, pp.39–58.

Hammond, Michael (1994). An OT account of variability in Walmatjari stress. *ROA* 20.

Hammond, Michael (1997). Parsing syllables: Modeling OT computationally. *ROA* 222.

Hammond, Michael (1999). *The phonology of English: A prosodic Optimality-Theoretic approach*. Oxford, OUP.

Hankamer, J. and J. Aissen (1974). The sonority hierarchy. In Anthony Bruck, Robert A. Fox and M. W. la Galy (eds.) *CLS 10.2: Papers from the parasession on Natural Phonology*. Chicago, Chicago Linguistic Society, pp.131–145.

Hansen, Kenneth C. and L. E. Hansen (1969). Pintupi phonology. *Oceanic Linguistics* 8: 153–170.

Hanson, Kristin & Paul Kiparsky (1996). A parametric theory of poetic meter. *Language* 72: 287–334.

Hansson, Gunnar (2001a). The phonologization of production constraints: evidence from consonant harmony. In Mary Andronis, Christopher Ball, Heidi Elston and Sylvain Neuvel (eds.) *CLS 37: The Main Session*. Chicago, CLS, pp.187–200.

Hansson, Gunnar (2001b). *Theoretical and typological issues in consonant harmony*. Doctoral dissertation, UCB.

Haraguchi, Shosuke (1977). *The tone pattern of Japanese: An autosegmental theory of tonology*. Tokyo, Kaitakusha.

Hargus, Sharon (1988). *The lexical phonology of Sekani*. New York, Garland.

Hargus, Sharon and Ellen M. Kaisse (1993). Introduction. In Sharon Hargus and Ellen M. Kaisse (eds.) *Studies in Lexical Phonology*. San Diego, Academic Press, pp.1–19.

Harnsberger, James D. (1999). *The effect of linguistic experience on perceptual similarity among nasal consonants: A multidimensional scaling analysis*. Research on spoken language processing 23, Indiana University.

Harris, James W. (1969). *Spanish Phonology*. Cambridge, MIT Press.

Harris, James W. (1983). *Syllable structure and stress in Spanish*. Cambridge, MA, MIT Press.

Harris, James W. (1984a). Autosegmental Phonology, Lexical Phonology, and Spanish nasals. In Mark Aronoff and Richard Oehrle (eds.) *Language Sound Structure*. Cambridge, MIT Press, pp.67–82.

Harris, James W. (1984b). Theories of Phonological Representation and Nasal Consonants in Spanish. In Phillip Baldi (ed.) *Papers from the XIIth Linguistic Symposium on Romance Languages*. Amsterdam, John Benjamins, pp.153–168.

Harris, James W. (1989). Towards a lexical analysis of a sound change in progress. *JL* 25: 35–56.

Harris, John (1990). Derived phonological contrasts. In Susan Ramsaran (ed.) *Studies in the pronunciation of English: A commemorative volume in honour of A. C. Gimson.* London, Routledge, pp.87–105.

Harris, John (1994). *English sound structure.* Oxford, Blackwell.

Harris, John (1997). Licensing Inheritance: an integrated theory of neutralisation. *Ph* 14: 315–370.

Harris, John (2004). Release the captive coda: the foot as a domain of phonetic interpretation. In J. Local, R. Ogden and R. Temple (eds.) *Phonetic interpretation.* Vol.6. Papers in Laboratory Phonology 6. Cambridge, CUP, pp.103–129.

Harris, John (2005). Vowel reduction as information loss. In P. Carr, J. Durand and C. J. Ewen (eds.) *Headhood, elements, specification and contrastivity.* Amsterdam, Benjamins, pp.119–132.

Harris, John and E. Gussmann (1998). Final codas: why the west was wrong. In Eugeniusz Cyran (ed.) *Structure and interpretation in phonology: studies in phonology.* Lublin, Folia, pp.139–162.

Harris, John and Geoff Lindsey (1995). The elements of phonological representation. In Jacques Durand and Francis Katamba (eds.) *Frontiers of phonology: atoms, structures, derivations.* Harlow, Essex, Longman, pp.34–79.

Harris, John and Geoff Lindsey (2000). Vowel patterns in mind and sound. In Noel Burton-Roberts, Philip Carr and Gerry Docherty (eds.) *Phonological knowledge: conceptual and empirical issues.* Oxford, OUP, pp.185–205.

Harris, Zellig (1951). *Methods in structural linguistics.* Chicago, Chicago University Press. [Reprinted in 1960 as *Structural Linguistics*].

Haugen, E. (1956). The syllable in linguistic description. In Morris Halle, H. G. Lunt and H. McClean (eds.) *For Roman Jakobson.* The Hague, Mouton, pp.213–221.

Hauser, Marc D., Noam Chomsky, and W. Tecumseh Fitch (2002). The Faculty of Language: What is it, who has it, and how did it evolve? *Science* 298.5598: 1569–1579.

Hay, Jennifer, Janet Pierrehumbert and Mary Beckman (2004). Speech perception, well-formedness and the statistics of the lexicon. In John Local, Richard Ogden and Rosalind Temple (eds.) *Phonetic Interpretation: Papers in Laboratory Phonology VI.* Cambridge, CUP, pp.58–74.

Hayes, Bruce (1980). *A metrical theory of stress rules.* Doctoral dissertation, MIT.

Hayes, Bruce (1982). Extrametricality and English stress. *LI* 13: 227–276.

Hayes, Bruce (1985). Iambic and trochaic rhythm in stress rules. In Mary Niepokuj, Mary VanClay, Vassiliki Nikiforidou and Deborah Feder (eds.) *BLS* 11: 429–446.

Hayes, Bruce (1986). Inalterability in CV phonology. *Lg* 62.2: 321–351.

Hayes, Bruce (1987). A revised parametric metrical theory. In Joyce McDonough and Bernadette Plunket (eds.) *NELS* 17, pp.274–289.

Hayes, Bruce (1989a). Compensatory lengthening in moraic phonology. *LI* 20: 253–306.

Hayes, Bruce (1989b). The prosodic hierarchy in meter. In Paul Kiparsky and Gilbert Youmans (eds.) *Rhythm and meter.* Orlando, FL, Academic Press, pp.201–260.

Hayes, Bruce (1995). *Metrical Stress Theory: principles and case studies*. Chicago, University of Chicago Press.

Hayes, Bruce (1999). Phonetically-driven phonology: the role of optimality theory and inductive grounding. In M. Darnell, Edith A. Moravscik, M. Noonan, F. Newmeyer and K. Wheatley (eds.) *Functionalism and Formalism in linguistics, vol. 1: General Papers*. Amsterdam, Benjamins, pp.243–285. [Also ROA 158].

Hayes, Bruce (2000). Gradient well-formedness in Optimality Theory. In Joost Dekkers, Frank van der Leeuw and Jeroen van de Weijer (eds.) *Optimality Theory: Phonology, syntax and acquisition*. Oxford, UK, OUP, pp.88–120.

Hayes, Bruce (2004a). Phonetically driven phonology: the role of Optimality Theory and inductive grounding. In John McCarthy (ed.) *Optimality Theory in phonology: A reader*. Oxford, Blackwell, pp.290–309.

Hayes, Bruce (2004b). Phonological acquisition in Optimality Theory: the early stages. In René Kager, Joe Pater and Wim Zonneveld (eds.) *Constraints on phonological acquisition*. Cambridge, UK, CUP, pp.158–203.

Hayes, Bruce (2004c). *Stochastic phonological knowledge: The case of Hungarian vowel harmony*. Handout from Colloquium at New York University (NYU), http://www.humnet.ucla.edu/humnet/linguistics/people/hayes/ HayesNYUHandout.pdf.

Hayes, Bruce and May Abad (1989). Reduplication and syllabification in Ilocano. *Ln* 77: 331–374.

Hayes, Bruce, Robert Kirchner and Donca Steriade (eds.) (2004). *Phonetically based phonology*. Cambridge, UK, CUP.

Hayes, Bruce and Aditi Lahiri (1991). Bengali intonational phonology. *NLLT* 9: 47–96.

Hayes, Bruce and Margaret McEachern (1998). Quatrain form in English folk verse. *Lg* 74.3: 473–507.

Hayes, Bruce and Donca Steriade (2004). Introduction: the phonetic bases of phonological markedness. In Bruce Hayes, Robert Kirchner and Donca Steriade (eds.) *Phonetically based phonology*. Cambridge, CUP, pp.1–33.

Hayes, Bruce, Bruce Tesar and Kie Zuraw (2003). *OTSoft: Optimality Theory Software, version 2.1*. http://www.linguistics.ucla.edu/people/hayes/otsoft.

Hayward, K. M. and R. J. Hayward (1989). "Guttural": arguments for a new distinctive feature. *Transactions of the Philological Society* 87: 179–193.

Heath, Jeffery (1999). *A grammar of Koyra Chiini, the Songhay of Timbuktu*. Berlin, Mouton de Gruyter.

Hegenscheidt, C., U. Janssen and Martina Penke (2002). *Agrammatic aphasia can lead to a deranking of phonological constraints*, Paper presented at the Third International Conference on the Mental Lexicon, Banff, Alberta, Canada, October 2002.

Heinz, Jeff, Greg Kobele, and Jason Riggle (2005). Exploring the typology of quantity insensitive stress systems without gradient constraints. Handout from talk presented at the Linguistic Society of America.

[http://www.linguistics.ucla.edu/people/grads/kobele/files/HeinzEtA105L-SA_Handout.pdf – 1 April 2006.

Helimski, E. (1998). Nganasan. In D. Abondolo (ed.) *The Uralic Languages.* London and New York, Routledge, pp.480–515.

Henderson, J. B. (1984). *Velopharyngeal function in oral and nasal vowels: A cross-language study.* Doctoral dissertation, University of Connecticut, Storrs.

Hendricks, Sean (1999). *Reduplication without template constraints: A study in bare-consonant reduplication.* Doctoral dissertation, University of Arizona.

Herbert, R. K. (1986). *Language universals, markedness theory, and natural phonetic processes.* Berlin, Mouton de Gruyter.

Hermans, Ben and Marc van Oostendorp (eds.) (1999). *The derivational residue in phonological Optimality Theory.* Amsterdam, John Benjamins.

Heuven, Vincent van and Judith Haan (2002). Temporal distribution of interrogativity markers in Dutch: A perceptual study. In Carlos Gussenhoven and Natasha Warner (eds.) *Laboratory Phonology 7.* Berlin and New York, Mouton de Gruyter, pp.61–86.

Hewitt, Mark (1992). *Vertical maximization and metrical theory.* Doctoral dissertation, Brandeis University.

Hinskins, Frans, Roeland van Hout and Leo Wetzels (eds.) (1997). *Variation, change and phonological theory.* Amsterdam and Philadelphia, PA, John Benjamins.

Hint, Mati (1973). *Eesti keele sonafonoloogia I.* Tallinn, Estonia, Eesti NSV Teaduste Akadeemia.

Hirose, H. (1997). Investigating the physiology of laryngeal structures. In W. J. Hardcastle and J. Laver, (eds.), *The handbook of phonetic sciences.* Oxford: Basil Blackwell, pp.116–136.

Hochberg, J. G. (1988a). First steps in the acquisition of Spanish stress. *JCL* 15.3: 273–292.

Hochberg, J. G. (1988b). Learning Spanish stress: Developmental and theoretical perspectives. *Lg* 64.4: 638–706.

Hockett, C. (1955). *A manual of phonology.* Chicago, University of Chicago Press.

Hollenbach, Barbara (1977). Phonetic vs phonemic correspondence in two Trique dialects. In William R. Merrifield (ed.) *Studies in Otomanguean Phonology.* Dallas, SIL, pp.35–67.

Holmer, Arthur (1996). *A parametric grammar of Seediq.* Lund, Lund University Press.

Holst, T., & Francis Nolan (1995). The influence of syntactic structure on [s] to [ʃ] assimilation, In B. Connell & A. Arvaniti (eds.), *Papers in Laboratory Phonology IV*, Cambridge, UK: Cambridge University Press, pp.315–333.

Holt, D. Eric (ed.) (2003). *Optimality Theory and language change.* Studies in NLLT. Dordrecht, Kluwer Academic Publishers.

Holt, L. L., A. J. Lotto and K. R. Kluender (2001). Influence of fundamental frequency on stop-consonant voicing perception: A case of learned covariation or auditory enhancement? *JASA* 109.2: 764–774.

Hombert, J.-M. (1987). Phonetic conditioning for the development of nasalization in Teke. *ICPhS 11 (Talinn)* 2: 273–276.

Hombert, J.-M., John J. Ohala and W. G. Ewan (1979). Phonetic explanations for the development of tones. *Lg* 55: 37–58.

Hong, Sung-Hoon (1994). *Issues in round harmony: Grounding, identity, and their interaction*. Doctoral dissertation, University of Arizona.

Honorof, Douglas (1999). *Articulatory gestures and Spanish nasal assimilation*. Doctoral dissertation, Yale University.

Hooper [Bybee], Joan (1976). *An introduction to Natural Generative Phonology*. New York, Academic Press.

Hooper [Bybee], Joan (1979). Substantive principles in Natural Generative Phonology. In Daniel A. Dinnsen (ed.) *Current approaches to phonological theory*. Bloomington, IN, Indiana University Press, pp.106–125.

Hore, Michael (1981). Syllable length and stress in Nunggubuyu. In Bruce Waters (ed.) *Australian phonologies: Collected papers*. Working papers of SIL-AAB. Darwin, Australia, SIL, pp.1–62.

Horwood, Graham (2002). Precedence faithfulness governs morpheme position. In L. Mikkelsen and C. Potts (eds.) *WCCFL 21*, Somerville, MA, Cascadilla Press, pp.166–179.

Houde, J. F. and M. I. Jordan (1998). Adaptation in speech production. *Science* 279: 1213–1216.

Houde, J. F. and M. I. Jordan (2002). Sensorimotor adaptation of speech I: Compensation and adaptation. *Journal of Speech, Language, and Hearing Research* 45: 239–262.

House, A. S. and K. N. Stevens (1956). Analog studies of the nasalization of vowels. *Journal of Speech and Hearing Disorders* 21: 218–232.

Howe, Darin and Douglas Pulleyblank (2004). Harmonic scales of faithfulness. *CJL* 49: 1–49.

Hsiao, Franny (2002). Tonal domains are stress domains in Taiwanese – evidence from focus. In Anikó Csirmaz, Zhiqiang Li, Andrew Nevins, Olga Vaysman and Michael Wagner (eds.) *MITWPL 42: Phonological answers (and their corresponding questions)*. Cambridge, MA, pp.109–140.

Hualde, José Ignacio (1987). On Basque affricates. *WCCFL* 6, pp.77–89.

Hualde, José Ignacio (1991). *Basque phonology*. New York, Routledge.

Hualde, José Ignacio, Gorka Elordieta, Iñaki Gaminde and Rajka Smiljani'ć (2002). From pitch accent to stress-accent in Basque. In Carlos Gussenhoven and Natasha Warner (eds.) *Laboratory Phonology* 7, pp.547–584.

Huang, James C.-T. (1980). The metrical structure of terraced level tones. *Cahiers Linguistiques d'Ottawa* 9: 257–270.

Huffman, M. K. and R. A. Krakow (eds.) (1993). *Nasals, nasalization and the velum*. Phonetics and Phonology 5. San Diego, Academic Press.

Hulst, Harry van der (1984). *Syllable structure and stress in Dutch*. Dordrecht, Germany, Foris.

Hulst, Harry van der (1989). Atoms of segmental structure: Components, gestures and dependency. *Ph* 6: 253–284.

Hulst, Harry van der and Colin J. Ewen (1991). Major class and manner features. In P. M. Bertinetto, Michael Kenstowicz and M. Loporcaro (eds.) *Certamen Phonologicum II: Papers from the 1990 Cortona Phonology Meeting*. Torino, Rosenberg and Sellier, pp.19–41.

Hulst, Harry van der and Marian Klamer (1996). The uneven trochee and the structure of Kambera roots. In Marina Nespor and Norval Smith (eds.) *Dam Phonology*. The Hague, Holland Academic Graphics.

Hulst, Harry van der and Norval Smith (eds.) (1988). *Features, segmental structure, and harmony processes, Vols. I & II*. Dordrecht, Foris.

Hulst, Harry van der and Ellis Visch (1992). Iambic lengthening in Carib. In Reineke Bok-Bennema and Roeland van Hout (eds.) *Linguistics in the Netherlands*. Amsterdam, John Benjamins, pp.113–124.

Hume, Elizabeth (1992). *Front vowels, coronal consonants and their interaction in non-linear phonology*. Doctoral dissertation, Cornell University.

Hume, Elizabeth (2003). Language specific markedness: The case of place of articulation. *Studies in phonetics, phonology and morphology* 9.2: 295–310.

Hume, Elizabeth (2004). Deconstructing markedness: A Predictability-based Approach. ms. Ohio State University, http://www.ling.ohio-state.edu/ ~ehume [1 April 2006].

Hume, Elizabeth and Keith Johnson (eds.) (2001). *The role of speech perception in phonology*. San Diego, Academic Press.

Hume, Elizabeth and David Odden (1996). Reconsidering [consonantal]. *Ph* 13.3: 345–376.

Hume, Elizabeth and George Tserdanelis (2002). Labial unmarkedness in Sri Lankan Portuguese Creole. *Ph* 19.3: 451–458.

Hung, Henrietta (1994). *The rhythmic and prosodic organization of edge constituents*. Doctoral dissertation, Brandeis University. [Also ROA 24].

Hyde, Brett (2002). A restrictive theory of metrical stress. *Ph* 19.3: 313–359.

Hyman, Larry (1973). The feature [grave] in phonological theory. *JPh* 1: 329–337.

Hyman, Larry (1975). *Phonological theory and analysis*. Fort Worth, TX, Holt, Rinheart and Winston.

Hyman, Larry (1976). Phonologization. In Alphonse Juilland, A. M. Devine and Laurence D. Stephens (eds.) *Linguistic studies offered to Joseph Greenberg on the occasion of his sixtieth birthday*. Saratoga, Anma Libri, pp.407–418.

Hyman, Larry (1977). On the nature of linguistic stress. In Larry Hyman (ed.) *Studies in stress and accent*. Southern California Occasional Papers in Linguistics. Los Angeles, CA, University of Southern California, pp.37–82.

Hyman, Larry (1985). *A theory of phonological weight*. Dordrecht, Foris.

Hyman, Larry (1988). Underspecification and vowel height transfer in Esimbi. *Ph* 5: 255–273.

Hyman, Larry (1993). Register tone and tonal geometry. In Harry van der Hulst and K. Snider (eds.) *The phonology of tone: The representation of tonal register*. Berlin, Mouton de Gruyter, pp.75–108.

Hyman, Larry (1995) Nasal consonant harmony at a distance: The case of Yaka. *Studies in African Linguistics* 24: 5–30.

Hyman, Larry (2001a). The limits of phonetic determinism in phonology: *NC revisited. In Elizabeth Hume and Keith Johnson (eds.) *The role of speech perception in phonology*. San Diego, Academic Press, pp.141–185.

Hyman, Larry (2001b). Privative tone in Bantu. In S. Kaji (ed.) *Cross-linguistic studies of tonal phenomena*. Tokyo, Institute for the study of languages and cultures, pp.237–257.

Hyman, Larry (2001c). Tone systems. In M. Haspelmath, E. König, W. Oesterreicher and W. Raible (eds.) *Language typology and language universals: An international handbook*. Vol.2. Berlin & New York, Walter de Gruyter, pp.1367–1380.

Hyman, Larry (2004). Why describe African languages? In Akinbiyi Akinlabi and Oluseye Adesola (eds.) *Proceedings of the 4th World Conference of African Linguistics*. Köln, Rüdiger Köppe Verlag, pp.21–41.

Hyman, Larry and E. R. Byarushengo (1984). A model of Haya tonology. In G. N. Clements and John Goldsmith (eds.) *Autosegmental studies in Bantu tone*. Dordrecht, Foris, pp.53–103.

Hyman, Larry M. and William R. Leben (2000). Suprasegmental processes. In Geert Booij, C. Lehmann and J. Mugdan (eds.) *A handbook on inflection and word formation*. Berlin, De Gruyter, pp.587–594.

Hyman, Larry and R. Schuh (1974). Universals of tone rules: Evidence from West Africa. *Linguistics Inquiry* 5: 81–115.

Idsardi, William (1992). *The computation of prosody*. Doctoral dissertation, MIT.

Idsardi, William (1998). Tiberian Hebrew spirantization and phonological derivations. *LI* 29: 37–73.

Idsardi, William (2000). Clarifying opacity. *The Linguistic Review* 17.2–4: 337–350.

Ingram, David (1974). Phonological rules in young children. *JCL* 1: 49–64.

Ingram, David (1980). A comparative study of phonological development in normal and linguistically delayed children. *Proceedings of the first Wisconsin symposium on research in child language disorders*. Vol.1, pp.23–33.

Ingram, David and B. Terselic (1983). Final ingression: A case of deviant child phonology. *Topics in Language Disorders* 3: 45–50.

Ingria, R. (1980). Compensatory lengthening as a metrical phenomenon. *LI* 11: 465–495.

Inkelas, Sharon (1996). The interaction of phrase and word rules in Turkish: an apparent paradox in the prosodic hierarchy. *The Linguistic Review* 13: 193–217.

Inkelas, Sharon (1998). The theoretical status of morphologically conditioned phonology: A case study of dominance effects. In Geert Booij and Jaap van Marle (eds.) *Yearbook of Morphology 1997*. Dordrecht, Kluwer, pp.121–155.

Inkelas, Sharon (1999). Exceptional stress-attracting suffixes in Turkish: representations vs. the grammar. In Harry van der Hulst, René Kager and Wim Zonneveld (eds.) *The Prosody-Morphology Interface*. Cambridge, UK, CUP, pp.134–187. [Also ROA 39].

Inkelas, Sharon, Cemil Orhan Orgun and Cheryl Zoll (1997). The implications of lexical exceptions for the nature of grammar. In Iggy Roca (ed.) *Derivations and constraints in phonology*. Oxford, UK, Clarendon Press, pp.393–418.

Inkelas, Sharon and Draga Zec (1988). Serbo-Croatian pitch accent. *Lg* 64: 227–248.

Inkelas, Sharon and Cheryl Zoll (1999). Reduplication as morphological doubling. *ROA* 412.

Inkelas, Sharon and Cheryl Zoll (2003). Is grammar dependence real? *ROA* 587.

Inkelas, Sharon and Cheryl Zoll (2005). *Reduplication: Doubling in morphology*. Cambridge, CUP.

Innes, D. (1969). *Mende-English dictionary*. Cambridge, UK, CUP.

Ishii, Toru (1996). An optimality theoretic approach to ternary stress systems. In Brian Agbayani and Naomi Harada (eds.) *Proceedings of the South Western Optimality Theory Workshop (SWOT II)*. UCI Working Papers in Linguistics. Irvine, CA, University of California, Irvine.

Itkonen, Erkki (1955). Ueber die Betonungsverhältnisse in den finnisch-ugrischen Sprachen. *Acta Linguistica Academiae Scientiarum Hungaricae* 5: 21–23.

Itô, Junko (1986). *Syllable theory in prosodic phonology*. Doctoral dissertation, UMass.

Itô, Junko (1989). A prosodic theory of epenthesis. *NLLT* 7: 217–259.

Itô, Junko, Yoshihisa Kitagawa and Armin Mester (1996). Prosodic faithfulness and correspondence: Evidence from a Japanese argot. *Journal of East Asian Linguistics* 5: 217–294.

Itô, Junko and Armin Mester (1986). The phonology of voicing in Japanese: Theoretical consequences for morphological accessibility. *LI* 17: 49–73.

Itô, Junko and Armin Mester (1992). *Weak layering and word binarity*, Manuscript. UCSC.

Itô, Junko and Armin Mester (1995). Japanese phonology. In John Goldsmith (ed.) *The handbook of phonological theory*. Oxford, UK, Blackwell, pp.817–838.

Itô, Junko and Armin Mester (1997). Correspondence and compositionality: The Ga-gyo variation in Japanese phonology. In Iggy Roca (ed.) *Derivations and constraints in phonology*. Oxford, UK, Clarendon Press, pp.419–462.

Itô, Junko and Armin Mester (1999). The phonological lexicon. In Matsuko Tsujimura (ed.) *The handbook of Japanese linguistics*. Oxford, UK, Blackwell, pp.62–100.

Itô, Junko and Armin Mester (2001). Structure preservation and stratal opacity in German. In Linda Lombardi (ed.) *Segmental phonology in Optimality Theory*. Cambridge, CUP, pp.261–295.

Itô, Junko and Armin Mester (2003). *Japanese morphophonemics: Markedness and Word Structure*. Cambridge, MA, MIT Press.

Itô, Junko, Armin Mester and Jaye Padgett (1995). Licensing and underspecification in Optimality Theory. *LI* 26: 571–613.

Iverson, Gregory (1995). Rule ordering. In John Goldsmith (ed.) *The handbook of phonological theory*. Oxford, Blackwell, pp.609–614.

Iverson, Gregory and Shinsook Lee (1995). Variation as optimality in Korean cluster reduction. In Janet Fuller, Ho Han and David Parkinson (eds.) *ESCOL* 11: 174–185.

Iverson, Gregory and J. Salmons (1995). Aspiration and laryngeal representation in Germanic. *Ph* 12: 369–396.

Iwai, Melissa (1989). *A prosodic analysis of Japanese loanwords*. BA thesis, UCSC.

Jackendoff, Ray (1972). *Semantic interpretation in generative grammar vol. 2: Studies in Linguistics Series*. Cambridge, MA, MIT Press.

Jackendoff, Ray (2002). *Foundations of language: brain, meaning, grammar, evolution*. Oxford, OUP.

Jacobs, Haike (1990). On Markedness and bounded stress systems. *The Linguistic Review* 7: 81–119.

Jacobs, Haike (2000). The revenge of the uneven trochee: Latin main stress, metrical constituency, stress-related phenomena and OT. In Lahiri, Aditi (ed.) *Analogy, levelling, markedness*. Mouton de Gruyter, Berlin, New York, pp.333–352.

Jacobs, Joachim (1993). Integration. In Marga Reis (ed.) *Wortstellung und Informationsstruktur*. Tübingen, Niemeyer, pp.63–116.

Jacobs, Joachim (1999). Informational autonomy. In Peter Bosch and Rob van der Sandt (eds.) *Focus: Linguistic, cognitive, and computational perspectives*. Cambridge, CUP, pp.56–81.

Jagger, P. (2001). *Hausa*. London Oriental and African Language Library 7. Amsterdam and Philadelphia, John Benjamins.

Jakobson, Roman (1931). Prinzipien der historischen Phonologie. *Travaux du Cercle Linguistique de Prague* 4: 247–267.

Jakobson, Roman (1941/1968). *Child language, aphasia and phonological universals*. The Hague and Paris, Mouton.

Jakobson, Roman (1962). Typological studies. *Selected writings 1: Phonological studies*. The Hague, Mouton & Co., pp.523–532.

Jakobson, Roman, Gunnar Fant and Morris Halle (1952). *Preliminaries to speech analysis*. Cambridge, MA, MIT Press.

Jakobson, Roman and Morris Halle (1956). *Fundamentals of language*. The Hague, Mouton.

James, D. J. (1994). Word tone in a Papuan language: an autosegmental solution. *Language and linguistics in Melanesia* 25: 125–148.

Jamieson, A. R. (1977). Chiquihuitlan Maxatec Tone. In William Merrifield (ed.) *Studies in Otomanguean Phonology*. Dallas, SIL, pp.107–136.

Janda, Richard (1999). Accounts of phonemic split have been greatly exaggerated – but not enough. *ICPhS* 14: 329–332.

Javkin, H. R. (1977). *Phonetic universals and phonological change.* Doctoral dissertation, UCB.

Jebbour, Abdelkrim (1985). *Dialecte Tachelhit (Parler de Tiznit),* Université Mahammed V, Rabat: Mémoire de Phonologie.

Jespersen, Otto (1904). *Lehrbuch der Phonetik.* Leipzig and Berlin.

Jha, Subhadra (1958). *The formation of the Maithili language.* London, Luzac.

Jiang-King, Ping (1996). *An Optimality account of tone-vowel interaction in Northern Min.* Doctoral dissertation, University of British Columbia. [Also ROA 266].

Johnson, C. Douglas (1972). *Formal aspects of phonological description.* The Hague, Mouton.

Johnson, Keith (1997). Speech perception without speaker normalization: An exemplar model. In Keith Johnson and John W. Mullennix (eds.) *Talker variability in speech processing.* San Diego, Academic Press, pp.145–165.

Johnson, Keith (2004). Cross-linguistic perceptual differences emerge from the lexicon. In Augustine Agwuele, Willis Warren and Sang-Hoon Park (eds.) *Proceedings of the 2003 Texas Linguistics Society Conference: Coarticulation in speech production and perception.* Somerville, MA, Cascadilla Press, pp.26–41.

Jones, A. (2002). A lexicon independent phonological well-formedness effect: Listeners' sensitivity to inappropriate aspiration in initial /st/ clusters. *UCLA Working Papers in Phonetics* 100: 33–72.

Jones, J. A. and K. G. Munhall (2002). The role of auditory feedback during phonation: Studies of Mandarin tone production. *JPh* 30: 303–320.

Jones, J. A. and K. G. Munhall (2003). Learning to produce speech with an altered vocal tract: The role of auditory feedback. *JASA* 113: 532–543.

Jongstra, Wenckje (2003). Variation in reduction strategies in Dutch word-initial consonant clusters. Doctoral Dissertation, University of Toronto.

Joos, Martin (1957). *Readings in linguistics I.* Chicago, University of Chicago Press.

Josephs, Lewis (1975). *Palauan reference grammar.* Honolulu, University Press of Hawaii.

Jun, Jongho (1995). *Perceptual and articulatory factors in place assimilation: An Optimality Theoretic approach.* Doctoral dissertation, UCLA.

Jun, Jongho (1996a). Place assimilation as the result of conflicting perceptual and articulatory constraints. In Jose Camacho, Lina Choueiri and Maki Watanabe (eds.) *WCCFL 14.* Stanford, CA, CSLI Publications, pp.221–237.

Jun, Jongho (1996b). Place assimilation is not the result of gestural overlap: evidence from Korean and English. *Ph* 13: 377–407.

Jun, Jongho (2004). A perception-based analysis of place assimilation. In B. Hayes, R. Kirchner and D. Steriade (eds.) *Phonetically based phonology.* Cambridge, CUP, pp.58–86.

Jun, Sun-Ah (1993). *The phonetics and phonology of Korean.* Doctoral dissertation, Ohio State University.

Jun, Sun-Ah (ed.) (2003). *Prosodic typology and transcription: A unified approach.* Oxford, UK, OUP.

Jun, Sun-Ah (ed.) (2005). *Prosodic typology: The phonology of intonation and phrasing.* Oxford, OUP.

Jurafsky, Daniel, Alan Bell and William D. Raymond (2001). Probabilistic relations between words: Evidence from reduction in lexical production. In Joan Bybee and Paul Hopper (eds.) *Frequency and the emergence of linguistic structure.* Amsterdam, John Benjamins, pp.229–254.

Jusczyk, Peter (1997). *The discovery of spoken language.* Cambridge, MA, MIT Press.

Jusczyk, Peter (1998). Constraining the search for structure in the input. *Ln* 106: 197–218.

Jusczyk, Peter and Richard N. Aslin (1995). Infants' detection of sound patterns of words in fluent speech. *Cognitive Psychology* 29: 1–23.

Jusczyk, Peter, A. D. Friederici, J. M. I. Wessels, V. Y. Svenkerud and A. Jusczyk (1993). Infants' sensitivity to the sound patterns of native language words. *Journal of Memory and Language* 32: 402–420.

Jusczyk, Peter, D. Houston and M. Newsome (1999). The beginnings of word segmentation in English-learning infants. *Cognitive Psychology* 39: 159–207.

Jusczyk, Peter, P. A. Luce and J. Charles-Luce (1994). Infants' sensitivity to phonotactic patterns in the native language. *Journal of Memory and Language* 33: 630–645.

Jusczyk, Peter, Paul Smolensky, and Theresa Allocco (2002). How English-learning infants respond to Markedness and Faithfulness constraints. *Language Acquisition* 10, 31–73.

Ka, Omar (1988). *Wolof phonology and morphology: A non-linear approach.* Doctoral dissertation, University of Illinois at Urbana-Champaign.

Kager, René (1989). *A metrical theory of stress and destressing in English and Dutch.* Dordrecht, Germany, Foris.

Kager, René (1992a). Are there any truly quantity-insensitive systems? In Laura Buszard-Welcher, L. Lee and William Weigel (eds.) *BLS* 18: 123–132.

Kager, René (1992b). Shapes of the generalized trochee. In Jonathan Mead (ed.) *WCCFL 11.* Chicago, IL, University of Chicago Press.

Kager, René (1993). Alternatives to the iambic-trochaic law. *NLLT* 11.3: 381–432.

Kager, René (1994). Ternary rhythm and alignment theory. *ROA* 35.

Kager, René (1995a). Consequences of catalexis. In Harry van der Hulst and Jeroen van de Weijer (eds.) *Leiden in las: HIL phonology papers.* Amsterdam, Holland Institute of Generative Linguistics.

Kager, René (1995b). Review of Hayes 1995. *Ph* 12.3: 437–464.

Kager, René (1996). On affix allomorphy and syllable counting. In Ursula Kleinhenz (ed.) *Interfaces in phonology.* Studia Grammatica. Berlin, Akademie Verlag, pp.155–171. [Also ROA 88].

Kager, René (1997a). Generalized alignment and morphological parsing. *Rivista di Linguistica* 9.2: 245–282.

Kager, René (1997b). Rhythmic vowel deletion in Optimality Theory. In Iggy Roca (ed.) *Derivations and constraints in phonology*, pp.463–499.

Kager, René (1999a). *Optimality Theory*. Cambridge, CUP.

Kager, René (1999b). Surface opacity of metrical structure in Optimality Theory. In Ben Hermans and Marc van Oostendorp (eds.) *The derivational residue in phonological Optimality Theory*. Amsterdam, John Benjamins, pp.207–245.

Kager, René (2001). Rhythmic directionality by positional licensing. *ROA* 514.

Kager, Rene (2003). *Lexical irregularity and the typology of contrast*, University of Utrecht.

Kager, René, Joe Pater and Wim Zonneveld (2004). *Constraints in phonological acquisition*. Cambridge, UK, CUP.

Kahn, Daniel (1976). *Syllable-based generalizations in English phonology*. Doctoral dissertation, MIT.

Kaisse, Ellen M. (1992). Can [consonantal] spread? *Lg* 68: 313–332.

Kaisse, Ellen M. and Sharon Hargus (1993). *Studies in Lexical Phonology*. San Diego, Academic Press.

Kaisse, Ellen M. and Patricia Shaw (1985). On the theory of Lexical Phonology. *Ph* 2: 1–30.

Kalmar, Michelle (2003). *Patterns of reduplication in Kʷakʷ'ʷala*. MA thesis, University of British Columbia.

Kanerva, Jonni M. (1989). *Focus and phrasing in Chicheŵa phonology*. Doctoral dissertation, Stanford University.

Kanerva, Jonni M. (1990). Focus on phonological phrases in Chicheŵa. In Sharon Inkelas and Draga Zec (eds.) *The phonology-syntax connection*. Chicago, IL, The University of Chicago Press, pp.145–161.

Kang, Hyeon-Seok (1994). Variation in past-marking and the question of the system in Trinidadian English. In Beals (ed.) *CLS 30, vol. 2: Parasession on variation in linguistic theory*. Chicago, IL, CLS, pp.150–164.

Kang, Yoonjung (2002). *Frequency of use and analogical change in Korean nouns: A case against abstract representation*, Cambridge, MA: MIT.

Kaplan, Ronald M. and Martin Kay (1994). Regular models of phonological rule systems. *Computational Linguistics* 20: 331–378.

Kappa, Iona (2002). On the acquisition of syllabic structure in Greek. *Journal of Greek Linguistics* 3: 1–52.

Kari, Ethelbert E. (1995). *The structure of the Degema verb*. MA thesis, University of Port Harcourt.

Kari, Ethelbert E. (1997). *Degema*. München-Newcastle, Lincom Europa.

Kari, James (1990). *Ahtna Athabaskan dictionary*. Fairbanks, Alaska, Alaska Native Language Center.

Karmiloff-Smith, Annette and commentators (1994). Précis and open peer commentary of Beyond modularity: A developmental perspective on cognitive science. *Behavioral and Brain Sciences* 17: 693–745.

Karttunen, Lauri (1993). Finite-state constraints. In John Goldsmith (ed.) *The last phonological rule: Reflections on constraints and derivations*. Chicago, University of Chicago Press, pp.173–194.

Kaun, Abigail (1995). *The typology of rounding harmony: An Optimality Theoretic approach.* Doctoral dissertation, UCLA.

Kaye, Jonathan (1973). Odawa stress and related phenomena. In G. L. Piggott & Jonathan Kaye (eds.) *Odawa Language Project: Second report.* University of Toronto: Centre for Linguistic Studies. pp.42–50.

Kaye, Jonathan (1974). Opacity and recoverability in phonology. *CJL* 19: 134–149.

Kaye, Jonathan (1975). A functional explanation of rule ordering in phonology. In R. Grossman, J. San and T. Vance (eds.) *Papers from the parasession on Functionalism.* Chicago, Chicago Linguistic Society, pp.244–252.

Kaye, Jonathan (1982). Harmony processes in Vata. In Harry van der Hulst and Norval Smith (eds.) *The structure of phonological representations II.* Dordrecht, Foris, pp.385–452.

Kaye, Jonathan, Jean Lowenstamm and Jean-Roger Vergnaud (1985). The internal structure of phonological elements: A theory of charm and government. *Phonology Yearbook* 2: 305–328.

Kaye, Jonathan, Jean Lowenstamm and Jean-Roger Vergnaud (1990). Constituent structure and government in phonology. *Ph* 7: 193–231.

Kean, Mary-Louise (1992). Markedness: An overview. In William Bright (ed.) *International Encyclopedia of Linguistics.* Vol.2. New York, OUP, pp.390–391.

Keating, Patricia A. (1988a). *A survey of phonological features.* Bloomington, IULC.

Keating, Patricia A. (1988b). Palatals as complex segments: x-ray evidence. *UCLA Working Papers in Phonetics* 69: 77–91.

Keating, Patricia A. (1988c). The phonology-phonetics interface. In Frederick J. Newmeyer (ed.) *Linguistic theory: Foundations.* Vol.1. Linguistics: The Cambridge survey. Cambridge, CUP, pp.281–302.

Keating, Patricia A. (1988d). Underspecification in phonetics. *Ph* 5: 275–292.

Keating, Patricia A. (1990a). Phonetic representations in a generative grammar. *JPh* 18: 321–334.

Keating, Patricia A. (1990b). The window model of coarticulation: Articulatory evidence. In John Kingston and Mary Beckman (eds.) *Papers in Laboratory Phonology I.* Cambridge, UK, CUP, pp.451–470.

Keating, Patricia A. (1996). The phonology-phonetics interface. In U. Kleinhenz (ed.) *Interfaces in Phonology.* Studia grammatica 41. Berlin, Akademie Verlag, pp.262–278.

Keating, Patricia A., T. Cho, C. Fougeron and C. Hsu (1999). Domain-initial articulatory strengthening in four languages. *UCLA Working Papers in Phonetics* 97: 139–156.

Keer, Edward (1999). *Geminates, the OCP and the Nature of CON.* Doctoral dissertation, Rutgers University. [Also ROA 350].

Kehoe, Margaret and Conxita Lleó (2003). The acquisition of syllable types in monolingual and bilingual German and Spanish children. In Barbara Beachley, Amanda Brown and Frances Conlin (eds.) *BUCLD 27: Proceedings of the 27th Annual Boston University Conference on Language Development.* Somerville, MA, Cascadilla Press, pp.402–413.

Kehrein, Wolfgan (2002). *Phonological representation and phonetic phrasing: Affricates and laryngeals.* Tübingen, Niemeyer.

Kelso, J. A. S. and B. Tuller (1983). 'Compensatory articulation' under conditions of reduced afferent information: A dynamic formulation. *Journal of Speech and Hearing Research* 26: 217–224.

Kenstowicz, Michael (1972). Lithuanian Phonology. *SLS* 2.2: 1–85.

Kenstowicz, Michael (1986). The phonology of Chukchee consonants. *SLS* 16.1: 79–96.

Kenstowicz, Michael (1989). *Comments on 'The structure of (complex) consonants' by H. van der Hulst and N. Smith.* Paper presented at the MIT Conference on Feature and Underspecification Theories, MIT.

Kenstowicz, Michael (1994). *Phonology in generative grammar.* Oxford, Basil Blackwell.

Kenstowicz, Michael (1996). Base-identity and uniform exponence: alternatives to cyclicity. In J. Durand and B. Laks (eds.) *Current trends in phonology: Models and methods.* Paris-X and Salford, University of Salford Publications, pp.363–393. [Also ROA 103].

Kenstowicz, Michael (1997). Quality-sensitive stress. *Rivista di Linguistica* 9.1: 157–188. [Also ROA 33].

Kenstowicz, Michael (2003). *Salience and similarity in loanword adaptation: A case study from Fijian.* Manuscript, http://web.mit.edu/linguistics/www/kenstowicz/bibliography.html.

Kenstowicz, Michael (2004). Quality-sensitive stress [abridged]. In John McCarthy (ed.) *Optimality Theory in Phonology: A Reader*, Blackwells, pp.191–201.

Kenstowicz, Michael and Kamal Abdul-Karim (1980). Cyclic stress in Levantine Arabic. *SLS* 10: 55–76.

Kenstowicz, Michael and Charles Kisseberth (1977). *Topics in phonological theory.* New York, Academic Press.

Kenstowicz, Michael and Charles Kisseberth (1979). *Generative phonology: Description and theory.* New York, Academic Press.

Kenstowicz, Michael and Charles Kisseberth (1990). Chizigula tonology: the word and beyond. In Sharon Inkelas and Draga Zec (eds.) *The phonology-syntax connection.* Vol.163–194. Chicago, CSLI.

Kenstowicz, Michael and Hyang-Sook Sohn (1997). Phrasing and focus in Northern Kyungsang Korean. In Pier Marco Bertinetto, Livio Gaeta, Georgi Jetchev and David Michaels (eds.) *Certamen Phonologicum III.* Turin, Italy, Rosenbery & Sellier, pp.137–156.

Kerkhoff, Annemarie (2004). Acquisition of voicing alternations. In Sergio Baauw and Jacqueline van Kampen (eds.) *Proceedings of GALA 2003.* Vol.2. Utrecht, LOT, pp.269–280.

Kessler, Brett and Rebecca Treiman (1997). Syllable structure and the distribution of phonemes in English syllables. *Journal of Memory and Language* 37: 295–311.

Ketner, Katherine (2003). *The Czech mobile 'e': An Optimality Theoretic approach.* MPhil thesis, University of Cambridge.

Key, Harold (1961). Phonotactics of Cayuvava. *IJAL* 27: 143–150.

Keyser, Samuel Jay and Paul Kiparsky (1984). Syllable structure in Finnish phonology. In Mark Aronoff and Richard T. Oerhle (eds.) *Language sound structure.* Cambridge, MA, MIT Press, pp.7–31.

Keyser, Samuel Jay and Kenneth Stevens (1994). Feature geometry and the vocal tract. *Ph* 11.2: 207–236.

Khubchandani, Lachman M. (1969). Stress in Sindhi. *Indian Linguistics* 30: 115–118.

Kientz, Albert (1979). *Dieu et les génies. Récits étiologiques senoufo (Côte-d'Ivoire),* Centre national de la recherché scientifique, Paris.

Kim, No-Ju (1997). *Tone, segments, and their interaction in North Kyungsang Korean: A Correspondence Theoretic account.* Doctoral dissertation, Ohio State University. [Also ROA 186].

Kingston, John (1982). Anchoring consonantal perturbation of fundamental frequency. *JASA* 71: S22–23 (Abstract).

Kingston, John (1985). *The phonetics and phonology of the timing of oral and glottal events.* Doctoral dissertation, UCB.

Kingston, John (1990). Articulatory binding. In John Kingston and Mary E. Beckman (eds.) *Papers in Laboratory Phonology I.* Cambridge, UK, CUP, pp.406–434.

Kingston, John (1991). Integrating articulations in the perception of vowel height. *Phonetica* 48: 149–179.

Kingston, John (2002). *Keeping and losing contrasts.* BLS 28S, pp. 155–176.

Kingston, John (2003). Learning foreign vowels. *Language and Speech* 46: 295–349.

Kingston, John (2004). Mechanisms of tone reversal. In S. Kaji (ed.) *Proceedings of the Third Symposium on Cross-linguistic Studies of Tone.* Tokyo, Institute of the Study of the Languages and Cultures of Asia and Africa, Tokyo University of Foreign Studies.

Kingston, John (2005). The phonetics of Athabaskan tonogenesis. In Sharon Hargus and Keren Rice (eds.) *Athabaskan prosody.* Amsterdam, John Benjamins.

Kingston, John and Randy Diehl (1994). Phonetic knowledge. *Lg* 70: 419–454.

Kingston, John and Randy Diehl (1995). Intermediate properties in the perception of distinctive feature values. In Bruce Connell and Amalia Arvaniti (eds.) *Phonology and phonetics: Papers in Laboratory Phonology IV.* Cambridge, UK, CUP, pp.7–27.

Kingston, John, R. L. Diehl, C. J. Kirk and W. A. Castleman (in preparation). *On the internal perceptual structure of distinctive features: The [voice] contrast.* Manuscript.

Kingston, John and N. A. Macmillan (1995). Integrality of nasalization and F1 in vowels in isolation and before oral and nasal consonants: A detection-theoretic application of the Garner paradigm. *JASA* 97: 1261–1285.

Kingston, John, N. A. Macmillan, L. Walsh Dickey, R. Thorburn and C. Bartels (1997). Integrality in the perception of tongue root position and voice quality in vowels. *JASA* 101: 1696–1709.

Kingston, John and D. Solnit (1989). The inadequacy of underspecification. In J. Carter and R.-M. Déchaine (eds.) *NELS 19*, Cascadilla Press.

Kiparsky, Paul (1968). Linguistic universals and linguistic change. In Emmon Bach and Robert Harms (eds.) *Universals in linguistic theory*. New York, Holt, Rinehart and Winston, pp.170–202.

Kiparsky, Paul (1971). Historical linguistics. In W. O. Dingwall (ed.) *A survey of linguistic science*. College Park, University of Maryland Linguistics Program, pp.579–642.

Kiparsky, Paul (1976). Abstractness, opacity, and global rules. In Andreas Koutsoudas (ed.) *The application and ordering of phonological rules*. The Hague, Mouton, pp.160–184.

Kiparsky, Paul (1979). Metrical structure assignment is cyclic. *LI* 10: 421–441.

Kiparsky, Paul (1981). Remarks on the metrical structure of the syllable. In W. Dressler, O. Pfeiffer and J. Rennison (eds.) *Phonologica 1980*. Innsbruck, Innsbrucker Beiträge zur Sprachwissenschaft, pp.245–256.

Kiparsky, Paul (1982a). From cyclic phonology to lexical phonology. In Harry van der Hulst and Norval Smith (eds.) *The structure of phonological representations*. Vol.1. Dordrecht, Foris, pp.131–175.

Kiparsky, Paul (1982b). Lexical morphology and phonology. In The Linguistic Society of Korea (ed.) Linguistics in the Morning Calm. Seoul, Hanshin, pp.3–91.

Kiparsky, Paul (1984). On the lexical phonology of Icelandic. In C. C. Elert, I. Johansson and E. Stangert (eds.) *Nordic prosody III*. Umeå, University of Umeå, pp.135–164.

Kiparsky, Paul (1985). Some consequences of Lexical Phonology. *Ph* 2: 85–138.

Kiparsky, Paul (1986). *The phonology of reduplication*. Manuscript, Stanford University.

Kiparsky, Paul (1988). Phonological change. In Frederick J. Newmeyer (ed.) *Linguistic theory: Foundations*. Vol.1. Linguistics: the Cambridge survey. Cambridge, CUP, pp.363–415.

Kiparsky, Paul (1991). Catalexis. Unpublished ms. Stanford University and Wissenschaftskolleg zu Berlin.

Kiparsky, Paul (1993). *Variable rules*. Handout, Rutgers Optimality Workshop 1.

Kiparsky, Paul (1995). The phonological basis of sound change. In John Goldsmith (ed.) *The handbook of phonological theory*. Oxford, UK, Blackwell, pp.640–670.

Kiparsky, Paul (2000). Opacity and cyclicity. *The Linguistic Review* 17: 351–367.

Kiparsky, Paul (2003). Syllables and moras in Arabic. In Caroline Féry and Ruben van de Vijver (eds.) *The syllable in Optimality Theory*. Cambridge, CUP, pp.147–182.

Kiparsky, Paul (2004). *Universals constrain change; change results in typological generalizations.* Manuscript, Stanford University: http://www.stanford.edu/~kiparsky/.

Kiparsky, Paul (2006) *Paradigmatic effects and opacity.* Chicago: University of Chicago Press.

Kiparsky, Paul and Morris Halle (1977). Towards a reconstruction of the Indo-European accent. In Larry Hyman (ed.) *Studies in stress and accent. Southern California Occasional Papers in Linguistics* 4, pp.209–238.

Kiparsky, Paul and Lise Menn (1977). On the acquisition of phonology. In John MacNamara (ed.) *Language and thought.* New York, NY, Academic Press, pp.47–78.

Kirchner, Robert (1993). Turkish vowel harmony and disharmony: An Optimality Theoretic account. *ROA* 4.

Kirchner, Robert (1996). Synchronic chain shifts in Optimality Theory *LI* 27: 341–350.

Kirchner, Robert (1997). Contrastiveness and faithfulness. *Ph* 14: 83–111.

Kirchner, Robert (1998). *An effort-based approach to consonant lenition.* Doctoral dissertation, UCLA.

Kirchner, Robert (1999). Preliminary thoughts on 'phonologization' within an exemplar-based speech processing system. *UCLA Working Papers in Linguistics 2: Papers in Phonology* 3, pp.207–231.

Kirchner, Robert (2001). Phonological contrast and articulatory effort. In Linda Lombardi (ed.) *Segmental phonology in Optimality Theory.* CUP, pp.79–117.

Kirchner, Robert (2004). Consonant lenition. In Bruce Hayes, Donca Steriade and Robert Kirchner (eds.) *Phonetically based phonology.* Cambridge, CUP pp.313–345.

Kirk, Cecilia (2001). *Phonological constraints on the segmentation of continuous speech.* Doctoral dissertation, UMass.

Kirk, Cecilia and Katherine Demuth (2003). Onset/coda asymmetries in the acquisition of clusters. In Barbara Beachley, Amanda Brown and Frances Conlin (eds.) *BUCLD 27: Proceedings of the 27th Annual Boston University Conference on Language Development.* Somerville, MA, Cascadilla Press, pp.437–448.

Kisseberth, Charles (1973). Is rule ordering necessary in phonology? In Braj B. Kachru, Robert B. Lees, Yakov Malkiel, Angelina Pietrangeli and Sol Saporta (eds.) *Issues in linguistics: papers in honor of Henry and Renée Kahane.* Urbana, IL, University of Illinois Press, pp.418–441.

Kisseberth, Charles (1984). Digo tonology. In G. N. Clements and John Goldsmith (eds.) *Studies in Bantu tonology.* Dordrecht, Foris, pp.105–182.

Kisseberth, Charles and Mohammad Imam Abasheikh (1974). Vowel length in Chi-Mwiːni: A case study of the role of grammar in phonology. In Michael W. LaGaly, Anthony Bruck and Robert A. Fox (eds.) *CLS 10: Parasession on natural phonology.* Chicago, IL, CLS, pp.193–209.

Kitto, Catherine and Paul de Lacy (1999). Correspondence and epenthetic quality. In Carolyn Smallwood and Catherine Kitto (eds.) *Proceedings of AFLA VI: The Sixth Meeting of the Austronesian Formal Linguistics Association.* Toronto, University of Toronto, pp.181–200.

Klein, Thomas (2005). Infixation and segmental constraint effects: UM and IN in Tagalog, Chamorro, and Toba Batak. *Ln* 115: 959–995.

Kluender, K. R. (1991). Effects of first formant onset properties on VOT judgments can be explained by auditory processes not specific to humans. *JASA* 90: 83–96.

Kluender, K. R. (1994). Speech perception as a tractable problem in cognitive science. In M. A. Gernsbacher (ed.) *Handbook of Psycholinguistics.* San Diego, CA, Academic Press, pp.173–217.

Kohler, Klaus J. (1994). Glottal stops and glottalization in German. *Phonetica: International Journal of Speech Science* 51: 38–51.

Koskenniemi, Kimmo (1983). *Two-level morphology: A general computational model for word-form recognition and production.* Helsinki, Department of General Linguistics, University of Helsinki.

Koutsoudas, Andreas, Gerald Sanders and Craig Noll (1974). On the application of phonological rules. *Lg* 50: 1–28.

Kraljic, Tanya and Susan E. Brennan (2005). Prosodic disambiguation of syntactic structure: For the speaker or for the addressee? *Cognitive Psychology* 50: 194–231.

Krämer, Martin (2001). *Vowel harmony and Correspondence Theory.* Doctoral dissertation, Heinrich-Heine-Universität, Düsseldorf.

Krause, Scott (1980). *Topics in Chukchee phonology and morphology.* Doctoral dissertation.

Krauss, M. (2005). Athabaskan tone. In Sharon Hargus and Keren Rice (eds.) *Athabaskan Prosody.* Amsterdam, John Benjamins.

Kroch, Anthony (1989). Reflexes of grammar in patterns of language change. *Language variation and change* 1.3: 199–244.

Kubozono, Haruo (1993). *The organization of Japanese prosody.* Tokyo, Kurosio Publishers.

Kuehn, D. P., J. W. Folkins and C. B. Cutting (1982). Relationship between muscle activity and velar position. *Cleft Palate Journal* 19.1: 25–35.

Kuhl, Patricia K. (2000). A new view of language acquisition. *Proceedings of the National Academy of Science* 97: 11850–11857.

Kuo, Yu-ching, Yi Xu, and Moira Yip (2007). The phonetics and phonology of apparent cases of iterative tonal change in Standard Chinese. In Carlos Gussenhoven and Thomas Riad (eds.) *Tones and tunes. Volume II: Phonetic and behavioural studies in word and sentence prosody.* Mouton de Gruyter.

Kurisu, Kazutaka (2001). *The phonology of morpheme realization.* Doctoral dissertation, UCSC. [Also ROA 490].

Kusumoto, K. and E. Moreton (1997). Native language determines parsing of nonlinguistic rhythmic stimuli. *JASA* 102: 3204 (Abstract).

Kuznecova, A. N., E. A. Helimskij, and E. V. Grushinka (1980) *Ocherki po sel'kupskomu jazyku (Studies on the Selkup Language)*. Moscow: Izdatel'stvo Moskovskogo Universiteta.

Laalo, Klaus (1988). *Imperfektimuotojen ti~si-vaihtelu suomen kielessa [The past tense ti~si alternation in Finnish]*. Suomalaisen Kirjallisuuden Seura 483. Helsinki, SKS.

Labov, William (1969). Contraction, deletion and inherent variability of the English copula. *Lg* 45: 715–762.

Labov, William (1981). Resolving the Neogrammarian controversy. *Lg* 57: 267–308.

Labov, William (1989). Exact description of the speech community: Short a in Philadelphia. In Ralph W. Fasold and Deborah Schiffrin (eds.) *Language change and variation*. Amsterdam, John Benjamins, pp.1–57.

Labov, William (1994). *Principles of linguistic change: Internal factors*. Oxford, UK, Blackwell.

Labov, William (1997). Resyllabification. In Frans Hinskins, Roeland van Hout and Leo Wetzels (eds.) *Variation, change and phonological theory*. Amsterdam and Philadelphia, PA, John Benjamins, pp.145–179.

Labov, William (2001). *Principles of linguistic change: Social factors*. Oxford, Blackwell.

Labov, William, Paul Cohen, Clarence Robins and John Lewis (1968). *A study of the nonstandard English of Negro and Puerto Rican speakers of New York City*. Cooperative Research Project No. 3288, Vol.2, Washington, DC: U.S. Office of Education.

LaCharité, Darlene (1993). *The internal structure of affricates*. Doctoral dissertation, University of Ottowa.

Ladd, D. Robert (1980). *The structure of intonational meaning: evidence from English*. Bloomington, IN, Indiana University Press.

Ladd, D. Robert (1983a). Even, focus and normal stress. *Journal of Semantics* 2.2: 257–270.

Ladd, D. Robert (1983b). Phonological features of intonational peaks. *Lg* 59: 721–759.

Ladd, D. Robert (1984). Declination: A review and some hypotheses. *Phonology Yearbook* 1, 53–74.

Ladd, D. Robert (1986). Intonational phrasing: The case for recursive prosodic structure. *Phonology Yearbook* 3: 311–340.

Ladd, D. Robert (1990). Metrical representation of pitch register. In John Kingston and Mary E. Beckman (eds.) *Papers in Laboratory Phonology I: Between the grammar and physics of speech*. Cambridge, CUP, pp.35–57.

Ladd, D. Robert (1993). In defense of a metrical theory of intonational downstep. In Harry van der Hulst and K. Snider (eds.) *The phonology of tone: The representation of tonal register*. Berlin and New York, Mouton de Gruyter, pp.109–132.

Ladd, D. Robert (1996). *Intonational phonology*. Cambridge, CUP.

Ladd, D. Robert, D. Faulkner, H. Faulkner and A. Schepman (1999). Constant 'segmental anchoring' of f0 movements under changes in speech rate. *JASA* 106: 1543–1554.

Ladd, D. Robert, I. Mennen and A. Schepman (2000). Phonological conditioning of peak alignment in rising pitch accents in Dutch. *JASA* 107.5: 2685–2696.

Ladd, D. Robert and R. Morton (1997). The perception of intonational emphasis: Continuous or categorical? *JPh* 25: 313–342.

Ladd, D. Robert and A. Schepman (2003). 'Sagging transitions' between high pitch accents in English: Experimental evidence. *JPh* 31: 81–112.

Ladd, D. Robert and James M. Scobbie (2003). External sandhi as gestural overlap? Counter-evidence from Sardinian. In John Local, Richard Ogden and Rosalind Temple (eds.) *Phonetic interpretation: Papers in Laboratory Phonology VI*. Cambridge, CUP, pp.164–182.

Ladefoged, Peter (1967). *Three areas of experimental phonetics*. London, OUP.

Ladefoged, Peter (1993). *A course in phonetics*. Fort Worth, TX, Harcourt Brace College Publishers.

Ladefoged, Peter and Ian Maddieson (1996). *The sounds of the world's languages*. Oxford, Blackwell.

Ladefoged, Peter and Theo Vennemann (1973). Phonetic features and phonological features. *Lingua* 32: 61–74.

Lahiri, A. (1995). *On resolving variation*. Manuscript, Universität Konstanz.

Lahiri, Aditi and Sheila E. Blumstein (1984). A re-evaluation of the feature coronal. *JPh* 12: 133–146.

Lahiri, Aditi and B. Elan Dresher (1999). Open Syllable Lengthening in West Germanic. *Lg* 75: 678–719.

Lahiri, Aditi and Vincent Evers (1991). Palatalization and coronality. In Carole Paradis and Jean-Francois Prunet (eds.) *The special status of coronals: Internal and external evidence*. Phonology and Phonetics 2. San Diego, CA, Academic Press, pp.79–100.

Lahiri, Aditi and William Marslen-Wilson (1991). The mental representation of lexical form: A phonological approach to the recognition lexicon. *Cognition* 38: 245–294.

Lahiri, A. and H. Reetz (2002). Underspecified recognition. In Carlos Gussenhoven and N. Warner (eds.) *Laboratory Phonology 7*. Berlin, Mouton de Gruyter, pp.637–675.

Lakoff, George (1993). Cognitive phonology. In John Goldsmith (ed.) *The last phonological rule: Reflections on constraints and derivations*. Chicago, University of Chicago Press, pp.117–145.

Laniran, Y. and G. N. Clements (2003). Downstep and high raising: Interacting factors in Yoruba tone production. *JPh* 31: 203–250.

LaPointe, S. G. and M. H. Feinstein (1982). Vowel deletion and epenthesis. In Harry van der Hulst and Norval Smith (eds.) *The structure of phonological representations*. Vol.2. Dordrecht, Foris, pp.69–120.

Larson, G. (1992). *Dynamic computational networks and the representation of phonological information*, University of Chicago.

Lass, Roger (1984). *Phonology: An introduction to basic concepts*. Cambridge, CUP.

Lawton, Ralph (1993). *Topics in the description of Kiriwina*. Canberra, Australian National University.

Leben, William R. (1973). *Suprasegmental phonology*. Doctoral dissertation, MIT.

Leben, William R. (1975). The tones in English intonation. *LI* 2: 69–107.

Lecours, A. R. and F. Lhermitte (1969). Phonemic paraphasias: Linguistic structures and tentative hypotheses. *Cortex* 5: 193–228.

Leer, Jeff (1979). *Proto-Athabaskan Verb Stem Variation, Part One: Phonology*. Alaska Native Language Center Research Papers 1. Fairbanks, University of Alaska.

Leer, Jeff (1985). Prosody in Alutiiq. In Michael Krauss (ed.) *Yupik Eskimo prosodic system: Descriptive and comparative studies*. Fairbanks, AL, Alaska Native Language Center, pp.77–133.

Leer, Jeff (1999). Tonogenesis in Athabaskan. In S. Kaji (ed.) *Cross-linguistic studies of tonal phenomena, tonogenesis, typology, and related topics vol. 1*. Tokyo, Institute of the Study of the Languages and Cultures of Asia and Africa, Tokyo University of Foreign Studies, pp.37–66.

Lehiste, Ilse (1961). The phonemes of Slovene. *International Journal of Slavic Linguistics and Poetics* 4: 48–66.

Lehiste, Ilse (1970). *Suprasegmentals*. Cambridge, UK, MIT Press.

Lehiste, Ilse (1985). An Estonian word game and phonematic status of long vowels. *LI* 16: 490–492.

Leonard, L. B. and K. K. MacGregor (1992). Grammatical morphology and speech perception in children with specific language impairment. *Journal of Speech and Hearing Research* 35: 1076–1085.

Leopold, Werner F. (1939–49). *Speech development of a bilingual child: a linguist's record*. Evanston, Northwestern University Press.

Lerdahl, Fred and Ray Jackendoff (1983). *A generative theory of tonal music*. Cambridge, MA, MIT Press.

Levelt, Clara (1994). *On the acquisition of place*. Doctoral dissertation, Holland Institute of Generative Linguistics (HIL), Leiden University.

Levelt, Clara, N. Schiller and W. Levelt (1999/2000). The acquisition of syllable types. *Language Acquisition* 8: 237–264.

Levelt, Clara and Ruben van de Vijver (2004). Syllable types in cross-linguistic and developmental grammars. In René Kager, Joe Pater and Wim Zonneveld (eds.) *Constraints in phonological acquisition*. Cambridge, UK, CUP, pp.204–218.

Levelt, W. J. M. (1989). *Speaking: From intention to articulation*. Cambridge, MA, MIT Press.

Levergood, Barbara (1984). Rule governed vowel harmony and the strict cycle. *NELS 14*, Amherst, MA, GLSA, pp.275–293.

Levin, Juliette (1985). *A metrical theory of syllabicity*. Doctoral dissertation, MIT.

Levin, Juliette (1988). Generating ternary feet. *Texas Linguistic Forum* 29: 97–113.

Leyden, K. van (2004). *Prosodic characteristics of Orkney and Shetland dialects: An experimental approach*. Utrecht, LOT, Netherlands Graduate School of Linguistics.

Li, C. and S. Thompson (1977). The acquisition of tone in Mandarin-speaking children. *JCL* 4: 185–199.

Liberman, A. M. and I. G. Mattingly (1985). The motor theory of speech perception revised. *Cognition* 21: 1–36.

Liberman, Mark (1975). *The intonational system of English*. Doctoral dissertation, MIT.

Liberman, Mark (1993). *Optionality and Optimality*. Manuscript, University of Pennsylvania.

Liberman, Mark Y. and J. B. Pierrehumbert (1984). Intonational invariance under changes in pitch range and length. In M. Aronoff and R. Oehrle (eds.) *Language sound structure*. Cambridge, MA, MIT Press, pp.157–233.

Liberman, Mark and Alan Prince (1977). On stress and linguistic rhythm. *LI* 8: 249–336.

Lichtenberk, Frantisek (1983). *A grammar of Manam*. Honolulu, University of Hawaii Press.

Lickley, R. J., A. Schepman and D. Robert Ladd (2005). Alignment of "phrase accent" lows in Dutch falling-rising questions: theoretical and methodological implications. *Language and Speech* 48.2: 157–183.

Lieber, Rochelle (1983). New developments in Autosegmental Morphology: Consonant mutation. In M. Barlow, D. Flickinger and M. Wescoat (eds.) *WCCFL 2*, Stanford Linguistic Association, pp.165–175.

Lieber, Rochelle (1984). Consonant Gradation in Fula: An Autosegmental approach. In Aronoff, Mark and Richard T. Oehrle (eds.) *Language sound structure*, Cambridge, MA: MIT. Press, pp. 329–345.

Lieber, Rochelle (1987). *An integrated theory of autosegmental processes*. Albany, NY, State University of New York Press.

Liljencrants, J. and B. Lindblom (1972). Numerical simulation of vowel quality systems: The role of perceptual contrast. *Lg* 48: 839–862.

Lin, Yen-Hwei (1989). The retroflex as a complex segment. In Anthony Green and Virginia Motapanyane (eds.) *ESCOL* 6: 182–193.

Lindblom, Björn (1963). Spectrographic study of vowel reduction. *JASA* 35: 1773–1781.

Lindblom, Björn (1986). Phonetic universals in vowel systems. In John J. Ohala and J. J. Jaeger (eds.) *Experimental phonology*. London, Academic Press, pp.13–44.

Lindblom, Björn (1990a). Explaining phonetic variation: A sketch of the H&H theory. In William Hardcastle and Alain Marchal (eds.) *Speech production and speech modelling*. Dordrecht, Kluwer, pp.403–439.

Lindblom, Björn (1990b). On the notion of "possible speech sound". *JPh* 18: 135–152.

Lindblom, Björn (1990c). Phonetic content in phonology. *Phonetic Experimental Research, Institute of Linguistics, University of Stockholm (PERILUS)* 11: 101–118.

Lindblom, Björn, J. Lubker and T. Gay (1979). Formant frequencies of some fixed-mandible vowels and a model of speech motor programmming by predictive simulation. *JPh* 7: 147–161.

Lindblom, Björn and Ian Maddieson (1988). Phonetic universals in consonant systems. In Larry Hyman and C. N. Li (eds.) *Language, speech and mind. Studies in honour of Victoria A. Fromkin*. London: Routledge, pp.62–78.

Lindblom, Björn and J. E. F. Sundberg (1971). Acoustical consequences of lip, tongue, jaw, and larynx movement. *JASA* 50: 1166–1179.

Lintz, L. B. and D. Sherman (1961). Phonetic elements and the perception of nasality. *Journal of Speech and Hearing Research* 4: 381–396.

Lisker, L. (1975). Is it VOT or a first-formant transition detector? *JASA* 57: 1547–1551.

Lleo, C., C. El Mogharbel and M. Prinz (1994). Babbling und Fruhwort-Produktion im Deutschen und Spanischen. *Linguistische Berichte* 151: 191–217.

Lloret, Maria-Rosa (1995). A re-evaluation of the feature coronal. *Ph* 13.2: 257–280.

Local, John and Ken Lodge (2004). Some auditory and acoustic observations on the phonetics of [ATR] harmony in a speaker of a dialect of Kalenjin. *JIPA* 34: 1–16.

Local, John, Richard Ogden and Rosalind Temple (eds.) (2003). *Phonetic interpretation: Papers in Laboratory Phonology VI*. Cambridge, CUP.

Lombardi, Linda (1990). The nonlinear organization of the affricate. *NLLT* 13.2: 257–280.

Lombardi, Linda (1991). *Laryngeal features and laryngeal neutralization*. Doctoral dissertation, UMass.

Lombardi, Linda (1995a). Laryngeal features and privativity. *The Linguistic Review* 12: 35–59.

Lombardi, Linda (1995b). Laryngeal neutralization and syllable well-formedness. *NLLT* 13: 39–74.

Lombardi, Linda (1996). Restrictions on direction of voicing assimilation: An OT account. *University of Maryland Working Papers in Linguistics* 4: 84–102. [Also ROA 247].

Lombardi, Linda (1999). Positional faithfulness and voicing assimilation in Optimality Theory. *NLLT* 17.2: 267–302.

Lombardi, Linda (2001). Why place and voice are different: Constraint-specific alternations in Optimality Theory. In Linda Lombardi (ed.)

Segmental phonology in Optimality Theory: Constraints and representations. Cambridge, CUP pp.13–45. [Also ROA 105].

Lombardi, Linda (2002). Coronal epenthesis and markedness. *Ph* 19: 219–251.

Lombardi, Linda (2003). Markedness and the typology of epenthetic vowels. *ROA* 578.

Lubker, J. (1968). An electromyographic-cineflourographic investigation of velar function during normal speech production. *Cleft Palate Journal* 5: 1–18.

Lubker, J. F., B. Fritzell and J. Lindqvist (1970). Velopharyngeal function: an electromyographic study. *Quarterly Progress and Status Report (KTH, Speech Transmission Laboratory)* 4: 9–20.

Łubowicz, Anna (2003). *Contrast preservation in phonological mappings.* Doctoral dissertation, UMass. [Also ROA 554].

Lynch, John (1974). *Lenakel phonology.* Doctoral dissertation, University of Hawaii.

Lynch, John (1978). *A Grammar of Lenakel.* Pacific Linguistics B. Canberra, Australian National University.

Lynch, John (2002). Iaai. In John Lynch, Malcolm Ross and Terry Crowley (eds.) *The Oceanic languages.* London, Curzon.

Macchi, M. (1988). Labial articulation patterns associated with segmental features and syllable structure in English. *Phonetica* 45: 109–121.

MacDonald, Lorna (1990). *A Grammar of Tauya.* New York, Mouton de Gruyter.

MacEachern, Margaret (1999). *Laryngeal cooccurrence restrictions.* New York, Garland.

MacKay, Carolyn (1999). *A grammar of Misantla Totonac.* Salt Lake City, University of Utah Press.

Macken, Marlys (1979). Developmental reorganization of phonology: a hierarchy of basic units of acquisition. *Ln* 49: 11–49.

Macken, Marlys (1995). Phonological acquisition. In John Goldsmith (ed.) *The handbook of phonological theory.* Cambridge, MA, Blackwell, pp.671–696.

Macken, Marlys and Charles A. Ferguson (1983). Cognitive aspects of phonological development: Model, evidence and issues. In Keith Nelson (ed.) *Children's language.* Vol.4. Hillsdale, NJ, Lawrence Erlbaum, pp.255–282.

Mackridge, P. (1985). *The Modern Greek language: A descriptive analysis of standard Modern Greek.* Oxford, OUP.

Macmillan, N. A., J. Kingston, R. Thorburn, L. Walsh Dickey and C. Bartels (1999). Integrality of nasalization and F1. II. Basic sensitivity and phonetic labeling measure distinct sensory and decision-rule interactions. *JASA* 106: 2913–2932.

MacNeilage, Peter and Barbara Davis (2000). Origin of the internal structure of word forms. *Science* 288: 527–531.

Maddieson, Ian (1978). Universals of tone. In Joseph H. Greenberg, Charles A. Ferguson and Edith A. Moravscik (eds.) *Universals of human language.* Vol.2: Phonology. Stanford, Calif., Stanford University Press, pp.335–366.

Maddieson, Ian (1984). *Patterns of sounds*. Cambridge, CUP.

Maddieson, Ian and K. Precoda (1992). *UCLA Phonological Segment Inventory Database*. Software, http://www.linguistics.ucla.edu/faciliti/sales/upsid.zip.

Maeda, S. (1993). Acoustics of vowel nasalization and articulatory shifts in French nasal vowels. In M. K. Huffman and R. A. Krakow (eds.) *Nasals, nasalization, and the velum*. San Diego, Academic Press, pp.147–167.

Major, E. and Barbara Bernhardt (1998). Metaphonological skills of children with phonological disorders before and after phonological and metaphonological intervention. *International Journal of Language and Communication Disorders* 33: 413–444.

Major, R. C. (1985). Stress and rhythm in Brazilian Portuguese. *Lg* 61: 259–282.

Marantz, Alec (1982). Re reduplication. *LI* 13: 435–482.

Marantz, Alec (1987). Phonologically induced bracketing paradoxes in full morpheme reduplication. In Megan Crowhurst (ed.) *WCCFL 6*. Stanford, SLA, pp.203–212.

Marcus, Gary (2001). *The algebraic mind*. Cambridge, MA, MIT Press.

Marlett, Stephen A. (1981). *The structure of Seri*. Doctoral dissertation, University of California, San Diego.

Marlett, Stephen A. and Joseph Stemberger (1983). Empty consonants in Seri. *LI* 5: 617–639.

Martens, M. and S. Tuominen (1977). A tentative phonemic statement of Yil in West Sepik Province. *Workpapers in Papua New Guinea Linguistics* 19: 29–48.

Martinet, Andre (1964). *Elements of general linguistics*. Chicago, University of Chicago Press.

Martinet, A. (1968). Phonetics and linguistic evolution. In B. Malmberg (ed.) *Manual of phonetics*. Amsterdam: North Holland, pp.464–87.

Mascaró, Joan (1976). *Catalan phonology and the phonological cycle*. Doctoral dissertation, MIT.

Massengill, R. and M. Bryson (1967). A study of velopharyngeal function as related to the perceived nasality of vowels using a cineflourographic television monitor. *Folia Phoniatrica* 19: 45–52.

Matteson, Esther (1965). *The Piro (Arawakan) language*. University of California Publications in Linguistics 22. Berkeley and Los Angeles, University of California Press.

Mattys, S. L. and P. W. Jusczyk (2001). Phonotactic cues for segmentation of fluent speech by infants. *Cognition* 78: 91–121.

Maye, Jessica, Janet Werker and LouAnn Gerken (2002). Infant sensitivity to distributional information can affect phonetic discrimination. *Cognition* 82: 1001–1111.

McCarthy, John J. (1979a). *Formal problems in Semitic phonology and morphology*. Doctoral dissertation, MIT.

McCarthy, John J. (1979b). On stress and syllabification. *LI* 10: 443–466.

McCarthy, John J. (1981). A prosodic theory of nonconcatenative morphology. *LI* 12: 373–418.

McCarthy, John J. (1982). Prosodic structure and expletive infixation. *Lg* 58: 574–590.

McCarthy, John J. (1986). OCP effects: Gemination and antigemination. *LI* 17: 207–263.

McCarthy, John J. (1988). Feature geometry and dependency: a review. *Phonetica* 43: 84–108.

McCarthy, John J. (1989). Linear order in phonological representation. *LI* 20: 71–99.

McCarthy, John J. (1993). Template form in prosodic morphology. In Laurel S. Stvan (ed.) *Papers from the Third Annual Formal Linguistics Society of Midamerica Conference*. Bloomington, IN, IULC, pp.187–218.

McCarthy, John J. (1994). The phonetics and phonology of Semitic pharyngeals. In Patricia A. Keating (ed.) *Papers in laboratory phonology III: Phonological structure and phonetic form*. Cambridge, CUP, pp.191–233.

McCarthy, John J. (1995). Expressions of faithfulness: Rotuman revisited. *ROA* 110.

McCarthy, John J. (1999). Sympathy and phonological opacity. *Ph* 16: 331–399.

McCarthy, John J. (2000a). Faithfulness and prosodic circumscription. In Joost Dekkers, Frank van der Leeuw and Jeroen van de Weijer (eds.) *Optimality Theory: Phonology, syntax, and acquisition*. Oxford, OUP, pp.151–189.

McCarthy, John J. (2000b). Harmonic serialism and parallelism. In Masako Hirotani, Andries Coetzee, Nancy Hall and Ji-yung Kim (eds.) *NELS 30*. Amherst, GLSA, pp.501–524.

McCarthy, John J. (2000c). The prosody of phase in Rotuman. *NLLT* 18: 147–197.

McCarthy, John J. (2002a). Comparative markedness [long version]. In Angela Carpenter, Andries Coetzee and Paul de Lacy (eds.) *UMOP 26: Papers in Optimality Theory II*. Amherst, MA, GLSA, pp.171–246. [Also ROA 489].

McCarthy, John J. (2002b). On targeted constraints and cluster simplification. *Ph* 19: 273–292.

McCarthy, John J. (2002c). *A thematic guide to Optimality Theory*. Cambridge, UK, CUP.

McCarthy, John J. (2003a). Comparative markedness. *Theoretical Linguistics* 29: 1–51.

McCarthy, John J. (2003b). OT constraints are categorical. *Ph* 20.1: 75–138.

McCarthy, John J. (2003c). Sympathy, cumulativity, and the Duke-of-York gambit. In Caroline Féry and Ruben van de Vijver (eds.) *The syllable in Optimality Theory*. Cambridge, CUP, pp.23–76.

McCarthy, John J. (2004a). Headed Spans and Autosegmental Spreading. *ROA* 685.

McCarthy, John J. (2004b). *Optimality Theory in phonology: a reader*. Malden, MA and Oxford, UK, Blackwell.

McCarthy, John J. (2005). Optimal paradigms. In Laura Downing, T. Alan Hall and Renate Raffelsiefen (eds.) *Paradigms in phonological theory*. Oxford, OUP, pp.170–210. [Also ROA 485].

McCarthy, John J. (2006). *Hidden generalizations: Phonological opacity in Optimality Theory*. London, Equinox Publishing.

McCarthy, John J. and Alan Prince (1986). *Prosodic morphology*. Rutgers Technical Report TR-32. New Brunswick, Rutgers University Center for Cognitive Science.

McCarthy, John J. and Alan Prince (1988). Quantitative transfer in reduplicative and templatic morphology. In Linguistic Society of Korea (ed.) *Linguistics in the morning calm 2*. Seoul, Hanshin Publishing Company, pp.3–35.

McCarthy, John J. and Alan Prince (1990). Foot and word in prosodic morphology: The Arabic broken plural. *NLLT* 8: 209–282.

McCarthy, John J. and Alan Prince (1993a). Generalized alignment. In Geert Booij and Jaap van Marle (eds.) *Yearbook of morphology*. Dordrecht, Kluwer, pp.79–153. [Also ROA 7; John Goldsmith (ed.) Essential readings in phonology. Oxford: Blackwell, pp.102–136; Excerpt in John J. McCarthy (ed.) Optimality Theory in phonology: a reader. Oxford and Malden, MA: Blackwell, pp.72–76.].

McCarthy, John J. and Alan Prince (1993b). *Prosodic morphology I: Constraint interaction and satisfaction*. Rutgers Technical Report TR-3. New Brunswick, Rutgers University Center for Cognitive Science. [Also ROA 482].

McCarthy, John J. and Alan Prince (1994). The emergence of the unmarked: Optimality in Prosodic Morphology. In Mercè Gonzàlez (ed.) *NELS 24*. Amherst, MA, GLSA, pp.333–379.

McCarthy, John J. and Alan Prince (1995a). Faithfulness and reduplicative identity. In Jill Beckman, Laura Walsh Dickey and Suzanne Urbanczyk (eds.) *UMOP 18: Papers in Optimality Theory*. Amherst, GLSA, UMass, pp.249–384. [Also ROA 60].

McCarthy, John J. and Alan Prince (1995b). Prosodic Morphology. In John Goldsmith (ed.) *Phonological theory: The essential readings*. Oxford, Blackwell, pp.238–288.

McCarthy, John J. and Alan Prince (1999). Faithfulness and identity in Prosodic Morphology. In Rene Kager, Harry van der Hulst and Wim Zonneveld (eds.) *The prosody-morphology Interface*. Cambridge, CUP, pp.218–309.

McCarthy, John J. and A. Taub (1992). Review of Carole Paradis and Jean-François Prunet (eds.) The special status of coronals: Internal and external evidence. *Ph* 9: 363–370.

McClelland, J. L., D. E. Rumelhart and The PDP Research Group (1986a). *Parallel distributed processing: Explorations in the microstructure of cognition, vol. 1: Explorations in the microstructure of cognition*. Cambridge, MA, MIT Press/Bradford Books.

McClelland, J. L., D. E. Rumelhart and The PDP Research Group (1986b). *Parallel distributed processing: Explorations in the microstructure of cognition, vol. 2: Psychological and biological models.* Cambridge, MA, MIT Press/Bradford Books.

McClelland, J. L., D. E. Rumelhart and G. E. Hinton (1986). The appeal of parallel distributed processing. In D. E. Rumelhart, J. L. McClelland and The PDP Research Group (eds.) *Parallel distributed processing: explorations in the microstructure of cognition, vol. 1: Explorations in the microstructure of cognition.* Vol.1. Cambridge, MA, MIT Press/Bradford Books, pp.3–44.

McDonough, Joyce (1999). Tone in Navajo. *Anthropological Linguistics* 41.4: 503–539.

McGarrity, Laura (2003). *Constraints on patterns of primary and secondary stress.* Doctoral dissertation, Indiana University.

McMahon, April (2000a). *Chance, change and optimality.* Oxford, OUP.

McMahon, April (2000b). *Lexical phonology and the history of English.* Cambridge, CUP.

Mehler, J., J. Y. Dommergues, U. Frauenfelder and J. Segui (1981). The syllable's role in speech segmentation. *Journal of Verbal Learning and Verbal Behavior* 20: 298–305.

Mellander, Evan (2001). Quantitative processes in trochaic systems. In K. Megerdoomian and L. A. Bar-el (eds.) *WCCFL 20.* Somerville, MA, Cascadilla Press, pp.414–427.

Mellander, Evan (2004). (HL)-creating processes in a theory of foot structure. *Linguistic Review* 20.2–4: 243–280.

Menn, Lise (1971). Phonological rules in beginning speech. *Ln* 26: 225–241.

Menn, Lise (1978). Phonological units in beginning speech. In Alan Bell and Joan Hooper [Bybee] (eds.) *Syllables and segments.* New York, NY, Elsevier-North Holland, pp.157–172.

Menn, Lise (1983). Developments of articulatory, phonetic and phonological capabilities. In B. Butterworth (ed.) *Language production 2.* London, UK, Academic Press, pp.3–50.

Menn, Lise and B. MacWhinney (1984). The repeated morph constraint: Toward an explanation. *Lg* 19: 519–541.

Menn, Lise and Edward Matthei (1992). The 'two-lexicon' account in child phonology. Looking back, looking ahead. In Charles A. Ferguson, Lise Menn and Carol Stoel-Gammon (eds.) *Phonological development: Models, research, implications.* Timonium, MD, York Press, pp.211–247.

Meredith, Scott (1990). *Issues in the phonology of prominence.* Doctoral dissertation, Issues in the phonology of prominence.

Mester, R. Armin (1986). *Studies in tier structure.* Doctoral dissertation, UMass.

Mester, R. Armin (1990). Patterns of truncation. *LI* 21.3: 478–485.

Mester, R. Armin (1991). *Some remarks on Tongan stress.* Manuscript, UCSC.

Mester, R. Armin (1994). The quantitative trochee in Latin. *NLLT* 12.1: 1–61.

Michelson, Karin (1981). Stress, epenthesis and syllable structure in Mohawk. In George Clements (ed.) *Harvard Studies in Phonology vol. 2.* Harvard, Harvard Linguistics Department, pp.311–353.

Miller, Wick (1996). Sketch of Shoshone, a Uto-Aztecan language. In Ives Goddard (ed.) *Handbook of American Indian Languages, vol. 17.* Washington, Smithsonian Institute, pp.693–720.

Minsky, Marvin and Seymour Papert (1969). *Perceptrons: An introduction to Computational Geometry.* Cambridge, MA, MIT Press.

Mitchell, T. F. (1960). Prominence and syllabification in Arabic. *Bulletin of the School of Oriental and African Studies* 23: 369–389. [Also In Mitchell, T. F. (1975) Principles of Firthian Linguistics. London: Longmans, pp.75–98].

Mohanan, K. P. (1982). *Lexical Phonology.* Doctoral dissertation, MIT.

Mohanan, K. P. (1986). *The theory of Lexical Phonology.* Dordrecht, Reidel.

Mohanan, K. P. (1991). On the bases of radical underspecification. *NLLT* 9: 285–325.

Mohanan, K. P. (1995). The organization of the grammar. In John A. Goldsmith (ed.) *Handbook of phonological theory.* Oxford: Blackwell, pp.24–69.

Mohanan, K. P. and Tara Mohanan (1984). Lexical Phonology of the Consonant System in Malayalam. *LI* 15.4: 575–603.

Moll, K. L. and T. Shriner (1967). Preliminary investigation of a new concept of velar activity in speech. *Cleft Palate Journal* 4: 58–69.

Monaghan, P. and R. Shillcock (2003). Connectionist modelling of the separable processing of consonants and vowels. *Brain and Language* 86: 83–98.

Montler, Timothy (1986). *An outline of the morphology and phonology of Saanich, North Straits Salish.* University of Montana Occasional Papers in Linguistics No.4. Montana, University of Montana Linguistics Department.

Moon, S.-J. and B. Lindblom (1994). Interaction between duration, context and speaking-style in English stressed vowels. *JASA* 96.1: 40–55.

Moon, S.-J. and B. Lindblom (2003). Two experiments on oxygen consumption during speech production: vocal effort and speaking tempo. *ICPhS 15* (Barcelona): 3129–3132.

Moravscik, Edith A. (1978). Reduplicative constructions. In Joseph H. Greenberg (ed.) *Universals of Human Language: Vol. 3: Word Structure.* Stanford, Stanford University Press, pp.297–334.

Morén, Bruce (1999). *Distinctiveness, coercion and sonority: A unified theory of weight.* Doctoral dissertation, University of Maryland, College Park.

Morén, Bruce (2003). The parallel structures model of feature geometry. *Working papers of the Cornell phonetics laboratory* 15: ch.5.

Morén, Bruce (2006). Consonant-vowel interactions in Serbian: Features, representations, and constraint interactions. *Ln* 116.8: 1198–1197.

Moreton, Elliott (1999). Evidence for phonological grammar in speech perception. In J. J. Ohala, Y. Hasegawa, M. Ohala, D. Granville and A. C. Bailey (eds.) *ICPhS 14 (San Francisco)*: 2215–2217.

Moreton, Elliott (2002). Structural constraints in the perception of English stop-sonorant clusters. *Cognition* 84: 55–71.

Moreton, Elliott (2004a). Non-computable functions in Optimality Theory. *Optimality Theory in phonology: A reader.* J. McCarthy. Oxford, Blackwell: 141–164.

Moreton, Elliott (2004b). Realization of the English postvocalic [voice] contrast in F1 and F2. *JPh* 32: 1–33.

Moreton, Elliott and S. Amano (1999). Phonotactics in the perception of Japanese vowel length: Evidence for long-distance dependencies. *Proceedings of the 6th European Conference on Speech Communication and Technology, Budapest.*

Moreton, Elliott and Paul Smolensky (2002). Typological consequences of local constraint conjunction. *ROA* 525.

Morris, Richard E. (1998). *Stylistic variation in Spanish phonology.* Doctoral dissertation, Ohio State University.

Mortensen, D. (2004). Abstract scales in phonology. *ROA* 667.

Moskowitz, Arlene J. (1973). The acquisition of phonology and syntax: a preliminary study. In K. Jaako Hintikka, J. M. E. Moravscik and P. Suppes (eds.) *Approaches to natural language. Proceedings of the 1970 Stanford Workshop on Grammar and Semantics.* Dordrecht, Germany, Reidel, pp.48–84.

Munro, Pamela and P. Benson (1973). Reduplication and rule ordering in Luiseño. *IJAL* 39: 15–21.

Mutaka, Ngessimo M. (1995). *Journal of West African Languages* 25 2: 41–55.

Mutaka, Ngessimo M. and Larry Hyman (1990). Syllable and morpheme integrity in Kinande reduplication. *Ph* 7: 73–120.

Myers, James (2003). Frequency effects in Optimality Theory. Manuscript, National Chung Cheng University.

Myers, James and Gregory Guy (1997). Frequency effects in Variable Lexical Phonology. In Alexis Dimitriadis, Laura Siegel, Clarissa Surek-Clark and Alexander Williams (eds.) *Proceedings of the 21st Annual Penn Linguistics Colloquium: University of Pennsylvania Working Papers in Linguistics.* Vol.4, pp.215–227.

Myers, Scott (1987a). *Tone and the structure of words in Shona.* Doctoral dissertation, UMass.

Myers, Scott (1987b). Vowel shortening in English. *NLLT* 5.4: 485–518.

Myers, Scott (1991). Persistent rules. *LI* 22: 315–344.

Myers, Scott (1997a). Expressing phonetic naturalness in phonology. In Iggy Roca (ed.) *Derivations and constraints in Phonology.* Oxford, OUP, pp.125–152.

Myers, Scott (1997b). OCP effects in Optimality Theory. *NLLT* 15.4: 847–892.

Myers, Scott (1999) Surface underspecification of tone in Chichewa. *Phonology* 15.3: 367–391.

Myers, Scott (2000). Boundary disputes: The distinction between phonetic and phonological sound patterns. In Noel Burton-Roberts, Philip Carr and Gerard Docherty (eds.) *Phonological knowledge: Conceptual and empirical issues.* Oxford, OUP, pp.245–272.

Nagy, Naomi and William Reynolds (1997). Optimality Theory and variable word-final deletion in Faetar. *Language variation and change* 9.1: 37–55.

Naigles, L. R. and E. Hoff-Ginsberg (1998). Why are some verbs learned before other verbs? Effects of input frequency and structure on children's early verb use. *JCL* 25: 95–120.

Navarro Tomás, Tomás (1957). *Manual de pronunciación española*. New York, Hafner Publishing Co.

Neeleman, Ad and Hans van de Koot (to appear). On syntactic and phonological representations. *Ln*.

Nelson, Nicole (2003). *Asymmetric anchoring*. Doctoral dissertation, Rutgers University.

Nespor, Marina and Irene Vogel (1986). *Prosodic phonology*. Studies in generative grammar vol. 28. Dordrecht, Germany, Foris.

Nespor, Marina and Irene Vogel (1989). On clashes and lapses. *Ph* 6: 69–116.

Neu, Helene (1980). Ranking of constraints on /t,d/ deletion in American English: a statistical analysis. In William Labov (ed.) *Locating language in time and space*. New York, NY, Academic Press, pp.37–54.

Newman, P. (1972). Syllable weight as a phonological variable. *Studies in African Linguistics* 3: 301–323.

Newman, P. (1995). Hausa tonology: Complexities in an 'easy' tone language. In John Goldsmith (ed.) *The handbook of phonological theory*. Cambridge, MA, Basil Blackwell, pp.762–781.

Newman, Stanley (1944). *The Yokuts language of California*. The Viking Fund Publications in Anthropology. New York, The Viking Fund.

Newmeyer, Frederick J. (ed.) (1988). *Linguistic theory: Foundations*. Linguistics: the Cambridge survey. Cambridge, CUP.

Newmeyer, Frederick J. (2003). Grammar is grammar and usage is usage. *Lg* 79: 682–707.

Ní Chiosáin, Máire (1994). Irish palatalization and the representation of place features. *Ph* 11: 89–106.

Ní Chiosáin, Máire and Jaye Padgett (1993). *Inherent VPlace*. Report no. LRC-93–09, Linguistics Research Center, UCSC.

Ní Chiosáin, Máire and Jaye Padgett (2001). Markedness, segment realization, and locality in spreading. In Linda Lombardi (ed.) *Segmental phonology in Optimality Theory: Constraints and representations*. New York, CUP, pp.118–158. [Also ROA 503].

Nickels, L. A. and D. Howard (2004). Dissociating effects of number of phonemes, number of syllables and syllabic complexity in aphasia: It's the number of phonemes that counts. *Cognitive Neuropsychology* 21: 57–78.

Nielsen, Konrad (1926). *Lærebok i lappisk*. Oslo, Brøgger.

Nolan, Francis (1992). The descriptive role of segments: Evidence from assimilation. In G. R. Docherty and D. R. Ladd (eds.) *Papers in Laboratory Phonology II*. Cambridge, UK, CUP, pp.261–280.

Nolan, Francis, T. Holst and B. Kühnert (1996). Modelling [s] to [ʃ] accommodation in English. *JPh* 24: 113–137.

Noonan, Michael (1992). *A grammar of Lango*. Berlin and New York, Mouton de Gruyter.

Nouveau, Dominique (1994). *Language acquisition, metrical theory and optimality*. Doctoral dissertation, Utrecht University.

Noyer, Rolf (1997). Attic Greek accentuation and intermediate derivational representations. In Iggy Roca (ed.) *Derivations and constraints in phonology*. Oxford, OUP, pp.501–528.

Oates, William and Lynette Oates (1964). Gugu-Yalanji linguistic and anthropological data. *Gugu-Yalanji and Wik-Mungan language studies*. Canberra, Australia, Australian Institute of Aboriginal Studies, pp.1–17.

O'Connor, J. D. and Gordon Arnold (1973). *Intonation of colloquial English*. London, UK, Longman.

Odden, David (1978). Further evidence for the feature [grave]. *LI* 9: 141–144.

Odden, David (1981). *Problems in tone assignment in Shona*. Doctoral dissertation, University of Illinois.

Odden, David (1984). Stem tone assignment in Shona. In G. N. Clements and John Goldsmith (eds.) *Autosegmental studies in Bantu tone*. Dordrecht, Foris, pp.255–280.

Odden, David (1986). On the role of the Obligatory Contour Principle in phonological theory. *Lg* 62: 353–383.

Odden, David (1987a). Dissimilation as deletion in Chukchi. *ESCOL 3*. Columbus, Ohio, Ohio State University, pp.235–246.

Odden, David (1987b). Kimatuumbi phrasal phonology. *Phonology Yearbook* 4: 13–36.

Odden, David (1991). Vowel geometry. *Ph* 8: 261–289.

Odden, David (1994). Adjacency parameters in phonology. *Lg* 70: 289–330.

Odden, David (1995). Tone: African languages. In John Goldsmith (ed.) *The handbook of phonological theory*. Oxford, Basil Blackwell, pp.444–475.

Odden, David (2005). *Introducing phonology*. Cambridge Introductions to Language and Linguistics. Cambridge, CUP.

Odden, David and Mary Odden (1985). Ordered reduplication in Kihehe. *LI* 16: 497–503.

Odé, Cecilia (2005). Neutralization or truncation? The perception of two Russian pitch accents on utterance-final syllables. *Speech Communication*.

Ohala, Diane (1995). *Cluster reduction and constraints in acquisition*. Doctoral dissertation, University of Arizona.

Ohala, John J. (1971). The role of physiological and acoustic models in explaining the direction of sound change. *Project on Linguistic Analysis Reports (UCB)* 15: 25–40.

Ohala, John J. (1972). How to represent natural sound patterns. *Project on Linguistic Analysis (Berkeley)* 16: 40–57. [http://trill.berkeley.edu/users/ohala/index3.html].

Ohala, John J. (1974). Experimental historical phonology. In J. M. Anderson and C. Jones (eds.) *Historical linguistics, II. Theory and description in phonology*. Amsterdam, North Holland, pp.353–389.

Ohala, John J. (1975). Phonetic explanations for nasal sound patterns. In C. A. Ferguson, L. M. Hyman and J. J. Ohala (eds.) *Nasalfest: Papers from a symposium on nasals and nasalization*. Stanford, Language Universals Project, pp.289–316.

Ohala, John J. (1976). A model of speech aerodynamics. *Report of the Phonology Laboratory (UCB)* 1: 93–107.

Ohala, John J. (1978). Production of tone. In Victoria Fromkin (ed.) *Tone: A linguistic survey*. New York, Academic Press, pp.5–40.

Ohala, John J. (1980). Moderator's introduction to the Symposium on Phonetic Universals in Phonological Systems and their Explanation. *ICPhS* 9, vol. 3 *(Copenhagen: Institute of Phonetics)*: 181–185.

Ohala, John J. (1981). The listener as a source of sound change. In Carrie Masek, Roberta Hendrick and Mary Frances Miller (eds.) *Papers from the parasession on language and behavior*. Chicago, Chicago Linguistics Society, pp.178–203.

Ohala, John J. (1983a). The origin of sound patterns in vocal tract constraints. In Peter MacNeilage (ed.) *The production of speech*. New York, Springer-Verlag, pp.189–216.

Ohala, John J. (1983b). The phonological end justifies any means. In S. Hattori and K. Inoue (eds.) *ICPhS 13* (Tokyo, Sanseido Shoten): 232–243.

Ohala, John J. (1989). Sound change is drawn from a pool of synchronic variation. In Leiv Egil Breivek and Ernst Håkon Jahr (eds.) *Language change: Contributions to the study of its causes*. Berlin, Mouton de Gruyter, pp.173–198.

Ohala, John J. (1990a). Alternatives to the sonority hierarchy for explaining segmental sequential constraints. In Michael Ziolkowski, Manuela Noske and Karen Deaton (eds.) *CLS 26: The parasession on the syllable in phonetics and phonology*. Vol.2. Chicago, CLS, pp.319–338.

Ohala, John J. (1990b). There is no interface between phonetics and phonology. A personal view. *JPh* 18: 153–171.

Ohala, John J. (1992). What's cognitive, what's not, in sound change. In G. Kellerman and M. D. Morrissey (eds.) *Diachrony within synchrony: Language history and cognition*. Frankfurt, Peter Lang Verlag, pp.309–355.

Ohala, John J. 1993. The phonetics of sound change. In C. Jones (ed.) Historical linguistics: Problems and perspectives. London: Longman Academic, pp. 237–278.

Ohala, John J. (1995). Phonetic explanations for sound patterns: Implications for grammars of competence. In K. Elenius and P. Branderud (eds.) *ICPhS* 13 (Stockholm), Vol.2, pp.52–59.

Ohala, John J. (1996). Speech perception is hearing sounds, not tongues. *JASA* 99: 1718–1725.

Ohala, John J. (1997). The relation between phonetics and phonology. In William Hardcastle and John Laver (eds.) *The handbook of phonetic sciences*. Oxford, Blackwell, pp.674–694.

Ohala, John J. and C. J. Riordan (1979). Passive vocal tract enlargement during voiced stops. In J. J. Wolf and D. H. Klatt (eds.) *Speech Communication Papers*. New York, Acoustical Society of America, pp.89–92.

Öhman, S (1966). Coarticulation in CVC utterances: Spectrographic measurements. *JASA* 66: 1691–1702.

Oostendorp, Marc van (1995). *Vowel quality and phonological projection*. Doctoral dissertation, Katolieke Universiteit Brabant.

Oostendorp, Marc van (1997). Style registers in conflict resolution. In Frans Hinskins, Roeland van Hout and Leo Wetzels (eds.) *Variation, change and phonological theory*. Amsterdam and Philadelphia, PA, John Benjamins, pp.207–229.

Orgun, C. Orhan (1996). *Sign-based morphology and phonology with special attention to Optimality Theory*. Doctoral dissertation, UCB. [Also ROA 171].

Orgun, C. Orhan and Ronald Sprouse (1999). From MParse to control: Deriving ungrammaticality. *Ph* 16: 191–220.

Osborn, Henry (1966). Warao I: Phonology and morphophonemics. *IJAL* 32: 108–123.

Osthoff, Hermann and Karl Brugmann (1878). *Morphologische Untersuchungen auf dem Gebiete der Indogermanischen Sprachen*. Leipzig, S. Hirzel.

Ota, Mitsuhiko (2003). *The development of prosodic structure in early words: Continuity, divergence and change*. Amsterdam, Benjamins.

Padgett, Jaye (1991). *Stricture in feature geometry*. Doctoral dissertation, UMass.

Padgett, Jaye (1994). Stricture and nasal place assimilation. *NLLT* 12: 463–513.

Padgett, Jaye (1995). *Stricture in feature geometry*. Dissertations in Linguistics Series. Stanford, CSLI Publications.

Padgett, Jaye (2001). Contrast dispersion and Russian palatalization. In Elizabeth Hume and Keith Johnson (eds.) *The role of speech perception in phonology*. San Diego, Academic Press, pp.187–218.

Padgett, Jaye (2002). On the characterization of feature classes in phonology. *Lg* 78.1: 81–110.

Padgett, Jaye (2003a). Contrast and post-velar fronting in Russian. *NLLT* 21: 39–87.

Padgett, Jaye (2003b). *Systemic contrast and Catalan rhotics*. Manuscript, UCSC: http://people.ucsc.edu/~padgett/papers.html.

Padgett, Jaye (2004). Russian vowel reduction and Dispersion Theory. *Phonological studies (Kaitakusha, Tokyo)* 7: 81–96.

Paine, T. (1776). *Common sense*. Philadelphia, PA, W. & T. Bradford.

Painter, Colin (1970). *Gonja: A phonological and grammatical study*. Bloomington, IN, Indiana University Publications.

Pais, A. (1983). *Subtle is the Lord: The science and the life of Albert Einstein*. Oxford, Oxford University Press.

Palmada, Bianca (1995). From place to continuancy. In Harry van der Hulst and J. van de Wiejer (eds.) *Leiden in Last: HIL phonology papers I*. The Hague, Holland Academic Graphics, pp.299–313.

Pankratz, Leo and Eunice V. Pike (1967). Phonology and morphotonemics of Ayutla Mixtec. *IJAL* 33: 287–289.

Paolillo, John C. (2002). *Analyzing linguistic variation: Statistical models and methods*. Stanford, CA, CSLI Publications.

Paradis, Carole (1986). *Phonologie et morphologie lexicales: Les classes nominales en pulaar (Fula)*. Doctoral dissertation, University of Montreal.

Paradis, Carole (1988). On constraints and repair strategies. *Linguistic Review* 6: 71–97.

Paradis, Carole (1997). Non-transparent constraint effects in Gere: from cycles to derivations. In Iggy Roca (ed.) *Derivations and constraints in phonology*. Oxford, OUP, pp.529–550.

Paradis, Carole and Darlene La Charité (2005). Category preservation and proximity versus phonetic approximation in loanword adaptation. *LI* 36.2: 223–258.

Paradis, Carole and Jean-François Prunet (1989). On coronal transparency. *Ph* 6: 317–348.

Paradis, Carole and Jean-François Prunet (1991a). Asymmetry and visibility in consonant articulations. In Carole Paradis and Jean-François Prunet (eds.) *The special status of coronals: Internal and external evidence*. San Diego, Academic Press, pp.1–28.

Paradis, Carole and Jean-François Prunet (eds.) (1991b). *The special status of coronals: Internal and external evidence*. Phonetics and phonology. San Diego, Academic Press.

Parker, E. M., R. L. Diehl and K. R. Kluender (1986). Trading relations in speech and non-speech. *Perception & Psychophysics* 39: 129–142.

Parker, Steve (2002). *Quantifying the sonority hierarchy*. Doctoral dissertation, UMass.

Patel, A. D., J. R. Iversen and K. Ohgushi (2004). Native language influences the perception of non-linguistic rhythm. In J. Slifka, S. Manuel and Melanie Matthies (eds.) *From sound to sense: 50+ years of discoveries in speech communication*. Cambridge, MA, Research Laboratory of Electronics.

Pater, Joe (1997). Minimal violation and phonological development. *Language Acquisition* 6.3: 201–253.

Pater, Joe (1999). Austronesian nasal substitution and other NÇ effects. In Rene Kager, Harry van der Hulst and Wim Zonneveld (eds.) *The prosody morphology interface*. Cambridge, MA, CUP, pp.310–343.

Pater, Joe (2000a) Unpublished course handout from Ling 751, University of Massachusetts, Amherst.

Pater, Joe (2000b). Nonuniformity in English secondary stress: the role of ranked and lexically specific constraints. *Ph* 17: 237–274. [Also ROA 107].

Pater, Joe (2003). *Balantak metathesis and theories of possible repair in Optimality Theory*. Manuscript, UMass.

Pater, Joe (2004). Bridging the gap between perception and production with minimally violable constraints. In R. Kager, J. Pater & W. Zonneveld (eds.) *Constraints in phonological acquisition*. Cambridge: Cambridge University Press. pp.219–244.

Pater, Joe, Christine Stager and Janet Werker (2004). The perceptual acquisition of phonological contrast. *Lg* 80.3: 384–402.

Pater, Joe and Adam Werle (2003). Direction of assimilation in child consonant harmony. *CJL* 48.3/4: 385–408.

Patrick, Peter (1991). Creoles at the intersection of variable processes: t, d deletion and past-marking in the Jamaican mesolect. *Language variation and change* 3.2: 171–189.

Pauliny, E. (1961). *Fonológia spisovnej slovenčiny*. Slovenské pedagogické nakladatel'stvo, Bratislava.

Paunonen, Heikki (1995). *Suomen kieli Helsingissa [The Finnish language in Helsinki]*. Helsingin yliopiston suomen kielen laitos. Helsinki.

Payne, David L. (1981). *The phonology and morphology of Axininca Campa*. Arlington, TX, The SIL and University of Texas at Arlington.

Payne, Judith (1990). Asheninca stress patterns. In Doris L. Payne (ed.) *Amazonian linguistics: Studies in Lowland South American languages*. Austin, University of Texas Press, pp.185–212.

Peng, S.-H. (1997). Production and perception of Taiwanese tones in different tonal and prosodic contexts. *JPh* 25: 371–400.

Peperkamp, Sharon (1997). *Prosodic words*. The Hague, Holland Academic Graphics.

Peperkamp, Sharon and E. Dupoux (2003). Reinterpreting loanword adaptations: The role of perception. *ICPhS* 15: 367–370.

Perkell, J. S., M. L. Matthies, M. A. Svirsky and M. I. Jordan (1993). Trading relations between tongue-body raising and lip rounding in production of the vowel /u/: A pilot motor equivalence study. *JASA* 93: 2948–2961.

Perkell, J. S., M. L. Matthies and M. Zandipour (1998). Motor equivalence in the production of /ʃ/. *JASA* 103: 3085 (Abstract).

Peters, Jörg (to appear a). Tone and intonation in the dialect of Hasselt. *Linguistics*.

Peters, Jörg (to appear b). Bitonal lexical pitch accents in the Limburgian dialect of Borgloon. In C. Gussenhoven and T. Riad (eds.) *Tones and tunes. Vol. II: Phonetic and behavioural studies*. Berlin: Mouton de Gruyter.

Pettersson, T. and S. Wood (1987a). Vowel reduction in Bulgarian and its implications for theories of vowel production: A review of the problem. *Folia Linguistica* 21: 261–279.

Pettersson, T. and S. Wood (1987b). Vowel reduction in Bulgarian: The phonetic data and model experiments. *Folia Linguistica* 22: 239–262.

Phillips, Betty S. (1984). Word frequency and the actuation of sound change. *Lg* 45: 9–25.

Phillips, Betty S. (1998). Lexical diffusion is not lexical analogy. *Word* 49: 369–380.

Phillips, Betty S. (2001). Lexical diffusion, lexical frequency and lexical analysis. In Joan Bybee and Paul Hopper (eds.) *Frequency and the emergence of linguistic structure*. Amsterdam, John Benjamins, pp.123–136.

Pierrehumbert, Janet (1980). *The phonology and phonetics of English intonation*. Doctoral dissertation, MIT.

Pierrehumbert, Janet (1990). Phonological and phonetic representations. *JPh* 18.3: 375–394.

Pierrehumbert, Janet (1993a). Alignment and prosodic heads. In Andreas Kathol and Michael Bernstein (eds.) *ESCOL 10*, Ithaca, NY: Cornell University Press, pp.268–286.

Pierrehumbert, Janet (1993b). Dissimilarity in the Arabic verbal roots. In A. Schafer (ed.) *NELS 23*. Amherst, MA, GLSA, pp.367–381.

Pierrehumbert, Janet (1994). Knowledge of variation. In K. Beals, J. Denton, R. Knippen, L. Melnar, H. Suzuki and E. Zeinfeld (eds.) *CLS 30 Vol.2: Papers from the parasession on variation*. Chicago, IL, CLS, pp.232–256.

Pierrehumbert, Janet (2001). Exemplar dynamics: Word frequency, lenition and contrast. In Joan L. Bybee and Paul Hopper (eds.) *Frequency and the emergence of language structure*. Amsterdam, John Benjamins, pp.137–157.

Pierrehumbert, Janet (2002). Word-specific phonetics. In Carlos Gussenhoven and Natasha Warner (eds.) *Laboratory Phonology 7*. Berlin, Mouton de Gruyter, pp.101–139.

Pierrehumbert, Janet (2003a). Phonetic diversity, statistical learning and acquisition of phonology. *Language and Speech* 46.2/3: 115–154.

Pierrehumbert, Janet (2003b). Probabilistic phonology: Discrimination and robustness. In Rens Bod, Jennifer Hay and Stefanie Jannedy (eds.) *Probabilistic linguistics*. Cambridge, MA, MIT Press, pp.177–228.

Pierrehumbert, Janet and Mary E. Beckman (1988). *Japanese tone structure*. LI Monograph Series No. 15. Cambridge, Mass., MIT Press.

Pierrehumbert, Janet, Mary E. Beckman and D. Robert Ladd (2000). Conceptual foundations of phonology as a laboratory science. In Noel Burton-Roberts, Philip Carr and Gerard Docherty (eds.) *Phonological knowledge: Conceptual and empirical issues*. Oxford, OUP, pp.273–303.

Piggott, Glyne (1974). *Aspects of Odawa morphophonemics*. Doctoral dissertation, University of Toronto.

Piggott, Glyne (1980). *Aspects of Odawa morphophonemics*. New York: Garland Publishing.

Piggott, Glyne (1992). Variability in feature dependency: the case of nasality. *NLLT* 10: 33–77.

Piggott, Glyne (1995). Epenthesis and syllable weight. *NLLT* 13.2: 283–326.

Pike, K. L. (1945). *The intonation of American English*. Ann Arbor, Michigan, University of Michigan Press.

Pike, Kenneth (1948). *Tone languages: A technique for determining the number and type of pitch contrasts in a language, with studies in tonemic substitution and fusion*. University of Michigan Publications in Linguistics, no.4. Ann Arbor, University of Michigan Press.

Pinker, Steven (1984). *Language learnability and language development*. Cambridge, MA, Harvard University Press.

Pinker, Steven (1999). *Words and rules: The ingredients of language*. London, Weidenfeld & Nicolson.

Pinker, Steven and Paul Bloom (1990). Natural language and natural selection. *Behavioral and Brain Sciences* 13.4: 707–784.

Pinker, S. and A. Prince (1988). On language and connectionism: Analysis of a parallel distributed processing model of language acquisition. *Cognition* 28: 73–193.

Plag, I. (1998). Morphological haplology in a constraint-based morphophonology. In W. Kehrein and R. Wiese (eds.) *Phonology and morphology of the Germanic languages.* Tübingen, Niemeyer, pp.199–215.

Plauché, M., C. Delogu and J. J. Ohala (1997). Asymmetries in consonant confusion. *Proceedings of Eurospeech '97: Fifth European Conference on Speech Perception and Technology* 4: 2187–2190.

Polome, E. (1967). *Swahili language handbook.* Washington, Center for Applied Linguistics.

Port, Robert and Adam Leary (2005). Against formal phonology. *Lg* 81.4: 927–964.

Poser, William (1984). *The phonetics and phonology of tone and intonation in Japanese.* Doctoral dissertation, MIT.

Poser, William (1989). The metrical foot in Diyari. *Ph* 6.1: 117–148.

Post, Brechtje (2000). *Tonal and phrasal structures in French intonation.* The Hague, Thesus (Holland Academic Graphics).

Potts, Christopher (2005). *The logic of conversational implicatures.* Oxford, OUP.

Powell, J. V. (1975). Proto-Chimakuan: Materials for a reconstruction. *Working Papers in Linguistics.* Vol.7.2, University of Hawaii.

Prieto, Pilar (2005). Syntactic and eurhythmic constraints on phrasing decisions in Catalan. In Merle Horne and Marc van Oostendorp (eds.) *Boundaries in intonational phonology.* Special Issue. Studia Linguistica 59.2/3: 194–222.

Prieto, Pilar, J. van Santen and J. Hirschberg (1995). Tonal alignment patterns in Spanish. *JPh* 23: 429–451.

Prince, Alan (1980). A metrical theory for Estonian quantity. *LI* 11.3: 511–562.

Prince, Alan (1983). Relating to the grid. *LI* 14.1: 19–100.

Prince, Alan (1987). Planes and copying. *LI* 18: 491–509.

Prince, Alan (1990). Quantitative consequences of rhythmic organization. In Michael Ziolkowski, Manuela Noske and Karen Deaton (eds.) *CLS 26: The parasession on the syllable in phonetics and phonology.* Vol.2. Chicago, CLS, pp.355–398.

Prince, Alan (1993). In defense of the number i: Anatomy of a linear dynamic model of linguistic generalizations. *Rutgers Technical Report TR-1.* http://ruccs.rutgers.edu/tech_rpt/dynlinmodel1.pdf.

Prince, Alan (1997). *Stringency and anti-Paninian hierarchies.* Handout from the LSA Linguistic Institute at Cornell, http://ling.rutgers.edu/people/faculty/prince.html.

Prince, Alan (1998). *Paninian relations.* Handout from talk at the University of Marburg, http://ling.rutgers.edu/people/faculty/prince.html.

Prince, Alan (2000). *The special and the general.* Handout from talk at the University of Pennsylvania, http://ling.rutgers.edu/people/faculty/prince.html.

Prince, Alan (2001). *Invariance under re-ranking*. Handout from *WCCFL* 20, http://ling.rutgers.edu/people/faculty/prince.html.

Prince, Alan (2002a). Arguing optimality. In Andries Coetzee, Angela Carpenter and Paul de Lacy (eds.) *Papers in Optimality Theory II*. Amherst, MA, GLSA [Also ROA 562].

Prince, Alan (2002b). Entailed ranking arguments. *ROA* 500.

Prince, A. and S. Pinker (1988). Wickelphone ambiguity. *Cognition* 30:189–190.

Prince, Alan and Paul Smolensky (2004). *Optimality Theory: Constraint interaction in generative grammar*. Oxford, Basil Blackwell. [Also TR 2, Rutgers University Cognitive Science Center (1993), also ROA 537].

Prince, Alan and Bruce Tesar (2004). Learning phonotactic distributions. In René Kager, Joe Pater and Wim Zonneveld (eds.) *Constraints in phonological acquisition*. Cambridge, UK, CUP, pp.245–291.

Pulleyblank, Douglas (1986). *Tone in Lexical Phonology*. Dordrecht, D. Reidel.

Pulleyblank, Douglas (1988). Underspecification, the feature hierarchy and Tiv vowels. *Ph* 5: 299–326.

Pulleyblank, Douglas (1996). Neutral vowels in Optimality Theory: A comparison of Yoruba and Wolof. *CJL* 41.4: 295–347.

Pulleyblank, Douglas (2002). Harmony drivers: No disagreement allowed. *BLS* 28: 249–267.

Pulleyblank, Douglas (2004). A note on tonal markedness in Yoruba. *Ph* 21: 409–425.

Pulleyblank, Douglas (in press). Patterns of reduplication in Yoruba. In Kristin Hanson and Sharon Inkelas (eds.) *The nature of the word: Essays in honor of Paul Kiparsky*. Cambridge, MA, MIT Press.

Pulleyblank, Douglas and William J. Turkel (2000). Learning phonology: Genetic algorithms and Yoruba tongue-root harmony. In Joost Dekkers, Frank van der Leeuw and Jeroen van de Weijer (eds.) *Optimality Theory: Phonology, syntax and acquisition*. Oxford, UK, OUP, pp.554–591.

Pulleyblank, Edwin G. (1989). The role of coronal in articulator based features. In Bradley Music, Randolph Graczyk and Caroline Wilshire (eds.) *CLS 25*. Chicago, Chicago Linguistics Society, pp.379–393.

Pullum, Geoffrey (1976). The Duke of York gambit. *JL* 12: 83–102.

Pycha, Anne, Pawel Nowak, Eurie Shin and Ryan Shosted (2003). Phonological rule-learning and its implications for a theory of vowel harmony. In G. Garding and M. Tsujimura (eds.) *WCCFL* 22. Cambridge, MA, Cascadilla Press, pp.423–435.

Pye, C., David Ingram and H. List (1987). A comparison of initial consonant acquisition in English and Quiché. In K. E. Nelson and A. van Kleek (eds.) *Children's language*. Vol.6. Hillsdale, NJ, Erlbaum, pp.175–190.

Raimy, Eric (2000). *The phonology and morphology of reduplication*. New York, Mouton de Gruyter.

Raphael, Lawrence J. (1981). Durations and contexts as cues to word-final cognate opposition in English. *Phonetica: International Journal of Speech Science* 38: 126–147.

Rehg, Kenneth and Damien Sohl (1981). *Ponapean reference grammar*. Honolulu, University of Hawaii Press.

Reilly, Ehren M. (to appear). Choosing just the right amount of overapplication in Texistepec Popoluca. In Leah Bateman and Adam Werle (eds.) *UMOP 32: Papers in Optimality Theory III*. Amherst, MA: GLSA.

Revithiadou, Anthi and Ruben van de Vijver (1997). Durational contrasts and the Iambic/Trochaic Law. In V. Samiian (ed.) *Proceedings of WECOL*. Department of Linguistics, California State University, Fresno, CA, pp.229–242.

Reynolds, William (1994). *Variation and phonological theory*. Doctoral dissertation, University of Pennsylvania.

Riad, Tomas (1992). *Structures in Germanic prosody: A diachronic study with special reference to Nordic languages*. Doctoral dissertation, Stockholm University.

Riad, Tomas (1998). Towards a Scandinavian accent typology. In W. Kehrein and R. Wiese (eds.) *Phonology and morphology of the Germanic languages*. Tübingen, Niemeyer, pp.77–109.

Rialland, A. (2001). Anticipatory raising in downstep realization: Evidence for preplanning in tone production. In S. Kaji (ed.) *Proceedings of the symposium on cross-linguistic studies of tonal phenomena: Tonogenesis, Japanese accentology, and other topics*. Tokyo, Tokyo University of Foreign Studies. Institute for the Study of Languages and Cultures of Asia and Africa, pp.301–321.

Rice, Curtis (1992). *Binarity and ternarity in metrical theory: Parametric extensions*. Doctoral dissertation, University of Texas, Austin.

Rice, Keren (1989). *A grammar of Slave*. Berlin, Mouton de Gruyter.

Rice, Keren (1993). A reexamination of the feature [sonorant]: The status of 'sonorant obstruents'. *Lg* 69.2: 308–344.

Rice, Keren (1994). Peripheral in consonants. *CJL* 39.3: 191–216.

Rice, Keren (1996). Default variability: The coronal-velar relationship. *NLLT* 14: 493–543.

Rice, Keren (1999a). Featural markedness in phonology: Variation. Part I. *GLOT* 4.7: 3–6.

Rice, Keren (1999b). Featural markedness in phonology: Variation. Part II. *GLOT* 4.8: 3–7.

Rice, Keren (2002). Featural markedness in phonology. In Lisa Cheng and Rint Sybesma (eds.) *The second GLOT International State-of-the-Article book*. Studies in Generative Grammar. Berlin, Mouton de Gruyter, pp.387–427.

Rice, Keren (to appear). *Featural markedness*. Cambridge, CUP.

Rice, Keren and Peter Avery (1991). On the relationship between laterality and coronality. In Carole Paradis and Jean-François Prunet (eds.) *The special status of coronals*. San Diego, Academic Press, pp.101–124.

Rice, Keren and Peter Avery (1995). Variability in a deterministic model of language acquisition: A theory of segmental acquisition. In J. Archibald (ed.) *Phonological acquisition and phonological theory*. Hillsdale, NJ, Lawrence Erlbaum, pp.23–42.

Rich, F. (1963). Arabela phonemes and high-level phonology. In B. Elson (ed.) *Studies in Peruvian Indian languages*. Vol.1. Norman, OK, SIL/University of Oklahoma, pp.193–206.

Rietveld, Toni and Carlos Gussenhoven (1995). Aligning pitch targets in speech synthesis: Effects of syllable structure. *JPh* 23: 375–385.

Riggle, Jason (2004). Contenders and learning. In Benjamin Schmeiser, Vineeta Chand, Ann Kelleher and Angelo Rodriguez (eds.) *WCCFL 23*. Somerville, MA, Cascadilla Press, pp.101–114.

Ringen, Catherine and Orvokki Heinamaki (1999). Variation in Finnish vowel harmony: an OT account. *NLLT* 17.2: 303–337.

Riordan, C. J. (1977). Control of vocal-tract length in speech. *JASA* 62: 998–1002.

Ristad, E. S. (1990). *The Computational structure of human language*. Doctoral dissertation, Massachusetts Institute of Technology.

Robins, R. H. (1957). Vowel nasality in Sundanese: a phonological and grammatical study. *Studies in Linguistics*. Oxford, Blackwell, pp.87–103.

Robinson, Orrin W. (2001). *Whose German? The ach/ich alternation and related phenomena in 'standard' and 'colloquial' German*. Amsterdam, John Benjamins.

Roca, Iggy (1994). *Generative phonology*. London, Routledge.

Roca, Iggy (ed.) (1997a). *Derivations and constraints in phonology*. Oxford, OUP.

Roca, Iggy (1997b). Derivations or constraints, or derivations and constraints? In Iggy Roca (ed.) *Derivations and constraints in phonology*. Oxford, OUP, pp.3–42.

Romani, C. and C. Galluzzi (2005). Effects of syllabic complexity in predicting accuracy of repetition and direction of errors in patients with articulatory and phonological difficulties. *Cognitive Neuropsychology* 22.

Rooth, Mats (1992). A theory of focus interpretation. *Natural language semantics* 1: 75–116.

Rose, Sharon (1993). Coronality and vocalic underspecification. In Carrie Dyck (ed.) *TWPL 12.2*. Toronto, University of Toronto Linguistics Department, pp.155–176.

Rose, Sharon (1996). Variable laryngeals and vowel lowering. *Ph* 13.1: 73–117.

Rose, Sharon (1997). *Theoretical issues in comparative Ethio-Semitic phonology and morphology*. Doctoral dissertation, McGill University.

Rose, Sharon (2000). Rethinking Geminates, Long-Distance Geminates, and the OCP. *LI* 31.1: 85–122.

Rose, Sharon and Rachel Walker (2004). A typology of consonant agreement as correspondence. *Lg* 80: 475–531.

Rose, Yvan (2000). *Headedness and prosodic licensing in the L1 acquisition of phonology*. Doctoral dissertation, McGill University.

Rose, Yvan (2003). ChildPhon: A database solution for the study of child phonology. In Barbara Beachley, Amanda Brown and Frances Conlin (eds.) *BUCLD 27: Proceedings of the 27th Annual Boston University Conference on Language Development*. Somerville, MA, Cascadilla Press, pp.674–685.

Rose, Yvan and Brian MacWhinney (2004). *Towards a solution for the sharing of phonological data*, Boston, MA: http://childes.psy.cmu.edu/phon/Phon.ppt.

Rosenblatt, Frank (1958). The Perceptron: A probabilistic model for information storage and organization in the brain. *Psychological Review* 65.6: 386–408.

Rosenthall, Samuel (1988). The representation of prenasalized consonants. In Hagit Borer (ed.) *WCCFL 7*. Stanford, CA, Stanford Linguistic Association, pp.277–291.

Rosenthall, Samuel (1994). *Vowel/Glide alternation in a theory of constraint interaction*. Doctoral dissertation, UMass.

Rosenthall, Samuel and Harry van der Hulst (1999). Weight-by-position by position. *NLLT* 17: 499–540.

Ross, Malcolm (2002). Takia. In John Lynch, Malcolm Ross and Terry Crowley (eds.) *The Oceanic languages*. Richmond, Curzon, pp.216–248.

Ross, Malcolm (2003). *Seminar on Takia, a Papuanised Austronesian language of Papua New Guinea*. Field Research Group, Institute of Linguistics, Academia Sinica, http://140.109.150.124/frg/frg_english/Tutorials/SAdelaar_tuto03.html.

Rubach, Jerzy (1984). *Cyclic and lexical phonology. The structure of Polish*. Dordrecht, Foris.

Rubach, Jerzy (1994). Affricates as strident stops in Polish. *LI* 25: 119–143.

Rubach, Jerzy (1997). Extrasyllabic consonants in Polish: derivational Optimality Theory. In Iggy Roca (ed.) *Derivations and constraints in phonology*. Oxford, OUP, pp.551–582.

Rubach, Jerzy (2000). Glide and glottal stop insertion in Slavic languages: a DOT analysis. *LI* 31: 271–317.

Rubach, Jerzy and Geert E. Booij (1985). A grid theory of stress in Polish. *Ln* 66.4: 281–319.

Ruhlen, Merritt (1978). Nasal vowels. In Joseph H. Greenberg (ed.) *Universals of human languages*. Vol.2, Stanford University Press, pp.203–241.

Rumelhart, David E. and James L. McClelland (1986). On learning the past tense of English verbs. In James L. McClelland, David E. Rumelhart and The PDP Research Group (eds.) *Parallel distributed processing: Explorations in the microstructure of cognition*. Vol.2. Cambridge, MA, MIT Press/Bradford Books, pp.7–57.

Russell, Kevin (1995). Morphemes and candidates in Optimality Theory. *ROA* 44.

Saari, D. (2001). *Decisions and elections: Explaining the unexpected*. Cambridge, UK, Cambridge University Press.

Saari, D. (2005). Collisions, rings and other Newtonian N-body problems. Providence, RI, American Mathematical Society.

Saeed, John (1999). *Somali*. The London Oriental and African Language Library. Amsterdam and Philadelphia, John Benjamins.

Sagey, Elizabeth (1986). *The representation of features and relations in nonlinear phonology*. Doctoral dissertation, MIT.

Sagey, Elizabeth (1988). On the ill-formedness of crossing association lines. *LI* 19: 109–118.

Sakas, William and Janet Dean Fodor (2001). The Structural Triggers Learner. In Stefano Bertolo (ed.) *Language acquisition and learnability*. Cambridge, UK, CUP, pp.172–233.

Salminen, Topani (1998). Nenets. In D. Abondolo (ed.) *Uralic languages*. London and New York, Routledge, pp.516–547.

Samek-Lodovici, Vieri (2005). Prosody-syntax interaction in the expression of focus. *NLLT* 23: 687–755.

Samek-Lodovici, Vieri and Alan Prince (1999). Optima. *ROA* 363.

Sandalo, Filomena and Hubert Truckenbrodt (2002). Some notes on phonological phrasing in Brazilian Portuguese. *Delta* 19.1: 1–30.

Sankoff, David (1988). Variable rules. In Ulrich Ammon, Norbert Dittmar and Klaus Mattheier (eds.) *Sociolinguistics: An international handbook of the science of language and society*. Vol.2. Berlin, Germany, Walter de Gruyter, pp.984–997.

Santa Ana, Otto (1991). *Phonetic simplification processes in the English of the Barrio: a cross-generational sociolinguistic study of the Chicanos of Los Angeles*. Doctoral dissertation, University of Pennsylvania.

Santa Ana, Otto (1992). Locating the linguistic cycle in vernacular speech: Chicano English and the Exponential Hypothesis. In Jeanette Marshall Denton, Grace P. Chan and Costas P. Canakis (eds.) *CLS 28, vol. 2: The cycle in linguistic theory*, pp.277–287.

Santa Ana, Otto (1996). Sonority and syllable structure in Chicano English. *Language variation and change* 8.1: 63–89.

Santen, Jan P. H. van and Julia Hirschberg (1994). Segmental effects on timing and height of pitch contours. *International Conference on Spoken Language Processing 94*, pp.719–722.

Santos, Raquel (2001). *A aquisição do acento primário no português brasileiro*. Doctoral dissertation, University of Campinas, Brazil (UNICAMP).

Santos, Raquel (2003). Bootstrapping in the acquisition of word stress in Brazilian Portuguese. *Journal of Portuguese linguistics* 2: 93–114.

Sapir, Edward (1922). The Takelma language of southwestern Oregon. *Bulletin of American Ethnology* 30.2: 1–296.

Sapir, Edward (1930). Southern Paiute, a Shoshonean language. *Proceedings of the American Academy of Arts and Sciences* 65: 1–3.

Sapir, Edward (1933/1949). The psychological reality of phonemes. In David Mandelbaum (ed.) *Selected Writings of Edward Sapir*. Berkeley and Los Angeles, University of California Press, pp.46–60.

Sapir, Edward and Morris Swadesh (1978). *Nootka texts: Tales and ethnological narratives, with grammatical notes and lexical material*. New York, AMS Press.

Sapir, J. D. (1965). *A grammar of Diola-Fogny*. West African Language Monographs. London, CUP.

Saussure, Ferdinand de (1916). *Cours de linguistique générale*. Lausanne and Paris, Payot.

Scatton, E. A. (1983). *A reference grammar of Modern Bulgarian*. Bloomington, IN, Slavica.

Schacter, Paul and Fe Otanes (1972). *Tagalog reference grammar*. Berkeley, University of California Press.

Schafer, Robin (1995). Headedness and the representation of affricates. *The Linguistic Review* 12: 61–87.

Schane, Sanford (1974). How abstract is abstract? In Anthony Bruck, Robert A. Fox and Michael W. LaGaly (eds.) *Papers from the parasession on Natural Phonology*. Chicago, Chicago Linguistic Society, pp.297–317.

Schane, Sanford (1984). The fundamentals of Particle Phonology. *Phonology Yearbook* 1: 129–156.

Scheer, Tobias (1998). A unified model of Proper Government. *The Linguistic Review* 15: 41–67.

Scheer, Tobias (2004). *A lateral theory of phonology: What is CVCV, and why should it be?* Studies in Generative Grammar 68.1, Mouton de Gruyter.

Schile, Perry and Ginny Schile (1993). A Kara phonology. In John M. Clifton (ed.) *Data papers on New Guinea linguistics: Phonologies of Austronesian languages 2*. Papua New Guinea, SIL Academic Publications, pp.99–130.

Schütz, A. (1985). *The Fijian language*. Honolulu, University of Hawaii Press.

Schwartz, J.-L., L.-J. Boë, N. Valleé and C. Abry (1997a). Major trends in vowel system inventories. *JPh* 25: 233–253.

Schwartz, J.-L., L.-J. Boë, N. Valleé and C. Abry (1997b). The dispersion-focalization theory of vowel systems. *JPh* 25: 255–286.

Schwarzschild, Roger (1999). Givenness, AvoidF and other constraints on the placement of accent. *Natural Language Semantics* 7.2: 141–177.

Scobbie, James (1992). Towards Declarative Phonology. *Edinburgh Working Papers in Cognitive Science* 7: 1–26.

Scobbie, James, John Coleman and Steven Bird (1996). Key aspects of Declarative Phonology. In J. Durand and B. Laks (eds.) *Current trends in phonology: Models and methods*. Manchester, England, European Studies Research Institute, University of Salford, pp.685–709.

Selkirk, Elisabeth O. (1978). On prosodic structure and its relation to syntactic structure. In T. Fretheim (ed.) *Nordic Prosody II*. Trondheim, TAPIR, pp.268–271.

Selkirk, Elisabeth O. (1980a). Prosodic domains in phonology: Sanskrit revisited. In Mark Aronoff and M.-L. Kean (eds.) *Juncture*. Saratoga, CA, Anma Libri, pp.107–129.

Selkirk, Elisabeth O. (1980b). The role of prosodic categories in English word stress. *LI* 11: 563–605.

Selkirk, Elisabeth O. (1981). Epenthesis and degenerate syllables in Cairean Arabic. In Hagit Borer and Joseph Aoun (eds.) *Theoretical issues in the grammar of the Semitic languages*. Cambridge, MA, MIT Press, pp.111–140.

Selkirk, Elizabeth O. (1982a). Syllables. In Harry van der Hulst and Norval Smith (eds.) *The structure of phonological representations, Part II.* Dordrecht, Foris, pp.337–383.

Selkirk, Elisabeth O. (1982b). *The syntax of words.* Cambridge, MA, MIT Press.

Selkirk, Elizabeth O. (1984a). On the major class features and syllable theory. In Mark Aronoff and Richard T. Oerhle (eds.) *Language sound structure: Studies in phonology presented to Morris Halle by his teacher and students.* Cambridge, MA, MIT Press, pp.107–136.

Selkirk, Elisabeth O. (1984b). *Phonology and syntax: The relation between sound and structure.* Cambridge, MA, MIT Press.

Selkirk, Elisabeth O. (1986). On derived domains in sentence phonology. *Phonology yearbook* 3: 371–405.

Selkirk, Elisabeth O. (1993). *[Labial] relations.* Manuscript, UMass.

Selkirk, Elisabeth O. (1995a). The prosodic structure of function words. In Jill Beckman, Laura Walsh Dickey and Suzanne Urbanczyk (eds.) *UMOP 18: Papers in Optimality Theory.* Amherst, MA, GLSA, pp.439–469.

Selkirk, Elisabeth O. (1995b). Sentence prosody: Intonation, stress and phrasing. In John Goldsmith (ed.) *The handbook of phonological theory.* Cambridge, MA, Blackwell, pp.550–569.

Selkirk, Elisabeth O. (2000). The interaction of constraints on prosodic phrasing. In Merle Horne (ed.) *Prosody: Theory and experiment.* Dordrecht: Kluwer. pp.231–261.

Selkirk, Elisabeth O. (2002). Contrastive FOCUS vs. presentational focus: Prosodic evidence from right node raising in English. In Bernard Bel and Isabelle Marlien (eds.) *Speech Prosody 2002: Proceedings of the First International Conference on Speech Prosody, Aix-en-Provence,* pp.643–646. [http://www.lpl.univ-aix.fr/sp2002/pdf/selkirk.pdf-1 April 2006]

Selkirk, Elisabeth O. (2004). Bengali intonation revisited: An optimality theoretic analysis in which FOCUS stress prominence drives FOCUS phrasing. In Chung-Min Lee, Matthew Gordon, and Daniel Büring (eds.) *Topic and Focus: A Cross-Linguistic Perspective.* Dordrecht, Kluwer, pp.217–246.

Selkirk, Elisabeth O. (2005). Comments on intonational phrasing in English. In Sónia Frota, Marina Vigário and Maria João Freitas (eds.) *Prosodies With Special reference to Iberian Languages.* Phonetics and Phonology Series, Mouton de Gruyter, pp.11–58.

Selkirk, Elisabeth O. and Tong Shen (1990). Prosodic domains in Shanghai Chinese. In Sharon Inkelas and Draga Zec (eds.) *The phonology-syntax connection.* Chicago, IL, University of Chicago Press, pp.313–337.

Selkirk, Elisabeth O. and Koichi Tateishi (1991). Syntax and downstep in Japanese. In Carol Georgopolous and Roberta Ishihara (eds.) *Interdisciplinary approaches to language: Essays in honor of S.-Y. Kuroda.* Dordrecht, Germany, Kluwer, pp.519–543.

Senft, Gunter (1986). *Kilivila: The language of the Trobriand islanders.* Berlin, Mouton de Gruyter.

Shaw, Patricia A. (1987). Non-conservation of melodic structure in reduplication. In A. Bosch, Barbara Need and Eric Schiller (eds.) *CLS 23, Part 2: Parasession on Autosegmental and Metrical Phonology*. Chicago, Chicago Linguistic Society, pp.291–306.

Shaw, Patricia A. (1989) The complex status of complex segments in Dakota. In Donna B. Gerdts and Karin Michelson (eds.) *Theoretical perspectives on Native American languages*. Albany, State University of New York Press, pp.3–37.

Shaw, Patricia A. (1991). Consonant harmony systems: The special status of coronal harmony. In Carole Paradis and Jean-François Prunet (eds.) *The special status of coronals*. San Diego, Academic Press, pp.125–157.

Shaw, Patricia A. (2005). Non-adjacency in reduplication. In Bernhard Hurch (ed.) *Studies on reduplication*. Empirical Approaches to Language Typology 28. Berlin, Mouton de Gruyter.

Shen, X.-N., S. (1990). *The prosody of Mandarin Chinese*. University of California Publications in Linguistics. Berkeley, University of California Press.

Sherer, T. (1994). *Prosodic phonotactics*. Doctoral dissertation, UMass.

Shih, Chi-lin (1997). Mandarin third tone sandhi and prosodic structure. In Jialing Wang and Norval Smith (eds.) *Studies in Chinese phonology*. New York, Mouton de Gruyter, pp.81–123.

Sievers, E. (1881). *Grudzüge der Phonetik*. Leipzig, Breitkopf and Hartel.

Silverman, David (1996). Phonology at the interface of phonetics and morphology: Root-final laryngeals in Chong, Korean and Sanskrit. *Journal of East Asian linguistics* 5.3: 301–322.

Silverman, David (1997a). Laryngeal complexity in Otomanguean vowels. *Ph* 14.2: 235–262.

Silverman, David (1997b). Tone sandhi in Comaltepec Chinantec. *Lg* 73.3: 473–492.

Silverman, K. E., M. Beckman, J. Pitrelli, M. Ostendorf, C. Wightman, P. Price, J. Pierrehumbert and J. Hirschberg (1992). ToBI: a standard for labelling English prosody. *Proceedings of the 1992 International Conference on Spoken Language Processing* (ICSLP), Vol.2, pp.867–870.

Silverman, K. E. and J. B. Pierrehumbert (1990). The timing of prenuclear high accents in English. In John Kingston and Mary E. Beckman (eds.) *Papers in Laboratory Phonology I: Between the grammar and physics of speech*. Cambridge, CUP, pp.72–106.

Skousen, Royal (1989). *Analogical modeling of language*. Dordrecht, Kluwer.

Slis, Iman (1986). Assimilation of voice in Dutch as a function of stress, word boundaries and sex of speaker and listener. *JPh* 14: 311–326.

Sloan, Kelly (1988). Bare consonant reduplication: Implications for a prosodic theory of reduplication. In Hagit Borer (ed.) *WCCFL 7*. Stanford, SLA, pp.319–330.

Smiljanić, Rajka and José Ignacio Hualde (2000). Lexical and pragmatic functions of tonal alignments in two Serbo-Croatian dialects. In Arika Okrent and John Boyle (eds.) *CLS 36*, Vol.1, pp.469–482.

Smith, Ian R. (1978). *Sri Lanka Portuguese Creole phonology*. Vanciyoor, Dravidian Linguistics Association.

Smith, Jennifer L. (1997). Noun faithfulness: On the privileged status of nouns in phonology. *ROA* 242.

Smith, Jennifer L. (2002). *Phonological augmentation in prominent positions*. Doctoral dissertation, UMass.

Smith, Jennifer L. (2003). Onset sonority constraints and syllable structure. *ROA* 608.

Smith, K. D. (1968). Laryngealization and de-laryngealization in Sedang phonemics. *Linguistics* 38: 52–69.

Smith, Neil V. (1973). *The acquisition of phonology: A case study*. London, UK, CUP.

Smith, Norval (2000). Dependency Theory meets OT: A proposal for a new approach to segmental structure. In Joost Dekkers, Frank van der Leeuw and Jeroen van de Weijer (eds.) *Optimality Theory: Phonology, syntax, and acquisition*, OUP, pp.234–277.

Smolensky, Paul (1993). Harmony, markedness, and phonological activity. *ROA* 87.

Smolensky, Paul (1995). On the internal structure of the constraint component Con of UG. *ROA* 86.

Smolensky, Paul (1996). The initial state and "richness of the base" in Optimality Theory. *ROA* 154.

Smolensky, Paul and G. Legendre (eds.) (2005). *The harmonic mind: From neutral computation to Optimality-Theoretic grammar; vol. 1: Cognitive architecture; vol. 2: Linguistic and philosophical implications*, Cambridge, MA: MIT Press.

Smolensky, Paul, Michael C. Mozer and David E. Rumelhart (eds.) (1996). *Mathematical perspectives on neural networks*. Mahwah: NJ, Lawrence Erlbaum Associates.

Snider, Keith (1990). Tonal upstep in Krachi: Evidence for a register tier. *Lg* 66: 453–474.

Snider, Keith (1999). *The geometry and features of tone*. Publications in Linguistics. Arlington, SIL and University of Texas.

So, L. K. H. and B. J. Dodd (1995). The acquisition of phonology by Cantonese-speaking children. *JCL* 22: 473–495.

Soh, Hooi Ling (2001). The syntax and semantics of phonological phrasing in Shanghai and Hokkien. *Journal of East Asian linguistics* 10: 37–80.

Sohn, Ho-Min and Byron W. Bender (1973). *A Ulithian Grammar*. Canberra, Australian National University.

Solnit, D. and J. Kingston (1988). *Voiced-high splits: Putting the blame on sonorants*. Talk, presented at the 63rd Annual Meeting of the Linguistic Society of America, New Orleans.

Spaelti, Phillip (1997). *Dimensions of Variation in Multi-Pattern Reduplication*. Doctoral dissertation, UCSC.

Spencer, Andrew (1984). Eliminating the feature [lateral]. *JL* 20: 23–43.

Spencer, Andrew (1996). *Phonology: Theory and description*. Oxford, Blackwell.

Spring, Cari (1990). *Implications of Axininca Campa for prosodic morphology and reduplication*. Doctoral dissertation, University of Arizona.

Sproat, Richard (1984). *On deriving the lexicon*. Doctoral dissertation, MIT.

Sproat, Richard and Osamu Fujimura (1993). Allophonic variation of English /l/ and its implications for phonetic implementation. *JPh* 21: 291–311.

Stampe, David (1973). *How I spent my summer vacation (A dissertation on Natural Generative Phonology)*. Doctoral dissertation, University of Chicago [Published 1979 by Garland Press].

Stemberger, Joseph P. (1981). Morphological haplology. *Lg* 57: 791–817.

Stemberger, Joseph P. (1990). Wordshape errors in language production. *Cognition* 35: 123–157.

Stemberger, Joseph P. (2003). *Possessor subjects in first language acquisition: The role of phonology*. Paper presented at the Workshop on the Form and Function of Pronouns, Vancouver, September 19–21, 2003.

Stemberger, Joseph P. and Barbara Bernhardt (1997). Optimality Theory. In M. Ball and R. Kent (eds.) *The new phonologies*. San Diego, CA, Singular Publishing Group, pp.211–245.

Stemberger, Joseph P. and B. MacWhinney (1986). Form-oriented inflectional errors in language processing. *Cognitive Psychology* 18: 163–180.

Stemberger, Joseph P. and Carol Stoel-Gammon (1991). The underspecification of coronals: Evidence from language acquisition and performance errors. In Carole Paradis and Jean-Francois Prunet (eds.) *Phonetics and phonology: Vol.2. The special status of coronals*. San Diego, CA, Academic Press, pp.181–199.

Stemberger, Joseph P. and R. Treiman (1986). The internal structure of word-initial consonant clusters. *Journal of Memory and Language* 25: 163–180.

Steriade, Donca (1977). Locality conditions and feature geometry. *NELS 17*. Amherst, Massachusetts, GLSA, pp.595–617.

Steriade, Donca (1982). *Greek prosodies and the nature of syllabification*. Doctoral dissertation, MIT.

Steriade, Donca (1987). Locality conditions and feature geometry. In Joyce McDonough and B. Plunkett (eds.) *NELS 17*. Somerville, MA, Cascadilla, pp.595–617.

Steriade, Donca (1988a). Greek accent: A case for preserving structure. *LI* 19: 271–314.

Steriade, Donca (1988b). Reduplication and syllable transfer in Sanskrit and elsewhere. *Ph* 5: 73–155.

Steriade, Donca (1988c). Review Article: Clements and Keyser, CV Phonology. *Lg* 64: 118–129.

Steriade, Donca (1991). Moras and other slots. In D. Meyer and S. Tomioka (eds.) *Proceedings of the 1st meeting of the Formal Linguistics Society of the Midwest*. Madison, University of Wisconsin, pp.254–280.

Steriade, Donca (1993). Closure, release, and nasal contours. In Marie K. Huffman and Rena A. Krakow (eds.) *Nasals, nasalization, and the velum*. San Diego, Academic Press, pp.401–470.

Steriade, Donca (1994). Complex onsets as single segments: The Mazateco pattern. In J. Cole and Charles Kisseberth (eds.) *Perspectives in phonology*. Stanford, CA, CSLI Publications, pp.203–291.

Steriade, Donca (1995). Underspecification and markedness. In John Goldsmith (ed.) *The handbook of phonological theory*. Cambridge, MA, Blackwell, pp.114–174.

Steriade, Donca (1997). Phonetics in phonology: the case of laryngeal neutralization. Ms, UCLA. [http://www.linguistics.ucla.edu/people/steriade/papers/phoneticsinphonology.pdf-1 April 2006].

Steriade, Donca (1999a). Alternatives to syllable-based accounts of consonantal phonotactics. In O. Fujimura, B. D. Joseph and B. Palek (eds.) *Proceedings of the 1998 Linguistics and Phonetics Conference*. Prague, Karolinum, pp.205–242.

Steriade, Donca (1999b). Phonetics in phonology: The case of laryngeal neutralization. In Matthew Gordon (ed.) *Papers in Phonology 3*. UCLA Working Papers in Linguistics 2. UCLA, UCLA linguistics department, pp.25–146. [Also at http://web.mit.edu/linguistics/www/bibliography/steriade.html].

Steriade, Donca (2000). Paradigm uniformity and the phonetics-phonology boundary. In Michael Broe and Janet Pierrehumbert (eds.) *Papers in laboratory phonology 5*. Cambridge, CUP, pp.313–334.

Steriade, Donca (2001a). Directional asymmetries in place assimilation: A perceptual account. In Elizabeth Hume and Keith Johnson (eds.) *The role of speech perception in phonology*. San Diego, Academic Press, pp.219–250.

Steriade, Donca (2001b). *The phonology of perceptibility effects: the P-map and its consequences for constraint organization*. Manuscript, MIT. http://web.mit.edu/linguistics/www/bibliography/steriade.html.

Stetson, Raymond H. (1928). *Motor Phonetics*. Amsterdam, North Holland.

Stevens, Alan M. (1968). *Madurese phonology and morphology*. American Oriental Series, American Oriental Society.

Stevens, Kenneth (1989). The quantal nature of speech. *JPh* 17: 3–46.

Stevens, Kenneth (1998). *Acoustic phonetics*. Cambridge, MA, MIT Press.

Stevens, Kenneth and S. E. Blumstein (1978). Invariant cues for place of articulation in stop consonants. *JASA* 64: 1358–1368.

Stevens, Kenneth, G. Fant and S. Hawkins (1987). Some acoustical and perceptual characteristics of nasal vowels. In R. Channon and L. Shockey (eds.) *In Honour of Ilse Lehiste*. Dordrecht, Foris, pp.241–254.

Stevens, Kenneth and Samuel J. Keyser (1989). Primary features and their enhancements in consonants. *Lg* 65: 81–106.

Stevens, Kenneth, Samuel J. Keyser and H. Kawasaki (1986). Toward a phonetic and phonological theory of redundant values. In J. Perkell and D. Klatt (eds.) *Invariance and variability in speech processes*. Hillsdale, NJ, Lawrence Erlbaum Associates, pp.426–449.

Stewart, John M. (1983). Downstep and floating low tones in Adioukrou. *Journal of African Languages and Linguistics* 5: 57–78.

Stoel, R. B. (2005). *Focus in Manado Malay*. Leiden, CNWS Publications.

Stoel-Gammon, Carol (1996). On the acquisition of velars in English. In Barbara Bernhardt, John Gilbert and David Ingram (eds.) *Proceedings of the UBC International Conference on Phonological Acquisition*. Somerville, MA, Cascadilla Press, pp.201–215.

Stoel-Gammon, Carol and J. Cooper (1984). Patterns of early lexical and phonological development. *JCL* 11: 247–271.

Stoel-Gammon, Carol and C. Dunn (1985). *Normal and disordered phonology in children*. Austin, TX, Pro-Ed.

Stoel-Gammon, Carol and Joseph P. Stemberger (1994). Consonant harmony and phonological underspecification in child speech. In M. Yavaş (ed.) *First and second language phonology*. San Diego, Singular Press, pp.63–80.

Street, J. C. (1963) *Khalkha Structure*. Bloomington: Indiana University.

Street, Chester and Gregory Mollinjin (1981). The phonology of Murinbata. In Bruce Waters (ed.) *Australian phonologies: Collected papers*. Working Papers of the SIL, Australian Aborigines Branch A 5. Darwin, Australia, *SIL*, pp.183–244.

Strik, H. and L. Boves (1995). Downtrend in F0 and Psb. *JPh* 23: 203–220.

Struijke, Caro (2000a). *Existential faithfulness: A study of reduplicative TETU, feature movement, and dissimilation*. Doctoral dissertation, University of Maryland, College Park.

Struijke, Caro (2000b). Why constraint conflict can disappear in reduplication. In M. Hirotani, Andries Coetzee, Nancy Hall and J.-Y. Kim (eds.) *NELS 30*. Amherst, GLSA, pp.613–626.

Sugahara, Mariko (2005). Post-FOCUS prosodic phrase boundaries in Tokyo Japanese: Asymmetric behavior of an F0 cue and domain-final lengthening. In Merle Horne and Marc van Oostendorp (eds.) *Boundaries in intonational phonology*. Special Issue. Studia Linguistica 59.2/3:144–173.

Summerfield, A. Q. and M. P. Haggard (1977). On the dissociation of spectral and temporal cues to the voicing distinction in initial stop consonants. *JASA* 62: 435–448.

Sussman, H. M., H. A. McCaffrey and S. A. Matthews (1991). An investigation of locus equations as a source of relational invariance for stop place categorization. *JASA* 90: 1309–1325.

Sussman, H. M., P. F. MacNeilage and R. J. Hanson (1973). Labial and mandiblar dynamics during the production of bilabial consonants: Preliminary observations. *Journal of Speech and Hearing Research* 16: 397–420.

Suzuki, Keiichiro (1998). *A typological investigation of dissimilation*. Doctoral dissertation, University of Arizona.

Taff, Alice (1997). Intonation patterns in Unangan. In Antonis Botinis, G. Kouroupetroglou and G. Carayannis (eds.) *Intonation: Theory, models and applications: Proceedings of an ESCA Workshop*. Athens, Greece, ESCA and University of Athens Department of Informatics, pp.301–304.

Taff, Alice (1999). *Phonetics and phonology of Unangan (Eastern Aleut) intonation*. Doctoral dissertation, University of Washington.

Taglicht, Josef (1998). Constraints on intonational phrasing in English. *JL* 34.1: 181–211.

Tarpent, Marie-Lucie (1987). *A grammar of the Nisgha language*. Doctoral dissertation, University of Victoria.

Ter Mors, Christine (1984). Affix to X: Broselow and McCarthy versus Marantz: A reinterpretation. *The Linguistic Review* 3: 275–298.

Tesar, Bruce (1995). *Computational Optimality Theory*. Doctoral dissertation, University of Colorado, Boulder, CO.

Tesar, Bruce (1996). An iterative strategy for learning metrical stress in Optimality Theory. In E. Hughes, M. Hughes and A. Greenhill (eds.) *The proceedings of the 21st annual Boston University Conference on Language Development*, pp.615–626. [Also ROA 177].

Tesar, Bruce (1997). Using the mutual inconsistency of structural descriptions to overcome ambiguity in language learning. In Pius N. Tamanji and Kiyomi Kusumoto (eds.) *NELS 28*. Amherst, MA, GLSA, pp.469–483.

Tesar, Bruce (1998). Error-driven learning in Optimality Theory via the efficient computation of optimal forms. In Pilar Barbosa, Danny Fox, Paul Hagstrom, Martha Jo McGinnis and David Pesetsky (eds.) *Is the best good enough? Optimality and competition in syntax*. Cambridge, MA, MIT Press, pp.421–435.

Tesar, Bruce (2002). Enforcing grammatical restrictiveness can help resolve structural ambiguity. In Line Mikkelsen and Christopher Potts (eds.) *WCCFL 21*. Somerville, MA, Cascadilla Press, pp.443–456. [Also ROA 618].

Tesar, Bruce (2004). Using inconsistency detection to overcome structural ambiguity. *LI* 35.2: 219–253.

Tesar, Bruce, John Alderete, Graham Horwood, Nazarré Merchant, Koichi Nishitani and Alan Prince (2003). Surgery in language learning. In G. Garding and M. Tsujimura (eds.) *WCCFL 22*. Somerville, MA, Cascadilla Press, pp.477–490. [Also ROA 619].

Tesar, Bruce and Alan Prince (to appear). Using phonotactics to learn phonological alternations. In Jonathan Cihlar, Amy Franklin, David Kaiser and Irene Kimbara (eds.) *CLS 39. Vol. II: the panels*. Chicago, CLS [Also ROA 620].

Tesar, Bruce and Paul Smolensky (1993). The learnability of Optimality Theory: An algorithm and some basic complexity results. *ROA 2*. [Also Computer Science Department Technical Report (University of Colorado, Boulder): CU-CS-678–93].

Tesar, Bruce and Paul Smolensky (1998). Learnability in Optimality Theory. *LI* 29.2: 229–268.

Tesar, Bruce and Paul Smolensky (2000). *Learnability in Optimality Theory*. Cambridge, MA, MIT Press.

't Hart, Johan, Rene Collier and A. Cohen (1990). *A Perceptual study of into-nation: An experimental-phonetic approach to speech melody*. Cambridge, CUP.

Thomas, E. R. (2000). Spectral differences in /ai/ offsets conditioned by voicing of the following consonant. *JPh* 28: 1–25.

Thompson, Lawrence (1965). *A Vietnamese grammar*. Seattle, University of Washington Press.

Topintzi, Nina (2006). *Moraic onsets*. Doctoral dissertation, University College London.

Trager, G. L. and H. L. Smith, Jr. (1951). *An outline of English structure*. Norman, OK, Battenburg Press.

Tranel, Bernard (1993). French liaison and elision revisited: A unified account within Optimality Theory. *ROA* 15.

Trask, R. L. (1996). *A dictionary of phonetics and phonology*. London and New York, Routledge.

Treiman, R. (1983). The structure of spoken syllables: Evidence from novel word games. *Cognition* 15: 49–74.

Treiman, R. and C. Danis (1988). Syllabification of intervocalic consonants. *Journal of Memory and Language* 27: 87–104.

Treiman, R. and A. Zukowski (1990). Toward an understanding of English syllabification. *Journal of Memory and Language* 29: 66–85.

Trigo, Loren (1991). On pharynx-larynx interactions. *Ph* 8: 113–136.

Trigo, Loren (1993). The inherent structure of nasal segments. In Marie Huffman and R. A. Krakow (eds.) *Nasals, nasalization, and the velum*. New York, Academic Press, pp.369–400.

Trubetzkoy, N. (1939). *Grundzüge der Phonologie*. Prague, Vandenhoeck and Ruprecht [Translation: C. A. M. Baltaxe (1969). *Principles of Phonology*, Berkeley: University of California Press].

Truckenbrodt, Hubert (1995). *Phonological phrases: Their relation to syntax, focus, and prominence*. Doctoral dissertation, MIT.

Truckenbrodt, Hubert (1999). On the relation between syntactic phrases and phonological phrases. *LI* 30.2: 219–255.

Truckenbrodt, Hubert (2002). Upstep and embedded register levels. *Ph* 19: 77–120.

Truckenbrodt, Hubert (2004). Final lowering in non-final position. *JPh* 32.3: 313–348.

Truckenbrodt, Hubert (2006). Phrasal stress. In Keith Brown (ed.) *Encyclopedia of Languages and Linguistics, 2nd Edition*, Elsevier Vol. 9, pp.572ff.

Truckenbrodt, Hubert (to appear). Upstep on edge tones and on nuclear accents. In Carlos Gussenhoven and Tomas Riad (eds.) *Tone and tunes, Vol. II: Phonetic and behavioural studies in word and sentence processing*. Berlin and New York, Mouton de Gruyter.

Tsay, Jane (1994). *Phonological pitch*. Doctoral dissertation, University of Arizona.

Tse, John K. P. (1978). Tone acquisition in Cantonese: A longitudinal study. *JCL* 5: 191–204.

Tucker, A. N. and M. A. Mpaayei (1955) *Linguistic analyses: The non-Bantu languages of North-Eastern Africa*. London:OUP.

Uhmann, Susanne (1991). *Fokusphonologie: Linguistische arbeiten 252*. Tübingen, Niemeyer.

Uhrbach, Amy (1987). *A formal analysis of reduplication and its interaction with phonological and morphological processes*. Doctoral dissertation, University of Texas, Austin.

Ullrich, A. (2004). *Nichtlineare Analyse des phonologischen Systems deutschsprachiger Kinder*. MA thesis, Julius-Maximilians-Universität Würzburg.

Underhill, Robert (1976). *Turkish grammar*. Cambridge, Massachusetts, MIT Press.

Urbanczyk, Suzanne (1996). *Patterns of reduplication in Lushootseed*. Doctoral dissertation, UMass.

Urbanczyk, Suzanne (1999a). A-templatic reduplication in Halq'eméylem. In Kimary N. Shahin, Susan Blake and Eun-Sook Kim (eds.) *WCCFL 17*. Stanford, CSLI, pp.655–669.

Urbanczyk, Suzanne (1999b). Echo vowels in Coast Salish. In Marion Caldicott, Suzanne Gessner and Eun-Sook Kim (eds.) *Proceedings of the Workshop on Structure and Constituency in the Languages of the Americas IV: UBC Working Papers in Linguistics*, pp.165–184.

Urbanczyk, Suzanne (2000). The bases of double reduplication. In Roger Billerey and Brook Danielle Lillehaugen (eds.) *WCCFL 19*. Somerville, MA, Cascadilla Press, pp.518–531.

Urbanczyk, Suzanne (2006). Reduplicative form and the root-affix asymmetry. *NLLT* 24.1: 179–240.

Ussishkin, Adam (2000). *The emergence of fixed prosody*. Doctoral dissertation, UCSC.

Ussishkin, Adam (2005). A fixed prosodic theory of nonconcatenative templatic morphology. *NLLT* 23: 169–218.

Vago, R. (1976). More evidence for the feature [grave]. *LI* 7: 671–674.

Vaissière, J. (2005). *Perception of intonation*. Malden, MA and Oxford, UK, Blackwell.

Vance, Timothy (1987). *An introduction to Japanese phonology*. Albany, SUNY Press.

Varga, L. (2002). *Stress and intonation: Evidence from Hungarian*. Basingstoke, UK: Palgrave.

Vaux, Bert (1998). The laryngeal specifications of fricatives. *LI* 29.3: 497–511.

Velten, Harry V. (1943). The growth of phonemic and lexical patterns in infant speech. *Lg* 19.4: 281–292.

Venditti, J. J. (2005). The j_ToBI model of Japanese intonation. In Sun-Ah Jun (ed.) *Typology: The phonology of intonation and phrasing*. Oxford, OUP, pp.172–200.

Vennemann, Theo (1972). On the theory of syllabic phonology. *Linguistische Berichte* 18: 1–18.

Vennemann, Theo (1974). Phonological concreteness in natural generative grammar. In Roger W. Shuy and C.-J. Bailey (eds.) *Towards tomorrow's linguistics*. Washington, DC, Georgetown University Press, pp.202–219.

Vennemann, Theo (1988). *Preference laws for syllable structure*. Berlin, Mouton de Gruyter.

Vigário, Marina (2003). *The prosodic word in European Portuguese*. Berlin: Mouton de Gruyter.

Vigário, Marina and Sónia Frota (2003). The intonation of Standard and Northen European Portuguese: A comparative and intonational phonology approach. *Journal of Portuguese Linguistics* 2: 115–137.

Vigário, Marina, Sónia Frota and Maria João Freitas (2003). From signal to grammar: Rhythm and the acquisition of syllable structure. In Barbara Beachley, Amanda Brown and Frances Conlin (eds.) *BUCLD 27: Proceedings of the 27th Annual Boston University Conference on Language Development.* Somerville, MA, Cascadilla Press, pp.809–821.

Vihman, Marilyn (1978). Consonant harmony: Its scope and function in child language. In Joseph H. Greenberg (ed.) *Universals of human language, Vol.2: Phonology.* Stanford, CA, Stanford University Press, pp.281–334.

Vihman, Marilyn (1992). Early syllables and the construction of phonology. In Charles A. Ferguson, Lise Menn and Carol Stoel-Gammon (eds.) *Phonological development: Models, research, implications.* Timonium, MA, York Press, pp.393–422.

Vihman, Marilyn (1996). *Phonological development: The origins of language in the child.* Oxford, UK, Blackwell.

Vihman, Marilyn, Shelley L. Velleman and Lorraine McCune (1994). How abstract is child phonology? Towards an integration of linguistic and psychological approaches. In Mehmet Yavaş (ed.) *First and second language phonology.* San Diego, CA, Singular Publishing Group, pp.9–44.

Vijver, Ruben van de (1998). *The iambic issue: Iambs as a result of constraint interaction,* Holland Institute of Generative Linguistics.

Voegelin, Charles (1935). Tübatulabal Grammar. *University of California Publications in American Archaeology and Ethnology 34, no.2.* Berkeley, University of California Press, pp.55–189.

Voorhoeve, Jan (1971) Tonology of the Bamileke noun. *Journal of African Languages* 10: 44–53.

Waksler, R. (1990). *A formal account of glide/vowel alternation in prosodic theory.* Doctoral dissertation, Harvard University.

Walker, Rachel (1997). Mongolian stress, licensing and factorial typology. *ROA* 172.

Walker, Rachel (1998). *Nasalization, neutral segments, and opacity effects.* Doctoral dissertation, UCSC. [Also ROA 405].

Walker, Rachel (2000a). Nasal reduplication in Mbe affixation. *Ph* 17: 65–115.

Walker, Rachel (2000b). *Nasalization, neutral segments, and opacity effects*, Garland Press.

Walker, Rachel (2001). Round licensing, harmony, and bisyllabic triggers in Altaic. *NLLT* 19: 827–878.

Walker, Rachel (2003a). *Nasal and oral consonant similarity in speech errors: Exploring parallels with long-distance nasal agreement.* Manuscript, University of Southern California: http://www-rcf.usc.edu/~rwalker/pubs.html.

Walker, Rachel (2003b). Reinterpreting transparency in nasal harmony. In Jeroen van de Weijer, Vincent van Heuven and Harry van der Hulst (eds.) *The phonological spectrum, Part I: Segmental structure.* Current Issues in Linguistic Theory 233. Amsterdam, John Benjamins, pp.37–72.

Walker, Rachel (2005). Weak triggers in vowel harmony. *NLLT* 23.4: 917–989.

Walsh Dickey, Laura (1997). *The phonology of liquids.* Doctoral dissertation, University of Amherst at Amherst.

Wang, William S.-Y. (1969). Competing changes as a cause of residue. *Lg* 45: 9–25.

Wang, William S.-Y. and C.-C. Cheng (1977). Implementation of phonological change: The Shaungfeng Chinese case. In W. S.-Y. Wang (ed.) *The lexicon in phonological change.* The Hague, Mouton, pp.148–158.

Wang, William S.-Y. and Chinfa Lien (eds.) (1993). Bidirectional diffusion in Sound Change. In C. Jones (ed.) *Historical linguistics.* Essex: Longman, pp.345–400.

Watanabe, Honoré (2000). *A morphological description of Sliammon, Mainland Comox Salish.* Doctoral dissertation, Kyoto University.

Watanabe, Honoré. (2003). *A morphological description of Sliammon, Mainland Comox Salish, with a sketch of syntax.* Endangered Languages of the Pacific Rim. Kyoto Japan: Nakanishi Printing Co. Ltd.

Waterson, Natalie (1971). Child phonology: a prosodic view. *JL* 7: 179–211.

Waterson, Natalie (1981). A tentative developmental model of phonological representation. In T. Myers, John Laver and J. Anderson (eds.) *The cognitive representation of speech.* Amsterdam, The North-Holland Publishing Company, pp.323–333.

Waterson, Natalie (1987). *Prosodic phonology: The theory and its application to language acquisition and speech processing.* Newcastle upon Tyne, Grevatt and Grevatt.

Watkins, L. J. (1984). *A grammar of Kiowa.* Lincoln and London, University of Nebraska Press.

Watson, Duane and Edward Gibson (2005). Intonational phrasing and constituency in language production and comprehension. In Merle Horne and Marc van Oostendorp (eds.) *Boundaries in intonational phonology.* Special Issue. Studia Linguistica 59.2/3: 279–300.

Wauquier-Gravelines, Sophie and Déborah Suet-Bouret (2004). *Acquisition des attaques syllabiques et 'palatal patterns'. Pourquoi yod?* Paper presented at Colloque du Réseau "Phonologie", 3 June 2004, Orleans.

Wedekind, Klaus (1983). A six-tone language of Ethiopia. *Journal of Ethiopian studies* 16: 129–156.

Wedel, Andrew (2004). *Self organization and categorical behaviour in phonology.* Doctoral dissertation, UCSC.

Weijer, Jeroen van de (1992). Basque affricates and the manner-place dependency. *Ln* 88: 129–147.

Weijer, Jeroen van de (1993). The manner-place dependency in complex segments. *Linguistics* 31: 87–110.

Weijer, Jeroen van de (1994). *Segmental structure and complex segments.* Doctoral dissertation, University of Leiden.

Welmers, William (1959). Tonemics, morphotonemics and tonal morphemes. *General Linguistics* 4: 1–19.

Welmers, William E. (1973) *African language structures.* Berkeley: University of California Press.

Werker, Janet, Christopher Fennell, Kathleen Corcoran and Christine Stager (2002). Age and vocabulary size influences on the phonological representation of newly learned words in infants aged 14 to 20 months. *Infancy* 3: 1–30.

Werker, Janet, D. Geoffrey Hall and Laurel Fais (2004). Restructuring U-shaped functions. *Journal of Cognition and Development* 5: 147–151.

Werker, Janet and Richard C. Tees (1984). Cross-language speech perception: Evidence for perceptual reorganization during the first year of life. *Infant behavior and development* 7: 49–63.

Westbury, J. R. (1983). Enlargement of the supraglottal cavity and its relation to stop consonant voicing. *JASA* 73: 1322–1336.

Westbury, J. R., M. Hashi and M. J. Lindstrom (1998). Differences among speakers in articulation of American English /r/. *Speech Communication* 26: 203–226.

Westbury, J. R. and P. A. Keating (1980). Central representation of vowel duration. *JASA* 67: S37A (Abstract).

Wetzels, W. Leo (1995). Mid-vowel alternations in the Brazilian Portuguese verb. *Ph* 12: 281–304.

Wetzels, W. Leo and Joan Mascaró (2001). The typology of voicing and devoicing. *Lg* 77.2: 207–244.

Wetzels, W. Leo and Engin Sezer (eds.) (1986). *Studies in compensatory lengthening.* Dordrecht, Foris.

Whalen, D. H. and P. S. Beddor (1989). Connections between nasality and vowel duration and height: elucidation of the Eastern Algonquian intrusive nasal. *Lg* 65: 457–486.

Whalen, D. H., C. T. Best and J. R. Irwin (1997). Lexical effects in the perception of American /p/ allophones. *JPh* 25: 501–528.

Wightman, C. W., S. Shattuck-Hufnagel, M. Ostendorf and P. J. Price (1992). Segmental durations in the vicinity of prosodic boundaries. *JASA* 91: 1707–1717.

Wilbur, Ronnie (1973). *The phonology of reduplication*. Doctoral dissertation, University of Illinois, Urbana-Champaign.

Wilkinson, Karina (1988). Prosodic structure and Lardil phonology. *LI* 19.2: 325–334.

Wilson, Colin (2000). *Targeted constraints: An approach to contextual neutralization in Optimality Theory*. Doctoral dissertation, Johns Hopkins University.

Wilson, Colin (2001). Consonant cluster neutralization and targeted constraints. *Ph* 18: 147–197.

Wilson, Colin (2003a). *Analyzing unbounded spreading with constraints: marks, targets, and derivations*. Manuscript, UCLA, Los Angeles.

Wilson, Colin (2003b). Experimental investigation of phonological naturalness. In G. Garding and M. Tsujimura (eds.) *WCCFL 22*. Cambridge, MA, Cascadilla Press, pp.533–546.

Woodbury, Anthony (1987). Meaningful phonological processes: A consideration of Central Alaskan Yupik Eskimo prosody. *Lg* 63: 685–740.

Wright, J. T. (1986). The behavior of nasalized vowels in the perceptual vowel space. In J. J. Ohala and J. J. Jaeger (eds.) *Experimental phonology*. Orlando, Academic Press, pp.45–67.

Wright, Richard (1996). *Consonant clusters and cue preservation in Tsou*. Doctoral dissertation, UCLA.

Wright, Richard (2003). Factors of lexical competition in vowel articulation. In John Local, Richard Ogden and Rosalind Temple (eds.) *Phonetic interpretation: Papers in Laboratory Phonology VI*. Oxford, OUP, pp.75–87.

Wright, Richard, S. Hargus and K. Davis (2002). On the categorization of ejectives: Data from Witsuwit'en. *JIPA* 32: 43–77.

Xu, Yi (1994). Production and perception of coarticulated tones. *JASA* 95.4: 2240–2253.

Xu, Yi (1998). Consistency of tone–syllable alignment across different syllable structures and speaking rates. *Phonetica* 55: 179–203.

Xu, Yi (1999). Effects of tone and focus on the formation and alignment of F0 contours. *JPh* 27: 55–105.

Xu, Yi (in press). Understanding tone from the perspective of production and perception. *Language and Linguistics*.

Xu, Yi and Q. Emily Wang (2001). Pitch targets and their realization: evidence from Mandarin Chinese. *Speech Communication* 33: 319–337.

Yavaş, M. (1998). *Phonology development and disorders*. San Diego, CA, Singular Publishing.

Yip, Moira (1980). *The tonal phonology of Chinese*. Doctoral dissertation, MIT.

Yip, Moira (1988). The Obligatory Contour Principle and phonological rules: A loss of identity. *LI* 19: 65–100.

Yip, Moira (1989a). Contour tones. *Ph* 6.1: 149–174.

Yip, Moira (1989b). Feature geometry and cooccurrence restrictions. *Ph* 6: 349–374.

Yip, Moira (1991). Coronals, consonant clusters, and the coda condition. In Carole Paradis and Jean-François Prunet (eds.) *The special status of coronals: Internal and external evidence*. Phonetics and Phonology. San Diego, Academic Press, pp.61–78.

Yip, Moira (1992). Reduplication with fixed melodic material. *NELS 21*. Amherst, MA, GLSA, pp.459–474.

Yip, Moira (1995). Tone in East Asian languages. In John Goldsmith (ed.) *The handbook of phonological theory*. Oxford, Basil Blackwell, pp.476–494.

Yip, Moira (1998). Identity avoidance in phonology and morphology. In Steven G. LaPointe, Diane K. Brentari and Patrick M. Farrell (eds.) *Morphology and its relation to phonology and syntax*. Stanford, CSLI, pp.216–246.

Yip, Moira (1999). Feet, tonal reduction and speech rate at the word and phrase level in Chinese. In René Kager and Wim Zonneveld (eds.) *Phrasal phonology*. Nijmegen, Nijmegen University Press, pp.171–194.

Yip, Moira (2001a). The complex interaction of tone and prominence. In M. Kim and U. Strauss (eds.) *NELS 31*. Amherst, MA, GLSA, pp.531–545.

Yip, Moira (2001b). Segmental unmarkedness versus input preservation in reduplication. In Linda Lombardi (ed.) *Segmental phonology in Optimality Theory: Constraints and representations*. Cambridge, CUP, pp.206–228.

Yip, Moira (2002). *Tone*. Cambridge, CUP.

Yip, Moira (2004). Lateral survival: An OT account. *International Journal of English Studies* 4.2: 25–51.

Yu, Alan (2003). *The morphology and phonology of infixation*. Doctoral dissertation, UCB.

Yu Cho, Young-Mee (1991). On the universality of the coronal articulator. In Carole Paradis and Jean-François Prunet (eds.) *The special status of coronals: Internal and external evidence*. San Diego, CA, Academic Press.

Zamuner, Tania (2003). *Input-based phonological acquisition*. New York, NY, Routledge.

Zamuner, Tania, LouAnn Gerken and Michael Hammond (2004). Phonotactic probabilities in young children's speech production. *JCL* 31.3: 515–536.

Zamuner, Tania, Annemarie Kerkhoff, Paula Fikkert and Ellen Westrek (2005). *Dutch children's acquisition of morpho-phonological alternations in plural formation*. Manuscript, Radboud University of Nijmegen and Utrecht University.

Zec, Draga (1988). *Sonority constraints on prosodic structure*. Doctoral dissertation, Stanford University.

Zec, Draga (1995). Sonority constraints on syllable structure. *Ph* 12: 85–129.

Zec, Draga (1999). Footed tones and tonal feet: rhythmic constituency in a pitch accent language. *Ph* 16: 225–264.

Zec, Draga (2000). Multiple sonority thresholds. In T. H. King and I. A. Sekerina (eds.) *The 8th Annual Workshop on Formal Approaches to Slavic Linguistics*. Ann Arbor, Michigan Slavic Publications, pp.382–413.

Zec, Draga (2003). Prosodic weight. In Caroline Féry and Ruben van de Vijver (eds.) *The syllable in Optimality Theory*. Cambridge, CUP, pp.123–143.

Zec, Draga (2005). Prosodic differences among function words. *Ph* 22. 1: 77–112.

Zhang, Jie (2000a). The phonetic basis for tonal melody mapping. *WCCFL 19*. Somerville, MA, Cascadilla Press, pp.603–616.

Zhang, Jie (2000b). Phonetic duration effects on contour tone distribution. In M. Hirotani, Andries Coetzee, Nancy Hall and J.-Y. Kim (eds.) *NELS 30*. Vol.2, pp.775–785.

Zhang, Jie (2001). *The effects of duration and sonority on contour tone distribution - typological survey and formal analysis*. Doctoral dissertation, UCLA. [Also ROA 452].

Zhang, Jie (2002). *The effects of duration and sonority on contour tone distribution: typological survey and formal analysis*. New York, Routledge.

Zhang, Jie (2004). The role of contrast-specific and language-specific phonetics in contour tone distribution. In Bruce Hayes, Donca Steriade and Robert Kirchner (eds.) *Phonetically based phonology*. Cambridge, CUP, pp.157–190.

Zhang, Jie and Yuwen Lai (2005). The psychological reality of Mandarin tone sandhi. *Poster presented at the annual LSA meeting*. Vol.5–9, Jan. 2005. Oakland, CA.

Zhang, Zheng-Sheng (1988). *Tone and tone sandhi in Chinese*. Doctoral dissertation, Ohio State University.

Ziervogel, D., P. J. Wetzel and T. N. Makuya (1972). *A Handbook of the Venda language*. Pretoria, University of South Africa Press.

Zoll, Cheryl (1996). *Parsing below the segment in a constraint based framework*. Doctoral dissertation, UCB. [Also ROA 143].

Zoll, Cheryl (1997). Conflicting directionality. *Ph* 14: 263–286.

Zoll, Cheryl (1998). *Positional markedness, positional faithfulness, and licensing*. Manuscript, MIT.

Zoll, Cheryl (2001). Constraints and representations in subsegmental phonology. In Linda Lombardi (ed.) *Segmental phonology in Optimality Theory*. Cambridge, CUP, pp.46–78.

Zoll, Cheryl (2003). Optimal tone mapping. *LI* 34.2: 225–268.

Zoll, Cheryl (2004). Positional asymmetries and licensing. In John McCarthy (ed.) *Optimality Theory in phonology: A reader*. Oxford, Blackwell, pp.365–378.

Zsiga, Elizabeth C. (1995). An acoustic and electropalatographic study of lexical and postlexical palatalization in American English. In Bruce Connell and Amalia Arvaniti (eds.) *Phonology and phonetic evidence: Papers in Laboratory Phonology IV*. Cambridge, CUP, pp.282–302.

Zsiga, Elizabeth C. (2000). Phonetic alignment constraints: Consonant overlap and palatalization in English and Russian. *JPh* 28: 69–102.

Zubizarreta, María Luisa (1994). On some prosodically governed syntactic operations. In Guglielmo Cinque, Jan Koster, Jean-Yves Pollock, Luigi Rizzi and Raffaella Zanuttini (eds.) *Paths toward Universal Grammar. Studies in honor of Richard S. Kayne*. Washington, Georgetown University Press, pp.473–485.

Zubizarreta, María Luisa (1998). *Prosody, focus and word order*. LI Monographs vol. 33. Cambridge, MA, MIT Press.

Zubritskaya, Katya (1997). Mechanism of sound change in Optimality Theory. *Language Variation and Change* 9.1: 121–48.

Zuraw, Kie (1996). *Floating phonotactics: Infixation and reduplication in Tagalog loanwords*. MA thesis, UCLA.

Zuraw, Kie (2000). *Patterned exceptions in phonology*. Doctoral dissertation, UCLA.

Zuraw, Kie (2003). Aggressive reduplication. *Ph* 19: 395–439.

Index of subjects

Index of languages and language families